Harvard Studies in Business History

XXV

Edited by Ralph W. Hidy
Isidor Straus Professor of Business History
Graduate School of Business Administration
George F. Baker Foundation
Harvard University

Investment Banking in America

A History

Vincent P. Carosso

Research Associates
Marian V. Sears
Irving Katz

Andrew S. Thomas Memorial Library
MORRIS HARVEY COLLEGE, CHARLESTON, W. VA.

Harvard University Press
Cambridge, Massachusetts
1970

74555

© Copyright 1970 by the President and Fellows of Harvard College
All rights reserved
Distributed in Great Britain by Oxford University Press, London
Library of Congress Catalog Card Number 70-99515
SBN 674-46574-1
Printed in the United States of America

332.66
C222i

For Rose and Steven

Editor's Introduction

With this study of the investment banker in the twentieth century a long step has been taken toward filling a gap in historical knowledge. Both general and economic historians have long known the major features of investment banking history in the United States up to World War I. Early in the century the behavior of the fraternity, being the subject of federal investigation, received much popular and semipopular analysis. By World War II, several authors, through articles and books of varying quality, had provided more comprehensive and better analyzed data on investment bankers from Nathaniel Prime to J. P. Morgan, the elder. Clearly needed, however, was an objective appraisal of the changing role of investment banking in the United States in the twentieth century.

During the five years after World War II historians at the Harvard Business School made some moves toward meeting the need. In discussions with men in a few firms Professor Henrietta M. Larson probed the possibilities of raising funds and of gaining access to the records of several private banking houses, but pressure of other obligations inhibited anything more than preliminary inquiries; she had to abandon an interest stimulated by her study of Jay Cooke. Although Professor Thomas R. Navin and Miss Marian V. Sears attempted no project covering all or major parts of the twentieth century, they did do some meaningful research and writing on segments of the topic. And later in the 1950's, Professor Barry Supple wrote an article on German-Jewish bankers in the United States in the nineteenth century.

Given such concern, it is not surprising that the historians at the School were quite interested when Kidder, Peabody & Co., Inc. suggested that it underwrite a scholarly history of the firm. After some discussion the topic for study was altered to the history of American investment banking in the twentieth century, data from the history of Kidder, Peabody & Co. to be used when appropriate. The School engaged Professor Vincent P. Carosso of New York University, at one time Business History Fellow at the School, to conduct the research and write the proposed book. It was understood that his work, both research and writing, would be carried on under my editorship. The views and interpretations expressed in the book were to be, and are, the author's alone.

Much discussion has revolved around shaping the questions to be answered and hypotheses to be tested. The major emphasis has been placed on the process of change through interaction of investment banks, including Kidder, Peabody & Co., with their environment. Special attention has been accorded adjustments and reactions of men and firms to shifts in the supply of investment funds, in the structure and size of the demand for them, and in public attitudes as well as actions of government agencies, both state and federal. Although three chapters deal with developments prior to 1900, the focus of the book is on the twentieth century. The study ends with an analysis of the extent of alteration in the structure of investment banking, in its function, and in the ways of performing the function. Overall, this provides an illustration of the process of change through interaction between business in general and the political, economic, and social "world" in which businessmen live and operate.

Personally, I am deeply grateful to several people for their aid in bringing the work to completion. Kidder, Peabody & Co. granted the funds to start the project and opened doors to numerous sources of information. Several executives of the firm critically read the manuscript for factual accuracy but suggested no changes in interpretation. The Business School's Division of Research, through Professor Bertrand Fox, then Director of Research, made supplementary grants to assure completion of the study. Professor Fox also applied his meticulous scholarship and deep knowledge of banking and finance to critical evaluation and refining of the manuscript's content and composition. Deepest appreciation goes to the author and his associates, who doggedly devoted several years of their lives, at times under stress from ill health, to producing this history. Together these individuals enable me to realize an ambition to publish a broad industry study in the series sponsored by the historians at the Harvard Business School.

November 1969   Ralph W. Hidy

Author's Preface

As a specialized middleman the investment banker is largely a development of the twentieth century. His job is to serve the users and suppliers of capital by providing the facilities through which savings are channeled into long-term investment. In the nineteenth century this function was performed by merchants, private bankers, and other intermediaries who carried on a large number of services concerned with marketing goods and securities.

The name "investment banker" itself is of recent general acceptance. Although it was used in England as early as the 1840's by traveling salesmen dealing in American railroad securities, it rarely was employed in the United States before the late 1880's except in reference to dealers in mortgages, western farms, or real estate. *The Bankers' Magazine* adopted the heading "Investment Bankers and Brokers" in its classified advertisements starting in January 1896; but in 1902, when investment bankers were close to the height of their influence and prestige, *Smith's Financial Dictionary*, a standard and respected reference work of the day, listed neither "investment banker" nor "investment banking" among its numerous entries. The 1902 *Rand-McNally Bankers' Directory*, a widely accepted listing of banks and trust companies in the United States, used the heading "Investment Banker" for New York City but under it failed to include some of Wall Street's outstanding firms, such as Kuhn, Loeb & Co. Eight years later the directory dropped the heading and substituted "Investment Securities and Bond Dealers."

In 1912, when the Investment Bankers Association of America (IBA) was established as an offshoot of the American Bankers Association, the organizers were not agreed as to what kinds of firms they should invite to join the new group. The difficulties encountered in establishing criteria of eligibility for membership in this, the first association "constituted purely of investment bankers," were very similar to those faced earlier by compilers of bank directories and financial dictionaries. As a result, the IBA's 347 charter members included many commercial banks and trust companies with bond departments performing some investment banking functions, as well as private bankers, brokers, and other dealers in securities.

Functional specialization among financial institutions still was blurred, and there was no agreement on a precise definition of an investment banker. Those engaged in the securities business rarely referred to themselves as such, and the investment banking function was performed by more firms than those specializing exclusively in the buying and selling of securities for resale. Nearly all the major pre-World War I investment houses, including such national leaders as J. P. Morgan & Co., Kuhn, Loeb & Co., and Kidder, Peabody & Co., conducted a general banking business — accepting deposits, trading in foreign exchange, issuing letters of credit, dealing in acceptances and commercial paper, and providing other financial services — as well as participating in the origination, purchase, underwriting, and distribution of new securities.

The old Boston house of Kidder, Peabody & Co. serves as an example. John R. Chapin, a partner who started with the firm in 1910, asserted that "a substantial proportion" of its business in the following decade was the "financing of imports and exports and the purchase and sale of foreign exchange." And even though by this time Kidder, Peabody had participated in financing numerous large railroad and industrial corporations, such as the Atchison, Topeka & Santa Fe Railroad Company and the American Telephone & Telegraph Company, the partners, like those in the House of Morgan, still looked upon themselves primarily as general bankers rather than as specialists serving the needs of a clientele composed largely of corporate borrowers and wealthy investors. Their views, shared by many other prominent bankers performing the investment banking function, reflected the diverse origins of the country's leading security houses and the fact that the need for specialized investment banking was a relatively recent development.

The purpose of this study is to analyze the changing role and practices of the investment banker in the American economy from the 1890's to the 1960's. To achieve this goal it is necessary to describe the function and status of investment banking at the turn of the century, to identify the forces that prompted change, and to discover the way security firms adapted their operations to alterations in the economic, social, and political environment.

The chapters that follow are not intended to provide a comprehensive review of the investment banking business, even though the need for such a survey has been recognized for some years. The concern of this work is more limited. It deals chiefly with a single, integrated phase of the investment banking business — the origination and merchandising of securities, including the financial and other advisory services rendered issuers. Other functions commonly performed by investment houses, such as trading in listed securities, maintaining markets for unlisted issues, handling secondary distributions, and acting as investment counselors for trusts and pension funds, are discussed only incidentally to indicate the range and variety of services provided by these firms.

Besides concentrating on a single function, the study is also limited geographically. The main focus is on the eastern United States, especially New York City, where, since the 1850's, much of the business of issuing new American securities has been concentrated. The rise of other investment banking centers, such as

Chicago and San Francisco, the growth of regional houses, and the relationship between these firms and those in the East are discussed only incidentally, not for any lack of appreciation of the importance of these developments, but because of the limitation of space and lack of evidence.

The overall thesis of the study is that despite the many profound economic and political changes of the last sixty years, the basic function of the investment banker has remained essentially unchanged. Today, as it was at the turn of the century, the investment banker's most important role is to channel savings into long-term investments. The services and merchandising functions involved in planning and distributing new security issues, with the possible exception of those sold at competitive bids, have remained largely what they were in the days of the elder J. Pierpont Morgan, when many of the industry's present-day practices and traditions became firmly established.

Economic and political pressures forced significant adaptations and alterations in the way investment bankers fulfilled their primary function of recruiting capital for industry and governments. In the course of adjusting to the needs and temper of the times the investment banker played many scenes on the American stage. Early in the century he strode across it, a figure of dominant economic influence. His role was so significant and pervasive that it invited attack. From time to time he was regarded as the villain, sometimes with justice, sometimes not, and his role became the basis for the rationalization of political action that set new parameters to his behavior. Throughout these years, investment bankers defended their policies and practices as valid and upright, while executing a strategic retreat. Between 1900 and 1960 investment bankers were forced to adapt their operations to many new legal requirements. Changes in investment banking methods that resulted from social and political pressures, with but few exceptions, appeared to have been no greater than those that grew out of the changes in the supply and demand for capital.

Neither public pressure nor economic change deprived the investment banker of his primary function. What changed, sometimes drastically, was the way he provided this all-important service. Equally important was the transformation that occurred in the investment banker's public image and relative status and influence in the economy.

Acknowledgments

Much of the material used in preparing this book was drawn from primary sources. When these were not obtainable, I tried to make as thorough an investigation as possible of the evidence available. But in a study of so large a subject, exhaustive research cannot be made into all the sources. Where my own investigations were relatively complete, I did not hesitate to reach conclusions differing from those of other writers; where they were not, I subordinated my views to those of students who probed more deeply. Among the scholars who preceded me in organizing certain periods and aspects of the subject, several deserve special mention. I relied upon Fritz Redlich's findings for much of the material on general nineteenth-century developments, and I also borrowed heavily from Ralph W. Hidy's study of the Barings and Henrietta M. Larson's account of Jay Cooke. Similarly, Louis Loss's monumental three-volume work, *Securities Regulation,* provided much of the legal information on that subject. For the period since the mid-1950's I have benefited from the work of Irwin Friend et al., *Investment Banking and the New Issues Market,* a study prepared by the Securities Research Unit of the University of Pennsylvania's Wharton School of Finance and Commerce. I owe a real debt to these and other authors whose monographs and articles are cited in the footnotes.

Many institutions assisted me in preparing this book. The staffs of several libraries, notably those of the New York Public, New York University, Columbia University, and New York Stock Exchange, searched their collections for relevant materials, both published and unpublished. Officials at the National Archives, the Library of Congress, and the Franklin D. Roosevelt Library also assisted me in finding important manuscripts. My greatest obligation, however, is to the Baker Library of the Harvard Graduate School of Business Administration. The expert knowledge and friendly assistance of its staff made working there a highly profitable and most enjoyable experience.

I also owe many acknowledgments to individuals. Henry G. Symonds, Jr., a former Research Associate at the Harvard Business School, helped me sift through and organize the extensive records of Kidder, Peabody & Co., Inc., in New York City, and David F. Hawkins, now Associate Professor of Business Administration at Harvard, assisted in investigating early state efforts at regulating the securities business. I benefited also from the findings of several of my graduate students at New York University who worked with me on various business and financial problems of the 1930's, particularly Dr. Helen M. Burns, now a legal librarian at the Federal Reserve Bank of New York, Philip J. Funigiello, Assistant Professor of History at the College of William and Mary, and Elwood D. Boynton, a Wall Street investment banker teaching at Pace College. Gordon L. Calvert, Executive Director and General Counsel of the Investment Bankers Association of America, answered innumerable questions and provided me with statistical and other information on the association's membership, activities, and programs, especially for the period since 1950. My greatest debt, as the entry on the title page indicates, is to Marian V. Sears, Research Associate at Harvard, and Irving Katz, Associate Professor of History at Indiana University. Both worked long and hard compiling bibliographies, gathering data, and revising the manuscript. Miss Sears also prepared preliminary drafts of several chapters and helped check footnotes and bibliographical citations. Without their diligent and painstaking assistance, it would have been impossible for me to investigate the voluminous documentary and other evidence available.

Nor could this book have been completed without the helpful cooperation of the officers and directors of Kidder, Peabody & Co., Inc., in particular Albert H. Gordon, Amyas Ames, and Alfred E. Borneman. I am greatly obligated to all of them, but especially to Mr. Borneman. Not only did he help me obtain countless private records, but he also arranged numerous interviews, cheerfully devoted many hours to answering my questions, and spent even more time reading various drafts of the manuscript. His generous and kindly assistance greatly lightened my labors.

Several other people also read the manuscript. Professors Bertrand D. Fox and Arthur M. Johnson of Harvard reviewed the text in its entirety and made suggestions for its improvement, as did Dr. Muriel E. Hidy of the Business History Foundation, Inc. Judge Harold R. Medina read the antitrust chapter, and numerous friends and colleagues gave me the benefit of their specialized knowledge. From Professor Ralph W. Hidy, under whose guidance the study was completed, I received the maximum of support, cooperation, and assistance. His constant advice, wide knowledge, and sympathetic encouragement were invaluable.

Two final acknowledgments remain to be made. Professor Bayrd Still, head of the History Department at New York University, arranged two leaves of absence when I needed them most, and my wife, Rose C. Carosso, took time from her own busy schedule to compile the bibliography and type most of the manuscript.

Whatever merit this study may have is due to the assistance and cooperation of many individuals. Its deficiencies are my own. Much research remains to be done in the history of investment banking. If this study helps encourage further investigation, it will have served a useful purpose.

Vincent P. Carosso

October 1969

Contents

1	Origins and Developments to 1873	1
2	From Railroads to Industrials, 1873–1900	29
3	The Development of the Syndicate to 1914	51
4	Investments, Investors, and Investment Bankers, 1900–1914	79
5	Prelude to Federal Investigation	110
6	Pujo	137
7	"Blue Sky": The Growth of Securities Regulation	156
8	Organizing for Defense: Formation of the Investment Bankers Association of America	165
9	The Passing of the Old Order	174
10	Investment Banking and Wilsonian Neutrality, 1914–1917	193
11	The War Years, 1917–1919	224
12	The Changing Investment and Financial Environment of the 1920's	240
13	Investment Banking Firms and the IBA in the 1920's	255
14	Three Types of Financial Institutions of the 1920's	271
15	Crash and Depression: The Investment Bankers' Image Transformed	300
16	The Investment Banker on Trial: The Gray-Pecora Investigation	322
17	The New Deal on Wall Street: I. Divorcement, Disclosure, Regulation	352
18	The New Deal on Wall Street: II. More Regulation and Further Adaptation	382
19	Pujo Revisited: The TNEC	408
20	Compulsory Competitive Bidding: Perennial Controversy	431
21	Antitrust	458
Epilogue: Mid-Century and Later		496
Bibliography		511
Index		543

Investment Banking in America

1 Origins and Developments to 1873

In the years after the Revolution investment banking in the United States evolved slowly and from various sources. Most investments did not require the services of an intermediary at first, but as the demand for investment capital grew, there was a gradual increase in the use of security issues, and more domestic and foreign investors were willing to risk their funds. The principal users of investment banking services were governments, which issued bonds to finance wars, new banks, internal improvements, and railroad companies — the nation's first big business enterprises.

Before the 1850's, when the financial needs of the railroads gave rise to some of the first investment banking houses, the business in securities was conducted by different kinds of unspecialized middlemen, all competing with one another.[1] In the United States, as in Europe, investment banking started out as a sideline or adjunct to some other business. One of the earliest and most important "ancestors of the modern investment banker" was the "loan contractor," who bought securities to resell to others at a profit. In America this role usually was filled by speculators and merchants, since relatively few other men of large wealth were willing to take the risks entailed in buying securities or had funds other than those invested in land or trade.

Merchants invested in securities not only because they promised income and capital gains, but also because stocks and bonds were used as collateral for bank loans, as a medium of domestic exchange, and for paying European creditors. When merchants acted as loan contractors, buying securities for resale, they added investment banking to their many other functions. One large-scale operation of this kind occurred in February 1813, when the Treasury raised $16 million to finance the war against England. Public subscriptions to this bond issue were so poor that the Treasury agreed to sell nearly $10 million of it to a group of three contractors, two of whom — Stephen Girard of Philadelphia and John Jacob Astor of New York — were probably the wealthiest merchants in America. David Parish, whom the English mercantile banking house of Baring Brothers & Co. of London had sent to the United States in 1805 to transact some of its affairs, was the third member of the group. Acting together, very much as investment banking syndicates were to do toward the end of the century, the group bought the bonds with its own and borrowed money and subsequently resold them at a profit through their widespread business and family connections.

1. Fritz Redlich, *The Molding of American Banking: Men and Ideas* (2 vols., New York, 1947, 1951), II, 304–26, 335.

Three years later, in May 1816, after the public had failed to subscribe to enough shares of the second Bank of the United States (BUS) to permit it to open, Stephen Girard took the entire amount ($3 million) required. Later he resold most of the shares.[2]

The investment banking function was performed also by incorporated commercial banks. Some of these institutions bought and sold securities because they were required by their charters to assist local enterprises, others because of local pride, but many more because it was profitable. Commercial bank participation was especially likely if the issuer also was a customer of the bank and used it as a depository for the funds received from the sale of the securities. By the mid-1830's chartered banks in several states were successfully bidding for new issues and reselling them in smaller lots either to subcontractors or directly to investors. Sometimes, for large issues, banks acted as co-contractors or with a foreign firm, like the Barings, who marketed numerous American state bonds in England and on the Continent.[3]

Of the many incorporated commercial banks performing an investment banking function before 1840, none was more deeply engaged in the business than the United States Bank of Pennsylvania, which took over the nongovernment affairs of the second BUS, when the latter's charter expired in 1836. In theory at least, this bank was similar to other state-chartered commercial banks, but Nicholas Biddle, its first president, hoped to make it into a national bank, performing all the central banking functions exercised earlier by the second BUS, as well as those of a leading international banking house. In the process of trying to realize these objectives, Biddle came very close to turning it into an "almost specialized" investment banking house. He contracted and negotiated for all kinds of public and private securities, including some of the first railroad issues. Like some large commercial banks doing an investment banking business a half century later, he tried to attract the deposits of the companies and government units whose securities he distributed. His one important innovation, and one that was partly responsible for the institution's ultimate collapse in 1841, was the practice of lending issuers money on securities he was trying to sell on commission.[4]

Biddle also was influential in directing into the investment business the Morris Canal and Banking Company, a New Jersey cor-

2. Redlich, *Molding of American Banking,* II, 316; Bray Hammond, *Banks and Politics in America from the Revolution to the Civil War* (Princeton, 1957), 245.
3. Redlich, *Molding of American Banking,* II, 317, 330–41; Merwin H. Waterman, *Investment Banking Functions: Their Evolution and Adaptation to Business Finance* (Ann Arbor, 1958), 18–20; Joseph E. Hedges, *Commercial Banking and the Stock Market before 1863* (Baltimore, 1938), 41; Thomas Payne Govan, *Nicholas Biddle: Nationalist and Public Banker, 1786–1844* (Chicago, 1959), 283, 287, 294–95.
4. Redlich, *Molding of American Banking,* II, 340.

poration. Chartered as an "improvement bank" to raise capital for state-sponsored internal improvements, this company became heavily involved in the securities business, buying and selling the stocks and bonds that states issued for public projects. Biddle's influence, starting about 1834, when his long-time friend Louis McLane, a former Secretary of the Treasury, became its president, grew enormously after 1837. The BUS of Pennsylvania secured a large block of the New Jersey corporation's stock, and several of Biddle's friends and relatives became officials. Excessive speculation and mismanagement, if not something worse, forced the Morris Canal and Banking Company into a scandalous bankruptcy, also in 1841.[5]

Many other incorporated banks also failed during the depression that followed the panic of 1837. The collapse of bond prices and debt repudiation by eight states and the territory of Florida shook the financial community at home and abroad. English bondholders condemned "the dishonesty and bad faith of the American people" and demanded a Parliamentary investigation.[6] In the United States there was widespread criticism of the banking system, especially of its close ties to the securities market. Strong demands for reform were raised, nearly all designed, in the word of *The Bankers' Magazine,* "to prevent banks from hazarding their capital, especially in stock jobbing, to which they are often strongly tempted, and from which disastrous consequences often follow."[7]

Although the depression loosened the incorporated banks' foothold in investment banking, it did not eliminate it entirely. Many of the new "free banks" established after 1838 continued to bid and contract for new federal and state issues.[8]

The depression also contributed to the decline of the lottery business, a commonly employed and generally accepted method of raising capital since the colonial era. During the first quarter of the nineteenth century lotteries were employed to raise money for community projects, such as roads, canals, rivers, churches, schools, and even jails. Some were conducted also for private purposes; one of the most famous of these was held to raise $80,000 for debt-ridden Thomas Jefferson, who was in danger of losing his beloved Monticello.[9]

5. *Ibid.,* II, 326, 341–42; George Rogers Taylor, *The Transportation Revolution, 1815–1860* (New York, 1951), 40.
6. Reginald C. McGrane, *Foreign Bondholders and American State Debts* (New York, 1935), 49–51.
7. Quoted in H. Parker Willis and Jules I. Bogen, *Investment Banking* (rev. ed., New York, 1936), 217.
8. Redlich, *Molding of American Banking,* II, 332, 344; Thomas C. Cochran, "The Entrepreneur in American Capital Formation," in National Bureau Committee for Economic Research, *Capital Formation and Economic Growth* (Princeton, 1955), 356.
9. John S. Ezell, *Fortune's Merry Wheel: The Lottery in America* (Cambridge, Mass., 1960), 77–82; Redlich, *Molding of American Banking,* II, 68–69, 327; Taylor, *Transportation Revolution,* 320–21.

At first, lotteries were simple affairs managed informally by citizens concerned with raising a relatively small sum for a specific local project, but as communities and states undertook more expensive improvements, many lotteries turned into large, organized, national operations, involving hundreds of thousands of dollars. In 1832, according to one estimate, "the value of lottery tickets authorized in nine eastern states . . . exceeded $53,000,000." [10] The lottery business increasingly became controlled by a few large contractors and ticket brokers, several of whom, such as S. and M. Allen, and Yates & McIntyre, built up national organizations with branch offices in at least a dozen states. Some of these operators gradually moved from selling lottery tickets to dealing in domestic exchange, to brokerage in stocks and bonds, and finally to private investment banking.[11]

During the first part of the nineteenth century, still another type of middleman in the investment process was the professional auctioneer, who sometimes specialized in stocks and bonds but often sold merchandise as well. These men handled securities just as they did any other property. Peter P. F. Degrand, one of Boston's leading auctioneers between 1825 and 1865, advertised regularly in the *Boston Daily Advertiser*; for example, in October 1834 he offered stock in 37 banks and 26 insurance companies. In the next decade, his advertisements, together with the reports of sales on the Boston Stock and Exchange Board, were the two sources of price quotations from which the *Boston Evening Transcript* compiled its lists.[12]

The importance of the auctioneer in the security markets is attested to by the fact that many stockbrokers, resenting his competition, tried to exclude him from membership in the stock exchanges. The distinction between auctioneer and broker, however, was not always very rigid or precise. Degrand, who advertised himself as an auctioneer, was listed in the *Boston Daily Advertiser* as a "Stock, Exchange, and Money Broker," and he was among the original thirteen brokers, "the oldest and best names in State-street," who organized the Boston Stock and Exchange Board. At once he became an active member of the new organization, and the first securities that were traded on the Boston Board came from his list.[13]

Degrand continued his auction business as did other members of

10. Taylor, *Transportation Revolution,* 321.
11. Ezell, *Fortune's Merry Wheel,* 82–83; Henrietta M. Larson, "S. & M. Allen — Lottery, Exchange, and Stock Brokerage," *Journal of Economic and Business History,* III (May 1931), 424–45; Redlich, *Molding of American Banking,* II, 68–69.
12. *Boston Daily Advertiser,* December 27, 1824; October 6, 1834; *Boston Evening Transcript,* June 8, 1846.
13. *Boston Daily Advertiser,* October 6, 1834; Boston Stock Exchange, *The Boston Stock Exchange* (Boston, 1930), 7–10; *The Bankers' Magazine,* XVIII (December 1863), 479; Joseph G. Martin, *Martin's Boston Stock Market* (Boston, 1886), 152.

the board, much to the annoyance of the regular brokers. They considered auctioneering a technique likely "to interfere with the business of the Board," as well as to deprive them of new commissions, at this time fixed at 2.5 percent on what was "usually considered the par value." [14] In March 1848 the brokers, "properly jealous of their rights," voted that any member of the board who attended a public sale of stocks should vacate his seat unless he had the special permission of the board or made a sale by order of executors, administrators, trustees, or corporations.[15] The Boston ruling was much less stringent than the one then in effect in New York.

The organization of stock and exchange boards, with their anti-auctioneering rules, led to a considerable decline in the stock auction business and caused many auctioneers to become brokers. After 1820 the latter probably constituted the largest single group of financial intermediaries. Nearly all the several principal types of brokers — exchange, money, note, and mortgage — traded in securities. Some of the merchant-exchange dealers also fulfilled a brokerage and investment banking service, dealing first in municipal bonds, and later adding bonds of local railroads.[16]

The stock and exchange brokers, supposedly the specialists in security trading on the exchanges, performed a diversity of functions. S. Gilbert & Sons, one of the founders of the Boston Stock and Exchange Board, traded in gold, currency, domestic exchange, and bank stocks.[17] In buying and selling new and old securities, brokers acted either on orders of investors, both large and small, or on their own account. A number of these brokers became respected members of the growing scurity markets, and occasionally they acted as investment counselors. Issuers of new securities, especially firms that expected to sell their bonds or stocks locally, placed great store in the broker's advice, friendship, and ability to place an entire issue directly or to divide it among his clients. In such cases, it was the custom for the issuer to offer "concessions to influential brokers, hoping to secure the advertising value of their names." But with or without concessions, nearly all brokers traded on a commission basis, not risking their own capital.[18]

During the 1840's, as the economy gradually recovered, many

14. [Clarence W. Barron and Joseph G. Martin] *The Boston Stock Exchange* (Boston, 1893), 1–3; *Boston Evening Transcript*, June 8, 1846.
15. *The Bankers' Magazine*, XIV (April 1860), 821. See also Joseph G. Martin, *Twenty-One Years in the Boston Stock Market* . . . (Boston, 1856), 30.
16. Willard E. Atkins *et al.*, *The Regulation of the Security Markets* (Washington, 1946), 23.
17. *Boston Daily Advertiser,* January 1, 2, 1824.
18. Atkins *et al.*, *Regulation of the Security Markets,* 23–24; Federal Reserve Bank of Boston, *Annual Report for 1960: A History of Investment Banking in New England* (Boston, 1961), 9; Henrietta M. Larson, *Jay Cooke: Private Banker* (Cambridge, Mass., 1936), 65; Jules I. Bogen, "A New Era of Investment Banking," *Investment Banking,* VIII (March 23, 1938), 124.

brokers became private bankers; the transition often was imperceptible. Like the broker, the private banker sold securities in large or small blocks; the former he usually placed with institutions or wealthy individuals, the latter, with less affluent clients who called at his office. Because the offices of most private bankers had counters over which customers bought and sold their securities, these operations came to be known as "over-the-counter" transactions.[19]

The chief difference between the broker and the private banker often was the fact that the latter accepted deposits, discounted loans, and traded extensively in foreign exchange.[20] The terms frequently were used interchangeably, not only by the uninitiated, but also by such informed groups as the banking commissioners of New York state and the compilers of professional directories. The fact that most private banks were partnerships and did not issue their own notes (paper money) distinguished them from incorporated banks. Lack of a charter also made it unnecessary for private banks to submit to state or federal inspection or disclose the amount of their capital, two privileges they guarded jealously. As in the case of brokerage houses, private banks also fulfilled numerous functions that were similar to, and in competition with, those of the incorporated banks.

One of the earliest brokers to turn private banker was Nathaniel Prime of New York City. He had started on Wall Street as a stock and commission broker in 1790, admitted his first partner eighteen years later, and, after adding and dropping several others, in 1826 established the firm of Prime, Ward & King. The firm is generally acknowledged to have been the "first large genuine private banking house" in the United States and "one of the first, if not the first, private bank to engage in embryonic investment banking activities."[21]

Prime, Ward & King competed with the second BUS in buying and selling foreign exchange, a business so dominated by Biddle's bank that few other private bankers dared enter it before 1840. Prime, Ward & King's ability to do so was a result of the great strength it drew from its very close ties with the Barings, dating from 1810.[22] In the 1820's the New York house started to negotiate and contract for securities. From then on, either alone or in alliance with other private and incorporated banks, it became increasingly involved in the security markets, bidding for new issues of federal and state bonds and trading in them extensively. Before the panic

19. John C. Loeser, *The Over-the-Counter Securities Market: What It Is and How It Operates* (New York, 1940), 7.
20. Redlich, *Molding of American Banking,* II, 60, 62, 64, 66, 81n.6.
21. *Ibid.,* II, 67.
22. *Ibid.,* Ralph W. Hidy, *The House of Baring in American Trade and Finance . . . 1763–1861* (Cambridge, Mass., 1949), 49.

of 1837 this firm was one of the principal houses from which the securities of American states crossed the Atlantic.[23]

Another important house with foreign ties was the Boston firm of John E. Thayer & Brother. Like many other private banks of that day, it grew out of a one-man organization, started in the 1820's by John Eliot Thayer.[24] His foreign exchange and brokerage office on Central Wharf was adjacent to some of the city's most prominent auctioneers, commodity brokers, and merchants. In 1826 Thayer moved to State Street, the financial center of Boston. The firm kept an address on or near that street even after John Thayer's death in 1857.[25]

Thayer's business grew rapidly and substantially. By 1834, when he participated in establishing the Boston Stock and Exchange Board, he was worth about $200,000 and considered to be an influential capitalist. In 1839 Thayer took his younger brother Nathaniel, who was a partner in a mercantile firm on Long Wharf, into a new house, John E. Thayer & Brother.[26] It provided a wide range of banking services, becoming "the agent and occasional banker of heavy capitalists in Salem, Providence, New York, Philadelphia and elsewhere."[27] Its principal activities included brokerage and banking as well as investing in, and trading in, railroads, savings banks, insurance, shipping, western lands, and Massachusetts real estate. It bid for government and state bonds and new and old corporate issues and sold them to both large and small investors. And it acted in numerous capacities for its issuing clients. Dealing in foreign exchange was probably one of its major activities; for a time it was the largest seller of exchange in Boston. Its principal English correspondent was McCalmont & Co., which, according to the Barings, was "a good second-rate house."[28] Such were the

23. Redlich, *Molding of American Banking*, II, 335; Larson, *Jay Cooke*, 65–66; Bray Hammond, "Long and Short Term Credit in Early American Banking," *Quarterly Journal of Economics*, XLIX (November 1934), 79–103.

24. Most of the primary source material for the Thayer story is based on an incomplete set of miscellaneous manuscripts, letterbooks, ledgers, and other accounts deposited in Baker Library, Harvard Graduate School of Business Administration, by Kidder, Peabody & Co., the successor firm to John E. Thayer & Brother.

25. *Boston Evening Transcript*, September 29, 1857; George E. Ellis, *Memoir of Nathaniel Thayer, A.M.* (Cambridge, Mass., 1885), 11; Writers' Program, Massachusetts, *Boston Looks Seaward, The Story of the Port, 1630–1940* (Boston, 1941), 101; [Abner Forbes] *The Rich Men of Massachusetts* . . . (2d ed., Boston, 1852), 66.

26. Various secondary works give different dates, ranging from 1834 to 1840, for the formation of this partnership. The account for John E. Thayer & Brother in John Thayer's personal ledger, however, has an opening entry for June 1839. John E. Thayer, "Ledger, 1836–1857," Thayer MSS.

27. Forbes, *Rich Men of Massachusetts*, 66.

28. Hidy, *House of Baring*, 394, 447–48, 463; Ralph W. Hidy, "The Organization and Functions of Anglo-American Merchant Bankers, 1815–1860," *The Journal of Economic History*, I (December 1941), 53–66.

functions and status of the firm in 1865. In that year Nathaniel Thayer retired and a new partnership (Kidder, Peabody & Co.) was organized by three employees to carry on the business.

Just as John E. Thayer & Brother and Prime, Ward, & King are examples of brokers and foreign exchange dealers who became private bankers fulfilling some modern-day investment banking functions, so Thomas Biddle & Co. of Philadelphia and Alexander Brown & Sons of Baltimore are illustrations of commercial and mercantile firms that made a similar transition and became successful private banking firms. Though probably less important and, as a group, certainly far less affluent than their counterparts in London, Paris, or Amsterdam, merchant bankers in America entered the securities business in much the same way. In both Europe and the United States the reputation and wealth of these firms grew out of their mercantile activities; and their various financial services, such as buying and selling bills of exchange, extending credit, and acquiring securities to use as a medium of exchange, were all essential functions for conducting their merchandise trade. Once these merchants started buying and selling securities, whether related to or independent of their mercantile affairs, they performed an investment banking function.

Thomas Biddle & Co. was founded on money originally accumulated by John Biddle, a pre-Revolutionary merchant and foreign trader. After the War of 1812 his heirs started contracting regularly for new federal and state issues, and by the 1830's Thomas Biddle had become a highly successful banking and brokerage house on the level of John E. Thayer.[29]

In contrast, Alexander Brown & Sons of Baltimore was a merchant-banking firm that, until the panic of 1837 at least, carried on both financial and mercantile operations simultaneously, in the manner of European houses. Established in 1800 as a linen merchant, the firm expanded into cotton shipping and exporting and then to dealing in exchange and issuing letters of credit, as well as buying securities for its own account. In 1813 William, the oldest son, opened W. & J. Brown & Co. in Liverpool, England, a firm that subsequently became Brown, Shipley & Co.; in 1818 another son, John A. Brown, started a branch in Philadelphia; and in 1826 the youngest opened a New York City office under the name of Brown Brothers & Co. Shortly thereafter, the Browns started cooperating with other commercial bankers and brokers in contracting for new securities, including state and railroad bonds, using their Liverpool branch to distribute them in England and on the Continent. Soon the Browns' banking business — dealing in new securities, operating in foreign exchange, issuing commercial and travelers' letters of credit, and accepting deposits — surpassed in importance their mer-

29. Redlich, *Molding of American Banking*, II, 69.

chandise trade. During the 1840's, Brown, Shipley competed strongly with the Barings in financing Anglo-American trade and in marketing American securities. By the end of the nineteenth century the New York and Baltimore firms ranked among the leading private banking houses in the United States specializing in investment services.[30]

While brokers and merchants moved into private banking, another highly important group of financial middlemen also operated extensively in the growing American securities markets. They were the agents, correspondents, and representatives in the United States of foreign, private banking houses. Every major European financial center, but particularly London, had several private banking houses that dealt heavily in American securities. Upon these firms the New York, Boston, Philadelphia, and Baltimore brokers and other middlemen depended to buy the issues for which they had contracted.[31]

The undisputed leader, especially during the years 1828 to 1843, was Baring Brothers & Co. Established in 1763, this firm originally was a manufacturer of serge cloth. It expanded into the import and export business, buying and selling wool and other commodities in the United Kingdom and on the Continent, and then it moved from and through foreign trade into international finance. Its connection with America predated the Revolution. In 1828 it added an American partner, Joshua Bates, who had more than a decade of experience in European business and numerous influential contacts in the United States. Two years later the firm appointed, as its resident agent in the United States, Thomas Wren Ward, a prominent Boston and New York businessman. At the same time it greatly increased the number of its financial correspondents.[32] Two of its most prominent American correspondents were the second BUS and Prime, Ward & King.

After 1835 N. M. Rothschild & Sons of London joined the ranks of the Barings' competitors by trading heavily in American securities. In 1837 the Frankfurt and Paris Rothschild firms sent the twenty-one-year-old, German-born August Belmont to the New World to investigate financial conditions. Belmont learned that the

---

30. *Ibid.*, II, 69, 335; Frank R. Kent, *The Story of Alexander Brown & Sons* (Baltimore, 1925), 133; Hedges, *Commercial Banking and the Stock Market before 1863*, 43; *Finance and Industry; The New York Stock Exchange: Banks, Bankers, Business Houses, and Moneyed Institutions of the Great Metropolis of the United States* (New York, 1886), 62; Hidy, *House of Baring*, 345–46, 366–67; Anna Rochester, *Rulers of America: A Study of Finance Capital* (New York, 1936), 79. Despite its Marxist slant, the Rochester book's facts are generally reliable. See also John Crosby Brown, *A Hundred Years of Merchant Banking: A History of Brown Brothers and Company* . . . (New York, 1909); Brown Brothers & Company, *Experiences of a Century, 1818–1918* (Philadelphia, 1919); John A. Kouwenhoven, *Partners in Banking: An Historical Portrait of a Great Private Bank, Brown Brothers Harriman & Co., 1818–1968* (Garden City, 1968).
31. Cochran, "Entrepreneur in American Capital Formation," 356.
32. Hidy, *House of Baring*, 8, 12, 78–79, 82–83, 97–101, 108–09.

Rothschilds' American representative, J. L. and S. I. Joseph & Co., had gone bankrupt in the panic of 1837, and he immediately persuaded the Rothschilds to recognize a new firm, August Belmont & Co. of New York City, as their agent in the United States. Belmont's rise on Wall Street was rapid; he profited from foreign exchange transactions; commercial and private loans; corporate, real estate, and railroad investments; and as one of the government's fiscal agents during the Mexican War.[33]

That same year George Peabody, a native of Massachusetts, but then a dry-goods merchant in Baltimore, moved to London, where he launched his investment banking career by selling Maryland bonds. After acting as an individual contractor for several years, in 1851 Peabody established his own banking house. Three years later he took in as his partner Junius Spencer Morgan, formerly a member of Beebe & Co., a dry-goods merchant of Boston. When Peabody retired in 1864, Morgan became head of the firm, changing the name to J. S. Morgan & Co.[34] Led by the Barings, these foreign banking houses provided the principal means by which English and Continental capital was transferred to the United States for investment.

In the generation before the Civil War, investment banking in the United States was conducted largely by private bankers, chiefly the agents of foreign banking houses or their principal American allies and competitors. Among them were old, well-established houses, such as Prime, Ward & King, and newer ones opened during the 1840's and 1850's, when the Mexican War and the railroads required large amounts of long-term capital.[35]

Corcoran & Riggs was one of the newer private banking houses that achieved national prominence in the 1840's. Established in 1837 in Washington, D.C., Corcoran & Riggs started in investment banking by subscribing to the federal loan of 1843 and made its reputation by bidding successfully for the largest portions of the Mexican War issues of 1847 and 1848, the latter in alliance with the Barings and several others. Corcoran & Riggs developed strong ties with European sources of capital, intimate political connections in Washington, and widespread business contacts. John E. Thayer, for example, was a close friend and associate of Corcoran. After the Mexican War, Corcoran & Riggs continued to play a major role in investment banking, expanding its dealings to include state issues and the new railroad bonds that were floated to pay for the pre-Civil

---

33. *Ibid.*, 79; Irving Katz, *August Belmont: A Political Biography* (New York, 1968), 5–8; Redlich, *Molding of American Banking,* II, 336–37.
34. Frederick Lewis Allen, *The Great Pierpont Morgan* (New York, 1949), 8–9; Redlich, *Molding of American Banking,* II, 350–53.
35. Redlich, *Molding of American Banking,* II, 70, 343–44.

War construction boom.[36] Another firm of the era was Duncan, Sherman & Co., the New York house in which J. P. Morgan started as a clerk in 1857, and which had close ties with George Peabody of London.[37]

Also prominent in the 1840's, but not so closely tied to European capital, was E. W. Clark & Co. of Philadelphia, established in 1837 by Enoch W. Clark, a distant relative of Solomon Allen of lottery fame. Clark had been a partner in S. & M. Allen, and when that firm collapsed in 1836 he opened a stock brokerage house in partnership with Edward Dodge, his brother-in-law. The firm was joined in 1839 by Jay Cooke, who became a partner in 1843. Clark and Dodge became "the first brokers in the city," enjoying "the unlimited confidence of the banks and merchants."[38] E. W. Clark kept "money all over the United States" and, in the tradition of S. & M. Allen, established several branch offices. During the Mexican War it was one of the principal outlets for government bonds, and after the war it bought and sold state, municipal, and railroad bonds. Forced into bankruptcy during the panic of 1857, the firm was immediately reorganized, and, under Edward W. Clark, the founder's son, E. W. Clark resumed business almost at once. Shortly thereafter, the former New York branch reopened as an independent firm under the name of Clark, Dodge & Co.[39]

An important Boston firm started in 1848 was Lee, Higginson & Co., brokers and domestic exchange dealers, "hustling" for customers in the street in competition with John E. Thayer, among others. After the Civil War, the firm became a private bank emphasizing investment services to a small and limited clientele of New England capitalists.[40] Others, like Speyer & Co., founded in 1845 by members of an old, famous international banking family of Frankfurt, made a similar transition, in this case from dealers in foreign exchange and merchandise importers; and Hallgarten & Co. started out in 1850 as brokers and general bankers.[41]

---

36. Thayer to Corcoran, March 26, 1851, April 22, 1851, August 12, 1855, in William Wilson Corcoran Papers, Library of Congress, Washington, D.C.

37. Redlich, *Molding of American Banking,* II, 347–48, 350–52; Hidy, *House of Baring,* 394; Frances Carpenter, ed., *Carp's Washington . . .* (New York, 1960), 143–44; Herbert L. Satterlee, *J. Pierpont Morgan: An Intimate Portrait* (New York, 1939), 92.

38. E. W. Clark & Co., brief typescript "History" in the possession of Professor Henrietta M. Larson; Redlich, *Molding of American Banking,* II, 71–72.

39. E. W. Clark & Co., "History," *passim;* Redlich, *Molding of American Banking,* II, 350.

40. "Lee, Higginson & Co., Boston," *The Bankers' Magazine,* LXXIV (May 1907), 813–14; Marshall W. Stevens, "History of Lee, Higginson and Company," 19–23, typescript in Baker Library. See also Henry G. Pearson, *Son of New England: James Jackson Storrow, 1864–1926* (Boston, 1932), 97–99; Bliss Perry, *Life and Letters of Henry Lee Higginson* (Boston, 1921), 268–76.

41. *The New York Times,* November 1, 1914; Paul H. Emden, *Money Powers*

Of all the private banks that existed in the United States before the Civil War, Winslow, Lanier & Co. probably came closer than any other to providing clients with most of the investment banking services commonly associated with the great banking houses of the latter part of the nineteenth and early twentieth centuries. Established in 1849, this firm, like many others at the time, was organized to do a general banking business, but its "chief object" from the very beginning, according to James F. D. Lanier, one of the founders, was "the negotiation of railway securities," especially those of the western lines, which up to this time had been sold almost exclusively to Boston bankers and investors. Within the next five years this firm, probably more than any other, contributed substantially toward making New York City the principal center of American railroad finance. Lanier established ties with some of the most distinguished and influential financiers in Europe, among them the Governor of the Bank of England, the heads of the Rothschild banks of London and Paris, and the manager of Hope & Co. of Amsterdam.[42]

The Lanier firm advertised extensively to reach the public, but also sold directly to private and institutional investors and to other bankers for resale abroad. Very often it sold issues by sealed bids, a method long employed by the federal government, but one rarely used up to this time for railroad bonds.[43] The firm assisted its clients in numerous ways, acting as purchasing agent, registrar, and transfer and fiscal agent. "At one period," Lanier asserted, "we paid the interest on fifty different classes of securities."[44] The partners accepted memberships on directorates, gave advice on financial matters, presided over reorganizations, and proposed policies designed to protect the value of the securities they had sponsored. At the time, these were novel functions for a banker to undertake.

By the end of 1854, when Winslow, Lanier "gradually withdrew from railway negotiations and confined itself almost entirely to banking," it was the leading railroad securities house in the United States, and its operations "extended to almost every State in the Union where railroads were in progress."[45] The firm continued to

---

of Europe in the Nineteenth and Twentieth Centuries (New York, 1938), 274; U.S. Senate, Committee on Finance, 72d Cong., 1st Sess., *Sale of Foreign Bonds or Securities in the United States: Hearings* . . . (4 pts., Washington, 1931–32), pt. 2, 1115–16.

42. J. F. D. Lanier, *Sketch of the Life of J. F. D. Lanier* (New York, 1870), 18, 41–43; Alfred D. Chandler, Jr., *Henry Varnum Poor: Business Editor, Analyst, and Reformer* (Cambridge, Mass., 1956), 88–89; Redlich, *Molding of American Banking*, II, 354–55.

43. Chandler, *Henry Varnum Poor*, 88. See, for example, the sealed-bid notice for a $400,000 issue of Michigan Southern Railroad Co. bonds in *American Railroad Journal*, XXIII (November 9, 1850), 712.

44. Lanier, *Sketch of the Life of J. F. D. Lanier*, 20.

45. *Ibid.*, 61.

provide various financial and advisory services to the companies whose securities it had negotiated and, after the Civil War, joined with other investment houses in bringing out many new railroad issues. Lanier's son Charles joined the firm in 1860 and, after his father retired, headed its operations.[46]

By the outbreak of the Civil War, investment banking in the United States, as practiced by such firms as Winslow, Lanier and a few others, had achieved a significant degree of maturity and specialization. The number of these quasi-modern investment houses, however, still was small. The variety of individuals and firms engaged in the business of buying and selling securities was almost as great in 1860 as it had been a half century earlier. Wealthy individuals, such as John Murray Forbes, the Boston capitalist who, together with a select group of friends, including John E. Thayer, helped to finance and manage several western railroads, continued to perform various investment banking functions, much as they had in the past.

Most of the firms and individuals engaged in buying and selling securities were either private bankers, stock brokers, auctioneers, or other bankers, very often commercial ones. All of them performed some of the functions now associated primarily with modern investment banking. The activities of many of these firms and individuals still were not very far removed from their original occupations and trades, some of which had been nonfinancial. The fact that most capital users, except for the railroads, did not need the services of an investment house accounts, of course, for the continued presence on the capital markets of so many types of unspecialized middlemen and the small number of banking houses that emphasized the business.

Even so, the number of firms providing investment banking services in 1860 was substantial and scattered in many cities. The leading houses, however, those with the reputation, connections, and ability to handle issues of as much as $1 million, were located in the large, mercantile centers of the eastern seaboard, notably New York, Boston, Philadelphia, and Baltimore, where most of the country's wealth was concentrated and where well-established stock exchanges were in operation.

The transition from unspecialized middleman to investment banker was greatly accelerated by the Civil War. Never before had the federal government been forced to raise so much money under such inauspicious circumstances. The methods devised to sell war loans brought about important changes in the size and operation of the country's investment banking community. Besides concentrating the securities business still further in the hands of the private banker

46. *The Commercial & Financial Chronicle,* CXXII (March 13, 1926), 1410; *The New York Times,* August 28, 1881.

and the stock broker, the war stimulated the rise of many new investment firms and the growth of new financial centers. It also forced bankers, brokers, and other dealers in government bonds to cooperate to a greater degree than ever before. Many of the business ties formed at this time were continued after the war, just as some of the practices developed during these years were employed later in refunding the government debt and in financing railroads and other large enterprises.

Abraham Lincoln's first Secretary of the Treasury, Salmon P. Chase, hoped to finance the war by loans distributed through the traditional method of calling for competitive bids. But the response was so poor and the need so pressing that he turned to the metropolitan banks and persuaded several in New York, Boston, and Philadelphia to take a $150 million bond issue at par. They failed to dispose of the whole issue, however, for the principal buyers of government bonds in the past objected to paying par. Yet Chase believed that accepting anything less would reflect on the country's credit.[47] Relations between the Treasury and the banking group were strained further by Chase's general distrust of banks and the conflicting views of the Treasury and the bankers over the method by which they were to pay for the bonds. The bankers expected the Treasury to keep its receipts on deposit with them, but Chase insisted that they pay in specie. The situation was complicated still further by unfavorable reports from the military front and fear that the diplomatic crisis over the *Trent* affair would lead to war with Great Britain.[48] These and other considerations precipitated a major financial crisis. In December 1861 the banks suspended specie payments, and the next month the government did likewise.

To meet the Treasury's pressing needs, Congress passed, late in February 1862, the Legal Tender Act. This law authorized the government to issue $150 million of Treasury notes, which the public quickly labeled "greenbacks," and $500 million 6 percent twenty-year bonds. Since these were callable in five years, they became popularly known as "five-twenties." Although Chase offered them at par, the fact that the public could pay for them in greenbacks soon made the par requirement more of a fiction than a reality. Even so, sales were discouragingly poor, and Chase called on Jay Cooke, who with his brother-in-law had opened a private banking house in Philadelphia in 1861.

Cooke proposed a hard-selling, well-organized campaign designed to appeal to the patriotism and self-interest of the small investor, who, he anticipated, would buy and hold on to the bonds. Chase's

---

47. Larson, *Jay Cooke*, 100, 105, 110; Edward C. Kirkland, *Industry Comes of Age, 1860–1897* (New York, 1961), 14–15; Redlich, *Molding of American Banking*, II, 357.

48. Larson, *Jay Cooke*, 118; Paul Studenski and Herman E. Krooss, *Financial History of the United States* (2d ed., New York, 1963), 141–43.

decision to adopt the Philadelphia banker's suggestion resulted partly from Cooke's persuasiveness and partly from the refusal of bankers and large investors to buy bonds at par. Lack of sympathy for the Union's cause among British bankers and government officials, moreover, strained financial ties with the London capital market and forced the government to cultivate new sources of domestic capital.[49]

Until the Civil War the small investor had not been a significant figure in the security markets. In the summer of 1861, Cooke, together with Drexel & Co. of Philadelphia,[50] succeeded in selling a $3 million Pennsylvania state defense issue at par. By aggressive salesmanship, extensive newspaper advertising, and effective use of agents on a statewide basis, Cooke reached both large institutional and small individual investors. Subscriptions ranged from $300,000 to as little as $50. The successful distribution of this loan at par, when few other bankers had thought it would be possible, was a major triumph for Cooke, although his methods shocked conservative bankers, including Drexel. Cooke's success with the Pennsylvania loan impressed Secretary Chase, however, and led him to appoint the Philadelphia banker as special agent responsible for marketing the unsold portion of "the great five-twenty loan."

In distributing these bonds Cooke employed all the methods he had used in selling the Pennsylvania loan, but on a far larger scale. He organized a nationwide sales force and directed it from his enlarged Philadelphia headquarters. In February 1862 he opened a Washington branch, both to make sales and to keep him informed of potential developments that might affect the progress of the bond drive. In New York, Boston, and other cities, Cooke recruited private bankers and brokers to act as his subagents. In the western states, where there were few private bankers or brokers, Cooke selected local businessmen, community leaders, or other volunteers. All in all, he gathered some 2,500 salesmen, in every state and territory. He aided this huge organization by a nationwide publicity campaign, which included the press as well as posters, handbills,

49. Larson, *Jay Cooke*, 116–17; Redlich, *Molding of American Banking*, II, 358.
50. In January 1838 Francis M. Drexel, an Austrian portrait painter, opened a brokerage office in Philadelphia primarily dealing in "uncurrent money." He soon turned to private banking and by the late 1840's was negotiating and contracting for securities. In 1847 his two oldest sons, Francis A. and Anthony J., entered the firm, and in June 1863, after their father's death, a third son, Joseph William, joined his brothers as a partner. During the Civil War, Drexel & Co. dealt heavily in government bonds and after 1865, under the very able and energetic leadership of Anthony J. Drexel, the firm developed into a specialized investment house, serving the financial needs of railroads and other corporations. See [Drexel & Co.] *A New Home for an Old House* (Philadelphia, 1927), 36–42; *Finance and Industry*, 110; *U.S. v. Henry S. Morgan et al.*, "Transcript of Trial, Defendant's Opening, Mr. [Arthur H.] Dean" (December 15, 1950), 1044–45; Witt Bowden's biographical sketches of Anthony J., Francis M., and Joseph W. Drexel in the *Dictionary of American Biography* (22 vols., New York, 1928–58), V, 455–57.

and educational literature. These reminded every social and economic group of its duty to country and self.[51]

Cooke's strategy proved successful. By mid-January 1864, when the loan was closed, his organization had sold nearly $362 million, the Treasury having disposed of the rest. His profit from selling the five-twenties amounted to only $\frac{1}{16}$ of 1 percent, which was very small, considering the risk and expense involved.[52] But close connections with the Treasury permitted the firm to make money by trading in five-twenties and other government securities on its own account, and greatly enhanced its prestige.

This close relationship aroused considerable criticism; and though charges made against Cooke were proved to be false, the Treasury did not engage him again as agent until January 1865. Then it asked him to take over the sale of a new loan, popularly known as "seven-thirties" because they bore 7.30 percent interest.

Cooke at once arranged to extend and refine the selling methods he had employed before. He opened "Working Men's Savings Banks," which were nothing more than night sales offices designed to accommodate laborers who could not buy bonds during the day. Cooke also employed the European practice of supporting the market price of the bonds during their initial distribution, using his own and Treasury funds. Though scarcely known in the United States before then, this technique later became common practice.

Cooke's bond drives were the first successful, large-scale effort to extend the security market to accommodate thousands of individuals with small savings, many of whom had never before owned a bond. The success of these operations made his firm the leading, most widely known banking house in the country. At the end of the war Cooke was as confident of his firm's future as he was that the nation's economic growth and progress would continue.

Adjustment to peacetime conditions, however, proved difficult. The anticipated sales of government securities never materialized to the extent to which Cooke had hoped. Public interest in government securities declined rapidly in the postwar years with the return of more familiar investment opportunities, such as improving farms, buying urban real estate, and expanding individually owned businesses.

To service the financial requirements of the Treasury alert businessmen established many new private banking and brokerage houses, not only in New York, Boston, and Philadelphia, but also in other northern and western cities as well.[53] Investment banking in

51. Larson, *Jay Cooke,* 105–08, 119–25, 128–32. Redlich, *Molding of American Banking,* II, 356.
52. Larson, *Jay Cooke,* 148.
53. Larson, *Jay Cooke,* 217. According to *Merchant's & Banker's Almanac, 1865* and *1870,* the number of brokers and private bankers in New York City increased by more than tenfold — from 170 in 1865 to 1,800 in 1870; the number of private

Chicago, for example, grew rapidly during the Civil War, when a number of new banking and brokerage houses were organized to sell government bonds. In 1850, according to one estimate, there were ten private banks in Chicago; by 1865, the number had doubled, if not trebled.[54]

Some of these new firms started out as agents or correspondents of Cooke. One of these, Fisk & Hatch, a private banking partnership, was organized in New York in 1862 by Harvey Fisk and Alfrederick Hatch, two Vermonters with considerable banking experience. The firm sold millions of bonds for Cooke in New York and New England. By 1865 it had established a national reputation.[55] Two other New York City investment houses also owed much of their financial strength and reputation to the war and their association with Cooke. Vermilye & Co., founded in 1830, was but relatively unimportant before 1860, and Livermore & Clews was the predecessor of Henry Clews & Co.[56]

Houses like Fisk & Hatch differed from most of the earlier banking or brokerage partnerships, which were primarily wholesalers of securities, usually with well-established foreign connections. Civil War bankers like Fisk & Hatch were essentially domestic retailers, large-scale marketers of government bonds in small amounts to individuals of modest means, many of whom they reached through intensive sales and advertising campaigns.[57]

The war also gave rise to a second and, as events were to prove, a much more durable group of investment houses — those estab-

---

bankers, excluding brokers, in Boston rose from 18 to 40, and in Philadelphia, from 36 to 43 (figures approximate).

54. Bessie Louise Pierce, *A History of Chicago* (3 vols., New York, 1937–57), II, 130, 134. See also *Merchant's & Banker's Almanac, 1865,* 47; F. Cyril James, *The Growth of Chicago Banks* (2 vols., New York, 1938), I, 339. James claims eighty-six private banking houses in Chicago for 1861. The difference between his figure and the one cited by Pierce is probably due, in part, to the fact that the compilers did not always separate private bankers from brokers and dealers in commercial paper. Sometimes compilers also listed the same firm under different categories, and often they omitted prominent investment firms. Furthermore, many private bankers called themselves brokers in order to avoid paying the special license and other taxes imposed on bankers. In Brooklyn alone the Commissioner of Internal Revenue filed more than a hundred suits in 1869, and his office was preparing others against that "certain class of men in what is called 'The Street,' who style themselves as brokers, but who transact a [banking] business." *The New York Times,* September 3, 1869.

55. Harvey E. Fisk, "Fisk & Hatch, Bankers and Dealers in Government Securities, 1862–1885," *Journal of Economic and Business History,* II (August 1930), 706–10. In 1884 the firm's name was changed to Harvey Fisk & Sons. See also the obituary of Pliny Fisk, *The New York Times,* March 31, 1939.

56. Larson, *Jay Cooke,* 124; Redlich, *Molding of American Banking,* II, 360–61. See also Matthew Hale Smith, *Twenty Years among the Bulls and Bears of Wall Street* (Hartford, 1870), 400–13; *Finance and Industry,* 70; *The Commercial & Financial Chronicle,* LXXV (November 15, 1902), 1067.

57. William L. Raymond, "Investment Banking in the United States: Its Historical Background and Development — The Wholesalers," *Barron's,* VI (May 31, 1926), 7; Bogen, "A New Era of Investment Banking," 124–25.

lished by German Jews. Most of these men had come to the United States in the late 1830's and early 1840's, usually in their late teens or early twenties, very often single, and with a small amount of money and almost no financial experience.[58] Very few of them started out as bankers. Philip Speyer, an immigrant from Frankfurt in 1837, was an outstanding exception. The son of a wealthy, established banking family and trained in foreign exchange and finance, Speyer was sent to the United States to establish an American office for his family's banking business.[59]

Nearly all the other German Jews who came to the United States before the Civil War, however, started out either as peddlers, wholesale and retail merchants, dry-goods importers, or commodity brokers. One of the first of these émigrés was Joseph Seligman, a native of Bavaria. Arriving in the United States in 1837 at the age of seventeen with less than $100, Seligman took a job as a store clerk in a small Pennsylvania mining town. He quit twelve months later to become a peddler. Within the next five years he was joined by seven brothers, all of whom started out as either peddlers, itinerant merchants, or storekeepers, selling domestic and imported dry goods. As their capital increased, the Seligmans extended their merchandising activities across the United States. By the time of the Civil War, they had established outlets in New York, St. Louis, and San Francisco. While the family was in the importing business, it shipped gold bars from San Francisco to New York and then sent them on to London to pay for their wool and silk imports.[60]

Profits from wartime government clothing contracts increased the brothers' already sizable wealth, so that by 1862, when they established the banking firm of J. & W. Seligman & Co. in New York, they were worth close to $1 million.[61] During the war the Seligmans sold government bonds, distributing some $200 million in Germany, where they had opened a branch in Frankfurt the year in which they started their New York bank. In 1864 they established a branch in London, and later still others in Paris, Amsterdam, Berlin, San Francisco, and New Orleans. In the tradition of the early Rothschilds, each Seligman bank was in the charge of a brother or some other close member of the family.[62] After the Civil War the Seligman banks expanded their investment business rapidly, and in 1869

58. Barry E. Supple, "A Business Elite: German-Jewish Financiers in Nineteenth-Century New York," *Business History Review,* XXXI (Summer 1957), 143–51.
59. Francis J. Oppenheimer, "James Speyer on Money and Railroad Problems," *The Magazine of Wall Street,* XXV (February 7, 1920), 435–36, 438.
60. Supple, "A Business Elite," 150, 153; Isaac Seligman, "Reminiscences" (typescript, dated July 1925), 3. I am indebted to Professor Henrietta M. Larson for permission to use this material.
61. Supple, "A Business Elite," 155.
62. Larson, *Jay Cooke,* 217–18; Seligman, "Reminiscences"; Redlich, *Molding of American Banking,* II, 362; *Finance and Industry,* 78.

James Seligman, the head of the New York bank, purchased a seat on the New York Stock Exchange.

Abraham Kuhn and Solomon Loeb, the brothers-in-law who founded Kuhn, Loeb & Co., entered finance in much the same way as did the Seligmans. About 1850 Kuhn and Loeb opened a general merchandise and clothing store in Lafayette, Indiana. A few years later they moved the business to Cincinnati, where there was a sizable German colony. In 1865 they dissolved the partnership. Two years later they opened a private bank in New York City. They soon were conducting an investment business as well, selling government and railroad bonds in the United States and Germany.[63] The firm prospered, but its rise to prominence did not occur until after 1875, when Jacob H. Schiff was admitted as a partner.

Jacob Schiff was to Kuhn, Loeb what the elder J. P. Morgan was to his firm. The son of an old, distinguished Frankfurt family of modest means with academic and mercantile ties, Schiff started his business career in 1861, when he was fourteen. In 1865 he emigrated to the United States and accepted a clerkship in a brokerage firm in New York. Two years later, after having been licensed as a broker, he became a partner in Budge, Schiff & Co., where he remained until 1872, when the firm was dissolved and he returned to Germany. Two years later, when Abraham Kuhn, the head of Kuhn, Loeb, offered him a partnership, Schiff returned to the United States. In 1885 Solomon Loeb, the last of the founders, retired, and Schiff, who had married one of Loeb's daughters, became head of the firm.[64]

Marcus Goldman, the founder of Goldman, Sachs, was a native of Bavaria. Arriving in the United States in 1848, he started out as a peddler in Philadelphia, and in 1869 moved to New York City, where he opened his own banking and brokerage house. Before 1882, when Samuel Sachs was admitted as a partner and the firm's name changed to M. Goldman & Sachs, this house dealt chiefly in commercial paper, buying short-term notes from small manufacturers and reselling them to banks and other institutional investors.[65]

63. [Kuhn, Loeb & Co.] *Investment Banking through Four Generations* (New York, 1955), 7, 14; Cyrus Adler, *Jacob H. Schiff: His Life and Letters* (2 vols., New York, 1929), I, 11–12; "Mr. Kuhn and Mr. Loeb," *Fortune*, I (March 1930), 116, 118; Redlich, *Molding of American Banking*, II, 362. See also John Moody and George K. Turner, "Wall Street: How Morgan Built the Money Power," *McClure's Magazine*, XXXVIII (June 1911), 186.

64. Cyrus Adler, "Jacob Henry Schiff," *Dictionary of American Biography*, XVI, 430–32; Redlich, *Molding of American Banking*, II, 385–87. See also Bertie C. Forbes, *Men Who Are Making America* (New York, 1921), 329–30; "Jacob H. Schiff," *The Magazine of Wall Street*, XXVI (October 16, 1920), 837–38, 869.

65. Supple, "A Business Elite," 147, 172. In 1885, when the first two partners started admitting their sons to the business and the firm's present name was adopted, Goldman, Sachs & Co. ceased being primarily a commercial paper house. Its activities were widened to include a foreign exchange and letter of credit business, and in the late 1890's the partners purchased a seat on the New York Stock Exchange.

The origins of Lehman Brothers date back to the 1840's, when Henry, Emanuel, and Mayer Lehman left Bavaria for the United States. Settling in Montgomery, Alabama, Henry Lehman, the oldest and the first of the three brothers to cross the Atlantic, spent his first year peddling. He then opened a general merchandise store and, after his brothers joined him, about 1847, entered the cotton brokerage business. In the 1850's the Lehmans opened a branch in New Orleans, and during the Civil War, Emanuel Lehman, while on a commission for the Confederacy, established another branch in New York City. After the war Lehman Brothers expanded its brokerage business to include other commodities, such as coffee, sugar, grain, and petroleum.[66]

The growth, financial strength, and durability of these German-Jewish houses rested largely on their access to European capital. Their success stemmed also from the close family, ethnic, religious, and business ties, and the care they employed in conserving their capital and maintaining its liquidity.

Just about the time when these German-Jewish émigrés were entering finance in New York, a third group of investment banking firms was being established there. These were the so-called "Yankee houses," since the founders were either native New Englanders or men who had received their early business experience in that region. Many of them had been merchants engaged in foreign and domestic trade, whose banking experience had grown out of dealing in gold, currency, and foreign exchange, or in extending mercantile credit. These Yankee firms also enjoyed strong international banking connections, especially with London.

It was this group that produced the greatest American investment banker of all time, John Pierpont Morgan. In 1854, when his father, Junius Spencer Morgan, left the United States to accept a partnership with George Peabody & Co. in London, Pierpont Morgan was seventeen years old and had just graduated from high school. After two years of further study in Switzerland and Germany, young Morgan gained some experience with George Peabody & Co. Then, in 1857, he was sent to New York as a clerk and junior accountant in Duncan, Sherman & Co., the firm's American representative.[67] Morgan remained with the firm for three years, learning the business.

In 1860 he left Duncan, Sherman to organize, with a partner,

---

66. See *ibid.*, 147, 152, 156; [Lehman Brothers] *A Centennial: Lehman Brothers, 1850–1950* (New York, 1950), 7–24; Arthur D. Howden Smith, *Men Who Run America* (New York, 1935), 111–12. As in the case of Goldman, Sachs, Lehman Brothers became an investment bank in the 1880's, when the sons of the founders were made partners.

67. Albert W. Atwood, "John Pierpont Morgan," *Dictionary of American Biography*, XIII, 175; Satterlee, *J. Pierpont Morgan*, 92; Muriel E. Hidy, "George Peabody: Merchant and Financier, 1759–1869" (unpub. diss., Harvard University, 1939), ch. xiii. See also Allen, *The Great Pierpont Morgan*, ch. ii.

J. Pierpont Morgan & Co., and this firm then became the American agent of George Peabody. During the next four years Morgan was largely on his own, receiving relatively little direct supervision from his father. It was at this time that he entered into certain "dubious enterprises." One was the well-known Hall Carbine Affair, which may have influenced the elder Morgan to provide his son with an older, more judicious partner.[68] In 1864 Charles H. Dabney, with whom Morgan had been closely associated in Duncan, Sherman, left that firm to join his former associate in establishing Dabney, Morgan & Co. The new firm's principal business was dealing in foreign exchange and gold; buying and selling securities, mostly on commission; and acting as the agent of the elder Morgan, who now headed his own firm in London (J. S. Morgan & Co.), Peabody having retired in 1864. In 1870 Dabney retired, and Morgan, who was then thirty-three and already had accumulated a comfortable fortune, also considered retirement. Early in 1871, however, Anthony J. Drexel persuaded him to reconsider retirement in favor of accepting a partnership in Drexel & Co., which then had branches in New York, London, and Paris. By having Morgan join his firm, Drexel strengthened his New York City connections and, even more important, acquired a close tie with J. S. Morgan & Co., whose position and prestige among international bankers at this time were high.[69] Alliance with Morgan thus transformed Drexel & Co. into an international banking house. The Morgans — both father and son — also benefited; association with the Drexels gave them a connection with one of the strongest private banking houses in the United States. Only Cooke appeared to surpass them.

Morgan became a full partner in Drexel & Co., and Drexel, Morgan & Co. was established in New York with the same partners as those of the Philadelphia house. The New York firm was a merger of Dabney, Morgan with the Drexel's New York branch, Reed, Drexel & Co. For the first few years the Drexels dominated both the New York City and Philadelphia firms, but in 1876, after the retirement of Joseph W. Drexel, his son Anthony J. Drexel headed the "parent firm," while Morgan assumed leadership in New York. Morgan's influence over policy, both in New York and in Philadelphia, grew steadily. In 1890 his father died, and three years later, Anthony Drexel, the last of founder Joseph W. Drexel's sons, died

68. Morgan is excoriated for his role in the "great scandal" involving the Hall carbines by Gustavus Myers, *History of the Great American Fortunes* (New York, 1936), 549–52. Years later R. Gordon Wasson, a Morgan partner, presented the facts of the case more completely and with greater objectivity in *The Hall Carbine Affair: A Study in Contemporary Folklore* (New York, 1948). See also Allen, *The Great Pierpont Morgan*, 19–20; Redlich, *Molding of American Banking*, II, 382.

69. Satterlee, *J. Pierpont Morgan*, 148–49; Allen, *The Great Pierpont Morgan*, 37. The elder Morgan's prestige was enhanced considerably by his successful flotation of a difficult $50 million loan for the defeated French government, which the Prussians had chased from Paris.

also. Morgan, who was then fifty-six and the preeminent investment banker in the United States, became the dominant figure in all the Drexel-Morgan banks.[70]

Just about the time Dabney, Morgan was organized there appeared on the New York financial scene another one-time Yankee merchant, Levi Parsons Morton, a former partner of Junius Morgan in the dry-goods business. In 1855 Morton had organized his own wholesale dry-goods company in New York City. When secession prevented him from collecting debts from his southern customers, he was forced into bankruptcy, but he recovered rapidly, paid his creditors, and in 1863 organized his own private bank on Wall Street, L. P. Morton & Co. One of his partners, Walter H. Burns, was Pierpont Morgan's brother-in-law. Burns soon left for London, however, where he established L. P. Morton, Burns & Co. In 1869 George Bliss became Morton's partner. He was the son of a poor Massachusetts farmer, but he had amassed several millions as a dry-goods merchant, and he contributed $2.5 million to the newly organized firm of Morton, Bliss & Co. About the same time, John Rose, a wealthy Canadian lawyer, businessman, and politician residing in London, became Morton's English partner. A new firm, Morton, Rose & Co., was organized to take over the business of L. P. Morton, Burns & Co.

During the 1870's the Morton firms were important chiefly as distributors of the Treasury's refunding loans. Morton's liberal campaign contributions, his close political friendship with high-ranking Republican leaders, and his relationship with the Morgans proved useful to his banking house, while the diplomatic activities of his English partner in facilitating the Anglo-American settlement of 1871–72 contributed further to the firm's growing prestige and influence. In the years between Appomattox and the panic of 1873, Morton emerged as one of Cooke's most powerful rivals.[71]

70. Satterlee, *J. Pierpont Morgan,* 148–49; Redlich, *Molding of American Banking,* II, 364, 382; Atwood, "John Pierpont Morgan," 175. See the testimony of Morgan's son in U.S. Senate, Special Committee Investigating the Munitions Industry, 73d and 74th Congs., *Munitions Industry: Hearings* . . . (40 pts., Washington, 1934–43), pt. 25, 7479. Consult also *U.S. v. Henry S. Morgan et al.,* "Transcript of Trial, Defendant's Opening" (December 15, 1950), 1045. At the time, the change involved no alteration in the original partnership agreement or in the name of the Philadelphia firm, which was purposely kept the same "in order to preserve the Drexel name." The New York partners continued to be, as before, partners in Drexel & Co., Philadelphia, or, as it was soon to become increasingly known, "the Philadelphia end of J. P. Morgan & Co."

71. Irving Katz, "Investment Bankers in American Government and Politics" (unpub. diss., New York University, 1964), ch. iv; Frederic L. Paxson, "Levi Parsons Morton," *Dictionary of American Biography,* XIII, 258–59; Redlich, *Molding of American Banking,* II, 362–64; H. Parker Willis, "George Bliss," *Dictionary of American Biography,* II, 372–73. Most of Bliss's fortune was made at the beginning and close of the Civil War. Believing that prices would rise appreciably if war broke out between the North and South, Bliss bought heavily before the onset of hostilities, making huge profits; subsequently, foreseeing the end of the war, he

Competing with these private bankers were a number of incorporated commercial banks. The most prominent among them was the First National Bank of New York, founded in 1863. Its first president, Samuel C. Thompson, was the son of a private banker who had conducted an active investment banking business prior to his failure during the panic of 1857. After a stint as compiler and publisher of the *Bank Note Detector,* a widely used periodical "listing and describing counterfeit or fraudulent [bank] notes in circulation," he and two sons opened a brokerage firm on Wall Street.[72] Subsequently, the Thompsons, together with a few others, became the principal organizers, officers, and employees of the First National Bank. George Fisher Baker, a twenty-three-year-old clerk in the New York State banking department in Albany, was one of the original incorporators, and he became the bank's first teller.[73]

From the beginning the First National engaged actively in investment banking. It sold war bonds, and after the Civil War the bank continued buying and selling government securities, sometimes taking entire issues and reselling them to brokers and bankers for further distribution. Together with Cooke and other investment firms, it participated in various refunding syndicates. After Cooke suspended operations, three of his partners, among them Harris C. Fahnestock, the manager of Cooke's New York City office, joined the First National and extended its investment banking business still further. In the year 1879, according to one of its commemorative pamphlets, it "handled" $780 million of federal bonds, "completing their receipt and delivery without error or loss." [74] By this time Thompson had retired, and Baker, who was not yet forty years old, had become president. A close friend of Pierpont Morgan, with whom he collaborated frequently, Baker developed the First National into a full-fledged investment house. By 1900 it was one of the half dozen leading investment banking institutions in the country.

The rapid rise to prominence of these new banking groups during the war led to increased competition. The rivalry among these houses to win the distribution of the government's postwar refunding issues was intense. Cooke's decision to finance the Northern Pacific Railroad was in part dictated by the postwar decline in the

---

sold before the first postwar price drop, thus augmenting his fortune still further. See also Robert McElroy, *Levi Parsons Morton: Banker, Diplomat and Statesman* (New York, 1930), 67, 84, and *passim.*

72. N. S. B. Gras and Henrietta M. Larson, *Casebook in American Business History* (New York, 1939), 512. See also Paul B. Trescott, *Financing American Enterprise: The Story of Commercial Banking* (New York, 1963), 35, 53.

73. N. S. B. Gras, "George Fisher Baker," *Dictionary of American Biography,* XXI, 44–45.

74. Quoted in Bertie C. Forbes, *Men Who Built America* (New York, 1927), 14–15.

government securities business. "If the business were always to be as now," one of his partners declared late in 1869, "we had better quit." [75] Other factors influencing Cooke's decision to move into railroad finance were his success in selling, in cooperation with E. W. Clark, a $2.5 million issue of Lake Superior & Mississippi Railroad bonds in 1869 and his wish to participate in the profits that some of his earlier wartime associates were earning in marketing railroad securities.

In January 1870 Cooke undertook to market the first of a series of bond issues for the Northern Pacific Railroad. The company gave him "exclusive control" over its bond offerings, chose him as its sole fiscal agent, and allowed him to appoint two of the railroad's directors and two members of its executive committee. In addition, he became purchasing agent for both building supplies and equipment. For these services Cooke's firm was to receive, at "nominal cost," shares equivalent to approximately 80 percent of the railroad's total capital stock of $100 million, the remaining shares being paid him as a bonus "at the rate of $200 for every $1,000 in bonds sold." Part of the stock bonus Cooke was to pass on as a bonus with the bonds.[76]

Cooke planned to seek the assistance of European bankers and to launch an aggressive, widespread sales campaign in the United States. His plan failed, however, partly as the result of poor timing and his inability to implement it effectively. Furthermore, he was unable to make the road's officials honor their contract to build only as fast as Cooke could dispose of the bonds. On several occasions the railroad overdrew its account, but Cooke continued to pay the road's bills, utilizing his depositors' funds.

Cooke's other major source of difficulty arose from his failure to win the cooperation of European bankers. He tried to interest the Rothschilds, sending his partner William Moorhead to Europe in the hope of persuading them to take $5 million of bonds. Moorhead promised to include the Rothschilds in the Treasury's next refunding loan, which Cooke hoped to win. He also offered to try to get the government to transfer to the Rothschild house its London deposit, which was held by the Barings. But the head of the London Rothschilds believed the Northern Pacific issue too risky, Moorhead

---

75. Quoted in Gras and Larson, *Casebook in American Business History*, 308.
76. *Ibid.*, 312. During the later decades of the nineteenth century it was common to give bond buyers a stock bonus. The practice contributed to the speculative character of equities. Conservative investment houses drew a very clear distinction between railroad bonds and stocks in describing them to investors. The former, according to Henry Clews, compared favorably with government securities, whereas the latter were "completely under the control of speculative directors and stock cliques." See Henry Clews & Co., *Railroad Investments* (New York 1870); U.S. Industrial Commission, *Report* . . . (19 vols., Washington, 1900–02), IV, pt. 2, 210.

wrote, "and no power in America, or England" could alter his view.[77] The same reasons motivated the other leading London houses, many of which already were loaded with American railroad issues. To add to Cooke's difficulties, the outbreak of the Franco-Prussian War in 1870 frightened European bankers and capitalists, making it impossible for him to sell many bonds on the Continent.

Finally, the domestic market also failed to respond to Cooke's aggressive salesmanship. The country's business and financial interests still were recovering from the bankruptcies, depressed conditions, and general loss of confidence that followed the Wall Street debacle on Black Friday, September 24, 1869. It was only after the most strenuous efforts that he was able to sell the first $5 million bond issue. A year later he launched a public sales campaign especially designed to attract small investors. He failed to realize, however, that many investors had bought war bonds largely for patriotic reasons. He could make no such stirring appeal on behalf of the Northern Pacific. Competition for investment funds, furthermore, came from more established and familiar enterprises. The money market was tight, and revelations of speculation and corruption in other railroads combined to defeat Cooke's hope of selling a sufficient quantity of bonds in the United States.

By mid-August 1873 the Northern Pacific's indebtedness to Jay Cooke's firm stood at $5.1 million. The market for bonds was poor, business conditions generally were no better, and Cooke's depositors grew uneasy and started to withdraw their money. Unable to stand the pressure of withdrawals, Cooke & Co., the "foremost American banking house," was forced to close its doors on September 18, 1873, triggering a severe panic on Wall Street. That catastrophe brought down numerous other well-known firms, among them Fisk & Hatch, E. W. Clark, and Henry Clews.[78]

The panic and depression resulted in far-reaching changes in the leadership of the investment banking community. Very few of the bond houses that had dominated the securities business in the 1860's survived the crisis without considerable loss, either in assets, influence, or prestige. Leadership now passed to international

---

77. Larson, *Jay Cooke,* 265–66. In 1871 the State Department dropped Baring Brothers as its financial agents. See *The New York Times,* September 2, 1871.

78. Larson, *Jay Cooke,* 409, 421–22. In December 1873 Charles D. Barney, Cooke's son-in-law, opened a brokerage firm of his own. Later he enlarged its activities to include underwriting, and soon thereafter it was performing all the functions of a "fully developed investment bank." On January 1, 1938, it merged with Edward B. Smith & Co., a Philadelphia firm established in 1892. The new partnership, organized in New York, resulted in the present-day firm of Smith, Barney & Co. See *U.S. v. Henry S. Morgan et al.,* "Corrected Opinion of Harold R. Medina (February 4, 1954), 65–66, 68. Fisk & Hatch reopened in December 1873, was forced to suspend again for two weeks in May 1884, and was dissolved in March 1885, twenty-three years after its founding. See Fisk, "Fisk & Hatch," 713, 717–18; *Boston Evening Transcript,* May 16, 1884.

bankers like Drexel, Morgan, Speyer, Seligman, and a few others, whose strength lay in their ability to mobilize large amounts of foreign and domestic capital and direct it into the building and improvement of railroads.[79] For the next forty years at least, the firms that these men headed, together with a few others, such as Lee, Higginson, and Kidder, Peabody in Boston, occupied a commanding position in American investment banking.

For instance, Lee, Higginson's strength stemmed largely from the close personal ties that existed between its partners and a select group of Boston investors, including the officers and directors of various New England financial institutions. The confidence these capitalists placed in this firm gave it access to a large, steady source of funds.[80] Kidder, Peabody also could count on similar sources of domestic capital, but its greatest advantage derived from its foreign connections, especially its close ties with Baring Brothers, for which it acted as agent and attorney. During the 1880's Kidder, Peabody advertised itself as "Foreign Bankers" and specialists in commercial and travelers letters of credit.[81]

Other firms rose to prominence, but very few large issues were distributed during these years without the participation of one or more of these strong, prestigious, and influential private banking houses. According to one listing, "the fourteen greatest private banking houses on Wall Street" in 1894 were of either German-Jewish or Yankee origin.[82]

The panic of 1873 also brought a speedy end to the first great effort of investment bankers to develop a large, permanent class of small investors. The security firms that had specialized in mass distribution during the war years were replaced by others concentrating on originating, underwriting, and distributing new issues abroad and to a select American clientele of large, individual and institutional buyers, including a number of smaller banking and brokerage

---

79. Lance E. Davis, "Capital Immobilities and Finance Capitalism: A Study of Economic Evolution in the United States, 1820–1920," *Explorations in Entrepreneurial History,* 2d ser., I (Fall 1963), 88–105. In 1932, while testifying before a Senate committee, James Speyer, the son of the founder of Speyer & Co., declared that after the Civil War "our firm sold millions of dollars of American railroad securities in Germany, Holland, Switzerland, and all over Europe, especially for railroads in California, such as the Southern Pacific and the Central Pacific, which were built with European money secured by us acting as intermediaries." See *Sale of Foreign Bonds or Securities, Hearings,* pt. 2, 609.

80. See George F. Redmond, *Financial Giants of America* (2 vols., Boston, 1922), I, 85; Frederic Haines Curtiss, *Fifty Years of Boston Finance, 1880–1930* (Boston, 1930), 2.

81. See, for example, the advertisements in *The Commercial & Financial Chronicle,* XLIV (January 1, 1887), iii; *The New York Times,* January 26, 1886.

82. See Edward G. Riggs *et al.,* "Wall Street," *Munsey's Magazine,* X (January 1894), 380–81; John Moody and George K. Turner, "Masters of Capital in America — Wall Street — The City Bank: The Federation of Great Merchants," *McClure's Magazine,* XXXVII (May 1911), 73–87.

houses.[83] Some of these wholesalers continued their retail business much as they had done earlier. Kidder, Peabody, for instance, had regular clients who appeared at its Devonshire Street office, in Boston, to buy railroad or other bonds that the firm sponsored. But the reputation of this firm, like that of Morgan and other leading international banking houses, rested on its ability to dispose of large blocs of securities. By the end of the 1870's, these were the bankers on whom large corporations relied for this service.[84]

Nearly all the methods that the investment banker employed in the conduct of his business before World War I were in use during the Cooke era. The growth of "active" investment banking, a term that Professor N. S. B. Gras used to describe the increasing influence of financiers over the policies of the corporations whose securities they sponsored, had its origins in the late 1840's and 1850's. Men like John Murray Forbes and firms like Winslow, Lanier started to assume a broader and a more permanent role in the affairs of the companies they assisted. After the Civil War, as issues grew larger and their flotation more risky, investment banking representation on railroads' boards of directors and finance committees became increasingly common. And though the kind of "directorial responsibility" that Cooke exercised over the Northern Pacific after 1870 was exceptional for the time, it became far less so by the end of the century.[85]

Similarly, the practice for an issuer to employ the same banking house repeatedly to market its securities also appears to have started during the late 1860's, when a number of railroads formed close ties with investment firms. In 1867, after Cooke had refused the job, the Union Pacific employed John J. Cisco & Son, a New York City firm, as its special agent in charge of bond sales. Fisk & Hatch became the fiscal agent of the Central Pacific and the Chesapeake & Ohio; the Rock Island relied heavily on Henry Clews; and the Pennsylvania Railroad employed Drexel until about 1880, when Kuhn, Loeb became this line's "principal bankers." [86]

83. During these years commercial and savings banks, trust companies, and life insurance companies were the investment bankers' principal customers. Bogen, "A New Era of Investment Banking," 125; Willis and Bogen, *Investment Banking,* 225. See also Raymond, "Investment Banking in the United States," 7, 20; Boston, FRB, *Annual Report, 1960,* 17; [Financial Advertisers Association, Investment Research Committee] *Advertising Investment Securities* (New York, 1928), 29.

84. Davis, "Capital Immobilities," 89, 94–95; Chandler Hovey to author, October 26, 1961. See also R. H. Inglis Palgrave, "An English View of Investments in the United States," *The Forum,* XV (April 1893), 198.

85. Thomas C. Cochran, *Railroad Leaders, 1845–1890: The Business Mind in Action* (Cambridge, Mass., 1953), 35, 70.

86. Larson, *Jay Cooke,* 245, 257; Redlich, *Molding of American Banking,* II, 360, 362, 417n.417; Fisk, "Fisk & Hatch," 706, 712; [Kuhn, Loeb & Co.] *Investment Banking Through Four Generations,* 8, 11; U.S. Senate, Committee on Interstate Commerce, 74th Cong., 2d Sess.–75th Cong., 3d Sess., *Investigation of Railroads,*

At first these arrangements were not looked upon by participants as at all exclusive or permanent. Most railroads continued to deal with several banking houses, and not a few of them appear to have sought to maintain the financial independence and advantages that came from being able to choose among several banking firms. The Union Pacific, for example, turned to Kidder, Peabody for a loan in 1869, using its securities as collateral;[87] and as late as 1881, John Murray Forbes, who was then president of the Chicago, Burlington, & Quincy, wrote of the benefits to be derived from having "two strings to our bow" and not being "*tied* to one House." [88]

The various financial services that Cooke performed for the Northern Pacific, like many of those that Winslow, Lanier provided some of its clients, marked a major stage in the evolution toward modern investment banking practices. The methods that these and a few other houses initiated and developed in the 1850's and 1860's became the accepted techniques that investment houses used to finance the railroad and industrial expansion of the later nineteenth and early twentieth centuries.

Holding Companies, and Affiliated Companies: Hearings . . . (29 pts., Washington, 1937–42), pt. 19, 8269. Between 1880 and 1899 Kuhn, Loeb marketed some $48.6 million of bonds for the Pennsylvania Railroad. For the details on these transactions see *Investigation of Railroads: Hearings,* pt. 19, 8552.

87. U.S. Pacific Railway Commission, *Report* . . . (10 vols., Washington, 1887), II, 767–68.

88. Quoted in Cochran, *Railroad Leaders,* 72.

2 From Railroads to Industrials, 1873–1900

Between 1870 and 1900 the burgeoning American economy provided investment bankers and other financial intermediaries with a host of challenges and opportunities. During these years both the supply and demand sides of the capital markets underwent numerous significant changes. Investment bankers, operating in a virtual regulatory vacuum, were largely free to respond as they saw fit to the changing market forces of the times. The policies and practices they developed during these years brought them to positions of power and influence that few, if any, had thought possible a decade earlier.

The greatest demand for investment banking services came from the railroad industry. The carriers were the largest corporate seekers of funds in the capital markets at the time and as such were the investment bankers' principal customers. Between the panic of 1873 and the beginning of recovery in 1878, some 400 banks collapsed and more than 47,000 businesses failed, including many railroads. New railroad construction dropped from 5,217 miles in 1873 to 1,606 miles two years later. By 1879 it had risen to 5,006 miles, and the expansion continued, with some interruption in the years 1883–1885, until the nation suffered another major setback in 1893. Between 1878 and 1893 total railroad mileage nearly tripled, and the combined total outstanding issues of railroad bonds and stocks more than doubled, increasing from $4.8 billion to $9.9 billion.[1]

Fluctuations in the business cycle largely determined the character of the railroads' needs for investment banking services. Depressions called for emphasis on one function, prosperity for stress on another. During the depressions of the 1870's and 1890's, the investment bankers' chief concern was reorganizing the capital structures of defaulting roads. In prosperity the carriers turned to investment houses for capital to expand and improve their rail systems.

Meanwhile, the need of a growing number of other large businesses, many of them new industrial combinations, also began to offer opportunities to investment bankers. After 1870 innumerable family-owned enterprises organized themselves as corporations, and the ambitions of many industrial leaders resulted in the formation of trusts and other combinations. Most of the capital for these large enterprises could not be supplied through reinvestment of earnings. The heads of these new industrial giants, like the railroad leaders

---

1. U.S. Bureau of the Census, *Historical Statistics of the United States, Colonial Times to 1957* (Washington, 1960), 427–29, 433, 636; Allan Nevins, *The Emergence of Modern America, 1865–1878* (New York, 1927), 298–304.

before them, turned to investment bankers for the funds they required.

Simultaneously, on the supply side of the capital markets, an increasing amount of funds seeking investment appeared on both sides of the Atlantic. Between 1870 and 1900, foreign investments in the United States more than doubled, increasing from approximately $1.4 billion to $3.3 billion.[2] At the same time capital accumulation was proceeding apace in the United States. In the nineteenth century "real saving per head . . . doubled every forty years," and there is "some evidence" to indicate that its rate of growth "was at a peak in the 1870's and 1880's."[3]

Two other changes in the capital markets of the late nineteenth century affected the behavior of investment bankers. The appearance of increasing numbers of railroad, industrial, and manufacturing companies resulted in the distribution of more equity issues than previously (see Exhibit 1). Before the panic of 1873, government and railroad bonds dominated the security markets; thereafter they increasingly shared the spotlight with corporate shares. A second parallel development was the continuing centralization of capital markets in New York, already clearly discernible in the 1850's, and, to a lesser extent, in Chicago and a few other growing regional urban centers.

A relatively small group of private, unincorporated banks handled the job of floating railroad securities, including various kinds of mortgage, equipment, and income bonds, as well as preferred and common stock. Most of these financial institutions, as noted before, had been established in the 1860's either by New Englanders or by German Jews. What distinguished these firms, such as Drexel, Morgan & Co. and J. & W. Seligman & Co., was their ability to recruit foreign capital. Some houses did this through branches of their own in Europe; others like Kidder, Peabody & Co. maintained close ties with a prominent London bank, in this case, Baring Brothers. These firms, together with several older houses, such as Winslow, Lanier & Co., Vermilye & Co., and Lee, Higginson & Co., underwrote and sold many of the railroad, government, and other corporate securities that were issued.

Despite the strength and reputation of these houses, they came nowhere near monopolizing the investment banking business. As in the pre-Civil War era, a substantial number of smaller private banks and brokerage firms, including several reorganized Civil War bond houses, as well as a growing number of commercial banks, such as

---

2. Eugene Staley, *War and the Private Investor: A Study in the Relations of International Politics and International Private Placement* (Garden City, 1935), 530. See also Edward C. Kirkland, *Industry Comes of Age: Business, Labor, and Public Policy, 1860–1897* (New York, 1961), 279, 304.

3. Raymond W. Goldsmith, *A Study of Saving in the United States* (3 vols., Princeton, 1955), I, 4.

Exhibit 1. Bond and stock offerings, 1885–1900 (in dollars)

Year	Issues for new capital	Old issues	Refunding issues	Total
		Bonds		
1885	103,844,000	27,700,000	65,715,000	197,259,000
1886	81,641,000	47,354,390	109,102,300	238,097,690
1887	180,386,000	16,304,000	146,787,321	343,477,321
1888	261,989,631	11,792,000	237,220,587	511,002,218
1889	206,864,000	6,050,000	176,806,000	389,720,000
1890	198,158,850	105,204,279	381,504,750	684,867,879
1891	191,397,700	16,187,000	80,061,000	287,645,700
1892	175,125,600	12,352,000	130,383,900	317,861,500
1893	139,272,000	42,178,000	107,353,400	288,803,400
1894	184,785,000	32,237,600	92,782,000	309,804,600
1895	166,526,300	15,587,000	75,162,100	257,275,400
1896	147,343,700	7,626,000	427,317,000	582,286,700
1897	87,720,502	15,713,500	253,981,900	357,415,902
1898	245,219,480	26,243,000	428,602,200	700,064,680
1899	156,304,760	22,908,000	346,171,480	525,384,240
1900	147,678,597	6,287,000	289,747,403	443,713,000
		Stocks		
1885	17,783,116	3,700,000	35,430,000	56,913,116
1886	54,006,350	67,236,800	208,226,200	329,469,350
1887	98,726,791	32,643,426	138,683,332	270,053,550
1888	62,408,357	10,872,475	175,447,443	248,228,275
1889	69,721,717	9,936,000	179,952,057	259,649,774
1890	161,461,729	10,490,747	263,039,854	437,992,330
1891	96,540,754	1,650,000	90,724,200	188,914,954
1892	99,905,900	48,364,850	88,765,355	237,036,105
1893	93,744,161	48,874,000	55,627,100	198,245,261
1894	36,616,253	4,800,000	209,776,750	251,193,003
1895	77,132,500	35,385,000	30,856,270	143,373,970
1896	76,573,572	–	514,158,643	590,732,215
1897	53,275,671	24,369,900	425,329,320	502,974,891
1898	69,754,130	52,646,600	405,753,266	528,153,996
1899	311,420,285	–	392,752,320	704,172,605
1900	296,550,572	130,205,000	194,179,428	620,935,000

Source: The Ticker, III (December 1908), 70.

the First National Bank of New York, continued to buy and sell securities.[4]

4. Fritz Redlich, *The Molding of American Banking: Men and Ideas* (2 vols., New York, 1947, 1951), II, 388–89.

Outside of New York, Boston, and Philadelphia, commercial banks often were the principal underwriters and distributors of new securities. In Chicago, for instance, incorporated banks floated most of the new issues that originated there. After the mid-1880's the First National Bank of Chicago became one of the leading distributors of middle western municipal and street railway bonds. By the beginning of the 1890's its bond department was originating local issues and underwriting and selling them through syndicates composed of Chicago and eastern banks and brokerage firms.[5]

Financing the railroad construction boom of the last two decades of the nineteenth century resulted in the extension and institutionalization of several investment banking practices that previously had been provided informally. The banker's relationships as the financial adviser and fiscal or transfer agent of the railroads he sponsored dated back to the late 1840's and early 1850's; the rise of railroad-banking alliances occurred in the 1860's, if not earlier; and the use of the syndicate to underwrite and distribute railroad bonds was introduced in the 1870's.

Bank representation on railroad directorates and finance committees after 1880 was an institutionalization of the close personal ties that commonly had existed between bankers and railroad officials before that date. In fact, some financiers continued to prefer the older, informal practices whereby the banker met with officials of the railroads he sponsored several times a year rather than serving as a director in formal meetings. Jacob H. Schiff, for one, deplored the inclination of many investment bankers to accept directorships and positions on key committees. The older way, he believed, was just as useful and less time-consuming, not to mention the fact that it allowed the banker to concentrate on more important business.[6]

Close, continuous relationships between railroads and the investment houses that financed them, whether formal or informal, were encouraged by both bankers and railroad officials because both benefited from them. The banker's presence on the board facilitated sales of a road's securities; it gave investors confidence that their interests were being better served; and it appeared to constitute either an endorsement of the issue's "investment quality" or "practically guaranteed" it.

The bankers desired this kind of representation in order to safeguard their own reputations. As the "financial watchdog" of the railroads he endorsed, the banker had the primary concern, as he saw it, of warning against corporate policies that might lead to

---

5. F. Cyril James, *The Growth of Chicago Banks* (2 vols., New York, 1938), I, 561–64.

6. Cyrus Adler, *Jacob H. Schiff: His Life and Letters* (2 vols., New York, 1929), I, 27–28.

financial difficulties and of encouraging those that promoted profits and stability. Very often this meant endorsing more conservative solutions to problems and rejecting unfamiliar ones, especially if they involved risking profits or threatening the value of the road's securities.[7]

The investment banker benefited in other ways as well. Usually the firm that originated an issue was appointed registrar of the railroad's securities; this meant that it kept the record of ownership, served as transfer agent, and usually acted as the corporation's bank of deposit. Even more important to the investment house than the fees and benefits it received was the knowledge it acquired of the railroad's operations and the friendships that developed with the road's officials. Whenever the railroad required additional capital it became common practice for it to call upon the banking house that had served it before and thus was most familiar with its current affairs. These advantages of banking representation were so important that many railroads included the names of the investment bankers on their boards in newspaper advertisements and prospectuses announcing new offerings.[8]

During the last two decades of the nineteenth century nearly all the major railroads in the United States developed close ties with one or more investment banking firms. Some of these associations continued well down into the 1920's. Around 1880 Kuhn, Loeb & Co. replaced the Drexels as the Pennsylvania Railroad's "principal bankers," or, to use a term more to the liking of a later president of this carrier, its "financial consultants." From that time on this railroad and all the companies that subsequently became part of its system relied almost exclusively upon Kuhn, Loeb for their major financing. Between 1880 and 1899 this banking firm, either alone or in cooperation with other investment houses, often Speyer & Co., floated nearly $49 million of this road's securities, and this sum was a mere trifle compared with the number and size of issues that Kuhn, Loeb handled for it during the first quarter of the twentieth century. Financing the Pennsylvania, together with managing the many sizable flotations for other lines, and the highly successful reorganization of the Union Pacific in 1897, made Kuhn, Loeb the leading banking house in the country specializing in railroad securities. By 1900 this firm was the principal banker of no fewer than ten major railroads, including some of the largest systems in the United States.[9]

7. Redlich, *Molding of American Banking*, II, 377.
8. *U.S. v. Henry S. Morgan et al.*, "Corrected Opinion of Harold R. Medina" (February 4, 1954), 24.
9. U.S. Senate, Committee on Interstate Commerce, 74th Cong., 2d Sess.–75th Cong., 3d Sess., *Investigation of Railroads, Holding Companies and Affiliated Companies: Hearings* . . . (29 pts., Washington, 1937–42), pt. 19, 8552. Between 1880 and 1926 the "major financial transactions" between Kuhn, Loeb and the

Kidder, Peabody's association with the Atchison, Topeka & Santa Fe illustrates the many activities of the investment banker as a railroad's "financial consultant." This Boston firm became banker for the road in 1870, when it launched a new construction program. With its principal office in Boston, and several of its directors and its president residents of that city, the management of the Santa Fe was, and for the next generation remained, closely tied to State Street. For a number of years its securities were owned almost entirely by Bostonians and listed only on the Boston Stock Exchange. In 1871 Francis H. Peabody, a Kidder, Peabody partner, joined the Santa Fe's board of directors and very shortly afterward became the chairman of its finance committee and subsequently the road's vice president. Between 1870 and 1888 Kidder, Peabody, usually with the assistance of its London correspondents, Baring Brothers, and sometimes with Winslow, Lanier, Lee, Higginson, or some other investment house, financed much of the Santa Fe's construction and acquisitions of new properties.[10] By 1888 the Santa Fe had developed from a sectional railroad, with most of its mileage in Kansas, into a full-fledged transcontinental, with 7,000 miles of track.

During the years of the Santa Fe's rapid growth, Kidder, Peabody had four principal responsibilities toward it. These were to provide new capital by floating the road's stocks and bonds, to act as its transfer agent, to serve as its bank of deposit, and to give financial advice to the management. In spite of these obligations, from 1879 the firm had not been represented on the directorate or in a management position. Since Kidder, Peabody and the Barings often were paid in stock, these two banking houses also were, for a time, among the Santa Fe's largest stockholders. Oliver W. Peabody, Francis's brother and partner, took an almost proprietary interest in this railroad. In March 1885 Oliver Peabody suggested to one of the road's directors and a large stockholder, that he use his influence with the Santa Fe's executives to have them build a line to the Pacific Coast and abandon their plans for one to the Gulf of Mexico.[11] On another occasion he recommended that Kidder, Pea-

---

Pennsylvania Railroad totaled $1.3 billion. See also *ibid.,* pt. 18, 7687–88; pt. 19, 8269–70, 8281; Adler, *Jacob H. Schiff,* I, 51–54, describes the principal roads that were financed by Kuhn, Loeb. See also the brief summary in "Mr. Kuhn and Mr. Loeb," *Fortune,* I (March 1930), 89. The story of the Union Pacific reorganization is told in George Kennan, *E. H. Harriman: A Biography* (2 vols., Boston, 1922), I, 116–30.

10. Francis H. Peabody to George C. Magoun, February 7, 1883, Kidder, Peabody & Co., "Confidential Letters," I, 3–5; Francis H. Peabody to Henry P. Kidder, August 9, 1863, *ibid.,* 7–9, Kidder, Peabody & Co. MSS., Baker Library, Harvard Graduate School of Business Administration. Sometimes wealthy Bostonians, usually personal friends of partners of Kidder, Peabody, some of whom were also depositors, were invited to participate in these flotations.

11. Oliver W. Peabody to Benjamin P. Cheney, March 4, 1885, Kidder, Peabody & Co., "Confidential Letters," I, 25–29.

body, the Barings, and Lee, Higginson form a syndicate to float securities to finance a further extension of the Santa Fe's line. "The property is increasing rapidly and largely in value and in influence," he wrote, "and has, on the whole, I think, the most honest and able management that I know of, of any railroad property here. We ought to keep it to ourselves." [12]

Building and consolidating the vast network of lines that made up the Santa Fe in the late 1880's imposed a heavy financial burden on the railroad. Its bonded debt nearly tripled between 1885 and 1888, jumping from $52 million to $154 million. Paying the interest put a serious strain on the railroad's resources, just when it faced a number of other problems, including a sharp decline in earnings.[13]

Kidder, Peabody's response to the Santa Fe's difficulties, first apparent late in 1887, was a three-part recommendation. The road should curtail expenditures, delay a new bond issue until its earnings had increased sufficiently to improve its credit, and reduce a proposed dividend. When these steps proved inadequate, and the road's financial condition worsened, Kidder, Peabody, consulted with the Barings.[14] The Boston firm then inaugurated a series of measures designed to save the road from bankruptcy. One recommendation was to remind the directors of their duty to pay all fixed charges out of available cash and curtail all expenditures. This was followed by other proposals that resulted in the road's giving Kidder, Peabody representation on its finance committee by appointing to it the firm's principal New York partner, George C. Magoun. The Boston bankers also required that all expenditures in excess of $25,000 be authorized by the Santa Fe's finance committee and that the road's accounting department adopt the uniform railroad bookkeeping system. Once these changes were made, Kidder, Peabody agreed to provide some much needed new capital by selling $7 million 6 percent three-year notes, secured by a second mortgage.[15]

Meanwhile Kidder, Peabody proposed and effected even more comprehensive reforms. The first of these the Santa Fe adopted at its annual meeting in May 1889, and it introduced others shortly thereafter. Together they involved nothing less than a complete re-

---

12. Oliver W. Peabody to Francis H. Peabody, September 20, 1886, *ibid.*, I, 46–47.
13. Arthur M. Johnson and Barry E. Supple, *Boston Capitalists and Western Railroads* (Cambridge, Mass., 1967), 320.
14. Kidder, Peabody & Co. to Atchison, Topeka & Santa Fe Finance Committee, July 30, 1888, Kidder, Peabody & Co., "Confidential Letters," II, 59; Kidder, Peabody & Co. to Wm. B. Strong, president, October 2, 1888, *ibid.*, 68–69; Kidder, Peabody & Co. to Baring Brothers & Co., October 9, 1888, *ibid.*, II, 69½.
15. Kidder, Peabody & Co. to William B. Strong, October 16, 1888, Kidder, Peabody & Co., "Confidential Letters," II, 70–71; Francis H. Peabody to J. J. McCook, October 20, 1888, *ibid.*, 72–73. A native of Cambridge, Massachusetts, Magoun had joined Kidder, Peabody as a clerk in 1865, when the firm was founded.

organization of the road's management and financial structure. Their net effect was to make Kidder, Peabody and the Barings the dominant influence in the Santa Fe's affairs. The first step was to draw up a new slate of directors and to get Thomas Baring, the American representative of his family's banking house and subsequently Magoun's New York partner, to vote his 442,520 shares in support of the "Kidder, Peabody ticket" at the annual meeting. Since less than 180,000 other shares were represented, the bankers' slate won easily. This included six new directors, two of whom were Kidder, Peabody partners. Four months later a third partner was added: Francis Peabody, who had previously served on the board. Magoun was made chairman and entrusted with all the Santa Fe's financial affairs; and the executive and finance committees also were reconstituted to give the bankers a clear majority.[16]

Once the Santa Fe's management had been changed to its satisfaction, Kidder, Peabody proceeded to reorganize the road's financial structure. Designed to "reduce fixed charges, consolidate a bewildering complexity of issues, simplify corporation structures, and fund the floating debt," the plan called for converting the more than three dozen kinds of outstanding bonds into two: general first mortgage and income bonds, the former paying 4 percent, the latter 5 percent. The exchange would not affect the bondholders' income, though they were asked to agree "to have part of their interest payments depend on current earnings, if available, rather than on a legal obligation." The railroad benefited from this plan because its fixed charges were reduced from $11.1 million to about $7.4 million.[17]

Kidder, Peabody also was searching for a way to prevent its reforms from being repudiated at a later date. In October 1889 Francis Peabody wrote to one of the newly appointed directors recommending that the stock be put into a voting trust vested in Kidder, Peabody "for protection of the property," with the trust set up in such a way as to guarantee the firm's control for three to five years.[18] Less than two months later, afraid that Jay Gould might try to win control of the road, Peabody made a similar suggestion to Magoun, this time proposing a ten-year voting trust, designed to assure Kidder, Peabody's control for a long enough period to dissuade speculators like Gould from trying to take the railroad away from them. "If he should do so," Peabody wrote, "it would not only be a great disaster to the property, but a terrible mortification for

---

16. Johnson and Supple, *Boston Capitalists and Western Railroads,* 325.
17. *Ibid.,* 326.
18. Francis H. Peabody to Edwin H. Abbott, October 23, 1889, Kidder, Peabody & Co., "Confidential Letters," II, 100–103.

K. P. & Co., who would practically have cooked the goose for him to eat." [19]

By the time Kidder, Peabody was intervening in the affairs of the Santa Fe and Kuhn, Loeb was becoming the banker of the Pennsylvania Railroad, J. P. Morgan's reputation as a railroad financier had been firmly established. In 1879 William H. Vanderbilt asked Morgan to sell 250,000 shares of the former's stock in the New York Central. By reducing his holdings from 87 percent to less than 50 percent, Vanderbilt hoped to quiet criticisms of his one-man rule. Concerned lest the sale of so large a block of securities publicly in New York would depress their price and arouse doubts about the property, he consulted Morgan. The latter agreed to market them privately in England through a syndicate headed by Drexel, Morgan and his father's firm, J. S. Morgan & Co. of London. The syndicate bought the shares from Vanderbilt at $120 and resold them at $130. In order to make the offering attractive, buyers were guaranteed an 8 percent dividend for five years and assured that their investment would be protected by having Morgan represent them on the Central's board of directors. When news of the sale reached Wall Street, it dominated conversation for a week. *The Commercial & Financial Chronicle* labeled it a "grand financial operation" and at once proclaimed the forty-year-old Morgan the leading railroad banker in the country.[20]

During the next fifteen years Morgan was concerned almost exclusively with railroad problems, financing new construction and reorganizing unprofitable lines. In 1880, operating through a syndicate headed by Drexel, Morgan, Winslow, Lanier, and August Belmont & Co., he sold a $40 million bond issue for the Northern Pacific. At that time this was "the largest transaction in railroad bonds ever made in the United States," according to *The Commercial & Financial Chronicle*. Five years later he negotiated a famous peace pact between the New York Central and the Pennsylvania that ended the prospect of a major railroad war between these two giant eastern trunk lines.[21] During the next few years he reorganized the Philadelphia & Reading, the Baltimore & Ohio, and the Chesapeake & Ohio, and arranged a conference among the heads of the

---

19. Francis H. Peabody to George C. Magoun, December 12, 1889, Kidder, Peabody & Co., *ibid.*, II, 106.

20. John K. Winkler, *Morgan the Magnificent: The Life of J. Pierpont Morgan (1837–1913)* (New York, 1930), 84–86. The other investment firms associated with Morgan in this transaction were August Belmont & Co. and Morton, Bliss & Co. See also Frederick Lewis Allen, *The Great Pierpont Morgan* (New York, 1949), 43–46; *The Commercial & Financial Chronicle*, XXIX (November 29, 1879), 554.

21. *The Commercial & Financial Chronicle*, XLI (October 17, 1885), 445–46. Morgan's career as a railroad financier is interestingly told in Allen, *The Great Pierpont Morgan*, chs. iv, vi.

principal anthracite carriers that resulted in their agreeing to limit the output of the mines they controlled and to maintain prices.

In all these transactions Morgan's primary concern was to protect both the interests of the investors and his own reputation. Like other responsible investment bankers, he realized that the success of his firm rested upon keeping the confidence of investors and other bankers. They held him accountable for the prosperity of the roads he endorsed, an obligation that Morgan accepted seriously, and he expected the managers of these lines to exercise a similar responsibility toward him. This meant putting an end to ruinous rate wars and senseless construction of parallel lines, as well as to the kind of financial buccaneering that had bankrupted many properties and undermined the reputation of railroad securities generally. What he expected of the roads he financed was prudent, conservative, honest management, and he was prepared to enforce such practices. He was not interested in managing the lines himself or building a railway empire that he could control to the benefit of his firm. Nor were these the reasons that led other reputable investment houses to intervene in the affairs of the railroads they assisted. Their purposes, like Morgan's, were to bring order and stability to an industry sorely in need of it, promote cooperation and harmony among competitors, and restore the investors' confidence in railroad securities.

To achieve these objectives, Morgan employed a variety of methods. "I never knew . . . a man who addressed himself more exclusively than Mr. Morgan did to the *ad hoc* situation and the *ad hoc* job that lay before him," one of his partners later declared. "He attempted simply to correct given situations which presented themselves to him as unsafe and destructive." [22] In the case of the Philadelphia & Reading and the Chesapeake & Ohio, he established voting trusts, appointing himself and other men in whom he had confidence as trustees. For instance, John C. Brown of Brown Brothers & Co. and George Bliss of Morton, Bliss & Co. served with Morgan as trustees of the Chesapeake & Ohio. By these voting trusts, most of which were set up to last five years, Morgan tried to make certain that the reorganized property would be managed by men he considered prudent. He hoped that once the voting trust had expired, the road's officials would have "become so confirmed in the practice of sound management that no such measures need be continued." [23]

When it was not possible to establish a voting trust, Morgan sought the same ends by informal means. In January 1889, in the

---

22. Thomas W. Lamont to R. Gordon Wasson, "Memorandum," dated March 27, 1939. I am indebted to Professor Henrietta M. Larson for permission to use this typescript.
23. *Ibid.*

hope of reducing rate wars and restoring profits to the major western roads, Morgan invited to a meeting in New York City the presidents of these lines, the heads of the principal eastern trunk lines, and the representatives of three other influential investment banking houses prominent in railroad finance. Besides Morgan, who represented both his own firm and his father's London house, present were John Brown and George Magoun, representing both Kidder, Peabody and the Barings, along with a few other large investors.[24]

Morgan had several reasons for calling this conference, officially known as the Interstate Commerce Railway Association. One was to organize a committee to enforce the Interstate Commerce Act, which Congress had passed two years earlier. Another was to reach agreement on rates that would ensure profits. A further purpose, Morgan said, "is to cause the members of this association to no longer take the law into their own hands when they suspect they have been wronged, as has been too much the practice heretofore. This is not elsewhere customary in civilized communities, and no good reason exists why such a practice should continue among railroads."[25] Whereas Morgan had opposed enactment of the Commerce Act, believing that the policies he advocated were more beneficial to everyone than those written into this statute, federal regulation was now a reality.

Morgan's effort to get the western roads to cooperate to everyone's advantage achieved little or nothing. They failed to honor the gentlemen's agreement that they had ratified at the New York meeting, and the era of "peace and plenty" that *The New York Times* somewhat cynically proclaimed would result from this conference did not follow.[26] Competition did not yield to cooperation; "suicidal rate cutting" continued much as before; and most railroad leaders displayed the same "covetousness, want of good faith, and low moral tone" that Charles Francis Adams, of the Union Pacific, had attributed to them on the first day of the meeting.[27]

Given the chance "to substitute law and arbitration for anarchy

24. Carl Hovey, *The Life Story of J. Pierpont Morgan* (New York, 1912), 137–45; Allen, *The Great Pierpont Morgan*, 59–62.
25. Quoted in Hovey, *The Life Story of J. Pierpont Morgan,* 139–40. See also Clarence E. Stedman, ed., *The New York Stock Exchange* (New York, 1905), 337.
26. Allen, *The Great Pierpont Morgan,* 62. Years later Gustavus Myers interpreted this agreement as marking the day when control of the nation's principal railroads passed into the hands of a small group of investment bankers. See his *History of the Great American Fortunes* (New York, 1937), 562–63, 568, 572–73; John Moody and George K. Turner, "Wall Street: How Morgan Built the Money Power," *McClure's Magazine,* XXXVIII (June 1911), 187–89, looked upon this conference, together with Morgan's previous railroad negotiations, as launching his firm on its long and profitable career in railroad finance or, as these two journalists preferred to label it, "tying up the railroad machinery of America into a working monopoly." See also George W. Edwards, *The Evolution of Finance Capitalism* (London, 1938), 174; Anna Rochester, *Rulers of America: A Study of Finance Capital* (New York, 1936), 27–28.
27. Quoted in Hovey, *The Life of J. Pierpont Morgan,* 141.

and might," to use the words of President George B. Roberts of the Pennsylvania, the railroad executives at the meeting in 1889 opted for the latter. Several years later, after the panic of 1893 and four years of depression had bankrupted nearly one-fourth of the country's railroads, the leaders of these lines accepted many of the very policies they previously had rejected. The reorganization plans that investment bankers now employed in rehabilitating distressed railroads were similar to those Kidder, Peabody had applied to the Santa Fe. They were designed, as one Kuhn, Loeb attorney later described them, to hold the whole railroad together by persuading the bondholders not to foreclose.[28]

The banker usually initiated these "rescue operations" by getting a federal court to appoint a receiver for the line and by working out a financial reorganization. The goal was to protect the bondholders' investment, restore the railroad's credit, provide it with new capital for improvements or for acquisition of competing lines, and establish the property on a profitable basis. To achieve these objectives sometimes required several years of difficult negotiations, involving a complete change in the road's capital structure and the consolidation of lines into a unified system.

Though no two reorganizations were exactly alike, most of them had certain features in common. This certainly was true of the ones worked out by Morgan's brilliant partner, Charles H. Coster. These plans involved a close study of the railroad's earnings, interest charges, dividends, operating and maintenance costs, equipment, and management. Next came calculation of "the extent and nature of the fixed charges that . . . [the railroad] might be able safely to undertake." Once this was settled, Coster devised a plan to reduce the road's bonded debt obligations to as close to its minimum earning capacity as practicable, thus making it possible to pay the interest even under adverse circumstances. Very often this reduction necessitated inducing the bondholders to exchange their bonds for others paying a lower rate, or for preferred or common stock, or a combination of all three. Stockholders frequently were assessed to provide working capital to pay outstanding short-term debts, acquire new equipment, or meet other current expenses. Finally, in order to "maintain a continuous policy of conservatism and prudent management for the initial period of the reorganization," a Morgan partner subsequently explained, a voting trust often was established "with men of eminence and probity as trustees." And when the trust expired, a Morgan partner or trusted business associate often was appointed a director and a member of the finance committee.[29] In

28. *Ibid.*, 140; Harold U. Faulkner, *The Decline of Laissez Faire, 1897–1917* (New York, 1951), 191; Kennan, *Harriman*, I, 117; *U.S. v. Henry S. Morgan et al.*, "Transcript of Trial, Defendants' Opening — Mr. [William Dwight] Whitney" (February 8, 1951), 2890–91.

29. Lamont to Wasson, "Memorandum," dated March 27, 1939. At the time of

this way Morgan sought to prevent the kind of mismanagement that had bankrupted many railroads, including several he had assisted previously, such as the Northern Pacific, the Philadelphia & Reading, and the Baltimore & Ohio.

The results of these reorganizations on the nation's railroads were mixed, at best. In some cases, such as Morgan's reorganization of the Southern Railway, they were highly beneficial to everyone concerned. Investors found this road's securities attractive, and its customers benefited from greatly improved service. But even the most well-conceived and conservatively executed reorganizations rarely resulted in lower rates. Indeed the reverse generally was true. "Five years ago," an Interstate Commerce Commissioner reported in 1903, "the crying evil in railway operations was discrimination, mainly discrimination between individual shippers. . . . Not so today. . . . The discrimination is disappearing, but in its place comes that other danger which always attends monopoly, the exaction of an unreasonable charge." [30]

Regardless of the long-term effects of these reorganizations upon the railroads themselves, in the short run they brought added prestige, influence, and alleged huge profits to the investment houses that negotiated them. Morgan's fee for reorganizing the Erie was reputed to have been $500,000. In addition, his firm received a commission on the bonds it sold.[31] Morgan's services, like those of other respected investment bankers, were expensive, and profits of a million dollars or more on a large transaction were not uncommon. The risk involved in a reorganization often was great; and the number of investment houses that could handle large projects of this kind was small. Corporations in need of their services and aware of the value of having their securities sponsored by a prestigious investment banking firm were prepared to pay the price. The public, learning of the bankers' "immense" profits, was shocked.

The bankers themselves, on the other hand, were convinced that their charges were justified, considering the risk, work, time, and responsibility involved. The reason why Morgan "commanded . . . confidence and a small moiety of . . . influence," according to one of his partners, "was that as a banker his charges were fair." The firm's profits on the many bond issues it sponsored, according to this source, "averaged less than ½ %." [32]

Coster's death in March 1900, *The Commercial & Financial Chronicle* described his work in rehabilitating distressed railroads as his most outstanding accomplishment. "We think the statement will not be questioned that next to the head of the concern, credit belongs chiefly to him for the successful reorganizations for which Mr. Morgan's house has become famous." *The Commercial & Financial Chronicle,* LXX (March 17, 1900), 502. See also Edward G. Campbell, *The Reorganization of the American Railroad System, 1893–1900* (New York, 1938), 148ff.

30. Quoted in Faulkner, *The Decline of Laissez Faire,* 199.
31. Allen, *The Great Pierpont Morgan,* 86.
32. Lamont to Wasson, "Memorandum," dated March 27, 1939.

During the 1890's, when most investment houses still concerned themselves primarily with reorganizing and consolidating railroads, a growing number of industrial companies also were seeking advice and assistance from investment bankers. Most manufacturing establishments were organized either as partnerships or closely held corporations, and only a few had capitalizations in excess of $5 million. A $10 million company was regarded as uncommonly large. The Pullman Palace Car Company and a few New England textile firms were the notable exceptions. The former was the only industrial company whose securities were widely traded on the New York Stock Exchange. The issues of the New England mill companies were traded almost exclusively on the Boston Stock Exchange, making it the leading market for industrial securities in the United States.[33]

Beginning late in the 1880's an increasing number of industrialists were seeking new capital to enlarge or improve their businesses. They wanted to buy new machinery and accumulate sufficient cash to operate large enterprises. "It is astonishing the amount of working capital you must have in a great concern," Andrew Carnegie recalled years later. "It is far more than the cost of the works."[34] Some large, successful corporations continued to finance expansion by reinvestment of profits. The phenomenal growth of the Standard Oil combination was accomplished in this way. "I think a concern so large as we are," John D. Rockefeller wrote in 1885, "should have its own money and be independent of the 'Street'."[35] Many other businessmen, however, sought outside capital. Some preferred to diversify their holdings, and others simply wanted to rid themselves of the inconvenience and legal limitations of the partnership form of organization.

Partnerships that recapitalized as corporations played a significant role in bringing industrial securities to the public's attention. One of the earliest and "most publicized" examples of this occurred in 1890, when John Claflin decided to incorporate his nationally known wholesale dry-goods firm, founded by his father.[36] Claflin's success in reorganizing H. B. Claflin & Co. and selling a large part of his holdings led other businessmen to follow his example; during the early 1890's a number of partnerships were recapitalized as corporations, some of the important ones being Procter & Gamble, P. Lorillard, and Westinghouse Electric.

Partnerships and corporations planning to "go public" took ad-

33. Thomas R. Navin and Marian V. Sears, "The Rise of a Market for Industrial Securities, 1887–1902," *Business History Review*, XXIX (June 1955), 105–38.
34. Quoted in Kirkland, *Industry Comes of Age*, 216.
35. Quoted in Ralph W. Hidy and Muriel E. Hidy, *Pioneering in Big Business, 1882–1911: History of the Standard Oil Company (New Jersey)* (New York, 1955), 607.
36. Navin and Sears, "The Rise of a Market for Industrial Securities," 123.

vantage of New Jersey's liberalized incorporation laws. In 1889 this state allowed the chartering of holding companies, a useful device through which stockholders might gain or retain control of an enterprise with a much smaller investment than otherwise would have been necessary. The holding company provided a convenient way for existing trusts to change their form of organization while keeping most of their advantages. The cotton oil refining trust was one of the first to use the holding company device, when in 1889 it became the American Cotton Oil Company. Two others, sugar and lead, did likewise in 1891. Meanwhile other large mergers, some of which earlier might have combined as trusts, were organized as holding companies.

The investment banker played an important and varied role in many of these transactions. In some cases he acted as a financial adviser, recommending the amount and type of stocks and bonds to be issued; in others, he distributed the securities. Kidder, Peabody assisted in organizing the incorporation of the sugar trust and distributed its preferred stock; and Winslow, Lanier performed the same services for the cotton oil trust. Lee, Higginson, the bankers of the Thomson-Houston Electric Company, together with J. P. Morgan, which had participated in the formation of the Edison Electric Company, arranged the consolidation of these two competitors into a new $50 million corporation, the General Electric Company.[37] The newly organized corporations generally issued few bonds. Security issues of $5 million or less almost never were underwritten. The common practice was for a single investment firm to buy the entire issue itself or jointly with another house and place the securities privately.[38]

Since most of the leading investment houses in the 1890's still were largely specialists in railroad bonds, those that agreed to handle industrials usually accepted only the larger transactions. These generally involved the conversions of trusts and large mergers requiring the issuing of bonds and preferred stock. As a rule these banking firms did not concern themselves with small mergers or those necessitating only the distribution of common stock. This business they left to individual promoters and brokerage firms, several of which, such as A. M. Kidder & Co., Blake Brothers, and John H. Davis & Co., became specialists in this type of work.[39]

The more conservative investment banking houses looked upon the common stock of most industrial companies as speculative. Jacob

---

37. Federal Reserve Bank of Boston, *Annual Report for 1960: A History of Investment Banking in New England* (Boston, 1961), 21. See also Forrest McDonald, *Insull* (Chicago, 1962), 41, 50.

38. Navin and Sears, "The Rise of a Market for Industrial Securities," 120–21.

39. *Ibid.*, 122, 124–26. See also "Is Speculation Declining?" *The Bankers' Magazine*, XLVII (December 1892), 415.

Schiff, for instance, regarded such issues with considerable skepticism, and Kuhn, Loeb did not participate actively in financing industrial corporations until the close of the century.[40] The clients of the leading investment firms, moreover, were unaccustomed to industrial common stock and reluctant to purchase it. Few manufacturers before 1900 considered it necessary or advisable to issue regular operating statements and balance sheets; and those that did too often published reports that either were incomplete or, because of the absence of standard accounting practices, were of "dubious value."[41] The *American Banker* attributed the low repute in which industrial common stock was held by commercial banks to the fact that most investors neither expected nor demanded that these corporations disclose their affairs to the public.[42]

Preferred stock, on the other hand, was popular with both investors and issuers. The former were familiar with those of railroad companies and appreciated the safety feature these securities possessed; and since most preferred stock carried no voting rights, issuers used them to raise new capital without losing control.

The Boston Stock Exchange was the principal market for industrial securities before 1900. Not surprisingly, the two leading investment banking firms of that city — Kidder, Peabody, and Lee, Higginson — were among the first private banking houses of established national reputation distributing such issues. The two principal firms selling industrials in New York were Baring, Magoun and August Belmont.[43]

After the depression of the mid-1890's demonstrated that industrial preferreds were not necessarily inferior to railroad bonds, public acceptance of these issues increased rapidly. During fifteen months beginning in 1897, after recovery had started and the merger movement regained momentum, more than a score of large industrial combinations were launched.[44] Most of these were organized by promoters and brokers who, together with other wealthy businessmen, formed their own syndicates to distribute the issues of these new companies. But after the Morgan firm organized and managed the syndicate establishing the Federal Steel Company in 1898,

---

40. Adler, *Jacob H. Schiff*, I, 27–28; [Kuhn, Loeb & Co.] *Investment Banking through Four Generations* (New York, 1955), 17–18.

41. David F. Hawkins, "The Development of Modern Financial Reporting Practices among American Manufacturing Corporations," *Business History Review*, XXXVII (Autumn 1963), 144. See also Richard D. Wyckoff, "Looking Forward — And Backward after Thirty-Five Years in Wall Street," *The Magazine of Wall Street*, XXXVIII (December 22, 1923), 300.

42. James B. Dill, "Industrials as Investments," *American Banker*, XLV (June 6, 1900), 995–96.

43. Navin and Sears, "The Rise of a Market for Industrial Securities," 124–25.

44. Luther Conant, Jr., "Industrial Consolidations in the United States," *Quarterly Publications of the American Statistical Association*, n.s. VII (March 1901), 1–20.

nearly all the other major investment houses participated in underwriting and distributing industrial bonds and preferred stock.[45]

By the first decade of the twentieth century the investment banker had replaced the promoter and the broker as the principal figure in financing industrial combinations and providing manufacturing companies with capital. In some cases the job was done by commercial banks, and several became very active in this field. The National City Bank of New York, together with William H. Rogers and William Rockefeller, two influential figures in the Standard Oil hierarchy, organized and launched the Amalgamated Copper Company, a combination including the Anaconda Mines and several other important properties. Thomas W. Lawson, a Boston stockbroker and speculator, who subsequently became widely known for his exposé "Frenzied Finance" (1904), was employed by them to advertise the new issues and make a market for them on the Boston exchange.[46]

Many of the consolidations that investment bankers organized after 1897 were overcapitalized. Much of the water represented the fees and charges of the promoters, brokers, and bankers who initiated and established them.[47] Witnesses appearing before the United States Industrial Commission, authorized by Congress in 1898 to hold hearings on recent economic developments in the United States, provided numerous specific illustrations of reputed and actual overcapitalization and the profits earned by promoters. William Griffiths, a tin-plate manufacturer whose business was consolidated in the merger creating the American Tin Plate Company as a $50 million corporation, declared that the promoters' fees were $10 million, out of which he believed they were to pay the organization expenses. N. Burton Rogers, a silver-plate manufacturer who refused to join the consolidation establishing the International Silver Company, testified that the promoters' fee, paid in common stock, amounted to 3 percent of the total capitalization of $20 million.[48] These were only two of several examples cited.

---

45. Navin and Sears, "The Rise of a Market for Industrial Securities," 130–31, 133, 138. See also U.S. Industrial Commission, *Report* . . . (19 vols., Washington, 1900–02), XIX, 600; I, pt. 1, 194–96, for Morgan's role; I, pt. 2, 986–89, 1003, for the testimony of Elbert H. Gary.

46. Richard D. Wyckoff, *Wall Street Ventures and Adventures through Forty Years* (New York, 1930), 66–68; Anna R. Burr, *The Portrait of a Banker: James Stillman, 1850–1918* (New York, 1927), 141–43; Stewart H. Holbrook, *The Age of the Moguls* (New York, 1954), 170–72. See also Edwin Lefevre, *Reminiscences of a Stock Operator* (New York, 1923).

47. U.S. Industrial Commission, *Report*, I, pt. 1, 12–13; I, pt. 2, 1021. See also Navin and Sears, "The Rise of a Market for Industrial Securities," 132–33; Henry Clews, "Current Concentration of Industrial Capital," *Lippincott's Monthly Magazine*, XLVI (September 1890), 382.

48. U.S. Industrial Commission, *Report*, I, pt. 2, 911–12, 1068. See also *ibid.*, 959–61 for the testimony of Judge William H. Moore on the methods and profits of promoting the American Tin Plate Company.

Payment in common stock, or a combination of common and preferred, was the usual way in which promoters were compensated for their services, though some of them demanded and received part of their fees in cash. Rarely, if ever, did an investment house receive a cash payment for promoting a merger. E. R. Chapman, a prominent New York City banker who sponsored several large consolidations, testified before the Industrial Commission that he had "never known any case where the bankers were paid any money or any specific amount. They take over a given percentage of the stock," he said, "and then settle up the claims of promoters and other people the best they can. They also settle with the lawyers, and perhaps have to pay them a very large amount in cash. Whatever stock is left after these accounts have been settled they appropriate for their own charges." [49] The banker earned his profit from selling the securities of the new corporation. It was, therefore, to his advantage to bring out as large an issue as he believed the market could absorb.

Whether mergers were sponsored by individual promoters or bankers, the results usually were the same. The new consolidations were overcapitalized.[50] In reviewing those of 1899, the *American Banker* estimated that 25 percent of the "aggregated capital" represented "pure inflation."[51] It was because of this, another writer for this journal reported, that the industrial stocks of 1900 generally were of poor investment quality and not the kind of securities "most desirable for collateral."[52]

Similar criticisms had been heard before, but a growing prosperity and optimistic predictions about the future of these new industrial giants caused such warnings to be ignored.[53] During the last two years of the nineteenth century industrial securities were in great demand by both investors and speculators. Trading in these issues flourished, as did the business of the brokers and bankers who dealt in them. Meanwhile the country's leading investment houses,

49. *Ibid.*, XIII, pt. 2, 96–97. See also *ibid.*, XIII, pt. I, vii–ix, for a review of the evidence the commission collected on the promotional methods used to finance mergers.

50. *Ibid.*, IX, pt. 2, 88. See also *ibid.*, I, pt. 2, 957, 1031–32; IX, pt. 2, 736. "On the whole," the commission concluded, "the inference seems a fair one that the capitalization of these companies is usually a sum considerably above the value of the plants together with patents.... In cases that are considered fairly conservative the amount of stock issued, including both preferred and common ... is from two to three times more than the value, while in not a few instances ... the capital stock seems to bear little relation to actual value of plants and patents." *Ibid.*, I, pt. 1, 15–16.

51. "The Old and the New Year," *American Banker,* LXV (January 3, 1900), 9. See also *ibid.,* XLV (January 24, 1900), 135–36; *The Commercial & Financial Chronicle,* LXX (January 6, 1900), 4.

52. Dill, "Industrials as Investments," 995–96.

53. See, for example, John F. Hume, "The Heart of Speculation," *The Forum,* II (October 1886), 130–41, and James A. Logan, "The Vice of Fictitious Corporate Capitalizations," *The American Journal of Politics,* II (February 1893), 203–10.

reluctant earlier to underwrite such issues, now were taking over the major responsibility for financing heavy industry and manufacturing, initiating mergers and consolidations, distributing industrial bonds and preferred stock, accepting representations on the directorates of these corporations, and generally assuming the same responsibilities for these companies that they did for railroads.

By the beginning of the twentieth century virtually all the principal railroads in the country and many of the largest industrial corporations looked to the investment banker for their long-term capital requirements. The number of private investment houses and commercial banks capable of meeting the financial needs of these large borrowers was very small, at most no more than a dozen institutions. Their services were eagerly solicited by a rapidly growing number of big businesses dependent upon raising capital from the public.[54] Smaller borrowers, such as public utility companies and corporations in the light industries in need of similar services, were financed by other, less well-known investment houses, some of which were just starting out as underwriters. The reputation and influence of the leading investment firms, such as J. P. Morgan, Kuhn, Loeb, and the First National Bank of New York, rested upon their ability to distribute large quantities of securities by selling them to their branches or correspondents abroad and to private and commercial banks, brokerage houses, and trust and life insurance companies in the United States; such firms then resold the stocks or bonds to the public or held them as investments.

The assistance of these financial institutions was vital in the distribution of large issues, and investment bankers sought to win and hold their support by investing in them or gaining representation on their directorates. "It has become quite a common practice in recent years for parties about to put through big deals to first obtain control of a bank, whereby their efforts could be facilitated," the *United States Investor* asserted in 1899. "Big deals are not possible if banking assistance is withheld."[55] Accordingly, the investment banker endeavored to assure himself of continuous access to new funds by developing close ties with officers of banks and trust companies; this move was as important as using his influence as a corporate director to protect the value of the securities he sponsored and to cultivate future business through acting as a company's financial doctor, to adopt a simile of Otto Kahn, a Kuhn, Loeb partner.[56]

Yet the influence of life insurance firms was increasing rapidly. Between 1875 and 1900 their resources almost quadrupled, jumping from $403 million to $1.7 billion.[57] Simultaneously, and even

54. Thomas C. Cochran, *The American Business System: A Historical Perspective, 1900–1955* (Cambridge, Mass., 1960), 79–81.
55. *United States Investor*, X (May 27, 1899), 705.
56. *Investigation of Railroads: Hearings*, XIX, 8272–73.
57. Edwards, *The Evolution of Finance Capitalism,* 184, Table 18.

more important, significant changes were taking place in their investment policies. Beginning in the early 1880's the leading life companies started putting their funds heavily into railroad bonds, and by 1904 these issues accounted for one-third of their total assets.

Realizing the extensive influence that control of this vast supply of capital brought them, the officers of these companies sought profits, prestige, and power by allying themselves closely with the leading investment houses, commercial banks, and trust companies. This they achieved either directly through investing in these institutions, or indirectly by accepting strategic positions on their directorates and finance committees.

The same objectives and methods that brought the insurance companies and their officials into the banking and securities business led investment bankers to penetrate the insurance companies. George W. Perkins's dual role as a partner in Morgan's bank and chairman of the New York Life Insurance Company's finance committee was typical of the kind of alliances that developed between the leading investment banking houses and the great life companies.[58]

Since most investment firms also borrowed regularly from commercial banks to carry their securities during a flotation, they sought to assure themselves continuous access to short-term capital.[59] Partners in the leading investment houses often were substantial stockholders in, or directors of, the major New York and Boston commercial banks. Under the National Banking Act country or local banks were allowed to deposit 60 percent of their reserves in reserve city banks, and the latter could deposit 50 percent of their reserves in a central reserve city bank. Before 1887 New York was the only central reserve city; but even after Chicago and St. Louis were so designated, the New York banks, by paying interest on these deposits, continued to attract most of them. These arrangements were profitable to both the out-of-town and the New York City banks. The former earned interest on that part of their reserves deposited in New York banks, and the latter enhanced their earnings by lending such funds on call to investment houses syndicating new securities and brokerage firms retailing them to the public.[60]

58. Morton Keller, *The Life Insurance Enterprise, 1885–1910: A Study in the Limits of Corporate Power* (Cambridge, Mass., 1963), 131, 177, ch. ix. See also John Moody, *The Masters of Capital: A Chronicle of Wall Street* (New Haven, 1921), 126–33; John A. Garraty, *Right-Hand Man: The Life of George W. Perkins* (New York, 1957).
59. Willard E. Atkins *et al., The Regulation of the Security Markets* (Washington, 1946), 28–29.
60. Kirkland, *Industry Comes of Age,* 31; Paul B. Trescott, *Financing American Enterprise: The Story of Commercial Banking* (New York, 1963), 149–50; Ross M. Robertson, "St. Louis as a Central Reserve City, 1887–1922," *Monthly Review,* Federal Reserve Bank of St. Louis, XXXVI (August 1954), 85–92.

The growing flow of these reserves into New York City was a powerful factor in concentrating the securities business in this city and with those investment banking houses that could secure loans from these banks.[61] Equally important was the fact that the courts and the Comptroller of the Currency interpreted the provisions of the National Banking Act so as to allow commercial banks to buy and sell "evidences of debt" and invest their own funds in municipal and corporate bonds; this permissive act provided still another incentive for investment firms to develop close ties with these institutions.[62]

By 1900 the passive, relatively detached merchandiser of securities typical of the pre-railroad era had been replaced by the active investment banker, the central figure in a more integrated stage of capitalistic development. Shortly before the turn of the century, Jacob Schiff attributed the growth of investment banking and the prominence of firms like his own to "the fact that they have been *more honest* than those who, thirty and twenty years ago, were among the leading banking firms. Not more honest, as construed in the literal sense of the word, but honest in their respect for the moral obligation assumed toward those who entrusted their financial affairs to them, be it investing in the securities of corporate enterprises which these bankers brought before the public, or otherwise; *more honest* in keeping their own capital from becoming immobile, so that their credit and prestige should not be called into question during times of financial peril and uncertainty; *more honest* in the ways which, not taking alone into account the monetary pecuniary profit, are certain, in the long run, to determine position, credit, and prestige."[63]

Unlike their earlier counterparts, the leading investment bankers of the late nineteenth and early twentieth centuries indirectly extended their influence far beyond the narrow confines of Wall Street. As the financial advisers to railroads and other large corporate enterprises, and as directors of the major banks and trust and life insurance companies, Morgan, Schiff, Baker, and a few others occupied a strategic position in the economy. The sociologist David Bell attributed the "breakup of family capitalism" during the years

---

61. Redlich, *Molding of American Banking*, II, 379; Sidney M. Robbins and Nestor E. Terleckyj, *Money Metropolis: A Locational Study of Financial Activities in the New York Region* (Cambridge, Mass., 1960), 12. Charles G. Washburn, *The Life of John W. Weeks* (Boston, 1928), 13–16, illustrates the kinds of assistance the Boston investment house of Hornblower & Weeks provided the Massachusetts National Bank in the crisis of 1898–1899.

62. Boston, FRB, *Annual Report, 1960*, 17–18; Redlich, *Molding of American Banking*, II, 389. The investments of national banks rose from $432 million in 1875 to $451 million in 1880, declining thereafter to $286 million in 1890. By 1900 they were up to $776 million. See William J. Shultz and M. R. Caine, *Financial Development of the United States* (New York, 1937), 384, 447.

63. Quoted in Adler, *Jacob H. Schiff*, I, 23–24.

1890 to 1910 to the activities of these men. "By their intervention," he pointed out, "the investment bankers, in effect, tore up the social roots of the capitalist order. By installing professional managers — with no proprietary stakes themselves in the enterprise, unable therefore to pass along their power automatically to their sons, and accountable to outside controllers — the bankers effected a radical separation of property and family." [64] More accurately, investment bankers implemented the desires of second and third generations of industrial families to dispose of a portion or all of their holdings in enterprises created by a father or a grandfather.

Many of the great investment houses continued to provide a variety of financial services, much as their predecessors had done a half century earlier; their place and influence, however, no longer depended upon these ancillary services, but rather upon their ability to mobilize large amounts of long-term capital. Because these amounts were so large and distribution problems became more complex, investment bankers increasingly joined together to pool their resources and talents and spread the risk involved in floating new security issues. Several types of these groups, or syndicates, developed in order to perform the various functions investment firms were now being called on to provide.

64. David Bell, *The End of Ideology* (new rev. ed., New York, 1962), 42–43.

3 The Development of the Syndicate to 1914

To perform more effectively the functions they assumed during the later decades of the nineteenth century, investment bankers adopted the syndicate, probably the most important and far-reaching change in their method of operations to be introduced in the period after the Civil War. Financing the vast economic expansion of these years, which transformed the United States from an agricultural, rural, loosely organized country into an industrial, urban, and highly organized nation, required huge outlays of capital. Since many enterprises needed more than any single banker could command or dared risk, investment bankers joined together in syndicates, as these groups came to be called, pooling their resources and talents and sharing the risk as widely as possible. They employed two general types of syndicates: those that were used to float specific issues of securities and those that were used to put through a merger, from acquiring the component companies to placing the securities of the new corporation.

By 1900 the investment bankers who organized and managed these syndicates emerged as the recognized specialists in servicing the financial requirements of large enterprises and the undisputed leaders in the business of buying and selling securities. Operated by "rich and able men," as *The New York Times* characterized them, the syndicate had become the "moving force" in the nation's security markets.[1]

Although the modern investment banking syndicate was developed largely during the last thirty years of the nineteenth century, some of its features have been traced as far back as the latter part of the Middle Ages and, with more certainty, to the seventeenth and eighteenth centuries. Professor Edward S. Meade, of the University of Pennsylvania, shortly after the turn of the century, found in the "original organization" of the Bank of England in 1694 several features of the bankers' syndicate of today."[2]

During the eighteenth and early part of the nineteenth centuries various types of group action were employed to market securities. The British and French governments sold their loans by calling for subscriptions. At first both investors and loan contractors were per-

1. Wallace B. Donham, "Underwriting Syndicates and the Purchase and Sale of Securities through Banking Houses" in Harvard Graduate School of Business Administration, "Corporation Finance" (mimeographed lecture notes, Baker Library, 1908), 177 (Donham was a vice president of the Old Colony Trust Company, a Boston institution actively engaged in the security business); Edward S. Meade, "Initial Stages of Organization" in *ibid.*, 47. See also *U.S. v. Henry S. Morgan et al.*, "Brief on General Points in Support of Motions to Dismiss," 42–50; *ibid.*, "Corrected Opinion of Harold R. Medina (February 4, 1954), 24–28; *The New York Times,* September 5, 1897; Martin Mayer, *Wall Street Men and Money* (rev. ed., New York, 1962), 163.
2. Quoted in *The New York Times,* May 4, 1902.

mitted to subscribe, but by the first decade of the nineteenth century only the latter were invited to do so. The ties formed by some of these contractors, such as those of the Barings, resulted in banking "alliances" and joint-account transactions. Out of these "stemmed the first embryonic syndicates" in both Europe and America.[3]

In the United States the origins of the modern syndicate date back to the days of David Parish, Stephen Girard, and John Jacob Astor. In 1813 Parish and Girard agreed to take, on joint account, some $7 million of federal bonds that the government had been unable to sell. Corcoran & Riggs employed much the same method in 1848, when, acting for itself and several other British and American private bankers, it bid for the entire $16 million Mexican War loan. Corcoran & Riggs's functions in this instance have been described as one of the earliest examples of an international syndicate led by an American house.[4] In both these cases, as in other similar joint-account transactions before the Civil War, the extent of the participants' cooperation involved little more than an agreement specifying the amount of the securities and the price at which each banker would buy or bid for them. As a rule, no provision was made for the group to cooperate in reselling the issue.

Cooperation in retailing securities, the distinguishing feature of the present-day selling syndicate, appears to have been employed first in the United States in February 1869. Jay Cooke & Co. and E. W. Clark & Co. agreed to buy, advertise, and sell on joint account and through joint management some $2.5 million of bonds of the Lake Superior & Mississippi Railroad. Working closely together, these two firms shared the Philadelphia market and assigned to each other exclusive rights to advertise and manage the distribution in New York and Boston. Sales in the former city were undertaken by Cooke; those in the latter by the Clarks. Commissions and a stock bonus were divided equally, each house keeping one-quarter and assigning half to a joint account to be divided later. The next year, again under Cooke's leadership, the syndicate was developed still further by the introduction of an underwriting commitment. If the issuer failed to sell its own securities, the syndicate guaranteed to buy and dispose of them.[5]

Although employed in England, underwriting appears to have been untried in the United States until Cooke first used it in March

3. Fritz Redlich, *The Molding of American Banking: Men and Ideas* (2 vols., New York, 1947, 1951), II, 358. See also Frederick Greenwood, "What Modern Underwriting Accomplishes," *The Magazine of Wall Street,* XII (September 1913), 353–56.

4. Redlich, *Molding of American Banking,* II, 316, 348, 358–59. See also Henrietta M. Larson, *Jay Cooke: Private Banker* (Cambridge, Mass., 1936), 315.

5. Larson, *Jay Cooke,* 251, 315, 475n.90. See also Redlich, *Molding of American Banking,* II, 358; Charles W. Gerstenberg, "The Underwriting of Securities by Syndicates," *Trust Companies,* X (June 1910), 328; Donham, "Underwriting Syndicates," 172–73.

1870, when he, together with seven other firms, underwrote a $2 million bond issue for the Pennsylvania Railroad. They guaranteed the railroad its money should the company fail to sell the securities by a certain date. It was this guarantee to the issuing corporation that originally distinguished underwriting from contracting, in which the banker bought and paid for the issue. This guarantee in itself was an important innovation in American investment banking; but just as important was the fact that the banking syndicate, by assigning to only five of its members the job of selling any bonds that the railroad itself had failed to market, also drew a clear distinction between underwriting (the risk-bearing function) and selling.[6] The distinguishing feature of underwriting of this type, indeed its very essence, was that the issuer itself, not the guaranteeing bankers, did the actual selling.

During the last three decades of the nineteenth century, syndicates took over many of the functions previously performed by individual bankers or small groups of investment firms acting jointly. At one time or another every Secretary of the Treasury between 1869 and 1877 made use of the device to refund the government's long-term debt, thus giving the term wide popular usage.[7] After 1879, when these transactions were largely completed, syndicates of various types were employed to distribute new railroad issues and, after the panic of 1893, to market securities issued in the reorganization of many bankrupt railroads. The success of these "reorganizing syndicates," in no small measure the result of returning prosperity, led investment bankers to employ them in financing the conversion of large, privately held industrial corporations into publicly owned enterprises.[8] The business of floating these issues was arranged and managed by many of the same banking syndicates that had reorganized the railroads.

By the beginning of the twentieth century investment bankers had moved away from underwriting as used in the strict sense of the term. The more common practice was for investment firms, operating through syndicates, to assume both the purchase and the sales functions. For a variety of reasons, fewer and fewer corporations

6. Larson, *Jay Cooke,* 315–16.
7. In the 1890's, when popular subscriptions proved inadequate, the federal government again called upon banking groups to assist the Treasury in selling its bonds, the most notable instance being the famous gold "contract" of February 1895, between the Treasury and the Morgan-Belmont syndicate. For the details of this well-known story see Redlich, *Molding of American Banking,* II, 370; Allen Nevins, *Grover Cleveland: A Study in Courage* (New York, 1944), 656–66; Matthew Simon, "The Morgan-Belmont Syndicate of 1895 and Intervention in the Foreign-Exchange Market," *Business History Review,* XLII (Winter 1968), 385–417.
8. "Syndicates as Promoters of Financial Enterprises," *The Bankers' Magazine,* LXVII (July 1903), 15–17. See also Alexander D. Noyes, "Finance," *The Forum,* XXXV (January 1904), 368; Paul Studenski and Herman E. Krooss, *Financial History of the United States* (2d ed., New York, 1963), 174.

chose to sell their own securities, as had been common a generation earlier, when an issuer's reputation often was greater than that of the banking house underwriting the flotation. By 1900 this was no longer the case; the prestige of certain banking houses exceeded by far that of most corporations. Moreover, bankers found it easier and more profitable to purchase an issue of securities and be responsible for selling it rather than to give a guarantee to the issuer should the corporation not succeed in marketing the securities itself. As a result, the underwriting syndicate, as originally defined and used, rarely was employed in issuing securities of established corporations.[9]

So rare was that type of syndicate that shortly after the turn of the century Wallace B. Donham, a leading Boston banker, found himself "at a loss to find examples . . . except in reorganizations."[10] Traditional underwriting in a reorganization this same Boston banker aptly described as "an effort to get somebody to subscribe to something he does not want, to protect something he wishes he had not got." It continued to be used by faltering or bankrupt enterprises seeking to induce the investor to accept the company's or the reorganization committee's proposal by assuring him that the plan's financial success was guaranteed by a syndicate of respected bankers.[11]

Traditional underwriting, however, continued to be employed by companies seeking to raise additional capital from their present security holders. In such cases an underwriting syndicate was organized to stand ready to take whatever securities investors failed to purchase.

By 1914, in response to changes in the issuers' financial requirements, investment bankers had effected corresponding alterations in the types of syndicates used. Environmental factors influencing syndicate changes were numerous. Among the most important developments were the large increase in the number and size of issues; the time and risk involved in selling them; the increasing difficulty and growing disinclination of corporations to finance themselves; and the fact that very few investment houses alone commanded sufficient resources or credit to finance large borrowers, such as the railroads, which were in constant need of millions of long-term capital to build, equip, and improve their systems.[12] Even a strong banking

9. Donham, "Underwriting Syndicates," 172, 180.
10. *Ibid.*, 180, 185. See also A. H. Joline, "Reorganization of Corporations: Reorganization and Underwriting Syndicates" in "Corporation Finance," 570–71. Donham asserted that traditional underwriting syndicates sometimes were used "when an issue of convertible bonds is being offered in order that the stockholders shall not have any chance to complain that they did not have a chance to subscribe their pro rata of the issue of stock which may be issued against the bonds, if they are ever converted."
11. Donham, "Underwriting Syndicates," 180.
12. Willard E. Atkins *et al., The Regulation of the Security Markets* (Washington, 1946), 26–27.

house was "reluctant to put all or a major portion of its resources in any one issue of securities."[13] The risk of failure was too great.

The syndicate provided the machinery through which a banker could participate in the profitable business of floating new securities while limiting his possible losses. One prominent Boston banker likened it to a "temporary" corporation. "It is formed," he said, "to handle something which is perhaps not conveniently handled by individual banking houses or by individuals."[14] By allowing investment bankers to "combine and limit themselves," the syndicate made it possible for them "to compete with the great aggregations of capital, such as the [commercial] banks and insurance companies," a consideration that became especially important during the first two decades of the twentieth century.[15]

Participation in a syndicate afforded the investment banker other advantages as well. It allowed him to diversify his commitments; permitted him to invest in several ventures simultaneously, thus accumulating a variety of securities suitable to the needs of different groups of investors; and provided a convenient way of developing new banking ties and strengthening old ones. Because of the syndicate's flexibility, it could be employed in every kind of flotation. Moreover, its use in no way altered the traditional relationship between the issuer and its banker. The syndicate dealt with a "corporation as a unit" through a manager who was almost always a member of the banking firm that originated the issue.[16]

The services performed by syndicates had become so diverse and the issues had become so large that investment bankers often found it necessary to establish several of these groups for a single flotation, one for each of the functions required. The range ran from the issuer's plan to put out a security to the delivery of a certificate to the investor. There were four main functions to be carried out: originating, purchasing or underwriting (sometimes used loosely), banking, and selling. The general scheme was for the issue to be sold to successive syndicates in the chain. Planning and organizing the distribution of a $100 million issue might require the formation of as many as four syndicates. For most flotations, however, functions were combined into two: one to originate, purchase, and perform the banking function, and the second to sell to dealers or investors.

The number and kinds of syndicates employed, as well as the size, structure, and operating methods of each depended upon numerous considerations. The major ones were the amount of

13. Lewis B. Franklin, "The Formation of Syndicates," *The Magazine of Wall Street*, XV (March 20, 1915), 452–53. See also the same author's article, "Syndicates," *The Bankers' Magazine*, LXXXVII (December 1913), 664–69.
14. Donham, "Underwriting Syndicates," 176.
15. *U.S. v. Henry S. Morgan et al.*, "Transcript of Trial, Plaintiff's Case" October 16, 1952), 17714–15.
16. Redlich, *Molding of American Banking*, II, 371; Donham, "Underwriting Syndicates," 173.

money that had to be raised, the risk involved, the kind of enterprise that was being financed, the reputation of the issuer, other financial commitments of the syndicate members at the time, and the general condition of the security and money markets.[17]

Origination, the first step in the process of floating a security issue, occurred when the borrower asked an investment house to assist it in raising capital, or when the investment house, learning that the corporation needed funds, took the initiative. Before accepting the assignment, the investment banker, investigated the corporation carefully, using his own and outside experts. The examination of an established industrial corporation might include inspection of the buildings, plant facilities, equipment, and machinery, and studies of the company's position in the industry, production methods, labor costs, sales performance, assets and liabilities, profit record, and management. The banker also might seek professional estimates of the company's potential growth, probable new sources of competition, and the likelihood of increased earnings.[18]

If the corporation seeking capital was a new enterprise, the investigation usually was even more comprehensive. The purchasing or underwriting syndicate might have to borrow from commercial banks to carry the securities, and these banks were less willing to make loans to syndicates financing untried companies. The investment banker often conferred with engineers, contractors, and builders, sometimes employing an independent construction firm to make an appraisal. By the beginning of the twentieth century it was not at all unusual for an investment house to spend two or three months and $10,000 or more to investigate a corporation planning a $2 million issue. Still haunted by the bankruptcies and defaults following the panic of 1893, the press cautioned even the most conservative investment bankers against looking at the enterprises they financed through "rose-colored glasses," and it urged them to employ more professional investigators.[19]

Once the examination was completed, and the investment banker was satisfied that the issue could be sold at a price satisfactory to

---

17. *U.S. v. Henry S. Morgan et al.*, "Transcript of Trial, Testimony of Harold L. Stuart" (April 30, 1952), 15183. See also Montgomery Rollins, "Underwritings," *The Magazine of Wall Street*, XVII (December 11, 1915), 288–92; Francis Cooper, *Financing an Enterprise* (2 vols., New York, 1906), II, 447. Cooper was a pseudonym of Hugh R. Conyngton, a longtime observer of corporate promotions and a participant in many.

18. Floyd F. Burtchett and Clifford M. Hicks, *Corporation Finance* (3d ed., Lincoln, 1959), 379. See also John H. Prime, "Private Negotiation in the Origination of Securities" in Investment Bankers Association, *Fundamentals of Investment Banking* (Englewood Cliffs, 1960), ch. xvi.

19. Donham, "Underwriting Syndicates," 204. See also James J. Storrow, "Management of Capital Account" in "Corporation Finance," 282–83. See, for example, Edward S. Mead, "How the Investment Banker Investigates Public Utilities," *Lippincott's Monthly Magazine*, XC (October 1912), 508–12. Consult also D. M. Means, "A New Profession," *The Nation*, LXV (August 26, 1897), 162–63.

the issuer, he proposed a detailed financial program. This program included a decision on the kinds and amounts of securities to be issued, the timing of the offering, the method to be employed in bringing it out, and whether it was to be underwritten or purchased.[20] If purchased, the originating banker bought the issue himself and immediately resold it to a purchase syndicate at an increase in price. Once such questions were resolved, the origination was said to have been completed.

Sometimes the originating banker called on one or two other investment houses to assist in the investigation and planning of the issue. When this occurred, the group sometimes was called an originating syndicate, and its functions were the same as those performed by a single banker.

By the time these preliminary steps had been completed, the originating banker already had decided whether to take the entire issue himself or to organize a purchase syndicate to buy the securities from the issuer. If he took them himself he did not have to share the profits. The decision was his alone. "Where there are only a few millions concerned," Jacob H. Schiff said, "there generally is no syndicate formed." There were no precise guidelines, but Kuhn, Loeb's policy was to organize a syndicate for any business that was larger than the firm wanted to keep entirely for itself.[21] Much the same view was expressed by James J. Storrow of Lee, Higginson & Co. If the overall economic "weather" looked "good," he explained, "and the issue was not too large" the banking house that originated it might purchase or underwrite the entire issue itself. If the weather appeared "squally," the originating banker decided to organize a purchase syndicate to buy the securities.[22]

When more than one banking house participated in an origination the members usually acted as co-managers.[23] Together they prepared the purchasing or underwriting agreement. That detailed document named the amount, conditions, time, and price that the syndicate was to pay the corporation for the securities. It stipulated the method of sale, whether the issue was to be listed on an exchange, and the obligations of the issuer in providing needed infor-

---

20. Burtchett and Hicks, *Corporation Finance*, 375–76; Gerstenberg, "Underwriting of Securities by Syndicates," 329. See also Prime, "Private Negotiation," ch. xvi; Percy M. Stewart, "Underwriting Syndicates" in IBA, *Fundamentals of Investment Banking*, ch. xviii.

21. New York, *Joint Committee of the Senate and Assembly . . . to Investigate and Examine into the Business and Affairs of Life Insurance Companies Doing Business in the State of New York* (7 vols., Albany, 1906), II, 1029.

22. Storrow, "Management of Capital Account," 283.

23. The exact origins of the term "manager" to describe the head of a group or syndicate is not certain. In 1952 Harold L. Stuart, who entered the investment banking business shortly after the turn of the century, testified that he "always regarded the head of a syndicate as the manager." *U.S. v. Henry S. Morgan et al.,* "Transcript of Trial, Testimony of Harold L. Stuart" (March 10, 1952), 13492.

mation and facilities. Many considerations affected the originating group's decisions. Among these were the condition of the domestic and international capital markets, the possibility that similar issues would appear at the same time, and the number and size of other commitments.

In organizing a purchase or underwriting syndicate, whichever was to be used, the originating banker, now acting as manager, either orally or by letter, sent out invitations to participate.[24] In either case, a contract, which came to be called the "syndicate agreement," was drawn up and signed by the manager and each participant. It covered details of the functions of managers and participants.

Rarely, if ever, was the corporation consulted about the provisions of such contracts. Indeed, the borrower's suggestions, when offered, usually were looked upon by the manager as unwarranted interference. "The internal management of the syndicate," a Boston banker declared in 1908, is a "matter of no moment to the corporation." [25]

Occasionally the issuer did, however, have a say in the size of the underwriting or purchasing syndicate and choice of members. Because it was difficult at times to find enough investment bankers to share the risk, the originating house and the issuer often arranged to include in the syndicate shareholders and officers of the corporation, wealthy individuals, and institutional investors, such as commercial banks and life insurance companies.[26] Jacob Schiff explained why Kuhn, Loeb allotted participations to the Equitable Life Assurance Society. The Equitable, or any other large insurance company or substantial "capitalist who wants to get, and properly get, the best return he can on his money," he explained, could afford to bear the risk entailed in buying securities at syndicate prices. If they were all sold immediately, the buyers made a quick profit; if they were not, the securities that Kuhn, Loeb sponsored, he continued, were "always good enough for any large insurance companies to hold." [27] Schiff's claim about the high quality of the securities brought out by his firm no doubt was true, but many wealthy investors and institutions found that being allowed to get in "on the ground floor" carried the risk, as one contemporary

24. Gerstenberg, "Underwriting of Securities by Syndicates," 329. Very often invitations to participate in a syndicate were extended orally and informally because, as a vice president of the Guaranty Trust Company put it, "the house originating the business does not like to make a formal proposition . . . unless it is quite sure that the proposition is going to be accepted, as a declination from any well established house may act as an argument against the business and influence some other house in declining it and thus throw cold water on the enterprise." See Franklin, "Syndicates," 665.
25. Donham, "Underwriting Syndicates," 176.
26. Ibid., 178–79; *U.S. v. Henry S. Morgan et al.,* "Corrected Opinion," 24.
27. New York, *Life Insurance Investigation,* II, 1018.

observer phrased it, that "underneath the ground floor there may be a basement, and besides that, a sub-cellar which is deeper yet." [28]

Besides the obvious requirement that participants possess the financial ability to make advances to the manager when called upon, or to take up their part of any unsold securities, the choice of syndicate members very often was influenced by the issuer's previous banking relationships. The result was that the same group of firms participated regularly in buying and selling the securities of the same corporations. The existence of these "communities of interest" was generally acknowledged by the financial press of the times, which explained their growth as an inevitable result of the rise of the large corporation and the syndicate as a device to finance it.[29]

Other observers interpreted the "remarkable development" of the underwriting syndicate during the last decade of the nineteenth century differently. It "made possible," *The New York Times* noted, "the formation of companies with hundreds of millions of dollars' capital; it . . . brought great banking houses into harmonious working agreements; it . . . brought American and foreign financial institutions into closer cooperation; and it . . . fixed a very snug berth for the stock market manipulator — the man who acts as a sort of selling agent for underwriting syndicates." A half century later, the Justice Department attributed the development of "traditional banker" relationships, as it called these communities of interest, to the efforts of certain investment bankers to monopolize the nation's security business.[30]

An equally compelling consideration in the selection of syndicate members was the desire of the originating banker to strengthen his ties with other investment houses.[31] Schiff declared that his firm's policy was "guided" by the size of its "circle of friends," but "nobody participates in a syndicate by any right; whoever participates, participates by the good will of Kuhn, Loeb & Company." [32] Another prominent banker explained the selection of syndicate members in these words: "Participations in syndicates are given for the sake of getting participations in syndicates," just as "participations in syndicates are taken for the sake of being able to offer participa-

28. Samuel A. Nelson, ed., *The Bond Buyers' Dictionary* (New York, 1907), 169–70.
29. A notable exception to this practice occurred in 1906, when Lee, Higginson, which had participated in distributing several AT&T issues, was not included in the $100 million syndicate of that year. See U.S. Temporary National Economic Committee, *Investigation of Concentration of Economic Power: Hearings* . . . (31 pts., Washington, 1939–41), pt. 23, 11830, 11837–38. Consult also Franklin, "Formation of Syndicates," 452.
30. *U.S. v. Henry S. Morgan et al.*, "Copy of Complaint" [1947], 14–15. See also *ibid.*, "Transcript of Trial, Plaintiff's Case — Deposition of [Charles E.] Mitchell" (November 2, 1951), 10395–402; *The New York Times*, March 4, 1902.
31. Storrow, "Management of Capital Account," 283–84; Franklin, "Formation of Syndicates," 452.
32. New York, *Life Insurance Investigation*, II, 1021–22.

tions in syndicates." [33] Some investment firms kept lists from which they selected their associates; others relied upon the memories of their partners. The results, as evidenced by the published announcements in the trade and financial press, were much the same. Each major originator had its friends and regular associates, whose names appeared repeatedly in its syndicates.[34]

The originating banker almost always determined the size of each syndicate member's participation. "We simply notify them how much has been allotted them," said Schiff, and the basis on which such decisions were made was "as suits Kuhn, Loeb & Company best." [35] One disgruntled Wall Street bond dealer attributed his inability to secure a participation in a popular, pre–World War I underwriting on the grounds that the originating banker, in this case J. P. Morgan & Co., sold the entire issue to friendly institutions, assigning each a specified amount. There was nothing "optional" about these transactions. "The bonds," he said, "were simply allotted. I believe in one or two instances the institution to which they were allotted had never heard of the . . . issue until that instant." [36] Years later, Thomas W. Lamont, a Morgan partner, called before the Senate Finance Committee to explain his firm's sale of foreign securities, testified that Morgan never coerced anyone to join its syndicates. "Every bank or banking house to whom we addressed the syndicate letter offering it participation in the syndicate has an absolute right to reject it," he said.[37]

No investment house could expect to be included only in syndicates of its own choice or dictate the size of its participation. *The New York Times* asserted that "firms and individuals who are permitted to participate in syndicates . . . cannot discriminate between promising and unpromising syndicates without being excluded altogether in the future. . . . Shrewd [syndicate] managers sometimes have a way of holding an inferior proposition back until several syndicates under their direction have turned out very profitably, and then the doubtful proposition is brought forward. Subscribers to other syndicates, with their profits still fresh, cannot well

33. Donham, "Underwriting Syndicates," 177. See also Mayer, *Wall Street: Men and Money,* 169.
34. Gerstenberg, "Underwriting of Securities by Syndicates," 329. See also W. R. Lawson, "The Financial Outlook in 1892," *The Bankers', Insurance Managers' & Agents' Magazine,* LIII (January 1892), 45–47, for illustrations of similar practices employed in London. Investment houses in that city, like the Barings, kept "red lists," containing the names of "special clients" who regularly were invited to participate in their flotations.
35. New York, *Life Insurance Investigation,* II, 1020.
36. Quoted in an unsigned article, "The Elusive Bogey: The Money Trust," *Current Literature,* LII (March 1912), 298.
37. U.S. Senate, Committee on Finance, 72d Cong., 1st Sess., *Sale of Foreign Bonds or Securities in the United States: Hearings* . . . (4 pts., Washington, 1931–32), pt. 1, 23.

refuse to take their share." [38] When Lamont was asked if a banking house that had refused to accept a participation in a risky venture might find itself at a "disadvantage with respect to the handling of any future bonds," the banker replied: "Oh, no; except on a common-sense basis — that is, if a house found itself consistently unable to place any bonds, eventually we would take that as an intimation that it did not care to have an invitation extended. That is all." [39]

Syndicates organized to purchase or underwrite an issue varied in size from fewer than a half dozen members to more than thirty. But whatever their size, they were almost always smaller than selling syndicates, which, by the first decade of the twentieth century, often included more than a hundred banking and brokerage firms.

Very often syndicate agreements were nothing more than an informal exchange of letters between the manager making the offer and the participants accepting it. Most business executives knew one another and were careful to join only those syndicates in which they had "confidence in the manager." "These things are so much a matter of custom and of business honor," one prominent corporation attorney and railroad executive wrote in 1909, "that legal questions rarely arise among the syndicate members or between them and the managers." [40] This probably more than anything else explains the lack of formality that characterized many of these agreements.

Whether long or short, formal or informal, the syndicate agreement gave the manager wide authority, very much like that conferred upon a trustee. "I do not know of a more absolute case of the delegation of power," said one investment banker, "than the typical syndicate agreement." [41] Limited entirely to questions concerning the internal operation and management of the syndicate, the agreement detailed the various responsibilities of the manager and the obligations of the participants. It specified, along with other things already noted, the duration of the syndicate, usually with a provision permitting the manager to extend it, if necessary; the brokerage commissions to be allowed the selling group, if one was formed; the time and method of payment to the company; and whether the members were to advance funds, and if so, whether directly to the corporation or to the syndicate manager. Very often the agreement also indicated the amount of the manager's "step up," the difference

38. *The New York Times*, September 24, 1905.
39. *Sale of Foreign Bonds: Hearings*, pt. 1, 55–56.
40. Joline, "Reorganization of Corporations," 571–72.
41. Donham, "Underwriting Syndicates," 190. See also "Legal Developments Significant in Business: The Relationship of Syndicate Managers and Members," *Harvard Business Review*, VIII (October 1929), 92; *The New York Times*, September 24, 1905; *U.S. v. Henry S. Morgan et al.*, "Transcript of Trial, Testimony of Harold L. Stuart: Colloquy" (March 12, 1952), 13663–73.

between what he as originator had paid the corporation for the securities and the price at which he was reselling them to the purchasing syndicate.[42]

Most agreements also authorized the manager to stabilize the market price of the issue during its distribution. Sometimes this entirely necessary and legitimate function was used to mislead potential buyers by creating a false impression that there was "a real and irresistible demand" for the issue, when actually there was none.[43] It was this kind of manipulation, when employed solely to allow a syndicate to unload its securities on an unsuspecting public, that increasingly came under attack during the first decade of the twentieth century.

Most syndicate agreements also authorized the manager to sell large blocks to institutional investors and to dealers at a specified price and for the account of the group, and they conferred upon him numerous other powers as well. He could assign exclusive sales territories to certain firms; permit participants to withdraw from the syndicate; if necessary, borrow from commercial banks; or sell the securities at a loss. Frederic Cromwell, treasurer of the Mutual Life Insurance Company, stated that "there were thousands of different forms of underwriting agreements." [44]

Syndicate members rarely questioned the manager's decision; fewer still dared break an agreement. "Should one of the participants fail to keep his promise," a New York attorney wrote in 1910, "the result would probably be not a suit for breach of contract, but banishment from the syndicate list," with all its attendant losses.[45] Participants understood the extent to which the success of a flotation depended upon the manager's judgment, experience, and ability. The desire to make a profit, the prestige of being associated with a prominent house of issue, and the customs that had developed combined to allow the manager to exercise "very nearly absolute power." The authority of the syndicate manager grew markedly

42. Franklin, "Formation of Syndicates," 453. As a result of several court decisions, the managers of New York syndicates were required to inform members whether the price they paid for their securities was higher than the one the originating house had paid the issuer. Before 1934, when the Securities Exchange Act revolutionized syndicate practices, the "step up" was the usual way managers were compensated for originating the issue, organizing the syndicate, keeping its books, and, after it had been terminated, settling accounts with the participants. See Burtchett and Hicks, *Corporation Finance,* 376–77; *U.S. v. Henry S. Morgan et al.,* "Transcript of Trial: Plaintiff's Case" (February 18, 1953), 20343–54.

43. Alexander D. Noyes, "Wall Street," *The Independent,* LVIII (January 26, 1905), 185. See also Franklin, "Formation of Syndicates," 453; Prime, "Private Negotiation," 485; Redlich, *Molding of American Banking,* II, 375.

44. Quoted in Gerstenberg, "Underwriting of Securities by Syndicates," 329. Sometimes a syndicate member was allowed either to take up his allotment and agree to hold onto it during the life of the syndicate, or to transfer it (though not his liability) to someone acceptable to the manager.

45. Gerstenberg, "Underwriting of Securities by Syndicates," 330.

after the beginning of the twentieth century, as the number and size of issues increased rapidly and risks multiplied.

For his services the manager generally charged the syndicate a commission in the form of a step up in price, usually the equivalent of ½ of 1 percent or 1 percent of the total par value of the issue. When Kuhn, Loeb organized and managed a purchase syndicate it generally charged 1 percent, except when the profit margin was exceptionally small. In such cases it cut its fee to ½ of 1 percent.[46] Sometimes other arrangements were made for compensating syndicate managers. In the flotation of a $150 million American Telephone and Telegraph Company (AT&T) bond issue in 1906, the managers of the underwriting syndicate, J. P. Morgan, Kuhn, Loeb, Kidder, Peabody, and Barings stated in the form letter they sent to prospective members that they made "no charge for their own services as Syndicate Managers, as they receive compensation from the Company." [47] Kidder, Peabody had received no fee for managing an underwriting syndicate for a smaller AT&T bond issue the previous year. When offering the Barings a participation in that syndicate the Boston firm had cabled London: "We recognize margin [between the suggested purchase and sale prices] small, but think underwriting desirable only to assist sales." [48]

Besides the profits to be earned, there were other advantages in being manager of a large, successful syndicate, the most important of which were the prestige associated with such enterprises and the opportunity to reward associates for past favors and to develop new ties.[49] The leading wholesale investment banking houses of the pre–World War I era, firms such as Morgan's and Kuhn, Loeb, as well as the smaller, newer ones just entering the underwriting business, like Goldman, Sachs & Co. and Lehman Brothers, were fully aware of the prestige and influence attached to managing issues; and they fought hard to win as many such assignments as were available within the limits of their resources.

The opportunity for added prestige, as well as profit, also explains why many syndicate participants attached great importance to the order in which their names appeared on "tombstone ads," the newspaper advertisements announcing new offerings. At the top of the list, usually on a level by itself, appeared the name of the manager, followed by those of the other syndicate members, on different lines, according to the size of their participations.

Judge Harold R. Medina attributed the investment bankers' great

46. New York, *Life Insurance Investigation,* I, 262, II, 1030–31.
47. Kidder, Peabody & Co., "Confidential Letters," III, 662, n.d. Kidder, Peabody & Co., MSS., Baker Library.
48. Kidder, Peabody & Co. to Baring Bros., March 3, 1905, "Confidential Letters," III, 617–18.
49. *U.S. v. Henry S. Morgan et al.,* "Transcript of Trial: Defendants' Opening — Mr. [William Dwight] Whitney" (February 15, 1951), 3164–65.

preoccupation with the position in which their names appeared in tombstone advertisements as a way of "inflating their egos," very much like the concern that Hollywood and Broadway stars have about the order in which their names appear on theater marquees.[50] The position a firm occupied on these advertisements involved more than just the kudos that went with appearing first or very close to the top of the list. It helped them attract new business. Some firms, Judge Medina observed, considered themselves "so high and mighty" that unless their names appeared first, they considered any other position "detrimental to their reputation" and refused to allow themselves to be listed at all.[51] Few firms, however, were so exclusive. If a syndicate promised to be profitable, most investment houses were ready to sacrifice a little prestige in order to make some money.

In the case of a very large or risky flotation, the originating banker might ask several commercial banks to form a banking syndicate to stand between him and the purchasing or underwriting group. Its function was to lend the purchasers or underwriters the funds necessary to meet their commitments to the issuer. If the corporation was an established one and there was every likelihood that investors would take up the issue quickly, the job of the banking syndicate was largely passive; it probably would not be called on to make any advance. In such cases the banking syndicate rarely investigated the issue carefully and was not concerned with the make-up of the purchasing or underwriting syndicate. If called upon, however, it would lend the amount it was committed to, accepting the securities being floated as collateral.

When the enterprise was new, the banking syndicate expected to be consulted more than was usual during the origination. Very often it insisted upon an exceptionally thorough investigation of the borrower's affairs, and it took an active part in selecting the purchasers or underwriters. Then, if called upon to make a loan, the banking syndicate very often required underwriting participants to pay in a considerable portion of their subscriptions — sometimes as much as 50 percent — and it supplied the rest.[52] The mere possibility that an underwriting or purchasing syndicate might have to borrow from a standby banking syndicate exerted a strong influence upon the originating banker's choice of associates, for the "borrowing

50. *Ibid.,* "Transcript of Trial: Defendant's Opening — Mr. Whitney" (February 15, 1951), 3164.
51. *Ibid.,* "Transcript of Trial: Plaintiff's Case (June 13, 1951), 8126. A firm's reputation was thought to be affected not only by how high its name appeared on the list, but also by its position on the line on which it appeared, the greatest prestige accruing to those whose name came first on each line, reading from left to right. At one time, when the practice was to read "tombstone ads" from right to left, the reverse was, of course, true.
52. Donham, "Underwriting Syndicates," 179, 184.

capacity" of an underwriting or purchasing syndicate depended almost entirely upon the credit and reputation of its members.

The final function in distribution was selling to ultimate investors. Once the underwriting or purchasing group was formed, and frequently at the very same time, a larger syndicate was organized to assume the risk and to handle the final distribution. Selling or distributing syndicates usually included most of the underwriters or purchasers, as well as other strong investment banking houses selected because of their ability to place sizable blocks of securities with institutions for investment as well as with small bankers, brokers, and dealers across the country. These retailers were brought together into a "selling syndicate," if they contracted for a specific allotment for which they were liable, or into a "selling group," if they assumed no risk and acted only as dealers receiving a commission on their sales. Neither of these two types of syndicate, however, appears to have been used extensively before World War I.[53]

The function of the distributing syndicate was essentially that of buying the securities at wholesale and retailing them at a slight increase in price, determined by the originating banker and maintained by agreement with him. Whatever securities the retailers failed to sell remained on their shelves. Such "floating supplies" of unsold bonds or stocks were referred to by financial commentators around the turn of the century as "undigested securities."[54] These dealers, or "merchants of securities," solicited large and small sales by circularizing their old customers and seeking new ones. Before World War I, only a few leading originators were equipped or inclined to sell to small investors. Those that were, such as Lee, Higginson, Kidder, Peabody, and three or four others, took up their allotments as underwriters and retailed most of these securities. The other great investment banking houses of the time, including Morgan and Kuhn, Loeb, allocated sales to brokers and dealers selected on the basis of past performance and the degree of participation in distributing a company's earlier offering. The kind of enterprise being financed, its location, and the types of securities being distributed also influenced the choice of retailers.[55]

53. Edward S. Meade, "Initial Stages of Organization," 47. See also *U.S. v. Henry S. Morgan et al.,* "Corrected Opinion," 25–26. Sometimes the distributing syndicate was called a "banking syndicate," though neither its make-up nor its purposes was in any way similar to that of the banking syndicate referred to above. Consult also Burtchett and Hicks, *Corporation Finance,* 374; American Council on Education, *A Study of Investment Banking* (n.p., 1927), 12–13; Marshall W. Stevens, "History of Lee, Higginson Company" (typescript in Baker Library), 38–39; Redlich, *Molding of American Banking,* II, 376.

54. *The New York Times,* October 18, 1903; *U.S. v. Henry S. Morgan et al.,* "Corrected Opinion," 26; See also "Syndicates as Promoters of Financial Enterprises," 15–16; Edward H. H. Simmons, *Modern Capitalism and Other Addresses* (n.p., 1927), 182–83.

55. Redlich, *Molding of American Banking,* II, 376; William L. Raymond, "Investment Banking in the United States: Its Historical Background and Development — The Wholesalers," *Barron's,* VI (May 31, 1926), 7.

Once the final distribution to investors was completed, the various syndicates were terminated. The manager then informed the participants, usually by letter or telegram, that the price restrictions were no longer in effect, and he distributed the syndicate's profits, making payment either in securities reserved for this purpose, in cash, or in both. Sometimes underwriting and distributing syndicates were kept together for several months after the issue had been sold so as to permit the participants to continue to manage the market and to sell the securities they received for their services at a satisfactory price.[56]

If payment to syndicate members was in cash, the manager sent each participant a check, the amount depending upon the size of his subscription. Rarely, if ever, did he send participants a detailed accounting of the group's profits and expenses. In questioning Edmund D. Randolph, the treasurer of the New York Life Insurance Company, on the way syndicate profits were distributed, Charles Evans Hughes, the counsel of the New York State (Armstrong) Investigating Committee, asked him whether he sought "to assure" himself that "a proper accounting" was made. "I have to admit to you," Randolph replied, "that we do not, nor does anyone else. . . . I don't know of . . . any of the houses who are syndicate leaders — that furnish a detailed statement at the conclusion of the syndicate." Participants placed their trust in "the well-known reputation and standing" of the houses with which they transacted their business, and it was not regarded as "good form" to ask for a detailed accounting. "I do not think you would be in the syndicate again," Randolph concluded, if you asked for one or "intimated distrust."[57]

Syndicates served the interests of the issuer just as advantageously as they did those of the investment banker. Among the many reasons that led more and more large corporations to sell their securities through such groups, one of the most important was that the syndicate could guarantee payment before the securities had been sold to investors, irrespective of the condition of the bond or stock market. This permitted the company to proceed with use of the funds without delay. Even if the syndicate failed to sell the securities, the corporation's credit was in no way adversely affected, as it would have been had the company itself tried and failed to sell them. The issuer, furthermore, was apprised early of exactly how much it would cost to market its securities. Very often both the issuer's reputation and the marketability of its securities were considerably improved by association with a group of influential banking houses. Sponsorship by such a banking house, whether acting alone or in a

56. *The New York Times,* May 4, 1902.
57. New York, *Life Insurance Investigation,* I, 260–61.

syndicate, weighed heavily with many investors, especially foreign buyers.[58]

The syndicate also assured the issuer a large, geographically widespread market for its securities, an advantage that became especially important early in the twentieth century. By that time the capital requirements of some corporations were outgrowing the resources of their traditional suppliers. The decision of AT&T in 1906 to add bankers in New York City and London to its Boston contingent in financing $100 million of its $150 million bond issue was motivated, in part, by the company's desire to widen the domestic market for its securities and to develop a foreign one.[59] Before then, with only one exception in 1902, AT&T, like its predecessor, the American Bell Telephone Company, had financed itself by either reinvesting profits or selling bonds. These went either directly to its stockholders, most of whom were New Englanders, or to four Boston investment houses, R. L. Day & Co., Estabrook & Co., Lee, Higginson, and Kidder, Peabody. After 1906, although the last-mentioned firm remained the company's principal Boston banker and the largest distributor of telephone securities in the United States,[60] leadership in underwriting new bond issues passed to Morgan's firm in New York.

58. Donham, "Underwriting Syndicates," 173–74. Arthur Crump, "The Baring Financial Crisis," *The Economic Journal,* I (June 1891), 392, which attributes the growing use of the underwriting syndicate in Great Britain after the Baring crisis to many of the same reasons. See also *U.S. v. Henry S. Morgan et al.,* "Transcript of Trial, Defendant's Opening — Mr. Whitney" (February 15, 1951), 3164–65; George Oliver May, "Flotation," in "Corporation Finance," 129.

59. Donham, "Underwriting Syndicates," 178. Donham declared in 1908 that "one of the very strong controlling factors" in AT&T's decision to seek the assistance of two influential New York City banking houses (J. P. Morgan and Kuhn, Loeb) and also of Baring Brothers of London in selling this issue was the company's desire to widen the market for its securities, especially since it was in need of large-scale financing and "found itself in a situation where New England had almost a saturated solution of telephone securities." Other reasons have been suggested for AT&T's decision to shift the center of its long-term financing from Boston to New York City. George D. Whitney, a clerk in Kidder, Peabody at the time and subsequently a partner in J. P. Morgan, declared that the decision was made by Robert Winsor (a Kidder, Peabody partner), on the grounds that the flotation was too large for his firm to handle alone. "It happens," Whitney testified in 1938, "that . . . one of the earliest recollections I have in my business life is of this transaction, so my historical recollection stems not only from what I knew then in office gossip — I was a very lowly clerk — but also from what I have learned since I moved and went into the employ of J. P. Morgan & Co." AT&T's decision also may have been influenced, as has been suggested by others, by the close ties that existed between Frederick P. Fish, the company's president at the time, and the heads of the two New York banking firms that were consulted. On the reasons for the change in the management of this issue see TNEC, *Hearings,* pt. 23, 11832–38, 11849, 11892–93; U.S. Federal Communications Commission, *Report on Telephone Investigation* (2 vols., Washington, 1939), I, 136–37; James W. Stehman, *The Financial History of the American Telephone and Telegraph Company* (Boston, 1925), 63.

60. Federal Reserve Bank of Boston, *Annual Report for 1960: A History of Investment Banking in New England* (Boston, 1961), 21.

Syndicates provided additional advantages to prospective borrowers of large amounts. Often they yielded better prices than dependence on either a few investment firms with sufficient resources to float a large issue or on direct sales to institutional investors, or on short-term loans from commercial banks.[61]

Occasionally an issuing corporation was skeptical of the theoretical advantages of underwriting or purchase syndicates and used another method. In 1901 the Lanston Monotype-Machine Company decided to sell a new stock issue directly to a few receptive capitalists; it "could not await the slow process of underwriting, public offer, subscriptions, and payments, and, prominent business gentlemen having offered to immediately purchase the entire amount for cash . . . this course was decided upon." [62]

The problems and costs of syndicating securities during the early 1900's were stressed by Judge Medina more than a half century later, after one of the lengthiest and most comprehensive reviews of the investment banking business ever conducted in the United States. He attributed the high syndicate charges of the pre–World War I era to "the excessively large capital resources" investment banking houses had to have in order to stay in business, and to "the slowness of distribution of a greatly increased volume of securities." [63] He commented, further, that prior to World War I, before the existence of a national "network of securities dealers," the job of reaching potential investors was slow, tedious, and risky. In 1905, for instance, it took N. W. Halsey & Co., a New York City firm specializing in utility bonds, "several months" to sell an issue of less than $1 million.[64]

Because of the time required to distribute securities, purchasing, banking, and distributing syndicates usually were organized to last anywhere from 15, 60, or 90 days to a year or more. Most of these groups were held together for about a year. Their managers, moreover, customarily reserved for themselves "broad powers" to extend them, and they frequently exercised this authority. A few syndicates were continued for five years or longer. Even when there was no underwriting or purchasing syndicate, as was customary when N. W. Halsey & Co. contracted for a small issue of public utility bonds, it still was common practice for the originating banker to get the dealers distributing the securities to agree "to maintain [the] price for a certain period," usually 15 days. Very often the firm reserved

---

61. *U.S. v. Henry S. Morgan et al.,* "Transcript of Trial" (March 29, 1951), 5332.

62. Lanston Monotype-Machine Company, *Annual Report,* year ending April 17, 1902, p. 9.

63. *U.S. v. Henry S. Morgan et al.,* "Corrected Opinion," 23.

64. *Ibid.,* 22; *ibid.,* "Transcript of Trial; Testimony of Harold L. Stuart" (March 11, 1952), 13594. See also *ibid.,* "Colloquy" (March 12, 1952), 13663–73; *ibid.,* "Corrected Opinion," 22–23.

for itself the right to extend the price agreement for another two weeks.[65]

Before World War I some of the more prominent New York City and Boston investment banking houses participated in twenty or twenty-five buying or underwriting syndicates a year. In the five years between 1907 and 1912, both Kidder, Peabody and Lee, Higginson purchased or underwrote, usually in conjunction with other bankers, more than a hundred issues, the total value of which amounted to $1 billion for each firm. The value of securities brought out by Morgan and Kuhn, Loeb was even larger. During the years 1902 to 1912 the House of Morgan sold more than $1.9 billion of securities for interstate corporations alone. In addition, it distributed "privately issued" securities, that is, those not publicly offered, and those sold for corporations in intrastate business. The volume of securities sponsored by Kuhn, Loeb between 1897 and 1906, either alone or acting with others, amounted to some $821 million. During the next six years, this firm jointly purchased or underwrote an additional $1.2 billion, of which it alone issued nearly $531 million.[66]

Besides the various specialized syndicates used to float new security issues, investment bankers also employed a second general type, those adapted expressly for launching mergers. In these syndicates they used many of the techniques common a generation earlier in financing railroads. Typically, the originating banker organized a syndicate to furnish the capital necessary to acquire the companies being merged and to provide working capital. Membership usually was limited to the promoters who initiated the combination — a few of the originating banker's wealthy friends and clients, selected because of their ability and willingness to assume the necessary risk as well as ownership of the properties being merged. The considerations applied in determining the size and membership of these syndicates were the same as those that decided the organization of those underwriting railroad mergers. Much the same was true of the selling syndicate,[67] and, as in the case of the railroads they spon-

65. *Ibid.*, "Transcript of Trial: Testimony of Harold L. Stuart" (March 17, 1952), 13907.
66. U.S. House, 62d Cong., 3d Sess., *Report of the Committee Appointed . . . to Investigate the Concentration of Control of Money and Credit* (Washington, 1913), 57, 75–78; Stevens, "History of Lee, Higginson and Company," 38.
67. Thomas R. Navin and Marian V. Sears, "The Rise of a Market for Industrial Securities, 1887–1902," *Business History Review*, XXIX (June 1955), 136–38; H. Parker Willis and Jules I. Bogen, *Investment Banking* (rev. ed., New York, 1936), 230–31; Nelson, *Bond Buyers' Dictionary*, 169. Some of the more well-known industrial consolidations that investment bankers organized at this time included United States Steel, International Harvester, American Can, American Car & Foundry, United Fruit, and International Silver. For a chronological listing of industrial consolidations capitalized at $1 million or more between 1897 and 1900, see Luther Conant, Jr., "Industrial Consolidations in the United States," *Quarterly Publications of the American Statistical Association*, n.s. VII (March

sored, the investment bankers also asked for and received representation on the new corporations' boards of directors.

A new corporation often was as anxious to have the banker who brought out the issue represented on its board as was the banker himself. The corporation's reputation among investors was improved by such an association, and the vendibility of its securities was enhanced. The investment banker, of course, also insisted upon this kind of representation as a safeguard.[68]

The merger creating the National Shawmut Bank of Boston (1898–1899) illustrates the many functions investment bankers fulfilled in negotiating one type of consolidation.[69] Unlike many other mergers of the time, this one was instigated by neither a promoter, the management of the banks concerned, nor individual stockholders. A group of Massachusetts savings banks, institutional stockholders, were dissatisfied with the recent dividends on their shares in Boston commercial banks, one of the few investment opportunities open to them and a highly favored one. The savings banks were convinced that one reason for the low return was an excess of commercial banking capital in Boston.[70] In order to correct this situation a committee representing the savings banks employed Kidder, Peabody to devise a consolidation plan. At a time when most mergers created corporations with reputedly inflated capitalizations, this one was designed to achieve just the opposite.

After lengthy deliberations a group of the city's leading financial men, closely associated with Kidder, Peabody and the savings institutions, worked out a plan to merge nine of Boston's fifty-seven commercial banks. The planners included Robert Winsor, who had recently become a partner in Kidder, Peabody; William A. Gaston, a member of the law firm of Gaston, Snow & Saltonstall; F. S. Moseley, a prominent broker; and representatives of the savings banks. The method chosen was for a syndicate headed by Kidder, Peabody to buy controlling shares in the banks, vote liquidation, and establish a successor corporation in which the savings banks then would invest. The nine institutions selected for liquidation had had differing histories of profitability, and the size of their capitals varied from $750,000 to $1 million. Kidder, Peabody was to buy

---

1901), 1–20. Consult also U.S. Industrial Commission, *Report* . . . (19 vols., Washington, 1900–02), XIII, pt. 2, 93–95, for the testimony of E. R. Chapman, a New York City broker, illustrating the methods used in organizing the American Smelting and Refining Co., established in 1899.

68. Donham, "Underwriting Syndicates," 183.

69. For a detailed study of this merger see Marian V. Sears, "The National Shawmut Bank Consolidation of 1898," *Business History Review*, XXXIX (Autumn 1965), 368–90.

70. N. S. B. Gras, *The Massachusetts First National Bank of Boston, 1784–1934* (Cambridge, 1937), 149; *Boston Evening Transcript*, September 30, 1898; *United States Investor*, IX (October 1, 15, 1898), 1429, 1436–37, 1486–87; *The Bankers' Magazine*, LVII (November 1898), 833–34. See also Frederic Haines Curtiss, *Fifty Years of Boston Finance, 1880–1930* (Boston, 1930), 4.

from the savings banks their investments in the nine banks and as much more as was necessary for control. The contract with the savings banks set the offering price at $12 a share above market. It also contained provisions to extend the offer to all savings banks in the state, to share with the stockholders any excess over this premium realized in liquidation, and to provide stockholders with an opportunity to subscribe to shares in the successor bank. Provision also was made to give displaced employees some compensation.[71]

Kidder, Peabody as sole manager now formed a syndicate to underwrite $13.5 million. That sum did not represent a new security issue, but the sum of the capitals of the nine banks to be merged, $8.5 million, plus the capital and surplus of the successor bank, $5 million. Syndicate members were responsible for advancing as much of their participations as was called for. The management fee was to be 4 percent of any sums Kidder, Peabody advanced to finance the merger plus 1 percent of the par value of all the bank shares owned by the syndicate after the banks had been liquidated. Profits to syndicate members were expected to come from liquidation of the banks' assets, which, it was anticipated, would yield more than the purchase price of the shares.[72]

The underwriting group was composed of sixteen Boston firms (some invited and some who asked to be included), three individuals, and three New York investment houses. The two Boston participants taking the largest share, after Kidder, Peabody itself ($3 million), were F. S. Moseley and R. L. Day, frequent syndicate associates of Kidder, Peabody. The largest New York participant was Price, McCormick & Co., which subscribed to $2.5 million. Other subscriptions ranged down to $20,000. Kidder, Peabody's New York affiliate, Baring, Magoun & Co., took only $200,000, whereas the House of Morgan accepted $1 million. A letter from Robert Bacon, a Morgan partner, to Robert Winsor shows the close, informal relations that existed between these two investment banking firms and the rather casual attitude they took toward the formalities of these transactions. Reminded that his firm had neglected to return the signed underwriting agreement, Bacon replied that the document had been "signed by Mr. Morgan himself"; failure to return it had resulted from "inadvertence." [73]

Carrying out the plans for consolidation brought unexpected

71. Kidder, Peabody & Co., "Bank Consolidation of 1898," "Agreement between Savings Bank Committee and Kidder, Peabody & Co.," dated September 21, 1898, in Kidder, Peabody & Co., MSS.; U.S. Comptroller of the Currency, *Annual Report . . . 1898* (2 vols., Washington, 1899), I, 532–34.

72. Kidder, Peabody & Co., "Bank Consolidation of 1898," "Agreement between Kidder, Peabody & Co. and Subscribers to Bank Underwriting Syndicate," dated September 26, 1898, in Kidder, Peabody & Co., MSS.

73. Kidder, Peabody & Co., "Bank Consolidation of 1898," Robert Bacon to Robert Winsor, letter dated October 14, 1898.

problems. There were protests from both the community and officials of the banks themselves. The general concept of eliminating solvent commercial banks was seen to be dangerous to the business community and the whole national banking system. The banks selected for dissolution were thought to have been poorly chosen (others were believed to need it more); and it was feared that the successor bank would cater to State Street brokers rather than to sound businessmen.[74] Officials of the banks were indignant because they had not been consulted; some advised their stockholders not to sell, or if they wanted to liquidate, to do so through the banks' own officers, who would carry out the proceedings with a greater return to the stockholders than if they used the services of expensive investment bankers.[75]

Kidder, Peabody proceeded to acquire controlling shares, however; to have the presidents of the banks hold stockholders' meetings to vote liquidation; and to carry out the liquidation process. The liquidators usually included a representative of Kidder, Peabody or its lawyers. The investment firm borrowed funds to finance these initial purchases and called for an advance from the underwriters of only 10 percent of their participation.[76]

The process of liquidation revealed that the affairs of one bank were not as reported in its financial statements, and losses resulted. Furthermore, this bank, as well as one other, succeeded in having some deposits and accounts transferred to outside banks before liquidation was voted. Officials of the other banks were more cooperative and were represented on the directorate of the new bank, the National Shawmut, which Kidder, Peabody now set up as a reorganization of an existing bank, the Shawmut National. Also on this directorate were Frank G. Webster, a partner in Kidder, Peabody, and representatives of F. S. Moseley and Lee, Higginson.[77] The profit to the underwriters was far less than had been anticipated, chiefly because of unexpected losses in liquidations.

The new bank now became the largest in Boston, with twice the capital of the next largest; but it was far smaller than the sum of its parts. Although its creation had achieved the purpose of reducing total banking capital, the reduction in total resources was much

74. *The Bankers' Magazine,* LVII (October 1898), 689; *United States Investor,* IX (October 15, 1898), 1486–87; Kidder, Peabody & Co., "Confidential Letters," III, 269; *Boston Daily Advertiser,* September 30, 1898.
75. *Boston Daily Advertiser,* September 30, 1898; *Boston Evening Transcript,* September 30, 1898; *The Banker and Tradesman and Massachusetts Law Reporter,* XXVI (October 5, 1898), 896.
76. Kidder, Peabody & Co., "Bank Consolidation of 1898" and "Confidential Letters," III.
77. *United States Investor,* IX (December 24, 1898), 1828; *Boston Daily Advertiser,* October 1, 29, November 1, 1898; *The Banker and Tradesman,* XXVI (November 23, 1898), 1065.

greater than had been expected, because of the transfers of deposits to competing banks.

Though vastly different in detail, the underwriting syndicate that the House of Morgan used to launch the United States Steel Corporation in 1901 was of the same general type as the one used by Kidder, Peabody to organize the National Shawmut Bank. The steel combination became notorious for the size of its nominal capitalization (the first billion dollar company), the proportion of its stated capital that was clear water, and the allegedly high return to the underwriters on their modest advances and small risk. The combination became the subject of its own federal investigations and a subsequent antitrust suit in 1911.[78]

Morgan's firm handled the whole process of merging the component companies. It assured their stockholders that it would determine the "entire Plan of Organization and Management" of the corporation.[79] There were more nonsteel than steel men on the new company's directorate. Four investment bankers were included among the former — three partners from Morgan's firm and one from Kidder, Peabody.

Morgan's functions were to organize a new corporation, exchange its securities for existing ones of the constituent companies, and supply new working capital. The firm had to decide on the amount and kinds of securities and the rates of exchange. The use of the different types was carefully discriminating. Andrew Carnegie had demanded bonds. The other companies exchanged shares for 7 percent preferred stock and common stock. The preferred was partly backed by assets, but the common had little behind it but prospects for future earnings.

The underwriting syndicate, composed of about three hundred members in the United States, Great Britain, and the Netherlands, included wealthy individuals, commercial bankers, and others, but only a very few representatives of investment firms. Among the twenty-six participants subscribing as much as $1.2 million were only two investment houses (Morgan and Kidder, Peabody), one commercial bank (First National Bank of New York), and one trust

---

78. See U.S. Bureau of Corporations, *Report . . . on the Steel Industry* (Washington, 1911–13); U.S. House, Committee on Rules, *Violations of Antitrust Act of 1890: Hearings . . .* (Washington, 1911); U.S. House, Committee on Investigation of United States Steel Corporation, *United States Steel Corporation: Hearings . . .* (Washington, 1912); U.S. House, Special Committee to Investigate Violations of Antitrust Act of 1890 and Other Acts, 62d Cong., 2d Sess., *Investigation of United States Steel Corporation, Report . . .* (Washington, 1912); *U.S. v. United States Steel Corporation and Others* [1911–1920].

79. J. P. Morgan & Co. [*Letter*] *To the Stockholders of the Federal Steel Company, National Steel Company, National Tube Company, American Steel and Wire Company of New Jersey, American Tin Plate Company, American Steel Hoop Company, American Sheet Steel Company* (March 2, 1901).

company (New York Security & Trust Company). Other subscribers in this selected group included individuals closely affiliated with the companies being merged; bankers and financiers long associated with these corporations; and other large capitalists, among them William Rockefeller, Marshall Field, William K. Vanderbilt, Thomas Fortune Ryan, and William Nelson Cromwell, the prominent and talented New York City corporation attorney soon to become involved in the negotiations leading to the acquisition of the Panama Canal site.[80] Participations, which correctly were expected to be very profitable, were so eagerly sought after that they actually were bought and sold.

The purpose of the underwriting syndicate was to guarantee the distribution of the new company's stock. The participants pledged a total of $200 million, but only $25 million was called up, and this was repaid shortly. For its services the syndicate was paid in stock which, when sold, amounted to about $60 million. Of this sum, the House of Morgan, as manager, received close to $12 million.[81]

Even expertly managed mergers occasionally resulted in serious losses, however. Such was the case in 1902 with Morgan's International Mercantile Marine Company (IMM), a giant holding company composed of the principal British and American steamship companies. The purpose of this corporation was to curb the costly and disorderly competition that existed in the North Atlantic traffic.

Originally scheduled to act only as banker, Morgan became a direct participant in order to complete the merger and to organize a syndicate to underwrite the new firm's $50 million bond issue. Its $60 million preferred stock and $60 million common were allotted as payment to original owners and as bonuses to the Morgan firm and the syndicate. The organization of this company followed directly after the highly profitable U.S. Steel merger, and syndicate memberships overlapped. Also, several of the larger subscribers were officials of the merged lines.

From the beginning the IMM syndicate met difficulties. Domestic and international complications combined to stifle demand for the new corporation's securities, and they were not offered publicly. Furthermore, syndicate members were called on for the entire amount of their participations. The syndicate's life was extended several times, and finally in 1906, the bonds, together with their bonuses in preferred and common stock, were distributed to members, at a time when prices at which they could be sold were far below the sums advanced. In the meantime the members had to

---

80. Frederick Lewis Allen, *The Great Pierpont Morgan* (New York, 1949), 292–93.

81. *Ibid.*, 292. Allen cites the original syndicate book as the source for the group's and the Morgan firm's profits.

stand the cost of advancing cash for the amount of their underwriting.[82]

While mergers and consolidations were booming, the syndicating of securities usually was highly remunerative to the participants. In 1899 the *United States Investor,* a respected Boston financial weekly, asserted that the underwriting syndicates of the past few years had provided investment banking houses with "a pleasant occupation, involving no great risk and entailing the most exaggerated fees." [83]

In truth, most syndicates during these years earned a profit, sometimes a very substantial one. Jacob Schiff asserted that not only did every syndicate managed by Kuhn, Loeb between 1904 and 1906 yield the participants a profit, but never once were participants called upon for any funds. The bonds this firm sponsored, he said, usually "were sold out before they were delivered." This was an exceptional record, for the very next year the firm experienced an embarrassing failure in disposing of a $75 million bond issue for the Union Pacific Railroad.[84]

The usual fees and commissions earned by underwriting syndicate members during these years were estimated to range between 2.5 percent and 10 percent of the total amount of their participations. A writer for *The New York Times* estimated underwriting profits in 1902 at 20 percent of the money guaranteed. "The profits to be divided from underwriting have grown to such an extent," this reporter concluded, "that many banks of considerable reputation in Wall Street rely almost entirely upon such profits for their income, letting the conventional banking business entirely alone." [85]

Similarly, syndicate " 'spread,' . . . the difference between the price paid . . . for the security and the price received for it . . . , was larger during this period than in later years." [86] Though evidence on this subject is scarce and incomplete, it has been estimated that during the years 1912 to 1915 bankers' spreads on railroad bonds ranged between 3.23 percent and 4.67 percent, whereas those on the bonds of public utility companies ranged between 5.36 percent and 6.78 percent, depending upon their quality. The spreads on preferred stock were even larger, a few amounting to as much as 14.25 percent.[87]

82. Thomas R. Navin and Marian V. Sears, "A Study in Merger: Formation of the International Mercantile Marine Company," *Business History Review,* XXVIII (December 1954), 320–24.
83. *United States Investor,* X (May 6, 1899), 584.
84. New York, *Life Insurance Investigation,* II, 1030; Gerstenberg, "Underwriting of Securities by Syndicates," 332. See also Redlich, *Molding of American Banking,* II, 373.
85. *The New York Times,* March 4, 1902. See also Gerstenberg, "Underwriting of Securities by Syndicates," 332.
86. *U.S. v. Henry S. Morgan et al.,* "Corrected Opinion," 23.
87. Merwin H. Waterman, *Investment Banking Functions: Their Evolution and Adaptation to Business Finance* (Ann Arbor, 1958), 75.

As the number and size of issues multiplied, syndicate operations became increasingly risky, especially for new securities, such as those issued to launch the huge new industrial combinations. These "trusts," the *United States Investor* explained in 1899, "have been underwritten with such astounding rapidity and in such appalling amounts in the last few months, and the [commercial] banks have so persistently refused to loan on the securities of new trusts, that the outlook for underwriters has become actually threatening." [88] In the decade before the panic of 1907, "the profits of underwriting," according to a knowledgeable contemporary, had become "as varied as the fortunes of the ventures it has been used to promote." [89]

The risk of having to take up a portion of an issue or the likelihood of an exceptionally slow sale, together with the possibility that the syndicate might not be able to borrow on unsold securities, made it necessary for investment houses to tie up substantial amounts of capital and to limit the number of syndicates in which they could participate. In explaining the high cost of syndicate charges in 1899, the *United States Investor* declared that "instead of turning their capital over with their usual frequency," the members of these groups "have locked it up for possibly a very long period, and they must be compensated for this." [90]

One of the earliest and most serious criticisms of the investment banker to gain widespread acceptance grew out of his activities in launching the great industrial combinations of the merger era. To many contemporary observers the practice of capitalizing earnings was an expensive and dangerous habit. "Heavy capitalization is, without question," the Industrial Commission concluded in its *Final Report*, "injurious to the interests of investors and the public at large; but to promoters and bankers it opens opportunities for great gains." The most commonly employed method, stock watering, the commission defined as "the issuing of securities that do not represent money invested in the property." [91] Professor Edward W. Bemis, an economist with the Bureau of Economic Research in New York City, testified that syndicates organized to float these securities were largely responsible for the vast amount of watered stock that was issued. "These banking syndicates want a profit," he said, "and the larger the stock issues the larger the commissions. . . . This statement has come to me from men very high up in corporate management." [92] Others testified similarly, and several witnesses asserted "that the amount of the stocks and bonds of most railways is far greater than their original cost or the cost of reproduction, and that

88. *United States Investor*, X (May 6, 1899), 584.
89. Nelson, *Bond Buyers' Dictionary*, 169.
90. *United States Investor*, X (May 6, 1899), 584.
91. U.S. Industrial Commission, *Report*, XIX, 405, 415.
92. *Ibid.*, IX, pt. 2, 88.

even the bonds in many cases exceed the actual cost of construction." [93]

The Industrial Commission described the usual practice employed in "financiering" mergers in these words: "The ordinary method of procedure is for a promoter to secure from the various companies which are to be consolidated options of purchase at fixed sums upon each plant. Then a new company is organized with a capitalization of possibly double the amount of the options. The companies are paid either in cash or in preferred stock of the new corporation, with perhaps some common stock thrown in as a bonus. The remainder of the capital stock then goes to the promoter as pay for his services in effecting the consolidation. In a word, promoters' profits come from watered stock. The extent of the promoter's gains in such a case depends upon his success in selling the new stock to the investors." [94]

When the promoter was not a banker, the securities were sold to an investment house, which then formed a syndicate to underwrite and distribute them to the public. In such cases the syndicate members' profits came from commissions, or from the difference between the price the banker paid for the securities and the one for which he sold them. Very often the syndicate also received an additional stock bonus, which the members sought to sell as quickly and profitably as possible.[95]

In order to arouse interest in the securities, the syndicate manager advertised them in newspapers, along with the names of respected and influential citizens associated with the enterprise. Prospectuses and circulars, neither of which provided the investor with sufficient information to permit him to reach an intelligent judgment, were distributed to promote still further interest in the securities. Rarely was the investor informed of the prices paid for the companies being merged, the promoters' profits, or the syndicate's charges. Only infrequently was he provided with a "careful estimate" of the new corporation's "tangible assets." [96] "Those things were really absurd," a Kidder, Peabody partner subsequently said of the prospectuses and circulars of the pre–World War I era.[97] The investor was entirely dependent upon whatever information was provided him by the investment house selling the issue.

Speculation in the securities of reorganized and newly consolidated companies was the rule rather than the exception. "Secrecy in promotion, combined with very large capitalization," the Industrial Commission reported, "gives a great advantage to directors and

93. *Ibid.*, IV, pt. 1, 19.
94. *Ibid.*, XIX, 415.
95. *Ibid.*, XIX, 416.
96. *Ibid.*, XIX, 619. See also [Roger W. Babson] *Actions and Reactions: An Autobiography* . . . (New York, 1935), 67.
97. Chandler Hovey to author, October 26, 1961.

officers of the combination and others associated with them in knowing the value of the shares. There seems to be no doubt that in many instances the promoters of combinations have been able to unload large blocks of stock at prices far above their values." [98] Too often, promoters of new enterprises were taking all the profits even before the new corporation started doing business, and the stockholders, instead of being considered "partners," were treated as "goats." [99]

By 1914 the syndicate, organized and led by an investment banking house, had become the commonly accepted method of underwriting and distributing large security issues of all kinds, including those used to launch combinations. Like many another twentieth-century investment banking practice, the syndicate originally was devised to meet the growing capital requirements of the federal government and the railroads and, after 1880, it was gradually adapted to satisfy the needs of other large private and public borrowers. The "evolution of the syndicate system," said Judge Medina, was "due entirely to the economic conditions in the midst of which investment bankers functioned. No single underwriter could have borne alone the underwriting risk involved in the purchase and sale of a large security issue. No single underwriter could have effected a successful public distribution of the issue. The various investment bankers combined and formed groups, and pooled their underwriting resources in order to compete for business." Without the syndicate, he concluded, "there would have been no underwriting and no distribution of new security issues." [100]

98. U.S. Industrial Commission, *Report,* XIX, 619.
99. Richard D. Wyckoff, "The Old vs. the New Idea in Capitalizing an Enterprise," *The Magazine of Wall Street,* XV (December 1914), 93.
100. *U.S. v. Henry S. Morgan et al.,* "Corrected Opinion," 27.

4 Investments, Investors, and Investment Bankers, 1900–1914

Between the 1890's and World War I, investment bankers responded positively to a variety of challenges, both inside and outside their industry. Their innovations and piecemeal adaptations to these environmental changes altered the structure of the industry and the pattern of competitive practices in it. "The most significant fact about the period prior to World War I," Judge Harold R. Medina wrote in 1954, "is that in it will be found the beginnings . . . from which in the course of time and by a gradual and traceable evolution there grew the elaborate and effective modern methods by which investment bankers, skilled in the application of their special techniques, perform the integrated services by which they earn their livelihood." [1]

One of the major changes that occurred in the securities business during these years was the relative decline in the importance of railroad issues, the former standby of the private bankers. The carriers' long-time dominance of the market was being challenged by the growing needs of industrial and utility corporations and, to a lesser extent, by those of foreign governments. Many of the new offerings brought out at this time, especially from 1901 to 1903, were those of recently organized combinations.

Nevertheless, while the number of industrials listed on the New York Stock Exchange rose steadily, from 20 in 1898 to 173 in 1915, railroad issues "dominated" the market for much of the period.[2] Between 1900 and 1902, for example, nearly $1.2 billion of new rail securities was floated, and the stocks and bonds of these companies accounted for a majority of the trading on the New York, Boston, and other major exchanges down to 1910. Not until then did industrials and utilities take the lead. At the same time, bonds gave way to preferred and common stock as the principal types of securities used by railroads and other enterprises.[3]

In addition, foreign governments borrowing in the United States were making more use of the services of American investment

---

1. *U.S. v. Henry S. Morgan et al.*, "Corrected Opinion of Harold R. Medina" (February 4, 1954), 27
2. William J. Shultz and M. R. Caine, *Financial Development of the United States* (New York, 1937), 441; H. Parker Willis and Jules I. Bogen, *Investment Banking* (rev. ed., New York, 1936), 232; Federal Reserve Bank of Boston, *Annual Report for 1960: A History of Investment Banking in New England* (Boston, 1961), 29.
3. Willis and Bogen, *Investment Banking,* 230; "Issues of Bonds in Place of Stocks," *American Banker,* LXVI (June 22, 1901), 2062; *The Commercial & Financial Chronicle,* LXXXIX (November 6, 1909), 1187. See also Myron T. Herrick, "The Government and the Bankers," *American Banker,* LXXV (June 25, 1910), 7712.

houses. "Our bankers," *The Commercial & Financial Chronicle* reported in 1901, "were able to make a departure and began to take part in the floating of European government loans, thus reversing our old-time position, where we had to seek rather than furnish capital abroad." [4] By 1900 some $185 million had been invested in Mexican railroads and mines, and an additional $150 million in Canadian securities. One prominent Boston investment banking house, E. H. Gay & Co., with offices in New York City, Philadelphia, and Montreal, announced that it was adding Canadian issues to its list of specialties.[5] What gave American investment bankers a new sense of pride and accomplishment was the fact that they had been called upon "to relieve Europe's loan requirements." [6]

Most of these foreign issues were floated between 1899 and 1905, when the English and Continental money markets were tight and disturbed and there was "an abundance of floating capital at New York." Public interest in these issues, moreover, was developing rapidly, according to informed opinion.[7] One of the earliest and largest foreign issues to attract widespread attention in the United States was the British National War Loan of March 1900, an outgrowth of the conflict in South Africa. J. P. Morgan & Co., acting as agent of the Bank of England, took subscriptions amounting to $12 million.[8] In the case of the British Exchequer loan of August 1900, J. P. Morgan, Drexel & Co., Kidder, Peabody & Co. and Baring, Magoun, the Boston firm's New York affiliate, received applications amounting to several times the $30 million awarded them for sale in the United States.

The next year the Bank of England authorized the same two New York houses, together with Kidder, Peabody of Boston and Drexel of Philadelphia, to accept subscriptions to a new loan amounting to £30 million. It, too, was greatly oversubscribed; the National City Bank and three insurance companies — New York

4. *The Commercial & Financial Chronicle*, LXXII (January 5, 1901), 6.
5. Nathaniel Bacon, "American International Indebtedness," *The Yale Review*, IX (November 1900), 265–85; George W. Edwards, *The Evolution of Finance Capitalism* (London, 1938), 182; *The Commercial & Financial Chronicle*, LXX (May 12, 1900), 925; Ralph A. Young, *Handbook on American Underwriting of Foreign Securities* (Washington, 1930), 9–10. Canada and Mexico accounted for nearly 73 percent of the total $460 million of foreign security holdings of Americans in 1900. The following figures, taken from Bacon, indicate the origins of the other foreign securities held by Americans at the time: Europe, $15 million; Cuba, $50 million; "other Antilles," $10 million; Latin America, $45 million; and Pacific, China, and Japan, $5 million.
6. *The Commercial & Financial Chronicle*, LXXI (September 22, 1900), 579; ibid., LXXII (January 5, 1901), 8; "The Financial Centre of the World," *The Bankers' Magazine*, LXIV (February 1902), 172–75.
7. *The Commercial & Financial Chronicle*, LXXII (April 27, 1901), 797; *American Banker*, LXV (July 4, 1900), 1168; Young, *Handbook on American Underwriting of Foreign Securities*, 10–11.
8. *The Commercial & Financial Chronicle*, LXX (March 10, 1900), 459; *ibid.*, LXXII (January 5, 1901), 8, 11.

Life, Mutual, and Equitable — each took £1 million, with smaller sums going to "large numbers of persons throughout the country." American subscriptions to this loan, including those from bankers in the United States who applied directly to London, amounted to about $150 million.[9] This transaction, according to one of Morgan's early biographers, established the United States "for the first time among the money powers of the world."[10]

Numerous smaller foreign issues also were floated in the United States. The obligations of German cities were especially attractive to American investors; their yield was generally higher than that of the same class of securities in the United States. C. I. Hudson & Co., a New York private banking firm, specialized in retailing these issues, leaving the job of underwriting to the larger investment houses.[11] Kuhn, Loeb & Co. was especially active in underwriting large blocks of Continental securities. In 1900, this firm, together with the National City Bank of New York, sold a large issue of German Imperial bonds, and in 1904 it performed the same service for the government of Sweden.[12]

A year later, Kuhn, Loeb participated in one of its largest and most important foreign flotations up to this time. Under the leadership of Jacob H. Schiff, it organized and managed the American syndicate distributing $75 million of Japanese war bonds in the United States. This loan, too, was greatly oversubscribed, the syndicate receiving applications amounting to $500 million.[13] In scaling down the bids the bankers gave first consideration to small investors and proportionally smaller amounts to financial interests whose single bids ran into millions.[14] In all, Kuhn, Loeb sent out nearly 15,000 allotment notices. The overwhelming success of this loan was especially gratifying to Schiff because, in his opinion, it would help defeat the anti-Semitic and tyrannical Russian government, which he labeled the "enemy of mankind."[15]

Between 1900 and 1913 nearly 250 foreign loans, with a par value of close to $1.1 billion, were placed in the United States. The

---

9. *The Commercial & Financial Chronicle*, LXXII (April 27, 1901), 796–97, 799–800; *ibid.* (May 4, 1901), 844; Margaret G. Myers, "Origins and Development" in Benjamin H. Beckhart, ed., *The New York Money Market* (4 vols., New York, 1931–32), I, 292. According to Lewis Corey, *The House of Morgan* (New York, 1930), 227, sale of these loans in the United States accounted for 20 percent of Britain's war costs.

10. Carl Hovey, *The Life Story of J. Pierpont Morgan* (New York, 1912), 281.

11. *The Commercial & Financial Chronicle*, LXXI (July 7, 1900), 9–10.

12. *Ibid.*, LXXII (January 5, 1901), 8; [Kuhn, Loeb & Co.] *Investment Banking through Four Generations* (New York, 1955), 17.

13. *The New York Times*, April 1, 1905; [Kuhn, Loeb & Co.] *Investment Banking through Four Generations*, 18; Cyrus Adler, *Jacob H. Schiff: His Life and Letters* (2 vols., New York, 1929), I, 212–40.

14. *The New York Times*, April 8, 1905, June 18, 1905.

15. [Kuhn, Loeb & Co.] *Investment Banking through Four Generations*, 18; Adler, *Schiff*, I, 212–40.

peak year was 1905, when issues totaling $175 million were floated.[16] Except for the British and Japanese war loans, most of these issues were either government refunding bonds, municipal obligations, or railroad securities. Kuhn, Loeb and Speyer, together with several other large New York City and German banking houses, reorganized and financed the consolidation of the Mexican railroads.[17] Among the more prominent British issues floated in the United States was one to help finance the construction of the London subway system, with Speyer winning from Morgan the management of the American distribution of these securities.[18]

Loans similar to these continued to be marketed in the United States until the outbreak of World War I, but beginning in 1906 they decreased in both number and size. By the end of 1913, according to one estimate, American holdings of European securities and property stood at about $350 million, of which $250 million was in English, German, and Swedish bonds.[19]

During the first decade of the twentieth century the growing financial needs of companies in light industry, retail stores, and other small enterprises seeking to go public were not being met by the major investment banking firms. This fact provided the opportunity for another group of private banking and brokerage houses to become underwriters.

Goldman, Sachs & Co. and Lehman Brothers were two such firms. Henry Goldman and Samuel Sachs, the two senior partners of Goldman, Sachs, believed there was a market for the securities of small, privately owned manufacturing and retail companies. Previously, the needs of such corporations had been "neglected or overlooked" by both the leading investment houses and the smaller firms that specialized in municipal and public utility issues.[20] Thus in 1906, when United Cigar Manufacturers and Sears, Roebuck & Co. needed substantial funds, the presidents of these concerns, both of whom were personal friends of the Goldman family, engaged Goldman, Sachs to float their issues.[21]

16. The geographical origin of these issues was as follows: Latin America (especially Mexico and Cuba), $374 million; Far East (chiefly Japan), $310 million; Europe, $278 million; and Canada, $175 million. Young, *Handbook on American Underwriting of Foreign Securities,* 10–11. See also M. F. Jolliffe, *The United States as a Financial Centre, 1919–1933* (Cardiff, Wales, 1935), 7.

17. Adler, *Schiff,* I, 197–211; U.S. Bureau of Foreign and Domestic Commerce, "A New Estimate of American Investments Abroad," *Trade Information Bulletin, No. 767* (Washington, 1931), 17.

18. Young, *Handbook on American Underwriting of Foreign Securities,* 10–11; Herbert L. Satterlee, *J. Pierpont Morgan: An Intimate Portrait* (New York, 1939), 381.

19. Shultz and Caine, *Financial Development of the United States,* 468.

20. *U.S. v. Henry S. Morgan et al.,* "Corrected Opinion," 19–21. See also George K. Turner, "Morgan's Partners," *McClure's Magazine,* XL (April 1913), 34–35.

21. *U.S. v. Henry S. Morgan et al.,* "Transcript of Trial: Plaintiff's Case —

The firm could not underwrite these issues alone, nor could it borrow on them from commercial banks; securities of this kind were generally unknown or viewed with suspicion. Accordingly, both Henry Goldman and Samuel Sachs, being close personal friends of Philip Lehman, the most influential member of Lehman Brothers, turned to his firm for assistance. They persuaded him to join them in underwriting for the two applicants. The issue for Sears, Roebuck amounted to $10 million of preferred and common stock. "I would like you to get the concept," Samuel Sachs's son testified nearly a half century later, "that it was . . . a difficult thing to accomplish [these flotations] and . . . the two firms together turned to individuals who were wealthy, the people that we knew in Europe. . . . We turned to them to find people who would . . . take this underwriting risk." [22]

Both ventures proved profitable, and the "informal, oral agreement" that Goldman, Sachs and Lehman Brothers entered upon at this time remained in effect for the next eighteen years.[23] Between 1906 and 1924 "the two firms were, in effect, a single partnership as to the heading of security issues." Together they managed 114 negotiated offerings for 56 issuers. On only four occasions during these years, all of them involving the B. F. Goodrich Rubber Co., did Goldman, Sachs bring out an issue without the participation of its usual associate.[24]

The entry of these two houses into the underwriting business in 1906 marked the beginning of a new type of investment house, one that was to grow rapidly during the next twenty years. Firms such as these established a special place for themselves, as more and more manufacturers and merchandisers of consumer goods, retail and variety store chains, and food packers and distributors went public.[25] As indicated before, the rapid rise of Goldman, Sachs and Lehman Brothers as major underwriters was greatly facilitated by the ties they had developed as foreign exchange dealers and commodity brokers.

Important changes also were taking place on the supply side of the capital markets. Both old and new sources of funds for investment grew considerably. Foreign capital continued to be important, but not as it had been in the previous half century.

Deposition of [Walter E.] Sachs" (May 10, 1951), 6652–55. See also Barry E. Supple, "A Business Elite: German-Jewish Financiers in Nineteenth-Century New York," *Business History Review*, XXXI (Summer 1957), 172.
  22. *U.S. v. Henry S. Morgan et al.*, "Transcript of Trial: Plaintiff's Case — Deposition of [Walter E.] Sachs" (May 10, 1951), 6653–54.
  23. *Ibid.*, "Corrected Opinion," 20–21. See also Supple, "A Business Elite," 173–74; [Lehman Brothers] *A Centennial: Lehman Brothers, 1850–1950* (New York, 1950), 32–33.
  24. *U.S. v. Henry S. Morgan et al.*, "Corrected Opinion," 313n.2.
  25. [Lehman Brothers] *A Centennial*, 35–38, 46–55, contains a list of the more important companies that this firm financed.

Nevertheless, many European investors continued to prefer American securities over those of their own countries. This circumstance prevailed in spite of the fact that Americans themselves were beginning to invest in foreign securities. Between 1896 and 1905 foreigners bought about $1.2 billion of American issues.[26] As in the past, the English were the largest buyers. Out of an estimated $3.1 billion of American securities held abroad in 1900, for example, they owned about $2.5 billion.[27]

One of the most widely discussed changes in the foreign market for American securities during the first decade of the twentieth century occurred after 1905. French bankers and investors began to display a growing interest in American issues. In 1906 Kuhn, Loeb placed a $50 million Pennsylvania Railroad bond issue entirely in Paris.[28] Many other American bankers wanted to draw on France's capital market, which, in their opinion, was one of the largest in the world and well known for its interest in foreign securities.[29] The existence of a tax on foreign securities listed on the Paris Bourse had not prevented several American investment houses, notably Morgan, Harjes & Co., the Paris partnership of the Morgan firm, from carrying on a "solid but unostentatious business in American securities with special clients."[30] Some American investment houses went so far as to issue investment circulars printed in French.[31] Later in 1906 Kuhn, Loeb floated another loan for the Pennsylvania Railroad in Paris and in 1909 a $5 million loan for the Southern Pacific. That same year Speyer placed a $10 million issue there for the St. Louis & San Francisco Railroad.[32]

During the first decade or so of the twentieth century the supply of domestic capital seeking investment also grew rapidly. Between 1900 and 1910 banking assets more than doubled, increasing from $10.7 billion to $22.4 billion, and many country banks in the Middle and Far West, which previously had invested almost exclusively in farm mortgages, started buying railroad, industrial, and utility

26. Shultz and Caine, *Financial Development of the United States*, 442.
27. Bacon, "American International Indebtedness," 265–74. See also U.S. Industrial Commission, *Reports* . . . (19 vols., Washington, 1900–02), XIX, 404; "The Amsterdam Stock Exchange," *The Ticker*, I (February 1908), 4–6. Excluding Britain, Bacon's estimate of the distribution of American securities abroad in 1900 was as follows: Holland, $241 million; Germany, $200 million; Switzerland, $75 million; France, $50 million; Belgium, $20 million; other European countries, $15 million; Latin America and Canada, $45 million.
28. [Kuhn, Loeb & Co.] *Investment Banking through Four Generations*, 17; *The Commercial & Financial Chronicle*, LXXXII (June 23, 1906), 1409–11.
29. *The Commercial & Financial Chronicle*, LXXXII (May 26, 1906), 1177; Charles A. Conant, "Selling American Securities Abroad," *North American Review*, CLXXXIII (September 21, 1906), 508. See also "French Investors and American Securities," *American Banker*, LXX (May 13, 1905), 871.
30. Conant, "Selling American Securities Abroad," 508.
31. *The Commercial & Financial Chronicle*, LXXXII (May 26, 1906), 1177. [Kuhn, Loeb & Co.] *Investment Banking through Four Generations*, 17.
32. *The Commercial & Financial Chronicle*, LXXXIX (July 10, 1909), 71.

bonds, and recommending these issues to farmers. The increase in funds for investment led to a growing interest in securities throughout the country. Meanwhile the assets of life insurance companies also expanded rapidly, climbing from $1.7 billion to $3.8 billion; and the number of individual investors increased too, according to one estimate, from about 4.4 million in 1900 to 7.4 million in 1910. In terms of population this growth represented an increase from approximately 5.8 percent to slightly more than 8 percent.[33]

During the fourteen years preceding the outbreak of World War I the investment banking business was conducted largely by some 250 institutions. Most of these were located in the eastern or middle eastern sections of the country.[34] In terms of capital, size, organization, functions, and clientele, the differences among them were as great as those among the businesses they served. Auctioneers continued to dispose of some issues in much the same way as their predecessors had done more than a half century earlier. Wealthy individuals and, before 1906, life insurance companies continued to appear regularly on syndicate lists. Most of the institutions engaged in underwriting, buying, and distributing new issues were either private banking or brokerage partnerships, or chartered commercial banks, their security affiliates, and trust companies.

Measured in terms of numbers alone, private bankers dominated the investment banking business down to the outbreak of World War I.[35] Though these firms differed significantly in numerous ways, nearly all of them were organized as partnerships. There were several reasons for this. Tradition had much to do with it. Most of them had started out this way and saw no good reason to incorporate. Indeed, there were at least two reasons that caused them to avoid

33. "Bonds Becoming Popular in the West," *American Banker*, LXXIV (August 14, 1910), 2917; Boston, FRB, *Annual Report, 1960*, 27; Edwards, *Evolution of Finance Capitalism*, 184; H. T. Warshaw, "The Distribution of Corporate Ownership in the United States," *The Quarterly Journal of Economics*, XXXIX (November 1924), 28. See also Shultz and Caine, *Financial Development of the United States*, 469.

34. *U.S. v. Henry S. Morgan et al.*, "Corrected Opinion," 22. Henry W. Sites, *Investment Bankers and Brokers of America* (New York, 1916), lists some 4,800 firms in 186 cities.

35. Available statistics on the number of private banks in the United States at the beginning of the twentieth century are widely conflicting. Usually they fail to distinguish between small, rural institutions that did no investment banking business, and large, urban ones, sometimes called "brokers' banks" or "financial banks," that were engaged actively in buying and selling securities. Many of the standard compilations, moreover, included brokerage firms and private banks in the same lists. In 1902 *Rand-McNally Bankers' Directory* cited the following figures on the number of private bankers and brokers in the major financial centers: New York City, 170; Boston, 184; Philadelphia, 183; Baltimore, 65; and Chicago, 73. Fritz Redlich's estimate of the number of private bankers in 1909 specializing in investment banking is considerably larger. According to his count there were close to 2,300 in New York, Pennsylvania, Massachusetts, and Illinois, the four states where private investment banking was most highly developed. See Redlich, *Molding of American Banking*, II, 74.

incorporation. As partnerships they did not have to disclose their capital to anyone, a fact made abundantly evident during the Pujo investigation, when Morgan, Kuhn, Loeb, and other private bankers refused to provide the committee with information about their resources or profits. Not even all the partners in a firm had access to this information; it was available only to a few senior members.[36] Private banks also avoided incorporation because they did not want to submit to inspection by state or federal authorities. They "don't wish to subject themselves to legislative interference," one prominent Boston trust company official explained. "They are afraid of it; they don't know what would happen." [37]

The organizational structure and internal operations of the old established private investment banking houses did not change much in the decade before World War I. During the early years of the twentieth century the number of partners in these firms usually ranged anywhere from four to a dozen.[38] Kidder, Peabody's Boston house, for example, in 1900 had four partners. One was added in 1901 and two others in October 1905, a month after the death of Francis H. Peabody, the last of the founders. Between 1905 and 1926, when several new members were admitted, six partners directed Kidder, Peabody's affairs in Boston and another managed the New York office.[39]

Like most other private investment houses, Kidder, Peabody recruited its partners from among the firm's employees, nearly all of whom originally were hired as clerks or messengers. It is "our invariable custom," Winsor wrote to a client, "to take only young men at the beginning of their business careers." [40]

It generally gave preference to members of the partners' families and the sons of friends or business associates. "A great deal of attention was paid to personal relationships," another Kidder, Peabody partner asserted.[41] Much the same was true of other private banks, especially the German-Jewish houses, many of whose partners were related by blood or marriage.

36. Chandler Hovey, retired partner in Kidder, Peabody & Co., to author, October 26, 1961. See also "What Constitutes Strength in a Brokerage House?" *The Ticker,* III (February 1909), 173–77.
37. Wallace B. Donham, "Underwriting Syndicates and the Purchase and Sale of Securities through Banking Houses," in Harvard Graduate School of Business Administration, "Corporation Finance" (mimeographed lecture notes, Baker Library, 1908), 206.
38. In 1912 the Morgan firm was composed of eleven partners; Kuhn, Loeb, six; Lee, Higginson, ten; and Kidder, Peabody, seven. See U.S. House, 62d Cong., 3d Sess., *Report of the Committee Appointed . . . to Investigate the Concentration of Control of Money and Credit* (Washington, 1913), 57, 75–77. See also Redlich, *Molding of American Banking,* II, 75.
39. Kidder, Peabody & Co., "Record of Clerks" [1880–1927?] 5 vols., Baker Library.
40. Robert Winsor to C. A. Wright, November 12, 1897, Kidder, Peabody & Co., "Confidential Letters," III, 224.
41. John R. Chapin to author, October 24, 1961.

In order to qualify for a partnership an employee usually had to accept a subordinate position for about ten years. Beginning salaries were low and rose slowly. "I joined the firm in 1900 at $4 a week as errand boy," said a subsequent Kidder, Peabody partner, "and after three years went up to $12."[42] Before being admitted to a partnership, promising employees were given "an interest" in the firm, usually 1 or 2 percent of the annual profits, a practice that made low stipends much more tolerable.[43]

Financial arrangements among the partners were arrived at orally. "I think it a wonderful record," Frank G. Webster, Kidder, Peabody's senior partner between 1905 and 1930, wrote to a partner in 1920, "that . . . all understandings have been verbal among the partners and at no time has any question arisen in respect to the partnership in which we were not all in accord."[44]

Partners often were admitted without having to invest in the firm if the members believed they "could add something," a Kidder, Peabody partner explained. "If he had some money, he might put some in."[45] Those who did not invest at the time they were admitted usually did so later. Partners received a percentage of the profits according to the size of their investment and their usefulness to the firm. This arrangement also was true of other well-established houses with ample working capital.

Before World War I the staff of most private banking houses was relatively small. Both Kidder, Peabody and Kuhn, Loeb had fewer than 50 employees, including a few women secretaries. Morgan's staff in 1913 numbered only 150.[46] It was composed of messengers, clerks, bookkeepers, tellers, cashiers, and statisticians, some of whom also served as security analysts.

Houses like Kidder, Peabody that were engaged in various banking activities usually assigned a partner to supervise each department. One partner represented it on the Boston Stock Exchange and another on the New York Stock Exchange. After 1919, Winsor was both "the pilot" of Kidder, Peabody's entire operations and the man principally responsible for cultivating new business, organizing syndicates, and negotiating participations with other investment houses. He enjoyed very close personal ties with the Morgan firm. Robert Bacon, a Morgan partner between 1894 and 1903, was Winsor's classmate at Harvard; and George Whitney, who became a Morgan partner in 1919, had been a clerk with Kidder, Peabody.

42. Hovey to author, October 26, 1961.
43. Chapin to author, October 24, 1961.
44. Frank G. Webster to Frank W. Remick, n.d. [1920?] Kidder, Peabody & Co., "Miscellaneous Records," Baker Library.
45. Hovey to author, October 26, 1961.
46. Chapin to author, October 24, 1961; Henrietta M. Larson, typescript of interview with George W. Bovenizer [a Kuhn, Loeb partner] dated December 18, 1951; George K. Turner, "Morgan's Partners," *McClure's Magazine,* XL (April 1913), 34–35.

Nearly every partner served on one or more of the boards of corporations in which the firm was financially interested. Francis Peabody was a director of the Santa Fe and the United States Steel Corporation; Frank Webster served on the boards of at least a half dozen companies, among them the National Shawmut Bank. The duties and responsibilities of Kidder, Peabody's partners were very similar to those of other private bankers.

Some firms had among their partners individuals who, because of seniority, ability, or force of personality ruled over the business almost single-handedly. These men made all the major decisions for their firms, often with little or no consultation with the other members. Such appeared to be the case with J. P. Morgan, especially after 1900, when many of the older partners had died or retired, and their successors "stood in such awe of him," one of them later wrote, "that they were sometimes hardly at their best with him."[47] The same came to be true of Winsor, who was sometimes called "the J. P. Morgan of Boston."[48] And so it was with Schiff at Kuhn, Loeb. He dominated this firm until his death in 1920, even though several forceful and very able partners were added after 1897.[49] George W. Bovenizer, a later partner, who started with the firm as an office boy and in 1911 took over the management of its syndicate operations, described Schiff as "the ablest of bankers" and "a tyrant."[50]

A contemporary observer of the Wall Street scene around 1910 described the atmosphere in a large private banking house in these words:[51]

There is an air of omniscience as if nothing unexpected could ever happen. Doors do not slam, men walk softly upon rugs, voices are never lifted in feverish excitement over profit and loss; no one is permitted even to call off prices from the tape. There is first a feeling of space, quite different from that sense of limited margins which pervades a broker's

---

47. Quoted in Redlich, *Molding of American Banking,* II, 385.
48. Chapin to author, October 24, 1961; Albert H. Gordon, chairman of Kidder, Peabody & Co., Inc., to author, April 22, 1965.
49. Between 1897 and 1902 four new partners were added, all of whom were related to existing ones by blood or marriage. Otto Kahn and Felix M. Warburg, who became partners in 1897, were the sons of prominent German bankers. Kahn was married to Adelaide Wolff, the daughter of Abraham Wolff, a partner since 1875, and Felix Warburg was married to Schiff's daughter. At the time these two men were made partners, Schiff also elevated his son Mortimer L. to a partnership. In 1902 Paul M. Warburg, who was then a member of his family's Hamburg banking house, M. M. Warburg & Co., and the husband of Solomon Loeb's younger daughter, arrived in the United States to join his brother as a partner in Kuhn, Loeb. No others were added until 1902, when Jerome H. Hanauer was admitted. He had started with the firm as an office boy and was the first partner "who was not one of the immediate family." See [Kuhn, Loeb & Co.] *Investment Banking through Four Generations,* 7, 14; Mary Jane Matz, *The Many Lives of Otto Kahn* (New York, 1963), 19–22.
50. "Larson-Bovenizer Typescript," dated December 18, 1951.
51. Garet Garrett, *Where the Money Grows* (New York, 1911), 49–50.

office. Ceilings in a banking house are higher than ceilings anywhere else, and that may account for it, but even before one is conscious of dimensions one gets the feeling of space from the manners of the person in uniform who attends to the noiseless opening and closing of the main portal and asks people what business they have to enter.

The responsibilities of private banking rest much more visibly upon this individual than upon the partners. He rules over all that probationary space lying between the entrance and the marble railing at which any trivial business may be transacted, and beyond which all important business must take place. . . . Nothing is concealed, not even the great bankers. Their degrees of greatness (or perhaps only their degrees of seniority) are known by the position of their desks.

The junior partner has the desk nearest the marble railing and most exposed to the scrutiny of all comers. The one of next greatness has the desk next farther removed, and so it goes, up to the senior partner, sometimes known reverentially in the back office as the "old man." His desk is at the big window. He himself is almost invisible; he is visible or invisible at will. Each partner's name is at the end of his desk on a brass plate. Why that is nobody ever knew. They certainly know each other; all the employees know them apart. No visitor is ever admitted to go wandering to and fro among the desks, looking for a man by his name-plate. It was probably an idea of the desk-makers.

When momentous things are forward, the atmosphere may be one of restrained expectancy, in which everybody shares to the degree of his station, though without being in the least excited. . . .

Within this calm and reserved interior the private banker performed a wide variety of functions. Most of these fell into two broad categories: general banking and investment banking. As general bankers they usually accepted deposits only from their corporate clients, friends, and employees, but rarely from the general public. Some firms, notably Kuhn, Loeb, did not even insist upon being made the depositories of the corporations whose securities they issued. Because of this, Kuhn, Loeb's deposits in 1913 amounted to only some $17.3 million, about one-tenth of those of Morgan's house.[52] Like commercial banks, private ones paid interest on deposits and imposed no service charges.[53] They used these funds to conduct their investment banking business and to invest in the short-term money markets.[54]

Private banks also provided other services. They created and dealt in bankers' acceptances, issued commercial and personal letters of credit, and carried on a vigorous commercial paper and foreign exchange business, for which they charged commissions. The range

---

52. *Money Trust Investigation: Report,* 78; Redlich, *Molding of American Banking,* II, 386.
53. Chapin to author, October 24, 1961.
54. John T. Madden and Marcus Nadler, *The International Money Markets* (New York, 1935), 155.

of their functions was comparable to that of merchant bankers of the Old World in an earlier day.

Not every private bank performed all these services, however; some specialized in one, others concentrated on a selected few. Kidder, Peabody, for instance, was known primarily as a foreign banking house, and its commercial letters of credit were employed extensively by New England wool importers. The firm also did a profitable business in personal letters of credit. At a time when few Americans traveled abroad and travelers checks still were uncommon, New Englanders visiting Europe relied upon Kidder, Peabody for such letters. Boston's large immigrant population also contributed to the firm's foreign banking business. "Young Italian fellows often came in with a sturdy roll of bills," a subsequent Kidder, Peabody partner explained, and "they would buy a draft to send some money back to Italy. We charged them a commission for this." The firm's profits from its foreign exchange and letter of credit business were sufficient to "take care of the overhead." [55]

In terms of its total yearly profits, however, Kidder, Peabody's general and foreign banking business was secondary to its earnings as an originator and distributor of securities. Its reputation and influence rested largely on its ability to provide long-term capital to railroads and industry. The same, of course, was true of the other major investment houses.

Nearly all the leading private banks were represented on one or more of the principal stock exchanges, and many of them did a substantial brokerage business. They traded in both listed and unlisted securities. Some firms, however, preferred to assign this business to brokerage houses. Although a partner in Lee, Higginson was a member of the New York Stock Exchange after 1888, the firm turned over all its transactions on this market to its New York City correspondents, Ladenburg, Thalmann & Co. and Clark, Dodge & Co.[56]

The increase in investment funds and the rise of new financial centers led some Atlantic Coast firms to establish branches in Chicago, San Francisco, and other western cities. Lee, Higginson opened a Chicago office in 1905, and soon other investment firms followed its lead.[57] Most of the other leading private bankers, however, continued to operate out of a single office and rely on correspondents to sell the issues they sponsored, much as they had done in the past. Meanwhile, several non-Atlantic Coast houses expanded into new areas. Some of the larger Chicago firms opened offices in New York City and Boston.

55. Hovey to author, October 26, 1961.
56. Chapin to author, October 24, 1961.
57. Marshall W. Stevens, "History of Lee Higginson and Company," typescript in Baker Library, 33; *The Commercial & Financial Chronicle,* LXXXI (September 16, 1905), 879.

Similarly, the importance of the British and Continental markets for American securities led almost all the leading private banking houses to employ foreign agents and correspondents. This, of course, was a long-time practice. In 1900 the London correspondent of August Belmont & Co. was N. M. Rothschild & Sons, the same house that the Belmont firm had represented in the United States since 1837. Winslow, Lanier & Co. transacted most of its European business through Glyn, Mills, Currie & Co. (London) and Hottinguer & Co. (Paris).

Several American houses maintained branches abroad or their members held individual partnerships in other firms operating under the same or similar names. J. & W. Seligman & Co., New York, had a partner in Seligman Brothers (London), Seligman Frères et Cie. (Paris), and Seligman & Stettheimer (Frankfurt). Brown Brothers & Co. (Baltimore) had branches with the same name in New York and Boston and was a partner in Brown, Shipley & Co. (London). The Morgan firm in New York City and Drexel & Co. (Philadelphia) were one and the same firm operating under different names in the two cities; in Europe, Morgan was a partner in Morgan, Harjes & Co. (Paris) and Morgan, Grenfell & Co., Ltd. (London).[58] Kidder, Peabody's close association with the Barings, dating back to 1885, made it unnecessary for this firm to open a branch in London or on the Continent.[59] Until 1906, when its principal competitor, Lee, Higginson, established a London office, Kidder,

---

58. See the testimony of J. P. Morgan, Jr., in U.S. Senate, Special Committee Investigating the Munitions Industry, 73d and 74th Congs., *Munitions Industry: Hearings* . . . (40 pts., Washington, 1934–43), pt. 25, 7479. Consult also *Money Trust Investigation: Report,* 57; George K. Turner, "Morgan's Partners," 25–35. On January 1, 1895, eighteen months after Anthony J. Drexel, the last of founder Francis W. Drexel's sons died, the name of the New York partnership was changed from Drexel, Morgan & Co. to J. P. Morgan & Co. and that of the Paris branch from Drexel, Harjes & Co. to Morgan, Harjes & Co. In 1926, after the death of Herman Harjes, it was changed to Morgan *et Cie.* See [Drexel & Co.] *A New Home for an Old House* (Philadelphia, 1927), 42. In December 1950 an attorney for Drexel & Co., which had been reorganized in April 1940 and made entirely independent of the Morgan firm in New York, described the old partnership arrangement that had existed between J. P. Morgan & Co. and Drexel & Co. before 1913 in these words: "In Philadelphia there were always two or three or four resident partners, but the New York partners were always, or usually, three times as many, and, of course, with Mr. Morgan over there, you can readily infer what his influence was." See *U.S. v. Henry S. Morgan et al.,* "Transcript of Trial, Defendants' Opening — Mr. [Arthur H.] Dean" (December 15, 1950), 1045.

59. On January 1, 1886, shortly after Kidder, Peabody had secured the exclusive American agency for Baring Brothers, Thomas Baring was made a partner in Kidder, Peabody's New York branch. In 1891 the Boston and New York offices were reorganized as separate partnerships; and the New York firm assumed the style of Baring, Magoun & Co. Each house continued to be the agent of the other. In 1906, thirteen years after Magoun's death, the name of the firm was changed to Baring & Co. Two years later it was changed back to Kidder, Peabody, and became the New York branch under a resident partner. See Kidder, Peabody & Co., "Record of Clerks"; *Finance and Industry* . . . (New York, 1886), 74; "Kidder, Peabody & Company," *The Bankers' Magazine,* LXXVI (February 1908), 263–70.

Peabody and Brown Brothers were the only two private investment banking houses in Boston with direct access to foreign credit and well-developed outlets for distributing American securities abroad.[60]

Kuhn, Loeb was one of the very few major private houses of issue that never opened any branches, either in the United States or abroad. This decision was based on Schiff's conviction that banking houses should cooperate rather than compete with one another. He was equally opposed to any kind of "exclusive arrangements" between banking firms. As his official biographer stated it, Schiff preferred having "intimate relations" with several leading houses in Europe and the United States rather than one or two permanent alliances.[61] Its foreign ties were excellent, nonetheless, and this firm's rise as a leading underwriter, second only to Morgan, was due in large part to Schiff's outstanding European connections. Especially important was his close friendship with such great financiers as Sir Ernest Cassel and Robert Fleming of London and Edouard Noetzlin of Paris.[62]

Investment bankers without these foreign connections cultivated the small investor. Not since the days of Jay Cooke had the investment banker shown so much interest in him. "A dozen or so years ago," a financial writer reported in 1912, "the small investor could hardly get anybody to look at him in Wall Street. Most of the New York Stock Exchange houses did not care to bother with orders for less than one hundred shares," and the bond buyer with less than $1,000 was virtually ignored. "His questions might be answered in a perfunctory way, but of real attention or carefully considered advice he got mighty little. . . . Bond and stock houses alike were busy in begging favors from the rich man's table."[63] By 1910 nearly the reverse was true. Only the great wholesalers ignored the small investor, the "master of the investment world," as one overly optimistic contemporary writer described him.[64]

During the years before World War I very few Atlantic Coast private investment houses were organized to distribute to investors the issues they originated. Most firms employed the same sales methods that had been common more than a half century earlier. They called for subscriptions through newspaper advertisements and circulars, distributed their securities in large blocks to a few institutional and large individual investors, or sold them through a few dealers

---

60. Stevens, "History of Lee Higginson and Company," 34–35.
61. Adler, *Schiff,* I, 194.
62. Paul H. Emden, *Money Powers of Europe in the Nineteenth and Twentieth Centuries* (New York, 1938), 331–32; Redlich, *Molding of American Banking,* II, 385–86.
63. William T. Connors, "The Day of the Small Investor," *The Magazine of Wall Street,* X (September 1912), 284. See also "Modern Bond Houses and Their Clients," *The Ticker,* I (March 1908), 2–4.
64. C. M. Keys, "Ten Years' Growth of the Investment Market," *The World's Work,* XXI (January 1911), 13843–45.

and brokers who fed them "slowly into a carefully manipulated market."[65] In 1905, when the American Telephone & Telegraph Co. brought out a $25 million bond issue, its largest such offering up to this time, Kidder, Peabody disposed of more than $5 million "at private sale" and sold the rest by calling for subscriptions. The House of Morgan did not retail any of the bonds it underwrote.[66]

Others, like Kuhn, Loeb, occasionally sold anywhere from one to five bonds to an individual, but like Morgan, Speyer, and other great wholesalers, Schiff's house made no "systematic attempt" to cultivate the small investor.[67] According to the head of its syndicate department, Kuhn, Loeb distributed nearly all its securities through a carefully selected list of some seven hundred institutions, wealthy investors, European bankers, and one or two dealers in each of the larger American cities.[68] Similarly, Roger W. Babson, who started his career with E. H. Gay in 1898 as an assorter and indexer of "a big pile of bond circulars," reported that most investment houses "depended largely on two or three big customers. The 'chicken feed' business was useful as scenery, but the big profits came from some insurance company, trust company, or large estate."[69]

The only two firms among the major underwriters of railroad and industrial securities that did both an extensive wholesale and retail business were Kidder, Peabody and Lee, Higginson. During the first dozen or so years of the twentieth century Kidder, Peabody employed six countermen at its State Street office in Boston to serve individuals with a few thousand dollars to invest. Many of these customers had never set foot in a private banking house before, but called upon Kidder, Peabody because of the confidence they had in its recommendations. As a result the firm developed a large, regular clientele of investors of modest means, most of whom were looking for income.[70]

The emergence of the small investor presented investment bankers with new problems and opportunities. Most individuals with limited funds to invest in securities preferred industrial stocks and public utility bonds over those of the railroads. The financial press attributed this to the fact that the interest rate on the latter usually was no better than that paid by savings banks.[71] Many of the older,

65. Redlich, *Molding of American Banking,* II, 376.
66. *The Commercial & Financial Chronicle,* LXXX (March 18, 1905), xiv; *Munitions Industry, Hearings,* pt. 27, 8154.
67. "Larson-Bovenizer Typescript," dated December 18, 1951. See also William L. Raymond, "Investment Banking in the United States: Its Historical Background and Development — The Wholesalers," *Barron's,* VI (May 31, 1926), 7.
68. "Larson-Bovenizer Typescript," dated December 18, 1951.
69. [Roger W. Babson] *Actions and Reactions: An Autobiography* . . . (New York, 1935), 76–77, 83.
70. Hovey to author, October 26, 1961.
71. *American Banker,* LXV (July 1900), 1218–19; "Public Utility Bonds," *ibid.,* LXXI (October 1906), 3291.

established eastern houses still looked upon themselves primarily as originators and distributors of railroad bonds, and they were neither equipped nor inclined to cultivate the small buyer interested in other types of issues. Most of them reacted very slowly to the needs of this group.

Lee, Higginson was one of the first large private Atlantic Coast firms to appreciate the importance of attracting small individual accounts. James Jackson Storrow, who became a partner in 1900, decided to tap this new source of capital by employing outside salesmen, establishing a new bond department, and developing it into a "retailing machine of such extent and efficiency" that Morgan, Kuhn, Loeb, and the other New York City wholesalers would want to include his firm in their syndicates.[72] Norwood P. Hallowell, who became a partner in 1906, was Lee, Higginson's first salesman. He traveled throughout New England making friends in various communities, advertising the firm's securities and, as business increased, hiring salesmen and assigning them to different cities.[73]

Most of those who bought their securities from Lee, Higginson, like many of the individuals who called upon Kidder, Peabody, were investors of modest and small means interested in income, not speculation. Whereas in 1900 almost 95 percent of Lee, Higginson's business was in railroad bonds, by 1913 these issues accounted for only about 25 percent of its sales.[74] Public utilities and industrials were now the firm's principal securities. "Even a person with a thousand dollars to save in those days," Harold Ben Clark, of White, Weld, and Co., recalled years later, "could afford to buy a bond because he would get five or six or seven per cent on it."[75]

Necessarily, investment counseling became one of the important ancillary functions of the alert investment banker. Before there were a large number of small investors, bankers could assume that large operators knew or could analyze the opportunities and market conditions. But the small investor had no such capacity. He needed assistance, and the house that helped him most efficiently got his business. At a time when there were fewer than a half dozen independent, professional investment counseling firms in the entire country, the investment banker and, to a lesser extent, brokers, attorneys, and trustees provided investors, large and small, with whatever financial advice they asked for.[76]

---

72. Henry G. Pearson, *Son of New England: James Jackson Storrow, 1864–1926* (Boston, 1932), 100; Stevens, "History of Lee, Higginson and Company," 7.

73. Stevens, "History of Lee, Higginson and Company," 12.

74. Pearson, *Storrow,* 101.

75. *U.S. v. Henry S. Morgan et al.,* "Transcript of Trial: Plaintiff's Case — Deposition of [Harold Ben] Clark" (May 8, 1951), 6432.

76. U.S. Securities and Exchange Commission, *Investment Trusts and Investment Companies: Report [on] Investment Counsel, Investment Management, Investment Supervisory, and Investment Advisory Services* (Washington, 1939), 3–4.

During the first decade of the twentieth century, few investment bankers were capable of handling the largest transactions. There were probably fewer than a half dozen houses that could both bring out a security issue of $20 million or more and also preside over the great mergers, consolidations, and reorganizations of the times. These were the "great international banking houses," the Morgan firm, Kuhn, Loeb, and Speyer in New York, followed by Kidder, Peabody and Lee, Higginson in Boston.[77]

Below the primary houses there were about two hundred important secondary firms, some of which specialized in certain types of issues, others in providing selected services.[78] There was a good deal of overlapping among the firms in this group. A house that was classified as a secondary one because of its limited ability as an underwriter might occupy a primary position as a sponsor of securities for a single type of issuer, such as a utility. Contemporary observers, however, usually classified private investment firms on their strength as underwriters.

There were at least three major categories of private banking firms below the select few at the top. One group was composed of firms sometimes labeled "good strong houses of secondary character." Very often the difference was based on nothing more than the size of the issues they sponsored or the prestige of the corporations they served. Firms in this category usually did not originate large railroad or industrial issues, though they participated regularly in the syndicates headed by the primary houses. Sometimes they bought substantial blocks of securities from the large issuers and, either alone or in syndicates, distributed them to small institutional investors and individuals. White, Weld, a New York City partnership established in 1895 under the name of Moffat & White, frequently served both Morgan and Kuhn, Loeb in this manner.[79] These latter two could not have managed their large flotations so effectively, if at all, without the assistance of these so-called secondary houses.

Another important and growing group of private banks were those specializing in financing municipalities and public utilities. N. W. Harris & Co., the Chicago private banking house that pio-

77. John Terret, "New York as a Bond Center," *Harper's Weekly*, LV (November 18, 1911), 13. See also Myers, "Origins and Development" I, 292–93; John Moody and George K. Turner, "Wall Street: How Morgan Built the Money Power," *McClure's Magazine*, XXXVII (June 1911), 201–02. Before Lee, Higginson opened its London branch, this firm's access to European capital appears to have been through its connection with Speyer & Co. See U.S. Temporary National Economic Committee, *Investigation of Concentration of Economic Power: Hearings . . .* (31 pts., Washington, 1939–41), pt. 23, 11837; U.S. Federal Communications Commission, *Report on Telephone Investigation* (2 vols., Washington, 1939), I, 152–53; Stevens, "History of Lee, Higginson and Company," 34–35.

78. *U.S. v. Henry S. Morgan et al.*, "Corrected Opinion," 22.

79. *Ibid.*, "Transcript of Trial: Plaintiff's Case — Deposition of [Harold Ben] Clark" (May 8, 1951), 6435.

neered the sale of these securities in the early 1880's, was the most prominent house dealing in these issues.[80] Several other similar firms were organized shortly after the turn of the century.

In 1901 Noah W. Halsey, a former Harris employee, established his own private bank in New York City — N. W. Halsey & Co. Two years later he hired Harold L. Stuart, also a former Harris employee, to manage the firm's recently opened Chicago office. Like the Harris organization, N. W. Halsey soon became an important municipal bond house, buying entire issues and reselling them "to individual investors" and "small . . . country banks." Next to municipals its principal business was in railroad bonds, mostly those originated by eastern houses. After 1910 its chief concern was underwriting and distributing public utility issues.[81]

At the time the private bank was being praised as the most "constructive force" in high finance and "the leading agency in all . . . operations involving the sale of securities," its primacy was being challenged by commercial banks.[82] As early as 1901 observers of financial developments were commenting upon the many significant changes that had occurred in "the character of commercial banking"; they pointed out that the larger banks in New York City, Boston, and other financial centers no longer were "doing the kind of business . . . [they had] transacted a decade ago."

Various reasons were given for this change. *The New York Financier* explained the shift from "commercial to syndicate banking" as the "inevitable outgrowth of industrial and financial expansion." *The Bankers' Magazine* asserted that "the day of small banks" had passed. "An institution with $1,000,000 capital and surplus for a similar amount is not apace with twentieth-century progress. Big men want big banks that can finance $10,000,000 deals at a week's, not a month's notice. . . . We shall have great banks for great enterprises, and the $10,000,000 institution with a string of affiliated banks is the logical outcome of existing tendencies in other

---

80. In February 1907 the assets, business, and goodwill of the Chicago office of N. W. Harris were transferred to the newly organized Harris Trust and Savings Bank. The New York City and Boston branches continued as partnerships operating under the name of N. W. Harris & Co. until January 1911, when the two became separate corporations, the New York firm taking the name Harris, Forbes & Co. and the Boston one assuming the corporate title N. W. Harris & Co., Inc. See *U.S. v. Henry S. Morgan et al.*, "Transcript of Trial: Plaintiff's Case" (May 1, 1951), 5757–58.

81. *Ibid.*, "Transcript of Trial: Testimony of Harold L. Stuart" (March 11, 1952), 13593, and (March 12, 1952), 13633.

82. Edward S. Meade, "Initial Stages of Organization" in "Corporation Finance," 47. See also Samuel A. Nelson, ed., *The Bond Buyers' Dictionary* (New York, 1907), 169; Samuel A. Nelson, "Wall Street As It Is," *The World's Work*, IX (February 1905), 5823. See also Hastings Lyon, "The Work of an Investment Banking House," *The Annals*, LXXXVIII (March 1920), 34–35; Alexander D. Noyes, "The Future of High Finance," *The Atlantic Monthly*, CV (February 1910), 229–39.

branches of activity."[83] By the beginning of the twentieth century the line between commercial and investment banking had become increasingly blurred and a subject of growing concern and controversy.[84]

Before 1900, commercial banks, whether holding a national or state charter, usually conducted their securities business through bond departments established to handle the bank's own investments. These departments subsequently were expanded to underwrite and syndicate securities for distribution to the bank's customers, brokerage firms, and other retail dealers.[85]

By the beginning of the twentieth century these bond departments were providing corporations and investors with all the facilities and services of private investment banking houses. Their staffs included appraisers, lawyers, and other specialists qualified to investigate and plan new issues and advise large and small investors. Many of them also offered general brokerage services as well. The bond department of the Mellon National Bank of Pittsburgh even had a "publicity bureau" which, according to its manager, was designed to assist the sales force in conducting "a campaign of education" for the benefit of the bank's clients and prospective investors.[86]

In 1902 the Comptroller of the Currency started restricting some of the investing activities of national banks. This decision forced institutions under his supervision to conform to his orders or get out of the investment banking business. In order to circumvent the new regulations, some national banks organized security affiliates. The first of these, The First Trust and Savings Bank of Chicago, was formed in 1903 by the First National Bank of that city. Five years later the First National Bank in New York organized its affiliate, the First Security Company. *The Bankers' Magazine* attributed the move to the bank's desire "for greater freedom of action" in conducting its investment banking business.[87]

---

83. *The New York Financier,* LXXVIII (October 28, 1901), 1448; *The Bankers' Magazine,* LXIV (February 1902), 178–79. Sereno S. Pratt, the associate editor of *The Wall Street Journal,* described commercial banks doing investment banking as being engaged in "department store banking." See Sereno S. Pratt, "New York's Great Financial Institutions and Their Presidents," *The Independent,* LVII (December 22, 1904), 1435–36.

84. John L. Blauss, "Commercial Banking and the Financing of Industry," *American Banker,* LXVI (March 2, 1901), 441. See also Anna Youngman, "The Growth of Financial Banking," *The Journal of Political Economy,* XIV (July 1906), 438–39; W. Nelson Peach, *The Security Affiliates of National Banks* (Baltimore, 1941), 10–11, 18–19.

85. Robert D. Coard, "Services Rendered to Investors by a Properly Conducted Bond Department," *The Bankers' Magazine,* LXXXIV (January 1912), 44–45.

86. *Ibid.,* 45.

87. William H. Steiner, "The Functions of the Investment Banker," *The Annals,* CLXXI (January 1934), 64; *The Bankers' Magazine,* LXXVI (March 1908), 322.

Security affiliates were state-chartered corporations owned by the stockholders of the national bank that sponsored them. They were "officered and directed" by the individuals who managed the bank.[88] To make certain that ownership of the affiliate and the bank always remained identical, stockholders could not buy or sell stock in one without also doing so in the other. Usually the same share of stock was used for both, one side bearing the name of the national bank and the other that of its affiliate.

Doubts about the legality of security affiliates failed to stop their use. In 1911, when the National City Bank organized its affiliate, the National City Co., to transact "business which though often very profitable may not be within the express corporate authority of a national bank," both Solicitor General Frederick W. Lehmann and Attorney General George W. Wickersham informed President Taft that security affiliates were illegal and dangerous. "Examples are recent and significant," Lehmann wrote Wickersham, "of the peril to a bank, incident to the dual and diverse interests of its officers and directors."[89] But since Treasury Secretary Franklin MacVeagh and Secretary of State Philander C. Knox thought otherwise, Taft chose not to challenge the national banks.

State-chartered commercial banks, of course, were not affected by federal rulings. Not surprisingly, they continued to conduct their investment banking business through bond departments.

The trust company was the other principal institution that engaged in the investment banking business. Incorporated under liberal state laws, trust companies quickly extended their activities far beyond those usually associated with the services of a fiduciary institution. Beginning in the 1890's, trust companies took on most of the functions of both commercial and private banks. They accepted deposits; made loans; participated extensively in reorganizing railroads and consolidating industrial corporations; acted as trustees, underwriters, and distributors of new securities; and served as the depositories of stocks, bonds, and titles.[90] Frequently they acted as attorneys for individuals and companies. Corporations regularly appointed them as registrars or fiscal and transfer agents. Very often they also owned and managed real estate. "The charters

---

88. Redlich, *Molding of American Banking*, II, 393.
89. Quoted in Henry F. Pringle, *The Life and Times of William Howard Taft* (2 vols., New York, 1939), II, 676–77. See also Ferdinand Lundberg, *America's 60 Families* (New York, 1937), 102–30. In 1912 George B. Caldwell, the first president of the Investment Bankers Association of America, warned both the private and the commercial bankers of the grave danger of excessive underwriting. If such occurred, he said, the public might very well classify all large-city bankers as being nothing more than "promoters." "Investment Bankers Organize," *The Bankers' Magazine*, LXXXV (September 1912), 285.
90. John E. Borne, "The Proper Conservative Attitude of Trust Companies toward Corporate Enterprises," *The Commercial & Financial Chronicle: Bankers' and Trust Supplement*, LXXI (October 13, 1900), 94.

which most of the states allow trust companies are so very liberal in their provisions," the *United States Investor* concluded, that they can "transact any kind of business whether it be financial, commercial, or manufacturing." [91]

Because of their huge assets, which grew at a phenomenally rapid rate between 1890 and 1910, trust companies were highly important institutional investors. The "aggregate resources" of trust companies chartered by New York State alone rose from about $280 million in 1891 to close to $800 million by the end of 1900, while their investments in stocks increased from $47 million to nearly $197 million.[92] These institutions were an important source of short-term loans. Private banks borrowed from them regularly to carry securities being syndicated, and the trust companies themselves found these loans a "favorite form of investment." [93] They also participated actively in underwriting and distributing securities, joining syndicates, and maintaining their own retail bond departments. "The name 'trust' seems to carry much more weight than that of a bank," the *United States Investor* declared, and it often was easier for a trust company than for a bank to sell a new issue.[94] By 1914 these institutions occupied a significant position in the securities business.

There were many differences among trust companies. As was to be expected, the largest ones were located east of the Mississippi River and most of them were in New York, Boston, Philadelphia, and Baltimore. Their operations, however, were nationwide. Several in New York City transacted more business for railroads and industrial corporations in the South and West than they did for companies in their own state, where competition from commercial and private banks was strongest. Some trust companies continued to provide a wide variety of financial and fiduciary services, but as the number of new security issues increased after 1897, many of them, realizing the profits that could be made from underwriting and distributing securities and from investing in the call market, came to concentrate their activities in these operations.

A number of trust companies closely associated themselves with certain large investment houses, commercial banks, and life insurance companies. Acting as the auxiliaries of these institutions, trust

---

91. "Trust Companies," *United States Investor,* IX (October 1, 1898), 1422.

92. *The Commercial & Financial Chronicle,* LXXII (February 23, 1901), 362–63; Edward T. Perine, "Trust Company Resources and Revenues: A Five-Year Summary," *ibid., Bankers' Convention Section,* LXXXIX (September 25, 1909), 178.

93. "Growth and Expansion of Trust Companies," *The Commercial & Financial Chronicle,* LXVII (August 6, 1898), 251–52.

94. "Trust Companies," 1422. See also Charles A. Conant, "The Existing Mechanism of the New York Money Market," *The Bankers' Magazine,* LXXV (July 1907), 20; the editorial "Investment Business of the Trust Companies," *ibid.,* LXXXIII (August 1911), 158–59.

companies provided them with the means to engage indirectly in various types of profitable operations that were either prohibited to them by law or, as the *United States Investor* put it, "not otherwise consistent with their regular business." [95] By 1914 some of the largest and "most successful" trust companies were the ones that specialized in providing commercial banks and life insurance companies with auxiliary services, the most important of which were the flotation and marketing of new security issues.

The growing participation of trust companies and security affiliates in the investment and securities business weakened the long-held primacy of the private banker as the principal source of new investment capital. This occurred just as J. P. Morgan came to be accused as one of the chief organizers and directors of an all-powerful "money trust." Affiliates and trust companies opened a large new domestic market for securities and made available great pools of underwriting capital. The investment banking activities of New York City's trust companies and commercial banks "revolutionized bond market conditions," *The Bankers' Magazine* reported in 1909. The "well-equipped and efficiently-officered bond departments" of these institutions made it possible for them, this journal concluded, "to bid for new issues and go into syndicates on a scale which was simply unheard of ten years ago." By 1914 the heads of two of these banks — Stillman of National City and Baker of the First National — occupied positions in the security markets comparable with Morgan's and Schiff's.[96]

Realizing that excessive competition was as unprofitable for them as it was for other businessmen, the leading investment bankers adhered to certain informal rules of interfirm behavior that to many people seemed purposely designed to promote monopoly.[97] When a major battle occurred among these firms, such as the 1901 struggle between the Morgan-Hill and Kuhn, Loeb-Harriman interests to win control of the Northern Pacific Railroad, the event was explained by the financial press as a mistake, an unfortunate breakdown in communications between these two great banking houses. Less friendly observers explained it as a typical Wall Street fight for supremacy. Several years later, at the time Kuhn, Loeb and Morgan jointly underwrote a $100 million bond issue for the Pennsylvania Railroad, the transaction was hailed as proof that "cordial relations" had been restored between these two banking houses.[98]

95. "Trust Companies as Banks," *United States Investor*, X (January 14, 1899), 71.
96. Franklin Escher, "Investments," *The Bankers' Magazine*, LXXVIII (June 1909), 1025; Redlich, *Molding of American Banking*, II, 382.
97. *Ibid.*, 379; Charles J. Bullock, "The Concentration of Banking Interests in the United States," *The Atlantic Monthly*, XCII (August 1903), 192.
98. *The New York Times*, March 29, 1905; *The Commercial & Financial Chronicle*, LXXX (April 1, 1905), 1201.

Since the 1880's many investment houses generally had honored one another's corporate clients unless the issuer was dissatisfied and seeking the services of another banker. It was "not good form," Schiff said, "to create unreasonable interference and competition. A large banking house or a small banking house — there is no difference between a large one and a small one — should respect itself. After the negotiation [of an issue] has once been begun, it should not endeavor to get it away from somebody else." [99] When Morgan in 1900 bought the Pennsylvania Coal Co. for the Erie Railroad, knowing that Schiff was negotiating to buy it for one of his lines, the event was an exception rather than the rule. And even then Morgan "insisted that Kuhn, Loeb & Co. share to a very substantial extent in the profits of the transaction." [100]

Corporation officials also preferred to continue to give their security business to firms that previously had served them satisfactorily. When Schiff was asked whether the Union Pacific Railroad, one of his firm's "recognized clients," would consider bringing out an issue of bonds through some other investment banking house, he replied that while there was nothing to prevent it from doing so, he believed it highly unlikely since, to the best of his knowledge, the Union Pacific's officers were "satisfied with the way Kuhn, Loeb & Co. have treated them." [101]

Investment bankers, in fact, also employed more formal means of assuring themselves of a client's future business. Very often the original purchase or underwriting contract included a clause requiring the corporation to offer all additional securities over a specified period through the originator's firm. These were called "first right of refusal" or "preferential right" clauses. Before World War I it was common for corporations to issue bonds in series, and it was generally understood "that at the time that one issue was offered . . . further financing would be done through the same bankers over a certain period." [102]

As the financial needs of railroads and industrial corporations increased, the banking groups upon which they had depended were enlarged to include firms heretofore excluded. Similarly, as new financial centers arose, investment bankers in these cities started competing for local and regional issues that previously had been brought out by Atlantic Coast houses. But the areas of greatest opportunity for new, smaller investment firms were those that had

99. U.S. House, 62d Cong., 3d Sess., *Investigation of Financial and Monetary Conditions in the United States* . . . (3 vols., Washington, 1913), III, 1665. See also Thomas C. Cochran, *Railroad Leaders, 1845–1890: The Business Mind in Action* (Cambridge, Mass., 1953), 70.
100. Adler, *Schiff*, I, 177.
101. *Money Trust Investigation, Hearings*, III, 1665.
102. *U.S. v. Henry S. Morgan et al.*, "Transcript of Trial: Testimony of Harold L. Stuart — Colloquy" (March 11, 1952), 13611.

been neglected by the older houses, such as public utilities, street railways, department stores, and family-owned corporations that were going public and as yet had formed no investment banking affiliations.

The future, according to an observer writing in 1911, rested with the young, "progressive" houses that were willing to finance new industries.[103] The greatest strides in developing efficient, well-organized retail organizations were made by these newer firms, without established clienteles, especially those specializing in municipal and public utility bonds — issues that were just beginning to gain wide acceptance.

Most of the firms selling these issues were both wholesalers and retailers. N. W. Halsey commonly sold the bonds it was syndicating in blocks to dealers at a slight concession in price and, at the same time, to individuals at the fixed, public offering price, making both types of sales for the benefit of the syndicate.[104] The same method was employed by N. W. Harris, which operated the largest and most highly developed distributing organization of any private investment house before World War I. This firm, with nine branches, was generally considered, according to George Whitney, "about the most effective and highest standing [retail] house in the whole country." [105] By 1911, only twenty-nine years after its founding, the Harris firms had sold about $1.2 billion of municipal, railroad, and public utility bonds; and it was not at all unusual for this partnership to "absorb a million or more of freshly-minted . . . securities" a day.[106]

Each of the Harris firms employed its own salesmen, who called upon prospective customers such as Cooke's agents had done. At first many of the established and more conservative houses were as disturbed by Harris's methods as their predecessors had been at Cooke's, but the organization's impressive sales record soon led other firms to employ the same practices. Stuart described the way N. W. Halsey sold an issue of $1 million or less, in small amounts, over several months. "All we had to work on in those days," Stuart recalled, "was a four-page circular and I would go into . . . [a small, country] bank, ask for the president, and if I could not see him I would see someone else, and tell him about the bonds and why they ought to put their money into them. Sometimes they agreed with me." Most of Stuart's sales, like those of other houses,

103. Keys, "Ten Years' Growth of the Investment Market," 13843–45.
104. *U.S. v. Henry S. Morgan et al.*, "Transcript of Trial: Testimony of Harold L. Stuart" (March 18, 1952), 13951.
105. *Munitions Industry, Hearings,* pt. 27, 8154. Besides its Wall Street office, the Harris organization had four other branches in New York State — Buffalo, Troy, Rochester, and Albany. The others were located in Boston, Philadelphia, Hartford, and Cleveland. See also *U.S. v. Henry S. Morgan et al.*, "Transcript of Trial: Plaintiff's Case — Deposition of [Harold Ben] Clark" (May 8, 1951), 6437.
106. *The Commercial & Financial Chronicle,* XCIII (September 9, 1911), 644.

were small, usually $2,000 or $3,000; $10,000 was "a big sale." [107]

To meet such competition an increasing number of private banking firms employed salesmen "to scour the land in search of investment funds." [108] Because a large number of the nation's security holders lived in New England, this region, which often was called the "Home of Investment Capital," was an especially lucrative market for salesmen; and several New York City houses dispatched a "small army of bond salesmen" to compete with those working for Boston firms, notably N. W. Harris and Lee, Higginson. [109]

The size of sales organizations varied widely. Some firms employed only one or two full-time salesmen, others ten times that many. About 1905 N. W. Halsey employed twenty in its New York City office and six in its Chicago branch. [110]

Salesmen were paid both a salary and a commission. "A good salesman," according to Harold Ben Clark of White, Weld, "had what we call a drawing account; that is, he was sure of a hundred dollars a month, or whatever it was, and then the rest of it depending on how many bonds he sold and how well he did." [111]

In selling an issue the retail security dealer operated like any other distributor. Each house had "a class of customers, sometimes running as high as the ten thousands — active, prospective or potential" — upon whom its salesmen would call. [112] Firms like New York City's White, Weld, which in 1910 had branches in Boston, Chicago, Cleveland, New Haven, and Buffalo, came close to being national retailers. The security affiliates of the commercial banks employed the same sales methods; their lists of customers included the bank's depositors. One contemporary observer attributed the declining volume of sales on the New York Stock Exchange in 1911 and 1912 to the success of the retail houses in persuading investors to buy new, unlisted issues or others traded over the counter. [113]

In order to accommodate the investor of moderate and small means and the odd-lot buyers, a number of security dealers introduced what popularly came to be known as the "partial payment plan," a system of buying securities on installments. Investors using this method were required to make an initial down payment of

107. *U.S. v. Henry S. Morgan et al.*, "Transcript of Trial: Testimony of Harold L. Stuart" (March 11, 1952), 13593–94.
108. George Carey, "The Investment Banker as an Educator," *Gunton's Magazine*, XXIII (December 1902), 511.
109. Franklin Escher, "New England: The Home of Investment Capital," *Harper's Weekly*, LIV (May 28, 1910), 34.
110. *U.S. v. Henry S. Morgan et al.*, "Transcript of Trial, Testimony of Harold L. Stuart" (March 11, 1952), 13603.
111. *Ibid.*, "Deposition of [Harold Ben] Clark" (May 8, 1951), 6432. See also Nelson, "Wall Street As It Is," 5823.
112. Meade, "Initial Stages of Organization," 47.
113. "Investment Bankers and the Stock Exchange," *The Literary Digest*, XLVI (April 26, 1913), 982; Edgar Van Deusen, "The Stock Exchange as the Investment Center," *The Bankers' Magazine*, LXXXIII (July 1911), 60–61.

25 percent of the purchase price and additional monthly payments that usually ranged between 5 percent and 10 percent. Designed primarily to meet the needs of salaried individuals "who wish to invest while . . . saving," the plan proved highly successful; and by 1914 it was being extolled in the financial press as "time-tried and panic-tested."[114] Most of the firms adopting the installment idea were New York City brokerage houses dealing in listed issues, but the plan had the strong endorsement of both large and small investment houses. In 1914 a leading spokesman for the country's investment bankers suggested similar and other ways of attracting new investors. One of his recommendations called for recruiting the assistance of bank officers throughout the country, the men best qualified to know who among their depositors might be interested in buying securities.[115]

Just as the new, smaller houses were the first to employ aggressive retailing methods, they too were the leaders in developing new ways of advertising securities. Before 1900 the chief way in which an investor or even dealers could learn about a new issue was to apply at the investment house sponsoring it or to follow the brief announcements of the offering bankers published in specialized financial weeklies, such as *The Commercial & Financial Chronicle,* or large metropolitan newspapers.[116] Those who wanted more information were advised to write to the president of the issuing company or to call at the investment house sponsoring the issue. In 1900 John Moody, a statistician formerly with Spencer, Trask & Co., a New York City banking and brokerage house, opened "a bureau of statistics for the use of bankers, bond-dealers and financial institutions generally." Its purpose was to collect and publish "information on all classes of corporation securities."[117]

Investment houses also made increasing use of the daily press to acquaint readers with the types of securities they were selling and to advertise free investment literature.[118] More important, they now employed both the press and circulars to educate readers on the wisdom of investing in securities and, in nonspecialized language, to acquaint them with the difference between a bond and a stock and the advantages of each.[119]

114. Paul S. Sheldon, "Buying Stocks on the Partial Payment Plan," *The Magazine of Wall Street,* XIV (September 1914), 455–57.
115. "Broadening the Bond Market," *The Bankers' Magazine,* LXXXIX (December 1914), 609.
116. A. E. Bryson, *Halsey, Stuart & Co. Inc., 1901–1937, 1938–1944: A History* . . . (Chicago, 1937, 1945), 5–6.
117. *The Commercial & Financial Chronicle,* LXXI (October 27, 1900), 868.
118. Financial Advertisers Association, *Advertising Investment Securities* (New York, 1928), 31. See also "Modern Bond Houses and Their Clients," 2–4; "The Investment Security Business," *The Ticker,* III (January 1909), 119–20.
119. "Some Good Bond Advertising," *The Bankers' Magazine,* LXXIV (March 1907), 425. See also "The Public Bond Market," *The American Banker,* LXX (August 26, 1905), 1921; Carey, "The Investment Banker as an Educator," 498.

The Halsey firm was a pioneer in this type of "vigorous, informative" advertisements, and soon its methods were copied by others. By 1914 a substantial number of investment houses not only advertised regularly in the daily and financial press, but in such widely read periodicals as *Scribner's, Harper's, The Outlook, McClure's,* and *The Saturday Evening Post.* A few investment houses even added to their staffs an advertising man charged with the responsibility of preparing interesting, informative, and confidence-inspiring copy.[120]

Between the end of the 1890's and the outbreak of World War I a few progressive firms had almost revolutionized the techniques of selling securities. Using advertising, brochures and circulars, personal letters, and frequent visits by salesmen, bond houses and other retail security dealers kept their customers informed of new issues and investment opportunities.

A different type of challenge to eastern leadership during these years came from the Middle West. Since the mid-1850's the securities business had become increasingly concentrated along the narrow and already overcrowded streets of lower Manhattan. By 1900 the leading investment banking firms, most of the major retail bond houses, the main offices of the largest commercial and savings banks, trust and life insurance companies, and the headquarters of some of the largest industrial corporations all were located in New York City. The New York Stock Exchange was the largest and most active market for securities in the United States. New York City's half century of undisputed financial leadership, however, was beginning to be challenged by Chicago, the only non-Atlantic Coast city in 1900 with banking facilities capable of floating sizable issues.[121]

The growth of Chicago's investment banking community had been remarkably rapid. After a brief flurry of activity during and immediately after the Civil War, lack of capital, poor foreign banking connections, and an inadequately developed money market prevented this city's private investment firms from growing into major, nationally recognized houses of issue. Business on the Chicago Stock Exchange fell to such a low point early in 1887 "that the Western Union Telegraph Company removed all its instruments from the floor of the Exchange. The few members in attendance had to rely upon newspapers, or private sources of information, for New York quotations."[122] Recovery from this low point followed rapidly, however, and during the next decade Chicago's investment banking

---

120. "The 'New Idea' in Bond Advertising," *The Bankers' Magazine,* LXXV (August 1907), 251–52.

121. *U.S. v. Henry S. Morgan et al.,* "Transcript of Trial: Defendants' Opening — Mr. [Arthur H.] Dean" (December 13, 1950), 877–78. See also Bullock, "The Concentration of Banking Interests in the United States," 183.

122. F. Cyril James, *The Growth of Chicago Banks* (2 vols., New York, 1938), I, 561–64.

community grew sufficiently to be able to handle small, local issues, mostly municipal and public utility bonds.

The city's two leading investment firms during the 1890's were the First National Bank of Chicago and the Harris firm. The first, a commercial bank, conducted its security business through its foreign exchange and bond departments. The second, a private banking and brokerage house, was founded in 1882 by Norman W. Harris, a native of Massachusetts who had started his banking career in Cincinnati.[123] In 1867 he helped organize the Central Life Insurance Company. As secretary and then manager of this company, he became convinced that carefully investigated municipal bonds were only slightly less safe than those of the federal government. Accordingly, when Harris opened his private banking house he made these issues his specialty, later adding railroad, public utility, and a few industrial securities to his list. By 1910 public utility bonds had become the firm's dominant interest.[124]

Harris was an aggressive innovator in marketing securities. Instead of selling municipals on commission, as was customary, he bought them outright. Since his was a new firm, had no established clientele, and was unlikely to develop one if it waited for prospective investors to call at his office, Harris decided to cultivate his own customers directly; he called on prospects personally or sent one of his clerks, a practice that was strongly frowned upon by some of the city's older bankers and brokers.[125] By 1900, with an estimated capital of $2 million and offices in New York and Boston, the Harris firm was the leading private investment banking house in the Middle West.[126]

Despite its remarkably rapid recovery, investment banking in Chicago at the turn of the century was still "limited in extent, and highly provincial in its interests."[127] The city's security houses, which numbered about seventy in 1900, excluding brokers, neither participated in the great railroad reorganization movement still going on nor took any significant part in financing the numerous major industrial consolidations then being organized. Very few Chicago houses were called upon even to distribute these issues,

---

123. *Ibid.*, I, 516, 561–64; *The Commercial & Financial Chronicle,* XCIII (September 9, 1911), 644; American Council on Education, *A Study of Investment Banking* (n.p., 1927), 22–23. See also Redlich, *Molding of American Banking,* II, 392; *U.S. v. Henry S. Morgan et al.,* "Corrected Opinion," 89, 105.

124. *U.S. v. Henry S. Morgan et al.,* "Transcript of Trial: Plaintiff's Case," (May 1, 1951), 5757–59; *ibid.,* "Testimony of Harold L. Stuart" (March 12, 1952), 13632–33. See also Raymond, "Investment Banking in the United States," 7.

125. American Council on Education, *A Study of Investment Banking,* 23; [Harris Trust & Savings Bank] *Forty Years of Investment Banking* (Chicago, 1922), 8–9. For having revived sales methods similar to those of Jay Cooke, Harris was dubbed "the father of the modern bond salesman."

126. James, *Growth of Chicago Banks,* II, 699.

127. *Ibid.,* II, 697.

their sale usually being left to the branch offices of New York and other eastern investment firms or entrusted to "ordinary bankers acting in the capacity of dealers." [128] Excluding state and municipal bonds, Chicago bankers in 1900 originated or headed syndicates offering a total of twelve new issues amounting to $7.3 million, of which ten, representing $6 million, were public utility bonds. The other two were industrial flotations.

Most of these issues were small and the securities of companies located within less than 200 miles of Chicago. Only one belonged to a corporation situated more than 400 miles from the city.[129]

Although the number of new issues originated by Chicago bankers increased considerably during the next decade (there were seventy-nine, amounting to $58.9 million in 1910), their size and character did not change greatly. In 1910 the largest issue underwritten in Chicago amounted to $4 million and, reflecting the trend of the times, the number of industrial offerings exceeded those of utility companies. That year Chicago bankers also brought out five railroad loans. None of these flotations, however, was associated with a major railroad reorganization or corporate consolidation.[130]

A much more significant development was the growth of the Chicago investment banking community's ties with prominent New York and other Atlantic Coast houses. Firms in both cities appreciated the advantages in such alliances. In order to sell large issues, primary investment bankers in New York needed to tap middle western savings. Chicago banks, realizing the profit and prestige associated with these transactions, welcomed the opportunity to act as intermediaries. The First National Bank of Chicago became a regular participant in numerous large flotations originated by Morgan, selling its share of these issues to individual depositors and smaller banks throughout the Middle West.[131]

The success of the First National in developing its securities business led other Chicago commercial banks to expand their bond departments and to develop New York ties. The Pujo Committee in 1913 cited Chicago's three largest commercial banks — the First National, the Illinois Trust & Savings Bank, and the Continental & Commercial National Bank — as "associates" of the small, powerful "inner group" of New York bankers who supposedly controlled the nation's money and credit.[132] Regardless of the validity of the

---

128. University of Illinois, Bureau of Economic and Business Research, Bulletin No. 39, *Investment Banking in Chicago* (Urbana, 1931), 7–9; *The Commercial & Financial Chronicle,* LXXXI (September 16, 1905), 879.

129. James, *Growth of Chicago Banks,* II, 697–98; *Investment Banking in Chicago,* 8–10, 15.

130. *Investment Banking in Chicago,* 8–9, 11–12; James, *Growth of Chicago Banks,* II, 698, 789.

131. James, *Growth of Chicago Banks,* II, 698.

132. *Money Trust Investigation: Report,* 131.

Pujo Committee's findings, its report served to illustrate the importance of Chicago as a regional investment banking center and the growing significance of the city's commercial banks in distributing securities in the Middle West.

Changing market conditions between 1900 and 1914 forced financial men of many types to effect a host of important changes in the organization of the investment banking community. The rise of Baker and Stillman to investment banking leadership by 1910, challenging Morgan and Schiff, epitomized the result of the response to fundamental changes in the capital markets and contributed to comparable alterations in the industry's institutional structure. These men and their competitors took advantage of the rapid growth of investment funds in the United States and helped to channel them into productive enterprises. In so doing, they speeded the declining importance of foreign capital and gave commercial banks a rapidly growing role in the security markets. During the same years, other men organized new private banking partnerships, and still others brought trust companies into the investment banking arena.

At the same time, the three principal groups engaged in underwriting and distributing securities — private and incorporated banks and trust companies — had greatly modified the ways they performed their functions. With but few exceptions, notably Morgan and a few others like Kuhn, Loeb and Speyer, nearly all investment banking firms had become both wholesalers and retailers, selling to institutions, dealers, other bankers, and individual investors. Most of the private banking firms established between 1900 and 1914 to finance public utilities and new industries also combined wholesaling and retailing functions, and many of them originated, underwrote, and sold small issues for local and regional companies as well. Security affiliates and trust companies were similarly organized to provide complete investment banking services. "Today," a writer for *The Bankers' Magazine* noted in 1909, "an issue of bonds is brought out by some big house, and the investor can get at them without having to pay the substantial commission the middleman used to make." [133]

As the number and size of issues increased, alert men organized new firms to meet local and regional needs and to cater to new investors with new services. Such actions changed the structure of the industry and competitive practices within it. Some of the older Atlantic Coast houses opened branches and developed extensive sales organizations. Firms like Harris, Forbes and N. W. Halsey, with branches in several major cities across the country, developed the first permanent, nationwide distributing systems. Besides sell-

---

133. Franklin Escher, "The Bond Broker's Hard Lot," *The Bankers' Magazine*, LXXIX (December 1909), 925–26.

ing the issues they originated, these and other recently established houses also sold large quantities of securities for the major underwriters who had no marketing facilities of their own.

While adding new firms and innovative techniques, the investment banking industry retained many practices introduced earlier in marketing railroad bonds. The syndicate and the practice of delegating broad powers to a manager authorized to maintain a fixed, public offering price and an orderly market now were employed extensively in financing the needs of new borrowers.[134]

In the process of fusing old and new firms and practices, investment bankers between 1900 and 1914 set the pattern for the securities business for years to come. Much of the organization and many of the methods developed during these years prevailed until the "Great Crash" of 1929 ushered in a new era. Even this cataclysmic event and the widespread changes that followed left the basic structure of the industry and its competitive practices much as they had existed in 1914.

134. *U.S. v. Henry S. Morgan et al.,* "Brief on General Points in Support of Motions to Dismiss," 42–50.

5 Prelude to Federal Investigation

While investment bankers were modifying their practices and the structure of their industry, they came under fire from critics and politicians on both the state and the federal levels. Fundamentally the attack was motivated by the same interacting forces that had contributed so much to the downfall of Nicholas Biddle almost a century earlier. Americans traditionally harbored hostility toward monopoly, privilege, and concentrated wealth. In all parts of the country small bankers and businessmen shared the farmers' antipathy against the great economic changes that had occurred in the nation since the close of the Civil War. They particularly feared and distrusted the giant corporate and financial institutions that had been organized by eastern businessmen and financiers.

Louis D. Brandeis's indictment of the "money trust" in *Other People's Money* (1914) climaxed more than a decade of growing popular concern with the rise of big business and the increasing concentration of economic and financial power in New York.[1] Isolated examples of criticism appeared early in the decade. In 1901 the president of the Ohio Bankers' Association launched a strong attack against Wall Street and the money trust. Two years later, writing in *The Atlantic Monthly,* Charles J. Bullock, a Harvard University economist, warned against the few wealthy and influential men who held the economic life of the country in their grip.[2]

Criticism and fear of the Wall Street money power were heightened by the short-lived panic of May 9, 1901, when a battle for control of the Northern Pacific Railroad drove the price of that stock from $350 to $1,000 a share in one hour. This famous fight was a major contest between the country's two greatest private investment banking houses, J. P. Morgan & Co., representing the interest of James J. Hill in the Northern Pacific and Great Northern, and Kuhn, Loeb & Co., representing that of Edward H. Harriman in the Union Pacific and Southern Pacific railroads. The prize was the Chicago, Burlington & Quincy, with its direct access to Chicago,

---

1. Louis D. Brandeis, *Other People's Money and How the Bankers Use It* (New York, 1914), 4. Most of the material in this book originally was published in *Harper's Weekly*. The first article appeared in November 1913, nine months after the Pujo Committee had made its *Report,* and at a time when the Interstate Commerce Commission was investigating the bankruptcy of Morgan's last great venture at consolidation, the New Haven Railroad, and the Senate was getting ready to vote on the Federal Reserve Act. Brandeis's association with the Money Trust Investigation is discussed in Alpheus T. Mason, *Brandeis: A Free Man's Life* (New York, 1946), ch. xxvii.

2. *The Bankers' Magazine,* LXIII (November 1901), 694–96; Charles J. Bullock, "The Concentration of Banking Interests in the United States," *The Atlantic Monthly,* XCII (August 1903), 182–92. La Follette reiterated and elaborated these charges in another Senate speech in 1911. See Alexander D. Noyes, *The Market Place: Reminiscences of a Financial Editor* (Boston, 1938), 242.

a road that both Hill and Harriman wanted to secure for their respective systems.

During this battle neither opponent succeeded in acquiring a clear majority of Northern Pacific shares, but between them they did. After a severe, but brief, stock market crash, in which short sellers suffered acutely, the opponents compromised their differences by turning their shares over to a holding company, the Northern Securities Company, organized in November 1901. In this corporation they both held shares.[3]

Many residents of the states through which the railroads crossed looked upon the Northern Securities Company as a dangerous monopoly. Reacting not only to their protests and the growing nationwide criticism against the consolidation movement generally, but also to the speculation and manipulation that accompanied the flotation of new issues, the governors and attorneys-general of several of these states prepared to test the legality of the Northern Securities Company in their courts. Meanwhile, the federal government, on the initiative of its new chief executive, started its own investigation.

Less than two months before the Northern Securities Company was organized, Theodore Roosevelt had become president, and in his first message to Congress, on December 3, 1901, he expressed his opinion about "the great corporations known as trusts." It was very close to the view held by a large majority of the American people. A substantial number of businessmen and bankers also were greatly disturbed by the consolidation movement and the growth of "financial banking." The latter was the term *The Bankers' Magazine* called "the operations of banks devoting themselves largely to the financing of great railway and industrial enterprises."[4] "We do not wish to destroy corporations," Roosevelt said, "but we do wish to make them subserve the public good. . . . The biggest corporation like the humblest private citizen must be held to strict compliance with the will of the people as expressed in the fundamental law."

Three months later, on March 10, 1902, the federal government filed suit against the Northern Securities Company for violation of the Sherman Antitrust Act, thus inaugurating TR's career as a "trust buster" and a new era in government-business relations. The Supreme Court reached its decision in 1904. By a five-to-four vote, it ruled against the Northern Securities Company. The decision,

---

3. U.S. House, Committee on Interstate and Foreign Commerce, 71st Cong., 3d Sess., *Regulation of Stock Ownership in Railroads* (3 vols., Washington, 1931), III, 1228–29, 1272–77, 1337–40; James C. Bonbright and Gardiner C. Means, *The Holding Company: Its Public Significance and Its Regulation* (New York, 1932), 235–41; Frederick Lewis Allen, *The Great Pierpont Morgan* (New York, 1949), ch. xi.

4. *The Bankers' Magazine*, LXIII (November 1901), 694–96; *ibid.*, LXXIV (February 1907), 179–80.

Roosevelt said later, had restored to the federal government, the "power to deal with industrial monopoly and suppress it and to control and regulate combinations." [5]

Taking their cue from Roosevelt, "muckrakers" and progressive reformers sought to improve business practices by exposing those they considered dangerous to the public interest. The close business and personal ties that existed among the members of the leading investment houses, the executives of the companies they served, and the officers of the other principal financial institutions caused increasing concern to trust-conscious Americans. The fact that a relatively few banking firms had sponsored most of the country's largest corporations emphasized still further the dominance of a few men over the economy. Most businessmen and financiers were well aware of the existence of these communities of interest. Not until 1904, however, did the public generally learn of the informal and subtle nature of these financial alliances, the extent of their influence, and the profits that were made in promoting and organizing mergers and consolidations.

In that year Thomas W. Lawson, a Boston stockbroker, promoter, and speculator turned muckraker, published the first of a series of articles under the general title "Frenzied Finance." Lawson was well qualified by personal experience to expose some of the shadier practices of "organized finance." In 1897 he had conceived the idea of setting up "a gigantic copper trust." Two years later, with the assistance of James Stillman of the National City Bank of New York and two Standard Oil tycoons, Henry H. Rogers and William Rockefeller, he organized the Amalgamated Copper Company. Launching this $75 million consolidation, composed principally of the Anaconda mining properties in Montana, for which the organizers had paid some $39 million, allegedly yielded the four promoters a $36 million profit.[6]

Lawson, who had distributed the securities, soon broke with his associates and embarked on a writing career. The break, combined with other personal grievances against the "great financiers," led him to accept an invitation from *Everybody's Magazine,* a recent convert to the muckraking crusade, to tell the true, "inside" story of Amalgamated Copper. Lawson's first article appeared in August 1904. It attracted immediate attention and, together with the others that followed, boosted *Everybody's* sales beyond those of all its competitors and won Lawson a permanent niche in the history of the muckraking era.

5. Theodore Roosevelt, *An Autobiography* (New York, 1926), 429.
6. U.S. Senate, Committee on Banking and Currency, 63d Cong., 2d Sess., *Regulation of the Stock Exchange: Hearings* . . . (Washington, 1914), 507–08; Alvin F. Harlow, "Thomas W. Lawson," *Dictionary of American Biography* (22 vols., New York, 1928–58), XI, 59–60; Louis Filler, *Crusaders for American Liberalism: The Story of the Muckrakers* (New York, 1961), ch. xiv.

In the September installment Lawson explained the extent to which financial control had become concentrated in the hands of a very few financiers through the use of interlocking directorships and similar devices.[7] He cited the New York Life Insurance Company as an example of a great company whose resources were controlled and used by bankers, in this case the National City Bank. Lawson's disclosures came as a frightening revelation to people who believed that life insurance companies were not in business for profit, but to protect the funds of their policyholders, as company officials repeatedly asserted.

His readers soon were shocked still further. In subsequent installments Lawson disclosed similarly close ties among other large life companies and the world of high finance. He pointed specifically to top officials of New York Life, Mutual, Equitable, and other companies, who profited personally from their relationships with investment houses. He indicated the ways in which these companies participated in the flotation of new securities, either directly or through the trust companies they owned or controlled, or with which they were affiliated. He covered the entire gamut of the life companies' activities in the security markets, including their investment policies.

Lawson's attack on the financial practices of the life companies aroused far more public indignation than did any of his charges against the "System," the term he used to describe the Standard Oil men with whom he formerly had been associated. It was one thing to issue watered stock and manipulate its price for the personal enrichment of a few insiders; only those who bought the securities stood to lose. But, as critics saw it, to use life insurance funds for speculative purposes jeopardized the welfare of thousands of innocent policyholders, who had entrusted their savings to these companies because they believed their funds would be managed conservatively.

Two subsequent events — a stock market decline and disclosure of mismanagement of the Equitable Life Assurance Society — gave added meaning to Lawson's charges. The "trust panic" of 1903 generally was attributed to an overabundance of new, overly inflated securities, more than the banks and trust companies could absorb; to loss of confidence in Wall Street's leaders and in the large enterprises they sponsored; and to widespread speculation. To this list Henry Clews added "revelations of fraud, chicanery, and excessive capitalization."[8] In one of his rare press interviews, however, J. P.

---

7. Filler, *Crusaders for American Liberalism*, 178, 185–95.
8. Henry Clews, *Fifty Years in Wall Street* (New York, 1908), 767–70, 776, and the same author's, "Wall Street's Wild Speculation: 1900–1904," *The Cosmopolitan*, XXXVII (August 1904), 410; Alexander D. Noyes, "Why There Has Been No Financial Crisis," *Yale Review*, XIII (November 1904); George W. Ed-

Morgan told a *New York Times* reporter that the mass of "undigested securities" that was depressing the market was "basically sound," and that when investors realized this, they would resume buying.[9]

Concern over "indigestible securities," as James J. Hill preferred calling them, and the 1903 decline in security prices caused nowhere near the public alarm that followed the disclosure of the fight for control of the Equitable. The contest was between James W. Alexander, its president, and James H. Hyde, the founder's son, a somewhat irresponsible and indiscreet young man. In 1899, at the time of his father's death, Hyde inherited a majority of the Equitable's outstanding stock. Increasingly thereafter he appeared to act as if the company and its resources were his personal property, to use as he saw fit.[10] On January 1, 1905, these resources amounted to about $412 million, second only to those of the Mutual Life Insurance Company.

The struggle between the two men broke into the open early in 1905, when Alexander sought to get his son appointed to the Equitable's executive committee. After that time, relations between Hyde and Alexander grew increasingly worse. The crisis in the Equitable's affairs, great as it was, assumed even wider significance because of the attempts, both real and rumored, by several Wall Street financiers or their representatives to buy Hyde's stock.[11]

During the first six months of 1905 two attempts were made to end the struggle, but both failed. Neither a committee of the Equitable's directors nor an investigation by the New York Superintendent of Insurance could produce a settlement. Indeed, their intervention served only to publicize the conflict, damaging the Equitable's reputation and increasing an already indignant public's demand for a thorough investigation of the life insurance business generally.

The report of the Superintendent of Insurance, published in June 1905, recommended numerous reforms, one of which was "the

---

wards, *The Evolution of Finance Capitalism* (London, 1938), 189. A spokesman for the Rothschilds attributed the crisis to the shrinkage of security values and a decline in the European market for American issues. *The New York Times*, January 12, 1903.

9. *The New York Times,* March 31, 1903.

10. R. Carlyle Buley, *The Equitable Life Assurance Society of the United States, 1859–1964* (2 vols., New York, 1967), I, 535; Morton Keller, *The Life Insurance Enterprise, 1885–1910: A Study in the Limits of Corporate Power* (Cambridge, Mass., 1963), ch. xv. See also the more contemporary account by Burton J. Hendrick, *The Story of Life Insurance* (New York, 1907).

11. Buley, *Equitable Life Assurance Society,* I, 643–44; Douglass C. North, "Life Insurance and Investment Banking at the Time of the Armstrong Investigation, 1905–1906," *The Journal of Economic History,* XIV (Summer 1954), 212. See also Harold F. Williamson and Orange A. Smalley, *Northwestern Mutual Life: A Century of Trusteeship* (Evanston, 1957), 133–34.

elimination of Wall Street control." [12] The press took up the demand for corrective legislation, and in July, Governor Frank W. Higgins called a special session of the legislature. It appointed State Senator William W. Armstrong chairman of a joint committee of the Senate and Assembly "to investigate and examine . . . the business and affairs of life insurance companies doing business in the state of New York." The next month Charles Evans Hughes, a well-known, forty-three-year-old corporation lawyer, who had just completed a successful investigation of gas rates in New York City, was appointed the committee's chief counsel. On September 6, 1905, hearings began in New York City. Before the first of the committee's fifty-five public sessions was called to order, almost everyone in the life insurance business faced the inquiry with complete self-confidence. Few, if any, of them foresaw the sweeping changes that would result from it.

Insofar as investment bankers were concerned, the Armstrong Committee was interested only in their activities as life insurance officials. But since these actions were so closely related to their responsibilities as bankers, the investigation ended by disclosing as much about the ways in which these men conducted their investment business as it did about the affairs of the life companies. Though Hughes questioned the bankers who appeared before him on a wide variety of subjects, he was concerned primarily with learning two things: the role they played in determining the investment policies of the companies with which they were associated, and how, as partners in investment houses selling securities and officials of companies buying them, they could serve the best interests of both. The ethics of such a relationship disturbed many people, not only then but for years thereafter.[13]

Under public questioning the nation's leading investment bankers seemed to have quite a limited perception of the implications of their actions. When Senator Armstrong queried George W. Perkins, a vice president of New York Life and chairman of its finance committee as well as a Morgan partner, the banker replied: "Mr. Chairman . . . I know when a transaction comes to me, whether it is in J. P. Morgan & Company, or the New York Life or the Steel Corporation, or whatever it may be, I take up that question and dispose of it as I see my duty." [14]

12. Keller, *Life Insurance Enterprise*, 247.
13. Edward S. Meade, "Initial Stages of Organization" in Harvard Graduate School of Business Administration, "Corporation Finance" (Boston, 1908), 47–48, and the same author's, *The Careful Investor* (Philadelphia, 1914), 70–71. The identical view was expressed by numerous other financial writers. See, for example, Franklin Escher, "The Great Open Market for Bonds," *The Bankers' Magazine*, LXXXIII (July 1911), 46; S. W. Straus, "The Ethics of Investment Banking," *ibid.*, LXXXVII (October 1913), 412–13; Samuel A. Nelson, ed., *The Bond Buyers' Dictionary* (New York, 1907), 171–72.
14. Quoted in John A. Garraty, *Right-Hand Man: The Life of George W. Perkins* (New York, 1957), 171.

Similar views were expressed by other investment bankers. Jacob H. Schiff, an Equitable director and the head of Kuhn, Loeb, declared that he had "never asked any favor" from the Society. "I have granted it many favors. I am not conscious of ever having done as [a] director of the Equitable . . . any wrong of commission. I may have done something . . . [by] omission. It is a case of hindsight and not of foresight, but my conscience frees me of any wrong [doing]. I have been as good a director as I knew how and I have done . . . my duty." [15]

Though neither Schiff nor Perkins, nor the other investment bankers who served as directors or trustees of these companies, was found to have used his position for his own personal profit or that of the banking house with which he was associated, to critics the conflict of interest was obvious. The propriety of having the same men whose firms issued securities recommending their purchase seemed definitely questionable. Also, the casualness with which some men invested company funds left them open to even greater criticism.

As in the case of railroads and other large corporations, life insurance companies welcomed investment banking representation on their boards and finance committees. The relationship was advantageous to both parties.

Rarely did a banker express his doubts about the propriety of interlocking responsibilities. In February 1901 Morgan invited Perkins to become a partner in his firm and urged him to resign from the insurance company in order to avoid a possible conflict of interest; New York Life was a large, regular buyer of Morgan-sponsored securities. Because of his long association with the company, Perkins refused to sever the connection, and Morgan reluctantly agreed to allow his new partner to continue with New York Life on a part-time basis.[16]

No such ethical consideration worried John A. McCall, the president of the life company. Indeed, once he had been reassured that Perkins would not sever his association with New York Life, McCall was, in the words of Perkins's biographer, "perfectly willing to see the chairman of his Finance Committee in the House of Morgan." [17] The executives of most other life companies shared similar views, with the result that it was not at all uncommon for more than one investment banking house to be represented on a company's board.[18]

Insurance companies had good reason for soliciting investment banking relationships of this kind. Close association with men like Morgan, Schiff, and Speyer added to the prestige of both the com-

15. Quoted in Cyrus Adler, *Jacob H. Schiff: His Life and Letters* (2 vols., New York, 1929), I, 192.
16. Garraty, *Right-Hand Man*, 85–87.
17. *Ibid.*, 87.
18. North, "Life Insurance and Investment Banking," 215–16.

pany and its officers. Even more important, the life companies needed the bankers' assistance in finding investment opportunities for their ever growing resources. Between 1900 and 1905 the assets of life insurance companies increased by nearly $1 billion.[19] Three companies, the Mutual, Equitable, and New York Life, all headquartered in New York City, held one-half of the assets. Despite their huge resources, these companies were neither disposed nor equipped to buy their securities directly from issuers. They "couldn't go to a railroad company that has a fifty million bond issue and say we will take that bond issue and market a part of it," Perkins told the Armstrong Committee, "because . . . [the companies] would assume the moral validity and legal validity and all that in that bond to other people." [20]

The banker foresaw that the situation might change. "When I was a boy the life insurance companies had to buy them at the second, third, or fourth hand. We have gradually moved up closer and closer, and the ultimate situation will be that those life insurance companies will get to the point where they will, between them, come more directly to the financial situation." [21]

The future proved Perkins right, but in 1905 the life companies were in no position to bypass the investment banker. The extent to which they were dependent upon him was brought out forcefully by the Armstrong inquiry. When Frederic Cromwell, the Mutual's treasurer, was asked whether the investment banker could float a large issue successfully without the assistance of the insurance companies, he replied: "Yes, Sir. . . . They sell more bonds in Europe in a week than we buy in a month." [22] Perkins confirmed this when he told Hughes that the Morgan firm had sold more bonds during the past "four years and a half . . . than New York Life and the Mutual and the Equitable have accumulated in 60 years." [23]

Borrowers found it too expensive and inconvenient to break up an issue into several blocks to accommodate buyers who were willing to take only a few million dollars. It was much easier for a corporation to dispose of an entire issue to an investment house and let it assume the responsibility for distribution. One of the reasons why insurance companies sought syndicate participations was to get large blocks of securities they wanted at reduced prices. It was in functioning as underwriters that their investment banking affiliations proved

19. *Ibid.*, 217; Keller, *Life Insurance Enterprise,* ch. viii.
20. New York, *Joint Committee of the Senate and Assembly of the State of New York to Investigate and Examine into the Business and Affairs of Life Insurance Companies Doing Business in the State of New York: Testimony* (7 vols., Albany, 1906), I, 599–600.
21. *Ibid.*
22. *Ibid.*, I, 489.
23. *Ibid.*, I, 599. See also the testimony of George Fisher Baker, president of the First National Bank of New York and a trustee of the Mutual Life Insurance Company, in *ibid.*, I, 486.

especially valuable. When Hughes asked Edmund B. Randolph, the treasurer of New York Life, why he preferred depending "on the favor of . . . banking houses in the allotment of syndicates" rather than buying the securities when they were offered publicly, Randolph said that it was "cheaper . . . decidedly cheaper."[24] Perkins later substantiated the point by saying that New York Life had saved some $400,000 by purchasing securities with a par value of $39.2 million and paying Morgan only $38.8 million for them.[25]

Buying at syndicate prices, however, was not at all common, because syndicate managers usually did not let insurance companies acquire their allotments at the stipulated rates. "They [the syndicate managers] won't give us a share in the syndicate if we do that [buy at syndicate prices] because they wish to make their profit in selling too," Cromwell asserted. Thus, most of the securities the life companies acquired for their portfolios they purchased at the public offering price. When they did take ownership of their allotments at syndicate prices, they did not participate in the syndicate's profit, no matter how large that was; nor were they allowed to sell the securities until the entire issue had been distributed. Sometimes this required waiting a year or longer and selling the securities "through a particular house."[26] Agreements such as these were essential if price maintenance during the flotation was to be effective.

Regular syndicate participations very often were highly profitable in themselves, not only to the life companies, but to their officers as well, many of whom regularly received participations of their own.[27] "My intention," Richard A. McCurdy, the president of Mutual Life, told Hughes, "was to avail myself of an opportunity of guaranteeing the sale of one lot by the bankers to the public and being compensated therefor as any other guarantor of an obligation upon the percentage that the bankers allowed to the guarantors, for that is all members of a syndicate are."[28]

A similar view was expressed by John Tatlock, the president of the Washington Life Insurance Company. "As a regular policy," Hughes asked, "you do not feel that a [life] company should buy securities with a view to resale for the purpose of making a profit on the rise in the market, do you?" "I think I do," Tatlock replied. "It seems to me that one of the functions of a life insurance com-

24. *Ibid.*, I, 261–62. See also Baker's testimony in *ibid.*, I, 486.
25. *Ibid.*, VII, pt. 2, 64. See also Garraty, *Right-Hand Man,* 169–70.
26. *New York Insurance Investigation,* I, 191, 234–35, 262.
27. *Ibid.*, I, 155. The Metropolitan Life Insurance Company and its president, John R. Hegeman, frequently participated in the same underwriting syndicates, many of which were managed by Vermilye & Co. "The company," Hughes reported, "has not only been a [syndicate] subscriber but it has bought bonds largely from the syndicate managers and in this way contributed to Mr. Hegeman's profits. He [Hegeman] figures the total amount of his profits from these transactions at $105,951.74." See *ibid.*, VII, pt. 2, 213.
28. *Ibid.*, II, 1647.

pany is that of a banker where it can make a legitimate profit in safe securities for the benefit of its policyholders."

Tatlock, like most other insurance officials who appeared before the Armstrong Committee, justified the syndicate participations of life companies as legitimate and necessary money-making operations. New York Life's profits from its syndicate participations during the ten years preceding the investigation had amounted to nearly $2.4 million.[29] When Hughes asked Tatlock if syndicate participations were not "tantamount to speculation," the insurance executive replied that if these activities, which he called "temporary investments," were conducted properly and with "good judgment," there was virtually no risk involved.[30]

When losses did occur, or if these "temporary investments" proved to be less successful than had been anticipated, the investment bankers with whom the companies were associated often assisted them in disguising their mistakes. The New York Life Insurance Company's participation in the $50 million International Mercantile Marine (IMM) syndicate illustrates this form of assistance and the informal way in which these transactions were conducted. In 1902 New York Life was allotted a $4 million participation in this Morgan-managed syndicate. (It originally had asked for $5 million.) Morgan could not make a market for the securities; the times were not favorable, and the public did not buy them. As a result, in this instance, syndicate subscribers had to pay for and hold their entire allotments, thereby losing the immediate earnings they had expected as guarantors and, even more, risking loss on later resale; New York Life was required to pay $3.2 million in 1902 and $800,000 the next year.[31] The company entered the $3.2 million IMM purchase on its 1902 financial statement to the New York Superintendent of Insurance, but it was reluctant to cite the $800,000 purchase on its 1903 statement; the report would show that the company had been forced to increase its holdings of an issue that investors had refused to take.

Perkins quietly solved the company's problem for that year. Acting for both the company and the House of Morgan, he arranged to have New York Life "sell" IMM bonds amounting to this sum to the bank. On December 31, 1903, the corporation received a check for $800,000 from the Morgan bank, deposited it in its account with

---

29. *Ibid.*, VII, pt. 2, 64.
30. *Ibid.*, V, 4175–76; VII, pt. 2, 133.
31. Payment was made somewhat easier for those who also had subscribed to the United States Steel syndicate, for it appears that Morgan conveniently timed the dividends paid to participants in that profitable syndicate with calls on the members of the unprofitable IMM one. There were many individuals and institutions, like New York Life, that had subscribed to both. See Thomas R. Navin and Marian V. Sears, "A Study in Merger: Formation of the International Mercantile Marine Company," *Business History Review*, XXVIII (December 1954), 291–328.

that institution, entered the transaction on its books as a sale, and reported to the Superintendent of Insurance its year-end holdings of IMM at $3.2 million. On January 2, 1904, Perkins repurchased the securities for New York Life, paying Morgan $800,266.67, the additional amount representing interest charges for two days.[32]

Perkins's solution delayed the final reckoning for a year. Just before the next report was due, New York Life sold its IMM bonds to Morgan's London house, J. S. Morgan & Co., Ltd. The loss on this sale totaled $160,000, Perkins assuming one-half of this amount himself.

Not only did the disclosure of transactions such as this disturb Hughes and the committee, they also were shocked to learn that the syndicate participations of some companies were intermixed with those of their directors and officers. The investment decisions of others too often appeared to have been reached circuitously, solely on the judgment of one or two individuals, and without the knowledge, much less the authorization, of other company officials.

On one occasion, in June 1904, Morgan refused to accept a one-half interest in a $2 million bond issue that Kidder, Peabody & Co. was bringing out for the Mexican Central Railroad. Perkins agreed to accept it himself on behalf of Nylic, the investment fund established for the benefit of New York Life's agency directors. "I presume," Perkins told Hughes, "the conversation between us [Perkins and Winsor, a Kidder, Peabody partner] did not last ten minutes. It was done very quickly. I made up my mind to undertake the business with the Nylic funds . . . for which I am trustee and manager. . . . Part of the transaction was that the Mexican Central Railway was to be immediately provided with $2,000,000, half of which I agreed to provide. And as the Nylic fund did not have that much money, [and] I did not wish to disturb the securities it did have, I arranged to have the Mexican Central bonds sent to the New York Life and that company to carry those bonds for the coupons, which were at the rate of five per cent. This was done. $1,000,000 of the bonds were delivered by Kidder, Peabody & Company to the New York Life on June 27th. The New York Life Insurance Company on that date by check paid Kidder, Peabody . . . $930,000 and held the balance until August, 1904, when Kidder, Peabody . . . sent the New York Life its check for $930,000 with interest on $1,000,000 at five per cent. for the time of the transaction. A little more than a month later, or on September 17th, Kidder, Peabody . . . rendered a statement to the New York Life of

---

32. *New York Insurance Investigation,* VII, pt. 2, 58–59. Garraty, *Right-Hand Man,* 172, states that Perkins later claimed that he had considered the original sale to Morgan a real one, but that his partners had objected to it. Because of this, Perkins "repurchased the bonds for the New York Life." See also Keller, *Life Insurance Enterprise,* 180–81.

the profits they had realized on the transaction amounting to $40,193.60, which check was cashed by the New York Life and the proceeds turned over to me." [33]

Looking upon his role in this transaction as entirely proper, Perkins defended his every action on the ground that it had been profitable. "I chose to do it for the Nylic fund," he said, because "I have the authority to do [so] without consulting anybody." His explanation for involving New York Life in the transaction was equally forthright. "I had to obtain the money somewhere, and as it was a bond transaction with the opportunity of realizing over five per cent interest on the money while in use, it was a perfectly natural thing, for two reasons, for me to have the New York Life Insurance Company furnish the money. First, because it furnished an excellent transaction for the New York Life at over 5 per cent. interest on absolutely safe securities. Second, because it was to be used in connection with an organization of agency directors . . . whose interests policyholders of the New York Life were vitally interested in promoting." The profits were paid to New York Life, Perkins explained, "because the whole transaction, so far as Kidder, Peabody & Company were concerned, was with the . . . Company." New York Life cashed the check and turned the money over to Perkins because it "in no way belonged to the New York Life." It was entitled only to the interest, which it received.[34]

When Hughes asked Perkins what he did with the money, the banker said that he reinvested it along with his own, "as I have with nearly all the Nylic money." "Don't you keep a separate fund of the Nylic money and invest it as trustee?" Hughes asked. "No, Sir, I do not," Perkins answered. "How do you discriminate between your individual interest and your duty as trustee in setting apart investments which you make indiscriminately?" "I do as my judgment dictates in each instance," Perkins said, "handling the money to make the most profit, and I think the best proof I have been successful is the amount I have earned." [35]

Schiff too defended his actions as a director of the Equitable by citing the profits this company had earned from the securities it had bought from Kuhn, Loeb. To be sure, the market value of some issues had declined, but "these . . . were the exception and not the rule." [36]

What disturbed Hughes and a growing number of the people who read the reports of the hearings was the almost limitless authority individuals like Perkins exercised over the investment policies of the great life companies. What was there to prevent these men from

---

33. *New York Insurance Investigation*, III, 2911. See also *ibid.*, IV, 2973–77; VI, 571–75.
34. *Ibid.*, III, 2912.
35. *Ibid.*, III, 2924. See also *ibid.*, VII, pt. 2, 62–63.
36. Adler, *Schiff*, I, 191–93.

using their positions to guarantee their firms a sure, steady market for the securities they issued? This was precisely what Brandeis charged when he stated that investment banking penetration of life insurance companies was purposely designed to "seek to control these never-failing reservoirs of capital."[37]

The Armstrong Committee uncovered no evidence that investment bankers dominated the financial policies of the companies with which they were associated. Schiff testified that his firm came nowhere near monopolizing the investments of the Equitable, of which he had been a director since 1893. Between 1900 and 1905 Kuhn, Loeb marketed nearly $1.4 billion in securities, of which about $33 million went to the Equitable, out of its total purchases of $197 million.[38] The Equitable, Schiff asserted, did not favor his firm over any other, nor did he expect it to do so; in fact, between 1900 and 1905 Kuhn, Loeb sold more securities ($42 million) to the Mutual, where Baker of the First National Bank and James Speyer of Speyer & Co. were represented, than it did to the Equitable; and it sold almost as many ($33 million) to New York Life. Whereas it was true that Kuhn, Loeb had not monopolized the Equitable's investments, the fact remained, one observer subsequently noted, that its "holdings reflected the railroad interests of Harriman-Kuhn, Loeb," just as those of New York Life showed a preponderance of Morgan-sponsored securities, and the Metropolitan Life Insurance Company's reflected heavy purchases of issues brought out by Vermilye & Co.[39]

Hughes was equally concerned about the life companies' stock purchases. He queried Schiff about the 17,800 shares of Union Pacific preferred that Kuhn, Loeb had sold to the Equitable. So far as he knew at the time, the banker explained, the transaction involved Hyde as an individual, not the company. And he went on to say that he learned that Hyde had transferred the stock to the Equitable only when the New York Superintendent of Insurance had informed him of the fact. Since Union Pacific preferred was "an investment of the highest order," he continued, the Equitable's finance committee certainly would have "approved of it as an investment of the Society."[40] This was no doubt true, but the danger in such transactions was great, Hughes pointed out in the committee's report. "Investments in stocks should be prohibited," he wrote. "They are fundamentally objectionable, as the corporation, instead of holding a secured obligation, acquires a proprietary interest in

37. Brandeis, *Other People's Money*, 15.
38. Adler, *Schiff*, I, 192. North, "Life Insurance and Investment Banking," 216n.31, states that Kuhn, Loeb sold to the Equitable "almost $50 million worth of securities."
39. North, "Life Insurance and Investment Banking," 221. See also *New York Insurance Investigation*, VII, pt. 2, 213.
40. Adler, *Schiff*, I, 190.

another business, with rights subject to all indebtedness which may be created in the conduct of it and often direct liabilities as stockholders." [41]

If the life companies profited by their close association with investment banking firms, the latter benefited even more from the relationship.[42] Through their associated and subsidiary trust companies, the life corporations provided investment houses with numerous services and opportunities. Not only did these institutions engage in many of the same kinds of investment functions as those of the life companies that influenced them, such as participating in underwriting syndicates and buying for their own account, but trust companies also provided additional, indirect means through which insurance companies could assist investment firms in placing new issues.[43] The Equitable received regular syndicate participations from its subsidiary, the Mercantile Trust Company; and the Prudential, which did not engage in any underwriting ventures itself, "made a considerable number of purchases" from the Fidelity Trust Co., whose officers had close connections with the life company.[44]

By keeping large deposits at low interest in associated trust companies, insurance corporations provided them with funds to lend investment houses in the form of collateral, or "Street," loans. Because the life companies themselves did not have "the machinery necessary for making collateral loans," and because these transactions involved "a good deal of labor and trouble," as Tatlock of Washington Life expressed it, insurance executives found it more convenient and just as profitable for their companies to participate in this business through their associated trust companies.[45]

These institutions also were useful channels through which life companies secured business they did not ordinarily get, such as making corporate loans. When Hughes questioned Cromwell's statement that a company like the Mutual needed assistance in finding corporate borrowers, this insurance officer replied: "But we don't hear of them, Mr. Hughes; we don't hear of them. They are brought to us by our own trust companies and by others." [46]

Trust companies also opened to the life firms and their associated investment bankers other avenues for profit. They brought to their attention prospective issuers in need of long-term financing. In addition, because there were so few statutory restrictions on the oper-

---

41. *New York Insurance Investigation,* VII, pt. 2, 295.
42. *Ibid.,* I, 196; North, "Life Insurance and Investment Banking," 218.
43. North, "Life Insurance and Investment Banking," 221–28.
44. *New York Insurance Investigation,* VII, pt. 2, 106, 251. New York Life, for example, owned a majority of the stock in the New York Security & Trust Company, of which Perkins was a trustee; and the Equitable owned 65 percent of the stock in the Mercantile Trust Co. See *ibid.,* VII, pt. 2, 61, 106.
45. *Ibid.,* V, 4176.
46. *Ibid.,* I, 196.

ations of trust companies, they participated in numerous other highly profitable investment activities that were legally barred to life corporations.[47]

The life companies assisted the investment banker in still another important way. The fact that these institutions associated themselves with an issue, either as underwriters, purchasers, or both, made the offering more attractive to the public. It always helped in selling an issue, Baker told Hughes, to have an insurance company interested in the securities. It gave them added respectability.[48]

The advisability of permitting life insurance companies to underwrite new issues had been questioned before. In 1903 Charles Bullock had declared: "The general tendency of the times seems to be to confuse the distinction between enterprises that are safe investments for funds held in a fiduciary capacity and ventures that should be undertaken only with capital that is otherwise provided. Underwriting projects in which a profit of two hundred per cent is considered none too large a compensation for the risks assumed do not furnish a good field for the conservative employment of trust funds." [49]

The Armstrong Committee was of the same opinion. After listening to the testimony of bankers like Perkins, Schiff, and Baker, and to company officials who looked upon themsleves more as financiers than as insurance executives, it condemned the underwriting activities of life companies and their officials as too hazardous and too easily susceptible to abuse. Even though the bankers and officers concerned had justified the practice by citing the profits that had been earned, the fact that many of them frequently profited personally was reason enough for the committee to recommend that life companies be prohibited from serving as underwriters, directly or through subsidiaries.[50] Referring to the syndicate activities of Mutual Life, the committee's report stated: "It is evident that those managing its financial affairs have been in a position by reason of relation to other companies and to financial enterprises, without violating the accepted traditions or departing from the standards of the company's management, to greatly advance their personal fortunes through the exercise of their discretion as trustees." [51] Bankers granted syndicate participations to life companies in order to win their "good will and favor," Hughes argued, and it was too much

---

47. Because of New York Life's policy of not buying stock, Perkins arranged to have this company participate in the syndicate underwriting the stock of the United States Steel Corporation through its subsidiary, the New York Security & Trust Company. See *ibid.*, VII, pt. 2, 61–62; Garraty, *Right-Hand Man*, 93–94.

48. *New York Insurance Investigation,* I, 486–87.

49. Charles J. Bullock, "The Concentration of Banking Interests in the United States," 192.

50. *New York Insurance Investigation,* VII, pt. 2, 31.

51. *Ibid.*

to expect that investment houses would offer them profitable ones if the companies refused to accept those involving more risk.[52]

Life insurance companies "were not incorporated to make money by speculation, by barter, by purchase for resale or by the development of industry," Hughes concluded. "They were chartered to furnish life insurance, and the true measure of their power and their duty in the handling of their funds is to invest them with due conservatism. . . . If in this manner they should make less money they would also be less likely to court disaster. They should not attempt, and should not be permitted to attempt, to undertake by indirection that which may not be done directly under provisions of their charters." [53]

In February the Armstrong Committee presented its recommendations, and the New York legislature immediately began putting them into effect, despite the strong opposition of the companies and their lobbyists, who at once descended upon Albany. Neither the companies, nor their spokesmen, nor the friendly business press, which cautioned against haste and the dangers of interfering with private enterprise, could stay the public's insistent demand for reform. Two months later, in April 1906, the New York legislature passed a series of comprehensive reform laws; and by the end of 1907, nineteen other states had enacted similar statutes.[54]

In the new laws, two provisions affected the investment banker most directly. They were those prohibiting life companies from underwriting the purchase or sale of securities, either alone or "jointly with any other person, firm, or corporation," and those barring such companies from investing in corporate stock and collateral trust bonds. The latter were defined as obligations for which "the greater part of the security consists of the hypothecated stocks of corporations." [55] Companies that held such securities were required to divest themselves of these holdings by December 31, 1911, later extended to 1916. The law also forbade an insurance company's making "any agreement" allowing it to "withhold from sale for any time, or subject to the discretion of others, any securities which it may own or acquire." Perhaps most significantly, no official of these companies was permitted to become "pecuniarily interested either as principal, co-principal, agent or beneficiary in any pur-

52. *Ibid.,* VII, pt. 2, 293.
53. *Ibid.,* VII, pt. 2, 294. See also William H. Price, "Life Insurance Reform in New York," *American Economic Association Quarterly,* X (December 1909), 22–23.
54. *The Commercial & Financial Chronicle,* LXXXII (March 3, 1906), 483–84; (March 17, 1906), 600–02; (March 24, 1906), 661–62; Keller, *Life Insurance Enterprise,* 257.
55. *New York Insurance Investigation,* VII, pt. 2, 296–97, 393. See also Williamson and Smalley, *Northwestern Mutual Life,* 136–37; Algernon A. Osborne, *Speculation on the New York Stock Exchange: September 1904–March 1907* (New York, 1913), 52–53.

chase, sale or loan made by the corporation, except in case of a loan upon his policy." [56]

Because life companies and their officers now were prohibited from underwriting securities, investment houses were forced to increase the size of their syndicates. The risk previously assumed by one or two insurance companies was distributed among other individuals, usually bank or trust company officials, the institutions with which they were affiliated, and private banking and brokerage firms that heretofore had not been regular participants in these groups. The result was that by 1914 both the make-up and size of syndicates were considerably different from what they had been ten years earlier. It was not at all uncommon for these groups to number a hundred or more individuals and firms.[57]

These laws also dealt a serious blow to the close ties that had developed between the life companies and the investment banking community. The provisions requiring insurance corporations to divest themselves of their stock holdings, much of which were in banks and trust companies, not only prohibited the life companies from using these institutions to engage in business they themselves were barred from transacting; it also weakened considerably, if it did not eliminate entirely, the "ties of common interest" that had "bound" them "to the world of high finance." [58]

After 1906 the relationship between insurance companies and the investment banking community became increasingly distant. The loosening of these ties occurred partly because of the changes in management forced upon the companies by the Armstrong Committee's revelations, but even more because of the necessity of having to distribute their bond purchases among a larger number of investment and brokerage firms. The extent to which the life companies had broken their previous investment banking affiliations was reflected in the amount of securities in their portfolios, which declined from 51.2 percent in 1905 to 41.9 percent in 1915. These connections, moreover, attracted relatively little attention during the Pujo investigation.[59]

The decline in bond purchases by life insurance companies that followed the Armstrong investigation contributed to the sluggishness that characterized the investment market in 1906. New loans were difficult to place, and investment houses found themselves loaded with undigested securities and, in several cases, unable to sell even "obligations of the very best sort, to which not a shadow of

---

56. *New York Insurance Investigation,* VII, pt. 2, 296.
57. Lewis B. Franklin, "Syndicates," *The Bankers' Magazine,* LXXXVII (December 1913), 665.
58. Keller, *Life Insurance Enterprise,* 281.
59. *Ibid.,* 283.

suspicion or discredit attaches." [60] *The Commercial & Financial Chronicle* attributed the "apathetic" condition of the investment markets almost entirely to that investigation. The new insurance laws, it reported, "have shorn the great life . . . companies of their energies as reproductive agents in the financial markets. Formerly there was scarcely a financial undertaking of any consequence in which these big life insurance concerns did not directly or indirectly take an active part. Many of such undertakings . . . were initiated by these concerns. They had large amounts of cash at command and almost unlimited resources. To have it known that one of these big companies was identified with or behind an undertaking was regarded as equivalent to an assurance of unbounded and unqualified success for the undertaking. But now all this has been changed." [61]

More significant than the immediate effects on the stock market was the fact that the investigation was one of the first major government probes into the conduct of an important group of large prestigious companies. The success with which this inquiry documented the close alliances and interlocking relationships between the life insurance companies and the investment banking community aroused widespread concern. Newspapers and periodicals publicized the committee's findings and elaborated upon the dangers of financial concentration and the growth of a money power. At the same time, muckraking magazines like *Everybody's* exposed the wrongdoings of some respected financiers as well as less reputable Wall Street operators, particularly those engaged in bucket-shopping, which was nothing more than gambling on the rise and fall in stock prices. [62]

To the swelling wave of criticism against the money power that was generated by investigators and muckrakers, Morgan gave unwitting support during the crisis of 1907. He played the role of a titan.

60. *The Commercial & Financial Chronicle*, LXXXII (June 30, 1906), 1468. See also Clews, *Fifty Years in Wall Street*, 778–79.
61. *The Commercial & Financial Chronicle*, LXXXII (June 30, 1906), 1468. See also *ibid.*, LXXXV (August 17, 1907), 370–71; (December 21, 1907), 1547.
62. Filler, *Crusaders for American Liberalism*, ch. xxiv. Bucket-shopping, whether conducted openly as such, or through a brokerage firm, involved betting on the price performance of listed stocks. No orders were executed. The bucket-shop operator simply accepted the customer's wager that certain stocks would increase or drop by a certain number of points. If the stocks reached the agreed-upon prices, the customer won and made a profit; if they did not, he was charged a loss. Most trades, as these transactions were euphemistically called, involved ten or twenty shares, and margins commonly were set at one or two points, usually requiring a deposit of less than $50. The customer paid a commission on each transaction. In 1908 the New York penal code was amended, making bucket-shop contracts illegal. See "Bucket Shops," *The Ticker*, II (May 1908), 12–23; "The New Bucket Shop Law in New York State," *ibid.*, II (August 1908), 177–78.

Pressures in American money markets had been increasing for several months. As early as January 1906 Schiff had warned against financial abuses and the dangers of speculation. A severe stock market break occurred a year later, in March 1907, forcing some of the highest grade stocks to tumble as much as twenty-nine points in less than a month. That shock was followed by two other serious setbacks in July and October.

Some financial leaders and their spokesmen immediately accused reformers like Roosevelt and Hughes, the latter now governor of New York, of having provoked the crisis by undermining business confidence. "The legislation of the last few years," *The Commercial & Financial Chronicle* asserted, "is responsible for the pass to which this country has been brought — where all classes and kinds of securities have become discredited, where security values have shrunk almost beyond precedent, and where the whole financial situation has been thrown into chaos and industrial affairs brought to the brink of ruin."[63] Lack of confidence certainly contributed significantly to the ten-month stock market decline that began in January 1907.

This lack, however, was attributable less to what Roosevelt had said or Hughes had done, Schiff remarked, than to the "general practices" of the times, notably the corporate and financial excesses of the previous year.[64] Most knowledgeable observers agreed. Revelations of gross dishonesty, business mismanagement, reckless speculation, heavy selling by large security holders, and the refusal of investors to be "baited" into buying by "numerous dividend increases," as another commentator put it, resulted in large numbers of new issues remaining unsold.[65] Early in June 1907 the *American Banker* discussed the growing number of unprofitable syndicates in which members had been forced to take up their participations and dispose of them at a loss to pay bank loans.[66]

The situation was made worse by the inelasticity of the nation's credit and currency. Neither the federal government nor the national banks could enlarge the supply of paper money to help sound and deserving banks meet the demands of their depositors.

---

63. *The Commercial & Financial Chronicle,* LXXXV (December 21, 1907), 1547. See also George L. Balgue, "The Big Panics since 1837," *The Magazine of Wall Street,* XIV (September 1914), 480–81.

64. Adler, *Schiff,* I, 36–37.

65. Charles F. Speare, "Wall Street's Crisis and the Country," *The American Monthly Review of Reviews,* XXXV (May 1907), 559. See also *The Bankers' Magazine,* LXXIV (April 1907), 506, which quotes *The* [London] *Economist's* explanation for the precipitous decline in railroad issues as "due to the [public's] conviction . . . that the small coterie of capitalists who control the railways . . . look upon the investor as a mere pawn." See also Osborne, *Speculation on the New York Stock Exchange,* 79–81.

66. "Peculiar State of the Bond Market," *American Banker,* LXXII (June 15, 1907), 1997; Clews, *Fifty Years in Wall Street,* 798–99, 885–86.

The panic broke on October 22, 1907, when the Knickerbocker Trust Company, with deposits of $60 million, was forced to suspend after paying out $8 million. Unlike commercial banks, trust companies were not required to maintain large cash reserves, nor were their investments so carefully regulated. Moreover, they were not members of the New York Clearing House Association and could not call upon it for assistance.

The Knickerbocker's failure caused the heads of other trust companies to fear similar runs on their institutions, and they rushed to Morgan for help.[67] Now seventy years old and semi-retired, the banker had been vacationing in Europe since March and during the first weeks of October, just before the storm broke, attending an Episcopal Convention in Richmond, Virginia. Returning to New York on Sunday, October 20, he was besieged by frightened bankers and financiers.

Once apprised of the facts, he devised a plan that prevented the panic from turning into a major disaster. He called together a group of young, able bankers to investigate the assets and condition of all institutions applying to him for assistance. The findings of this group would determine which trust companies he would help. The Knickerbocker Trust Company did not pass the test, and, even though Morgan himself was one of its stockholders, on Tuesday, October 22, he took no steps to prevent its failure.

That evening he organized a second group of bankers, with himself, Stillman of the National City Bank, and Baker of the First National Bank of New York, as presiding officers. The members of this "rescue party," as Thomas W. Lamont called it, agreed to provide Morgan with statements of their financial condition and, in his son-in-law's words, allow him "to allocate to each one the sum of money which he felt was appropriate and necessary to make up the total amount needed to carry the weaker institutions through the panic."[68] Meanwhile, Secretary of the Treasury George B. Cortelyou arrived in New York City and, after conferring with the Morgan group, ordered government funds deposited in the national banks, thus providing them with money to lend to sound trust companies temporarily unable to satisfy the demands of their depositors.

For two weeks Morgan led "the forces of defense" through one crisis after another. On Wednesday, October 23, less than an hour before closing time, it appeared as though the Trust Company of America, one of the largest in the city, would have to suspend; the rescue party supplied it with enough cash to remain open. The next

---

67. Morgan's role in the panic of 1907 is ably told in Allen, *The Great Pierpont Morgan*, ch. xii; Herbert L. Satterlee, *J. Pierpont Morgan: An Intimate Portrait* (New York, 1939), ch. xvi; more briefly in Thomas W. Lamont, *Across World Frontiers* (New York, 1951), 36–39; John A. Garraty, "Lion in the Street," *American Heritage*, VIII (June 1957), 33–35, 97–101.

68. Satterlee, *J. Pierpont Morgan*, 466.

day the committee raised $25 million to prevent the New York Stock Exchange from closing, and on Friday, October 25, turned over to it another $13 million. "If twenty millions had been needed that day," Perkins testified later, "the Stock Exchange and a hundred or more firms would have gone up, it was just that close. It was touch and go."[69] The weekend provided a brief respite, but on Monday depositors once again lined up at banks and trust companies demanding their money, which they then hoarded at home or in safe deposit boxes.

Just when money was at a premium, the city of New York needed $30 million to meet current debts, and it saw no possibility of borrowing such a sum. City officials turned to Morgan's firm, and on Tuesday, October 29, it agreed to underwrite and sell a $30 million bond issue, which would yield the investor 6 percent. This dramatic display of confidence did more than save New York City from bankruptcy; it boosted morale and strengthened hopes that the worst of the panic was over.[70]

A few days later Morgan faced an even more serious crisis, one that threatened to undo everything he had accomplished thus far. The brokerage house of Moore & Schley was in serious difficulty, and some feared that its collapse would cause a new wave of bankruptcies.[71] The firm had borrowed heavily from banks; its loans were about due; and it had no funds with which to pay them. Among the securities it had used as collateral was a sizable block of Tennessee Coal, Iron & Railroad Co. (TCI&R) stock which the firm itself held as collateral for loans it had granted its senior partner, Grant B. Schley, the brother-in-law of George F. Baker. If the banks were forced to sell Moore & Schley's TCI&R stock, the price at which buyers would take it would be so disastrously low as to force the firm's downfall.

The solution that Morgan finally decided upon was suggested to him by Lewis Cass Ledyard, TCI&R's attorney. The United States Steel Corporation would buy the TCI&R stock and pay for it with its own bonds, whose value no one questioned. Moore & Schley would be saved, the possibility of another Wall Street shock would be eliminated, and the steel corporation would absorb a competitor. Most important, the plan could be effected without the use of any scarce cash.[72] Morgan, of course, would have to win the steel corporation's approval. At the same time he had to persuade the

69. Quoted in Allen, *The Great Pierpont Morgan,* 255.
70. *Ibid.,* 258.
71. This account follows closely the ones given in Allen, *The Great Pierpont Morgan,* 259–66, and Garraty, "Lion in the Street," 99–101.
72. Critics of big business and Wall Street subsequently charged that Morgan and Gary deliberately had made use of the crisis to acquire TCI&R for United States Steel for much less than its real value and that they had misled Roosevelt as to the facts of the situation. Roosevelt strongly defended his action as "emphatically for the public good." See Roosevelt, *Autobiography,* 438–43.

heads of the principal trust companies to subscribe to another $25 million to save the Trust Company of America and other similarly "imperiled institutions."

Morgan solved both problems. The trust companies agreed to raise the necessary money, and the steel corporation's finance committee, after first rejecting the proposal, subsequently decided in favor of Ledyard's plan. Elbert H. Gary, the head of the steel corporation, insisted on President Roosevelt's approval, for Big Steel hoped to forestall a possible antitrust suit. Consultation with the White House had proved useful before, and it was hoped that negotiation with Roosevelt would strengthen the spirit of friendly cooperation that had been developed between the executive and Wall Street.[73] On Monday, November 5, Henry Clay Frick and Gary, of United States Steel, called on Roosevelt, who interrupted his breakfast to confer with them. In the presence of Secretary of State Elihu Root, Gary described, somewhat hastily and without many details, the dangerous situation that still existed and the "great benefit to financial conditions" that would result from the purchase. Roosevelt gave his assent, and Gary immediately communicated the decision to the House of Morgan, which passed it on to the New York Stock Exchange, minutes before it opened. During the next two days, arrangements were made to put the plan into effect, and when the banks opened on Wednesday, November 6, the worst of the panic was over.

Morgan's role had been decisive. He was, Frederick Lewis Allen later said, a "one-man Federal Reserve Bank." For two weeks, while other bankers were running for cover, Morgan and the men around him "stood like a Gibraltar of strength." His able and forceful leadership, which reached its height at this time, prevented the panic from degenerating into a full-scale crash. To supporter and critic alike his display of power was awesome.

Morgan's success, and the realization of the extent to which he had "controlled and dominated the situation," one congressman later stated, aroused increased fears of a "money trust" and renewed agitation for government reform of the financial system. During the congressional debate on the Aldrich-Vreeland proposal to increase the elasticity of the currency by allowing national banks to issue notes secured by other than federal bonds, Senator Robert M. La Follette denounced the "group of financiers who withhold and dispense prosperity," and charged them with having been "deliberately" responsible for having "brought on the late panic, to serve their own ends." [74] Thus was sounded the call that soon led to the Pujo investigation.

73. Robert H. Wiebe, "The House of Morgan and the Executive, 1905–1913," *American Historical Review*, LXV (October 1959), 56.
74. *The Bankers' Magazine*, LXXVI (April 1908), 480; *The Commercial & Financial Chronicle*, XCVI (March 8, 1913), 680–81.

Before that event occurred Morgan's services to the New York, New Haven, and Hartford Railroad (the New Haven) provided additional data that critics interpreted as evidences of the dangers of "banker-management" and of the existence of monopoly and vested interests. Morgan's long connection with this carrier gave him an intimate knowledge of its affairs, which he used to plan a major reorganization. He had presided over its reorganization in the 1890's and had been a director since 1892. He intended to make this road the nucleus of a unified transportation system for all New England; the idea was to consolidate the region's interurban trolley lines and coastal steamship companies, the Boston & Maine Railroad, and the Maine Central under the management of the New Haven.

In August 1903 Morgan persuaded Charles S. Mellen to become the New Haven's president. Head of the Northern Pacific since 1897, Mellen was widely respected as a railroad executive. Roosevelt considered him "a first class fellow," and in 1905 wrote his close friend Attorney General William H. Moody that "what he [Mellen] asks is almost always right." [75]

Under Mellen's leadership, and with the full support and assistance of Morgan, the New Haven launched an expansion program that proved to be exorbitantly costly. In ten years the company increased its capitalization by more than four times, from $93 million in 1903 to $417 million in 1913. That the road was in financial difficulties became apparent by 1910. Besides paying exaggerated prices for the properties acquired — far more than their future earning capacity warranted — Mellen used methods in securing them that aroused widespread criticism and opposition. He finally was forced to resign.

In its report on the New Haven, published in July 1914, the Interstate Commerce Commission (ICC) criticized the officials of the road in language rarely used in government reports. It accused them of an "indefensible standard of business ethics and the absence of financial acumen," and it described their policies as "loose, extravagant and improvident" examples of "financial legerdemain" of the worst kind.[76] Brandeis attributed the New Haven's financial plight to "banker-management." When on December 10, 1913, the company failed to pay its regular dividend, the first one it had passed in forty years, he called this action the "final confession of ten years' mismanagement . . . under banker-control." [77] Morgan was dead by

75. Quoted in Richard M. Abrams, "Brandeis and the New Haven-Boston & Maine Merger Battle Revisited," *Business History Review*, XXXVI (Winter 1962), 408–09. See also Harold U. Faulkner, *The Decline of Laissez Faire, 1897–1917* (New York, 1951), 198–202.

76. Quoted in Faulkner, *Decline of Laissez Faire*, 201–02.

77. Quoted in Mason, *Brandeis*, 211. The New Haven did not pay another dividend until 1928.

this time, and one of his biographers suggested that it was "highly unlikely" that "he even had any direct knowledge" of the scandals that the ICC had uncovered.⁷⁸ Its report did not hold Morgan or his firm responsible for the "reckless and profligate" way in which the New Haven was financed.

Still the fact remained that Morgan had erred seriously. Besides misjudging Mellen and failing to keep adequately informed of what he was doing, Morgan overestimated the region's future growth and the New Haven's ability to earn enough to support the heavy capitalization his ambitious program imposed upon it. He also discounted entirely the potential threat posed by the infant automobile industry, an excusable oversight at the time.⁷⁹ More important was his failure to appreciate the changing mood of the country, especially the public's growing suspicion of big business, fear of monopoly, and distaste for the speculative orgies that occasionally convulsed the stock market.

Roosevelt, in a special message to Congress in January 1908, had asked for federal legislation regulating speculation on the stock exchanges and trading on margin, but nothing came of his request. The responsibility of policing the stock market, Congress decided, belonged to the states.

In December 1908, New York's Governor Hughes appointed a special ten-man committee to investigate speculation on the state's securities and commodities markets and, if necessary, to recommend legislation designed to protect investors.⁸⁰ It was headed by Horace White, a well-known seventy-four-year-old journalist, editor, and economist, whose reputation as a newspaperman dated back to the days when he reported the Lincoln-Douglas debates for the *Chicago Tribune*. The committee concerned itself primarily with eliminating flagrant abuses and "wasteful and morally destructive" speculation.⁸¹

Undesirable speculation, like many of the other practices the committee criticized, proved difficult to distinguish from what it considered legitimate and necessary activities. As a result, most of the recommendations in the committee's report, issued in 1909, were so carefully guarded as to be almost meaningless. On the subject of speculation, for instance, the committee lamented "the practical impossibility of distinguishing what is virtually gambling from

78. Allen, *The Great Pierpont Morgan*, 237.
79. In 1908, when William C. Durant was organizing the General Motors Corporation, he sought J. P. Morgan & Co's assistance. Perkins scoffed at the automobile manufacturer's claim that the time would come when 500,000 cars would be sold yearly, and Durant was forced to go elsewhere for help. He received it from Lee, Higginson and J. & W. Seligman. See Edwards, *Evolution of Finance Capitalism*, 178; Stewart H. Holbrook, *The Age of the Moguls* (New York, 1954), 204–05.
80. *The Commercial & Financial Chronicle*, LXXXVII (December 19, 1908), 1572–74, 1581.
81. Louis Loss, *Securities Regulation* (2d ed., 3 vols., Boston, 1961), II, 1165.

legitimate speculation." It endorsed legitimate speculation as "a necessary incident of productive operations" but was "unable to see how the State could distinguish by law between proper and improper transactions, since the forms and the mechanisms used are identical." Legislation "directed against the latter would seriously interfere with the former." Accordingly, the committee recommended that the stock exchange itself determine and enforce whatever "correctives" it deemed necessary to reduce "the volume of speculation of the gambling type." [82]

The committee's strongest criticisms were directed against three disapproved practices. One was "pyramiding," which it defined as "the use of paper profits in stock transactions as a margin for further commitments." The second was fictitious or "wash" sales, which already were forbidden. The committee also frowned upon the growing practice of brokerage houses' opening branches in New York City, "often luxuriously furnished and sometimes equipped with lunch rooms, cards, and liquor." Establishments of this kind, the committee declared, should be prohibited, for they served only "to increase the lure of the ticker by the temptation of creature comforts." [83]

To be sure, the committee recognized the existence of other abuses, notably those accompanying margin accounts, short sales, and price manipulation, but it refused to recommend their prohibition or limitation by statute. Like speculation, these practices were necessary and useful, often beneficial. It suggested that investment and brokerage houses "discourage speculation upon small margins" and called upon the New York Stock Exchange "to use its influence, and, if necessary, its power, to prevent members from soliciting and generally accepting business on a less margin than 20 per cent." Although "strongly urged" to oppose short sales as morally wrong and economically unjustifiable, the committee refused to do so, since, it said, "short-selling tends to produce steadiness in prices, which is an advantage to the community." [84]

On the equally controversial and oft-debated question of price manipulation the committee very carefully distinguished between two types of practice. It strongly endorsed the technique when used in making a market for new issues, that is, as a means "of bringing new investments into public notice." It just as emphatically denounced price manipulation "designed to serve merely speculative purposes in the endeavor to make a profit as the result of fluctuations which have been planned in advance." Acknowledging that

---

82. New York, Committee on Speculation in Securities and Commodities, *Report . . . June 7, 1909* (Albany, 1910), 4–8. See also Horace White, "The Hughes Investigation," *The Journal of Political Economy*, XVII (October 1909), 528–40; *The Commercial & Financial Chronicle*, LXXXVIII (June 19, 1909), 1533–34.

83. New York, Committee on Speculation, *Report*, 9, 18.

84. *Ibid.*, 9–10.

this kind of manipulation was "open to serious criticism," the committee nevertheless found itself "unable to discover any complete remedy short of abolishing the Stock Exchange itself." It left the entire problem up to the exchange, convinced that it was better qualified than any legislature to "prevent the worst forms of this evil by exercising its influence and authority over the members." [85]

The report of the committee, with its strong emphasis upon self-regulation rather than corrective state legislation, met with a mixed reception. It was hailed by such journals as *The Commercial & Financial Chronicle* as "a conservative and meritorious document," but the report did nothing to satisfy the critics of high finance. They called its defense of so many current Wall Street practices a "whitewash," a "travesty," and a "grim jest." [86] Critics of the report vehemently denounced the committee's readiness to accept the views of the stock exchange as eternal verities. They condemned its unwillingness to endorse what it called "radical changes" that might disturb the "nicely adjusted" mechanism of the exchange. One of the more responsible financial analysts particularly complained of the committee's failure to stress that many of the practices it defended — price manipulation, for instance — too often were employed solely for the benefit of a few insiders.[87]

Although the New York Stock Exchange implemented nearly all the committee's suggestions, the demand for effective legislative safeguards against abuses and for restricting the powers of finance capitalism became even more insistent.[88] Fear and antipathy of Wall Street embittered the debate over monetary and currency reform. Western and southern bankers were almost as vehement in their denunciations of the eastern moneyed interests as were the muckrakers. The Aldrich-Vreeland Act of 1908 was strongly criticized in *The Bankers' Magazine* by a writer who claimed that the statute would be of chief benefit to stock speculators and bond syndicates. "Should the principle of this law be permanently embodied in our banking law," he asserted, "there need no longer be any 'indigestible securities.' . . . The syndicates will buy these bonds, turn them over to their banks, and these in turn will put them up with the

85. *Ibid.*, 11–12.
86. *The Commercial & Financial Chronicle*, LXXXVIII (June 19, 1909), 1529–31; Franklin Escher, "Finance: The Wall Street Investigation," *Harper's Weekly*, LII (July 3, 1909), 28; John T. Flynn, "The Marines Land in Wall Street," *Harper's Magazine*, CLXIX (July 1934), 150; Rudolph L. Weissman, *The New Wall Street* (New York, 1939), 138.
87. Escher, "Finance: The Wall Street Investigation," 28; White, "Hughes Investigation," 539; [New York Stock Exchange] *Answers of the New York Stock Exchange to the Questions of Governor Hughes' Committee* (New York, 1909).
88. "The Stock Exchange and the Pujo Committee," *The Magazine of Wall Street*, XI (February 1913), 221–26; "Probable Stock Exchange Legislation," *ibid.*, XIII (November 1913), 24–27; "The Bill for the Control of Stock Exchanges," *ibid.*, XIII (March 1914), 351–54; "Should the Government Regulate the Exchange?" *ibid.*, XV (January 23, 1915), 224.

Treasury for so-called bank notes . . . and these will be handed out to the people instead of money." [89] Wall Street and specifically the great investment houses increasingly became identified with "the promoting and speculating movement of the day." [90]

Criticisms such as these, combined with reports of large underwriting profits and market manipulations, gave rise to calls for testing the charge that a few powerful investment bankers controlled the nation's economic life. In 1911 Charles A. Lindbergh, the Minnesota Republican reformer and father of the future world-famous aviator, asked Congress to investigate the money trust, which he and many others looked upon as the most powerful and dangerous "trust" of all.[91] Woodrow Wilson took up the charge and made it a part of his preconvention campaign. The stage was set for a thorough airing of the issue.

89. "The New Currency Law," *The Bankers' Magazine,* LXXVI (June 1908), 817–19. On the various sectional and other conflicts among the members of the American Bankers Association, see Robert H. Wiebe, *Businessmen and Reform: A Study of the Progressive Movement* (Cambridge, Mass., 1962), 11, 15, 24, 154–55. Consult also "The Money Trust," *American Banker,* LXXVII (February 3, 1912), 326–27; "Investigating the Money Trust," *The Bankers' Magazine,* LXXXIV (March 1912), 285–86; "The Bank Investigation — What It Might Reveal," *ibid.,* (June 1912), 751–52.

90. Alexander D. Noyes, "The Future of High Finance," *The Atlantic Monthly,* CV (February 1910), 237.

91. See the editorial comments in the *American Banker,* LXXVII (June 8, 1912), 1830–31; *ibid.,* LXXVII (May 3, 1913), 1400.

6 Pujo

On April 25, 1912, the House Banking and Currency Committee passed a resolution establishing a subcommittee to investigate "the concentration of money and credit."[1] Hearings started three weeks later and, as the Democratic leaders had agreed earlier, were adjourned at the end of June in order to avoid any "sensationalism" that might occur during "the heat and excitement of a political campaign." Resumed on December 9, they continued until February 26, 1913.[2] Although the politicians succeeded in postponing "sensationalism" in 1912, the probe became one of the most widely cited and important investigations in the history of American investment banking.

The subcommittee was headed by Arsène P. Pujo, a relatively unknown fifty-two-year-old Louisiana lawyer and Democrat of French descent. First elected to the House of Representatives in 1902, Pujo had served on the National Monetary Commission and, after the Democrats won control of the House in the midterm elections of 1910, had become chairman of the Banking and Currency Committee. While serving as head of the subcommittee named after him, he was defeated in his effort to win nomination to the Senate; refusing to run again for his House seat, he retired in 1913, a few days after submitting the subcommittee's report.[3] As head of this subcommittee Pujo became a national figure, even though his contribution to the conduct of this inquiry was far less important than that of the subcommittee's counsel, Samuel Untermyer.

Indeed, the subcommittee might more properly bear the counsel's name than that of its chairman. Born on January 6, 1858, in Lynchburg, Virginia, of German-Jewish parents, Untermyer grew up in New York City, graduating from Columbia University Law School in 1878.[4] A few years later he opened a law office with his brother

1. The original Resolution, number 429, passed February 24, 1912, called for an investigation designed "to obtain full and complete information of the banking and currency conditions of the United States for the purpose of determining what legislation is needed." Two months later, on April 22, House Resolution 504 was introduced. It called for a more extensive probe into financial abuses. Before its adoption the Democratic leaders sought the views of Champ Clark, William Jennings Bryan, and Woodrow Wilson, the party's principal contenders for the presidential nomination, all of whom declared themselves in favor of the investigation. It was on the basis of this second resolution that the Pujo subcommittee was organized. See Henry Parker Willis, *The Federal Reserve System: Legislation, Organization and Operation* (New York, 1923), 105–09.
2. "The Untermyer Inquiry," *The American Review of Reviews*, XLVII (February 1913), 136–37.
3. Willis, *Federal Reserve System*, 137–38; George B. Tindall, "Arsène Paulin Pujo," *Dictionary of American Biography* (22 vols., New York, 1928–58), XXII, 544–45.
4. Samuel F. Howard, Jr., "Samuel Untermyer," *Dictionary of American Biography*, XXII, 674–76.

and half-brother and soon became one of the city's busiest and most respected trial lawyers. His practice and work in organizing industrial consolidations gave him an intimate knowledge of business and finance. The large fees he received for his services, together with his investments, made him a multimillionaire. Early in the twentieth century Untermyer revised many of his previous ideas about corporate practices and the combination movement. By 1912, when he was asked to serve as counsel for the Pujo Committee, he had become an outspoken critic of big business and high finance and a strong advocate of government regulation. Meanwhile, his own interests appear to have turned toward a career in politics. It was rumored that he was seeking a seat in the United States Senate.[5] Knowledge, experience, and an infinite capacity for work made Untermyer a formidable adversary in the courtroom and, as witnesses before the committee soon learned, an equally vigorous and fearless examiner.[6]

Untermyer made the Pujo investigation much more comprehensive and thorough than the probe Hughes had ordered four years earlier in New York State. Unlike the latter, which confined itself almost entirely to speculation and abuses on the stock exchanges, the Pujo inquiry concerned itself with the much larger problem of investigating the nation's financial and monetary condition and, more specifically, with seeking to ascertain whether a money trust actually existed.

Neither inquiry was an impartial one.[7] The Hughes Committee, composed mostly of individuals friendly to business and financial interests, based its recommendations largely on evidence supplied by the exchanges themselves, without questioning it very seriously. The Pujo Committee, and especially its chief counsel, Untermyer, represented the views of those who believed in Adam Smith's maxim that competition is the most effective "regulator of economic activity." That principle George W. Perkins had denied publicly a half dozen years earlier, when testifying before the Armstrong Committee. "The old idea that we were raised under," Perkins had said then, "that competition is the life of trade, is exploded. Competition is no longer the life of trade, it is co-operation."[8]

The Pujo Committee rejected Perkins's argument, believing it to

5. *The Magazine of Wall Street,* XI (February 1913), 233.
6. Howard, "Samuel Untermyer," 674–76.
7. On the one-sidedness of the Pujo investigation consult *U.S. v. Henry S. Morgan et al.,* "Transcript of Trial: Defendants' Opening — Mr. [Arthur H.] Dean" (December 11, 1950), 708–13; *ibid.,* "Mr. [Ralph M.] Carson" (January 16, 1951), 1752–53. See also *ibid.,* "Mr. [William Dwight] Whitney" (February 1, 1951), 2618–20; *ibid.* (February 2, 1951), 2663–87; the editorial, "The Late Pujo Committee," *The Outlook,* CIII (March 15, 1913), 568–69.
8. New York, *Joint Committee of the Senate and Assembly of the State of New York to Investigate and Examine into the Business and Affairs of Life Insurance Companies Doing Business in the State of New York* (7 vols., Albany, 1906), I, 600.

be an excuse to allow a small group of eastern financiers to dominate the economic life of the country. Untermyer asserted as much two months before the House of Representatives authorized the investigation. "If it is expected that any Congressional or other investigation will expose the existence of a 'money trust' in the sense in which we use the word 'trust' as applied to unlawful industrial combinations, that expectation will not be realized," he told the Finance Forum of the West Side YMCA in New York City. "Of course there is no such thing. . . . There certainly is none that can be said to be in violation of existing law. If, however, we mean by this loose, elastic term 'trust' as applied to the concentration of the 'Money Power,' that there is a close and well-defined 'community of interest' and understanding among the men who dominate the financial destinies of our country and who wield fabulous power over the fortunes of others through their control of corporate funds belonging to other people, our investigators will find a situation confronting us more serious than is popularly supposed to exist." [9]

The investigation covered a broad range of subjects, but mostly it was concerned with the role and functions of the investment banker in the economy. It probed the methods he employed in financing transportation and industry, the influence he exercised over the corporations whose securities he issued, and his relationship to the banks and trust companies with which he was affiliated. Prior to the hearings the committee had sent the leading investment bankers of New York and Boston a lengthy questionnaire. It asked them, among other things, for such information as the size and number of deposits they held for customers, and for whom held; the number of their joint purchases and underwritings of corporate securities since 1907 and the names of their associates in these transactions; a list of the directorships held by the bankers' partners or officers; and a statement indicating their individual as well as their firms' investments in other financial institutions. Untermyer used this material in interrogating the witnesses and preparing the majority report.[10]

Both bankers and others were reluctant to supply this information, but in the end all answered most of the questions submitted. Gardiner M. Lane, of Lee, Higginson & Co., told Untermyer: "I do not think there is anything we should be asked to disclose." [11] Frank W. Remick, a partner in Kidder, Peabody & Co., wrote Untermyer

9. Quoted in *The Commercial & Financial Chronicle*, XCIII (December 30, 1911), 1756.
10. *Ibid.*, XCV (December 7, 1912), 1508. See also "Investigating the Money Trust," *American Banker*, LXXVII (May 4, 1912), 1382–83; "The 'Money Trust' Inquiry," *ibid.* (May 18, 1912), 1559.
11. U.S. House, 62d Cong., 3d Sess., *Investigation of Financial and Monetary Conditions in the United States: Hearings* . . . (3 vols., Washington, 1913), III, 2010.

on December 5, 1912, that his firm was collecting the data he had requested "in order not to unnecessarily delay the Committee," but he added: "we wish it clearly understood that we do not admit the right of the Committee to require the production from us of any of the information desired, and we reserve the right if we are so advised to refuse to produce before the Committee any or all of the information asked for until the Courts have decided that the Committee have the right to require its production." [12] George G. Henry, a partner in William Salomon & Co., was indicted for contempt of Congress and released on $2,000 bail for refusing to name "certain bank officers who participated individually as underwriters in the sale of the stock of the California Petroleum Co." and for failing to identify one of the firms that had participated in the original syndicate.[13] The Comptroller of the Currency also challenged the committee's demand that he supply it with information concerning the investment banking activities of national banks, but, on the advice of the Attorney General, President Taft instructed the Comptroller to provide Untermyer with whatever material he had available.[14]

The most important phase of the investigation occurred during December 1912, after the presidential election, when many of the nation's leading investment bankers were called to testify.[15] Morgan, Schiff, Baker, Winsor, and a host of others were asked to explain how they conducted their affairs. Untermyer's purpose was twofold: to document the extent of financial concentration that existed among a very few Atlantic Coast banks, and to show the ways in which these institutions had achieved and maintained their dominant position.

Six banks were identified as being "the most active agents in forwarding and bringing about the concentration of control of money and credit" in the United States. They were J. P. Morgan & Co., the First National Bank of New York, the National City Bank of New York, Lee, Higginson & Co., Kidder, Peabody & Co., and Kuhn, Loeb & Co.[16] The first three, together with their two con-

12. Frank W. Remick to Samuel Untermyer, December 5, 1912, Kidder, Peabody & Co., "Confidential Letters," VI, 17. Kidder, Peabody & Co., MSS., Baker Library. The text of Untermyer's letter requesting information from the bankers is reprinted in *The Commercial & Financial Chronicle,* XCV (December 7, 1912), 1508.

13. *The Commercial & Financial Chronicle,* XCVI (January 11, 1913), 98; (February 15, 1913), 456.

14. *Ibid.,* XCIV (June 15, 1912), 1595; XCV (September 7, 1912), 590–91; (September 21, 1912), 721–22; (September 28, 1912), 788–89; (October 5, 1912), 864; (November 23, 1912), 1369; XCVI (January 4, 1913), 40.

15. *Ibid.,* XCV (November 23, 1912), 1369. Prior to this time most of the committee's energy was spent questioning members of the New York Stock Exchange and the Clearing House Association, which *The Nation* called "entirely unnecessary." See "The 'Money Trust' Inquiry," *The Nation,* XCIV (June 6, 1912), 575.

16. U.S. House, 62d Cong., 3d Sess., *Report of the Committee Appointed . . . to Investigate the Concentration of Control of Money and Credit* (Washington,

trolled trust companies — Guaranty Trust and Bankers Trust — were said to constitute the "inner group"; the next two, along with Chicago's three largest commercial banks, made up the inner group's chief allies; and the last, Kuhn, Loeb, was classified as being "qualifiedly allied with the inner group and only in isolated transactions."[17] Together these institutions were, according to the majority report, "the principal banking agencies through which the greater corporate enterprises of the United States obtain capital for their operations." Although the members of the subgroup were not always so firmly tied to each other as those in the inner group, they allegedly cooperated with the latter so frequently and so closely that virtually no competition existed among them.[18]

Intimately associated with the inner category and its principal "friends" and associates was another group composed of important, lesser houses, such as Kissel, Kinnicutt & Co., White, Weld & Co., and Harvey Fisk & Sons. These firms, according to the majority report, "receive large and lucrative patronage from the dominating groups and are used by the latter as jobbers or distributors of securities the issuing of which they control, but which for reasons of their own they prefer not to have issued or distributed under their own names."[19] Because of its strong sales organization, Lee, Higginson frequently joined these lesser firms as a distributor for the inner group.

Besides these major jobbers and distributors, there were several hundred banks and smaller investment firms scattered across the country that cooperated with the inner group and the other great houses of issue in underwriting and selling securities. The profits of these bankers, the majority report asserted, were dependent upon the goodwill and patronage of the inner group and its associates. Without their assistance and cooperation these smaller bankers received neither syndicate participations nor securities to sell to their clients.

Except for certain small issues that the larger houses refused to handle, so said the committee, the securities business was monopolized by a few Atlantic Coast investment bankers. To a very large extent, the same firms also allegedly controlled the largest users of capital — the major American railroads and industrial corporations. "The powerful grip of these gentlemen," the majority report concluded, "is upon the throttle that controls the wheels of credit and upon their signal those wheels will turn or stop."[20] The committee

---

1913), 56. See also *U.S. v. Henry S. Morgan et al.,* "Transcript of Trial: Defendants' Opening — Mr. Whitney" (February 1, 1951), 2616–17.

17. The three Chicago banks cited were the First National Bank of Chicago, the Illinois Trust & Savings Bank, and the Continental & Commercial National Bank.
18. *Money Trust Investigation: Report,* 90.
19. *Ibid.,* 131–32.
20. *Ibid.,* 131–33.

buttressed these assertions with an impressive array of statistics, charts, and diagrams showing how these great investment bankers maintained their near-monopoly of the nation's credit and their reputed control over the largest corporations in the country.

According to the majority report, the financial power of these men stemmed from their control of "other people's money." An important source of their strength came from holding the deposits of the corporations they financed. Half of J. P. Morgan's deposits, Untermyer brought out, belonged to seventy-eight interstate corporations, thirty-two of which had a Morgan partner on their boards.[21] "When J. P. Morgan & Co. buy an issue of securities," Brandeis later asserted, "the purchase money, instead of being paid over to the corporation, is retained by the banker for the corporation, to be drawn upon only as the funds are needed by the corporation. And as the securities are issued in large blocks, and the money raised is often not all spent until long thereafter, the aggregate of the balances remaining in the banker's hands are huge."[22] The two outstanding exceptions were Kuhn, Loeb and Lee, Higginson, neither of which required corporations to keep on deposit with them the purchase money of the securities they sold.[23]

The investment banker also accomplished his control over "other people's money," the committee concluded, by investing in the stock of other financial institutions. Though this was an expensive device, all the members of the inner group and their principal associates were substantial stockholders in several banks, trust companies, and life insurance companies. The Morgan firm and its "nominees," Untermyer detailed, controlled or influenced banks and trust companies in New York City with resources of $723 million. Next to Baker and his son, who owned 25,050 shares of the First National Bank of New York, the Morgan firm, with 14,500, was the single largest stockholder in that institution, whose resources in 1913 were estimated at $105 million. The House of Morgan also held 15,000 shares of National City Bank stock and was a majority stockholder in the Equitable Life Assurance Society, with resources of $503 million. These, together with the firm's own deposits of nearly $162.5 million, gave Morgan, according to Untermyer, control of resources in excess of $1.3 billion.[24]

Numerous other examples of such investments were disclosed. The First Security Co., the wholly owned, directed, and officered affiliate of the First National Bank, owned a majority of the stock of the Chase National Bank and sizable blocks of shares in the

21. *Ibid.*, 56–57.
22. Louis D. Brandeis, *Other People's Money and How the Bankers Use It* (New York, 1914), 22.
23. *Money Trust Investigation: Report,* 75, 78.
24. *Ibid.,* 57, 60, 66.

National Bank of Commerce and the Bankers Trust Co.²⁵ Kuhn, Loeb was a major stockholder in the Fourth National Bank of New York and the Equitable Trust Co., and Schiff himself owned 500 shares of National City Bank stock.

The same situation existed in Boston's banks and trust companies, where Kidder, Peabody and Lee, Higginson were alleged to control that city's banking resources. Kidder, Peabody owned a substantial block of stock of the National Shawmut Bank, the city's largest commercial bank, and nearly as large an amount in the Old Colony Trust Co., the largest such institution in New England. The investment house also was a stockholder in two other Massachusetts trust companies, a Boston bank, and the National City Bank of New York. Lee, Higginson's investments in Boston banks and trust companies were smaller than Kidder, Peabody's, and they were concentrated largely in three institutions — the National Shawmut Bank, the First National Bank of Boston, and the Old Colony Trust Co. These three institutions, the majority report alleged, controlled "at least more than half of the banking resources" of the city.²⁶

Voting trusts and interlocking directorships, it was alleged, were just as effective instruments of control as direct investments and far less expensive. Untermyer illustrated the way Morgan and Baker used voting-trust agreements to "control" both the Bankers Trust and the Guaranty Trust of New York. In questioning a director of the former company, Untermyer brought out the fact that that company was controlled by three trustees, one of whom, Henry P. Davison, was a Morgan partner and another, George F. Baker, was chairman of the board and head of the executive committee of the First National Bank of New York. The third member was an attorney in the law firm employed by Baker's bank. The Guaranty was governed by the same kind of voting trust, empowering three trustees to vote all the company's stock. Davison and Baker also were trustees of this institution, along with William H. Porter, another Morgan partner.²⁷

These men, like the partners in the other investment banking houses singled out by the Pujo Committee, also held a number of bank directorships and were members of the finance or executive committees of several trust and life insurance companies. Morgan and two of his partners, Davison and Lamont, were among the fourteen directors of the First National Bank of New York, and Morgan's son, a partner in his father's firm, was a director of the National City Bank of New York.²⁸ Schiff and his partners held directorships

25. *Ibid.*, 67–68.
26. *Ibid.*, 75–78.
27. *The Commercial & Financial Chronicle,* XCV (December 14, 1912), 1581; (December 21, 1912), 1659.
28. *Ibid.*, XCV (December 21, 1912), 1659, summarizes the common directorships held by J. P. Morgan & Co. and the First National Bank of New York in

in a half dozen New York City banks and trust companies; several of Kidder, Peabody's partners were officers or board members of six similar institutions in Massachusetts; and Lee, Higginson was represented on three Boston banks and trust companies.[29]

Investment bankers held numerous directorships in nonfinancial institutions as well. Nearly all the principal railroads and large industrial and public service corporations had at least one banker on their boards. According to the committee, the Morgan firm dominated the board of the United States Steel Corporation. That banking house, along with the First National Bank of New York and Kidder, Peabody, three of the underwriters of the corporation's first bond issue, were represented on its directorate, as was Lee, Higginson. One or more of the partners in Kuhn, Loeb sat on the boards of the sixteen major railroad systems whose securities this firm had sponsored.[30]

These corporations, according to Untermyer and Brandeis, like most of the country's principal financial institutions, were captives of the investment bankers upon whom they depended.[31] The system of interlocking directorates, Brandeis asserted, gave investment bankers effective control over most of the country's transportation and industrial corporations and the financial institutions that held the vast "reservoir of other people's money." They and their associates not only used these resources to extend their dominion, but "what is often even more important," he affirmed, the directorships they held entrusted a small group of men with "the power to prevent the funds [they controlled from] being lent to any rival interests." [32]

Evidence presented at the hearings indicated that the power and influence of the inner group and its chief allies were maintained and extended by the arrangements and understandings that existed among them when purchasing, underwriting, and distributing securities, especially the larger issues of the major interstate corporations.[33] Untermyer emphasized the extent to which large borrowers were dependent upon these bankers when Baker, whom he was questioning, was unable "to name a single transaction in the last [5 or] 10 years of over $10,000,000" that had not been financed

---

various New York City banks and trust companies; *Money Trust Investigation: Report*, 66, 71–72.

29. *Money Trust Investigation: Report*, 75–80.
30. *Ibid.*, 63–64, 75–80.
31. Brandeis, *Other People's Money*, 10–12.
32. *Ibid.*, 19–20. See also Henry H. Klein, *Dynastic America and Those Who Own It* (New York, 1921), 105–08, for a brief summary of the financial interests that the Pujo Committee indicated "controlled" the nation's "leading banks."
33. *Money Trust Investigation: Report,* 92–100, contains a lengthy, detailed table showing the "joint purchases and underwritings of corporate securities" of the "inner group" and its seven principal associates.

by one or more members of the inner group or its close associates.[34] The syndicate, originally devised to spread the risk, now frequently was employed, Untermyer asserted, to stifle competition, exclude rival investment houses, reward former associates for past favors, and cultivate new ones. These practices, together with the custom of awarding syndicate allotments to firms that previously had participated in bringing out the securities of the same corporation, led to the organization of overly large syndicates, with underwriting strength far in excess of the risk involved. Moreover, the custom whereby investment houses recognized each others' corporate clients, commonly called "banking ethics," eliminated whatever investment banking competition still remained; this practice resulted in exorbitant underwriting charges and excessive commissions, which the borrower passed on to the consumer in the form of higher prices and rates.[35]

The bankers who appeared before the committee denied all these charges. They asserted that they employed neither the syndicate nor any other investment banking practice or custom so as to exclude rival firms or to monopolize the securities business.

Baker explained the close community of interest that existed among the principal firms and their close associates in one syndicate after another as perfectly natural and understandable. "We have always tried," he said, in describing the First National Bank's choice of underwriting partners, "to deal with our friends rather than people we do not know." [36] Schiff testified that Kuhn, Loeb chose its underwriting partners from a list of 75, 100, or 125 banking houses, depending upon "the nature and character of the business." Very often many of these were foreign firms and, not infrequently, all of them were English or Continental houses. "We make alliances for the occasion," Schiff said. "We have no standing alliances." [37]

34. *Money Trust Investigation: Hearings,* II, 1540–41.
35. *Money Trust Investigation: Report,* 56, 101–02, 104–05. The charge that investment bankers demanded and received too much for their services was an old one, going back to the railroad reorganizations of the 1890's and the Industrial Commission's investigation. Alexander Dana Noyes warned against "the scattering of the money of corporations on so lavish a scale that it fairly staggered the observer's mind. Sums which would have equipped a great corporation a dozen years ago, and which might do so again, are, month by month disbursed outright to syndicates for the mere service of guaranteeing the sale of new securities." See Noyes's article, "Financial Signs of the Times," *The Nation,* LXXIV (May 1, 1902), 340. Brandeis made use of this and similar information, such as the fee Morgan paid James R. Keene for making a market for United States Steel common stock, to illustrate his charge that investment bankers exacted fees and commissions amounting to as much as 10 percent of the total cash raised. See Brandeis, *Other People's Money,* 23–26, 95–96. The Pujo Committee revealed similarly high bankers' profits, when it reviewed the distribution of the California Petroleum Company's stock. See *The Commercial & Financial Chronicle,* XCVI (January 11, 1913), 98; John T. Flynn, *Security Speculation: Its Economic Effects* (New York, 1934), 179–82.
36. *Money Trust Investigation: Hearings,* II, 1542.
37. *Ibid.,* III, 1662–63.

Partners in the Morgan firm gave similar testimony. Morgan himself testified that his firm had no "regular list" of underwriters to whom it offered syndicate participations. Like most other houses, Morgan & Co. chose its partners from the same group of firms and individuals with which it had done business in the past.[38] Morgan's partner Davison told Untermyer that it was customary, when organizing a syndicate, to include the same parties who had participated in floating a corporation's earlier issues. If a previous transaction for a company had been satisfactory, "the natural way of handling" the next one was to do what had been done before.[39]

This practice, the bankers held, did not prevent them from competing with one another on some later occasion. Schiff told Untermyer that he disapproved of bankers' competing for one another's clients, but he ruefully admitted that it was done.[40] Schiff spoke from experience; some of his most prestigious clients once had been financed by Winslow, Lanier & Co. and Speyer & Co.[41]

Similarly, the fact that an investment house had sponsored a corporation's earlier issues did not mean that it was the captive of that banker, as Untermyer suggested when questioning Davison. The lawyer had asked whether the American Telephone & Telegraph Co. could finance a $67 million bond issue without calling upon the same group of bankers that it had depended upon before. "There are 10 houses in New York City that could get up a syndicate in 24 hours, irrespective of any one of those houses," Davison asserted. Untermyer was unconvinced. "I know and you know," he told Untermyer, "that there are a great many houses in New York doing a very large volume of business that have no relation or connection with those houses you have named there," referring to the inner group and its allies. "You know it just as well as I do, and it can be proved," Davison repeated. The colloquy ended there, each man convinced of the other's dissimulation.[42]

Requiring interstate corporations to sell their securities by competitive bidding was another practice whose merits were debated in the Pujo hearings. Not until later did it become an important issue in controversies over proper distribution methods. Morgan said the practice would neither assure issuers a better price nor serve their own or the buyers' best interests.[43]

38. *Ibid.*, II, 1029–30.
39. *Ibid.*, III, 1858.
40. *Ibid.*, III, 1666.
41. *U.S. v. Henry S. Morgan et al.*, "Transcript of Trial: Defendants' Opening — Mr. Whitney" (February 2, 1951), 2669.
42. *Money Trust Investigation: Hearings*, III, 1858–63. Some of the investment houses that Davison cited as being able to handle substantial transactions independently of the ones named by Untermyer were William Salomon & Co., Lehman Brothers, Heidelbach, Ickelheimer & Co., and Goldman, Sachs & Co.
43. *Money Trust Investigation: Hearings*, II, 1020–21. See also Davison's testimony in *ibid.*, III, 1978–80.

In a letter to the committee, Morgan explained why the securities of private corporations rarely were sold at competitive bids. "The reasons against such practice are plain. Such corporate issues have neither the security, the steadiness nor the general confidence possessed by municipal bonds [which regularly were sold at competitive bids], and while in good times it is possible that they [private corporate securities] might be subscribed for at public auction, in bad times there would be no one to bid for them. . . . Should these . . . [railroad and industrial corporations] appeal directly to the proverbially timid investor there can be little question that, in times of stress, support would be totally lacking. We should have the spectacle of numberless corporations failing for lack of strong financial or banking support." [44]

Competitive bidding also imposed other disadvantages. Corporations would lose the benefit of the financial advice and counsel that resulted from close, continuous association with a banking house. The reputation of the securities themselves would suffer from lack of banking endorsement. Close identity between the banker and the corporation he served was as desirable for the latter as it was for the former and the public.

None of the bankers questioned considered it at all improper for them to be on the boards or finance committees of corporations whose securities they purchased. Nor did these men see any danger in an investment firm's selling securities to banks and trust companies on which one or more of its partners was an officer or director. The evils of interlocking directorates were grossly exaggerated, they asserted. Winsor testified that these institutions were not dependent upon the invstment houses represented on their boards. Prohibiting investment bankers from serving as directors of other financial institutions would deprive them of the services of some "very valuable people." [45] Davison and Schiff were of the same opinion. "I know of no bank or trust company," said Schiff, "that is absolutely controlled by one banking house." [46] Davison argued that without these representations the private banker would make more money. "I think," he told Untermyer, "a connection of that kind always militates against the man who is doing the business." [47]

The most positive, straightforward, and emphatic defense of investment banking practices and ethics was made by the seventy-six-

44. J. P. Morgan & Co., "Letter from Messrs. J. P. Morgan & Co., in Response to the Invitation of the Sub-Committee (Hon. A. P. Pujo, Chairman) of the Committee on Banking and Currency of the House of Representatives" (New York, 1913), 20.
45. *Money Trust Investigation: Hearings,* III, 2002.
46. *Ibid.,* III, 1682. See also Thomas W. Lamont, *Henry P. Davison: The Record of a Useful Life* (New York, 1933), 137–47.
47. *Money Trust Investigation: Hearings,* III, 1980.

year-old Morgan. Unlike many other financiers who were called to testify, "Old Jupiter" was neither evasive, guarded, curt, nor ill-humored. He knew what Untermyer was after, and he answered the attorney's questions fully and authoritatively. For nearly two full days Morgan defended his actions and the policies of his banking house knowledgeably and with conviction.[48] When Morgan was asked about the propriety of investment bankers appointing corporate directors, he defended the policy as necessary and desirable.[49]

Mr. Untermyer: You think, therefore, that where you name a board of directors that is to remain in existence only a year and you have the power to name another board next year, that his [sic] board so named is in an independent position to deal with your banking house as would be a board named by the stockholders themselves?
Mr. Morgan: I think it would be better.
Mr. Untermyer: You think it is a great deal better?
Mr. Morgan: Yes, sir.
Mr. Untermyer: More independent?
Mr. Morgan: Better.
Mr. Untermyer: Will you tell us why?
Mr. Morgan: Simply because we select the best people that we can find for the positions.
Mr. Untermyer: Yes; but do you not see, taking the subject in a general aspect, rather than with respect to your particular banking house. . . .
Mr. Morgan: I am not doing that Mr. Counsel. I am speaking from a broad point of view.
Mr. Untermyer: Yes. Well, speaking from a broad point of view, do you not realize that a board thus selected is under the domination of the people who name it?
Mr. Morgan: My experience is quite otherwise, sir.
Mr. Untermyer: It is?
Mr. Morgan: Yes, sir.
Mr. Untermyer: Is it your experience, then, that the people who name a board of directors and have the right to rename them, or to drop them, have less power with them than people who have no connection in naming them?
Mr. Morgan: Very much so, sir.

48. Frederick Lewis Allen, *The Great Pierpont Morgan* (New York, 1949), 272–77, describes Morgan's appearance and testimony before the Pujo Committee. See also *The Magazine of Wall Street*, XI (February 1913), 233, and "J. P. Morgan Before the Pujo Committee," *Current Opinion*, LIV (February 1913), 90–92, for a brief summary of various newspaper comments on Morgan's testimony.
49. *Money Trust Investigation: Hearings*, II, 1019–20.

Morgan was just as emphatic and certain that combination and concentration did not lead to control, and he denied categorically that a money trust existed or that he wielded great power.[50]

Mr. Untermyer: You are an advocate of combination and cooperation as against competition, are you not?
Mr. Morgan: Yes. Cooperation I should favor.
Mr. Untermyer: Combination as against competition?
Mr. Morgan: I do not object to competition, either. I like a little competition.
Mr. Untermyer: You like a little if it does not hurt you? Competition that hurts you, you do not believe in?
Mr. Morgan: I do not mind it. . . . Now, another point. . . . This may be a sensitive subject. I do not want to talk of it. This is probably the only chance I will have to speak of it.
Mr. Untermyer: You mean the subject of combination and concentration?
Mr. Morgan: Yes; the question of control. Without you have control you can not do anything.

. . . . .

Mr. Untermyer: Well, I guess that is right. Is that the reason you want to control everything?
Mr. Morgan: I want to control nothing.

. . . . .

Mr. Untermyer: What is the point, Mr. Morgan, you want to make, because I do not quite gather it?
Mr. Morgan: What I say is this, that control is a thing, particularly in money, and you are talking about a money control — now, there is nothing in the world that you can make a trust on money [sic].
Mr. Untermyer: What you mean is that there is no way one man can get it all?
Mr. Morgan: Or any of it . . . or control of it.
Mr. Untermyer: He can make a try at it?
Mr. Morgan: No, sir; he cannot. He may have all the money in Christendom, but he can not do it.

. . . . .

Mr. Untermyer: Now, suppose you owned all the banks and trust companies, or controlled them. . . . And somebody wanted to start up in the steel business, you understand, against the United States Steel Corporation.

50. *Ibid.*, II, 1050–53. See also *The Commercial & Financial Chronicle,* XCV (December 21, 1912), 1659; Frederick Lewis Allen, *The Lords of Creation* (New York, 1935), ch. vi; "Mr. Morgan's Denial of a Money Trust," *The Literary Digest,* XLV (December 28, 1912), 1213–14.

	. . . . .
	You would be under a duty, would you not, to the United States Steel Corporation, to see that it was not subjected to ruinous competition?
Mr. Morgan:	No, sir; it has nothing to do with it.
	. . . . .
Mr. Untermyer:	You would welcome competition?
Mr. Morgan:	I would welcome competition.
Mr. Untermyer:	The more of it the better?
Mr. Morgan:	Yes.
	. . . . .
Mr. Untermyer:	. . . Your idea is that when a man has got a vast power, such as you have — you admit you have, do you not?
	. . . . .
Mr. Morgan:	I do not think I have.
Mr. Untermyer:	You do not feel it at all?
Mr. Morgan:	No; I do not feel it at all.
	. . . . .
Mr. Untermyer:	. . . Your idea is that when a man abuses it, he loses it?
Mr. Morgan:	Yes; and he never gets it back again, either.
	. . . . .
Mr. Untermyer:	. . . Do you think that a competitive condition in the banks and trust companies of New York is more or less preferable than a concentrated control over those banks?
	. . . . .
Mr. Morgan:	I would rather have competition.

Somewhat later Morgan repeated his conviction that money could not be controlled. The question of control, in the United States at least, was personal. The same was true of credit; money could not buy credit. And again a little later:[51]

Mr. Untermyer:	Is not commercial credit based primarily upon money or property?
Mr. Morgan:	No, sir; the first thing is character.
Mr. Untermyer:	Before money or property?
Mr. Morgan:	Before money or anything else. Money can not buy it.

On February 28, 1913, three days before the last session of the Sixty-second Congress adjourned, the committee submitted its re-

51. *Money Trust Investigation: Hearings,* II, 1082–84.

port. The majority report, signed by the seven Democratic members, found that there was "an established and well-defined identity and community of interest between a few leaders of finance, created and held together through stock ownership, interlocking directorates, partnership and joint account transactions, and other forms of domination over banks, trust companies, railroads, and public-service and industrial corporations, which has resulted in great and rapidly growing concentration of the control of money and credit in the hands of these few men." In this sense, the majority concluded, a money trust existed.[52]

There were two minority reports, both largely ignored in later discussions. One, signed by three Republicans, stated that although "the testimony had not disclosed the existence of any so-called Money Trust," it did reveal "a dangerous concentration of credit in New York City and to some extent in Boston and Chicago." The other, signed by Henry McMorran, a Michigan Republican, condemned the investigation for having cast "a sinister light . . . over many banking practices which was not justified by the facts, that no effort has been made to show the reasonable and commendable explanation of these practices, and that in many cases an impression has been given to the country as to the character and motives of leading bankers which is altogether unfair."

The majority report did not prove the existence of a money trust, not even in the sense in which Untermyer defined it. The concentration of banking capital in a few New York City institutions was neither planned nor brought about by a few financiers. It was the result of the growing needs of a burgeoning economy, especially the emergence of large corporations, an inadequate and poorly functioning banking system, the absence of any federal regulation, and, as Morgan and Davison had suggested, the natural consequence of "economic laws which in every country create some one city as the great financial centre."[53] Moreover, during the very years when the inner group was accused of building its money monopoly, the banking resources of New York City, when compared with those of the rest of the country, actually had declined, from 23.2 percent in 1900 to 18.9 percent in 1912.[54]

The committee's detailed tables and charts on interlocking directorates were equally misleading. The fact that the 180 bankers and directors of the inner circle served on the boards of 341 financial and other corporations with total resources in excess of $25 billion did not mean that these funds were theirs to command as they saw

---

52. *Money Trust Investigation: Report,* 129, 133–35, 160–61. See also *The Commercial & Financial Chronicle,* XCVI (March 8, 1913), 689.
53. "Morgan to Pujo Letter," 2–3. See also *The Commercial & Financial Chronicle,* XCVI (March 1, 1913), 589, 604.
54. "Morgan to Pujo Letter," 9–10.

fit. Much of this vast wealth represented investments in land, factories, and equipment. It was not, as Morgan informed Pujo, "in cash or liquid form, subject to the selfish use or abuse of individuals." [55] Nor did these men, many of whom rarely saw each other, support the same policies or purposely act together; and even if they had, they would have been unable to impose their will upon the other directors, who were always more numerous than the representatives of Wall Street.[56] Banker control, which Untermyer and Brandeis denounced so vehemently, was potential, at best, rather than actual; its extent varied widely; and it was effected most frequently when corporations found themselves in financial trouble. The bankers, on the other hand, could be faulted for accumulating more directorships than they could manage to stay abreast of, as the testimony of Baker, Davison, and others revealed.

The committee's findings also failed to prove that the inner group and its principal allies had eliminated competition in the issuing and marketing of securities. During the very years when these top firms were supposedly in control, new ones were entering the industry. Several of the leading present-day investment houses started underwriting and distributing securities during the very years that Pujo investigated. It was these firms, together with others, rather than those singled out by Untermyer, that financed most public utilities, light manufactures, and other new enterprises. The inner group concerned itself almost exclusively with financing railroads and large industrial combinations.[57] But even in these areas competition was not entirely lacking, Schiff explained. He told Untermyer that there was "very frequently interference or attempted interference." [58]

Competition within the inner group, however, was less frequent and more restrained than it was among the smaller and newer houses. To a certain extent each of the great houses had its "recognized clients," and so long as the borrower believed his interests were well served by his banker, he was not interested in seeking another. Schiff may have been displeased to learn that at various times one or another of his rivals sought to take the Union Pacific account from his house, but he was not much concerned about it because, he said, the officers and directors of this railroad "would

---

55. *Ibid.*, 9.
56. Thomas C. Cochran, *The American Business System: A Historical Perspective, 1900–1955* (Cambridge, Mass., 1960), 84–85. See also *The Magazine of Wall Street*, XII (May 1913), 14.
57. *U.S. v. Henry S. Morgan et al.*, "Corrected Opinion of Harold R. Medina" (February 4, 1954), 18–20.
58. *Money Trust Investigation: Hearings*, III, 1666. See also Fritz Redlich, *The Molding of American Banking: Men and Ideas* (2 vols., New York, 1947, 1951), II, 380.

not like to invite anybody else [to bid for its securities], because they are satisfied with the way Kuhn, Loeb & Co. have treated them." [59]

The existence of close, continuous ties of this kind led Untermyer to conclude that the leading investment houses deprived the clients' competitors of needed funds, "to the detriment of interstate commerce and of the general public." The committee offered no evidence to substantiate this charge, and it ignored entirely Morgan's rejoinder that, "except under unfavorable money market conditions, we have never heard of any responsible and deserving individual, firm or corporation being unable to secure ample credit." [60]

Despite some of its exaggerated and misleading conclusions, the Pujo investigation revealed a high degree of financial concentration in New York City, a fact that both Baker and Morgan admitted. It also showed that the business of underwriting and distributing securities, especially those of the great interstate corporations was, as it had been and continued to be, the occupation of a relatively few firms. It was this centralization of financial power, the diverse, subtle, and personal nature of its influence, and the absence of any public control over it that worried the committee and disturbed so many Americans.[61]

It was not so much that the inner group had misused or abused its authority and influence. On the whole it had exercised both very well. "We are not unmindful of the important and valuable part that the gentlemen who dominate this inner group and their allies have played in the development of our prosperity," the committee report asserted. "Without the aid of their invaluable enterprise and initiative and their credit and financial power the many requirements of our vast ventures could not have been financed in the past, and much less so in the future." [62]

The committee's long list of recommendations was designed to prevent further financial concentration, restore competition in the capital markets, decentralize high finance, and bring Wall Street under government regulation. Some of these objectives were to be achieved by reforming the stock exchanges, requiring their incorporation under state law, placing them under federal supervision, prohibiting certain practices, and tightening controls over others. "The Exchange is a wholesome public necessity," Untermyer asserted. "It is not healthful or desirable that a few banking houses should monopolize the prestige and profit of acting as intermediaries between those who need capital . . . and the investors who are

59. *Money Trust Investigation: Hearings*, III, 1665.
60. "Morgan to Pujo Letter," 16.
61. Cochran, *American Business System*, 85–86.
62. *Money Trust Investigation: Report*, 159.

able to supply it. The need should be supplied by a public market for securities." [63]

The committee's proposals designed to regulate investment banking activities were even more radical. In order to break the power of the inner group, especially its alleged control over the issuing and marketing of securities of large corporations, the committee recommended that the Interstate Commerce Commission (ICC) supervise the bond and stock issues of all interstate railroads and that the securities be offered only at competitive bids, either public or private. The committee would have required the ICC to regulate the security issues of industrial corporations engaged in interstate commerce as well, but since it was uncertain whether Congress had the authority to empower the ICC to do so, the committee did not include this proposal in its final recommendations.[64]

The inner group's domination of the principal users and institutional suppliers of capital was to be destroyed by outlawing other allegedly noncompetitive practices and customs. Interstate corporations were to be barred from designating "any bank, banker, or trust company their sole fiscal agent to dispose of their security issues" and from depositing their funds in private banks; this would prevent these institutions from using their clients' funds to lend on the call market or to finance syndicates. National banks and their security affiliates were to be prohibited from underwriting and selling securities. The officers and directors of these institutions, like those of life insurance companies, were to be barred "from participating in syndicates, promotions, or underwritings of securities in which their banks are or may become interested as underwriters or owners or as lenders thereon." [65] No person might be a director of more than one national bank serving the same community. The stock of national banks was not to be "owned or held, directly or indirectly," by any other bank or trust company or holding company. National banks were to be prohibited from turning over their stock to voting trusts. All bank consolidations were to be approved by the Comptroller of the Currency.[66]

Criticism of investment bankers was not limited to the Congress. At the very time Untermyer was interrogating the top leaders of American finance, state legislators were enacting regulatory statutes

---

63. Samuel Untermyer, "Speculation on the Stock Exchanges and Public Regulation of the Exchanges," *The American Economic Review*, V, suppl. (March 1915), 24–68. See also [Henry K. Pomroy] "An Ex-president of the Stock Exchange Replies to Miss Tarbell," *The American Magazine*, LXXV (June 1913), 29–32; the editorial, "Reforming the Stock Exchange," *Current Opinion*, LIV (March 1913), 246.
64. *Money Trust Investigation: Report*, 150–51.
65. *Ibid.*, 164–65.
66. *The Commercial & Financial Chronicle*, XCVI (March 8, 1913), 682. See also the editorial, "The 'Money Trust' Investigation," *The Outlook*, CIII (January 4, 1913), 2.

of their own. Many of the same groups that applauded the work of the Pujo Committee — farmers, small businessmen, aggrieved investors — also demanded compulsory disclosure laws and more effective state supervision of the securities business. Never before had investment bankers been under such a many-sided attack as they were during the first and second decades of the twentieth century. The demand for reform and government supervision of the securities industry was incessant. "The time is coming," Morgan told a friend, shortly before his death, "when all business will have to be done with glass pockets." [67] The "Blue Sky" movement that spread across the country after 1911 seemed to mark the beginning of the new era to which Morgan referred.

67. Quoted in Alexander D. Noyes, *The Market Place: Reminiscences of a Financial Editor* (Boston, 1938), 202.

7 "Blue Sky": The Growth of Securities Regulation

Criticism of investment bankers reached a peak during the years 1910 to 1913. The demand for reform focused chiefly on two areas: financial concentration and abuses and deception in the issuing and marketing of securities. Relief was sought from both the federal and state governments. Congress concerned itself largely with restraining the power and influence of the "financial oligarchy" that Louis D. Brandeis accused of controlling the economic life of the country, and the states limited themselves principally to enacting better disclosure and more effective antifraud laws.

Kansas launched the new era in state regulation of the securities industry. On March 10, 1911, fourteen months before the Pujo Committee opened its investigation, the Kansas legislature enacted the "first comprehensive licensing system" in the country. The law marked the beginning of a more formal and effective era in the regulation of the securities business. This and similar statutes passed by other states were generally known as "blue sky" laws because they were designed to protect potential investors from fraudulent promotions and securities salesmen who "would sell building lots in the blue sky in fee simple."[1]

Before the states adopted blue-sky laws the investment banking business had been almost entirely free from government regulation. The only federal statutes that applied to individuals dealing in securities were the postal fraud laws, under which the government prosecuted swindlers convicted of using the mails to mislead and defraud the public. The states had been regulating the securities of corporations they chartered since the middle of the nineteenth century, in some cases even earlier. These regulations, however, did not protect investors of one state who had purchased securities issued by corporations of other states. Most state efforts, moreover, were aimed at controlling the capitalization of railroads and public utilities rather than the practices of the bankers and brokers who dealt in the securities of these corporations. Furthermore, many of these laws were inadequate or poorly enforced. This was especially true in states without strong commissions or other independent and competently staffed agencies to administer them. But even states

---

1. Much of the material in this chapter is based upon Louis Loss, *Securities Regulation* (2d ed., 3 vols., Boston, 1961), I, 23–67, and Gerald D. Nash, "Government and Business: A Case Study of State Regulation of Corporate Securities, 1850–1933," *Business History Review,* XXXVIII (Summer 1964), 144–62. See also the briefer accounts in William C. Breed, "Public Regulation in Origination and Distribution of Securities," *Investment Banking,* III (February 21, 1933), 183–96; David Saperstein, "Governmental Regulation of Investment Banking," in Investment Bankers Association, *Fundamentals of Investment Banking* (Englewood Cliffs, 1960), 620–29.

with vigorous commissions did not regulate the way in which securities were sold. Once the investment banker received the commission's approval to bring out an issue, he was entirely free to distribute it as he saw fit.²

Blue-sky laws grew out of this earlier experience. Their purpose was to supplement the special and general incorporation laws of the various states. These statutes included some of the first security regulations written into American law. State incorporation laws varied widely, but nearly all of them sought to insure honest capitalization by stipulating the amount of stock and bonds that a corporation could issue. In 1852 the Massachusetts legislature passed a law prohibiting a railroad chartered in that state from beginning construction until "a certificate shall have been filed in the office of the secretary of the Commonwealth." This document had to state "that all of the stock named in the charter has been subscribed for by responsible parties, and that twenty per cent. of the par value of each and every share of the stock thereof" had been "actually paid" into the treasury of the company.³

Other states imposed similar requirements. Examples are numerous. In 1855 a special Illinois law chartering the Wabash Mining Company established this corporation's maximum allowable capitalization, stipulated the amount of stock that had to be sold and paid in before the company could borrow, limited the size of its indebtedness, and fixed the term and selection of its directors. That same year the Texas legislature wrote almost identical restrictions in the charters of three corporations, a telegraph and two railroad companies. In 1859, after many of its citizens had been defrauded by unscrupulous promoters, Indiana enacted a general incorporation law for bridge companies, setting standards for these corporations. By the end of the Civil War most state incorporation laws included provisions fixing the capitalization of new corporations, regulating subsequent issues of new securities, and stipulating the rights of stockholders.⁴

Enforcement of these laws, however, proved increasingly difficult, especially after 1870, when the number and size of corporations increased rapidly, and their activities grew more complex and diverse. These developments soon stimulated growing public demand for more effective regulation of business. Much of the pressure, directed particularly against the railroads, came from such farm groups as the Grangers and Populists, but many other interest groups also contributed to it.

Responding to popular demand, the states adopted more forceful

2. Mary L. Barron, "State Regulation of the Securities of Railroads and Public Service Companies," *The Annals*, LXXVI (March 1918), 167–90.
3. Quoted in Loss, *Securities Regulation*, I, 23.
4. Nash, "Government and Business," 146–48.

methods of administering their corporation laws. This responsibility the legislatures commonly assigned to a special bureau, board, or commission. "Work hitherto badly done, spasmodically done, superficially done, and too often corruptly done by temporary and irresponsible legislative committees," Charles Francis Adams, Jr., wrote optimistically in 1868, "is in [the] future, to be reduced to order and science by the labors of permanent bureaus and placed by them before legislatures for intelligent action."[5]

Such use of boards and commissions for administrative purposes was an adaptation of an old technique to a new problem. Several states had utilized them to supervise internal improvement projects. Later, as railroads became more important, special commissions were organized to regulate these carriers. The earliest regulatory commissions were established in New England, the section with the most highly developed railway system. Rhode Island led the way in 1839, and by the end of the century more than half the states had established railroad commissions.[6]

Like earlier special committees of legislatures, the railroad commissions concerned themselves primarily with regulating rates, services, and capitalizations. By controlling the latter, the states hoped to eliminate stock watering, a common post–civil War practice that probably more than any other aroused the widest public criticism in both the United States and Britain.[7] Massachusetts made the transition from legislative to commission regulation of railroad securities in 1869; it tightened the provisions of an earlier law controlling the issue of railroad stock and entrusted enforcement of the increased restrictions to a newly organized railroad commission. In 1894 the legislature strengthened the commission's authority by passing an "anti-stock watering act" prohibiting railroads from issuing stock other than at market value and then only with the approval of the commission.[8] Similar regulatory boards were established in other states across the country. For instance, in 1893 Texas passed a Stock and Bond Law requiring the state railroad commission to authorize, approve, and register all new railroad issues.[9]

5. Quoted in Edward C. Kirkland, *Industry Comes of Age: Business, Labor, and Public Policy, 1860–1897* (New York, 1961), 117.

6. John F. Stover, *American Railroads* (Chicago, 1961), 125; Kirkland, *Industry Comes of Age*, 117–18, credits New Hampshire with establishing the first railroad commission; Nash, "Government and Business," 148.

7. See, for example, the three articles, "Would It Pay To Be Honest in Company Promotion?" *The Statist*, XXXV (February 9, 1895), 185; (February 23, 1895), 245–46; (April 27, 1895), 537–38; James A. Logan, "The Vice of Fictitious Corporate Capitalizations," *The American Journal of Politics*, II (February 1893), 203–10.

8. Edward C. Kirkland, *Men, Cities and Transportation* (2 vols., Cambridge, Mass., 1948), II, 323–24; Nash, "Government and Business," 148–49.

9. William Z. Ripley, *Railroads: Finance & Organization* (New York, 1915), 301; Nash, "Government and Business," 149. See also U.S. Industrial Commission, *Report* . . . (19 vols., Washington, 1900–02), IX, 935–36.

The authority of these commissions varied widely, as did their effectiveness in regulating railroad capitalization. Although generally they fell considerably short of expectations, such agencies continued to be established.

Moreover, after 1900 the practice of regulating security issues by commission was extended to the rapidly growing public utilities industry. The regulation of such issues started in New York in 1906 with the passage of a gas and electric commission bill. The next year, under the forceful and progressive leadership of Governor Charles Evans Hughes, the legislature passed two public service commission laws, one for New York City and the other to exercise authority over the rest of the state. The Gas and Electric Commission and the Board of Railroad Commissioners were combined into a single Public Service Commission, vested with wide investigative and regulatory authority, including the power to pass upon all new public utility issues. The latter provision was designed specifically to prevent overcapitalization.[10]

In 1908 the commission shocked the New York City investment banking community by announcing that it intended to "revolutionize" the method of financing public utility corporations. Instead of allowing the utility companies to sell their securities "privately" to a single investment house or a syndicate, as they had done in the past, the commission proposed requiring them to offer their bonds publicly at competitive bids.[11] Though nothing came of this proposal at the time, compulsory competitive bidding remained a hotly debated issue among investment bankers and public officials.

Meanwhile other states followed New York's lead. They established public service commissions with regulatory powers over utility issues or, as in the case of Wisconsin in 1907, brought the corporations offering these securities under the control of railroad commissions. By 1917 more than half the states had enacted laws regulating the securities of public service companies.[12]

During the first decade of the twentieth century the demand for effective regulation of the securities business grew more and more insistent. Investors were told of the extent to which many corporations were being overcapitalized and their inflated stock being advertised as safe, promising investments by reputable bankers and brokers.[13] The stock market panic of 1901 and the glut of undigested securities that depressed stock and bond prices in 1903 piled up additional data for critics. To these were added the secrecy

10. *The Bankers' Magazine,* LXXV (September 1907), 324.
11. "The Public Bond Market," *American Banker,* LXXIII (June 20, 1908), 2184.
12. George W. Edwards, *The Evolution of Finance Capitalism* (London, 1938), 194–95.
13. [Roger W. Babson] *Actions and Reactions: An Autobiography* . . . (New York, 1935), 88–89.

that surrounded the organization, financing, and management of most great corporations as well as the public's growing fear of monopoly power that a few financiers seemed to exercise over much of the economy. All these circumstances contributed still further toward agitation for more accurate financial information from corporations and greater protection for investors. The fact that Britain enacted a new securities law in 1900 also strengthened the demand for similar regulatory legislation in the United States.[14]

The English Companies Act of 1900 reaffirmed the principle of compulsory disclosure, originally introduced in 1844. In that year, for the first time, Parliament had required every issuer to file a prospectus with the Board of Trade, where it would be available to the public. The new law increased substantially the amount of information that had to be included in a prospectus or any other notice offering stocks and bonds to the public.[15] The statute was intended to protect investors by requiring issuers to provide them with full, accurate information about the company, its sponsors, and its bankers as well as the securities themselves. The government assumed no responsibility for the quality of the securities; its sole function was to make certain that the corporation and its bankers supplied potential investors with the kind of information necessary for them to make an intelligent decision.

The advisability of enacting a similar law in the United States had been discussed in hearings before the Industrial Commission. Charles R. Flint, the organizer of the United States Rubber Company, the American Woolen Company, and many other large consolidations, spoke against it. "My idea is that affairs of trade are best regulated by natural laws," he told the commission. "While I think it is desirable that there should be a system sustained for proper auditing and accounting, and regulation as to the issuing of securities, the evils which have developed in connection with the organization of industries are being corrected by natural laws. The careless banker has lost his reputation; the careless investor has lost his money; and the result of it is, more care will be taken." [16] Other witnesses, realizing the extent to which the public was being cheated by the sale of watered and fictitious securities, were unwilling to leave the protection of the investor to the "natural laws" of the marketplace; they recommended that the states or, if "constitutionally possible," the Congress supervise the issue and sale of securities.[17]

Many other Americans — businessmen, bankers, and financial

14. U.S. Industrial Commission, *Report,* XIX, 416.
15. Loss, *Securities Regulation,* I, 5–6. See also Andrew Ten Eyck, "Some Precedents in British Law and Practice for Safeguarding Securities," *Harvard Business Review,* II (July 1924), 385–97.
16. U.S. Industrial Commission, *Report,* XIII, pt. 2, 92–93.
17. *Ibid.,* IV, pt. 1, 19.

editors, as well as public officials and reformers like Brandeis — urged and supported greater disclosure and more effective regulation.[18] Early in 1907 a St. Paul judge warned the Great Northern Railway Company that the "issue of stock by a railroad corporation is a matter of public concern, and the state has a right to insist that when a corporation increases its stock there should be value behind the stock." A writer for *The Bankers' Magazine* applauded the action, calling it a wise and moral doctrine.[19] A few months later, Henry Clews, the head of the well-known investment banking house of Henry Clews & Co., asserted that overcapitalization had "run riot and produced an overplus of undigested securities. This system of financing will surely lead to disaster if not curbed." The only way to stop stock watering, Clews declared, was to compel corporations "to state exactly and definitely for what purpose" they were issuing securities, and "to make a clear and definite report."[20]

Responding to widespread criticism against stock watering and the growing protests of investors, state legislators first adopted more effective notification laws to protect the investing public. In 1903 Connecticut, the initiator, required mining and oil corporations offering securities in that state to file with the Secretary of State a statement "showing its financial condition, the location and plans of its properties, the amount of work done and cash expended for improvements, and the condition of its plant and machinery." The law was framed so that it would not "in any way affect any corporation all of whose mines are situated within this state."[21]

Nevada passed a similar notification statute in 1909. This law aimed principally at achieving "full disclosure in the sale of mining stock." It required every Nevada mining corporation offering and selling stock in the state to file semi-annually "a sworn statement containing specified information as to its mining property and development, its use of the proceeds from the sale of stock, its capital structure, compensation paid to its officers, and other expenditures."[22] The Attorney General and recorder of every county where the company was working or developing mining property was to receive a copy, as was every stockholder. The law drew a distinction between treasury and promotion stock, its classification depending upon whether the money received from its sale was "to be used for the actual development of the mineral resources of any mining claim or for the purpose of making necessary improvements thereon." It also required that every stock certificate be clearly and conspicu-

18. See, for example, *American Banker,* LXIV (August 23, 1899); Nash, "Government and Business," 150; Louis D. Brandeis, *Other People's Money and How the Bankers Use It* (New York, 1914), 103–05.
19. *The Bankers' Magazine,* LXXIV (February 1907), 177.
20. Henry Clews, "The Overcapitalization of Railroads," *The Bankers' Magazine,* LXXV (July 1907), 123.
21. Loss, *Securities Regulation,* I, 25.
22. *Ibid.,* I, 26.

ously labeled as such.[23] Two years later these requirements were relaxed considerably, and in 1915 the law itself was repealed.

Rhode Island was the third state to adopt a general notification statute. In 1910 the state's corporation law was amended to include a general securities provision regulating the issue of "stock, shares, or installment shares, in any investment company or in any real estate, mining, or co-operative corporation, society, association, or organization, other than building and loan associations, or notes or bonds or other securities thereof." [24] None of these companies, nor their agents or brokers, could offer or sell any of these securities in Rhode Island without first filing with the Secretary of State a statement disclosing its financial condition as well as plans and location of its properties, "the amount of work thereon, the amount of cash expended for improvements . . . and the condition of the plant and machinery, if any, connected therewith." A similar statement had to be filed annually thereafter.[25] The only exempt corporations were those holding a Rhode Island charter and having at least 90 percent of their property located in the state.

Meanwhile, Kansans moved toward adopting a more stringent securities law. During the first decade of the twentieth century Kansas, along with other middle western farm states, enjoyed a period of unprecedented prosperity. Between 1900 and 1910 the total estimated value of farm land and buildings in the United States more than doubled, while the index of wholesale prices for all farm products rose approximately 50 percent. Many farmers paid off their debts and accumulated cash savings. Prosperity attracted to Kansas numerous promoters, swindlers, and "blue sky merchants" determined to separate the affluent farmer from his savings by enticing him to invest in fraudulent, financially unsound, or highly speculative enterprises. Suffering heavy losses, the victims of these frauds and misrepresentations agitated for protection, then joined with other dissatisfied midwesterners to elect reform administrations that promised them relief from such abuses. Voters also wanted more effective laws regulating railroads and other corporations, the same vested interests that the Populists had inveighed against earlier and that now were being denounced by progressives in both the Democratic and Republican parties. In Kansas, overproduction of crude oil precipitated a sharp price decline, causing many small, poorly financed, local companies to skip dividend payments. Accordingly, the demand for reform focused on trimming the power of the Standard Oil Company and, among other things, protecting investors.[26]

23. Quoted in *ibid*.
24. Quoted in *ibid*.
25. Quoted in *ibid*., I, 25–26.
26. Ralph W. Hidy and Muriel E. Hidy, *Pioneering in Big Business, 1882–1911: History of the Standard Oil Company (New Jersey)* (New York, 1955), 671–72.

In 1910 Walter R. Stubbs, a wealthy, reform-minded Republican businessman and admirer of Theodore Roosevelt, was reelected governor of Kansas. For his bank commissioner, Stubbs chose one of his political allies, J. N. Dolley, a former grocer, who had served as chairman of the Republican state committee and speaker of the state House of Representatives.

Once in office, Dolley immediately organized a special department under his supervision to investigate all securities publicly offered in Kansas, to expose those considered fraudulent, and to advise investors seeking information. Rejecting the commonly held belief that "the people do not need a guardian to supervise their investments," Dolley argued that a firm selling securities should be regulated like a bank. "History and statistics show," he declared, "that losses through banks are but a drop in the bucket compared with the money which is lost through investment in worthless stocks and bonds." [27] Meanwhile he pressed for legal authority to continue his department's work; largely as a result of his efforts, strengthened by a widespread belief that thousands of Kansans were being victimized by unscrupulous promoters of worthless securities and watered stock, the legislature enacted his recommendations into law.

Because of its greater comprehensiveness, more effective enforcement procedures, and subsequent widespread impact, the Kansas blue-sky law is generally regarded as inaugurating the modern era of securities regulation. The Rhode Island, Nevada, and Connecticut statutes were primarily notification laws, with no special administrative agency to enforce them. In contrast, the Kansas act required the registration of all securities, except a few specifically exempted ones, such as notes secured by mortgages on Kansas land, and government bonds — federal, state, and municipal. The law also called for the licensing of investment bankers, brokers, and dealers selling stocks and bonds in the state.[28] The Bank Commissioner was authorized to enforce the law. Issuers were required to file with him a detailed statement describing in full the condition of their business. Any false statements were punishable by fine or imprisonment.

In addition to disclosure requirements the law introduced an entirely new regulatory principle, one without precedent in either British or American statutes. No security covered by the act could be issued or sold without a permit from the Bank Commissioner. Grounds for denial were defined broadly. Anything in the registration statement or accompanying documents that appeared to him to be "unfair, unjust, inequitable or oppressive to any class of contributors" was sufficient to outlaw sale of the issue in the state. If,

---

27. Quoted in Louis Loss and Edward M. Cowett, *Blue Sky Law* (Boston, 1958), 9n.27.
28. Loss, *Securities Regulation,* I, 27. See also Breed, "Public Regulation," 186.

after examining its affairs, the commissioner decided that a company was insolvent, did not "intend to do a fair and honest business," or that its securities did not "promise a fair return," he was authorized to prevent it from doing "any further business" in Kansas.[29]

These and other provisions made the Kansas law the most comprehensive and vigorously enforced securities statute enacted in the United States up to that time. Never before had a state sought to prevent its citizens from making unwise investments. The law went far beyond the fraud and disclosure principles incorporated in the British Companies Act or earlier state statutes regulating securities.

Confronted with attacks on both the state and federal levels, security dealers and investment bankers took formal steps to counter their critics, improve their image, and raise standards of practice. They hoped that such a program would satisfy disgruntled investors and check the demand for further regulation. To achieve these objectives, investment bankers proposed organizing a national association of security dealers. The financial and daily press welcomed the move. Such an organization, the *American Banker* editorialized, was long overdue and sorely needed. Had one been in existence earlier, this journal continued, investors could have been saved countless losses and the investment banking business might have been spared "a black eye." [30]

29. Quoted in Loss, *Securities Regulation,* I, 27n.22.
30. "National Bond Dealers' Association," *American Banker,* LXXVI (June 17, 1911), 1941; (July 22, 1911), 2484; "That Bond Dealers' Organization," LXXVI (September 30, 1911), 3284; "Investment Bankers Organize," LXXVII (August 10, 1912), 2694.

8 Organizing for Defense: Formation of the Investment Bankers Association of America

The Investment Bankers Association of America (IBA), formally organized in August 1912, was the industry's united response to mounting public criticism and increasing demands for regulatory legislation. Group action through trade associations was common in other fields of enterprise. To promote their mutual interests, commercial and savings banks and trust companies belonged to the American Bankers Association (ABA), founded in 1875. The IBA was a splinter group from that organization. The new association was the means through which investment bankers sought to establish their identity and proclaim the importance of their function, their high ethical standards, and their intention to improve their operations and extend their services.

Although New York City was the most important investment banking center in the United States, the IBA had its real origin in Chicago two years before it was formally organized, and for many years it kept its headquarters there. George B. Caldwell, vice president of that city's Continental & Commercial Trust and Savings Bank, was the leading spirit behind the organization. He was chairman of the organizing meeting and became the first president, serving for two terms.

At the 1912 meeting Caldwell described the preliminary steps in the formation of the association, the attendant frustrations, and the need for the industry to present a united front before a hostile public.[1] Caldwell recounted that at a Chicago dinner meeting of "bond bankers" in 1910, a group of those present discussed the feasibility of asking the ABA for the privilege of organizing as a section of that body. The ABA, which then numbered over 12,000 members, included about 400 investment bankers but did not have among its officers, or as a member of its large executive council, a single private banker. Although the proposal found many friends, informal inquiry revealed that a majority of the executive council thought that the existing six sections of the ABA already were too many and that there were no funds available to carry on the work of another. Some ABA members believed that "investment banking was not banking in the broadest sense, and that some concerns were

---

1. Investment Bankers Association of America, *Proceedings . . . 1912* (Chicago, 1912), 16–18. Much of the material for this chapter is based on this source. See also *U.S. v. Henry S. Morgan et al.*, "Transcript of Trial: Government's Opening" (December 4, 1950), 292–308; *ibid.*, "Defendants' Opening" (March 13, 1951), 4423–26; *The Commercial & Financial Chronicle,* XCVI (March 15, 1913), 764.

unscrupulous and might bring heavy loss upon innocent people and discredit upon the American Bankers Association." [2]

Investment bankers were unimpressed with the negative arguments. They interpreted these views as a stamp of disapproval upon their specialty. As to the plea of lack of funds to pay the expenses of a separate section, it was proposed to raise the dues of the private bankers and also to increase the membership. In answer to the other objection, membership in the proposed section could be sufficiently safeguarded to keep out undesirable investment bankers, just as the ABA kept out undesirable bankers of other classes.

Nor was the ABA convinced by the Chicago group's more positive arguments. The facts that some investment bankers took deposits, that some banks of deposit dealt in securities, that each class was essential to the other, and that both kinds of banking carried the maximum responsibility in granting credits, Caldwell said, "did not as we then hoped find enough support and we were defeated. I make this statement so no one can truthfully say or assume we are either insurgents or radicals."

In the same speech Caldwell outlined the advantages of the new association and defined its proposed relation to its parent organization. The IBA would have control of its own funds through its own officers and, being a less unwieldy group, would accomplish a great deal more than if organized as a section of the ABA. His bank would continue to be a member of the larger group, and he hoped that the new IBA would emulate the dignity of the ABA and be worthy of its approval. Investment bankers could not be regarded as competitors, he held, but must cooperate with the ABA whenever possible and "maintain the most friendly relations, recognizing that we are both important branches of our financial system."

The Commercial & Financial Chronicle commended the group forming the new association, pointing out its social usefulness and the emerging concept of the investment banker as a specialist. The *Chronicle* agreed that investment bankers could accomplish more outside the ABA than they could within it. For one thing, they would be less circumscribed in their endeavors and would not have to defer to the views of those having divided interests. Investment bankers, it said, had a distinct field of their own, and it should be their purpose to develop it to the utmost. Since banks and trust companies also were engaged in the securities business, they were as deeply interested as the investment bankers themselves in seeing the new organization flourish.[3]

---

2. IBA, *Proceedings . . . 1912*, 16–18.
3. "The Coming Meeting of the Investment Bankers," *The Commercial & Financial Chronicle,* XCV (August 3, 1912), 268–69. See also "Prospects of the Investment Bankers' Association," *The Magazine of Wall Street,* X (September 1912), 250–51; "Investment Bankers Organize," *The Bankers' Magazine,* LXXXV (Sep-

The letter of the organizing secretary inviting banks to send representatives to the formal organizing meeting referred to the large number of responses already received from the bond houses and banks with bond departments all over the country. The meeting was expected to be well attended, and the new association would start out with "a very representative membership." The organizers were anxious to have the cooperation of those invited to join this "high grade organization, which will have for its purpose the betterment of the investment banking business." [4]

Initial membership was modest in size, widely distributed geographically, and included different types of banks and bankers. Charter members, those joining by the end of 1912, included representatives of Pujo's inner group and other industry leaders as well as many smaller houses. Altogether they numbered nearly 375, including branches of parent firms. Forty-two cities were represented, from Chicago to New Orleans, and from Portland, Maine, to Los Angeles (see Exhibit 2).

Members' affiliations indicated a broad definition of "investment banker." Even the bankers in the organizing group still were not agreed on the functions or the type of financial firms that they should invite to join. The Foreword to the first volume of *Proceedings* said that the association was the first one "consituted purely of investment bankers," as though they were a clearly defined group; yet at least three definitions appeared in this volume. President Caldwell said in his initial address: "investment banking . . . broadly speaking, has to do with the organization and distribution of a secured form of credit known as bonds." He did not mention stocks or spell out the distribution function.[5]

The membership committee's tentative definition of those eligible to join was broader than the president's: "Any National or State bank, trust company, private banker, banking firm or corporation in good standing, having a paid-in capital of $50,000 or more, and which makes a practice of buying bonds or investment stocks and publicly offers the same as dealers therein, shall be eligible to membership in this Association." [6]

Some included social responsibilities along with business and economic services as part of the investment bankers' functions. Eugene E. Prussing, a Chicago lawyer, told the IBA's members that the function of the investment banker was "the care of the communities' financial reserve against panics, misfortune, old age and the helplessness of the infirm, young and incompetent. . . . He is the

---

tember 1912), 281–91; "Investment Bankers and Bankers' Association," *The Literary Digest*, XLIV (May 25, 1912), 1126.
  4. IBA, *Proceedings . . . 1912*, 11.
  5. *Ibid.*, 5, 12.
  6. *Ibid.*, 150.

Exhibit 2. Number of offices (including branches) of charter members in the Investment Bankers Association of America, by city, 1912

City	Number	City	Number
New York	108	Indianapolis	2
Chicago	65	Oklahoma City	2
Philadelphia	31	Spokane	2
Boston	23	Atlanta	1
Baltimore	22	Richmond	1
St. Louis	15	Washington, D.C.	1
Cincinnati	14	St. Paul	1
San Francisco	11	Louisville	1
Cleveland	9	Rochester	1
Pittsburgh	8	Columbus	1
Denver	7	Dayton	1
Detroit	5	Bridgeport	1
Toledo	5	Davenport	1
New Orleans	5	Portland, Maine	1
Kansas City	5	Augusta	1
Minneapolis	5	Madison	1
Milwaukee	3	West Chester, Pa.	1
Los Angeles	3	Mason City	1
Seattle	3	Buffalo	1
Providence	3	Toronto	1
Portland, Oregon	3	Halifax, N.S.	1
Totals Cities,	42	Firms, including branches,	373

Source: Investment Bankers Association, *Proceedings . . . 1912* (Chicago, 1912), 239–49.

pioneer of enterprise, the agent of prosperity and the hope and reliance of the wise as well as the dependent." [7]

The speaker looked upon John Murray Forbes as the model for investment bankers. He spoke of that financier as "the great merchant and investment banker of Boston," whose actions in performing his duties in his seventy-year career "brought their reward in the development of a great character, public confidence and esteem seldom, if ever, surpassed in his community, as well as a colossal fortune."

Lack of agreement on an acceptable definition of "investment banker" complicated setting standards for membership. Originally the organizers had planned to restrict membership to actual dealers in bonds. The idea was abandoned quickly when it became apparent that such a policy would limit greatly the growth of the association

7. *Ibid.,* 28–29.

and the funds available to it for carrying on its work. Careful selectivity as to character and size of firm was adopted as the guideline for admission. Such a policy, it was hoped, would satisfy the need to establish and maintain high standards of operation and attract enough members to finance the IBA's many planned activities. "By a conservative extending of its membership," Caldwell explained, the association could acquire added strength from various types of high-grade investment bankers. There was no good reason why this should not be done, especially since it was hoped the organization would become national in character.[8]

Membership in the IBA included commercial banks, savings banks, and trust companies. The association excluded only dealers in commercial paper, brokers, and dealers in mortgages. Only a small percentage of the membership, however, was connected with organized banks; so the IBA was bringing together "for the first time a new class of bankers engaged in creating, buying and selling a specialized form of credit." Since the association's responsibilities were large and bound to increase, and since it already could see more to do than it could wisely undertake, considering its age and means, Caldwell believed that it would be well to move slowly on the question of broadening the membership further. He saw one exception: "we should include Canadian investment bankers as eligible to membership in any association truly American."[9]

The association's finances were modest. Annual dues were $50, and for members joining after January 1, 1913, the membership fee was $100. Receipts for 1912 and 1913 were about $13,000 and $6,000, respectively — used mostly for getting established, current expenses, and meetings. Not until 1914 did the association start spending for external activities, such as lobbying.

Although the IBA looked upon investment banking essentially as a business with "dignity and character," its members recognized that there were weaknesses in operations that should be and could be overcome by the formation of an effective trade association. Members would work together for the best interests of the industry. Among the problems to be faced were occasional uncooperative relations among banking firms, organization of new ones with inadequate capital and experience and lower ethical standards, and increased competition. At the organization meeting the president had stressed the general goals that the founders had in mind. They hoped to make the association "a vital constructive force in the realm

---

8. *Ibid.*, 78. Later the organizers thought that perhaps they had been too hasty in their initial invitations and not sufficiently selective. In 1913 the president said that before the association was formed the founders "did not know enough about the business of those engaged in investment banking, so that our membership at our organization meeting could not be as carefully selected as it should be from now on." See *ibid., 1913,* 18.

9. *Ibid., 1912,* 78.

of conservative investment," which would not "hazard prophecies as to the course of the investment market, nor unduly emphasize any particular securities. Realizing that the number of investors in high-grade bonds and mortgages increase in direct proportions to the dissemination of investment knowledge," he went on, "I believe . . . that through an association of this kind we can expect to receive and extend to one another some support and deal with investment banking and business problems from a scientific standpoint." In more specific vein he proposed that the organization set forth "salient and pertinent facts bearing upon the development of municipalities, the railroads and public utilities of our country, the governmental safeguards surrounding invested capital and other matters of interest for the public good." [10]

The president assured his audience at the first convention that "the ethics of trading among bond and stock houses are highly developed — more so than among any other class of merchants. There is, however, a chance for improvement in this respect and it seems to me that as an association we should try to encourage this. I want to see the day when confidences between our members will not be abused, but increased, and selling agreements more generally respected." Quoting a recent accusation that the banker had "ceased to be reputable," and was "satisfied with the creed 'Caveat Emptor'," he urged "the co-operation of those houses, East and West, North and South, that bring out and make the first distribution of any large issues" to unite to sustain markets as well as to make offerings, so as to earn the public's confidence in the security and in the representations made to them. Although listing upon some exchange tended to inspire confidence, "a bond offered on the Exchange without a buyer or a friend always makes a bad showing — even worse than an unlisted bond, because of the greater publicity given it." One of the problems of the association was to find out how to inspire public confidence and reach broader markets. He hoped that the IBA would "educate the public to know that fair trading, as well as the greatest protection from sharp practice which it can have, will come through its dealing with members of this Association." [11]

The following year the IBA framed a "creed," citing three problems of greatest current concern to investment bankers. These were the need for greater protection of investors, improved methods of distributing securities, and uniform state regulatory laws. In dealing with these questions the association assigned itself a twofold function: to provide information for members and to lobby for change when necessary.[12]

10. *Ibid.,* 12–14, 77.
11. *Ibid.,* 78–79.
12. *Ibid., 1913,* 218.

One of the first tasks the IBA assumed for itself was to bring about uniformity in matters affecting security issues. This involved campaigning for uniform state laws governing the issuance of municipal securities, statutes relating to public utility offerings and state regulatory commissions, tax-exempt municipal bonds, and laws governing other types of government bonds, such as those for drainage and reclamation. Industrial securities presented a special problem because indenture provisions for bonds and the annual reports of issuers varied widely among companies and were not susceptible to generalized and analytical review. The IBA worked hard to bring about uniformity in this area also, and it campaigned just as vigorously to achieve uniform listing requirements.

The IBA declared itself in favor of laws designed to protect investors and require issuers to provide the public with more financial information. What it opposed was the lack of uniformity among these statutes and the haphazard provisions made to enforce them. The association recognized, Caldwell asserted, the "change of public sentiment," and warned that "with a surplus of ideas there will be a surplus of laws, some of which will of necessity require amendment or repeal." He also warned that unless investment bankers, especially those in the larger cities, exercised greater responsibility and self-discipline, they would become so commonly classed as promoters that suspicion and discredit would attach to them and prove harmful to the entire industry.[13]

One of the IBA's principal tasks, Caldwell declared, was to provide information and guidance to bankers, legislators, and the public generally. Education was the key to improving the investment bankers' image and the means to save the industry from unfriendly legislation. If a law similar to the English Companies Act were passed in the United States, as some critics of high finance proposed, corporations might find it more advantageous to sell their securities directly to the public or large institutional buyers. "First class" underwriting houses already faced the problem of finding issues of quality. The supply might be reduced still further if issuers decided to bypass the investment banker.[14]

The IBA's leaders expressed particular concern over the plight of the railroads, in the past the investment bankers' mainstay. Faced with falling freight rates and forced to compete for funds with industrial corporations, public utilities, and foreign borrowers, the carriers had to offer higher interest rates in order to sell their securities, just at a time when they could least afford to do so. To add to their problems, the public had lost confidence in the railroads and their managements. Recognizing this, the IBA saw as one of

13. *Ibid., 1912*, 19–20.
14. *Ibid.*, 20–21.

its immediate tasks the need to come to the railroads' assistance. "Is it not time for us to recognize the value and importance of public sentiment and lend a hand to support markets for our securities at home and abroad, at least when public sentiment runs against us?" Caldwell asked. The current prejudice attached to railroad securities might be directed against other types of issues. The job of a trade association like the IBA was to unite with other similar groups to assist such industries through a campaign of "honest publicity and a broader education." [15]

As part of its education and service functions for members, the association maintained a statistical library and issued a bulletin reporting proposed legislation and recent court decisions. Readers also were informed of money lost by investors in issues floated by nonmembers, and they were urged to correct abuses in their own practices.

The association had the usual roster of officials and a board of governors composed of three groups, each with eight members. Each group (except for the original ones, of course) was elected for a three-year term, one group terminating each year. These groups set general policy and were influential in determining the association's activities. Selected so as to represent both the various types of firms that were members and their wide geographical coverage, they were expected to report regional ideas to the central management and to carry back to their local areas the ideas of the central organization.[16]

Committees were the chief functioning arm of the association. Aside from those entrusted with running it, like the committee on finance, the others generally had twofold functions: (1) to collect and impart information pertinent to their assigned responsibilities and (2) to take action, for example, to lobby, although this term was not used. The constitution provided for seven committees, six of which had to do with running the association: membership, finance, auditing, annual meeting, publicity, and constitution and by-laws; the seventh was the committee on legislation. All additional ones appointed by the president in 1912 or 1913 were concerned with the activities of members: there was a committee on taxation and one on monetary legislation; and five were concerned with problems related to the types of security issues that members distributed, namely, industrial, public utility, municipal, foreign, and railroad.

By the end of 1912 the IBA stood ready to speak for the industry and defend it against attack. The program of the legislative com-

15. *Ibid.*, 21. In spite of the value the IBA attached to presenting a unified front and improving the image of the investment banker, the association was not prepared to allow members to use its name on their letterheads or in advertising, and adopted a bylaw to this effect.
16. The membership in 1912 is given in IBA, *Proceedings . . . 1912*, 7.

mittee epitomized the philosophy of the association. The projects the IBA supported were designed to protect investors from unscrupulous security dealers in the hope, it said, that "by helping others we can help ourselves." [17] The IBA was, *The Magazine of Wall Street* reported, essentially educational and directional.[18] Investors demanded relief and reform; politicians on both the federal and state levels promised them corrective legislation. The task of the IBA was to see that the proposed laws protected investors and prevented the issuance of fraudulent and worthless securities without burdening legitimate dealers or disrupting the industry's established practices. The job of educating the public and guiding legislation proved to be exceptionally difficult, as the leaders of the IBA soon learned.

17. *Ibid.*, 154–56.
18. "The Investment Bankers' Association: What It Proposes to Do," *The Magazine of Wall Street*, XI (January 1913), 184.

9   The Passing of the Old Order

On February 28, 1913, one week before Woodrow Wilson was inaugurated president, the Pujo Committee released its *Report*. Publication of that document climaxed almost a decade of agitation for financial reform, just as the passage of the Kansas blue-sky law two years earlier had marked a new departure in state regulation of the securities business. The years between these two events and American entry into World War I were a time of profound and rapid change, not only for investment bankers but for American society generally. For investment bankers it was the beginning of a new era. Never again would they be so free to conduct their affairs as they had been at the turn of the century, when J. P. Morgan presided over the securities industry. His death in Rome on March 31, 1913, proved to be far more of a dividing line in the history of American high finance than was generally acknowledged at the time.[1]

A few observers noted the significance of the changes that were taking place in American finance. Walter Hines Page, the journalist-publisher whom Wilson appointed ambassador to Great Britain, declared that Morgan's death marked the close of an epoch. "In spite of the constructive work and the masterful leadership of Mr. Morgan and of his great deeds in the era that we are now passing out of," Page wrote, "a revision of the currency and banking laws, if a wise revision be made, will prevent any other such career, even if another such strong personality were to arise. The possession of such great power — or the possibility of its possession — does not fit into the American scheme of life or business."[2] Publication of the Pujo Committee's findings caused many Americans to agree with Page's assessment.

Public reaction to the majority report ranged widely. Some newspapers and journals agreed with Samuel Untermyer and Louis D. Brandeis that "a few men control the business of America." Others like *The New York Times* found much of the majority report unconvincing. The evidence uncovered, this newspaper reported, showed that the existence of a money trust was "shadowy, its powers . . . doubtful, and its ill deeds unproved."[3]

As was to be expected, much of the financial press criticized the committee's findings. *The Commercial & Financial Chronicle* de-

---

1. Henry F. May, *The End of American Innocence: A Study of the First Years of Our Own Time* (New York, 1959), vii–xi.
2. Quoted in Sigmund Diamond, *The Reputation of the American Businessman* (Cambridge, Mass., 1955), 90.
3. *The New York Times,* March 1, 1913. For brief samplings of other opinions see: "The Money-Trust Evidence," *The Literary Digest,* XLVI (January 4, 1913), 1–3; "The 'Money Trust' Recommendations," *The Journal of Political Economy,* XXI (April 1913), 355–57.

scribed the majority report as having "fallen extremely flat." The *American Banker,* which had labeled the probe a "foolish investigation" and had described the hearings as an "absurd performance," attributed banking and financial concentration in New York City to the growth of business and industry rather than the machinations of investment bankers.[4] *The Magazine of Wall Street* took a more moderate position, pointing out that whereas the investigation failed to uncover a money trust, it did suggest the need for investment bankers to review some of their practices and eliminate those that caused the public to lose confidence in the country's financial leaders.

This view was shared by some of the nonfinancial press as well. The editor of *The Nation* found worthy of very serious consideration the committee's proposals prohibiting national banks from underwriting and selling securities and making it illegal for their officers and directors to accept individual participations in transactions in which their institutions had an interest.[5] By the end of the year Untermyer himself favored calling "a general amnesty." "Let us wipe the slate and begin the work of so re-framing and strengthening our laws," he said, "that there can be no repetition of the past without the certainty of prompt detection and punishment."[6]

Most investment bankers said little publicly, though they resented the way the investigation had been conducted.[7] Some of them believed they had been badly abused, and nearly all of them were certain that their activities had been misrepresented. Few were as outspoken as Henry Lee Higginson, the seventy-nine-year-old senior partner of Lee, Higginson & Co. He denounced Pujo as "a contemptible fellow" interested only in making headlines rather than in finding facts.

The recently organized Investment Bankers Association (IBA) protested Brandeis's articles in *Harper's Weekly* interpreting and summarizing the committee's findings. The association especially disliked the Boston lawyer's use of the term investment banker,

---

4. *The Commercial & Financial Chronicle,* XCVI (March 8, 1913), 681; "The Barren Money Trust Inquiry," *American Banker,* LXXVII (June 22, 1912), 2022; "The Pujo Committee Inquiry," *ibid.* (December 21, 1912), 4360–61. See also "The Public and the Banks," *The Bankers' Magazine,* LXXXVI (February 1913), 135–36; "The 'Money Trust,'" *The Nation,* XCV (December 19, 1912), 599; *ibid.,* XCVI (January 16, 1913), 67, criticizing Senator Robert M. La Follette and Congressmen Charles A. Lindbergh of Minnesota and Robert L. Henry of Texas for their "wildly extravagant" conception of Wall Street.

5. *The Magazine of Wall Street,* XI (January 1913), 189; "The Pujo Report," *The Nation,* XCVI (March 6, 1913), 224–25.

6. Quoted in *The Commercial & Financial Chronicle,* XCVII (December 6, 1913), 1636.

7. *The New York Times,* March 2, 1913. See also H. L. Higginson, "The Real 'Money Trust' Consists of the Trust of One's Fellow-Men," *The Bankers' Magazine,* LXXXVI (April 1913), 450.

which its counsel argued led the public to believe all IBA members approved of and were engaged in the practices the committee had condemned.

The IBA's effort to dissociate itself from some of its own charter members, all of whom were outstanding leaders of the investment banking community, proved to be a very poor stratagem. Norman Hapgood, the editor of *Harper's Weekly,* countered it effectively. "Are not J. P. Morgan & Co., Kuhn, Loeb & Co., Lee, Higginson & Co., Kidder, Peabody & Co. . . . among the leading and most honored investment bankers? And, if so," he asked, "is it not fair to judge the propriety of the practices of this profession from the practices of the recognized leaders?" [8]

Three months later, after the committee's report had been published, another IBA spokesman presented a more careful defense of the investment banking business. In a letter to *The Outlook,* Lawrence Chamberlain, the association's general counsel, sought to explain investment banking fees in terms of the risk, time, labor, and costs involved in selling securities. Part of the bankers' charges, Chamberlain asserted, represented the many years of work and expense that went into developing a clientele and cultivating goodwill. These, much more than its capital, were an investment house's greatest assets.[9]

Meeting in special session on April 7, 1913, the Sixty-third Congress failed to enact any of the Pujo Committee's twenty or more recommendations. It also refused to approve a continuation of the inquiry or the publication of an additional 100,000 copies of the *Report.*[10]

Several factors accounted for Congress's reluctance to act. President Wilson kept it preoccupied with more pressing business, and many senators and representatives disapproved of the way the investigation had been conducted.

At the same time Congress did not ignore the Pujo Committee's findings altogether. Far from it. Both the Federal Reserve Act of 1913 and, to an even greater degree, the 1914 Clayton Antitrust

---

8. *The New York Times,* December 22, 1913. See also Alpheus T. Mason, *Brandeis: A Free Man's Life* (New York, 1946), 415–18.

9. Lawrence Chamberlain, "Are Investment Bankers Public Servants?" *The Outlook,* CVI (March 14, 1914), 604–05; the same author's "A Reply to Mr. Brandeis," *Harper's Weekly,* LVIII (April 4, 1914), 22.

10. *The Commercial & Financial Chronicle,* XCVI (June 21, 1913), 1746; "The 'Money Trust' Recommendations," 355. On June 13, 1913, Representative Robert L. Henry of Texas, the leader of the southern agrarian wing of the Democratic party, introduced a bill amending the National Banking Act. Its purpose was to empower Congress to force the Comptroller of the Currency to provide Congress with whatever information it requested concerning the business affairs of national banks. Henry hoped that this measure would assist Congress in continuing its investigation of the money trust. "The Pujo Committee," Henry declared, "barely scratched the surface of facts underlying the concentration of control of money and credit." Quoted in *The Commercial & Financial Chronicle* article cited above.

Act reflected the impact of the money trust investigation. By rejecting a single central bank, which many commercial bankers wanted, in favor of a decentralized system of twelve regional banks, the Federal Reserve Act bowed to the demands of all those who wanted to check the concentration of financial power in the Northeast. Similarly, the provisions creating a Federal Reserve Board, appointed by the president, to regulate and supervise the banking system and money supply revealed the influence of men like Brandeis, William Jennings Bryan, and other progressive Democrats who insisted upon public rather than private control.[11]

The influence of the money trust investigation on the Clayton Act was even more direct. Indeed, it was only because Wilson promised the more radical southern agrarian Democrats, "the inheritors of the Jacksonian-Populist tradition," that he would include a provision prohibiting interlocking bank directorates in the administration's antitrust bill that he was able to win their votes for the Federal Reserve Act.[12] True to Wilson's word, Section VII of the Clayton Act made it illegal for corporations to acquire the stock of other corporations, "where the effect of such acquisition was to substantially lessen competition." Section VIII outlawed interlocking directorates among banks and trust companies with resources in excess of $5 million and interstate corporations with assets of more than $1 million. And Section X forbade "common carriers" from having "any dealings in securities" amounting to more than $50,000 a year with any bank or trust company "with which they had any interlocking officers or directors, except through competitive bidding in accordance with regulations to be prescribed by the ICC."[13]

Two other bills strongly recommended by the Pujo Committee failed to pass Congress. Robert L. Owen, the Oklahoma Democrat and co-sponsor of the Federal Reserve Act, introduced one; it incorporated Untermyer's recommendations concerning federal regulation of the stock exchanges and a full-disclosure provision similar to the one subsequently incorporated in the Securities Act of 1933. The advisability of such a law had been discussed before the turn of the century. Several witnesses before the Industrial Commission had testified to its necessity. The Wilson administration failed to endorse the measure, and it never came to a vote.[14]

The other bill, empowering the Interstate Commerce Commission (ICC) to supervise and regulate the issuance of railroad securi-

---

11. Arthur S. Link, *Wilson: The New Freedom* (Princeton, 1956), ch. vii.
12. Arthur S. Link, *Woodrow Wilson and the Progressive Era, 1910–1917* (New York, 1954), 48–49.
13. Louis Loss, *Securities Regulation* (2d ed., 3 vols., Boston, 1961), I, 388n.60. See also Link, *Wilson: The New Freedom*, 425.
14. Link, *Wilson: The New Freedom*, 426.

ties, was introduced in the House by Sam Rayburn of Texas. Similar proposals had been introduced and rejected before.

In his December 1905 message to Congress, President Theodore Roosevelt had stressed the need for legislation regulating the great interstate corporations, especially the railroads. A provision authorizing the ICC to supervise the issuance of railroad securities was considered during the congressional debate on the Hepburn Act (1906) but was not included in the approved version. The omission was a rebuff for Roosevelt; he had called for federal regulation of corporate securities two months earlier in a speech to the Gridiron Club.[15] The next year, the president again raised the question with the ICC, asking it to provide him with information on the best way of accomplishing this objective. On May 30, 1907, he asked for federal regulation of railroad securities, and repeated the demand, to no effect, in his last message to Congress in December 1908.

President William Howard Taft shared Roosevelt's views on the need for regulation. A provision to this effect was included in the original version of the Mann-Elkins Act, but a combination of stalwart Republicans and conservative Democratic senators succeeded in writing it out of the final bill that became law on June 18, 1910.[16] The Senate then established a Railroad Securities Commission to study the question further, and the next year President Taft appointed another special investigatory commission. Both were headed by Arthur T. Hadley, an economist, long-time student of railroad problems, and then president of Yale University.

Each commission sought the advice of railroad officials, investment bankers, and corporation lawyers. Many witnesses opposed any kind of railroad securities law, but nearly everyone recognized the probability that one would pass. The only question was whether the states or the federal government should be the regulator, and on this witnesses were as divided as the Congress. Jacob H. Schiff, the leading railroad banker in the country, declared himself strongly in favor of federal supervision; Francis Lynde Stetson, J. P. Morgan's personal attorney and an expert on mergers and corporate reorganizations, endorsed state regulation just as emphatically. Untermyer argued for a system of controls modeled after that of Britain, where Parliament supervised railroad incorporations and finance. In the United States the ICC should be vested with this authority, Untermyer believed.[17]

The Hadley Commission's report, issued in 1911, refused to

15. George E. Mowry, *The Era of Theodore Roosevelt, 1900–1912* (New York, 1958), 206.
16. *Ibid.*, 260–61. See also Harold U. Faulkner, *The Decline of Laissez Faire, 1897–1917* (New York, 1951), 207–08.
17. "Government Regulation of Bond and Stock Issue," *Moody's Magazine*, XI (January 1911), 53–54.

recommend federal regulation of railroad securities. It held that such authority raised too many constitutional questions and that full publicity of the road's financial affairs was a more effective guarantee against stock watering and similar abuses than government supervision of their security issues.[18]

This was the background to the Rayburn bill, introduced on June 5, 1914. The measure passed the House only to die in the Senate, a victim of the stock market panic that followed the outbreak of the war in Europe, the objections of railroad leaders and others who feared the delays and red tape necessary to legalize an issue, and the opposition of states' righters and "extreme progressives" who were afraid that ICC approval might be construed as government endorsement and guarantee of an issue.[19] Three weeks after the House voted the bill, even Brandeis, who had assisted Rayburn in drafting it, was reported as being opposed to it for this very reason. The liberal lawyer also thought that the ICC was overburdened and not sufficiently informed to judge the quality of every new railroad issue.[20] Six years later, at the specific request of the railroads, Congress, in the Transportation Act of 1920, authorized the ICC to regulate the issuance of their securities.

Although Congress failed to enact any of the Pujo Committee's recommendations, the investigation caused investment bankers to reconsider some of their policies. Reacting to the change in public attitude toward their close affiliation with so many corporations, several of the major firms announced their voluntary withdrawal from numerous directorships. On January 3, 1914, J. P. Morgan, Jr., who had become head of the firm upon his father's death, announced that he and his partners would resign from the boards of twenty-seven corporations.[21] "An apparent change in public sentiment in regard to directorships seems now to warrant us in seeking to resign from some of these connections," he explained. "Indeed it may be, in view of the change in sentiment upon this subject, that we

18. "Federal Control of Railroad Securities," *American Banker*, LXXVI (December 16, 1911), 4338–39; Faulkner, *Decline of Laissez Faire*, 208.
19. Link, *Wilson: The New Freedom*, 426; *The Commercial & Financial Chronicle*, XCVIII (May 16, 1914), 1484–85.
20. *The Commercial & Financial Chronicle*, XCVIII (June 27, 1914), 1962.
21. *The Commercial & Financial Chronicle* blamed the Pujo Committee and its counsel for the elder Morgan's death in Rome on March 31, 1913, as did a Boston banker, who apparently forgot he had predicted it once before, nineteen years earlier. Neither the *American Banker* nor *The Magazine of Wall Street* accepted the *Chronicle's* explanation; the former found sufficient medical reasons for the great financier's death, and the latter questioned whether an "old war horse" like Morgan was "seriously disturbed" by appearing on the witness stand. See *The Commercial & Financial Chronicle*, XCVI (April 5, 1913), 975; *ibid.*, XCVIII (January 10, 1914), 101; Diamond, *Reputation of the American Businessman*, 85, rency, 63d Cong., 2d Sess., *Regulation of the Stock Exchange: Hearings . . .* 192n.17; *American Banker*, LXXVIII (April 5, 1913), 1078–79; *The Magazine of Wall Street*, XII (May 1913), 22; U.S. Senate, Committee on Banking and Cur- (Washington, 1914), 76–77.

shall be in a better position to serve such properties and their security holders if we are not directors." [22] George F. Baker and other members of the inner group did likewise. Kuhn, Loeb & Co., whose partners had resigned from several of their railroad directorships in 1906 after the New York life insurance investigation,[23] had not suffered any great loss from this action and, Morgan intimated, he did not anticipate any either.

Public reaction to Morgan's announcement was generally favorable. *The Commercial & Financial Chronicle* regretted the decision, believing that it would deprive corporations of able advisers, but most other newspapers and periodicals agreed with *Harper's Weekly* that the firm had shown "good judgment." [24] Attributing the decision to the revelations of the Pujo Committee and the recent New Haven bankruptcy, this journal concluded that Morgan's action was "a striking example of the truth that . . . much good can often be brought out of misfortune." Some newspapers, like *The New York Times,* were more skeptical, pointing out that "the withdrawals were so arranged as to leave the bankers with one member on most of the boards with which they had been affiliated." More optimistically, President Wilson, after being reassured of the sincerity of Morgan's action by his trusted adviser, Colonel Edward M. House, and his secretary, Joseph P. Tumulty, subsequently told the Congress, in his antitrust message of January 20, 1914, that the "antagonism between business and government is over." [25]

Thanks as much to Brandeis's *Other People's Money* as to anything else, the impact of the Pujo Committee's findings long outlived the Wilson administration. The Boston lawyer's criticism of the investment banker as the dominant force and "directing power" in American business and finance became part of the accepted folklore. The idea that a few Atlantic Coast bankers controlled the great railroad, industrial, and public utility corporations, and that the nation's largest banks, trust companies, and life insurance concerns, the "reservoirs of the people's savings," were "tools" of the investment banker hung over all subsequent Wall Street investigations.[26] Many aspects of investment banking behavior that Brandeis and Untermyer had raised were criticized repeatedly during the next thirty years. For example, the practice of a single banking house becoming the "exclusive agent to dispose of a corporation's security

22. Quoted in Ray Stannard Baker, *Woodrow Wilson: Life and Letters* (8 vols., Garden City, 1927–39), IV, 367.
23. *The Commercial & Financial Chronicle,* LXXXII (March 3, 1906), 476.
24. *Ibid.,* XCVIII (January 10, 1914), 101; the editorial, "A Good Example," *Harper's Weekly,* LVIII (January 17, 1914), 3.
25. Baker, *Wilson,* IV, 368–70. See also Mason, *Brandeis,* 401; *The Magazine of Wall Street,* XIII (February 1914), 270–71.
26. Humphrey B. Neill, *The Inside Story of the Stock Exchange* (New York, 1950), 180–81; *U.S. v. Henry S. Morgan et al.,* "Transcript of Trial: Defendants' Opening — Mr. [Ralph M] Carson" (January 16, 1951), 1752–53.

issues" was argued before the Temporary National Economic Committee (TNEC) in 1939 and, together with other widely employed investment banking methods first questioned by the Pujo Committee, was debated once again during the lengthy antitrust case that started in 1947.[27]

The Pujo *Report* appeared just at the time when investment bankers were under widespread criticism from state legislatures across the country. The investment banking community's reaction to these attacks differed considerably from its response to those of Pujo and Untermyer. The IBA said little and did even less to counter Pujo's charges. This job it left entirely to the firms the committee had accused of directing the money trust. But the association took a very active role in trying to stem the flow of new state laws. In 1913 this was no small task; that year, according to the IBA, was one of "epidemic" regulation.

Some investment bankers and financial journals had responded to the Kansas act and similar laws with vehement hostility. "There is little ground for government intervention to save the fool and the knave from the consequences of his own folly and knavery," argued the editors of *The Bankers' Magazine*. With so many sound and safe securities available, anyone who invested in projects that promised more than a fair return deserved to lose his funds, they insisted.[28]

Most investment bankers took a more moderate position than *The Bankers' Magazine*. They sympathized fully with laws designed to eliminate fraud and "nonmeritorious securities," as the first president of the IBA reported in 1912. The association disliked being "compelled to take the lead in attacking the chief laws that had been enacted with this ostensible object" in mind.[29] "As an association," President Caldwell declared, "we have in no wise disapproved of any law wisely drawn to suppress the sale of 'wild cat' securities and losses yearly borne by honest but ignorant investors. We have been on the defensive only when these laws or proposed laws unnecessarily and unjustly hamper legitimate business." [30]

What investment bankers resented was the implication that the entire industry was guilty of the serious abuses attributed to the knavery of a few. Statutes like the Kansas act, they argued, were not the answer to this problem; they were unnecessarily restrictive, burdensome, and discriminatory, and a serious threat to the free

27. *U.S. v. Henry S. Morgan et al.*, "Transcript of Trial: Defendants' Opening — Mr. [William Dwight] Whitney" (February 1, 1951), 2618–20; (February 2, 1951), 2663–87.
28. "The 'Blue-Sky' Laws," *The Bankers' Magazine*, LXXXIV (May 1912), 635–37.
29. Quoted in *The Magazine of Wall Street*, XIV (June 1914), 115. See also *The Commercial & Financial Chronicle*, XCV (November 23, 1912), 1367–68; *ibid.*, XCVIII (April 25, 1914), 1288–89.
30. Quoted in *The Commercial & Financial Chronicle*, XCVI (May 24, 1913), 1461. The complete text is in *I.B.A. of A. Bulletin*, II (April 10, 1914), 4–5.

flow of capital across state lines. The investment banking community also argued that no commission or other public agency possessed the necessary qualifications to judge the merits of an issue and that speculative securities fulfilled a legitimate, useful purpose in attracting capital to new industries. Spokesmen were convinced, furthermore, that commission supervision of new issues would not deter fraudulent promoters and that the licensing of securities dealers would not exclude swindlers and other undesirable persons from entering the stock and bond business. In fact, regulations of this kind might very well promote rather than prevent fraud, since the unscrupulous dealer would not be deterred from violating them. At the same time the public would interpret his possession of a license as a sign of his having received official approval to engage in the securities business.[31]

These and other objections led a number of investment houses, encouraged and assisted by the IBA, to challenge the constitutionality of several blue-sky laws.[32] The association's general counsel cooperated with local attorneys in preparing briefs and assisted them in pleading their cases before the courts. The fight was carried on for almost four years in both state and federal courts.

At the same time the IBA was leading the court attack, it also was preparing for more constructive action. Its legislative committee was drafting a model blue-sky law that the association hoped would be adopted instead of the "crude, paternalistic measures" then being enacted or considered by so many states.[33]

Caldwell outlined what the ideal law should avoid and what it should aim to do. It should not "infringe" on the rights of buyers and sellers to determine for themselves whether a security was sound and promised a fair return. It should not exercise a paternalistic judgment "through one man as to what the people of that State shall trade in and with whom they shall trade." The duty of the state, Caldwell asserted, was to expose the peddler of fraudulent securities, license legitimate dealers, and establish laws guaranteeing "publicity and truthfulness." [34]

For years Brandeis had been advocating full-disclosure laws as

---

31. William C. Breed, "Public Regulation in Origination and Distribution of Securities," *Investment Banking*, III (February 21, 1933), 189–91. See also *The Magazine of Wall Street*, XIV (June 1914), 115. When, early in 1913, a bill was introduced in the New York legislature proposing to establish the office of Examiner of Securities with authority to determine who should be allowed to sell stocks and bonds in the state, and making it legal for investors "to scrutinize" the affairs of dealers, the financial press denounced the measure as one of the most objectionable laws ever proposed. See *The Magazine of Wall Street*, XII (May 1913), 12; the editorial, "Blue Sky Laws in New York," *American Banker*, LXXVIII (March 29, 1913), 1000.

32. *The New York Times*, October 5, 1913.

33. "Blue Sky Laws," *American Banker*, LXXVIII (April 12, 1913), 1158–59.

34. *The Commercial & Financial Chronicle*, XCVI (January 25, 1913), 246–49.

the best guarantee against fraud. Without apparent discomfort, Caldwell agreed fully with the statement of the famous Boston attorney, now a close adviser to President Wilson, that the state "should not seek to prevent investors from making bad bargains." [35]

The IBA's model blue-sky law was designed to prevent fraud and misrepresentation without interfering with the investment bankers' business or requiring them to modify the practices they had developed for distributing securities. Investment banking had become an interstate business. Large bond issues originating in New York City, Boston, Philadelphia, and Chicago were underwritten, sold, and traded not only by investment and brokerage firms in those cities but by many others across the country. In states with restrictive blue-sky laws of the Kansas type all nonexempt issues had to be approved by a public official. Sometimes temporary approvals expedited the procedure, but differing state requirements imposed a heavy burden on the banker distributing a large issue through dealers in a dozen or more states.

In order to facilitate and expedite the "blue-skying" of securities, Warren S. Hayden, a partner in the Cleveland firm of Hayden, Miller & Co., suggested that investment bankers counter political attacks with a bill of their own. At the IBA's first convention, in 1912, he proposed that the association's legislative committee study the subject of state regulation carefully, draft a workable and effective statute, and present it to the membership. When a state was considering adopting a blue-sky law the members who lived there would then be ready to recommend passage of the IBA's model act. "It is always an awkward thing to be on the defensive, trying to tear down what someone had painfully built up, particularly if those building it up are working with good intentions, even though their information is rather scant," Hayden concluded. "We ought . . . to formulate our own ideas so that we can offer an affirmative program to those who are seeking to accomplish what, really, is an entirely praiseworthy object." [36]

The IBA endorsed Hayden's suggestion enthusiastically. By unanimous vote, members adopted a resolution authorizing the committee to draft a model law. Earlier that year Hayden and some of his associates had worked on a law to submit to the Ohio legislature, which was then planning to enact one. Several of its features subsequently were incorporated in the IBA's model statute.

Based on Hayden's recommendations, the association proposed a measure containing three general types of provisions: licenses,

---

35. Louis D. Brandeis, *Other People's Money and How the Bankers Use It* (New York, 1914), 103.
36. Investment Bankers Association, *Proceedings . . . 1912* (Chicago, 1912), 147–48. See also "Regulating the Sale of Securities," *The Magazine of Wall Street*, XI (March 1913), 326.

publicity, and penalties. The IBA's bill authorized state banking authorities to license everyone offering securities within state borders. Licenses were to be granted on the basis of the applicant's character, reputation, and standing, and they were to be revoked if the holders engaged in any improper practices. The proposed law required that the state furnish investors with the means of obtaining information on all new offerings, but in order to avoid burdensome filing requirements, it exempted most transactions from this provision. Hayden estimated that only about 10 percent of the issues offered by the IBA's members would be affected by this feature of the measure which, though clearly intended to bear down heavily on "get-rich-quick" schemes, also sought to interfere as little as possible with the freedom of the investment banker.[37] Finally, the model bill imposed heavy penalties on fraud and misrepresentation. Effective enforcement of this provision, more than anything else, the IBA argued, would give the investor all the protection he required.

Blue-sky laws, the association's general counsel explained, should "be confined to those against whom they were first intended to be directed." The "first step toward the right path in dealing with this subject," he told the National Association of State Bank Supervisors (NASBS) in 1914, many of whose members were charged with enforcing blue-sky laws, "[is that] . . . you put out of consideration the idea of asserting an executive control over the business of the dealer in investment securities." [38]

The IBA's stand, as expressed by its counsel and revealed in its model law, was strongly criticized by Donald R. Richberg, a young progressive Chicago lawyer, who later served President Franklin D. Roosevelt as general counsel for the National Recovery Administration. Richberg condemned the IBA's statute, saying it afforded the investor little, if any, protection. "The state authority invested with the alleged power of protection was made nearly powerless, and . . . the only result of such a law would be to deceive investors into the notion that the state supervision guaranteed honest securities when . . . there was no supervision and no guarantee." Richberg was surprised that the sponsors of this law, "the gentlemen who are supposedly most interested in cultivating the market for honest securities by restoring the public's confidence," should propose such an ineffective measure. "This appears to be," he concluded, "another case where actions merit greater attention than words." [39]

37. IBA, *Proceedings . . . 1912*, 145–47.
38. [Robert R. Reed] "Regulation of the Business of the Investment Banker," *I.B.A. of A. Bulletin*, II (July 15, 1914), 9–17. See also *The Commercial & Financial Chronicle*, XCIX (September 19, 1914), 790–92.
39. [Donald R. Richberg] "Mr. Brandeis and Investment Banking," *Harper's Weekly*, LVIII (January 17, 1914), 25.

Richberg's doubts were shared by a good many others, including many state legislators. Of the twenty states that enacted blue-sky laws in 1913, only Maine adopted one embodying the type of fraud and dealer-licensing provisions recommended by Hayden and the IBA.

Most other blue-sky laws enacted that year, even those that included similar provisions, did so in conjunction with other, more stringent, requirements. Georgia's securities law, which became effective January 1, 1914, provided a case in point. It required every dealer to file a detailed statement with the Secretary of State, giving his name and place of business and the names, residences, and business addresses of all persons interested in his securities as principals, officers, directors, or trustees, and of any agent resident in Georgia. Nonresident dealers had to file a power of attorney, designating some state resident to receive service of process in all proceedings instituted against them in any Georgia court. The law also required that the securities themselves be registered.[40]

In 1914 the NASBS appointed a special committee to work with the investment bankers to prepare a uniform statute, one that both groups could recommend enthusiastically to legislators. The move was motivated by the IBA's appeal for cooperation and the general dissatisfaction of the state bank supervisors with existing blue-sky laws. The next year, the two organizations presented a "Proposed Blue Sky Act" that was almost identical to the one Hayden had endorsed in 1912. This draft contained stiff antifraud provisions, very much like those in the postal laws, and required all securities dealers to register annually with an appropriate state official. It included a notification provision requiring bankers, brokers, and other individuals planning to offer securities in a state to notify the proper authorities in advance and to file with them copies of all circulars and prospectuses used in promoting sales. If, upon investigating the issue, the state official charged with enforcing the law deemed it advisable, he could require the filing of more information. No notification had to be given if the securities were traded on one of the state's recognized stock exchanges or if they had been advertised in out-of-state magazines or newspapers.[41]

The IBA considered the fraud and notification provisions to be the proposed law's most important features, as effective in protecting the investor as those contained in the original Kansas act. Publicity and disclosure rather than cumbersome regulation were all that was needed to drive the "blue sky merchants" out of business. Much the same view was expressed a few years later by a partner in Kuhn, Loeb & Co. Speaking before the Association of Stock Exchange

40. *The Commercial & Financial Chronicle,* XCVII (November 8, 1913), 1324–25.
41. IBA, *Proceedings . . . 1915,* 192–94.

Brokers, Otto Kahn called for legislation prohibiting "any public dealing in any industrial security . . . unless its introduction is accompanied by a prospectus setting forth every material detail about the company concerned and the security offered, such prospectus to be signed by persons who are to be held responsible at law for any willful omission or misstatement therein." He specifically excluded railroad and public utility issues from this requirement, since most of these already were regulated by state commissions, a fact which, in his opinion, afforded the public "ample protection." [42]

Few others outside the investment banking business shared the IBA's faith in the efficacy of the type of disclosure-and-fraud law it had drafted. A great many people, including the editors of *The Bankers' Magazine,* questioned whether the states were able to supervise effectively a business that involved so many interstate transactions. "In our judgment," this financial monthly observed, "the sale of securities should, if practicable, be brought under Federal regulation rather than be committed to the numerous States with their varying standards of legislation and administration." [43]

While the advisability of a federal securities law was being debated in and out of Congress, the IBA was fighting the spread of state regulation in the courts. The association's fire was directed specifically against statutes of the Kansas type. The requirements of this law were "so drastic," the IBA's legislative committee declared, that the most reputable bankers were "virtually prevented from doing business" in that state.[44]

Between 1914 and 1916, while some state courts were upholding blue-sky laws, four federal tribunals were declaring them void. Early in 1914 a Michigan federal court invalidated that state's blue-sky law on the grounds that it interfered with the freedom of individuals, exceeded the police power of the states, and burdened interstate commerce.[45] Later that year a West Virginia federal court voided that state's blue-sky law as "unlawfully discriminatory," citing it as a violation of the due process, privileges and immunities, and equal protection of the law clauses of the federal Constitution. The court

42. Otto H. Kahn, *Our Economic and Other Problems: A Financier's Point of View* (New York, 1920), 152.
43. "Regulation of the Sale of Securities," *The Bankers' Magazine,* LXXXVI (April 1913), 418–19. See also "Why Not a Federal Law?" *The Magazine of Wall Street,* XII (May 1913), 12–13.
44. IBA, *Proceedings . . . 1912,* 156.
45. *The Commercial & Financial Chronicle,* XCVIII (February 7, 1914), 414–15; *The New York Times,* January 30, 1914. "The issuing of commercial paper, stocks or bonds by a private company to get money for its own business, no one can suppose is a public or quasi-public enterprise; the business of buying and selling stocks and bonds and other securities is no more 'affected by a public interest,'" the court ruled, "than is the business of buying and selling groceries." Quoted in a speech by the IBA's general counsel, in *I.B.A. of A. Bulletin,* II (July 15, 1914), 10.

also condemned the law as a burden on interstate commerce.[46] Subsequently the Iowa and Ohio laws were invalidated on similar grounds. In all four cases the courts held that these laws were excessively paternalistic; went far beyond their stated purpose, to prevent fraud; and as a result were an invalid exercise of the state's police powers.

The next year the Michigan legislature, assisted by a special committee appointed by the National Association of Attorneys-General, enacted a revised statute. It was designed to overcome the objections that the court had raised to its original law and required only a minimum of inspection and supervision of securities and dealers. The IBA had volunteered to cooperate in drafting the bill, but its offer was declined.

Shortly afterward the new law was tested in a federal court in Michigan and declared unconstitutional. The judges ruled that "like the old one [it] impresses upon interstate commerce a burden which is direct and which is beyond the limits of the [state's] police power." The case, together with two others, involving the South Dakota and Ohio laws, was appealed to the Supreme Court, where all three were decided together.[47]

At the time these three cases were being argued before the Supreme Court, twenty-seven states had enacted general securities laws. All these statutes, except Rhode Island's, contained some type of licensing provision. Moreover, similar statutes were being considered by several other states, and their legislatures, like everyone in the securities business, anxiously awaited the Supreme Court's decision.

The justices rendered it on January 22, 1917. They ruled that the police power enabled the states to enact comprehensive licensing laws in order to protect their citizens. "In the exercise of its power to prevent fraud and imposition," the Court declared, "a State may regulate trading in securities within its borders, require a license of those engaging in such dealing, make issuance of a license dependent on a public officer's being satisfied of the good repute of the applicants, and permit him, subject to judicial review of his findings, to revoke the same." [48]

The "Blue Sky Cases" opened the way for other states to enact similar comprehensive licensing laws. Objections to them persisted, and the constitutionality of specific clauses and sections continued

---

46. *The Commercial & Financial Chronicle,* XCIX (December 19, 1914), 1789–91.

47. *Hall v. Geiger-Jones Co.,* 242 U.S. 539 (1917); *Caldwell v. Sioux Falls Stock Yards Co.,* 242 U.S. 559 (1917); *Merrick v. N. W. Halsey & Co.,* 242 U.S. 568 (1917). See Louis Loss and Edward M. Cowett, *Blue Sky Law* (Boston, 1958), 10–17.

48. Quoted in Edward S. Corwin, ed., *The Constitution of the United States of America: Analysis and Interpretation, Annotation of Cases Decided by the Supreme Court of the United States to June 30, 1952* (Washington, 1953), 1019.

to be tested in the courts, but no further widespread attack occurred. Between 1917 and 1920 eight states passed such laws, and by 1933 every state except Nevada had adopted a blue-sky law.[49]

The IBA's efforts to secure passage of uniform state laws proved a disappointment. The states saw little merit in the association's model law and ignored most of its recommendations. The blue-sky laws enacted between 1911 and 1920 differed widely in scope, types of securities exempted, amount of information that had to be filed, and methods of enforcement, but all of them had at least one objective in common: protection of the investor against fraud. Many states, following the example set by Kansas, also assumed the responsibility of passing upon the quality and soundness of the securities offered within their borders. The British had rejected this principle in the 1890's, when Parliament was considering a new companies act, and the federal government refused to accept it in 1933, as the Securities Act demonstrated.[50]

Though no two laws were alike, all contained certain common features. They can be classified into three broad groups: (1) antifraud acts; (2) statutes requiring the registration or licensing of securities, sometimes called "specific-approval" laws; and (3) acts calling for the licensing or registration of individuals engaged in the securities business, commonly known as "dealer-licensing" laws.[51] All three types were intended to protect the investor.

What distinguished them was the method employed to achieve this common objective. Antifraud laws authorized the state to investigate suspicious transactions and warn the public against them; the state could issue injunctions or other orders to prevent threatened frauds, prosecute swindlers, and, if enforcement officials were convicted, impose criminal penalties. Specific-approval and dealer-licensing laws, the two types of blue-sky laws most commonly employed, sought to prevent fraud before its occurrence. The former type allowed the state to impose qualitative standards on the securities that could be sold within its borders, and the latter was designed to prohibit dishonest, negligent, and unqualified brokers and dealers from doing business in the state. The first dealer-licensing statute was adopted by Maine in 1913. From there it spread to other states, where it usually was included to strengthen existing statutes.[52]

49. Loss, *Securities Regulation,* I, 28–29; Breed, "Public Regulation," 186. Nevada, the second state to enact a securities law, passed one in 1909 and repealed it in 1915.
50. Loss, *Securities Regulation,* I, 57.
51. *Ibid.,* I, 33. See also Forrest Bee Ashby, *The Economic Effect of Blue Sky Laws* (Philadelphia, 1926). Ashby classified blue-sky laws into two groups: (1) fraud acts and (2) regulatory acts, the latter composed of two subcategories, "dealer-licensing" and "specific-approval" laws.
52. Loss, *Securities Regulation,* I, 34; Ashby, *Economic Effect of Blue Sky Laws,* 7; Jacob Murray Edelman, *Securities Regulation in the 48 States* (Chicago, 1942), 5.

The effectiveness of the blue-sky laws varied widely, but generally the most restrictive and vigorously enforced were those enacted in the Middle West. There Populist doctrines still were strong and the success of the Kansas act was widely publicized. J. N. Dolley, the state's bank commissioner, advertised the "wonderful results" that his office had accomplished. Eighteen months after the law had been passed, he issued a report stating that it had saved the citizens of Kansas "at least six million dollars." Out of some fourteen or fifteen hundred companies investigated by this office, "less than one hundred have been granted permits to sell their securities in Kansas."[53] Though his claims proved to be overly optimistic, as a subsequent examination of his department's records revealed, Dolley's assertion that the Kansas blue-sky law was "rapidly gaining fame all over the world" was not far from the truth. Few laws were so well advertised. It was largely because of his efforts that so many states adopted the highly regulatory approach that came to be typical of most specific-approval laws.[54]

The blue-sky movement brought the investment banking business under the supervision of a multiplicity of dissimilar state laws. The regulations of one state very often conflicted with those of another; inconsistencies among them were common and revisions frequent. Investment houses preparing an offering for national distribution had to make certain that the issue satisfied the legal requirements of every state in which the securities were to be sold. This lack of uniformity in laws, though failing to curb the unscrupulous peddler of fraudulent securities, imposed unaccustomed hardships on legitimate houses.[55]

Investment bankers, however, quickly devised ways of conforming to the new state laws. The existence of the IBA made the task easier. To keep members informed of changes, the association distributed a comprehensive survey of all blue-sky laws in effect and provided other pertinent instructional materials. As more and more states adopted such statutes, investment houses soon decided to assign the job of "blue-skying" an issue to law firms that specialized in this work.[56]

Faced with public pressure for even more effective protection and the opposition of its members to increased regulation, the IBA tried to satisfy both by urging the adoption of stringent, uniform antifraud laws.[57] When in 1917 the Supreme Court upheld the

53. Quoted in Loss and Cowett, *Blue Sky Law*, 9.
54. Loss and Cowett, *Blue Sky Law*, 9.
55. Arthur G. Davis, "A Multiplicity of Laws," *Investment Banking*, I (September 1931), 30–31, 41. See also Henry R. Hayes, "Public Aspects of the Securities Business," *ibid.*, I (October 1931), 27–29, 41–42.
56. *The Commercial & Financial Chronicle*, XCVI (May 10, 1913), 1340–41; Loss, *Securities Regulation*, I, 33.
57. IBA, *Proceedings . . . 1913*, 53–56.

constitutionality of blue-sky laws, no general agreement had been reached on either the type of legislation that was required or whether its enforcement should be entrusted to the states or the federal government.

The blue-sky movement concerned itself chiefly with protecting investors from unscrupulous security dealers. The Pujo Committee, on the other hand, directed its attention largely to documenting the existence of an allegedly all-powerful money trust. Together they focused the nation's attention on the investment banker as the central figure in the economy and the chief agent in financing the huge transportation and industrial developments of the later nineteenth and early twentieth centuries. This, together with the secrecy with which investment houses conducted their affairs, the disclosure of financial favoritism, and the lack of responsibility of some firms toward investors, and several brief but sharp stock market crises, resulted in the first major effort on the part of the state and federal governments to regulate and supervise the securities business.

The laws that were passed in the half decade or so preceding America's entry into World War I accomplished few of the objectives for which they were intended. Financial concentration was not markedly reduced. Nor were the ties between big business and Wall Street significantly loosened. And the protection afforded investors was not greatly improved by the multiplicity of state laws that were enacted between 1911 and 1917.

The real significance of these statutes was that they changed the political and legal environment in which investment bankers had to operate. The blue-sky laws and the New Freedom legislation of the Wilson administration forced investment bankers to adjust to new pressures and conditions. The IBA's preoccupation with state and federal regulation reflected the industry's new concern with government and the need to improve its image. Neither one of these problems had worried investment bankers in 1900. By 1910 they had become sufficiently important to cause investment bankers to organize their own trade association and entrust it with the dual responsibility of "combatting iniquitous or unreasonable measures" and moderating the public's demand for reform.

Public criticism of financial concentration and the demand for more effective regulation obscured other important changes occurring within the investment banking industry itself. These developments, as much as the Pujo revelations and the blue-sky movement, also indicated the passing of an era.

During the second decade of the twentieth century the public image and leadership of the investment banking community changed significantly. In 1913, when the Pujo Committee published its findings, the investment banker as the "symbol of economic power" stood near the zenith of his prestige and influence. Never again, not even during the great stock market boom of the late 1920's, did he enjoy the prestige or exercise the authority he had in the first decade of the twentieth century, when J. P. Morgan, George F. Baker, Jacob Schiff, James Stillman, and a few others presided over American finance. By the time Wilson left the White House all these titans, and lesser ones like Frank Vanderlip of the National City Bank of New York, Henry Lee Higginson, and his partner Gardiner M. Lane, were either dead or retired. Except for Robert Winsor of Kidder, Peabody & Co., who continued to dominate this firm until his death in 1930, the leadership of the securities business passed to a new generation, none of whom came to occupy the outstanding position previously held by Morgan or Schiff.

Many of the problems investment bankers were to face in the 1920's first appeared in the years just before America's entry into World War I. The rise of new firms, the growth of Chicago and other investment banking centers, the changing needs and preferences of capital users and investors upset accustomed investment banking practices and relationships.

The controversy over syndicate practices that occurred during the immediate prewar years was symptomatic of new developments within the industry. It grew out of the fact that more and more firms in different parts of the country were being included in New York syndicates. Many of these houses were unaccustomed to the way Wall Street and other leading Atlantic Coast bankers managed these operations. The problem of settling joint syndicate accounts was raised at the IBA's annual meeting in 1915. The topic proved to be of great interest to middle western members. At their request the association ordered a special pamphlet prepared on the subject, saying it was intended to assist those houses that "undertake the larger ratio of their joint adventures by telegraph or telephone with firms in distant cities." [58]

The major points at issue were that the several parties to joint accounts often did not make clear to one another the terms of joint syndicate agreements. This often resulted in disputes at the time of settlement. But there was also real disagreement over the nature of the terms themselves. Controversies arose when syndicates were dissolved with unsold bonds on their hands and when not all members had disposed of equal proportions of their participations.[59]

To deal with the first point, the pamphlet defined terms and offered a model agreement, but did not suggest that the form necessarily reflected the official view of the association. Problems in the second area of controversy arose when accounts were "divided as to liability and undivided as to selling." In a simple divided account each participant took his own bonds and sold them and took his

58. *Ibid., 1915*, 58.
59. *Ibid.*, 134–41.

own profit. But when there was an undivided feature, profits or losses were not distributed until the syndicate dissolved.

Two practices had developed in the industry. They were known as the New York and the Chicago plans, the latter being an innovation arising from dissatisfaction with the more common New York plan. Under the New York system, at the expiration of a syndicate, any bonds remaining were redistributed to syndicate members on the same pro rata basis as their original participation contract. Members who had distributed their share of bonds had to take an additional amount. They received the selling commission on these, it was true, but having to sell more than their original commitment was a hardship if the issue was not going well.

The Chicago plan, in contrast, permitted the members to complete their obligation when they had sold their allotted shares; members who had not sold their shares took up the unsold portion at the minimum selling price. Total syndicate profits or losses then were distributed pro rata to the members.

The convention reached no consensus on the matter. One Chicago commentator pointed out that some of the reasons for the adoption of the New York plan no longer applied and that it had become "repugnant" to bond dealers, a title which many members still preferred over investment banker. The plan had been used at first in distributions from an original buyer to a larger group, many of whom did not intend to sell. They were included for their carrying capacity. The selling then was done by a comparatively smaller number of houses that were paid for distributing the securities.

The controversy over syndicate practices, one of the most important issues of the time, remained unresolved. Nor was any satisfactory solution reached concerning the industry's other problems. The need for standardizing practices and improving business conduct was debated by the IBA, but no significant action was taken. The association devoted itself largely to fighting the spread of regulation and increases in federal income and excess profits taxes.[60] Adjustment to the changes and innovations of these years was delayed and complicated by the outbreak of war in August 1914. For the next few years the attention of investment bankers was dominated by the pressures, challenges, and opportunities of global war.

60. *The New York Times,* February 13, 1914, December 29, 1929.

10 Investment Banking and Wilsonian Neutrality, 1914–1917

Between August 1914 and April 1917 American investment bankers faced more radically different problems than at any time since the Civil War. The outbreak of hostilities in Europe precipitated an immediate crisis in the world's financial centers; the continuation of the conflict presented investment houses with heightened demands for their services and unusual opportunities for profit. "Make Hay While the Sun Shines," a writer for *The Magazine of Wall Street* advised bankers and businessmen at the time of the *Lusitania* sinking, in May 1915. Not to do so, he warned, "would be a mistake so great as to amount to an irreparable blunder," especially since the war might very well be followed by a depression.[1]

In meeting the challenges and opportunities of war, investment bankers employed old techniques and devised new ones. In some instances they took the initiative and in others responded to Washington's requests. Many of the services investment houses were required to provide were new to them. These new services, together with uncertainty about the duration of the war, brought forth increased cooperation among individual firms and between the firms and the government.

The first of the many new, pressing problems investment bankers had to confront involved the New York Stock Exchange. "In every financial crisis, great or small, it is the stock exchanges which first have to face the shock," observed Alexander D. Noyes, the noted New York City financial reporter. "They met it this time [1914] by closing their doors in every market of the world."[2] Jittery since the assassination of Austrian Archduke Franz Ferdinand on June 28, managers of stock exchanges everywhere, including London, stopped operations when Russia announced general mobilization on July 30. These actions left the New York Stock Exchange the last major market to continue unrestricted business and, *The Commercial & Financial Chronicle* recorded, it was suffering "huge unloadings of American securities from all sections of the world."

The issues sold during the preceding week had included many top-quality American stocks and bonds. To experienced observers, reported the *Chronicle,* such selling indicated that "the liquidation was much more important than mere selling of floating supplies," and that it was not "essentially speculative" in origin. "It repre-

---

1. Paul Clay, "American Business and The Great War," *The Magazine of Wall Street,* XVI (May 1, 1915), 6–9.
2. Alexander D. Noyes, *The War Period of American Finance, 1908–1925* (New York, 1926), 56.

sented, rather, the outpouring of securities that had been locked up as permanent investments." [3]

J. P. Morgan, Jr., promptly called two conferences of bankers and stock exchange officials to review the situation and decide whether to keep New York's exchange open. At the meeting on Thursday, July 30, the group decided not to close. But during the night of July 30 a deluge of selling orders reached New York by cable. Their execution the next day, the *Chronicle* observed, might easily have resulted in "widespread disaster in financial circles as a whole." Meanwhile, another distressing fact was uncovered. The conference that Morgan called on the morning of July 31 learned that $30 million of credit would be needed that day by member houses of the New York Stock Exchange to avoid "embarrassments," and the reserves of New York banks, drained by gold exports earlier that year, were near depletion. Knowledge of these facts finally convinced the group that the exchange should not open for business. They reached the decision just before the scheduled time for opening.[4]

The essential role of America's stock exchanges in facilitating the functioning of the economy became increasingly evident as the duration of their closing lengthened. *The Commercial & Financial Chronicle* editorialized: "No one not familiar with the situation can understand to what extent the business of the country is hampered and restricted by the lack of an open market or a market of any kind for securities." [5] Not only was it a place to exchange securities, it also set values — a matter of special interest to institutional holders of securities as collateral. The closing, furthermore, stopped the flotation of new issues.

The *Chronicle* compared the current crisis to those of 1895 and 1907. On those occasions J. P. Morgan, Sr., had stepped in to save the financial markets. This time, however, the situation was different, for dumping of still more American securities was threatened. The periodical suggested, with its usual confidence in the unlimited capacity of J. P. Morgan & Co., that this great firm should head a syndicate to buy up the overhanging securities and thus free the market for regular business.[6] The suggestion was not followed, and with the market already stagnant, the exchange remained closed, and investment and commercial bankers drafted emergency procedures until normal activities could be resumed.

Executives of the exchange promptly set about establishing facilities for handling essential transactions in securities, preventing a

3. *The Commercial & Financial Chronicle,* XCIX (August 1, 1914), 297.
4. *Ibid.,* 297, 314; U.S. Treasury, *Annual Report . . . 1914* (Washington, 1915), 481.
5. *The Commercial & Financial Chronicle,* XCIX (September 5, 1914), 667.
6. *Ibid.,* 629–30.

collapse in prices, and deciding where and under what conditions they should authorize reopening. The New York Stock Exchange assigned these responsibilities to an appointed Committee of Five. H. G. S. Noble, president of the exchange and a partner in the brokerage house of De Coppett & Doremus, was made chairman.[7]

One of the committee's routine activities was to approve and arrange cash purchases for members at prices no lower, or only slightly lower, than those of July 30. It also arranged for completing contracts undertaken by members before the exchange closed, for disposing of securities sold earlier in Europe but returned to this country after the exchange had closed, and for handling hardship cases.

When the committee decided that it was feasible, it allowed gradual reopening. Bond trading on a restricted basis began late in November, and stock trading in mid-December.[8] This committee thereupon disbanded, although two others had charge during the continuing period of restrictions that lasted until April 1, 1915.

The New York Curb Exchange and the New York Consolidated Exchange also closed, but the restrictions imposed by these two groups were not universally observed. A "gutter" market operated, with price quotations at first passed by word of mouth and later in daily printed circulars. Although sales were not in significantly large amounts, the feared price declines did occur: United States Steel, for example, fell from $51\frac{7}{8}$, just before the New York Stock Exchange closed, to a low of $38\frac{1}{2}$ bid, on October 23.[9]

Investment and commercial bankers also set up a committee to decide on appropriate activities for themselves and to confer with the Committee of Five. The bankers' Committee of Seven was composed entirely of representatives of firms that belonged to the Investment Bankers Association (IBA). After insisting on an initial ban on trading in securities, the group soon approved a gradual resumption on a limited scale. No impression was to be given that there was an active trading market, however, and salesmen were not to return to their usual activities. Dealings were chiefly in unlisted securities.[10]

When new issues began to be floated, the currently popular securities were short-term notes. In October 1914 Morgan offered $20 million of one-year notes and the same amount of six-month notes for the New York Central Railroad; and in November, a syndicate

---

7. *Ibid.*, XCIX (August 8, 1914), 386. The other members represented both brokerage and investment firms. They included Donald G. Geddes (Clark, Dodge), Ernest Groesbeck (Groesbeck & Co.), Henry K. Pomroy (Pomroy Bros.), and Samuel F. Streit (H. T. Carey & Co.).

8. *The Commercial & Financial Chronicle*, XCIX (December 5, 1914), 1620.

9. *Ibid.*, XCIX (December 26, 1914), 1864; *ibid.*, C (January 16, 1915), 194.

10. The firms represented on the Committee of Seven included Harris, Forbes & Co., Guaranty Trust Co., White, Weld & Co., Brown Bros., Kissel, Kinnicutt & Co., William A. Read, and Remick, Hodges & Co.

that had underwritten an earlier $40 million issue of bonds was dissolved with $8 million still on its hands.[11]

Since marketing new offerings as well as trading in existing issues were at a near standstill, many firms cut their staffs. Christmas in Wall Street reflected these effects on different types of financial firms: brokers had been most severely hit; next were bond houses; and banks felt the impact least of all. Several firms had failed. All had suffered from general business depression, the war, and "political legislation." Although by the year's end conditions had improved enough for some houses to pay bonuses, unemployment was so extensive that investment bankers and brokers organized a Wall Street Employees' Relief Committee to try to find positions for former employees.[12]

Throughout the country stock exchanges followed the example of New York, but the duration of their closing varied. They too appointed similar special committees to act during the shutdown. And auctioneers, still providing some investment banking services, followed the example of the organized exchanges.

In Chicago a serious controversy over early resumption in trading arose between investment bankers and commercial banks, which also were important bond dealers. The commercial bankers opposed it, fearing that price declines would jeopardize loans secured by stocks or bonds; yet they themselves were selling securities. Ultimately they compromised along lines established in New York. Houses could sell, at any price, unlisted securities held in their inventories, as well as other unlisted securities subject to the approval of special committees. Maintenance of July 30 prices was the aim, but it was not always achieved.[13]

In spite of the New York Stock Exchange's closing, investment bankers gradually resumed a few of their usual activities in the fall. In mid-October, Harris, Forbes & Co. issued its first circular of bond offerings since the start of the war, acting as did other houses to offer unlisted bonds in its inventory. It stated that it had reduced prices to what it considered the present value and added this sales appeal: "In many cases issues which have our full recommendation as intrinsically safe and sound in every respect can now be purchased at prices yielding approximately 6% over a period of ten to twenty years, and we advise the purchase of such bonds at this time."[14] By

11. *The Commercial & Financial Chronicle*, C (January 16, 1915), 199, 202.
12. *Ibid.*, XCIX (December 26, 1914), 1882–83. One firm that suspended was A. H. Combs & Co., one of the oldest exchange firms, having been admitted to the exchange in 1869. The cause of its failure was the suspension of Flower & Co., which owed money to Combs & Co. In recent years Combs had acted chiefly as a brokers' broker; earlier it had been more important in the financial district, having been broker for such notorious traders as James R. Keene and Jay Gould. *The Commercial & Financial Chronicle*, XCIX (December 12, 1914), 1727.
13. Cyril James, *The Growth of Chicago Banks* (2 vols., New York, 1938), II, 854–58.
14. *The Commercial & Financial Chronicle*, XCIX (October 10, 1914), 1932.

mid-November a well-established market appeared to exist for unlisted bonds and some stocks. Since there no longer seemed a danger of serious price declines, the Committee of Seven was dissolved. Other signs of restored confidence appeared in the *Chronicle* late in December. This influential weekly called attention to the fact that the "national investment firm" of E. W. Clark & Co., founded in 1837 and a member of the New York, Philadelphia, and Chicago stock exchanges, was soliciting inquiries from bankers and brokers wanting to buy original issues of high-grade public utility bonds, obligations of properties under the firm's management.[15]

While their usual business activities were stalled, investment bankers were responding to a series of emergency demands. One of the first of these was to ship gold to stranded American tourists in Europe who could not cash their letters of credit or travelers checks because of the disruption in foreign exchange markets. On August 5, 1914, Congress approved an appropriation of $1.5 million to be sent in gold to London on the *U.S.S. Tennessee,* and New York investment bankers sent an additional $3 million for their clients. The committee arranging this shipment included representatives of the Morgan firm; Kidder, Peabody & Co.; Brown Brothers; and American Express, plus several commercial banks. The bankers had been prepared to ship $2 million more, but withdrew the offer when France appointed Morgan its financial representative in the United States and transferred gold directly to Morgan's Paris house. The United States government also received deposits from individuals and transmitted them to beneficiaries abroad.[16]

Investment bankers also assisted in the immediate settlement of municipal debts due abroad. In the hysteria of the early days of the war the value of the dollar in terms of sterling declined sharply. There was widespread suspicion that the United States, a debtor nation, would not meet its international obligations, among which was payment of $80 million due on New York City notes, payable in London and Paris in installments before the end of the year. The first payment of $12 million was due by October 1, and the English were pressing for payment in gold. The comptroller of New York City, with the counsel and cooperation of Morgan, decided to issue $100 million refunding gold notes and to appeal to all New York commercial banks to buy them for resale, using their gold reserves. Subscriptions were to be payable as the foreign obligations became due. The gold was to be deposited in Canada for the account of the Bank of England.[17]

15. *Ibid.,* XCIX (December 26, 1914), 1916.
16. U.S. Treasury, *Annual Report, 1914,* 24–25; *The Commercial & Financial Chronicle,* XCIX (August 8, 1914), 385.
17. Thomas W. Lamont, *Henry P. Davison: The Record of a Useful Life* (New York, 1933), 173–82; *The Commercial & Financial Chronicle,* XCIX (August 22, 1914), 505; (September 5, 1914), 635.

The Morgan house formed a syndicate to buy the issue and invited Kuhn, Loeb & Co. to become joint manager. "Of course *we* did all the work," Dwight Morrow, a Morgan partner, wrote later. "It seemed desirable to have them in at the time in order to have an entirely united front. . . . I recall distinctly the feeling that I had of the very great power that the House had in leadership." [18] Kuhn, Loeb had been associate manager with William A. Read in underwriting a $65 million loan put out by New York City in April.[19] That gold should be paid, as the English requested, was urged by Jacob H. Schiff, of Kuhn, Loeb. This fact was important, the *Chronicle* reported, "as indicating the sense of honor existing among bankers here, for Mr. Schiff is supposed to have German sympathies, while the act he was advocating could benefit only the English." [20]

The arduous job of obtaining subscriptions from 126 New York City banks, in the proportions deemed appropriate for each, was largely the work of Morgan partner Henry P. Davison.[21] Inviting all the banks was called a democratic plan, not "the work of any coterie or faction." Only four small banks in the city did not participate.[22]

The syndicate managers offered half the issue to the public. Morgan alone received over 5,000 applications, amounting to over $116 million,[23] and some subscriptions came from abroad. The firm thus had to scale down allotments. The notes immediately were traded at a premium. The *Chronicle* had observed: "The maturing obligations of New York City, which were made the basis of extravagant predictions of default, are being worked out in an entirely orderly manner through bankers. No calm-minded person has entertained from the first any idea of a different result." [24]

Unexpectedly, coupons for a $3.8 million interest payment due on September 1 on another issue, for which the option existed for payment in London, were presented in New York. "With the easier situation prevailing . . . in their own market," said the *Chronicle,* "London bankers are not calling so loudly for the payment of American balances by the shipment of gold. . . . Great Britain needs not so much our gold as our food supplies." [25]

During the autumn Morgan carried through the payment plan

18. Quoted in Harold Nicolson, *Dwight Morrow* (New York, 1935), 168–69.
19. *The Commercial & Financial Chronicle,* XCIX (October 17, 1914), 1157. The *Chronicle,* reporting the dissolution of this syndicate in mid-October, said it was rumored that only 60 perecnt of the issue had been placed with investors.
20. *Ibid.,* XCIX (December 12, 1914), 1701.
21. Lamont, *Davison,* 180–82.
22. *The Commercial & Financial Chronicle,* XCIX (September 12, 1914), 709; (September 19, 1914), 792.
23. Lamont, *Davison,* 182.
24. *The Commercial & Financial Chronicle,* XCIX (September 26, 1914), 871; (September 5, 1914), 635.
25. *Ibid.,* XCIX (September 5, 1914), 635; (September 12, 1914), 697.

for the city. The firm made about a dozen calls for installments from the syndicate. At first, payments were made principally in gold, and the rest in exchange. But as the financial situation eased and the price of British exchange fell in terms of dollars, the proportion of gold called for decreased. The final calls were payable by check, since exchange was purchasable at advantageous rates.

By early December the operation was completed. The total called up approximated the $80 million originally estimated as necessary. This amount was made up of about $35 million in gold, $12 million in exchange, and $33 million in checks. As the successive calls were made, gold and exchange were sent to Ottawa as had been arranged. Deposits were credited to the Bank of England for the account of Morgan's London house, Morgan, Grenfell & Co., which used the credit in London to take up the New York City notes as they fell due.[26]

The managers received no compensation for their services. Morgan stated that he did not wish to make any money out of the city, and he rejected the usual $\frac{1}{2}$ percent commission. The participating banks received a 2 percent selling commission, and New York City a return of between $400,000 and $500,000 derived from the profit from exchange.[27]

Prompt, joint action by government and bankers was taken in additional ways to restore the value of the dollar in foreign exchange and thus to facilitate resumption of foreign trade. Even before the New York City plan had been worked out, Wall Street bankers, representatives of clearinghouses, and the Treasury had proposed establishing a $150 million gold pool. The money was to be placed in Canada for the credit of the Bank of England. Before the plan was completed, however, arrangements had been made for paying the New York City debt. Once this was accomplished, there seemed to be less urgency for sending gold to Canada, and the proposed $150 million pool was temporarily abandoned.

Shortly thereafter the proposal was revived. This time the goal was $100 million, and a pool was organized under a Gold Fund Committee composed of commercial bankers. It secured pledges of subscriptions from banks throughout the United States. New York's 117 banks — already involved in the City syndicate — were to furnish 45 percent of the total amount. About twenty other cities had smaller commitments, some less than $1 million. When the pool became operative, gold contributions were called up in installments and shipped to Ottawa to serve as the basis for drawing checks on London. But since conditions improved in the fall, only $25 million

26. *Ibid.*, XCIX (September 19, 1914), 792; (October 31, 1914), 1252; (December 5, 1914), 1620, 1637; Lamont, *Davison*, 183.
27. *The Commercial & Financial Chronicle*, XCIX (September 12, 1914), 709; C (January 2, 1915), 13; C (January 16, 1915), 203.

was called, and only $12 million actually shipped out. Of the advance, 30 percent had been returned to the contributors by December. The role of investment bankers in this project was chiefly advisory.[28]

Investment bankers also were called on for assistance to relieve the domestic economic crisis in the cotton market. This project involved foreign trade, transportation, and domestic production, as well as government-banker cooperation and bankers acting both as advisers and as money lenders. In the face of the war-induced demoralization in foreign exchange and ocean transport, the United States had a record-breaking cotton crop, and the means of export were abruptly cut off for this major export item.

Treasury Secretary William G. McAdoo called a series of conferences, starting the first week in August. It was decided to "restore through the bankers the market for foreign bills of exchange" and for the shipping men to provide vessels. Among the conferees were shippers, shipping men, foreign exchange bankers, businessmen from all over the country, and Cabinet officials, as well as members of Congress and the new Federal Reserve Board. Among the participating bankers and brokers were Morgan, James Speyer, William L. Benedict of Kidder, Peabody, and H. L. Ickelheimer of Heidelbach, Ickelheimer & Co.[29]

Both government and bankers furnished financial aid in this endeavor. The government deposited funds in southern banks to increase the credit base by over $12 million. The Federal Reserve Board issued over $75 million in emergency currency to southern banks and gave banks permission to issue currency on the basis of notes secured by cotton. The group of cooperating bankers agreed to raise a $135 million loan fund, a scheme that received the approval of the Federal Reserve Board and the Attorney General, the latter clearing it of any violation of antitrust laws.

Subscriptions came from commercial and investment bankers throughout the country, quotas being set for different areas. New York agreed to provide $50 million if other sections took their share.[30] Secretary McAdoo put pressure on localities where, he believed, subscriptions were too small. He chided Major Henry Lee Higginson on Boston's participation of only $2 million, since that city had benefited from the gold fund, to which southern states had subscribed even more. "It seems particularly narrow," he telegraphed, "and a mistaken policy, for the Boston banks to fail to reciprocate when the South needs assistance and asks Boston to do

28. U.S. Treasury, *Annual Report, 1914*, 6; *The Commercial & Financial Chronicle*, XCIX (August 8, 1914), 373; (September 12, 1914), 700, 711; (September 19, 1914), 795; (October 3, 1914), 929, 939; (October 17, 1914), 1106; (December 12, 1914), 1701, 1706.
29. U.S. Treasury, *Annual Report, 1914*, 4–17; *The Commercial & Financial Chronicle*, XXCIX (August 15, 1914), 450–51.
30. U.S. Treasury, *Annual Report, 1914*, 11–16.

so little."[31] When only about $97.3 million had been subscribed by November 17, the deadline for the plan to become operative, the deficiency was made up by Kuhn, Loeb ($2 million) and Bernard Baruch ($1 million). Among the larger subscribers in New York City was the House of Morgan.[32]

Secretary McAdoo gave assurances that the services of the Treasury in bringing about these aids to the economy were not part of its official duties, but a patriotic service. "It is a pleasure," he added, "to testify to the patriotism and broadmindedness of the banks and bankers who have so cheerfully supported . . . the organization of this fund."[33]

The calls on American gold reserves and the economic slowdown soon were reversed, and within a year industrial prosperity had returned. The United States became a creditor nation with a gold stock larger than any ever before held by one country.[34] "It must be a source of profound satisfaction to the people . . . regardless of political affiliations, to contrast the conditions [in December 1915] with those prevailing in this country in December, 1914," McAdoo observed.[35]

The different activities of investment bankers to meet domestic emergencies soon were overshadowed by their involvement in much larger operations. The first of these transactions was on behalf of the Allied powers.

Before the United States entered the war, the attitudes of American investment bankers toward the Allied cause were almost as important as their activities. Although the great majority had no direct part in foreign placements of American securities, the largest of the investment houses, especially those in New York City, had very close business or family ties with English, French, Dutch, and German bankers. It was only natural, therefore, that these firms should be called upon to play an important role in furnishing credit for the belligerents and in acting as their purchasing agents in this country. Most of these firms were ready to serve the Allies even before the United States government decided that financing belligerents did not violate the policy of neutrality, though no major financing was undertaken until it was acceptable to Washington.

As might be expected in an all-embracing organization, the attitude of the IBA toward foreign loans reflected the ambivalence of

31. *The Commercial & Financial Chronicle*, XCIX (November 21, 1914), 1498.
32. U.S. Treasury, *Annual Report, 1914*, 15.
33. *Ibid.*, 16.
34. To cover their purchases and facilitate floating loans, the British and French shipped "a steady stream of gold" to the United States. Among these shipments were some of the original bags and their contents that the French had paid as indemnity to Berlin in 1871 and that subsequently returned to France and some that Morgan had shipped to Paris in 1904 in settlement of the Panama Canal purchase. See *The Magazine of Wall Street*, XIX (January 20, 1917), 508; Lamont, *Davison*, 209.
35. U.S. Treasury, *Annual Report, 1915*, 1.

its members. Some opinions represented the viewpoints of bankers with less close European ties; in November 1914 President George B. Caldwell told the IBA convention that he feared that European loans would use up available credit and strain the domestic security markets. Yet one of the invited speakers at that meeting was Sir George Paish, joint editor of *The Statist* and an adviser to the Chancellor of the Exchequer and the British Treasury. Paish had been sent to the United States to negotiate British credits. He described his country's financial problems and warned that Americans must buy back issues floated abroad.[36]

By the next year the association appeared to favor lending abroad, for Europe now was a valued customer. Lewis B. Franklin, a vice president of the Guaranty Trust Co. and the new IBA president said: "We will do business with anybody who does business in the right way." The convention then passed a resolution approving military preparedness and another one endorsing neutrality. A guest speaker, former Republican senator from Ohio, Theodore E. Burton, spoke on the investment bankers' responsibilities for placing foreign issues here. "Not force, but common interest in finance and trade, will best promote friendship and peace," he said. "The investment banker must always have an abiding consciousness of the new duties imposed upon the citizens of Greater America as the leaders in the world's civilization." Investment bankers must not let "the eager desire for success supplant the finer qualities of cosmopolitanism and due regard for all, which are the crowning distinctions in the enlargement of a nation's financial life."[37]

Some Americans criticized the country's plunge into international finance. For example, Edward S. Meade, Professor of Finance at the University of Pennsylvania, thought the nation should keep its money at home, that there was not enough for both domestic and foreign needs, and that the government should be giving employment to its own people, not foreigners. The United States should be building highways, developing drainage and irrigation projects, building canals and railroads, and improving housing. Floating foreign issues here, Meade argued, would have disastrous effects on the domestic securities markets.[38]

Although the Wilson administration soon made it possible for Americans to lend to foreign governments, investors still had to be educated in the advantages of owning foreign bonds. "Investors in this country are rather provincial," asserted two writers for *The Magazine of Wall Street*. They noted that some people hesitated to buy foreign bonds, believing that such purchases would lengthen

---

36. Investment Bankers Association, *Proceedings . . . 1914* (Chicago, 1914), 19–20, 203–10.
37. *Ibid., 1915*, 93–94, 176, 217, 246.
38. Quoted in *The Magazine of Wall Street*, XVII (October 30, 1915), 84.

the war. They also raised other penetrating questions: were the "returns on these foreign bonds any better than returns on American bonds now offering, and are the countries at war who are asking support from American investors going to be able to pay their debts when the war, which has already cost a tremendous sum and is progressively expensive, ends?" It was not "an entirely fanciful idea" that Europe might repudiate its debts after the close of the war. Such events had occurred "after struggles much less devastating than the present one." They feared also a strong socialistic trend that might "produce demands similar to those made by the people of France after some of their great conflicts." [39]

Writing on other aspects of the same question, Paul Clay, another contributor to *The Magazine of Wall Street,* observed that it would pay better in the end to put domestic investment funds into financing America's export trade rather than into Canadian municipals or foreign government bonds or notes. In his view the investor who bought the bond or note of a company that was building or enlarging plants to produce goods for export not only was obtaining the desired income, but also was contributing to the prosperity of the United States. He pointed out, further, that Americans should learn the methods that England and Germany practiced in foreign markets in recent years, namely, that in order to get a big export trade one must lend foreign governments the money with which to pay for the goods. The lender gained both the return on the loan and the profit from the exports. As to the belligerents' borrowing power, measured by their existing debt compared to resources, Germany's was the greatest, but that country had lost nearly all its foreign trade. The basic soundness of securities of the United Kingdom, France, and Germany seemed to Clay more certain than that of other European countries.[40]

As the need for American credits became more urgent, the dispatch of foreign representatives to New York City to negotiate loans aroused still more apprehension. "The bankers of the United States have recently been confronted with a more staggering problem in finance than has ever been presented for solution in the past," another writer warned. "The representatives of England, France and Russia are here endeavoring to arrange for a credit estimated between a half a billion and a billion dollars. . . . The important point to be considered by the investor" was " 'what effect, if any, will this loan have on the securities which I own'?" He concluded that the financing would be advantageous for companies making war supplies, clothing materials, and all other products being or-

---

39. Charles F. Speare and Paul Clay, "Foreign War Loans and the Investor," *The Magazine of Wall Street,* XVI (July 24, 1915), 415–19. [Each is author of a separate part.]
40. *Ibid.*

dered by the Allies, but disadvantageous to most nonspeculative, fixed income securities.[41]

In spite of the misgivings and criticisms of some commentators and the opposition of various peace groups, the House of Morgan plunged into and led practically all the public loan operations of the British and French governments in the United States during the first three years of the war.[42] As Davison expressed it, "Some of us in America realized that this was our war from the very start." [43] He made numerous trips to England and France to negotiate transactions and to give to those governments advice and information on financial markets. The Morgan firm became purchasing agent for both Britain and France. The Allies, as well as Morgan's house, gained from these arrangements. The total assets of Morgan's New York and Philadelphia houses increased from about $228 million on December 31, 1914, to $481 million on December 31, 1917.[44]

The largest single foreign bond issue that J. P. Morgan marketed in the United States was the $500 million Anglo-French loan of October 1915. The biographer of a Morgan partner characterized this flotation as "one of the most difficult that the house of Morgan ever attempted to place," partly because of the strenuous opposition of "the German and Irish elements" in the United States.[45]

The preliminary arrangements for the loan were not conducted exclusively with Morgan. A special commission visiting the United States in the summer of 1915 to conclude negotiations consulted other investment bankers also. But whereas these other bankers warned the visitors that they could raise no more than $250 million in the United States and that collateral would be necessary, Otto Kahn and Mortimer Schiff of Kuhn, Loeb advised them that they could raise $500 million and that collateral would not be required. Incidentally, Kuhn, Loeb did not join in the underwriting, because Jacob Schiff was afraid that some of the proceeds would be used to help Czarist Russia, the scene of anti-Jewish pogroms in previous years. Not until Russia was out of the war and the United States had become a belligerent did that house support Anglo-French

41. Norman Merriman, "The Big Loan: Its Probable Effect on Security Markets," *The Magazine of Wall Street*, XVI (October 2, 1915), 762–64.

42. Lamont, *Davison*, 187.

43. George W. Edwards, *The Evolution of Finance Capitalism* (London, 1938), 203, quoting James Kerney, *The Political Education of Woodrow Wilson* (New York, 1936), 395.

44. U.S. Senate, Special Committee Investigating the Munitions Industry, 73d and 74th Congs., *Munitions Industry: Hearings* . . . (40 pts., Washington, 1934–43), pt. 25, 7657–58.

45. Nicolson, *Morrow*, 174. The arrangements for syndicating this loan were used thirty-five years later in the government's antitrust suit as precedent setting and evidence of the start of the alleged conspiracy among certain investment bankers to restrain trade.

financing, although individual partners had done so from the beginning.[46]

In spite of an assassination attempt, believed to have been made "by either cranks or German sympathizers," Morgan proceeded in his preliminary negotiations with the issuing governments. He formed an underwriting syndicate but did not charge the usual fee for organizing and managing it. The managing group included 61 commercial banks, trust companies, and investment houses in New York City, and the distributing organization was composed of 1570 members throughout the country. Although the managers carried out a nationwide educational campaign, they failed to obtain subscriptions to the full amount, and the Morgan and Drexel firms subscribed to $30 million themselves.[47] Among other large individual subscribers were the Guggenheims, James Stillman, George F. Baker, Andrew Carnegie, Vincent Astor, Otto H. Kahn, and Samuel Untermyer. Insurance companies, banks, and industrial corporations also subscribed. *The Magazine of Wall Street* reported that du Pont interests had taken $35 million; Bethlehem Steel, $20 million; and Westinghouse, $15 million.[48]

Only one Chicago bank, the Central Trust Company, headed by Charles G. Dawes, was courageous enough to resist local pro-German and antiwar sentiment to become an underwriter. Even so, some of the bank's officers resigned, and over four hundred accounts were withdrawn. Dawes received so much threatening mail that he had his house guarded.[49]

At the conclusion of the underwriting phase Morgan told the bond salesmen who would be distributing the securities that he did not consider them "war bonds," but simply a device for giving America's customers an extension of time to pay for the merchandise they were buying in the United States. Britain and France were the most resourceful nations the world had produced, and their bonds were safe, for an external loan always was understood as a first mortgage on the resources of the debtor nations and would be taken care of regardless of what arrangements were made to care for internal obligations.[50]

---

46. Cyrus Adler, *Jacob H. Schiff: His Life and Letters* (2 vols., New York, 1929), II, 250–53.
47. Lamont, *Davison*, 193–97.
48. *The Magazine of Wall Street,* XVII (December 11, 1915), 295.
49. James, *Growth of Chicago Banks,* II, 891.
50. *The Magazine of Wall Street,* XVII (October 16, 1915), 14. Another defender of the loan, IBA counsel Robert R. Reed, pointed out the economic value of supporting it. He believed that businessmen would read with interest the names of the banks, trust companies, and bankers participating in the so-called "war credit." The depositors of banks, furthermore, would be the chief beneficiaries of the loan, the effect of which would be to maintain and improve American prosperity by providing a market for American products. See *U.S. v. Henry S. Morgan*

The general public was not persuaded by these arguments. Unconvinced that lending to the Allies was a neutral act, it remained aloof. Had the loan been dependent upon their purchases, it would have failed badly.[51] Part of the loan subsequently was disbursed as dividends by manufacturers of explosives.

One important purpose of the Anglo-French loan of 1915 was to restore foreign exchange rates to their normal levels and stabilize them. The "enormous" funds the loan made available gave the market a steadiness it had not enjoyed since the outbreak of hostilities. As a further step to support exchange, in December 1915 England arranged for a $50 million credit to be granted by a syndicate of American bankers to eight leading British joint stock banks to facilitate private transactions. The credit was secured by a deposit of British government securities and was used in the form of acceptances given in payment for American exports.[52] In 1916 and 1917 Morgan marketed four additional issues for Great Britain, totaling $950 million.[53]

Meanwhile Morgan had been performing many services for France. Early in August 1914 the firm was appointed the American representative of the French government and arranged for the transfer of $6 million in gold from the Bank of France to Morgan, Harjes in Paris. This transfer gave the French government credit in this country and gave to Morgan a gold deposit that made unnecessary the planned gold shipment from the United States. In less than a month France added $10 million to this deposit. In still another transaction in August, Morgan extended a $12 million loan to the French government.[54]

The following year Morgan arranged for an additional $100 million loan to France. For this one, collateral was demanded by the underwriting bankers as essential to making the issue attractive for resale. The American Foreign Securities Company was organized to lend the money. It was chartered in New York State with capital stock of $10 million and a three-year 5 percent note issue of $95

---

et al., "Plaintiff's Exhibits (39–82)," 44-B, No. 1924, 7443–44, quoting *The Wall Street Journal,* October 1, 1915.

51. Arthur S. Link, *Wilson: The Struggle for Neutrality, 1914–1915* (Princeton, 1960), 625–28; Ferdinand Lundberg, *America's 60 Families* (New York, 1937), 140–41; Gordon Blythe Anderson, "The Effect of the War on New Security Issues in the United States," and Thomas Conway, Jr., "Financing American War Orders," *America's Changing Investment Market, The Annals,* LXVIII (November 1916), 129, 142.

52. George Zimmer, "Foreign Exchange during the War," *America's Changing Investment Market, The Annals,* LXVIII (November 1916), 156–57.

53. Nicolson, *Morrow,* 177–78n.7.

54. *The Commercial & Financial Chronicle,* XCIX (August 8, 1914), 385–86; (August 22, 1914), 514. In October 1914 the National City Bank headed a syndicate to establish an additional $10 million credit for France. See *The Commercial & Financial Chronicle,* XCIX (October 31, 1914), 1252.

million. France put up collateral, which was to be maintained at a margin of 20 percent above the loan amount and made up of securities issued by the neutral governments of Argentina, Sweden, Norway, Denmark, Switzerland, Holland, Uruguay, Egypt, Brazil, Spain, and Quebec province, plus shares of the Suez Canal Company and bonds and stocks of American corporations. The corporation's president was Robert Bacon, former ambassador to France and a former partner of J. P. Morgan.[55]

The note issue was marketed by a syndicate managed by Morgan and Brown Brothers. It was announced in a full-page advertisement in the *Chronicle* over the names of the firms with which the new corporation's directors were affiliated. Small and large investors were served. Available denominations of the notes were $100, $1,000, $5,000, and $10,000.[56] The prospectus appeared over thirty-two names, headed by Morgan and including several firms in the Midwest. Kidder, Peabody, which participated in the various French loans marketed in this country, recommended the notes to its clients as an attractive and safe investment.[57]

Further urging to lend funds to the Allies came when the United States was about to enter the war. The government was planning its first war loan to cover, in part, direct loans to the Allies. Thomas Lamont pointed out the "enormous value to America" of war sales to the Allies. He believed this warranted further credits — subscribing to a United States war loan would be an indirect way to extend help to these nations, which had been "fighting our battles for us. . . . If the Treasurer [*sic*] should decide to issue a Government obligation tomorrow for a billion dollars," he said, "the whole sum would be waiting for it."[58]

One anticipated effect of extending liberal credits was to attract world trade after the war was over and thus to maintain the current high level of industrial production. In preparation for this, industrialists and financiers in the United States were becoming more familiar with trade acceptances, financial instruments little used here

---

55. *The Commercial & Financial Chronicle,* CIII (July 15, 1916), 196. The directors were as follows: James S. Alexander, National Bank of Commerce; George F. Baker, First National Bank; James Brown, Brown Brothers; T. DeWitt Cuyler, Commercial Trust Co., Philadelphia; Charles G. Dawes, Central Trust Co., Chicago; Clarence Dillon, Wm. A. Read & Co.; Allen B. Forbes, Harris, Forbes & Co.; Henry L. Higginson, Lee, Higginson & Co.; Louis W. Hill, First National Bank of St. Paul; Edwin S. Marston, Farmers' Loan & Trust Co.; A. W. Mellon, Mellon National Bank of Pittsburgh; Edwin G. Merrill, Union Trust Co.; J. P. Morgan, J. P. Morgan & Co.; Seward Prosser, Bankers Trust Co.; Charles H. Sabin, Guaranty Trust Co.; Henry Seligman, J. & W. Seligman & Co.; Frank A. Vanderlip, National City Bank; Albert H. Wiggin, Chase National Bank; Robert Winsor, Kidder, Peabody & Co.; William Woodward, Hanover National Bank.

56. *The Commercial & Financial Chronicle,* CIII (July 22, 1916), xvi.

57. Kidder, Peabody & Co., "Circulars," [1895–1927] (10 vols., Baker Library), II, 171, 196, 197.

58. Quoted in *The Magazine of Wall Street,* XIX (March 31, 1917), 877.

before the war. Facilities for discounting them were provided by the new Federal Reserve System.

The involvement of investment bankers in Allied purchases became complicated as they began performing a variety of services centered around a single company: agent for customers, supplier of funds, marketer of securities, and corporate director and financial counselor. Morgan, for instance, negotiated contracts with the Winchester Repeating Arms Company of Connecticut for guns and ammunition for Britain and Russia. The company itself also solicited business from both countries. For initial necessary expansion Morgan lent the company about $8 million and Britain advanced another $8 million.[59] When this amount proved inadequate, Morgan turned over to Kidder, Peabody the business of raising further sums. In March 1916 Kidder, Peabody floated a $16 million two-year note issue, heading a syndicate including Morgan and William P. Bonbright. Part of the proceeds were to pay off the earlier loan.[60] One of the New York partners of Kidder, Peabody, Charles S. Sargent, joined the Winchester board.[61] In its description of the issue, Kidder, Peabody said that the company had "a unique and steadily increasing business carried on at a handsome profit," and the company had never yet been able to fill the demand for its output.[62]

At almost the same time, Kidder, Peabody also attempted to negotiate sale of control of Winchester to E. I. du Pont de Nemours, obtaining from the arms company's stockholders an option on 55 percent of the stock at $2,250 a share ($100 par).[63] A recent market quotation had been $2,500, and average dividends for the past eleven years had been 55 percent.[64]

The sale was not completed, because the seller could not furnish evidence of adequate contracts on hand to suit the prospective buyer. Delays in production, difficulties in getting inspection approvals, and increasing British production of arms led to a lower volume of orders than had been anticipated. But the pressure Morgan put on the British helped to maintain the level of Winchester's orders.[65] Britain was at this time negotiating with Morgan to place a new $300 million government loan here.[66] When the Winchester notes became due in 1918, half had been paid, and Kidder, Pea-

---

59. Harold F. Williamson, *Winchester: The Gun That Won the West* (Washington, 1952), 218–24.
60. *Munitions Industry: Hearings,* pt. 25, 7578; *The Commercial & Financial Chronicle,* CII (February 26, 1916), 810.
61. Williamson, *Winchester,* 260.
62. Kidder, Peabody & Co., "Circulars," II, 167.
63. *Munitions Industry: Hearings,* pt. 25, 7584.
64. *The Commercial & Financial Chronicle,* CII (January 29, 1916), 443; (March 4, 1916), 891.
65. Williamson, *Winchester,* 226–29, 233.
66. Lamont, *Davison,* 205.

body handled a refunding issue for the remainder.[67] Throughout the period the company carried on its usual production for domestic orders.

Investment bankers' acceptance of deposit accounts tended to increase during the war as European clients increased their balances in the United States.[68] This was particularly the case with houses acting as purchasing agents for foreign governments, such as the Morgan firm, but it applied also to those handling individual accounts. Kidder, Peabody, for example, writing to Baring Brothers & Co. on January 27, 1916, to make its annual report of profits and results of joint ventures, said, "We are glad to be able to say that we have had a good year. . . . Of course we understand that it is a temporary increase [in foreign deposits] and we have guarded ourselves against it by keeping a large amount of cash in banks and by the purchase of the quickest kind of short time notes and quick securities." [69]

By 1918 the distribution of foreign securities had become an important but still new role for investment bankers. In this year the IBA appointed a permanent Committee on Foreign Securities. Its purposes were to maintain contacts with American and foreign governments, with counterpart bodies in other countries, and with foreign agencies directly concerned with particular security issues. The association hoped the mere presence of such a body would prevent exploitation of American investors and serve directly the holders of a given security issue.[70]

By the end of the war the government was heartily encouraging private flotation of Allied loans. Treasury Secretary Carter Glass, McAdoo's successor, stated that the Treasury favored American loans to European countries and cities, for they contributed to relieving the exchanges. "I am sure that when peace is consummated, and the political risk measurably removed, American exporters and European importers will lay the basis of credit in sound business transactions, and I know that American bankers will not fail then

67. Kidder, Peabody & Co., "Histories," [1911–1943] (16 vols., Baker Library), I, Winchester Repeating Arms Company, One year 7% Notes Syndicate, February 5, 1918.
68. *The Commercial & Financial Chronicle,* C (January 16, 1915), 199.
69. Kidder, Peabody & Co., "Confidential Letters," VI, 101.
70. The members of the committee and their banking affiliations were as follows: Thomas W. Lamont, J. P. Morgan & Co.; Moreau Delano, Brown Bros. & Co.; Allen B. Forbes, Harris, Forbes & Co.; Alvin W. Krech, Equitable Trust Co.; Charles E. Mitchell, The National City Co.; Charles H. Sabin, Guaranty Trust Co.; Charles S. Sargent, Jr., Kidder, Peabody & Co.; Mortimer L. Schiff, Kuhn, Loeb & Co.; Albert H. Wiggin, Chase Securities Corp.; Seward Prosser, Bankers Trust Co.; William P. Bonbright, Bonbright & Co., Inc.; Clarence Dillon, Wm. A. Read & Co.; H. L. Stuart, Halsey, Stuart & Co., Chicago; Francis L. Higginson, Jr., Lee, Higginson & Co.; H. C. McEldowney, Union Trust Co., Pittsburgh; John Evans, International Trust Co., Denver; Lewis H. Parsons, Graham, Parsons & Co., Philadelphia; Herbert Fleishacker, Anglo & London Paris National Bank, San Francisco. IBA, *Proceedings . . . 1918,* 193–94.

to devise means of financing the needs of the situation nor American investors to respond to Europe's demand for capital on a sound investment basis." [71]

Investment bankers with established relations with the Central Powers continued to carry on correspondence with them until the United States entered the war. For instance, Kuhn, Loeb and the National City Bank, which had marketed a $25 million note issue for the Austrian government in 1912, were somewhat surprised when half of these notes were paid on July 1, 1914, and the remainder on January 1, 1915. Schiff wrote to the German banker Max Warburg: "I must say frankly that we here feel fortunate, not only because we had large holdings ourselves, but even more because the Notes had been placed through us." [72] Kidder, Peabody had taken 10 percent of the issue in 1912, at which time it had offered a fifth of its share to Barings, who had declined the offer with thanks, saying: "We foresee so many calls on our resources in connection with European finance, fear we must decline; but business looks attractive. Wish you every success." [73]

Speyer & Co., with branches in England and Germany, continued for a time to carry on business with the Frankfurt house and with others in Germany. But in October 1914 Sir Edgar Speyer, a British subject, member of the Privy Council, and head of the London house, temporarily retired from the New York firm following a royal proclamation forbidding British businessmen and bankers from having commercial relations with persons in Germany.[74]

In September 1914 it was reported that plans for placing a German loan in the United States were dropped when the State Department's attitude toward floating a French one became known.[75] But later on Germany did place several issues in this country, mostly short-term notes. In March 1915 Chandler & Co., of New York and Philadelphia, sold $10 million of German Treasury notes, about half to banks and trust companies in New York and half to individuals in Philadelphia, Cincinnati, and other cities. It later offered the issue to the public.[76] In 1916 the firm offered $10 million more short-term 6 percent Treasury notes payable in gold at the Central Trust Company, New York. The announcement of the offer stated

71. U.S. Treasury, *Annual Report, 1919,* 14.
72. Adler, *Schiff,* II, 259.
73. Kidder, Peabody, & Co., "Confidential Letters," VI, 22.
74. *The Commercial & Financial Chronicle,* XCIX (October 10, 1914), 1031.
75. *Ibid.,* XCIX (September 12, 1914), 698–99.
76. *Ibid.,* CII (January 8, 1916), 111. Chandler Brothers & Co. had recently taken over the business of Edward Sweet & Co., founded in 1854. It had been prominent in financial and social circles and was known as a Vanderbilt and Rockefeller house. E. H. Harriman had been its broker, and he was a customer after he became a railroad tycoon. See *The Commercial & Financial Chronicle,* XCIX (December 12, 1914), 1728.

that the notes would be placed with banks in the East and Middle West "according to the actual requirements" for use of credits in this country. There was no public offering.[77] And in September 1915, Zimmerman & Forshay, of New York, offered part of the third German war loan, at about 84. This low price was due in part to the low exchange rate. The firm's advertisement for this issue in the *Chronicle* stressed its security and yield.[78]

Writing in October 1915, the "frankly pro-German" Siegfried Strauss analyzed the security of investments in the war loans of the various belligerents. France and Russia, he judged, would soon have debts of nearly 30 percent of their wealth, whereas England and Germany would have less than 20 percent. "The cautious American investor will thus come to the conclusion that both the German war loan and the Allied war loan are safe investments, the latter on the strength of the English promise to pay." [79]

Although Schiff maintained friendly relations with individuals in Germany until the United States entered the war, his firm did no financing for the Kaiser's government or its allies. In the fall of 1916 a projected bond issue for the cities of Hamburg, Frankfurt, and Berlin, to be marketed by Kuhn, Loeb, was dropped because of opposition by the Federal Reserve Board and the president. Wilson wrote to Colonel House on November 24, 1916, suggesting that he convey to Kuhn, Loeb, through Schiff, who would be sure of the president's personal friendship, the intimation that America's relations with Germany were now "in a very unsatisfactory and doubtful state, and that it would be most unwise at this time to risk a loan." [80] However, the firm did join in the French cities loan of 1916.[81]

Between 1914 and 1917 American investment bankers marketed loans for both sides as well as for neutrals, and in addition individual firms granted credits that were not publicly offered security issues. The great majority of the issues floated, however, were for the Allied governments. The first large loan was the $500 million five-year Anglo-French bond issue of October 1915, negotiated soon after President Wilson had reversed the State Department's original policy on such loans. This was the largest single bond issue marketed up to this time in the United States, and for its distribution there was assembled the largest underwriting group ever gathered together. Other large foreign issues followed, but there were fewer of them after American entry into the war and after the government started granting direct loans to the Allies. Loans to the Central Powers, of

77. *The Commercial & Financial Chronicle,* CII (May 27, 1916), 1942.
78. *Ibid.,* CI (September 25, 1915), xiii.
79. Siegfried Strauss, "Safety of War Loans," *The Magazine of Wall Street,* XVI (October 2, 1915), 765–66.
80. *Munitions Industry: Hearings,* pt. 28, 8570.
81. Adler, *Schiff,* II, 249.

course, were stopped altogether. The extent of American loans, amounting to nearly $3 billion, is summarized in Exhibit 3.[82]

Exhibit 3. Foreign loans marketed in the United States from the summer of 1914 to April 1917

Country	Amount (millions)
England	1,250
France	640
Russia	107
Japan	102
Italy	25
Central Powers	35

Source: William J. Shultz and M. R. Caine, *Financial Development of the United States* (New York, 1937), 505–06. (Adapted by permission of Prentice-Hall, Inc., Englewood Cliffs, New Jersey.)
Note: Loans to Canada, China, Latin American countries, European neutrals, foreign municipalities and state governments, and foreign public utilities and industrial enterprises brought the grand total to $2,997,395,287.

Sales of repatriated securities also furnished a substantial amount of credits for England and France. Arrangements for orderly sales through investment bankers prevented the damaging effects that would have come from dumping, as had happened at the very start of the war. Negotiations for the return of these securities were carried out in large part by Davison and British and French bankers and officials. The total volume of securities so distributed amounted to nearly $3 billion for the British and over $50 million for the French. Started on what later turned out to be a small scale, although regarded as large at the time, the first major shipment was made in August 1915, preliminary to the placement of the major Anglo-French loan of October, already being negotiated by Morgan. Securities were arriving in New York "by the bale and finding final lodgment in the hands of thrifty American investors," a Morgan partner declared.[83] Other securities already were held by New York bankers for European owners.

The technique for accomplishing this organized marketing was for the British and French governments to buy securities from private holders in their countries and pay for them with their own government bonds. The respective governments then sold the issues for cash in New York or used them as collateral for loans. When

---

82. William J. Shultz and M. R. Caine, *Financial Development of the United States* (New York, 1937), 505–06.
83. Lamont, *Davison,* 201, 212–13.

voluntary participation in the scheme proved to be slow, Britain levied a tax on foreign securities in order to stimulate these exchanges.[84] One purpose served by having these assets in New York was to strengthen exchange rates for the currencies of these countries. By the end of 1915 the pound had been restored to about $4.73 from its low point of $4.50.[85]

"This plan was on the whole an advantageous one for American investors," a Morgan partner observed. It gave them "a fresh opportunity" to invest in "the bonds and shares of the very American corporations which, just then, were beginning to realize increasingly satisfactory profits through the increasingly heavy purchases of the Allied Governments."[86] When the securities were offered here in 1915 the market had become bullish, and prices rose to new highs.[87] President A. B. Leach of the IBA commented that these repatriations could not have been presented at a better time, for never before had Americans been in a position to absorb them. Furthermore, the interest and dividends now would be paid to them instead of to foreigners.[88]

Germany also liquidated holdings of American securities. Many American railroad issues had been floated in Germany, and active trading in them continued during the war. In 1914 about thirty-five bond and two stock issues were traded on the Berlin, Frankfurt, and Hamburg stock exchanges. Of the more than $1.5 billion of American securities repatriated by the end of 1915, 20 percent were credited to Germans. "The nations of Europe not only willingly sacrificed their lives in this terrible struggle," Siegfried Strauss observed, "but they also put their wealth at the disposition of their governments to secure a victorious peace. *England and Germany are a shining example of not only physical courage but the financial power of strong nations.*" German-held American securities, having been declared contraband, could not be shipped to the United States, but a technique was proposed to accomplish the same result and at the same time to give Americans a chance to profit from the wartime situation. Having bought marks at depreciated rates, Americans cabled them to Germany, and took delivery of the securities after the war or through "one of the prominent banks of Holland or Switzerland."[89]

84. Zimmer, "Foreign Exchange during the War," 155–57.
85. G. C. Selden, "Striking England's Balance Sheet," *The Magazine of Wall Street*, XVII (January 8, 1916), 434.
86. Lamont, *Davison*, 187.
87. Shultz and Caine, *Financial Development of the United States*, 504.
88. *The New York Times*, September 21, 1915.
89. Siegfried Strauss, "The War Loans," *The Magazine of Wall Street*, XVII (January 8, 1916), 453; Siegfried Strauss, "Profits in 'Interned' Securities: How the Investor Who Is Willing to Wait for the End of the War May Make Money — Securities Interned in Germany," *The Magazine of Wall Street*, XIX (December 23, 1916), 385–86.

One source of business and management activity for investment bankers during the war was the refinancing in 1915–16 of Sulzberger & Sons of Chicago, successor firm to one organized in 1853 and one of the Big Five meat packers. The owners of the company were reputed to be pro-German; France made formal protests against its shipments abroad; and England seized four cargoes of beef that the company was shipping to Scandinavia under an arrangement with the Deutsche Bank of Berlin.[90] Through diplomatic channels the State Department protested this British action and eventually obtained a settlement. This came about largely because, in the meantime, control of the Sulzberger company had been placed with New York bankers, one of which was Guaranty Trust. Since Britain was borrowing from this bank at the time and did not want to jeopardize its status as debtor, it agreed to Washington's request for settlement.[91]

The company's problems were complicated by the fact that it was in financial difficulties. These stemmed from unprofitable expansion in the United States and South America. The firm called on investment bankers for assistance, and they helped solve the meat packer's problem. In the summer of 1915 the Sulzbergers arranged to have an $8 million issue of debentures, maturing in 1916, refinanced by William Salomon & Co.; Hallgarten & Co. acting for itself and for Kuhn, Loeb; Chase National Bank; and Guaranty Trust. In the course of the negotiations disagreements led to the bankers' acquiring a substantial common stock interest and all the common being placed in a five-year voting trust, composed of three bankers from the firms named above, plus two Sulzbergers. Thomas E. Wilson, former president of Morris & Company, another of the Big Five, became president, and the name of the company was changed to Wilson & Company, Inc., a name more acceptable to the English and French. The locus of interest in the company shifted from New York to Chicago. Headquarters were moved to that city, and the public offer of a new stock issue received special response there.[92] The bankers, investment and commercial, served the company in various and profitable ways and were firmly in control.

Before the United States entered the war, the government had given tangible assistance to domestic businessmen and bankers endeavoring to take over Europe's role in financing Latin American trade. Before 1914 even the direct trade of the United States had been financed chiefly through London. Secretary McAdoo saw the war situation as "an extraordinary opportunity to enlarge our trade

---

90. Robert Taylor Swaine, *The Cravath Firm and Its Predecessors, 1819–1948* (3 vols., New York, 1946–1948), II, 155.
91. Lloyd C. Griscom, *Diplomatically Speaking* (Boston, 1940), 355, 363.
92. *Moody's Manual, Industrials, 1916,* 3563–65; *The Commercial & Financial Chronicle,* CIII (November 4, 1916), 1709.

interests and financial influence in all of the Central and South American countries." [93]

In 1914 Congress authorized the president to invite representatives of twenty of these countries to visit the United States for a formal Pan American Financial Conference. The visitors included finance ministers and bankers. They were entertained first in New York by representatives of such organizations as the New York Stock Exchange and mercantile and financial groups, and by such individual commercial and investment bankers as Davison and Willard D. Straight, of the Morgan firm; Jacob Schiff; Franklin Q. Brown of Redmond & Co.; and S. R. Bertron of Bertron, Griscom & Co. And on the committee appointed to participate in discussions were Straight, Davison, Schiff, James Speyer, James Brown, and William Loeb, Jr.

The meeting made decisions on the improvement of banking, exchange, credit, discount, and other matters involved in trade between the two areas. President Wilson addressed the gathering and alarmed some domestic financiers by stating that if private capital did not soon establish necessary inter-American shipping facilities, the federal government would. Schiff advised the visitors that Latin American securities likely to appeal to United States investors would have to be doubly secured bonds, secured by the issuer and endorsed by its government.[94] These meetings led to the organization of the more permanent International High Commission.

In 1915, in accord with the growing spirit of national financial self-consciousness, the engineering firm of Stone & Webster organized the American International Corporation (AIC), a conglomerate holding company. The new corporation was set up "on a scale transcending anything America has ever known." Charles A. Stone became president.[95] Behind the scheme were Kuhn, Loeb, the National City Bank, the Rockefellers, and other important firms and individuals. Capital stock of $49 million common and $1 million preferred was oversubscribed. Of the common stock, $25 million was set aside to be offered to stockholders of the National City Bank. This bank also was the new corporation's transfer agent, and Frank A. Vanderlip, National City's president, was chairman of AIC's board.[96] Bertie Charles Forbes, the founder and editor of *Forbes Magazine,* expected the new corporation to be the culmination of the idea that "every robust American would like to see the United States become the greatest financial and commercial nation on earth." [97] The company acquired holdings in Morgan's International Mercantile Marine Company, recently put in receivership,

93. U.S. Treasury, *Annual Report, 1915,* 15.
94. *The Commercial & Financial Chronicle,* C (May 29, 1915), 1799, 1801.
95. Bertie C. Forbes, *Men Who Are Making America* (New York, 1921), 396.
96. *Moody's Manual, Industrials, 1916,* 2068.
97. Forbes, *Men Who Are Making America,* 396.

the United Fruit Company, and others. At the end of its first year AIC announced that it had investigated opportunities for investment in over 1,200 projects in twelve major areas throughout the world and in seven major lines of activity, from finance to mining; it had declined about 900 of these and others were pending.[98]

By 1918, through wholly or partly owned subsidiaries, many of which the parent company had established, AIC was carrying on operations in over seventeen countries in Central and South America, the Far East, and Europe. Operations were chiefly in industrial construction, construction machinery, public utilities, shipping and shipbuilding, plus such nonrelated activities as importing tea and forging shells. Capital subscribed by that time amounted to $50 million, but only 80 percent had been called up.[99]

During the years of American neutrality the chief focus of investment banking activity shifted from domestic to foreign business. Most of the leading houses became heavily engaged in financing the Allied governments. Kidder, Peabody, for example, distributed numerous foreign issues. Included among these were the important British and French government loans under Morgan; the French cities loan and the Paris loan of 1916, under the management of Kuhn, Loeb; and the $50 million Russian government loan of 1916, underwritten by Morgan, National City Bank, Guaranty Trust Co., Lee, Higginson, and Kidder, Peabody itself. Of the Russian loan it was said that the success of the Czar's armies on the battlefield and the St. Petersburg government's large purchases in the United States would cause a heavy demand for the issue; and, indeed, it was fully subscribed. As part of the negotiation for this issue the underwriting syndicate obtained an option on a subsequent Russian dollar bond offering with a $4\frac{1}{2}$ percent commission and an opportunity to profit from exchange.[100]

For almost three years America's leading investment houses were occupied almost entirely with servicing the financial needs of the Allied and neutral powers. Between July 1914 and April 1917 investment bankers arranged the resale of more than $3 billion of American securities held in Europe and marketed almost $2.2 billion of Allied bonds. The functions investment houses performed in facilitating these and other related transactions played a vital role in transforming the United States from a debtor to a creditor nation and in shifting the financial capital of the world from London to New York.[101]

The war relegated the domestic, new issues business to a secondary position. The total volume of new, domestic corporate securi-

---

98. *The Commercial & Financial Chronicle*, CIII (December 23, 1916), 2338.
99. *Moody's Industrials, 1918*, 1949–52; *1919*, 2104–08.
100. *The Commercial & Financial Chronicle*, CII (June 17, 1916), 2211.
101. Harold U. Faulkner, *The Decline of Laissez Faire, 1897–1917* (New York, 1951), 86–89.

Exhibit 4. Changing sources of corporate funds, 1914–1917 (in millions)

Year	Bonds and notes	Stocks	Total	Loans all banks
1914	1,175	262	1,437	15,502
1915	1,111	325	1,436	15,976
1916	1,405	782	2,187	18,263
1917	1,076	455	1,531	20,902

Source: U.S. Bureau of the Census, *Historical Statistics of the United States, Colonial Times to 1957* (Washington, 1960), 624, 658.
Note: All banks = all banks reporting to the Comptroller of the Currency: national, state, and private.

ties offered remained at a relatively low level during the years 1914 to 1917 (see Exhibit 4). Total issues had been declining since 1912 ($2.2 billion) and continued at this lower volume except for a rise in 1916 to nearly the 1912 rate. Much of the increase in the later year, however, was accounted for by stocks, which more than doubled between 1915 ($324.7 million) and 1916 ($781.5 million). Bonds and notes, on the other hand, remained relatively stable, but with the latter steadily growing in popularity. Most of the domestic issues in which Kidder, Peabody participated between 1914 and 1917 were short-term notes.[102]

The most significant change occurred in the volume of commercial bank credit. Even before the outbreak of war, temporary financing through bank loans was replacing long-term borrowing through security issues. In August 1914 the *Chronicle* reported "a practical cessation of great consolidations and re-capitalization of industrial enterprises" and noted that "the bulk of the 100 millions of miscellaneous stocks listed during the half-year just closed were of this variety, though dating back to the preceding year or earlier."[103] The use of commercial bank credit increased markedly during the years of American neutrality. Between 1914 and 1917 loans and discounts jumped by almost 35 percent.

During these years other changes occurred in the domestic securities market. Financial advisers were beginning to realize that some securities other than bonds were suitable for conservative investors. A financial reporter writing in *The Magazine of Wall Street* in 1915 boldly made a case for the investment value of high-grade preferred stocks of public utilities and railroads, but cautioned: "We must 'soft pedal' in comparing good bonds with these stocks."[104]

102. Kidder, Peabody & Co., "Histories" and "Confidential Letters."
103. *The Commercial & Financial Chronicle*, XCIX (August 1, 1914), 306–07.
104. Howard Thompson, "When Stocks Are Better than Bonds," *The Magazine of Wall Street*, XVI (September 18, 1915), 726–30.

As the war caused domestic industry to expand, industrial securities became more acceptable to distributors and investors.[105] "Probably never before were rumors of immense orders and prophecies of unheard-of profits so persistently paraded before the reading public day after day," another financial observer reported in 1916.[106] But utilities of all kinds lagged, for rate regulation limited profits, and prospects were less inviting in spite of wartime expansion of demand for their services.

Extreme fluctuations in prices and shares of securities traded were additional factors in the uncertain environment in which investment bankers were operating. (Exhibit 5 gives figures for common

Exhibit 5. Index of common stock prices (1941–1943 = 10) and number of shares traded on New York Stock Exchange, 1914–1917

	Common stock prices				Number of shares traded (millions)
Year	Total	Industrial	Railroad	Utilities	
1914	8.08	4.50	27.39	18.14	48
1915	8.31	5.22	26.38	18.65	173
1916	9.47	6.62	28.35	20.26	233
1917	8.50	6.15	24.89	18.24	186

Source: Historical Statistics to 1957, 657, 659.

stocks traded on the New York Stock Exchange.) Although the price indexes do not reveal the extent of fluctuations of individual stocks, they do indicate a 1914 decline, caused in part by the panic at the start of the war and the closing of the exchanges, the peak in 1916, and the fall after the United States entered the war. By 1916 security prices were advancing along with the general price level, which was rising because of shortages and high profits. The Comptroller of the Currency cited levels "undreamed of": Bethlehem Steel, from a 1914–15 low of 30 to 700 in 1916, followed by a severe drop in December 1916, when there was a rumor of German surrender.[107] Thereafter the price continued down through 1917.

A mid-period analysis of important changes in the security markets commented on a variety of them. Among these were the "aston-

105. A. E. Bryson, *Halsey, Stuart & Co. Inc., 1901–1937, 1938–1944: A History* . . . ([Chicago, 1937, 1945]), 10.
106. S. S. Huebner, "The American Security Market during the War," *America's Changing Investment Market, The Annals*, LXVIII (November 1916), 99.
107. U.S. Treasury, *Annual Report, 1917*, 536.

ishing" volume of issues so far absorbed; the increase in speculative offerings, the rising interest rates and yields demanded by investors, the sluggishness of some issues in reaching ultimate investors — some remaining on the shelves of the underwriters — the investors' search for bargains, speculation in war stocks, and the difficulties that railroads had in finding new capital. "Under the stimulating influences which have existed since the advent of war orders and the return of industrial prosperity, the power of absorption of new securities is as great as in any previous period of our history," reported a knowledgeable observer. "This record is all the more astonishing when we consider that since August, 1914, American investors have been called upon to absorb in addition over $1,740,000,000 of European war loans and approximately $1,300,000,000 of American securities formerly held abroad." [108]

The chief effect of the war upon established American corporations seeking funds through new security issues was to force them to pay higher interest rates. Large corporations had to compete with foreign governments, which had been constantly increasing the rate that they would pay. While banks were lending at comparatively low rates, the investment market was looking for a higher yield. Railroads were not bidding strongly for investment funds because their business in 1915 was depressed and as yet had not started to share in the prosperity that affected a few industries. Tremendous speculation in stocks of munitions and automobile companies induced industrial combinations and new corporations. And early in 1916 municipal bonds and public securities generally were popular because they were tax exempt.

Particularly depressing for investment bankers was the state of the market for railroad securities. There was no demand for this staple commodity. The diagnosis of Lewis G. Franklin, speaking before the Society of Railway Financial Officers, was that railroads had an excess of bonded debt in relation to common stock, and although the carriers needed new financing, public prejudice against railroad securities raised difficult problems.[109]

A few new railroad bond offerings were sold, however. Kuhn, Loeb placed several large issues. In 1915 it underwrote two, one for the Illinois Central and one for the Baltimore & Ohio; the latter, for $60 million, was promptly oversubscribed. In 1915 also as part of an agreement under an earlier syndicate formed with Kidder, Peabody and the Central Trust Company of New York, Kuhn, Loeb took up an option on the remainder of an issue of gold notes of the Brooklyn Rapid Transit subway system, amounting to $20 million.[110]

108. Anderson, "The Effect of the War on New Security Issues," 120–30.
109. *The Commercial & Financial Chronicle*, XCIX (September 19, 1914), 785–86.
110. *The New York Times*, October 7, 1915.

Most important were this firm's services for the Pennsylvania Railroad. In February and June 1915, Kuhn, Loeb bought two of the road's bond issues, the first for nearly $50 million, for which it paid in full by the largest check up to that time ever drawn in the United States; and the second, for $65 million, also paid for by one check.[111] Still another service that Kuhn, Loeb performed for this railroad in 1915 was the conversion into dollar bonds of an issue that it originally had floated in Paris in 1906, the first American railroad issue listed on the Paris Bourse. At the time this marketing had been considered a great achievement. The French now wished to sell it in the United States in order to build up their credits here. In this transaction Kuhn, Loeb placed some $37 million in this country. Two years later the firm placed another $60 million bond issue for the railroad.[112]

Despite Kuhn, Loeb's success in selling the Pennsylvania's bond offerings, most railroad securities remained depressed, and new issues were difficult to sell. The railroads were in "a desperate plight," *The Commercial & Financial Chronicle* reported early in 1915, "their earnings shrinking and their credit impaired."[113] The roads' operators and the investment bankers who had financed and helped manage the lines were not entirely without blame for the critical condition in which this industry found itself. An even more important consideration, according to this conservative weekly, was excessive government interference and the threat of even more federal intervention. Burdensome regulations, low rates, wage increases, and climbing operating and replacement costs combined to limit profits and contribute to severe declines in the price of railroad issues. The devaluation of railroad securities became so critical that in 1917 the Comptroller of the Currency did not require national banks holding these issues to record on their books the full extent of their losses.[114]

Convinced that their interests were being threatened, the holders of railroad securities organized themselves as the National Association of Owners of Railroad Securities. In May 1917, 300 of them, representing individuals, insurance companies, and savings banks, met in Baltimore. The group represented almost 18 percent ($3 billion) of the total amount of securities issued by all American railroads (see Exhibit 6).

111. A spokesman for J. S. Bache & Co. commented that the $50 million Pennsylvania bond issue of February 1915 had been subscribed for five times over and that 80 percent of the money that had been ready to take up the issue was idle and seeking employment. *The Magazine of Wall Street*, XV (February 20, 1915), 307.
112. Adler, *Schiff*, II, 263–64. In 1918, after restrictions on private financing had been relaxed, Kuhn, Loeb marketed an additional $50 million issue for the Pennsylvania.
113. *The Commercial & Financial Chronicle*, C (January 9, 1915), 84.
114. U.S. Treasury, *Annual Report, 1917*, 538.

Exhibit 6. Distribution of railroad securities, 1917

By individuals outright, numbering about 1,000,000, owning in excess of	$10,000,000,000
By life insurance companies with 46,000,000 policies in force	1,550,000,000
By savings banks, with 10,000,000 depositors	847,000,000
By fire, marine, casualty and surety companies	649,000,000
By benevolent societies, colleges, charitable institutions and schools	350,000,000
By trust companies, state and national banks	865,000,000
In channels not enumerated, mostly abroad	2,739,000,000
Total	$17,000,000,000

Source: Walter McNaughton, "Organizing the Railroad Investor," *The Magazine of Wall Street,* XX (June 9, 1917), 308.

S. Davies Warfield, president of the Continental Trust Company of Baltimore, addressing the meeting, pointed out that the ICC would have to increase rates in order to offset rising costs; and he also warned of public hostility: "Through years of abuse of the railroads a 'state of mind' has been created which seems to forbid the consideration, in a spirit of fairness, of questions of vital consequence to the railroads and those who in good faith have invested their money in their securities." [115]

The final blow came near the end of 1917, when the government leased the roads. A majority of the IBA considered this step an ideological and practical catastrophe. The Committee on Railroad Securities recommended that the association put itself "squarely on record" as opposed to public ownership of railroads or permanent public operation and in favor of an early return to private ownership under such altered methods of regulation as would ensure sound railroad credit and an adequate transportation system.[116]

A profit squeeze comparable to that in railroad operations also had hurt public utilities and had led to a similarly inefficient state of operations. Complaints over rates and services, moreover, had made these companies "favorite targets for sneers and savage criticisms from large parts of the public and the press." In the war situation, when their services were extended, they had difficulty attracting investment capital, and federal aid was advocated in some quarters for both railroads and public utilities.[117]

The securities of domestic companies profiting most from the

115. Walter McNaughton, "Organizing the Railroad Investor," *The Magazine of Wall Street,* XX (June 9, 1917), 307–09.
116. IBA, *Proceedings . . . 1918,* 36.
117. U.S. Treasury, *Annual Report, 1917,* 540.

war were the so-called "War Brides." These issues boomed, and financial analysts, at first quite forthright in welcoming opportunities for profit-making in these issues, soon became more wary. "The public has been warned by newspapers, magazines, bankers, brokers, in fact by nearly all conservatively thinking people, to beware of these skyrocketing stocks, and the warning seems to have finally taken effect to a certain extent," observed a writer for *The Magazine of Wall Street*. "A frequent nightmare of the holder of a war stock has been a sudden cessation of hostilities resulting in a dizzy drop in the securities of the munition companies." [118]

Whether securities were good for the long pull depended largely on whether the issuers had had the foresight to get "cast iron clauses in their contracts, providing against cancellation of any of their orders." Bethlehem Steel had had such foresight, and its prices were said to have been figured to yield profits of at least a modest 30 percent. And if the war should end at once, its profits for the next two or three years would be $500 a share. Many others were equally fortunate. "New companies are being formed to get into what might be called the American end of the war game. . . . Do the securities of any of these companies look attractive as a permanent investment? We are inclined to answer this in the affirmative," remarked a writer for *The Magazine of Wall Street* in November 1915.[119]

The reporter's optimism proved more than justified. As the war continued, the nation's wealth increased "with wonderful rapidity," and the world acknowledged America's new role in international finance. "From present indications," the Treasury reported at the end of 1916, "it is probable that we will be required to finance not only our own enterprises, our preparations to make ourselves a formidable and therefore respected power, and the commerce which is unfolding for us on this hemisphere, but also the endless complications and demands of readjustment and reestablishment that will follow the close of the great war." [120] *The Magazine of Wall Street* editorialized at length on the great importance of America's transformation from debtor to creditor nation.[121]

Investment bankers were fully conscious of the decisive role they had played in that transformation. They had participated in all the great international transactions that helped make the United States the financial leader of the world. They had contributed much to the Allied war effort, had assisted the huge expansion in America's foreign trade, and had helped to expedite and finance the preparedness program. These accomplishments, together with their leader-

---

118. M. Frederick Lewis, "Europe's Golden Flood," *The Magazine of Wall Street*, XVII (November 27, 1915), 219.
119. *Ibid.*, 219–21, 277–78.
120. U.S. Treasury, *Annual Report, 1916*, 579–80.
121. *The Magazine of Wall Street*, XIX (November 11, 1916), 148–49.

ship in restoring order and stability to the securities markets after the closing of the exchanges, gave investment bankers added prestige and confidence. By the time Wilson appeared before Congress, on April 2, 1917, to ask for a declaration of war against Germany, the investment banking community was certain of its ability to satisfy the financial needs of both Europe and America.

11 The War Years, 1917–1919

Once the United States entered the war, on April 6, 1917, investment bankers faced a situation far different from that previously prevailing. Along with all other citizens they were expected to give primary attention to winning the war. Washington called on investment bankers and other financial intermediaries to assist in the task of raising money to carry on the conflict. To that demand men and firms in the industry responded strongly; in doing so, many of them played fleeting and unaccustomed roles.

The major change in the economic environment of investment bankers was the sheer size of the government's demand for funds. This fact, coupled with new procedures in distribution, forced them to alter familiar modes of behavior. During 1917 and 1918, through four Liberty Loans, the United States Treasury issued bonds totaling $17 billion. To that sum was added a $4.5 billion Victory Loan in April 1919. Such enormous calls on savings were unprecedented, and their impact was enhanced by the fact that they were all made in a two-year period.

Secretary of the Treasury William G. McAdoo sought advice from bankers, investment houses, other businessmen, and investors in all parts of the country.[1] The suggestions advanced covered such major matters as choice in size of issues, terms of payment, and methods of distribution. Many of the larger investment houses still believed that Wall Street was "no place for the average salaried man without a surplus." In December 1916 a writer for *The Magazine of Wall Street* confirmed this view. He advised uninitiated investors to stick to bonds issued in $100 denominations and regretted the relatively short supply of such offerings.[2] The Treasury's war bonds soon filled the need.

The first Liberty Loan Act, passed by Congress on April 24, 1917, authorized the Treasury to borrow up to $5 billion. Many men "experienced in large bond operations" believed that no more than $500 million or $1 billion could be sold in a single operation. McAdoo was not convinced by the bankers' arguments and decided to offer $2 billion. He believed that amount could be sold and that it was necessary for America's own needs, plus those of foreign governments to which Congress had just authorized credit extensions.

At the outset subscriptions lagged. "Investors were temporarily paralyzed by the idea of raising $5,000,000,000 for bonds, in addition to being called upon to pay very heavy current taxes," the

---

1. U.S. Treasury, *Annual Report, 1917* (Washington, 1918), 6.
2. Roger H. Woods, "Investment Situation and the Small Investor," *The Magazine of Wall Street*, XIX (December 23, 1916), 369–71.

Treasury reported.³ "The idea held by many optimists that the Liberty Loan would practically sell itself and that the popular rush to subscribe would result in a heavy oversubscription has had to be abandoned. The U.S. Treasury Department, especially, has all along been a victim of overconfidence in regard to the practical methods of floating the loan. Uncertainty in regard to details, such as the maturity of the bonds, the terms of conversion into a later issue bearing a higher rate of interest, and the face value of the smallest bonds, has tended to restrict subscriptions," a financial writer commented.⁴

The Treasury immediately decided to mount an intensive nationwide sales effort.⁵ Advertisements and thousands of spokesmen emphasized the security, high yield, and probable appreciation of the new Liberty bonds. Established techniques were put aside. Instead of selling substantial amounts of large denominations for holding in relatively few hands, the government issued bonds in small denominations, utilized war saving stamps extensively, and permitted installment payments. All the foregoing "new" departures were designed to appeal to individuals not considered potential investors since the Civil War days of Jay Cooke.

So successful was the campaign that the amount offered was oversubscribed by one-half, much of the excess coming from New York City. The eventual popularity of the loan was attributed in part to the widespread adoption of the partial payment plan, similar to the one used for several years by at least one investment house. "Bankers, businessmen, bond houses, newspapers, press associations, and citizens generally cooperated in a great movement that vibrated with energy and patriotism and swept the country from coast to coast in the greatest bond-selling campaign ever launched by any nation," reported the Treasury.⁶

An even more comprehensive appeal was instituted for the second Liberty bond drive, launched on October 1, 1917. The marketing of this and subsequent loans was entrusted to the War Loan Organization (WLO), organized in April 1917. Assistant Treasury Secretary Russell C. Leffingwell, later a partner in J. P. Morgan & Co., supervised the agency's activities. The drive itself was directed by Lewis B. Franklin of the Guaranty Trust Co. and, at the time, president of the Investment Bankers Association (IBA). Special effort was made to reach the prosperous, well-to-do, but not wealthy owners of property who had responded sluggishly to the first drive. Special messages were directed to the farmers of the West and

3. U.S. Treasury, *Annual Report, 1917*, 6.
4. *The Magazine of Wall Street*, XX (May 26, 1917), 219.
5. U.S. Treasury, *Annual Report, 1917*, 6.
6. Gardiner S. Dresser, "The Liberty Loan and the Partial Payment Plan," *The Magazine of Wall Street*, XX (July 7, 1917), 461; U.S. Treasury, *Annual Report, 1917*, 6.

South.⁷ The same general advertising and sales techniques were used in the remaining drives, and all were oversubscribed.

The Treasury labeled the successful sale of its $4.5 billion Victory Loan of March 1919 "the greatest financial achievement in all history and a wonderful manifestation of the strength and purpose of the American people." ⁸ The campaign was without parallel. "Every avenue of publicity and propaganda" was used. And although the final drive was launched after the close of the war, the loan was oversubscribed, again in the face of predictions of failure.⁹

Distribution of the securities began with their transmittal by the Treasury to the Federal Reserve banks, which passed them on to the ultimate sellers, namely, commercial banks, investment houses, brokerage firms, and other financial intermediaries. The sales force included volunteer amateurs as well as professional investment bankers, most of whom were experienced bond dealers. The IBA looked on the whole program as its particular province, cooperating heartily with the Treasury and other officials in planning and executing the drives. Not surprisingly, some members of the association believed that they should be paid a selling commission, particularly since their own business was being curtailed by the war and also because Britain paid one. No such concession was granted to American bankers.

Participation in this major selling job familiarized investment bankers not only with the use of high-pressure selling techniques but also with a tremendous number of new potential buyers of securities. Whereas bankers had estimated the bond market in 1917 at 350,000 individuals, the number subscribing to the first Liberty Loan was over 4 million and was much larger for the second, third, fourth, and fifth loans — 9.4, 18.4, 22.8, and 11.8 million, respectively.¹⁰ War bonds provided millions of Americans with their first experience in owning intangible property, and they soon learned that "money could be made by the simple process of holding paper securities until they went up in value." ¹¹

Because of recent investigations and laws, the administration originally had hesitated to call on Wall Street for assistance in distributing Liberty bonds, but it soon changed its attitude. Investment bankers were called to serve the Treasury's special wartime agencies, such as the WLO; the National War Savings Committee, established in November 1917 to promote the sale of thrift stamps and war savings certificates; and the Liberty Loan Committees, one of

7. William T. Connors, "Striking Features of the New Liberty Loan," *The Magazine of Wall Street*, XX (September 29, 1917), 857.
8. U.S. Treasury, *Annual Report, 1918,* 18.
9. *Ibid., 1919,* 70.
10. *Ibid., 1918,* and *ibid., 1919, passim.*
11. Benjamin Ginzburg, "Wall Street Under the New Deal," *The North American Review*, CCXLV (Spring 1938), 70.

which was organized in each Federal Reserve district. The purpose of these committees, which operated through local, state, city, and county subgroups, was to help the Treasury sell its loans. They publicized the drives, accepted subscriptions, and provided facilities for receiving, exchanging, and converting bonds from one issue to another. Investment bankers participated in all these organizations. Frank A. Vanderlip headed the National War Savings Committee, the seventy-year-old Jacob H. Schiff took an active part in various Liberty Loan committees, as did Thomas W. Lamont, George F. Baker, and other prominent financiers. The Treasury's choice of these men, many of whom had been recently criticized by the Pujo Committee, was, in the words of a writer for *The Magazine of Wall Street,* "a signal recognition of the importance and necessity of the financial district and financial leaders in the flotation of the Liberty Loan."[12]

The practices of Kidder, Peabody & Co. illustrate how a major investment banking house promoted the sale of Liberty bonds. Anticipating the first offering, the firm sent out letters to its clients on April 27, 1917, making an interim offer of short-term government notes:[13]

If you intend to purchase some of the long-term $3\frac{1}{2}$'s, when issued, and have the money on hand now, we suggest your purchasing Treasury Notes which will be received in payment for the Bonds, and which will yield in the meantime 3%.

We have bought of the Secretary of the Treasury and have on hand $10,000,000. of the Treasury Notes, and shall be glad to let you have such an amount as you may wish at cost to us.

Three days later the firm sent a follow-up letter, emphasizing the fact that Liberty bonds were *"free from all taxation"* and that Kidder, Peabody was prepared to furnish its own "participation receipts for smaller amounts" than the stated denomination of the notes.[14] The firm employed the same practices in subsequent loans, actively promoting all of them.

A major concern of the Treasury, financial intermediaries, and investors alike was that several factors tended to depress prices of many nongovernment securities. The huge volume of the Liberty Loans was enough to absorb a large proportion of investible funds. In addition, the tax-free feature of government issues in the context of the new and seemingly high income taxes led to selling of nongovernments and further decline in prices. Another depressing factor was that existing federal and state regulation, plus the imposition

12. Barnard Powers, "Wall Street's Patriotism," *The Magazine of Wall Street,* XX (June 23, 1917), 363.
13. Kidder, Peabody & Co., "Circulars," [1895–1927] (10 vols., Baker Library), II, 193.
14. *Ibid.,* II, 194.

of higher labor costs by the Adamson Act and the United States Railroad Administration, appeared to limit profits of railroads; investors tended to sell securities of carriers for the purpose of putting their money into unregulated industrials and government bonds that offered greater prospects for profit.[15]

To cushion the impact of such shifts in investor preference, the Federal Reserve Board adopted a course of action that aroused still further fears. It endeavored to place Liberty Loans at times, and under conditions, that would cause least disturbance to established financial markets, yet would result in the highest return to the government. This led investment bankers to believe that the Federal Reserve Board was "systematically and methodically" taking charge of the money market.[16]

Financial writers sought to reassure those who feared that Liberty bonds, being tax free, would so appeal to investors that they would put money in them and curtail their businesses. "There seems to be nothing in this contention and the possible danger of adoption of such a course has been pretty well dissipated," one author observed in June 1917.[17]

To assess the impact of the Liberty Loans, *The Magazine of Wall Street* sought the views of Charles E. Mitchell, head of the National City Co. In ordinary times this affiliate was the largest distributor of investment securities in the country. Mitchell foresaw that the effect of the Liberty Loan flotation would be a period of "sound inflation," with the Federal Reserve System ensuring credit and currency elasticity even in the face of heavy borrowing. He paid a tribute to investment bankers, who were giving up their ordinary business to push the loan. The one commercial reward to them would come, he correctly expected, from "the development of a large, new army of investors in this country who have never heretofore known what it means to own a coupon bond and who may in the future be developed into savers and bond buyers."[18] The incoming president of the IBA, Warren S. Hayden, phrased the same idea more succinctly: in encouraging thrift, and strongly endorsing bonds as a form of investment, he observed, "the government will have done in a year or two what our private enterprise as it was before the war could not have done in decades."[19]

Recognizing that the Liberty Loans were disturbing normal capital flows, the government assumed the responsibility for making

15. [James H. Oliphant & Co.] *The Problem of Depreciated Investment Securities* (New York [1920]), 13–14.
16. Connors, "Striking Features of the New Liberty Loan," 856.
17. Richard H. Tingley, "Lessons of Other Wars," *The Magazine of Wall Street,* XX (June 9, 1917), 297.
18. Charles E. Mitchell, "Sound Inflation," *The Magazine of Wall Street,* XX (June 9, 1917), 295–96.
19. Investment Bankers Association, *Proceedings . . . 1917,* 208.

adequate amounts of money available to essential industries and to farmers. Some of the measures adversely affected investment bankers, others provided new opportunities for profitable service.

To provide long-term loans to farmers, Congress had passed the Federal Farm Loan Act in July 1916. The law divided the country into twelve districts, each with its own land bank. Although authorized by the government, these banks were to be financed largely by private capital. Partly because the commercial banks at first opposed the establishment of the new institutions, the initial public subscription to their capital stock was so inadequate that the government was forced to supply most of the initial funds.[20]

In 1918 investment bankers were finally called in to give counsel and aid in getting the banks' bonds distributed to private investors. Benjamin H. Griswold, head of Alexander Brown & Sons, was asked to form a "national group of the most conservative investment houses in every section of the country which would be willing to say the bonds were good and willing to sell them to their customers."[21] The group he assembled included his firm, Brown Brothers; Harris, Forbes & Co.; Lee, Higginson; and the National City Company. Their endorsement proved to be effective, and they placed the bonds satisfactorily.

To mitigate the impact of the changed financial conditions on selected segments of the economy Congress created the War Finance Corporation (WFC) in April 1918. Its direction was entrusted to William P. G. Harding of the Federal Reserve Board, and its $500 million authorized capital was to be subscribed by the United States Treasury as needed. The WFC was potentially competitive with the investment banking industry in that, through commercial banks, it was empowered to supply credit to essential war industries that might have used the established capital markets. It also was authorized to offer credit to savings banks that might otherwise have had to sell their investments in an unfavorable market. In exceptional cases, the law stipulated, the WFC could furnish direct loans to essential industries that were allegedly being discriminated against by commercial banks.

The first two services, credit to industry through banks and directly to savings banks, turned out to be used only to a slight extent. The Secretary of the Treasury attributed this fact to the psychological effect of mere availability and to the services of the Federal Reserve System. By October 31, 1918, only $140 million in capital had been called up and $67.7 million had been lent, of which $64.7 million had been for "exceptional" direct loans. The secretary believed that the project, which was an entirely new de-

20. U.S. Treasury, *Annual Report, 1917,* 38.
21. Frank R. Kent, *The Story of Alexander Brown & Sons* (Baltimore, 1925), 189–90.

parture in the financial operations of the government, had proved successful.[22] In spite of its limited use, the corporation was continued after the war's end, and its functions were extended to include financing of foreign trade.

Before it acted in this new area the WFC took a step that proved to be of great assistance to important clients of the investment banking industry. Leaders of the corporation rationalized that the scope of its functions could include extending credit to railroads in the interim period when Congress had failed to pass an appropriation bill with essential aid for them. The WFC stepped into the breach and advanced the carriers $50 million. The move immediately brought forth the "prompt and patriotic cooperation" of the nation's investment bankers.[23]

During the years 1917 and 1918 investment bankers also aided the federal government in its effort to control or direct the allocation of private investment capital. The objective was to prevent its diversion into enterprises deemed unnecessary to the war effort. In September 1917 a subcommittee of the New York Liberty Loan Committee, composed of leading bankers, had tried voluntarily to limit funds available to the stock market, to provide those needed to protect the market, and to protect Liberty Loans. Its device was to peg the call money rate at 6 percent to brokers and hold down the supply, giving precedence to the needs of the government and commercial borrowers. Collateral loans to brokers were required to have a 30 percent margin in contrast to the previous 20 percent. The stock market thus was restricted as a competitor for funds, yet it was not strangled.[24]

Key men in controlling the nation's capital flows deemed the voluntary measures inadequate. Addressing the IBA's November 1917 convention, Treasury Secretary McAdoo and Reserve Board Governor James F. Curtis both pointed out the government's need for funds in competition with business. Curtis spoke particularly on the need to control capital issues.

At once the IBA responded affirmatively. Retiring president Franklin urged members to join a "Suicide Club" to make effective the proposed restriction on investments, recognizing that they would be supporting a policy that would severely cut into their regular business.[25] "The activities of investment banking have paused, and we may fairly expect that while the war goes on they will be intermittent and restricted," incoming President Warren S. Hayden observed. "It is only necessary to compare the saving capacity of the

22. U.S. Treasury, *Annual Report, 1918,* 57–58.
23. *Ibid., 1919,* 105.
24. Benjamin M. Anderson, *Economics and the Public Welfare: Financial and Economic History of the United States, 1914–1946* (New York, 1949), 36.
25. IBA, *Proceedings . . . 1917,* 39.

country with its war requirement to be convinced that as a rule strictly private demands for fixed capital must be denied. Investment bankers understand this and their attitude toward the situation is not reluctant submission to superior force but rather recognition that derangement of their business is incidental to that victory for the nation which for them, as for all lovers of their country, is the paramount aim." [26]

The convention resolved that capital conservation was necessary. President Hayden immediately appointed a committee to study the question and to confer with other organizations and government officials on appropriate measures.[27] Allen B. Forbes of Harris, Forbes, who was a member of this group, became a member of the government's committee when that was established. The IBA's proposal had the support of the American Bankers Association and the New York Stock Exchange.[28]

Implementing the IBA's suggestions, the Federal Reserve Board (FRB), early in 1918, set up an informal Capital Issues Committee (CIC). It was composed of three FRB members and an advisory group made up of representative commercial and investment bankers. Similar committees were organized in each Federal Reserve district to assist in deciding local cases. All served without pay.

The CIC was given formal status in April 1918 under Title II of the War Finance Corporation Act.[29] The British had had such a committee since 1915, when the London Stock Exchange reopened. The functions of the CIC, which had no enforcement powers, were to review proposed industry and government capital issues. If they were for more than the $100,000 minimum amount, it was to determine whether they qualified as necessary for the war effort. New issues, moreover, had to give evidence of being likely to be profitable, and management had to be of good character. "The operation of this little-known organization was of deep significance, since it constituted a general regulation of both the quality and the quantity of the demand for capital," one observer later noted.[30]

The committee endeavored in its decision-making to develop a "scientific method of dealing with applications" and "a scientific distribution of labor." It reported cooperation from all quarters.[31]

Illustrative of the way prospectuses for new issues were phrased

26. *Ibid.*, 205.
27. *Ibid.*, 152.
28. *The New York Times,* March 8, 1918.
29. "Report of the Capital Issues Committee," *Federal Reserve Bulletin,* IV (August 1, 1918), 704–08. See also Allen B. Forbes, "Supervision of Security Issues by the United States," *The Nation,* CVI (March 28, 1918), 372; Woodbury Willoughby, *The Capital Issues Committee and the War Finance Corporation* (Baltimore, 1934).
30. George W. Edwards, *The Evolution of Finance Capitalism* (London, 1938), 309.
31. "Report of the Capital Issues Committee," 706–07.

to satisfy the requirements of the WFC and CIC are these excerpts from one put out by Kidder, Peabody, for a $50 million 7 percent Serial Gold Note offering of the Bethlehem Steel Corporation, dated July 15, 1918.[32]

> The War Finance Corporation has agreed to make a direct advance to Bethlehem Steel Corporation through the purchase of $20,000,000 of the Notes, which will be used to complete certain construction undertaken at the request of the Government and required for the production of commercial steel products essential to the Government's war program.
>
> As a result of the present financing, the liquidation of $37,600,000 British Treasury Bills, due February 1, 1919, and appropriations from earnings, the Corporation will be placed in funds sufficient to complete the construction program . . . , provide adequate additional working capital, and pay off the $50,000,000 [maturing notes]. . . .

To this application the CIC gave qualified endorsement. In its enumeration of facts about the company's business, Kidder, Peabody pointed to the spectacular increases in orders on hand. These had grown from $14.4 million in 1905 to $46.5 million in 1914, then jumped to $453 million three years later and currently stood at $650 million. Less than $12\frac{1}{2}$ percent of the latter were for war materials. The CIC passed the application as "not incompatible with the national interest, but without approval of legality, validity, worth or security."

Notable about this issue were its terms. The company had to pay 7 percent interest, and the notes were offered at $99\frac{1}{2}$ to 97, depending on their duration, which was for one to five years. This was a remarkably high interest rate for a company booming from war orders, but a reflection of the prevailing high cost of capital.

Prior to and during the sale of the fourth Liberty Loan, in September 1918, the CIC strongly restricted private financing. It announced that it would not pass any application respecting the sale or offer for sale of shares or securities during the period from September 15 until after the close of the campaign, except applications deemed urgently necessary. It asked investment houses, brokers, corporations, and others offering unsold portions of security issues already approved by the committee to withdraw them during the period. This action was not intended to prohibit counter sales or the ordinary business of stock exchanges. The IBA telegraphed its approval.[33]

Carter Glass, who in 1918 succeeded McAdoo as Secretary of the Treasury, gave the CIC a strong encomium for its work. It had performed, he declared, "a most important function during the war and served an imperative purpose in conserving investment capital,

32. Kidder, Peabody & Co., "Circulars," III, 56.
33. *I.B.A. of A. Bulletin,* VII (October 1, 1918), 20.

labor, and material" for use of the government and essential industries.³⁴ By December 31, 1918, when it stopped active operation, the CIC had passed on over 3,000 applications involving new securities valued at more than $3.7 billion. The total amount disapproved was nearly $920 million. Not surprisingly, new corporate issues dropped from a peak of $2.2 billion in 1916 to $1.5 billion a year later, then to $1.3 billion in 1918.³⁵

The CIC interpreted its duties as extending beyond simple discouragement of the flotation of nonessential or poorly timed issues. Of broader and in the long run of much more lasting significance were its efforts to control the sale of fraudulent securities. The experience of the CIC subsequently was cited repeatedly as proof of the urgent need for a federal disclosure law.

As soon as the first Liberty Loan was marketed, unscrupulous promoters began to take advantage of credulous new investors. Some bought the new bonds from naive owners at less than current prices, paying in cash or in other securities often found to be worthless, a kind of behavior reminiscent of post–Civil War days. The practice became so notorious as to attract the attention of the government as well as banking groups.³⁶ Newspapers, Liberty Loan committees, and investment bankers all warned the public about this continuing danger.

The CIC rationalized that a fraudulent issue was not "compatible with the national interest" and that protection against such practices came under its jurisdiction. The IBA, furthermore, recommended that the CIC take direct action against the increasing numbers of nonessential and fraudulent issues: "The traffic in exchanging Liberty Bonds for worthless oil stock, industrial and mining shares, has reached a point almost unbelievable in its magnitude." ³⁷

To combat such "traffic," the director of the CIC's Enforcement Division proposed to the head of a special IBA group that in each Federal Reserve district an "Economic Vigilance Committee" be organized. The new body would have at least one member in every community to represent it directly. He would obtain and distribute "information respecting the operation of persons and corporations offering securities without the authority of the Capital Issues Committee." ³⁸

Steps for enforcement were approved by Secretary McAdoo, and the CIC press announcement read: "It should be understood by the people everywhere that while the motive may be different, it is as unpatriotic to buy securities not passed by the Capital Issues Com-

34. U.S. Treasury, *Annual Report, 1919,* 107.
35. U.S. Bureau of the Census, *Historical Statistics of the United States, Colonial Times to 1957* (Washington, 1960), 658.
36. U.S. Treasury, *Annual Report, 1918,* 93; ibid., *1919,* 95–96.
37. *I.B.A. of A. Bulletin,* VII (October 1, 1918), 23.
38. *Ibid.,* 21.

mittee as it is to sell them, and that in no case is the country served by exchanging Liberty Bonds for the stocks or bonds of any private enterprise." Members of the CIC were confident that with the assistance of the Department of Justice, United States Railroad Administration, Postmaster General, War Industries Board, Fuel Administration, and other government and outside agencies, they would "be able to break up speedily the traffic in unauthorized issues" which had "assumed such proportions as to be a real menace." [39]

Before effective action could be taken, the war ended; but in its final report to the Senate the CIC urgently called for continued conservation of capital in peace as well as in war. It warned the public of "the enormous losses sustained by the nation through the sale of worthless and fraudulent securities." Furthermore, it strongly advocated that Congress establish "adequate machinery to put a stop to this traffic." The CIC had in preparation a further report recommending a law to prevent "existing abuses." A covering comment by Secretary Glass also proposed immediate and speedy legislation to protect the millions of buyers of Liberty bonds who were being swindled by unscrupulous promoters.[40] The New York Stock Exchange and the IBA joined Glass and the CIC in stressing this responsibility and urged immediate congressional action to protect investors against false and misleading security advertising.[41]

Unfortunately, federal legislators chose to disregard the recommendations of the financial community at this time. This action left regulation of fraud where it had been before the outbreak of the war, to "blue sky" commissions and agencies in the various states.

In addition to fraudulent securities, financial intermediaries also perceived, with varying degrees of clarity, other areas for concern. Under the pressures before and after America's entry into the war, some brokerage firms began to recognize that they were inefficiently run. As early as the stock market boom in 1916, their machinery for handling sales became so clogged that the processing of orders nearly stopped on some days. "The larger wire houses presented the appearance of gambling hells in the morning, just before the cards and chips had been swept away by the attendants," according to one contemporary observer. "From a booking [sic] view point, very few brokerage firms had any conception of just how they 'stood,' and it was a fortunate firm whose clerks kept them up-to-date." [42]

This same analyst also saw other weaknesses in brokerage practices. "The firms which pay a real salary for the work done by their

39. *Ibid.*, 22.
40. "Capital Issues Committee Terminates Its Work," *Federal Reserve Bulletin*, V (January 1, 1919), 18–19.
41. IBA, *Proceedings . . . 1918,* 72–73.
42. Robert L. Smitley, "Wall Street's Red Tape," *The Magazine of Wall Street*, XIX (February 3, 1917), 592.

human machinery are really very few," he commented. "The so-called bonus and profit sharing plans are installed to protect the broker, for when times become dull again employees must be dismissed, salaries reduced to a proportionate consideration with business done, and they who have received the bonus are worse off than before. In plain words, the brokerage business as it is conducted today is carried on with make-shift machinery and there is no stability. This condition steps from clerk to partner to firm and then to customer." Although this analyst perceived the human problems and weak practices, he failed to see how machines could be utilized to improve conditions. "Electrical devices, typewriting machines which add, subtract and multiply, figure interest and make copies for every department are theoretically wonderful but actually most impracticable," he wrote.

Evasive tactics by some investment firms on commissions might have earned, but did not receive, criticism at the time. Although the investment bankers' usual sources of income were curtailed during the war, some managers found ways of tapping new ones. One of them was to obtain a special commission for negotiating the sale of an issue, a provision that did not appear on the face of the contract and varied from $\frac{1}{2}$ of 1 percent to 3 percent. Especially in 1917 and 1918 these "secret commissions" were quite customary. They had the advantage of giving the bond house an extra profit of which its own salesmen and its associates were unaware. The issuer had the advantage of a "capital expense" that it did not need to amortize and could enter in its accounting records under names other than "Bond Discount"; "Legal Expenses" was a ruse often used to disguise this charge.[43]

During the war years, however, investment bankers made several important and lasting changes in their own practices. One of the most important of these was the great expansion in the size of selling syndicates. The need to reach a broad market for the enormous and unfamiliar issues floated for foreign and domestic governments induced the managers of underwriting syndicates to build up nationwide organizations. "It was obviously impossible," one financial observer commented in 1921, "for a banker or combination of local dealers to maintain staffs sufficiently large to extend into every section of the country where there were surplus funds, and therefore the assistance of out-of-town dealers was obtained. In this way, the countrywide syndicates now commonly formed came into existence."[44]

---

43. T. Kenneth Haven, *Investment Banking under the Securities and Exchange Commission* (Ann Arbor, 1940), 32fn.b.

44. Graham Ashmead, "Syndicate Management and Operation: The Machinery for Distribution and Marketing of Industrial Securities," *Trust Companies*, XXXIII (September 1921), 232.

Exigencies of war finance also accentuated the trend for commercial banks to establish affiliates to carry on investment banking functions, a forerunner of the much greater swell that soon was to follow. One factor behind this change was the experience that these banks had in distributing Liberty Loans. They had become familiar both with distribution techniques and with investors who later became customers, when the banks elected to continue the distribution function for nongovernment securities. In New York the Guaranty Trust Company's great success in organizing its activities to sell Liberty bonds contributed to its later leadership in underwriting. Such institutions continued to develop the business of originating, underwriting, and distributing security issues. In reaction against specialization, numerous other banks also established bond departments and became "department-store" banks, advertising "complete banking facilities." [45]

Opportunities in the rapidly expanding securities business prompted some men to form new houses. In response to one of the growing financial markets in the southern United States, for example, Caldwell & Co. was established in Nashville, Tennessee, in 1917. The firm specialized in southern municipal bonds. It prospered for a time, although it started under the inauspicious circumstance of having to compete for funds with Liberty Loans, and its principal commodity was relatively less acceptable to the general public than were northern bonds. It soon carried on an active brokerage and underwriting business through the New York branch of Kidder, Peabody, the latter firm often carrying Caldwell's participations until the new house could find a market for them. In conjunction with its operations, Caldwell established a commercial bank, the Bank of Tennessee, in which the investment house often required that customers deposit the proceeds of securities sales.[46]

Some distributing firms of the 1920's had their origin in associations formed solely to sell Liberty bonds. For instance, the Federal Securities Corporation was organized in Chicago in 1919 by five individuals who had been in the investment business for many years. The new firm not only had a special women's department, headed by the former vice chairman of the local Women's Liberty Loan organization, but also one to specialize in selling securities to Chicago's foreign-born investors. Led by Felix J. Streyckmans, former manager of the foreign language division of the Federal Reserve's seventh district, the latter department was designed to cater to a special "class of patronage" that never had been "systematically

---

45. W. Nelson Peach, *The Security Affiliates of National Banks* (Baltimore, 1941), 13, 32–33, 71–72.

46. John Berry McFerrin, *Caldwell and Company: A Southern Financial Empire* (Chapel Hill, 1939), 1, 11–12, 30–31.

solicited by any high grade investment house." The company soon became national in scope.⁴⁷

During the war, adjustment to loss of employees to the armed services and other activities became a major concern for many houses, but it was taken in stride. Because investment firms typically recruited young men, the departure of employees for military service caused some severe hardships. As replacements, investment houses had to hire inexperienced personnel, unfamiliar with the services and standards that their employers had maintained.⁴⁸ For example, Kidder, Peabody's turnover of clerks was substantial, about 65 leaving and over 125 being hired in the five years between 1914 and 1919.⁴⁹ The firm's loss by death of Frank E. Peabody, son of an original partner, came at a difficult time. Other houses were disrupted by partners' leaving to go to Washington to staff new government agencies. Herbert H. Lehman of Lehman Brothers, for instance, went to work for the War Industries Board under Bernard Baruch.⁵⁰

In spite of continued maladjustments, participation of members of the IBA in patriotic activities was a source of pride. "I dare say," observed President Hayden in 1917, "that from the floor of this convention we could obtain headquarters reports upon the Liberty Loan, Red Cross, conservation and camp morale campaigns in nearly every great center of the United States." ⁵¹ At that time 36 percent of the IBA's members were in the army.

In fact the wartime activities of investment bankers made IBA President Hayden optimistic about their future role. The services they provided were "indispensable to the public interest." "Very possibly," he said, "we shall come to look upon the history prior to 1917 as within the pioneer period of investment banking. It is to be expected that costs will be highest in the pioneer period and equally to be expected that costs will fall as market widens, system develops and risk decreases. . . . Here we stand, knowing what conditions have been; certain that deep-reaching changes are in the making; seeing the broadening base of future markets; looking toward the coming of a personnel of extraordinary efficiency [returning from the army]." The association would continue to give its counsel to government bodies "in affairs of which it had special means of knowledge." Members would conduct their own businesses according to the "best methods attainable." "I take it to be true," he added,

47. *The Commercial & Financial Chronicle*, CIX (August 23, 1919), 749–50.
48. A. E. Bryson, *Halsey, Stuart & Co. Inc., 1901–1937, 1938–1944: A History* . . . ([Chicago, 1937, 1945]), 11.
49. Kidder, Peabody & Co., "Record of Clerks," V.
50. [Lehman Brothers] *A Centennial: Lehman Brothers, 1850–1950* (New York, 1950), 33.
51. IBA, *Proceedings* . . . *1917,* 206.

"that the advantage of the public and of the vocation [of investment banking] lie together." [52]

Experience in distributing Liberty Loans revealed that some traditional investment banking functions could be bypassed, and not a few individuals were apprehensive that this example might be followed in corporate financing. A writer in *The World's Work* in 1918, however, reached the conclusion that investment bankers still would be needed for the "proper leading" of future investors, lest they "be abandoned to the temptations of the unprincipled promoter." Furthermore, after the war, foreign countries would be needing American financial aid and American investors would need the educational services of investment bankers who, probably, could place issues more cheaply than could others.[53]

By the close of the war investment bankers operated in a new environment, one only partly of their own making. The United States had become a major international financial power, and investment bankers were deeply committed in ways with which many had not been accustomed. Worldwide demand for goods pressured for America's increasing involvement.

Government assistance to, as well as regulation of, business had become well established, and although it then was tapering off, there were fears of its continuation. Industry had become more widely dispersed, and investment banking houses were proliferating. Industrial common stocks were becoming more popular, and security salesmanship was becoming high pressure.

Paul M. Warburg also found a change in the "quality and the quantity" of investors. "Where heretofore investment banking addressed itself primarily to the comparatively few possessed of large incomes, taxation today strikes so heavily at the revenues and inheritances of the so-called well-to-do classes, and interferes so drastically with the accumulation of investment funds on their part, that successful distribution of large volumes of new securities can only be carried on by following wealth into the millions of small rivulets and channels into which it now flows, and where it is less subjected to the exactions of the tax-collector." [54]

A vast new group of investors had been revealed throughout the land. "The war fervor . . . placed government bonds in the hands of millions of people who never before had possessed such instruments of credits," later wrote Harvard University's economic historian Edwin F. Gay. "They were not . . . educated in the use of credit; they simply received a new vision of its possibilities. The

---

52. *Ibid.,* 206–09.
53. "Merchants of Credit and the Pirates of Promotion," *The World's Work,* XXXVI (September 1918), 539.
54. Paul M. Warburg, "Some Problems of the Investment Banker," an address delivered before the Bond Club of New York, May 23, 1919, 3.

basis was thus laid for the vast and credulous post-war market for credit which culminated in the portentous speculation of 1928 and 1929." [55]

55. Edwin F. Gay, "The Great Depression," *Foreign Affairs,* X (July 1932), 533–34.

12 The Changing Investment and Financial Environment of the 1920's

The spectacular growth of the American economy during the 1920's provided investment bankers with a highly stimulating and expansive environment. The number of borrowers, both corporate and public and domestic and foreign, increased sharply, as did the number of investors, both actual and potential. The government's wartime bond drives had made the American people more securities-conscious than ever before. Their continued readiness to invest in stocks and bonds after the war provided investment bankers with the mass market necessary to absorb the unprecedented supply of domestic and foreign issues that were sold after 1922, when the nation started its recovery from a relatively brief but severe postwar depression. From early 1922 until the stock market collapse of October 1929, except for slight interruptions, most Americans enjoyed prosperity. The security markets flourished and investment bankers enjoyed an unprecedented volume of business. The number of firms in the industry increased significantly as did the volume of capital they employed.

The decade of the 1920's also witnessed important changes in the character of the securities markets. Some of these developments had been in the making before World War I, others grew out of the conflict itself, and still others were the result of postwar developments. Stocks, for example, became more popular than bonds; securities of new industries outranked those of railroads, and the distribution of foreign and repatriated issues grew appreciably. The increase in America's foreign trade, moreover, also called for new services from investment bankers and attracted the competition of other financial intermediaries. Many of these developments were beyond the investment bankers' control, but the changes they brought about caused investment houses to alter some of their traditional ways of doing business. The rapid rise of the United States as a capital exporter, the impressive growth of the economy, and the quick relaxation of government regulation after the war gave rise to a national psychology of optimism and confidence. Developments in the economy and practices in the securities markets became so extreme that by the end of the decade they turned the great stock market boom into a huge bust and invited federal investigation and regulation.

World War I had left the United States rich and physically unharmed. As Treasury Secretary Carter Glass said: "The impious hand of the enemy has not touched any part of her fair land and there are no waste places here to restore." The United States had become the world's banker. "Virtually all the nations on earth, large and small," looked to America for "credit or aid, of one kind or another."[1] No one doubted the country's ability to meet these demands. All that was needed, according to business and financial spokesmen, was sound, safe leadership in Washington.

The election of Warren G. Harding to the presidency in 1920 appeared to provide just what these advocates and millions of other Americans believed necessary: a return to the simpler, more settled and familiar times of prewar America. The country was tired of Wilsonian reform and idealism. Harding promised it release from both, and his landslide victory was widely applauded as a return to "safe" government in Washington. Four years later, after the voters had repulsed an even more serious threat to order and stability by returning Calvin Coolidge to the White House, Treasury Secretary Andrew W. Mellon reaffirmed the close association between sound government and prosperity. Together with many other conservatives, he congratulated the voters for rejecting the dangerous economic theories espoused by reformers and radicals who had supported the presidential bid of Robert M. La Follette, the Wisconsin Progressive. "The sober judgment of a great majority of our people has in the election just past repudiated these theories and expressed itself in favor of a constructive and orderly program of handling our governmental affairs," he reported. "It is only through work, economy, and sound policies that we have a right to expect true progress."[2]

The economic advance and prosperity to which Mellon referred were easily documented. In March 1921, when he was sworn into office, the nation was in a depression. Many of the wartime goals that Glass had cited in his last *Annual Report* as Secretary of the Treasury had been wiped out or drastically reduced. By 1924 the losses had been more than recouped and the country appeared to be well on its way to a "new era" of widespread and permanent prosperity. The total resources of all reporting banks, which had stood at about $53 billion in 1920 and fell to $50 billion the following year, started their upward climb in 1922 and continued in that direction for the rest of the decade, reaching some $72 billion in 1929. This rise of about 35 percent occurred at a time when the population was growing at less than half that rate. Total bank clearings at principal cities revealed a similar pattern. After a 1921 drop of some $90 billion from the previous year's all-time high of almost $440 billion, they, too, started to move up again in 1922, reaching almost $716 billion by 1929.[3]

1. U.S. Treasury, *Annual Report, 1919* (Washington, 1920), 1901.
2. *Ibid., 1924*, 1.
3. U.S. Bureau of the Census, *Historical Statistics of the United States, Colonial Times to 1957* (Washington, 1960), 624, 640.

The growth pattern of the nation's banks in the 1920's also showed important changes. The new characteristic of the era was combination and concentration in the larger cities. The Comptroller of the Currency commented on this development with approval. "Banking is following in the wake of the trend in business in general toward larger operating units with stronger capital funds and more experienced and highly trained management," he wrote in 1929. By that time some 250 metropolitan banks held over $33 billion in resources out of the national total of $72 billion. This growth had come through both mergers and generally increasing business.[4]

In contrast to the growth in resources, there had been a substantial decrease in the number of banks. Suspensions added significantly to the number. No large city bank failed in the 1920's, but 5,000 small country ones closed their doors, tying up approximately $1.5 billion in deposits. In seven states more than 40 percent of all the banks in existence in 1920 had failed. The suspension rate of state and private institutions (4,228) far exceeded that of the national banks (697). The greatest number of all bank failures occurred in the South (1,170), the Middle West (1,241), and West (1,572). The farm depression was the principal reason for most of these failures. Important too, however, was the growing trend toward concentration among local utility and industrial companies. These corporations previously had been the prime customers of country banks. In the 1920's the deposits of these businesses increasingly moved to the cities, where the parent or holding companies that owned or controlled them were headquartered.[5]

Another important development of the 1920's contributing to the decline of independent bank units was the growth of branch banking. In 1900 only 87 commercial banks had operated branches. By 1920 the number had grown to 530. The high point of the decade was reached in 1928, with 775 banks operating 3,138 branches.[6] The leader in this development was a Californian, A. P. Giannini, the son of Italian immigrants. In 1904 he founded the Bank of Italy in San Francisco, now the Bank of America. By the beginning of 1927 the bank operated 276 branches in 199 California communities.[7]

The most spectacular financial developments of the decade, however, occurred in the securities industry. They were the result of several circumstances, some indicating fundamental changes in financial practices. During the 1920's, as business profits rose, corporations increasingly relied on the security markets not only for their long-term capital requirements, but for their current needs as

---

4. U.S. Treasury, *Annual Report, 1929,* 679.
5. *Ibid., 1929,* 679–82; *Historical Statistics to 1957,* 624.
6. *Historical Statistics to 1957,* 635.
7. Marquis James and Bessie R. James, *Biography of a Bank: The Story of Bank of America, N.T. & S.A.* (New York, 1954), 198.

well. Rising profits, moreover, made many businesses less dependent than previously upon short-term bank credit. Demand deposits, the chief source of commercial bank loans, increased only slightly during the decade, those of all national banks climbing from $8.7 billion in 1921 to $10.9 billion in 1930.[8] Corporations either deposited their surplus earnings in savings banks, which paid interest on them, or invested them in the stock market. Commercial banks, faced with more funds than they could profitably employ in commercial loans, also turned to the stock market, making loans as well as buying securities. These developments, together with others, not the least of which was the desire of hundreds of thousands of Americans to get rich quickly by investing and speculating in securities, resulted in huge annual increases in the volume of new stock and bond offerings.

During the 1920's the yearly total issues of domestic corporate securities more than tripled, soaring from about $2.8 billion in 1920 to over $9 billion in 1929. Except for the 1921 slump, which resulted in about a $500 million decline from the previous year, the growth was continuous, with a rapid rise after 1925 (see Exhibit 7).

Exhibit 7. Corporate issues, by class of security, 1919–1929 (in millions)

Year	Bonds and notes	Stocks	Total
1919	1,122	1,546	2,668
1920	1,750	1,038	2,788
1921	1,994	275	2,269
1922	2,329	621	2,950
1923	2,430	736	3,166
1924	2,655	865	3,520
1925	2,975	1,247	4,222
1926	3,354	1,220	4,574
1927	4,769	1,738	6,507
1928	3,439	3,491	6,930
1929	2,620	6,757	9,377

Source: U.S. Bureau of the Census, *Historical Statistics of the United States, Colonial Times to 1957*, (Washington, 1960), 658

Until 1928 debt issues exceeded equities by far. In that year the two series came closer together, but in 1929 stocks finally exceeded bonds. The number of shares traded on the New York Stock Exchange during the 1920's also was generally at higher levels than it had been before. The first peak of the century was reached in 1919, when 317 million shares changed hands. The next year the

8. George Soule, *Prosperity Decade, from War to Depression: 1917–1929* (New York, 1947), 155.

figure dropped to 227 million, and in 1921 it fell still further, to 173 million. From then on, except for two small declines in 1923 and 1926, the number of shares traded grew steadily and quite spectacularly in 1928 and reached a high of over a billion shares in 1929 (see Exhibit 8).

The indexes of stock prices did more than register the brief recessions of the decade. They revealed other significant developments as well. One of the more important of these was the relative valuations investors placed on securities of different industries. During the 1920's rails fell in favor in relation to industrials and utilities. The greatest gain was registered by the latter. Not only did the index price of utility stocks increase steadily from 1920 to 1929, and spectacularly in 1928 and 1929, but it was also the only index that registered an advance during the 1921 slump (see Exhibit 8).

Exhibit 8. Index of common stock prices (1941–1943 = 10) and number of shares traded on New York Stock Exchange, 1919–1929

Year	Common stock prices				Number of shares traded (millions)
	Total	Industrial	Railroad	Utilities	
1919	8.78	7.13	22.94	14.79	317
1920	7.98	6.50	20.86	13.36	227
1921	6.86	5.07	20.15	14.18	173
1922	8.41	6.35	23.71	17.39	259
1923	8.57	6.54	23.45	18.11	236
1924	9.05	6.83	25.02	19.34	282
1925	11.15	8.69	29.21	23.28	454
1926	12.59	10.04	32.72	24.11	451
1927	15.34	12.53	38.17	27.63	577
1928	19.95	16.92	40.40	36.86	920
1929	26.02	21.35	46.15	59.33	1,125

Source: Historical Statistics to 1957, 657, 659.

The supply of securities came from both domestic and foreign sources. The formation of new domestic corporations increased, and old companies funded floating debt incurred during the prewar years and sought new funds for expansion.[9] Corporations that had

9. Joseph L. Snider, "Security Issues in the United States: 1909–1920," *The Review of Economic Statistics*, III (May 25, 1921), 100.

postponed marketing securities because of the restrictions imposed by the Capital Issues Committee now proceeded to offer them.

State and municipal financing, which also had been curtailed during the war, increased substantially after 1920. In 1921 new state and municipal issues passed the billion dollar mark for the first time; yet investment bankers had difficulty in finding enough to satisfy their customers. By 1927 the annual volume had risen to almost $1.5 billion, where it remained through 1929.[10] Local governments were building streets, schools, and other necessary urban and suburban facilities, and the states were financing highways, public buildings, and soldiers' bonuses. Debt limitations were constantly being reached, but land values, on which debt limits generally were based, also were rising. By 1930 outstanding state debt was about $1.8 billion and that of local governments stood at $12.7 billion.[11]

Serial bonds, compulsory in many states, became increasingly popular and the generally accepted method of financing many public improvements. Unlike most other types of securities, which were sold privately to investment houses, state and municipal bonds commonly were sold by public sealed bidding. The only other type of security generally sold by this method in the 1920's was railroad equipment trust certificates. In 1926 the Interstate Commerce Commission required that these issues be sold by competitive bidding.[12]

The tax-free feature of municipals attracted many wealthy investors, to the alarm of some individuals who feared that investment in essential industry would be neglected. Interpreting the significance of reports of recently probated wills of wealthy individuals, Secretary Mellon said: "These cases are remarkable for the way they show how men noted for their business ability and initiative have withdrawn their capital from productive business and placed it in municipal and other tax-free bonds." [13]

Augmenting these developments in domestic securities was an expansion in the placement of foreign issues. America's third underwriting boom in foreign securities started in 1924, when the previous records of the early 1900's and the war years were exceeded. Much of this volume was refunding of government short-term credits. From 1922 through 1929 Americans made a net investment in foreign issues of $4.6 billion, surpassing Englishmen as the world's leading exporters of capital. Investments flowed in both directions: foreign holdings of American securities were repatriated here,

---

10. John B. McFerrin, *Caldwell and Company: A Southern Financial Empire* (Chapel Hill, 1939), 9.
11. William J. Shultz and M. R. Caine, *Financial Development of the United States* (New York, 1937), 624–27.
12. *Ibid., U.S. v. Henry S. Morgan et al.,* "Brief for Kuhn, Loeb & Co. in Support of its Motion to Dismiss" (April 15, 1953), 3.
13. U.S. Treasury, *Annual Report, 1923,* 5.

American holdings of foreign issues were repatriated abroad, and foreigners were buying new issues in the United States.[14]

The trend to repatriation of American issues, plus American purchases of foreign securities, were important influences in rectifying adverse exchange rates. Immediately after the war, sterling, francs, and lire sold at substantial discounts. Secretary Glass attributed the "extreme depression" in 1920 in high-grade American securities largely to heavy selling in the United States of issues held abroad by investors taking advantage of exchange differences. American purchases of repatriated securities provided Europe with much needed capital. The United States, Glass said, in referring to these transactions, now was aiding Europe just as the Old World previously had assisted America in its period of growth and times of monetary troubles.[15]

Repatriation of American issues was one feature of the international postwar business in securities; the other was the resumption of foreign purchases of American issues, which began immediately after the armistice and continued throughout the 1920's. Between 1919 and 1930 foreign holdings of long-term American securities increased from $1.6 billion to $4.3 billion. During the same period American holdings of long-term foreign securities grew from $2.6 billion to $7.2 billion. In 1930 these investments alone accounted for approximately 33 percent of America's net credit position.[16]

Americans invested in foreign stocks as well as bonds. Stock offerings were small and irregular until 1928, when they began to rise appreciably; bond flotations rose in 1922, fell in 1923, and by 1927 were more than double the 1920 amount. They then fell sharply to 1929 [17] (see Exhibit 9).

New capital issues for external purposes sold in the United States between 1920 and 1929, as a percentage of total issues, fluctuated moderately until 1929. Up to that time the percentage ranged between 10 and 18. In 1929 it fell sharply to 6 percent from the 1928 figure of 15 percent (see Exhibit 10).

Europe supplied most of the foreign securities sold in the United States during the 1920's. By the end of the decade these accounted for 41 percent of the total. Canada provided the next largest amount (almost 25 percent), followed by Central and South America (nearly 22 percent). The rest of the world, principally the Far East, supplied the remainder (12 percent). National and provincial government loans constituted the single largest kind of foreign securi-

14. Ralph A. Young, *Handbook on American Underwriting of Foreign Securities* (Washington, 1930), 12, 14, 16; Shultz and Caine, *Financial Development of the United States*, 605, 607.
15. U.S. Treasury, *Annual Report, 1919*, 14; ibid., *1920*, 60, 77.
16. *Historical Statistics to 1957*, 565.
17. Ilse S. Mintz, *Deterioration in the Quality of Foreign Bonds Issued in the United States, 1920–1930* (New York, 1951), 24–27.

Exhibit 9. Foreign common stock and foreign government bonds issued in the United States, 1920–1929 (in millions)

Year	Stocks	Bonds
1920	7	439
1921	0	532
1922	0	660
1923	10	303
1924	0	912
1925	10	818
1926	11	673
1927	9	1,023
1928	41	875
1929	34	253

Source: Ilse S. Mintz, *Deterioration in the Quality of Foreign Bonds Issued in the United States, 1920–1930* (New York, 1951), 28.

ties sold in the United States, followed by corporate and municipal issues.[18]

The proceeds from these loans generally were used to rebuild currencies and devastated areas or increase productive capacity. The latter was the case with most of the funds Americans invested

Exhibit 10. Foreign capital issues compared with total capital issues offered in the United States, 1920–1929 (in millions)

Year	New foreign issues	Total new issues	Foreign in percent of total
1920	485	3,635	13
1921	631	3,577	18
1922	728	4,304	17
1923	413	4,304	10
1924	1,001	5,593	18
1925	1,072	6,220	17
1926	1,130	6,344	18
1927	1,302	7,776	17
1928	1,246	8,050	15
1929	779	11,604	6

Source: Allin W. Dakin, "Foreign Securities in the American Money Market, 1914–1930," *Harvard Business Review*, X (January 1932), 229.

18. The figures used to calculate the percentages were taken from Cleona Lewis, *America's Stake in International Investments* (Washington, 1938), 652–53.

in Canada. Many of the loans, notably some of those going to Latin America, however, were wasteful and speculative, the very kind that Herbert Hoover, then Secretary of Commerce, deplored and warned against.[19]

Foreign bonds were popular with both investors and bankers. Their high yield attracted buyers, while the substantial discounts, commissions, and fiscal agency fees investment firms charged to negotiate and handle foreign loans brought handsome profits to the houses that sponsored and distributed them. Competition among American bankers to underwrite and distribute these issues was lively.[20]

The sale of foreign securities was endorsed by government officials and by many business and financial leaders. Some believed that investments in overseas loans would improve public understanding of America's new role and responsibilities in world affairs and assist the development of an enlightened, far-sighted foreign economic policy.[21] In December 1920, speaking at a meeting of the American Bankers Association, Hoover stressed the imperative need of assisting the European countries to stabilize their currencies. The prosperity of the United States, he said, depended upon Europe's recovery. Private credits, not government loans, provided the means to achieve both. Three months later, as Secretary of Commerce, Hoover put his ideas into practice. Under his leadership the Commerce Department conducted an extensive educational and advisory program aimed to educate Americans about the advantages as well as the dangers of investing in foreign securities and to encourage bankers to sponsor only sound, productive loans that would "bless both the borrower and the lender."[22]

In 1921 Hoover persuaded President Harding to call a White House conference to consider the subject of foreign loans. Its purpose was twofold: to devise ways of protecting Americans investing in these issues and to see to it that the loans themselves were in the national interest. Representatives of the country's leading investment houses attended the meeting. The government was represented by two other cabinet members besides Hoover: Charles Evans Hughes, the Secretary of State, and Secretary Mellon, of the Treasury. Hoover had hoped to get the conference to agree on definite guidelines and procedures, but neither Hughes nor the bankers considered it necessary or desirable. Instead of a formal loan-approval program the group agreed upon an informal system whereby the State Department was to be kept informed of all projected private

19. Soule, *Prosperity Decade,* 269; Joseph Brandes, *Herbert Hoover and Economic Diplomacy: Department of Commerce Policy, 1921–1928* (Pittsburgh, 1962), 155–57.
20. Soule, *Prosperity Decade,* 269.
21. Allin W. Dakin, "Foreign Securities in the American Money Market, 1914–1930" *Harvard Business Review,* X (January 1932), 232, 235.
22. Brandes, *Herbert Hoover and Economic Diplomacy,* 155

foreign financings. It would review the details of the offering, consult with the Commerce and Treasury departments, and decide whether loans were in accordance with national policy. Although proposed, legislation to enforce these goals was not enacted. Former Treasury Secretary Glass, a United States Senator since 1920, believed such a law was unconstitutional, and he opposed any State Department review of private foreign financings. The fact that the government did not disapprove of a loan was, in his opinion, tantamount to its endorsement of the quality of the issue. State Department review of private foreign offerings, furthermore, was a usurpation of the banking function. Actual controls proved to be slight, and no international controversies arose over the direction of investment. As a public service, various government offices, most notably the Commerce Department, collected and disseminated information on foreign financial conditions.[23]

Unsettled conditions abroad also led to some private probing of America's growingly complex role in international finance. Siegfried Stern, vice president of the Seaboard National Bank of New York, recommended caution in the extension of private credits, with careful scrutiny of an offering country's political stability and solvency and the security behind the issue. A decision to lend would call for "mature judgment and conservative aggressiveness," he said. But his conclusion was that by assisting the nations that already were our debtors, the United States could promote its foreign commerce and compete successfully in the "imminent struggle for world trade." [24]

Another notable characteristic of the postwar decade was the spread of ownership of securities. The pressure of demand for domestic and foreign investment capital was drawing out small buyers, who became an important element in the boom of the late 1920's.[25] Expansion in normal domestic capital sources resulted from the growing population as well as rising incomes. No accurate figures are available for the number of persons owning securities, but many writers hazarded estimates, and the conclusions reached varied widely. Illustrative, but not necessarily the gamut, were figures of almost three million for 1927, made by government actuary Joseph S. McCoy, using federal income tax returns for 1924,[26] to nearly 14 million for 1922, by Robert R. Doane.[27] Another analysis of

23. *Ibid.*, 153–54; George W. Edwards, *The Evolution of Finance Capitalism* (London, 1938), 307–08.
24. S. Stern, "Has the Time Come for the American Banker to Help Finance Europe?" *The Magazine of Wall Street*, XXXII (September 29, 1923), 1013, 1056.
25. Charles C. Abbott, *The New York Bond Market: 1920–1930* (Cambridge, Mass., 1937), 53.
26. Joseph S. McCoy, "The U.S. Legion of Capitalists," *American Bankers Association Journal*, XIX (February 1927), 560, 626–28.
27. Robert R. Doane, *The Anatomy of American Wealth* (New York, 1940), 138–39.

internal revenue statistics gave an estimate of about 15 million, with 75 percent of the dollar amount of holdings owned by only 600,000 individuals. The author of this view saw no "proletarian" control existing among corporations, although some employees' purchase plans had been much publicized as such.[28]

In spite of wide differences, estimators did agree that spread of stock ownership was substantial, and for several reasons specifically arising from the current situation. First, the wartime experience with Liberty bonds revealed to bankers an unexpectedly large investing group and to investors the profits from security ownership. There was also a continuing trend toward issuing smaller denominations of bonds to attract small purchasers, even though some investment dealers believed these sales were unprofitable to distributors. By 1927 many municipals and most corporate bonds were available in $500 and $100 denominations. These involved more work for issuers and distributors, increased the vendor's selling costs, and resulted in higher prices to the consumer. Some houses, nonetheless, specialized in these denominations.[29]

The small investor was indeed the popular figure in current writing. He was seen in many roles of varying importance. Whereas some commentators looked to this group as the necessary source of capital for an expanding economy, others viewed it as an exploited one, and still others even considered it responsible for the "speculative orgy" of 1919 and 1920.[30] Treasury Secretary Mellon in 1926 expressed encouragement at the extent of security investments held by small investors, who were buying foreign as well as domestic issues. The average investment in recently offered foreign issues, Mellon reported, was about $3,000. It represented "an intelligent and widespread body of our citizenship." He saw no harm in seeking the high return that these issues offered.[31] In 1925 *Moody's Investors Service* reported that the most striking current financial development was the great increase in purchasing power of American investors and businessmen. This had not even been paralleled, relatively, by the situation in the United States after the Civil War or that in Great Britain after the Napoleonic wars. "This vast new buying power is almost dominating the security market," the report read, "and is seeking new avenues of expansion in all domestic industries and in foreign fields." [32]

Another variation on the small investor theme was a theory that

---

28. Lewis Corey, "How Is Ownership Distributed?" *The New Republic,* XLVI (May 5, 1926), 323–24.

29. Lawrence Chamberlain and George W. Edwards, *The Principles of Bond Investment* (rev. ed., New York, 1927), 24.

30. Victor DeVilliers, "The Growing Army of 'Small Investors.' " *The Magazine of Wall Street,* XXVII (November 13, 1920), 30.

31. U.S. Treasury, *Annual Report, 1926,* 2–5.

32. *Moody's Investors Service,* January 8, 1925, 9.

democratizing of industry and general goodwill would follow labor's participation in industry, banking, and securities. Three prominent men, described as typical American business executives, were interviewed for *The Magazine of Wall Street*. These three — Samuel Insull, then the highly respected Chicago utility magnate, F. Edson White of Armour & Co., and M. A. Traylor of Chicago's First Trust and Savings Bank — foresaw a new era of peaceful industrial relations.[33]

"We are living in the day of the small investor, and the small investor is the real owner of Wall Street," another writer reported in *The Magazine of Wall Street*. The "typical" investor he described was one who subscribed to "the reputable financial reporting agencies and to the better class of financial magazines." [34] This conclusion, like many others concerning the small investor of the 1920's, proved to be more fancy than fact.

Some corporations were selling stock to customers and employees, and these purchasers partly replaced the capitalists who now sought tax-free issues.[35] Paul M. Warburg urged "modern investment and deposit corporations" to seek the patronage of the "smallest customers" by catering to immigrants and others of the "working classes." He warned in 1920 that increasing taxation had "decreased the importance of the one-time class of professional capitalists as the exclusive field to cultivate for the purpose of placing investment securities. The savings of the masses will become an element of growing importance in this regard, if private enterprise is to successfully finance the future of our country." [36]

An editorial in *The Magazine of Wall Street* in 1924 warned small investors — "the school teachers, doctors, small retailers and others of but average means" — that the safest place for their funds was in the domestic market. It pointed out that the risks of foreign issues were suitable only for large corporations, which, doing an international business, could accept foreign securities in payment for goods, or for wealthy individuals seeking diversification and able to risk their funds for the sake of a high return.[37]

Prevention of the exploitation of the small investor still was an important concern in government, financial, and other circles. The Treasury, for example, continued to issue warnings about the dangers, commenting in 1919 on the unscrupulous persons who were

33. Theodore M. Knappen, "The Silent Revolution in American Finance," *The Magazine of Wall Street*, XXXV (December 20, 1924), 262.
34. Barnard Powers, "Who Are the Real Owners of Wall Street?" *The Magazine of Wall Street*, XXXIII (April 26, 1924), 1106.
35. Gardiner C. Means, "The Diffusion of Stock Ownership in the United States," *The Quarterly Journal of Economics*, XLIV (August 1930), 591.
36. "Paul M. Warburg Says: 'Immigrants Art Potential Capitalists'," *The Magazine of Wall Street*, XXVI (June 26, 1920), 226.
37. "Is It Safe to Buy Foreign Securities?" *The Magazine of Wall Street*, XXXIII (April 26, 1924), 1112–13.

swindling the holders of government obligations. In 1926 it observed that "sound securities" were being sought by the small investor.[38] The Federal Trade Commission took jurisdiction in some cases of issuance of wildcat securities, but generally the harm was done before the commission could act.[39]

Throughout the period the question of federal regulation of security issues was in the mill. At House hearings in 1919 Paul M. Warburg had testified to the extent of the danger of fraudulent issues and the urgent need for action. He believed that reputable investment houses should be willing to submit to a certain amount of red tape in the interest of protecting the general public. "It is only a question of time for some grave disappointments or scandals to occur discrediting future issues and interfering with the free and healthy development of our security market." [40] And Congressman George S. Graham, a Pennsylvania Republican, vividly described the tactics of the individuals he sought to guard against.[41]

> I want to protect the average unwary citizen from the reckless and unscrupulous promoters, the hot-air projectors who ought to be in jail, and who by all manners of devices, including moving picture shows, flamboyant and deceptive talk, and bombastic figures and advertisements, inveigle and flimflam their victims into buying stocks. . . . It seems that all of the bubble blowers of other days, the moonshine promoters, green goods, and gold bricks, and shell game men, financial pan-handlers and wildcat exploiters, and skin-game fakers . . . are now engaged in the stock selling game. For a generation to come there will be hundreds of thousands of our people who will sadly remember this period as the time in which they were unmercifully stung on "a golden opportunity to grasp riches beyond the wildest dreams of avarice" and all they will have to show for their credulity will be the luridly lithographed certificates bearing marvelous artists' dreams of the fabulous wealth in which the bearer was soon to participate.

So much of the publicity about fraudulent financial practices was being associated with New York City's financial district that *The Magazine of Wall Street* undertook its defense. In articles and advertisements it attempted to give the side of the legitimate dealers. It chided them, furthermore, for not departing from their traditional advertising practices to undertake a major campaign to fight back. Such a campaign, it stated, not only would clear the standing of the banking and brokerage profession but also could be effective in

---

38. U.S. Treasury, *Annual Report, 1919,* 93–95; *ibid., 1926,* 2.
39. U.S. Federal Trade Commission, *Annual Report . . . 1919* (Washington, 1920), 47–48.
40. *Ibid., 1922,* 54; U.S. House, Committee on the Judiciary, 66th Cong., 1st Sess., *Proposed Federal "Blue Sky" Law: Hearings . . .* (Washington, 1919), 123.
41. *Proposed Federal "Blue Sky" Law: Hearings,* 123–24.

educating the gullible victims who, the magazine estimated, were losing some $500 million annually.[42]

As the decade proceeded to its disastrous close, security markets claimed universal attention, much beyond that directed toward the investment banking profession. A warning of possible dangers ahead came from Secretary Mellon in 1928. Reporting on the ineffectiveness of the action that the Federal Reserve System already had taken in trying to curb speculation on the stock exchanges, he explained that the reason for failure was "partly due to the activities of powerful groups of speculators, and partly due to the fact that the public in general believed and acted as if the price of securities would indefinitely advance." [43]

As the boom was building up in the late 1920's some analysts began to probe the relations of general business and the stock market, to look to historical parallels in earlier periods of speculative excesses, and to find warning signals. In July 1928 Alexander Dana Noyes called attention to the fact that throughout the country, discussions of business had been superseded by talk of the "extraordinary stock market." Buying orders from all over the country were pouring into New York in such volume that brokerage houses could not keep up with them. Hours of trading on the New York Stock Exchange were shortened so as to reduce the amount of business transacted. Some of the most spectacular stock price increases were found in issues paying trivial or no dividends at all; he cited those of radio and airplane companies. And he observed that if "the speculator dismisses from mind both the official reports and the state of the trade in which the company operates, he has parted completely with the realities." Speculating in certain stocks, he warned, was not the same as speculating in the future of the United States.[44]

"Financial and psychological phenomena," Noyes observed, had been seen before when economic forces had supplied an adequate basis for the belief that rising stock prices must indicate the future of trade and industry. But the situation this time was comparable with that of 1901, when "the sober banking community lost its head completely." The public now "had taken the bit in its teeth." [45]

To those in the investment business, also, the opportunities of the "prosperity decade" appeared limitless. The public demand for securities, stimulated by advertising and promotional campaigns, was insatiable, and the profits to be made in underwriting and

42. John Read, "Bringing Wall Street to the People," *The Magazine of Wall Street*, XXVIII (June 11, 1921), 153, 211–12.
43. U.S. Treasury, *Annual Report, 1928*, 5.
44. Alexander D. Noyes, "The Course of a Great Stock-Exchange Speculation," reprint from *Scribner's Magazine*, (July 1928), n.p.
45. *Ibid.*

distributing new issues lucrative. The result was a marked decline in banking judgment and ethics and unscrupulous exploitation of public gullibility and avarice. The few financiers and business leaders who dared to condemn publicly the wild speculation and to urge caution and responsibility were ignored, if not ridiculed. With few exceptions, investment and brokerage houses scrambled to win new offerings and earn greater profits. The securities industry, like much of the public and many government leaders, including President Coolidge, was convinced that the spanking good times would continue and improve still further. In December 1928, less than three months before leaving the White House, Coolidge told the country it could "regard the present with satisfaction and anticipate the future with optimism."

13 Investment Banking Firms and the IBA in the 1920's

Faced with favorable conditions of unparalleled proportions on both the demand and supply side of the securities market during the 1920's, investment bankers engaged in a veritable orgy of competition. Old respected Atlantic Coast houses, the so-called "Establishment," fought for their share of the business against rising young or new firms, many led by able, aggressive, and imaginative financiers. Given the competitive, speculative climate of operations and the existence of minimal, largely ineffectual, external restraints, investment bankers had to rely almost entirely on their own values and judgment in setting individual standards of firm conduct. The result was a range of behavior running from the high norms of most established firms to the excesses, even fraud, of some old and many new houses. For investment bankers the 1920's were years of unequally shared, unhealthy expansion.

The two principal conservative forces of the decade were some of the older firms and the Investment Bankers Association (IBA). They were the ones that urged restraint and tried to uphold the high standards that had proved advantageous to both investors and bankers. Their appeals were ignored; their leadership contested, if not totally rejected.

Against the decade's many varied pressures for change, most long-established houses, while continuing to grow, maintained their conservative policies in the face of growing competition. They did not adopt aggressive sales tactics or openly solicit business. They sold few common stocks even though these were becoming the more popular securities. An important characteristic of many of these old houses was that they continued their well-established foreign ties as international investment bankers and financiers of foreign trade; yet here too the newcomers became more active and more aggressive.

The principal business of J. P. Morgan & Co. remained private banking.[1] Its investment business was less important than formerly, as were its dealings in foreign exchange and letters of credit, and its other functions. Its net worth at the end of 1929 was about $118.6 million, whereas deposits were about $492.3 million, and total assets were about $680.4 million. The firm kept its interlocking partnership ties with Drexel & Co., Philadelphia; Morgan, Grenfell & Co., London; and Morgan *et Cie.,* Paris; but did not branch out further, as many of its competitors were doing.

1. The chief source for material on J. P. Morgan & Co. is U.S. Senate, Committee on Banking and Currency, 72d and 73d Congs., *Stock Exchange Practices: Hearings* . . . (20 pts., Washington, 1933–34), pts. 1 and 2, 7, 22, 165–66, 168–69, 223–24, 879–81.

During the 1920's the Morgan firm continued to be the country's leading private investment banking house. Its sponsorship of senior securities exceeded that of all other private firms. Between January 1919 and May 1933 the House of Morgan offered to the public over $6 billion of securities, generally in association with others and divided roughly as follows: foreign government and foreign corporation bonds, over $2 billion; railroad bonds, nearly $2 billion; public utility company and public utility holding company bonds, over $1 billion; industrial bonds and preferred stocks, nearly $600 million; municipal bonds, $160 million; and railroad holding company bonds, about $130 million. Common stock amounted to about $3\frac{1}{3}$ percent of all securities it distributed, and usually it did not offer these directly to the general public, but to experienced investors who, Morgan explained, knew the risks of common stock and were prepared to run them.

The Morgan firm itself remained a wholesaler, although its selling syndicates or groups sometimes included as many as 1,200 retailers, large and small, located throughout the country. This represented considerable expansion in the size of these groups compared to what they had been before World War I. The Morgan firm selected syndicate members for their selling ability, previous association with the issuer, and standing in their communities.

The firm continued its previous practice of being represented on the directorates of many of the companies for which it floated securities. The corporations so served remained numerous and became a subject for Senate investigations.

Goaded into making defensive statements concerning the firm's relations with customers, Morgan told Senate questioners in 1933 that being a client of Morgan never had been held to be discreditable. And he described the contemporary image of the firm in these words: "Our business comes to us because our depositors, relying upon a banking experience covering more than three generations, put more faith in our banking reputation, our resources, and our methods of doing business than they put in the work of bank examiners, or even in the not always illuminating published statements of institutions."

Kuhn, Loeb & Co.[2] also remained a conservative private banker, generally letting customers seek it out, rather than competing for accounts. In its investment business it continued to specialize in railroad securities. The firm had established such close ties with several roads that it became influential in their management policy and even in the selection of managers. It also held an important

---

2. The source for most of the material on Kuhn, Loeb & Co. is *U.S. v. Henry S. Morgan et al.*, "Brief for Kuhn, Loeb & Co. in Support of Its Motion to Dismiss," 2, 3, 11–13; *ibid.*, "Plaintiff's Exhibit," 1,222–B, 1,029–B, 1,030–B; *Stock Exchange Practices: Hearings*, pt. 3, 958–60, 964, 967, 981, 990, 1,085.

place in the distribution of foreign issues. As with some other investment bankers, its functions included services depending on personal qualities rather than capital. Otto H. Kahn explained that the firm catered to clients — as distinguished from the general public — buying and selling securities for them and advising them about their financial affairs. Clients were diverse in type and location; many depositors were foreign banks.

The relative importance of Kuhn, Loeb's banking business is shown in its balance sheets for the year ending December 31, 1929. Of total liabilities of over $120 million, $25 million was capital and $88.5 million was deposits. Of total assets, nearly $50 million was in time and call loans. The number of partners remained relatively small, most of them being members of the family. It had only one office in the United States, at the corner of William and Pine streets, in New York City's financial district, but there was a resident partner in London.

To a limited extent Kuhn, Loeb, too, succumbed to the competitive pressures of the 1920's. It bowed to them slightly late in the decade. From 1927 to 1930 the firm operated a wholly owned London subsidiary, European Merchants Banking Co., Ltd., a private banking partnership organized to assist Kuhn, Loeb's international financings.

Among the especially close railroad clients for whom Kuhn, Loeb served as investment banker were the Pennsylvania, the Missouri Pacific, and the Chicago, Milwaukee, and St. Paul. The firm's involvement in the receivership and reorganization of the latter in the 1920's went so far as to include selection of judge, lawyers, receivers, and various other individuals concerned in the receivership proceedings. Such services were the source of substantial fees as well as considerable criticism.[3]

Like the Morgan firm, Kuhn, Loeb prided itself on its professional aloofness. As Kahn remarked, "It has long been our policy and our effort to get our clients, not by chasing after them, not by praising our own wares, but by an attempt to establish a reputation which would make clients feel that if they have a problem of a financial nature, Dr. Kuhn, Loeb & Co. is a pretty good doctor to go to." Kahn deplored the current cutthroat competition of investment bankers for foreign issues, saying, "15 American bankers sat in Belgrade, Yugoslavia, making bids, and a dozen American bankers sat in a half a dozen South and Central American States, or in Balkan States . . . one outbidding the other foolishly, recklessly, to the detriment of the public, compelling him to force bonds upon the public at a price which is not determined by the value of that security so much as by his eagerness to get it."

3. Max Lowenthal, *The Investor Pays* (New York, 1933).

Kidder, Peabody & Co., like the other long-established firms, was feeling the effects of increased competition, in spite of the general rise in the investment business. It shared in fewer of Morgan's and Kuhn, Loeb's offerings than previously and was the principal in fewer issues.[4] Moreover, it was experiencing increasing competition from commercial banks in financing foreign trade. A further harassment was a lengthy, but unsuccessful, lawsuit against it, based on methods it had used in arranging an industrial merger.[5]

Kidder, Peabody bent to the competitive pressures of the decade more than some of the other old houses, but without abandoning entirely all its traditional standards and practices. In some respects it was unchanging, in others it adapted its operations to the optimism of the times. The firm's old conservatism was reflected in the decision to keep the main office in Boston when most of its business was in New York City and to rely heavily for most of its new offerings on old New England corporations with which it had been long associated. Kidder, Peabody continued its joint accounts with the Barings in London and Hottinguer *et Cie* in Paris and maintained its prewar ties with investment firms in other cities, such as Mitchum, Tully & Co. in San Francisco.[6]

The dichotomy in Kidder, Peabody's operations in the 1920's was revealed in the character of its underwritings. At a time when common stocks were gaining in favor, the firm continued to offer principally bonds. On the other hand, it sponsored more equities than did other old-line houses. Its common stock offerings grew from 9 percent of total offerings in 1927 to 25 percent in 1929. In the tradition of the times, Kidder, Peabody also expanded its sales function, opening small branch offices in and around Boston and in Providence, New York City, and Newark. The firm's commitment to the new sales practices of the 1920's did not extend to Robert Winsor, the undisputed head of the house. He considered it beneath his dignity to solicit new business and made no effort to compete for new underwritings. The most startling example of Kidder, Peabody's acceptance of the "New Era's" financial practices was the decision to sponsor its own investment trusts. This, more than anything else, set Kidder, Peabody apart from the other old established houses like Morgan and Kuhn, Loeb. Kidder, Peabody succumbed to the investment trust mania of the late 1920's because of competitive pressures and the desire to share in the profits to be made from organizing and managing these institutions.

The dominant positions of the older eastern investment banking

4. *U.S. v. Henry S. Morgan et al.,* "Plaintiff's Exhibit" 326–B, No. 1,135.
5. George S. Gibb, *The Saco-Lowell Shops: Textile Machinery Building in New England, 1813–1949* (Cambridge, Mass., 1950), 514–15.
6. Kidder, Peabody & Co. MSS., Baker Library; Kidder, Peabody & Co. Records, New York City.

houses were successfully challenged in this period by firms originating in other parts of the country. Among the challengers were Halsey, Stuart & Co., Inc., of Chicago, and Blyth & Co., of San Francisco. The former, a corporation, evolved from a Chicago branch, set up in 1903 under Harold L. Stuart, of N. W. Halsey & Co. of New York, which had been started two years earlier. By the time the United States went to war, the New York firm had grown to have branches in eleven American cities and two abroad. When Halsey died in 1911, the firm was split three ways, each part incorporated: one in New York to include the eastern and foreign branches; one in Illinois to cover Chicago, Detroit, St. Louis, and Milwaukee; and another in California, to include Pacific Coast branches. The Illinois corporation, still under Stuart, became Halsey, Stuart & Co.[7]

The Halsey, Stuart firms began concentrating on public utility bonds when these still were novel and other investment bankers were wary of them. With the Insull companies, Stuart established relations that later became very close. Immediately after the war Halsey, Stuart also started broadening its offerings. In 1918 it obtained a $60 million Armour Company debenture issue, when that corporation already had well-established relations with eastern bankers. At the time this was the largest transaction ever negotiated outside of New York City. Later, Halsey, Stuart added industrials and foreign issues, although it never actively solicited foreign accounts. Among the European countries it did represent were Great Britain, France, Germany, the Scandinavian states, and Italy. It also distributed South American securities. It handled important issues for motion picture companies and for publication and newsprint corporations. But throughout the period it confined itself to fixed income securities. As might be expected of an aggressive, young house, Halsey, Stuart also took part in the currently popular pastime of starting affiliated firms to carry on activities that it chose not to perform itself.[8] In 1919 it organized and owned the Corporation Securities Company to deal in preferred stocks, which then were popular, but this company never was very active. Ten years later the affiliate consolidated with Western Securities Company, owned by Insull interests, to become Corporation Securities Company of Illinois, which held substantial amounts of common stocks for control purposes. Halsey, Stuart marketed issues for the company, and several officers of the house went on the board of the corporation.

Whereas Halsey, Stuart and N. W. Halsey were conservative in

7. Source for this firm is A. E. Bryson, *Halsey, Stuart & Co. Inc., 1901–1937, 1938–1944: A History* . . . ([Chicago, 1937, 1945]), 6–36.
8. When Halsey, Stuart & Co. was organized as a separate company in 1916, the New York and West Coast corporations were absorbed by the National City Bank of New York as part of its security affiliate, the National City Co.

the type of securities they handled, that is, bonds, they adopted many novel policies and aggressive sales methods. In 1904 N. W. Halsey had started national advertising in periodicals, a practice continued by Halsey, Stuart; in 1928 it was one of the very first investment houses to use radio advertising. In 1918 it had installed the first private wire system to connect offices in different cities. It started a formal training school for salesmen, and a partial payment plan for customers, modeled after such plans used in the Liberty Loan distributions of World War I. Stuart had been Director of Sales for Liberty Loans for the entire Federal Reserve seventh district.

Throughout the period 1916 to 1930 Halsey, Stuart grew in size and prestige. It opened offices in New York City, Boston, and Philadelphia in 1917, when other firms were retrenching. Its staff grew from about 100 in that year to about 1,000 in 1930. The firm established new buying contacts, handled new types of bonds, and established a high reputation with issuers, dealers, and the public. It broadened its financial activities, also; for example, it held accounts as fiscal agent. The amounts so held increased from about $60,000 in 1916 to over $11 million in 1929. During the fifteen years before 1930 its offerings totaled hundreds of millions of dollars and "provided a rich heritage of sound, aggressive policies and fruitful experience." By 1930 Halsey, Stuart had gained a position of "positive leadership," ranking third, as syndicate head, and ahead of Morgan, in total volume of issues managed in the boom period of 1927-1931.

Blyth & Co., Inc.[9] originated in San Francisco and by the early 1930's had become one of the major principals in the distribution of securities won in public sealed bidding. It had its origin in 1914 and in a small corporation, Blyth, Witter & Co., started by Charles R. Blyth and Dean Witter, president and vice president. It did a general investment banking business but concentrated on issues of power and light companies of the Pacific Coast. Soon it branched out to open offices in Los Angeles, Portland, Seattle, and even New Orleans. By 1925 it had an office in New York City, "thereby bringing to the attention of investment banking houses in the East that there was a market for securities in San Francisco" and that Blyth, Witter was a good underwriter and distributor on the Coast. One of its particular problems in the East was to try to offset lingering Atlantic Coast fears of recurring earthquakes in California.

Changes within the firm came when Dean Witter left it in 1924 to form Dean Witter & Co. But Blyth, Witter retained its name until 1928, when it became a partnership and entered the brokerage business. And then, largely because of the 1929 crash, the partner-

9. Source for this firm is *U.S. v. Henry S. Morgan et al.,* "Corrected Opinion of Harold R. Medina" (February 4, 1954), 94–96, 100, 363.

ship was dissolved, and Blyth & Co. was incorporated in Delaware to continue the investment banking business. It made changes also in its offerings—in size and character; it added nonutilities and securities of corporations not located on the West Coast.

Blyth and Halsey, Stuart are examples of an important type of relatively young firm that emerged into major national investment houses during the 1920's. Unlike the members of the old Atlantic Coast "Establishment," this new group grew in size and prominence not because of its access to European capital but from its success in financing regional enterprises, very often utility or traction companies, and to a lesser extent small manufacturers and retailers. Their reputation also stemmed from their demonstrated ability to tap new sources of local capital, both individual and institutional, and usually in relatively small amounts. These firms, together with scores of smaller, newer, and financially weaker houses, competed with the older eastern houses for new issues, both domestic and foreign.

The great increase in the quantity of foreign securities floated in the United States during the 1920's challenged the standards of old and new houses and forced both to focus on the new problems created by these issues. Sponsorship of foreign securities increased an investment firm's prestige, and there was much competition to win these flotations. Many of them, usually those of better quality, fell to established, conservative firms with well-developed foreign connections. During the 1920's American investment houses, for the first time, became active promoters and underwriters of foreign issues on an extensive scale. Foreign nations, provinces, and cities all issued securities in the United States through investment bankers, some with widely scattered clients and others with very limited clienteles.[10]

Some foreign government issues were distributed through large syndicates and others through a few bankers. Most foreign loans were sold through groups organized by New York banks or private investment firms. Some governments relied more on one banking house than another, but no one firm monopolized the issues of any one country. France, for instance, depended heavily on syndicates headed by Morgan, Guaranty Trust Company, and Kuhn, Loeb, whereas Germany in 1924 and 1925 used many more bankers for its national loans. Its largest offering, the Dawes Plan loan, was sold through a syndicate managed by Morgan, but Germany's provincial and municipal loans were brought out by groups headed by seven New York City houses ranging in size from the very large National City Co. to the much smaller, old and respected house of Speyer & Co. National governments, whether in Europe, Latin

10. Much of the material for this section is taken from Robert W. Dunn, *American Foreign Investments* (New York, 1926), 18–33, 106.

America, or the Far East, used different bankers at different times. The number of houses they employed to head their offerings was limited. No government appears to have had its various issues sponsored by more than three or four houses. Foreign municipalities, on the other hand, sold their securities through a larger number of firms. Norwegian government bonds were sold by Morgan, but Norway's cities borrowed through at least a half dozen bankers, different houses heading the various offerings.

Many of the same bankers who distributed foreign government bonds also sold those of overseas corporations. The major difference in the marketing of foreign corporate bonds was that a considerably larger number of houses were engaged in sponsoring these issues. Also, many younger, smaller firms in and out of New York City headed groups distributing foreign corporate offerings. A dozen or more American bankers served French corporations in the 1920's. The size of these banking firms ranged widely, from the largest and most prestigious Wall Street banks and firms to smaller, less experienced ones in other cities.

The expectation of large profits, as noted before, was the major inducement that attracted bankers to these issues. "An investment banker, especially, pays himself fat commissions for the questionable service he renders . . . as a go-between," recorded a critic of these loans in 1934. "These commissions were the motive for the investments made in Germany after 1923. It was in fact such a potent motive that bankrupt German municipalities and disrupted German industries had not to beg foreign bankers for advances; they were actually besieged by those bankers until they accepted loans." [11] Similar instances of bankers persuading foreign governments and corporations to issue bonds to finance unnecessary expenditures were commonplace.

The marked increase in foreign offerings during the 1920's together with the much greater rise in domestic issues resulted in significant modifications of the syndicate system, the investment bankers' traditional method of marketing securities. The prewar trend away from strict underwriting, whereby bankers only guaranteed the sale of an issue but did not actually sell it themselves, continued steadily in the 1920's. The large amounts of available investment funds, the great demand for stocks and bonds, and the adoption of new syndicate procedures made for the speedy placement of large issues, thus reducing the risk of having to carry unsold securities.[12]

During the 1920's changes occurred in the type, number, and

11. Robert Valeur, "Foreign Investments in Germany and the Problem of Inter-Governmental Debts," *The Annals,* CLXXIV (July 1934), 32–33.
12. Willard E. Atkins *et al., The Regulation of the Security Markets* (Washington, 1946), 35–37. See also *U.S. v. Henry S. Morgan et al.,* "Corrected Opinion," 30.

size of syndicates employed to float new issues. Syndicates were larger, and they lasted for shorter periods — that is, distribution was speeded up. Selling syndicates were used much more frequently than before, and they tended to be larger and more dispersed than previously. These results stemmed from various economic changes: more corporations were being formed, existing ones were growing, the investor group was expanding, investment banking firms also were expanding, and new ones were being formed.[13]

Harold Stuart described the types of selling syndicates during the 1920's as follows:[14]

There were three types of selling syndicates. While they represented successive steps in the development of investment banking, and while there were shifts in the type that was most extensively used, all three were used throughout the 1920's.

The first form was known as the "unlimited liability selling syndicate." This was a group in which each participant agreed to have a pro rata share in the purchase by the selling syndicate from the previous group, at a stated price, and to take up his share of any unsold bonds remaining in the syndicate upon its expiration. The syndicate agreement stated the terms on which the offering to the public was to be made, and the participant was given the right to offer bonds to the public, receiving a stated commission on all confirmed sales. However, no matter what amount he sold, he still retained his liability to take up his proportionate share of unsold securities. The undivided syndicate combined selling with the assumption of risk; hence both houses with distributing power and those with financial capacity but without selling ability were included in the syndicate.* . . .

This caused objection on the part of the dealers who did the actual selling, and there subsequently evolved the second form, called the "limited liability selling syndicate." This syndicate operated much the same as the undivided syndicate except that each member's obligation was limited to the amount of his participation, and distribution of that amount relieved him of further liability.† The participant retained his proportionate liability for the costs of carrying the securities, shared in the profits or losses of the trading account, and was liable for such other expenses as occurred after the purchase from the banking or purchase group.

The "limited liability selling syndicate" gradually evolved into a third

---

13. *U.S. v. Henry S. Morgan et al.*, "Brief on General Points . . . in Support of Motions to Dismiss of Defendants Blyth & Co., Inc., The First Boston Corporation, Glore, Forgan & Co., Goldman, Sachs & Co., and Lehman Brothers," n.d., 61–64; Paul P. Gourrich, "Investment Banking Methods Prior to and since the Securities Act of 1933," *Law and Contemporary Problems*, IV (January 1937), 52.

14. *U.S. v. Henry S. Morgan et al.*, "Brief on General Points," 64–66. Compare New York and Chicago plans, described in chapter ix.

* Usually a banking group was not used with this form of selling syndicate. The purchase group sold the securities directly to the selling syndicate.

† A banking group was usually used with the limited liability syndicate. It paid the costs of carrying the securities, shared in the profits or losses of the trading account, and was liable for the other expenses of underwriting.

form known simply as the "selling group," which differed from the limited syndicate in that its member[s] did not take over the liabilities for carrying costs, trading account, etc. The dealer relieved himself of all liabilities except those connected with the actual retail distribution of securities.* The member's financial liability was restricted to selling or taking up the amount of bonds for which he subscribed.

With the growing complexities of issuing securities, Stuart also noted, "the syndicate operation became larger and as the number of firms participating . . . increased, the contracts became more detailed and explicit." [15]

The agreements of selling syndicates, like many of those before World War I, included mechanisms for controlling the price of securities during the distribution period. The managers of selling syndicates customarily traded in the securities in the open market in order to maintain or "stabilize" the offering price. If a dealer's bonds came back on the market and tended to depress it, they were bought for the syndicate's trading account. Members whose stock so appeared were considered not to have performed their placing function and might be penalized, for instance, by loss of their selling commissions.

Among the methods used to stabilize prices was to take a short position until distribution was completed or to stand ready to buy until the offering was "thoroughly absorbed." Sometimes comparable issues also were stabilized, thus avoiding a price difference that would appear to place the new securities at a disadvantage. In theory the stabilizing procedure benefited both issuer and investor.[16]

An example of the several groups employed in floating a foreign loan was the one set up in 1925 to sell a $20 million $6\frac{1}{2}$ percent gold bond issue for the Mortgage Bank of Chile. Kuhn, Loeb and the Guaranty Co. were the originators. On the day they signed the purchase contract with the bank they granted a participation on the original terms to Lehman Brothers. And on the same day they also started (and shortly completed) organizing a banking syndicate. Members of this group paid nothing to the originators but assumed risks to the extent of their participations. While the banking group was being organized, letters were sent to a great many dealers inviting them to join a selling syndicate. This group assumed no risk but merely undertook to sell the bonds to the public for a commission. Within twenty-four hours after the original syndicate

---

* As a general rule a large banking group was organized when the "selling group" was to be used. The banking group took over the liability for carrying costs, traders' account, and other expenses.

15. *Ibid.*, 68.

16. U.S. Senate, Committee on Banking and Currency, 72d and 73d Congs., *Stock Exchange Practices, Report* . . . (Washington, 1934), 95, 100.

had bought the bonds, the one organized to sell the bonds had obtained subscriptions for the whole issue.[17]

The speed with which the Chilean bank issue and many others were handled created grave problems for security dealers. Rapid distributions left them with no time to investigate the merits of the bonds and stocks they sold. They had to rely entirely on the integrity and word of the originating bankers. Dealers realized that if they did not accept participations they might not be asked to join future syndicates.[18] The responsibilities of dealers to their clients was a subject of industry-wide debate during the 1920's.

The IBA deplored the spread of hasty, slipshod, irresponsible syndicate practices. "At the present time," one of its committees reported as early as 1920, "when large syndicates are the rule and offerings are made at once on receipt of a syndicate letter or a telegram, it is little exaggeration to say that in some cases the distributing banker knows no more about the issue than does his customer." [19]

Criticism of syndicate practices, especially as they affected interfirm relations, was not new. It had been heard in 1915, and even earlier. It increased sufficiently after the war so that in 1921 the IBA formed a Committee on Syndicate Agreements. Its first report included by implication or direct assertion a number of complaints of members in regard to prevailing syndicate procedures, some in violation of syndicate agreements. The committee recommended specific remedies and the establishment of a permanent Committee on Business Practice to perform what amounted to a policing function, although it had no real enforcing power. "The committee believed," it reported as tactfully as it could, "that the standards of business practice set by the Association and its individual members were very high, but that the large number of new houses in the business and insufficient knowledge of syndicate matters on the part of juniors and salesmen, even in some of the older houses, had led to some misunderstandings and misconceptions of syndicate practice, which it might hope to correct in some measure by calling specific attention of members thereto." [20]

The principal source of interfirm difficulties — the one that most likely prompted the greatest criticism from dealers — stemmed from the fact that the growth in syndicate size exceeded the increase in the supply of securities. Syndicates had become so large, the committee reported, that they were "frequently a source of great embarrassment to managers." It estimated that in 1920, when about

17. *Ibid.*, 94.
18. *Ibid.*, 100.
19. Investment Bankers Association, *Proceedings . . . 1920* (Chicago, 1920), 162.
20. *Ibid., 1921,* 337.

thirty nationwide syndicates had averaged placements of $18 million each, the originating firms and a few of the "greatest national distributing houses" took about a third of this to retail, leaving only $25,000 each for the remaining dealers, approximately 500. Some of these were very large houses, and they were "almost sure to be dissatisfied with the size of their participation."[21] Without the cooperation of originating houses intent upon speedy distribution of securities, there was little the committee could do to assist disgruntled dealers.

For other complaints the IBA committee offered tentative remedies. Some syndicate members allegedly cut prices in order to unload securities they had not sold at the close of a syndicate; the committee recommended that syndicate managers or other members cooperate with such dealers to secure distribution, for the benefit of all. A second complaint was that members were not given adequate advance information about the issues they were to sell; the solution to this was obvious. A third complaint stemmed from the widespread memberships in syndicates, bringing problems resulting from location in different time zones and delayed communications. The committee suggested that a day elapse between the time of offering participations and the release of securities for public offering. Fourth, some syndicate members objected to the inclusion, as fellow members, of persons "not regularly engaged in the distribution of securities and without proper responsibility." Exclusion of such individuals from the lists was the answer, but the practice continued throughout the decade.[22]

The committee suggested that although it could not set up a model syndicate agreement form, it would recommend that such contracts be made clear and specific and that their provisions be enforced by managers. It was in the latter regard that the association could perform the policing function most effectively. Departure from high business standards, the committee asserted, "would have a tendency to destroy the confidence of the public, which is the greatest pride and the greatest asset of the investment banking business."[23]

A few years later, however, a financial observer writing under the auspices of the IBA acknowledged the continued existence of certain violations of syndicate agreements. The most prevalent one was price cutting. Participants deliberately cut prices or split commissions to individuals, to investors, or to other dealers or banks. Common explanations were that the issues did not sell rapidly enough and the participants did not have the resources to hold securities for better market conditions. If managers learned of such

---

21. *Ibid.*, 336.
22. *Ibid.*, 337; *U.S. v. Henry S. Morgan et al.*, "Corrected Opinion," 34–35.
23. IBA, *Proceedings . . . 1921*, 339.

violations, they were likely to drop the offender from later syndicates.[24]

The tremendous growth in the investment banking business during the 1920's was not accurately reflected in the enlarged size and expanded activities of the IBA, the industry's trade association.[25] This arose from the fact that throughout the decade the IBA maintained the same attitude of exclusiveness that it had taken at the time of its organization. In 1929, for example, it was estimated that there were some 6,445 security dealers in the United States, of which approximately 3,000 later were classified as investment bankers. The IBA's membership that year was about 650.[26] The association declared that it extended "a cordial welcome to all deserving firms that prove themselves worthy of a place" in its midst, but its increasingly stringent standards of admission excluded hundreds of firms and slowed down its growth. There was nonetheless a steady gain up to 1928, followed by a slight drop in 1929, attributable to a few resignations. There were some every year; occasionally they involved a major house. In May 1925 the National City Co. resigned but rejoined in November 1931.[27]

The association's growth did reflect the rise of new investment banking centers. The number of cities represented by members increased greatly, as did the number of firms or branches in cities already included (see Exhibit 11). By 1929 there were thirty-three cities with fifteen or more houses; in 1920 there had been only eleven.

The presidency went more frequently to large New York firms than it had in the years before American entry into World War I, when the Wall Street money power was under attack. The men who held the office, however, came from firms other than those the Pujo Committee had cited as belonging to the inner circle of American finance. Not a single representative of those firms held the presidency of the association during the 1920's, though one or two of these houses almost always were represented on the Board of Governors, the IBA's policy-making group. There was, nonetheless, wide geographic representation. The rise of new investment banking centers and the country-wide location of members was reflected in the make-up of the Board of Governors.

The work of the association was conducted by its committees. Standing and special ones were added or dropped from time to time, depending on the industry's changing interests. They were

---

24. Arthur Galston, *Security Syndicate Operations: Organization, Management and Accounting* (rev. enl. ed., New York, 1928), 116–19.
25. The activities of the IBA are recorded in its annual *Proceedings,* from which most of the material for this section has been drawn.
26. Irwin Friend, James R. Longstreet *et al., Investment Banking and the New Issues Market* (Cleveland, 1967), 94.
27. *The New York Times,* May 6, 1925; October 23, November 8, 1931.

Exhibit 11. Offices of member firms of Investment Bankers Association of America with fifteen or more members, by city, 1929

City	Number of offices	City	Number of offices
New York	233	Providence	25
Chicago	134	Kansas City	23
Philadelphia	102	Albany	22
Boston	79	Scranton	21
St. Louis	61	Denver	20
Pittsburgh	55	New Orleans	20
Detroit	53	Portland, Oregon	20
Los Angeles	52	St. Paul	20
San Francisco	49	Newark	20
Baltimore	46	Hartford	19
Cleveland	42	Rochester	18
Milwaukee	42	Springfield	16
Cincinnati	39	Portland, Maine	15
Minneapolis	37	Worcester	15
Buffalo	31	Louisville	15
Seattle	30	Toledo	15
Washington, D.C.	27		

Source: Investment Bankers Association, *Proceedings . . . 1929* (Chicago, 1929).

selected, according to a 1925 report by the IBA's secretary, to represent every section of the country and every aspect of investment banking. By 1929 there were nearly 30 of them, with over 350 members.

The functions and activities of the IBA committees during the 1920's reflected the range of concerns in the industry and the association. Apart from those involved with the operation of the IBA itself, the most important committees, as determined by their size, were those concerned with various kinds of securities, such as railroads, industrials, utilities, and foreign issues. Some, such as those reporting on foreign and municipal issues, dated back to the time of the IBA's organization; others were more recent, reflecting new, postwar trends and interests. The committee on industrials, for instance, though originally set up in 1912, did not become active until after the close of the war; and the committee on industrial trusts was established in 1927.

Other committees were concerned with more general problems. They dealt with protecting and improving the investment banker's public image and preventing the enactment of unfriendly regulatory laws, such as the more restrictive types of blue-sky statutes.

Originally the IBA had declared itself opposed to lobbying. "The Association maintains no lobby at Washington or elsewhere in the interests of special legislation," it asserted in 1921. "Our public position is well known — we seek no private advantage. We represent the investors of the country as distributors of legitimate securities. When legislation comes up for consideration and it is felt the investment bankers should be heard a special committee is appointed." [28]

Three years later the association reversed itself. It assigned a permanent representative in Washington to attend congressional hearings and provide the membership with information concerning the Treasury's flow of new rulings. By 1929 the association's outlays for counsel, lobbying, and related activities accounted for most of its nonoperating expenses.

The IBA did not concern itself solely with protecting and promoting the interest of its members. The association also sought to safeguard those of "the great army of uninformed investors." It stood for conservatism and restraint in an industry sorely in need of both. Its objectives and programs, designed to educate and protect investors, combat fraud, and expose unscrupulous security dealers were praiseworthy, as were its efforts to establish ethical and enforceable standards of interfirm behavior. These goals were more easily proclaimed than achieved.

One of the IBA's most difficult tasks was to police the conduct of its own members. The association had established its first business practices committee in 1914. Its purpose was to supervise the external ethics of the association's members. The committee made no reports to the general membership and remained anonymous until 1922. During this time it acted as a quasi-court, settling differences among members. In 1925 its name was changed to business conduct committee, and it was assigned the responsibility of overlooking the practice of its members in their relations with one another and with the public. The committee formalized and applied standards of conduct for members, but it had few real disciplinary powers. Like its predecessor, it continued to act as a quasi-court concerned with establishing and enforcing acceptable syndicate practices. It emphasized the need for "frank and fair" dealings among members and, in the hope of minimizing interfirm disputes, urged the acceptance of uniform trade practices and the adoption of higher standards for securities circulars and financial reporting. In 1929, reflecting the confidence and optimism characteristic of the times, as well as a considerable amount of self-delusion, the committee reported that the "business conduct of our membership in their relations with the public and between themselves is

---

28. IBA, *Proceedings . . . 1921*, 38.

on a higher plane than at any time in the history of the Association, and we therefore look forward to 1930 with the greatest of confidence."

The leadership of the IBA in the 1920's reflected the declining influence of the old established Atlantic Coast investment banking houses of the prewar era and the growing number and importance of newer firms, many of them located in the Middle and Far West. The altered status of the older firms was due, in part, to their reluctance to finance new industries or to compete with the more aggressive newcomers. Much of the strength of the established houses had come from their ability to tap European sources of capital. In the 1920's the lenders had become borrowers, and the small American investor, previously neglected by the great Atlantic Coast houses, assumed increasing importance.

In the 1920's a firm's underwriting capacity often was less important than its ability to distribute an issue quickly. This emphasis upon sales was reflected in the growing use of selling groups, a device that rarely had been employed before the war. A speaker at an IBA convention described the pressure to sell that possessed the securities industry in the 1920's. There was, he said, a "continuous ringing of doorbells and telephones throughout the land."

The rise of new firms, the expansion of syndicates, and the growth in the number of security holders created many new difficult problems for investment bankers. The purpose of the IBA was to assist them in resolving interfirm disputes by establishing high operating standards for the industry, policing their conformance and thus fulfilling the association's stated objective: "to protect the public and broaden the bond market." The IBA spent much time and money to bring about legislation, on state and national levels, that would prevent the distribution of fraudulent securities without interfering with issuers and their bankers. Self-regulation proved difficult to enforce, and many investment bankers generally failed to live up to the standards of practice urged by their own trade association. No better proof of this can be found than in the record of some of the more popular financial institutions of the decade.

14 Three Types of Financial Institutions of the 1920's

While some leaders of old-line private investment firms and the Investment Bankers Association (IBA) tried to uphold high standards of conduct during the 1920's, many of them easily succumbed to the speculative fever of the times and the opportunities for quick, easy profits which it promised. To achieve these goals, established banking houses often employed some of the same practices and institutions of their younger competitors.

Three types of financial institutions achieved great popularity in the 1920's, only to collapse in the next decade and become the subject of federal investigation and regulation. These were the security affiliates of commercial banks, whose functions largely resembled those of private investment bankers; investment trusts, some of which had characteristics and functions similar to those of security affiliates; and public utility holding companies, which were a special category of investment trust. Not one of the three was an innovation of the time, but all suddenly increased in numbers and activities and participated in the prevailing speculative fever.

In 1931, at the time when they were under investigation, the United States Senate Banking and Currency Committee defined security affiliates as "any corporation" established by a commercial bank in which the latter "directly or indirectly controls the election of a majority of . . . [the affiliate's] board of directors."[1] There were several ways in which these institutions were affiliated with their founders. In some instances, all or part of the affiliate's stock was deposited in trust for the benefit of the bank's depositors. In others, the affiliate's stock was sold with that of the bank, as a unit. In still others, a controlling amount of their stock was held by the same interests that controlled the bank's stock, or by the bank itself, or by another affiliate of the bank.

There were four common methods of organizing affiliated companies of the type here discussed. First, a bank declared a cash dividend that stockholders used to buy shares in the affiliate. The Senate Banking Committee found no instance where a stockholder refused to go along with such a plan. Second, a bank organized a wholly owned subsidiary. This plan was used only in states where banks could own such stock; in New York, for instance, trust companies could do this. Third, a bank offered stock to stockholders at a large premium over par, part or all of the premium being subscribed to the stock of the affiliate. Fourth, a bank sold stock of the

---

1. U.S. Senate, Committee on Banking and Currency, 71st Cong., 3d Sess., *Operation of the National and Federal Reserve Banking Systems: Hearings* . . . (8 pts., Washington, 1931–32), pt. 7, 1054–55.

affiliate directly to its stockholders. This method was less common, except for investment trusts.²

Several devices were used to ensure that stockholders of the two corporations were identical. When the stock of an affiliate was held in trust by the bank for the stockholders, this interest was indicated on the bank's own stock certificates and the two could not be separated. In many cases stock certificates of the affiliate were printed on the same document as the bank's certificate. Often affiliates were interlocked through loans and stock holdings.

Although many affiliates were chartered in the state where the parent bank was located, many others were chartered in Delaware to take advantage of its liberal incorporation laws, which permitted more varied activities than did some states. The Guaranty Trust Company's affiliate, the Guaranty Co., for instance, was chartered in Delaware, which allowed these companies to establish branches in other states and countries. The Guaranty Co. operated offices in St. Louis and Montreal. The Delaware charter of the Union Commerce Investment Company, the affiliate of the Union Trust Company of Detroit, which started in 1928, was said to let the company "do everything except solemnize marriages and hold religious services."³

A few security affiliates had been organized before World War I, and in the decade before the 1920's most of the large banks in New York City and other financial centers had established them. Although their numbers had increased substantially by 1930, it was not until the Bank of the United States, with fifty-nine such affiliates, failed in December of that year that much became generally known about them.⁴

Although the federal courts had not decided on the legality of affiliates organized by national banks engaging in the investment banking business, some states had ruled on the matter. In Michigan they had been upheld, whereas in Texas it had been decided that it was a violation of its antitrust laws for stock of an affiliate to be held jointly by stockholders of a parent bank.⁵

As early as 1920 John Skelton Williams, Comptroller of the Currency, had issued a warning against these companies, similar to the one that had been suppressed during the Taft administration, but it went unheeded. The Comptroller headed a section of his report for 1920: " 'Securities Companies' as Adjuncts to National Banks Often a Menace." Such affiliates, he said, already "have become instruments of speculation, and headquarters for promo-

2. *Ibid.,* 1055–57.
3. W. Nelson Peach, *The Security Affiliates of National Banks* (Baltimore, 1941), 65.
4. *Operation of the National and Federal Reserve Banking Systems: Hearings,* pt. 7, 1054.
5. Peach, *Security Affiliates,* 143.

tions of all kinds of financial schemes." Many flotations had been "disastrous," whereas many others had made large profits. He warned that the quality of conservatism essential in officers of national banks did not fit with that suitable for managing the "speculative ventures and promotions of the ancillary institutions." Among their abuses, he noted, were borrowing from their parents and other national banks "in an endless chain . . . for the accommodation of speculative cliques." Holding such positions diverted attention from their banking activities and sometimes led them to make unjustified loans. He asked for legislation to stop the practice as well as to prevent officers of national banks from becoming directors in other corporations.[6]

The Comptroller's report was ignored and no protective legislation followed this appeal. And the attitude of his office soon changed completely. It came to hold that unless national banks could compete with state and private banks, they probably would leave the national banking system, an event to be avoided. The McFadden Act of 1927, in fact, authorized branch banking and certain types of securities business. Not until the 1929 crash did Congress's attitude change.[7]

Contributing to the move of national banks into investment banking was the current tendency for their traditional customers for short-term loans to seek long-term capital. As industrial corporations grew, they became less dependent on banks except for "mechanical banking services."[8]

Many national banks originally had entered the securities business through their bond departments. Most of these had been established before World War I to manage the bank's own bond holdings, having acquired them as secondary reserves. From that situation they developed into bond merchants. The distribution of Liberty bonds during the war gave the banks further experience in selling securities. Most affiliates grew out of such bond departments, and in the 1920's they added common and preferred stocks to their offerings.[9]

There were numerous motivations and functions for these affiliates. One of the first to be started was the First Security Company in New York, with capital of $10 million, incorporated in 1908 by the First National Bank of New York. Because of J. P. Morgan's close relationship with this bank, it had the endorsement of an investment banking firm. President George F. Baker's letter to the bank's stockholders asking their approval of the plan to start the

6. U.S. Treasury, *Annual Report . . . 1920* (Washington, 1921), 1223–24.
7. Peach, *Security Affiliates*, 150ff.
8. Theodore M. Knappen, "A New Deal in Banking," *The Magazine of Wall Street*, LI (March 18, 1933), 566.
9. H. H. Preston and Allan R. Finlay, "Investment Affiliates Thrive," *American Bankers Association Journal*, XXII (May 1930), 1027–28.

affiliate gave its purpose as "transacting for its patrons certain lines of profitable business, which, though often transacted by bankers, are not expressly included with the corporate powers of national banks. Among these are the acquiring and holding of real estate, securities, stocks, and other property." His letter added that several other banks had found such affiliates "advantageous" and that the form of affiliation was agreed to by Morgan and others, who were acting for the stockholders. Stock of this affiliate was held by trustees for the benefit of the shareholders of the First National, which had declared a 100 percent dividend to provide the purchase money.[10]

The National City Bank's affiliate, the National City Co., was started in 1911 for purposes different from those of New York's First National, but it evolved into an organization similar to most others. It began as a holding company to acquire stock in other banks and became the largest concentration of holdings of bank stock anywhere. When the legality of this action was questioned by the Solicitor General, the affiliate disposed of its bank stock and turned to more general investment business. In 1916 it absorbed the private investment banking firm of N. W. Halsey & Co. and combined with it the work of the National City Bank's bond department. Under Charles E. Mitchell the affiliate became the "largest agency in the world for the distribution of securities." [11]

State-chartered commercial banks and trust companies also started affiliates. New York City's Guaranty Trust Co. organized the Guaranty Co. in 1920 as a wholly owned subsidiary. The trust company carried the stock as an investment. The affiliate was a spin-off of the bank's bond department, which was separated "for easier operation"; that is, as a separate corporation it could have offices in various states throughout the country and engage in operations not generally open to trust companies. It proceeded to open offices in Chicago, Philadelphia, and Boston and offered a broad range of investment services. Guaranty Trust's success in marketing Liberty Loans paved the way for its subsequent leadership in underwriting private security issues. By 1930 it had three New York branches and twenty-four others out of town.[12]

The First National Corporation, the affiliate of the First National Bank of Boston, was started in 1918 as a wholly owned subsidiary to participate in the huge increase in foreign business. Its first operations were in letters of credit and foreign acceptances and generally to promote New England import and export trade, but when these

10. *Operation of the National and Federal Reserve Banking Systems: Hearings*, pt. 7, 1052–53.
11. Peach, *Security Affiliates*, 20, 143–46.
12. U.S. Senate, Committee on Finance, 72d Cong., 1st Sess., *Sale of Foreign Bonds or Securities in the United States: Hearings* . . . (4 pts., Washington, 1931–32), pt. 2, 866–68; Peach, *Security Affiliates*, 33, 99.

fell off, it turned to domestic bankers' acceptances and dealing in United States government loans. The acceptance business familiarized this affiliate with customers throughout the country and opened up possibilities for expansion. In 1921 the stock was transferred to trustees for the beneficial interest of the First National's stockholders, and subsequently this became The First Boston Corporation.[13]

Frequently banks took over private investment houses and converted them into branches of their security affiliates. The National City Co.'s absorption of N. W. Halsey, as noted before, was an example of this arrangement.[14]

Some affiliates made slow starts. The First National Investment Company of Chicago, for instance, organized by the First National Bank of Chicago in 1919, expected to participate in underwriting and distributing high-grade stock and thus to "serve a good purpose to . . . customers." But in its early days the imposition of income taxes drove customers to tax-exempt securities.[15]

Another midwestern affiliate, started in 1920, had broader aims. The First Wisconsin National Bank formed the First Wisconsin Co. to take over its bond and investment business and that of the First Wisconsin Trust Company. It also was to underwrite, purchase, and sell bonds and preferred stock and to give special attention to municipal and government securities, domestic and foreign. The national bank was acting to meet the current need to make facilities available for supplying long-term capital to replace short-term.[16]

Accounting in part for the growth in popularity of the affiliate form of organization were the existing business practices of commercial banks. Their regular functions brought officers in close touch with companies issuing securities. As the bond and stock business boomed, commercial banks wishing to participate found that an affiliated organization served the purpose. Customers for short-term loans told bankers of their long-term requirements, and the bankers already knew the issuers' credit standing. Bank officers thought it only fair to let their stockholders benefit from the ownership of an affiliate whose services arose from the bank's sponsorship.[17]

Another factor contributing to the growth of affiliates was the fact that the sales staffs and the capital of existing private investment banking firms were not adequate to handle the great volume of securities being issued. Commercial banks could participate in

13. The First National Bank of Boston, *The First National Corporation* (Boston, May 25, 1918), n.p.; The First National Bank of Boston, *Report to the Stockholders,* January 14, 1919, April 16, 1921.
14. Peach, *Security Affiliates,* 21.
15. James B. Forgan, *Recollections of a Busy Life* (New York, 1924), 157–58.
16. Peach, *Security Affiliates,* 35.
17. *Ibid.,* 21, 34.

this business by lending to brokers and dealers or by participating themselves through their affiliates. They did both, and the fashion became "irresistible." [18]

The functions of affiliates became so varied that, together with their sponsors, they could offer so-called "department store" banking facilities. The more active ones developed large sales organizations and actively solicited business, seeking the securities business as an end in itself.[19] The variety of types of affiliates developed has been summarized as follows:[20]

(1) Wholesalers of security issues, purchasing entire offerings or participating in purchase and banking groups which acquire whole issues of securities from governmental bodies or corporations.

(2) Retailers of securities, maintaining corps of salesmen and often branches in other States than that in which the bank operates for the distribution of stocks and bonds to institutions and private investors.

(3) Holding and finance companies, carrying blocks of securities for control or otherwise, which the bank could not or would not list among its own investments.

(4) Investment trusts, buying and selling securities acquired purely for investment or speculative purposes.

(5) An asset realization company, to take over from the parent bank loans and investments which prove doubtful or nonliquid.

(6) A medium for supporting the market for the bank's own stock.

(7) A real estate holding company.

For large city banks underwriting became the most important function of their affiliates, but the activity most familiar to the public was retail distribution. People commonly associated the affiliate with the parent, the parent with the security issue, and eventually the success or failure of an issue with the parent bank.

Other functions of affiliates were less generally known to the public. Some were organized as a means for securing control of another corporation or for long-time speculation, either because the parent bank was not allowed to carry out this function itself or did not wish to appear as owner.[21]

One important activity of the National City Co. was to act in a service capacity for its parent bank. The National City Bank bought a substantial portion of its investment portfolio through its own affiliate. But it was not the parent's policy to have its trust department or its trust affiliate, the City Bank Farmers Trust Company, also located in New York City, buy their investments through the

18. Raymond W. Goldschmidt, *Changing Structure of American Banking* (London, 1933), 131–32.
19. Peach, *Security Affiliates*, 72, 74.
20. *Operation of the National and Federal Reserve Banking Systems: Hearings*, pt. 7, 1053.
21. Steven L. Osterweis, "Security Affiliates and Security Operations of Commercial Banks," *Harvard Business Review*, XI (October 1932), 126–28.

National City Co. Another function of the affiliate was to trade in the stock of the parent with the aim of leveling price fluctuations; it did not buy for permanent investment, a matter about which the bank had an agreement with the Comptroller of the Currency.[22]

Some banks without actual affiliates or bond departments also offered a variety of investment banking services. They provided advice and executed orders for customers; others distributed only government bonds. Some specialized in selling municipal securities to serve their local areas, as did the Atlas National Bank of Cincinnati. Some borderline banks performed these distribution functions reluctantly, and only as a service to customers who had come to expect it because other banks offered it. Some reluctant banks formed affiliates to obtain syndicate participations that would permit them to buy securities for their own account at preferred prices.[23]

The 1929 collapse stimulated publication of positive and negative appraisals of the affiliate form. In favor was the argument that affiliates could deal in stocks, "an important factor in view of the trend toward this type of investment medium during the past few years." Also, the banks could participate in the "profitable rewards" of such investments. Affiliates could borrow from parents to increase their own purchases. A bank could establish an unlimited number of branches through this device. The separation of corporations allowed a separation of managements, each specializing in the separate and different management qualifications required and receiving different and appropriate compensation; investment banking naturally received higher rewards and thus became "more adequately recognized." Separate organizations, furthermore, facilitated separate kinds of bookkeeping. Affiliates established research departments for their own and the parents' use.[24]

Affiliates of national banks, it was argued, were likely to be larger and more conservative than nonaffiliated investment bankers, with more resources at their command and better able to withstand market fluctuations. Banks lending on collateral would be good judges of its value because of contact with their affiliates. Affiliates, furthermore, would bring business to their parents.[25]

On the contrary side the arguments were equally strong if not stronger than those in favor of security affiliates. The parent increased its risks if it had an affiliate, it was no longer disinterested in the securities it offered, and often it competed with its customers.

22. *Operation of the National and Federal Reserve Banking Systems: Hearings*, pt. 2, 300–01. Testimony of Charles E. Mitchell.
23. Peach, *Security Affiliates*, 73–75.
24. H. H. Preston and Allan R. Finlay, "Era Favors Investment Affiliates," *American Bankers Association Journal*, XXII (June 1930), 1153–54; Osterweis, "Security Affiliates," 128–29.
25. *Ibid.*

There were other features of affiliates that were actually or potentially detrimental to the parent bank. An affiliate could borrow from the parent, and it could sell securities to the bank under a repurchase agreement. The public's association of the two institutions in its own mind would make the parent prevent its affiliate's failure. The parent might buy its affiliate's excess holdings and lend too freely to customers on issues sponsored by an affiliate. The goodwill of the bank's depositors would be jeopardized if they suffered losses on issues of the affiliate, which could use lists of depositors for its prospective clients.

There were other dangers as well. Operations of affiliates in the bank's own stock might cause disadvantageous fluctuations. Similarly, wide variations in the net asset value of the affiliate would tend to make the parent's securities fluctuate. The ability to shift a commitment to its affiliate might make the bank less careful in its original obligations. The effects of these considerations on the trust department of a bank might be adverse to the independence of its fiduciary responsibilities. Lastly, the affiliate's ties to its parent might make it less cautious than a private investment house.[26]

Although a relatively small proportion of all commercial banks had such affiliates, or even bond departments, the larger banks in important financial centers generally did have them. Since these affiliates often had branches widely scattered throughout the country and abroad, their influence became significant. In addition, bank mergers led to wider geographical distribution and broader functions. Some affiliates merged with private investment firms or became closely associated with them. Some affiliates actually were holding companies controlling chains of banks, using them as outlets for securities as they would employ branches.[27]

By 1921 the trend for commercial banks and trust companies to establish security affiliates was well under way. In 1922 there were 10 affiliates underwriting and distributing securities; 62 national banks had bond departments; 8 state banks and trust companies had such affiliates; and 197 state banks and trust companies conducted a securities business through bond departments. In the decade they continued to grow, especially in 1928 and 1929, when, it was estimated, a third of those in existence in 1930 had been established. By 1929 nearly every large urban bank had one or several affiliates, usually with a name slightly altered from that of the parent. The models most frequently followed were those of the First Security Co., National City Co., and Chase Securities Corporation, the latter organized in 1917 as the affiliate of New York City's Chase National Bank. Many banks, in their letters to stockholders, referred to

26. *Operation of the National and Federal Reserve Banking Systems: Hearings*, pt. 7, 1063–64.
27. Peach, *Security Affiliates*, 85–86.

the fact that they were following models and practices first used by these three prominent institutions.[28]

By the end of the decade commercial banks and their affiliates were equal in importance to all investment bankers in the distribution of long-term capital and in the facilities and value of their business. In 1930, eleven large affiliates had combined assets of $535 million.[29]

Through their bond departments or affiliates, commercial banks originated 22 percent of new issues in 1927; in 1930 it was 44.6 percent. Their participations in new issues in 1927 accounted for nearly 37 percent of all such participations, and in 1930, over 60 percent. Their role in distribution made commercial banks by far the most important element in the investment banking business.[30] They relied heavily on salesmen and advertising, and the affiliates appealed directly to the parent's deposit customers, with whose accounts and habits they were familiar.[31]

Although there was some contemporary criticism of both the theory and the practice of having such affiliates, not until the 1929 crash was the question of regulating them seriously faced. "The particular event which marked the beginning of widespread hostility toward the affiliate system was the failure of the Bank of the United States in New York City." The officers and directors of this bank, it was disclosed later, had abused their trust — "a horrifying spectacle of the misuse of depositors' funds."[32] But not until the federal investigations made prior to the Securities acts of 1933 and 1934 were their many real abuses revealed. Some of these, not inherent in the affiliate relationship, were marketing unsound securities, publishing misleading prospectuses, and engaging in high-pressure selling. Private investment bankers were subject to the same criticisms. Directly connected with the affiliate relationship, however, were bank officers' use of affiliates for personal profit, banks' use of affiliates to take frozen loans or affiliates' use of banks to take unsuccessful promotions, and participation by affiliates in pool operations in the stock of parent banks.[33]

Even if affiliates had limited themselves to distribution, they would have experienced losses in the 1929 crash, but many entered into extremely speculative ventures. Some were involved in disastrous real estate speculation, and some manipulated the stock of their parents. When the crash came, they suffered the consequences.[34]

28. *Ibid.*, 64; Preston and Finlay, "Investment Affiliates Thrive," 1027–28.
29. Goldschmidt, *Changing Structure of American Banking*, 135.
30. George W. Edwards, *The Evolution of Finance Capitalism* (London, 1938), 226; Osterweis, "Security Affiliates," 126.
31. Goldschmidt, *Changing Structure of American Banking*, 134–35.
32. Peach, *Security Affiliates*, 151.
33. *Ibid.*, 113–14.
34. Goldschmidt, *Changing Structure of American Banking*, 139.

Their lack of regard for the public interest has been described thus: "From being investment counsel they not infrequently became investment merchants, with little more regard for the customer's interest than an automobile salesman has for a [prospective customer]." [35] Among their activities that were dangerous to themselves was playing the market on their own account, and for their parents, lending on pledged collateral that was inferior in quality and amount.[36]

The system had its defenders, however, even after the crash. For example, Bernard W. Trafford, of the First National Bank of Boston, thought affiliates had done well and filled a need. Abuses that occurred, he believed, stemmed from bad management, not from the system.[37]

Some banks stayed out of the popular movement because they did not approve of the practice, and so advertised. They asserted that they thus were able to give unbiased investment advice. New York City's old and respected Farmers' Loan and Trust Company, for example, did not even have a bond-selling department. It did have a securities department, but its function was solely analysis of securities, not dealing in them. Some banks that did have affiliates took pains to point out that they would continue to operate on safe and conservative lines.[38]

A 1934 study published in the *Harvard Business Review* explored the relative successes of security originations of affiliates and those of private investment bankers.[39] The span covered the period 1921 to 1932 and it included the eight largest private investment houses and eight largest affiliates of national banks.

Private Investment Banks	*Affiliates of National Banks*
J. P. Morgan & Co.	Guaranty Co.
Bonbright & Co., Inc.	Continental Illinois
Harris, Forbes & Co.	National City Co.
Kuhn, Loeb & Co.	Chase Securities
Dillon, Read & Co.	Bankers Trust
Blair & Co.	First National–Old Colony
Halsey, Stuart & Co.	Equitable Trust
Lee, Higginson & Co.	Union Trust

The securities included amounted to about $28 billion and over 2,500 issues. This was between one-third to one-half of the total

---

35. Knappen, "New Deal in Banking," 566.
36. Edwards, *Evolution of Finance Capitalism*, 226.
37. *Operation of the National and Federal Reserve Banking Systems: Hearings*, pt. 1, 231.
38. Peach, *Security Affiliates*, 72.
39. Terris Moore, "Security Affiliates Versus Private Investment Banker — A Study in Security Originations," *Harvard Business Review*, XII (July 1934), 478–84.

dollar value and one-tenth of the total number of issues in the twelve years. Since many more private houses than security affiliates originated new issues, the eight largest investment firms represented a smaller proportion of the total in their group than did the eight affiliates. By far the larger number of all new issues were brought out by many small houses, and the offerings were not large. Many of these smaller issues were of questionable character.

The study made separate analyses for bonds and notes and for preferred stock. Bonds and notes were judged on the basis of price change, preferreds on their dividend record. The firms studied floated so few common issues that these were not included in the analysis.

The study disclosed that the records of private houses with the best showings were superior to those of the best affiliates. On the other hand, the findings also demonstrated that the records of the poorest private houses were inferior to those of the corresponding affiliates. The fact that some houses specialized in securities of single industries influenced their records. Kuhn, Loeb & Co., a railroad house, made a poor showing, whereas a public utility specialist like Bonbright & Co. had a "happy" record. The Morgan firm, which diversified, had the best record of all.

The study concluded that there was little to choose between the two types of financial firms. "The banks, despite their closer association with the corporations whose securities were being floated, have decidedly not performed the security origination function any better than have the private investment bankers. One can now say that there has been no significant difference in the quality of the new security originations of these two groups." [40]

The prominence and activities of commercial banks and their affiliates in the securities industry during the 1920's were rivaled by those of another type of financial institution, the investment trust. During the 1920's these companies, like the security affiliates, grew from relative obscurity to "a recognized position in the field of finance and investment." The spread of the investment trust idea, *Moody's Manual of Investments* reported in 1928, "seems almost phenomenal." [41]

In 1925, when still only a few investment trusts had been established and before their potentialities for good and bad had been demonstrated, another writer for the *Harvard Business Review* provided the readers of this respected publication with an optimistic definition of the purposes of these increasingly popular organizations. An investment trust, he said, was a "financial institution set up for the purpose of making it possible for the investor to obtain a high degree of safety in his investment by buying securities of the

40. *Ibid.,* 484.
41. *Moody's Manual of Investments: Banks . . . 1928,* xvii.

trust, which securities in turn are backed by various other securities — stocks and bonds." Investment trusts differed from holding companies in that they did not seek to acquire control of the companies they invested in, but to hold securities as collateral for their own issues. The diversification of their holdings lent stability to their own securities.[42]

There were two main types of trusts: management and fixed. In the former, directors or trustees controlled the portfolio and made investments as they saw fit; in the latter, the portfolio, once determined, was not changed. Many trusts also dealt in securities, participated in underwriting, made short-term loans, and engaged in other financial activities. Until 1926 participation in underwritings was uncommon, but by 1929 it often was written into charters.[43] As the decade progressed, investment trust functions expanded and these organizations spread throughout the country.

Investment trusts put funds into a variety of types of securities and themselves issued a variety of securities: bonds, preferreds of several classes, and common stock. Many trusts invested only in domestic issues, but some also bought foreign securities. Others specialized in a single industry, some were diversified, some specified limits to the amount of any one security in which they would invest, and some prohibited underwriting and brokerage.[44]

Management trusts supposedly relied on income from securities to cover expenses and give a return on investment. To do so successfully, however, the trust had to be large enough so that the expenses would be a relatively small proportion of income. When income was inadequate to provide an attractive enough return to satisfy the managers, they tended to seek speculative gains by buying and selling. The smaller the trust, the greater this temptation. As opportunities for speculative profits increased later in the decade, the tendency to exploit them often became irresistible, with the result that many of these trusts turned out to be nothing more than "blind pools" manipulated by managers.[45] The problem of reinvesting funds was aggravated by the market boom. Some managers solved it by buying speculative issues; others built up cash reserves. The high market prices for the trusts' own securities, often beyond "any reasonable proportion to either liquidating value or earnings," gave rise to an unwarranted assumption of continued high earnings.[46]

42. Russell D. Kilborne, "American Investment Trusts," *Harvard Business Review*, III (January 1925), 160–61.
43. William H. Steiner, *Investment Trusts: American Experience* (New York, 1929), 171.
44. John F. Fowler, *American Investment Trusts* (New York, 1928), 65–66.
45. Arthur S. Dewing, "Investment Trusts," *Harvard Business Review*, X (October 1931), 24–25.
46. Joseph A. Thomas, "Ten Investment Trusts in America — A Three-Year Record," *Harvard Business Review*, IX (October 1930), 83.

Fixed trusts generally were established by bankers who wanted something to sell. They invested in blue chip securities, increasing the demand for them and thus tending to push up prices. In a market upswing, if trustees could borrow, they were likely to do so to build up their investable funds. In the boom years 1927 to 1929, shares of fixed trusts were not popular, but after the stock market crash and the poor administration of many managed trusts was revealed, the public reversed its judgment.[47]

The organization of investment trusts varied greatly among the different investment banking firms and over the period. Many were incorporated in Delaware because this state did not tax the estates of nonresident decedents and because regular meetings of stockholders and directors could be held outside its borders.

The investment trusts of the 1920's can be classified into four groups according to the types of their sponsors. There were trusts started by professional managers, who concentrated on the business of the trust. An example was the International Securities Trust of America (ISTA), organized in Massachusetts in 1921. It was not dominated by any investment house, probably not from choice, but because banking firms at first were skeptical of investment trusts. The fact that ISTA bought only seasoned securities was an exception to the later common practice of these institutions. This trust was reorganized in 1927 and incorporated in Maryland under a slightly different name, International Securities Corporation of America, to operate as a management trust.[48]

Investment consultants and trustees provided a second type of sponsorship. These men usually established and managed fund-type trusts while they continued to work at their regular professions. These trusts were especially common in Boston.[49]

Sponsors of the third type were investment bankers. Kidder, Peabody & Co., for instance, started Kidder Participations, Inc., which was officered by the firm's partners and typically invested in Kidder, Peabody's underwritings.[50]

The fourth group included investment trusts sponsored by commercial banks, trust companies, and their security affiliates. An example of this type was the Shawmut Association of Boston. The National Shawmut Bank furnished the association with supervisory and other services but did not own stock in it.[51]

None of these types of trusts, nor any other, was popular in the United States at the close of World War I. Few were in existence. They had not been promoted actively, and the investing public gen-

47. Dewing, "Investment Trusts," 25–26.
48. Steiner, *Investment Trusts,* 51, 120–21, 171; *Moody's Manual of Investments: Banks, 1928,* 2016.
49. Steiner, *Investment Trusts,* 62, 121.
50. *Ibid.;* Kidder, Peabody & Co., MSS., Baker Library.
51. Steiner, *Investment Trusts,* 62, 121, 218.

erally was unfamiliar with them, even though they were very common in Britain and on the Continent. The British especially had had a long and favorable experience with them, much more so than had other Europeans.[52]

Several factors contributed to launching the investment trust movement in America. Immediately after the war American bankers interested in foreign markets turned to these institutions as a device to acquire foreign securities. In 1919 Paul M. Warburg, who had just returned to his partnership in Kuhn, Loeb & Co. after serving on the Federal Reserve Board for five years as one of Woodrow Wilson's original appointees, advocated the formation of "powerful investment trusts" to specialize in foreign securities. Such trusts, he said, would enable the " 'little fellow', in a modest and safe manner to become the holder of foreign securities." He believed investment bankers should become interested in such companies and lend their experienced judgment to them. He suggested that they form a "huge investment trust" first to distribute bonds for the War Finance Corporation and then go on to other types of issues.[53]

Investment opportunities in Europe after the war attracted many investment trusts to the issues of former creditor nations, currently undervalued because of lack of capital in those countries. Purchases by American trusts tended to raise the prices of those securities nearer to their actual values, as well as to raise exchange rates beyond the gold export point for dollars, thus causing gold to flow out of the United States. European central banks, which looked on American purchases of their countries' bonds as short-term loans, tried to maintain the stability of their currencies, anticipating that a reverse flow soon would occur.[54]

Some observers at the time looked upon the investment trusts' purchases of foreign securities as a means of overcoming the American public's distrust of them. These trusts were being given considerable publicity, and it was expected, rightly, that their issues, and foreign securities generally, would become popular.[55]

There also were other considerations favoring the establishment of investment trusts. The fact that various states had relaxed their restrictions on the ownership of one company by another, that the supply of securities was ample, and that investors had capital to place all contributed to the growth of these institutions.[56]

Circumstances were especially favorable for launching new trusts after 1926. The principal stimulating factors were the rising

52. Kilborne, "American Investment Trusts," 161.
53. Paul M. Warburg, "Some Problems of the Investment Banker," an address delivered before the Bond Club of New York, May 23, 1919, 6–7.
54. Steiner, *Investment Trusts,* 172–73.
55. Kilborne, "American Investment Trusts," 160.
56. U.S. Securities and Exchange Commission, *Investment Trusts and Investment Companies: Report* . . . (5 pts., Washington, 1939–42), pt. 1, 37.

stock market and the easy availability of capital. The freedom of management enjoyed by these institutions and the fact that they provided "a safety-deposit box in the form of a strong call-loan demand" also were contributing factors.[57] Equally important was the public's growing interest in equities, especially common stock. War industries had issued common, and much publicity was given to stocks in the 1920's. Listing of new issues was widely publicized; books, articles, and pamphlets appeared on the topic. Common stocks even became the subject of college courses. Everything was done "to remove the prejudice of the small investor against common stock," the Securities and Exchange Commission reported later. Issuers advertised in general as well as financial publications. "Bankers Planning Rich Man's Trust," "The Investment Trust and the Small Investor," "Art of Investing Fast Developing into a Science" were a few of the titles of articles used to advertise trusts.[58]

The fact that the New York Stock Exchange had no formal ruling against listing investment trust shares also contributed to their growth and popularity. Its stated policy was to judge each application on its merits. Early in the decade it passed a resolution stating that if a member took part in a trust that did not properly protect the interest of investors, it would consider such an act detrimental to the exchange and call for sanctions.[59] By 1929 it had drawn up listing requirements for trusts, including one calling for disclosure of security portfolios.[60]

Investment bankers and other financiers finally became heavily involved in the trust movement to exploit a waiting market. After 1926 they began wholesale sponsorship of these institutions. They distributed the trusts' securities, receiving management fees as well as fees for acting as custodian, transfer agent, and registrar. Trusts lent money to, or deposited funds with, their sponsors and bought securities that the latter offered. Often they gave the sponsor an indirect control of large blocks of securities; and trusts also were a means of establishing contacts between bankers and companies whose issues the trusts held. The sponsor's prestige was associated with the trust, and he assumed that he was well qualified to take on these new functions.[61]

A large proportion of managed investment companies were organized by investment bankers or security companies to take advantage of opportunities in underwriting. As of the end of 1929, 109 out of 162 closed-end management investment trusts were launched, principally by houses of issue, bank affiliates, brokers,

57. Thomas, "Ten Investment Trusts in America," 83.
58. *Investment Trusts and Investment Companies: Report,* pt. 1, 57–59.
59. Kilborne, "American Investment Trusts," 167.
60. Edward H. H. Simmons, *Financing American Industry and Other Addresses* (n.p. [1930]), 319.
61. *Investment Trusts and Investment Companies: Report,* pt. 1, 76–77.

or dealers. Some trusts acted as co-entrepreneurs in the purchase, distribution, and underwriting of issues. The investment banking sponsors determined the functions and structure of the trusts, power was centralized in the organizer, and contracts were made in which dominant individuals in the sponsoring firm were personally interested.[62]

The sponsoring investment bankers actively promoted their trusts, created a demand for their securities, and profited from both distribution and management. Among the means they used were to issue special management stock, options, and bonuses; to charge underwriting fees and commissions; to benefit from direct dealings with trusts; and to receive "all the other emoluments attendant on the control of substantial liquid funds and blocks of securities of other corporations." [63]

As new and refunding issues increased during the 1920's, investment bankers came to regard trusts as receptacles for their new flotations. Trusts also served to expand the bankers' financial capacity. Most investment company issues did not supply operating companies with capital, but simply provided business to the investment bankers. Sponsors controlled their trusts by holding voting stock, controlling proxy machinery, setting up voting trusts and management contracts, and by pyramiding — the piling of one trust upon another with power firmly entrenched among a few organizers at the top. Some trusts were affiliated with one another through interlocking directorates, stock ownership, or other similar arrangements.[64]

Investment bankers also formed trusts in order to render additional services to clients and to retain their patronage. They believed that they would incur little additional work; they could run their trusts from "a corner of the office." Other bankers joined in the movement because it was sweeping the country, and they used the new sales device to reach new clients. Investment counselors also formed affiliated investment trusts, as did "Boston trustees," who established funds in which they wanted the public to participate. Some trusts were practically subsidiaries. Sometimes investment houses jointly established trusts, occasionally with foreign houses.[65] Others were said to have formed trusts simply to get promoters' profits and assure themselves of a customer for slow securities.[66]

Investment bankers brought experience to the operation of trusts and lent their statistical facilities in ways that placed trusts in strong competitive positions. Investment trusts became an important chan-

62. *Ibid.*, pt. 3, 879.
63. *Ibid.*, pt. 1, 62.
64. *Ibid.*, pt. 1, 62; Steiner, *Investment Trusts*, 120.
65. Steiner, *Investment Trusts*, 62.
66. George W. Dowrie, *Money and Banking* (New York, 1936), 397–98.

nel for the absorption of new issues, maintaining an equilibrium in the markets while the securities were seasoning.[67] Issuers were in a position to offer clients securities of companies they managed and to create and maintain a device for investing in blocks of attractive, diversified, current issues. Not only did these dealings strengthen market prices, but trusts participating in underwriting could receive price concessions on purchases for their own account.[68]

The public came to identify an investment trust with its sponsor, as was the case with affiliates of commercial banks. A classified directory of investment trusts gave this piece of advice to users: "In directing correspondence to investment trusts, it is desirable to insert the names of the affiliations below the address, since there are a substantial number of investment trusts with no addresses other than those of the principal banking or underwriting affiliations or fiscal agent." [69]

The investment trust movement started slowly early in the decade, picked up momentum in 1926, and was racing by 1929. Before 1921 only about 40 of these institutions had been established; by the end of 1929 there were 770 in existence, 265 of which had been launched in 1929 (see Exhibit 12). The total assets of all these

Exhibit 12. Number of investment trusts organized, 1921–1929

Year	Number organized
Before 1921	40
1921–1926	139
1927	140
1928	186
1929	265
	770

Source: U.S. Securities and Exchange Commission, *Investment Trusts and Investment Companies: Report*, I, 36.

companies by the end of 1926 amounted to about $1 billion; by the close of 1929 they exceeded $7 billion.[70]

The huge volume of investment trust and holding company issues marketed in September 1929 — about $650 million — would have seemed excessive in ordinary times, said the president of the New York Stock Exchange. "But the idea seemed to prevail that invest-

67. Fowler, *American Investment Trusts*, 26, 28, 247.
68. Leland R. Robinson, *Investment Trust Organization and Management* (rev. ed., New York, 1929), 23–24.
69. Fowler, *American Investment Trusts*, 251.
70. *Investment Trusts and Investment Companies: Report*, pt. 1, 36.

ment trust and finance company issues did not actually absorb any new public capital, because the proceeds of these issues would be used to purchase other outstanding issues." [71]

Not until after the 1929 crash, and subsequent investigations, did the public know much about the actual operations of investment trusts. Although many articles were written about them while they were booming, much of their content was theoretical, if not irrelevant. As late as 1929, one writer commented on their function as supplementary to investment bankers rather than competitive; he declared that trust securities were stable and that they could be put under the hammer without appreciable loss.[72]

Often trusts did not publish much financial information, and there was current debate over whether to publish portfolio holdings. Whereas publicity, then and later, was believed to be a great preventive of abuses, many arguments against it were advanced. Pointing to British practice (about half of British investment trusts did publish their holdings) one author summarized some persuasive reasons for secrecy: ill-informed investors might exaggerate market effects; disclosure would give away a valuable asset; other firms might be attracted to an issue in which the trust itself wished to increase its holdings, or selling might become more difficult; requests for information would be invited; portfolio lists soon would become out of date, misleading, or, in some cases, reveal the personal interests of directors; and omission of a security might be misinterpreted as a judgment that it was not worth buying.[73]

Even before the crash, opportunities for abuses were recognized by some writers, but the usual response to these warnings, however, was that such opportunities always existed for individuals looking for them.[74]

Although blue-sky laws were being advocated more and more during these years, there was, in fact, little state or federal regulation of trusts. The Attorney General of New York had proposed that the state banking department should pass on the operating plans of investment trusts and supervise them. Others called for a combination of public control and self-policing as an "ideal" situation.[75] Scant attention was given to these proposals.

When the crash came, investment trusts went down with a "deadening thud."[76] Portfolio values shrank, revenues decreased, and abuses ranging from poor judgment to outright dishonesty were revealed. Weaknesses also were disclosed in organizational

71. Simmons, *Financing American Industry*, 319.
72. Robinson, *Investment Trust Organization*, 521–22.
73. Steiner, *Investment Trusts*, 174–75.
74. Robinson, *Investment Trust Organization*, 24.
75. Steiner, *Investment Trusts*, 305.
76. Carl Williams, "Investment Trusts under the Microscope," *The Magazine of Wall Street*, LI (October 29, 1932), 26.

structures and general operations. The mushroom growth of 1928–29, it was later recognized, "was bound to bring a great deal of grief and humiliation." In those years there were not enough good securities to go around, and even some of the best were not good enough. Some trusts bought shares in other trusts, a type of transaction that became "a definite pathology." Stock in A rose because B was buying it, and B rose because A was buying its shares. One notable exception to the dismal investment trust record of late 1929 was the Lehman Corporation, which was afraid of the market and kept its funds largely in cash.[77]

Even as far back as 1925, it was said, investment bankers had begun to lose their heads; before that time they had done their work well. Cheap money and urgent demands for securities caused them to relax their credit standards, and with renewed cheap money in 1927 and after, they badly lost perspective.[78]

Three prominent investment trusts organized by investment bankers serve to illustrate the uses and abuses of these institutions. The organizers were Goldman, Sachs & Co., Dillon, Read & Co., and Kidder, Peabody & Co.

The Goldman Sachs Trading Corporation provided an excellent example of pyramiding.[79] It was organized to invest in securities, and it published its portfolio. Incorporated in Delaware in December 1928, it issued only common stock, a million shares. The sponsor firm took 100,000 shares at 100 and sold the rest to the public at 104, making about $3 million profit. Subsequently the company floated more securities. Upon its organization it proceeded to make the following investments:

Holdings of Goldman Sachs Trading Corporation	Capital (Millions)
Shenandoah Corporation	34
Pacific American Associates	83
Frosted Foods	13
Central States Electric	10
Banks and trust companies	42
Insurance companies	19
Total	201

The first step in the Goldman Sachs Trading Corporation's dramatic rise to national prominence occurred two months after its organization. It involved a merger with another investment trust, the Financial and Industrial Securities Corporation. This move in-

77. Benjamin M. Anderson, *Economics and the Public Welfare: Financial and Economic History of the United States, 1914–1946* (New York, 1949), 204–05.
78. *Ibid.*
79. John T. Flynn, *Investment Trusts Gone Wrong!* (New York, 1931), 78–91.

creased the Trading Corporation's assets to $235 million, more than double what they had been three months earlier.

After a brief respite, during which time it boomed its own stock, the Trading Corporation entered upon the most spectacular phase of its career. In July it joined with the Central States Electric Corporation, a public utility holding company, to launch a new investment trust, the Shenandoah Corporation. The initial stock offering of this company was $102.5 million, and it was heavily oversubscribed.

Shenandoah, like the Trading Corporation that created it, immediately gave birth to an offspring of its own. In August 1929 it organized and invested in the Blue Ridge Corporation, an investment trust, holding, and finance company. The Blue Ridge Company did invest part of its money in a productive enterprise, but it also put part in Central States Electric. That company, in turn, invested in North American Company and American Cities Power and Light Company, both holding or finance companies. The latter company held securities of Chain Stores, Inc., another investment company that held shares in Metropolitan Chain Stores in New York, a company actually in business. The flow of dividends from Metropolitan Chain had eight separate steps of management waiting for their shares and, according to John T. Flynn, a critic of this trust, "serving absolutely no useful purpose in industry, in finance, in society." [80] Although some of the trusts in the series made no management charge, they received managerial profits through their compensation for floating securities in the several firms, obtaining shares at special prices, or through stock options.

On the same day that Shenandoah launched the Blue Ridge Corporation, the Trading Corporation, which controlled both of them, acquired another investment trust, Pacific American Associates. This West Coast corporation controlled another holding company that owned all the stock in a trust company that owned a security holding company that owned the American Securities Company. In this chain the trust company itself was a merger of San Francisco banks and had 96 branches in the area.

Another finance company owned by Goldman, Sachs controlled a group of banks in New York City, including the Manufacturers Trust Company. The latter owned a number of insurance companies.

Goldman, Sachs was not the first investment banking house to involve itself with investment trusts. This honor belonged to Dillon, Read, the "most active investment banking house in the country." In 1924 it organized the United States & Foreign Securities Company (US&FS), the "most eminent" of investment trusts. The move

80. *Ibid.*, 87. See also Hugh Bullock, *The Story of Investment Companies* (New York, 1959), 19–20.

was seen as "an opportunity to let the public in on Dillon's investment brains." [81]

The opportunity for an investment banking firm to profit from its affiliated trust was illustrated in Dillon, Read's promotion of US&FS. The trust issued two classes of preferred stock as well as common, all no par. The 250,000 shares of $6 first preferred Dillon, Read sold to the public for $100, each share carrying a bonus of one share of common. The 50,000 shares of $6 second preferred the banking house itself bought for $5 million, and it received as a bonus 750,000 shares of common, the remainder of the authorized 1 million shares. Thus for putting up one-sixth of the cash Dillon, Read became entitled to $6 dividends on the second preferred plus three-fourths of the net profit after preferred dividends. This enviable position proved to be more theoretical than actual, however, for US&FS never paid any common dividends. Typically, the trust bought into issues floated by Dillon, Read, and there were interlocking directorates. Furthermore, there was reciprocal stock ownership with International Securities Corporation, another Dillon, Read investment trust.[82]

Kidder, Peabody, one of the long-established, eminently respectable investment banking houses, also succumbed to the investment trust mania that swept American finance in the late 1920's. Making ingenious use of an industrial corporation, a merger it had promoted at the turn of the century and with which it had become more and more closely associated, this private banking firm had responded to previous changes in the financial environment by converting that organization from a manufacturer into a holding company, then into an acceptance dealer, and lastly into an investment trust and participant in Kidder, Peabody's promotions. And to widen the trust's activities still further, the bankers established additional corporations with parallel functions and finally set up a trust company to serve the investment companies.

Starting with the New England Cotton Yarn Company, a merger of 1899, the bankers in 1916 turned it into the New England Investment Corporation, a textile holding company. In 1922 they made it into the Kidder, Peabody Acceptance Corporation, which specialized at first in dealing in dollar acceptances and finally in industrial promotions. Then to join in these promotions, the bankers

---

81. Bullock, *The Story of Investment Companies,* 19–20.
82. Flynn, *Investment Trusts Gone Wrong!* 5, 57, 60; Steiner, *Investment Trusts,* 134; *Moody's Manual of Investments, Banks . . . 1929,* 2755; Ferdinand Pecora, *Wall Street Under Oath: The Story of Our Modern Money Changers* (New York, 1939), 209. On its balance sheet US&FS assigned the first preferred a value of $100 a share and the second preferred and common $1 each. It carried also a General Reserve account of $4,950,000, explaining that this was set up out of the $5 million paid in cash by the subscribers to the second preferred. *Moody's, 1929,* 2755.

floated three Kidder, Peabody Participations, Inc., Numbers 1, 2, and 3, in 1926 and 1927, and Mitchum Tully Participations, Inc., on the West Coast, also in 1927. And in that year too they established the Kidder, Peabody Trust Company, Inc.[83]

The firms became increasingly close in top management so that eventually Kidder, Peabody partners were nearly identical with the directorates and executives of the affiliates. Kidder, Peabody generally held control through ownership of common stock and added millions to its capital resources by marketing the affiliates' preferred issues. The affiliates joined in Kidder, Peabody's underwritings and invested in its promotions. Through ownership of the preferred stock, the public could participate in Kidder, Peabody's managerial experience, and through its affiliates, Kidder, Peabody broadened its investment and promotion policy to include issues that were more speculative than had been customary for this firm. All participated in the subsequent boom and crash.[84]

The investment bankers' activities in promoting and organizing investment trusts contrasted sharply with their previously sound practices and reputation for financial conservatism. In general the leading firms formerly had scrutinized the safety of investments before offering them to the public. Representing the buyers of an issue, they had acted at arm's length with issuers and usually had charged only a reasonable fee for raising capital. But during the boom of the later 1920's many firms contravened the criteria for reputable flotations. They sold new, unseasoned issues; for their affiliated investment trusts, management and financiers were identical; compensation was determined by interested individuals; and the buyers' interests were not protected. In 1928 and 1929 the effects of "egotistical views [were] prevalent in the financial world."[85]

Investment trusts that were affiliates of commercial banks engaged in the securities business were revealed also to have been subject to abuses. Such trusts and holding companies showed a greater tendency to operate with borrowed funds than did such organizations when independent of banks. Identity of management tended to make them use funds that were available. When an investment trust was the receptacle for slow-moving issues, it helped to keep the sponsor liquid, but if the bank then lent to the affiliate, it was advancing funds on doubtful assets. The availability of the affiliate made bankers less cautious.[86]

83. *Investment Trusts and Investment Companies: Report,* pt. 1, 81–83; Kidder, Peabody & Co., "Circulars" [1895–1927], 10 vols., Baker Library, various dates.
84. Kidder, Peabody & Co., "Circulars," various dates.
85. Benjamin Graham and David L. Dodd, *Security Analysis: Principles and Technique* (2d ed., New York, 1940), 651–52.
86. *Operation of the National and Federal Reserve Banking Systems: Hearings,* pt. 7, 1058.

The investment trust boom, according to a Marxist view, greatly increased the bankers' control over the modest savings of small investors. "Salaried workers and small capitalists would buy the non-voting stock of the investment trust — control remaining with a small block of voting stock held by the promoters. Some three billions of dollars of stock and bonds in investment trusts were sold to the petty capitalist world during the boom and added that much more to the controlled market for new securities." [87]

One of the earliest efforts to appraise the performance of investment trusts was made in 1930. In that year a study was conducted of the operations of ten large investment trusts. It compared their forms of organization, their operating policies from 1926 to 1928, and the effects of the crash on the prices of their own securities.[88] In this period of rising stock prices, the Dow-Jones average of industrials went from a 1926 low of 135.20 to 300 in 1928. Call money went from $3\frac{1}{2}$ percent to 12 percent, "thus providing a safe, convenient, profitable market for excess funds awaiting investment." Capital was easy to come by and investors were eager.

Exhibit 13 Ten investment trusts: percentage of decline in common stock prices in market break in October and November 1929

Name	1929 high	1929 low	Percent decline
State Street Investment Corporation	290	132	54.5
U.S. & Foreign Securities Corporation	72	17	76
General Public Service Corporation	98	20	79.5
United Bond & Share Corporation	n.a.	n.a.	–
Railway & Light Securities Corporation	116	55	52.5
American British & Continental	22	5	77.6
Overseas Securities Corporation	59	19½	66.9
Massachusetts Investors Trust	129	80	38
Guardian Investors	18	4	78
Securities Corporation General	915	265	71

Source: Joseph A. Thomas, "Ten Investment Trusts in America — A Three-Year Record," *Harvard Business Review*, IX (October 1930), 83.

The ten investment trusts, listed in Exhibit 13, each had at least $1 million in capital. They were general management types, organized to invest and reinvest funds according to the managers' judg-

---

87. Anna Rochester, *Rulers of America: A Study of Finance Capital* (New York, 1936), 97.
88. Thomas, "Ten Investment Trusts in America," 78–88. See also Fowler, *American Investment Trusts,* Appendix A.

ment, subject in some cases to formal protective restrictions. All had been organized by 1925, one as early as 1904. None had issued bonds at first, but by 1928, as their credit had become established, six had floated bonds, although none for as much as 50 percent of its capital. Five used debentures and one, collateral trust bonds, mostly 5 percent issues. Seven had preferred stock. General practice was to raise from 20 percent to 50 percent of capital through preferreds. When investment trusts still were a novelty, preferred stock had been easier to sell than bonds or common, and promoters generally wanted to keep common for themselves. In several instances common was given as a bonus with the preferred. Two Massachusetts companies had common stock only. All the common stocks had no par value.

Typical returns on invested capital of these ten companies (outstanding capital stock and bonds plus earned surplus) showed spectacular rises. In 1926 the figure was 8.7 percent; in 1927, as earnings rose, the average was 10 percent, but the range was from 4.8 percent to 23.1 percent. Further rises in 1928 gave one firm 35.4 percent. These high returns showed an "aggressive policy" of realizing on capital gains; in 1928 one company received 90 percent of its income from such profits. For these firms a negligible part of profits came from underwriting.

Exhibit 14 compares the effects of contrasting policies of three of these firms. State Street Investment Corporation, for example, which paid management a percentage of net worth, paid out in dividends a relatively low percentage of its total earnings. In general the firms tended to become increasingly conservative in their dividend payments and to build up reserves. In 1928 only three distributed more than half the year's net profits, but earnings were so great that dividend rates were raised or extras declared.

When this study was made it was too soon after the 1929 crash to draw definite conclusions about the ten companies. The author attributed their success to the skill of management. Their growth had been healthy, he believed, and management had been "alert and yet not reckless." Policies had been "tempered with conservatism," and he concluded that the companies had justified "their place in American finance and their worth to American investors." [89]

The investment trust was not the only spectacular financial institution of the 1920's. The exalted status in which it was held by the public and the many practical purposes to which it lent itself were rivaled only by the public utility holding company. It too was a manifestation of an era of proliferating firms performing investment banking functions. Public utility holding companies had many characteristics of general purpose investment trusts and also often were affiliates of financial institutions.

89. Thomas, "Ten Investment Trusts in America," 88.

Exhibit 14. Selected statistics for three investment trusts, 1928

	State Street Investment Corporation	Massachusetts Investors Trust	General Public Service Corporation
Management compensation	1 percent average net worth	6 percent annual income	Salaries
Total expenses (percent total income 1928)	21.2	8.1	10.5
Capital structure (December 1928)	100 percent common	100 percent common	Bonds $4.9 mil. Pfd. $3.5 mil. Com. 542,539 shares
Percent net return on invested capital, 1928	35.4	8.3	9.6
Percent total income from securities sales, 1928	90.7	36.1	48
Percent decline in common, 1929	54.5	38	79.5
Percent net earnings paid out	14	68.5	8 percent stock div. Pfd. 34.7
Earned per share, 1928	$23.00	$3.32	$1.18
Dividend (common), 1928	$ 5.00	$4.72	8 percent stock

Source: Thomas, "Ten Investment Trusts in America," 79, 80, 83, 84, 86, 87.

The history of public utility holding companies in the United States dates back to the 1890's, when public utilities of various kinds were beginning to be promoted on a national scale. Many public utility companies had an economically productive role, actually starting out as devices for raising new capital for an industry still judged as very risky. Electric light and power companies and electric railways — city and interurban — still were having to prove themselves worthy reservoirs of investment.

Public utility holding companies fell into three main classes. Some were formed as affiliates of engineering or electrical companies and received technical assistance from their sponsors. Others were created to facilitate raising capital for productive uses. By the 1920's many more were formed and floated as a source of profits for promoters, and by the end of the decade they had developed the pyramiding features of other investment trusts.

The early public utility holding companies had been started as a means of placing bonds of small, local, little-known utilities. Securities of a holding company, generally collateral trust bonds, were more marketable than those of the utility itself. In the 1890's, for instance, a predecessor company to General Electric had taken securities of local users of its equipment in payment, then sought ways of liquidating those holdings. It did this by forming a corporation to take over these diversified issues, then selling the corporation's own securities, using the portfolios as collateral. Through this process the securities of the small operating companies were marketed and funds elicited from the public.[90]

In 1905 General Electric took the next step by organizing the Electric Bond & Share Company (EB&S). The purpose of this corporation was to hold shares in operating companies. General Electric held the common stock of EB&S, but sold $1 million of its 6 percent first preferred. EB&S later established a service engineering department that sold its services to clients at about cost. By September 1925 this department had grown to employ about nine hundred people. It was not regarded as a direct source of profits, however, though it did contribute to the earning capacity of the operating companies.[91]

Many holding companies were formed as affiliates of firms active in engineering and construction for utilities. Stone & Webster, for example, had many widely scattered power companies as clients and furnished them with managerial as well as investment banking services. Following the practice of other organizations in the public utility field, Stone & Webster began "in self-defense" to use the holding company device to acquire control of power companies. It formed Engineers Public Service Company and General Public Service Corporation, which acquired diversified but noncontrolling interests in power companies.[92]

A related development was that of H. M. Byllesby & Co., investment bankers. This firm not only offered engineering and management services for its clients, but also provided them with investment banking services. It then acquired large blocks of its clients' securities. A common theme in many of these offers of engineering, construction, managerial, and financial services was "the endeavor of rival service organizations to obtain clients and to retain clients." [93]

In the several flotations made in mid-1929, intraholding company underwritings were common, and these firms could be classed with the more general types performing functions of little economic

90. U.S. Federal Trade Commission, *Electric-Power Industry, Control of Power Companies . . . : A Report Relative to the Organization, Control and Ownership of Commercial Electric Power Companies* (Washington, 1927), 70–71.
91. *Ibid.*, 75.
92. *Ibid.*, 169–70.
93. *Ibid.*, 171–72.

worth. For example, Associated Gas & Electric Securities Company, Inc., underwrote a common stock issue of Metropolitan Edison Company, an operating company in the Associated System. The underwriter was a subsidiary of Associated Gas & Electric Company, and an Associated System subholding company subscribed for most of the issue. The transaction was summed up as follows: "No effort was expended — or indeed could have been expended — by the Securities Co. in guaranteeing that an affiliated subholding company would purchase its proportion, or, failing the same, purchase the stock itself. The management in both cases was the same, although separate corporate entities existed, and the effect as far as actual underwriting was concerned, was a farce. The practical result, however, was to take a fee from the operating company for which little or no service was rendered." [94]

Two of the largest investment banking houses made use of affiliated investment trusts to obtain a controlling interest in utilities, namely, Goldman, Sachs and Harris, Forbes. The two firms also were joint investors in a holding company, Electrical Shareholdings Corporation.[95]

In contrast some public utilities organized their own bond houses to distribute the securities they issued to finance their expanding services, thereby saving selling commissions. When these firms were not selling securities for their parent companies, they took on the distributing function for outside issues.[96]

Even the House of Morgan joined the race in 1929, when the pace became "frantic." In January this old firm, together with Drexel & Co. and Bonbright, organized the United Corporation, with assets exceeding $300 million.[97] By this date investment bankers, caught up in the hysteria of the times, actually were competing with one another in launching new utility holding companies. The pyramiding of these corporations provided the bankers that promoted and financed them with huge profits and freshly minted securities to satisfy the public's seemingly insatiable demand.

One of the dangers of investment banking control of utilities was that the bankers too often paid excessively high prices for securities in companies they acquired and then brought pressure for rate increases without regard for the public interest. As with many other types of corporations at the time, public utility holding companies

---

94. U.S. Federal Trade Commission, *Utility Corporations: Summary Report . . . on Economic, Financial and Corporate Phases of Holding and Operating Companies of Electric and Gas Utilities* (96 pts., Washington, 1928–1937), pt. 72-A, 352.

95. James C. Bonbright and Gardiner C. Means, *The Holding Company: Its Public Significance and Its Regulation* (New York, 1932), 139–40.

96. Albert S. Keister, *Our Financial System: An Introductory Text* (New York, 1930), 279–80.

97. Hugh Bullock, *The Story of Investment Companies*, 39.

tended to float much larger issues than their earnings justified. For years thereafter, hundreds of millions of dollars in preferred stock paid no dividends.[98]

Commercial banks also acquired control of public utility holding companies. Having advanced funds against pledged securities as collateral, the bankers continued to exert control even after the loans had been repaid, and in some cases they made heavy financing charges. In one instance, it was reported, there was "also substantial evidence of hard bargaining and coercive measures to bring about complete bank dominance of the policies and acts of this utility . . . and its parent company set up at the bank's instance." "Clearly," the report concluded, "management of utilities is not a banking function." [99]

Public utility holding companies, investment trusts, and security affiliates of national banks so increased in number during the 1920's that they became important both as competitors and affiliates of traditional investment bankers. All three types had existed earlier in small numbers, but the vast opportunities for middlemen provided by the financial environment and psychology of the decade caused ambitious financiers to multiply them rapidly. Like almost every firm in the securities business during the boom years, these institutions not only responded to the changing patterns and practices of the times but very often took advantage of them, as they did of the growing number of ready buyers anxious to invest in a rising market.

There were many characteristics of these institutions that made them very useful devices for facilitating the investment process, but all three proved to be easily susceptible to misuse, deliberate and inadvertent. That they were overused is incontrovertible, as the investigations following the stock market collapse soon made clear. Very few realized or cared to admit this during the boom of early 1929.

Those who believed in the usefulness of these institutions, like most other leaders of American finance at the time, failed to appreciate the extent to which investment trusts and holding companies were supporting the stock market boom. *Moody's Investors Service* asserted as much in January 1929 but tempered its observation by saying that the "immense sums" these institutions were pouring into securities and lending on the call market made them a "specific factor" against a "shake out." There were significant counter forces to be watched, this respected journal warned, but it too erroneously concluded that there would be no collapse in 1929.[100]

---

98. William O. Douglas, *Democracy and Finance* (New Haven, 1940), 134; Felix Frankfurter, *The Public and Its Government* (New Haven, 1930), 109.
99. *Utility Corporations: Summary Report*, pt. 84–A, 600, 617.
100. *Moody's Investors Service,* January 3, 1929, 5.

Carried away by the extremes of competition and the pursuit of short-term profits, large segments of the investment banking industry, including some respected old-line firms, lowered their own criteria of proper conduct and displayed considerable lack of judgment. The excessive promotion of investment companies and the mad scramble to originate and distribute securities of little worth and dubious quality fed the speculative fire that spread across the nation in the late 1920's. Investment bankers did nothing to dampen it; even worse, some of them helped fan the blaze to greater intensity by new promotions and optimistic forecasts. The situation they helped create contributed directly and significantly to the debacle of October 1929.

15 Crash and Depression: The Investment Bankers' Image Transformed

The reputation of the investment banker, which the elder Morgan once said took years to cultivate, was destroyed by the 1929 stock market debacle and the events that followed it. The crash and the depression transformed the image of the investment banker from one with halo to one with horns and spiked tail. The shortsighted, occasionally two-faced behavior of financial leaders during and immediately following the crisis shook the public's confidence in bankers as expert custodians of other people's money. The subsequent failure of hundreds of firms, including some of the strongest ones, damaged still further the investment bankers' image by demonstrating how incompetent many of them had been in managing their own affairs. Not only that, but the events of that fateful autumn also disclosed that Wall Street was no better a prognosticator of economic events than was the public generally. The bankers' optimistic forecasts of early October came back to haunt them in the pessimistic months that followed.

On October 13, 1929, eleven days before "Black Thursday," the Investment Bankers Association (IBA) met in Quebec for its annual convention, confident that the securities business would continue to prosper and that stock prices would climb to new highs. The *Proceedings* made no mention of the fact that the stock market already had suffered several serious declines and that prices generally had been ragged and irregular since September 5, when the drop of that day had sent *The New York Times*'s industrial averages down 10 points.[1] Like almost everyone else, most investment bankers interpreted this break, and every other decline that had occurred during the past six weeks, as a "technical correction" or a "temporarily overbought condition" rather than the prelude to a crash.[2]

Prominent commentators reflected the variety and confusion of current perceptions. Roger W. Babson, the Massachusetts business and financial statistician, said on September 5, "Sooner or later a crash is coming, and it may be terrific."[3] Irving Fisher, the respected Yale economist, stood at the opposite pole. "There may be a recession in stock prices," he said, "but not anything in the nature of a crash."[4]

1. Investment Bankers Association, *Proceedings . . . 1929* (Chicago 1929), *passim*.
2. See, for instance, *The Wall Street Journal*, September 5, 10, 12, 1929.
3. Quoted in John Kenneth Galbraith, *The Great Crash, 1929* (Boston, 1955), 89.
4. Quoted in *ibid.*, 90–91.

The president of the IBA reiterated the conviction that "speculation in its proper sense is a laudable and necessary function."[5] Eight months earlier, in March, the Federal Reserve Board had sought to pressure the banks into limiting brokers' loans. The object was to check what Paul M. Warburg of Kuhn, Loeb & Co. had labeled the "orgy of unrestrained speculation," which he predicted would "bring about a general depression involving the entire country." As might be expected from the IBA president's views, Wall Street greeted this distinguished banker's warning with the same disrespect that it showed toward Babson's pessimistic forecast.[6]

In point of fact it was neither the "colossal volume of brokers' loans," nor the extent of speculation, nor the prices of common stocks that concerned the investment bankers that October. What disturbed them most was the fact that the bond business had been suffering seriously for more than a year. Investors, attracted by the great bull market, were buying stocks rather than bonds. The volume of stock issues had increased some 250 percent since 1927, while bond offerings had dropped 38 percent. Since most members of the IBA still looked upon themselves primarily as originators and distributors of senior securities rather than of common stocks, many of them were worried that investors' growing preference for equities was more than just a current fad, one fed by a desire for capital gains rather than safety and income.

Apart from this concern the problems that occupied the bankers' attention related to the internal management of firms. Among other topics of considerable interest were staffing and cost accounting; the conduct of interfirm relationships, such as syndicate procedures; and the perennial question of the proper relationship between an investment house and its customers. In this latter area the association voiced its continued concern with the maintenance of the highest ethical standards.

None of the speakers nor any of the association's officials intimated that there was anything in the foreseeable future that seriously threatened the securities market or the permanence of prosperity. Indeed, there were signs that both might continue indefinitely. Two of these which many IBA members found especially encouraging were the continuing surplus in the federal budget and the steady reduction of the government debt. Another twenty-five years and the burden would be eliminated entirely, so some of them believed. With this happy thought and the confident reassurances of Charles E. Mitchell, head of the National City Bank, and Professor Fisher that the stock market was sound and that it would go even higher,

---

5. IBA, *Proceedings . . . 1929*, 13.
6. Quoted in Alexander D. Noyes, *The Market Place: Reminiscences of a Financial Editor* (Boston, 1938), 324.

the IBA's eighteenth annual convention came to a close on October 18.

The next day the stock market suffered another sharp decline. Speculative issues plunged badly, and blue chips also were hit hard. By noon that Saturday, when the New York Stock Exchange closed for the day, nearly 3.5 million shares had been traded.

Monday, October 21, was even worse, with sales reaching close to 6.1 million shares, making it the third busiest day in the exchange's history. "The market has had a very bad break," *The Wall Street Journal* reported the next morning, "the most severe in a number of years." Some good values were available, this paper observed, and it would be strange indeed if investors did not take advantage of them.[7]

Reassurances that the decline was only temporary, similar to previous setbacks, appeared at once. In a featured, page 1 item, the *Journal* announced: "Stocks Resist Selling Wave; Supporting Orders from Influential Circles Apparent for First Time Since Break; Nine of 20 Leaders Up."[8] For those who preferred a more exalted and sophisticated opinion, Professor Fisher explained Monday's decline as nothing more than a "shaking out of the lunatic fringe."[9]

The next day proved to be somewhat better. That morning Mitchell, on arriving from Europe, announced that "the decline had gone too far." The situation was "fundamentally sound," he said, and recovery was certain.[10]

The market quickly proved these optimistic forecasts wrong. On Wednesday it slumped badly. Over 6 million shares changed hands, of which some 2.6 million were traded during the hour before the exchange closed.[11] By the end of the day, *The New York Times*'s financial editor, one of the few observers who had been predicting a bust for a long time, reported that "the averages stood 50 points below the high mark of September."[12]

Worse was to come. On the next day, "Black Thursday," October 24, the deluge started in earnest and quickly turned into a full-fledged panic as millions of shares were dumped at steadily falling prices.

The day's losses, however, were not so heavy as they might have been, largely because of the timely intervention of a small group of powerful Wall Street bankers called together by Thomas W. Lamont of J. P. Morgan & Co. It included Mitchell, Albert H.

7. *The Wall Street Journal*, October 22, 1929. See also Galbraith, *The Great Crash*, 101–02; Frederick Lewis Allen, *Since Yesterday: The Nineteen-Thirties in America* . . . (New York, 1940), 23.
   8. *The Wall Street Journal*, October 22, 1929.
   9. Quoted in Galbraith, *The Great Crash*, 102.
   10. *Ibid.*
   11. Galbraith, *The Great Crash*, 103; Broadus Mitchell, *Depression Decade: From New Era through New Deal, 1929–1941* (New York, 1947), 27.
   12. Noyes, *The Market Place*, 329.

Wiggin of the Chase National Bank, Seward Prosser of the Bankers Trust Co., and William C. Potter of the Guaranty Trust Co. The banking resources of these five institutions exceeded $6 billion.[13] Subsequently George Fisher Baker, Jr., of the First National Bank, joined the consortium.

The prestige and influence of these financiers was such that as soon as word of their meeting reached the New York Stock Exchange, fear gave way to hope, tensions eased, and the panic subsided. At one-thirty that afternoon the bankers' representative, Richard Whitney, the acting president of the exchange and younger brother of a Morgan partner, appeared on the floor offering to buy 10,000 shares of United States Steel at 205, several points above the last bid.[14] By this time the market had begun to rally, and when the exchange closed many stocks had made impressive recoveries. Like the elder Morgan, who had stopped the panic of 1907 before it engulfed the Trust Company of America, Lamont's group had succeeded in averting a major disaster on the exchange. *The Wall Street Journal* headlined the extent of their accomplishment: "Bankers Halt Stock Debacle: 2-Hour Selling Deluge Stopped After Conference at Morgan's Office; $1,000,000,000 for Support." [15]

The funds available to the group were far less than the amount this newspaper reported. The bankers themselves never revealed the exact figure, but years later *The New York Times* indicated that it may have been between $20 million and $30 million.[16] Whatever the amount was, knowledge that this powerful consortium of bankers was prepared to prevent another panic restored considerable confidence, especially on Wall Street and in brokerage offices across the country. For the next two days the market was steady and orderly, and the bankers, so it was believed, took advantage of the respite to resell the stocks they had purchased on Black Thursday.

Meanwhile, reassuring statements and optimistic forecasts continued to fill the press. *The Wall Street Journal,* in a featured, page 1 item, announced that the bankers had organized a "Stock Support Plan" to "Prevent Needless Sacrifice of Values." From the White House, President Herbert Hoover reassured everyone that "the fundamental business of the country, that is production and distribution of commodities, is on a sound and prosperous basis." [17] He

13. *The New York Times,* October 25, 1929; *The Commercial & Financial Chronicle,* CXXIX (October 26, 1929), 2617.
14. Galbraith, *The Great Crash,* 107; Allen, *Since Yesterday,* 24–25.
15. *The Wall Street Journal,* October 25, 1929.
16. Galbraith cites Frederick Lewis Allen, *Only Yesterday,* 329–30, as source for claims that bankers had agreed to put up $40 million apiece. But he discounts the total figure of $240 million as "much too large to be plausible," and refers to *The New York Times,* March 9, 1938. Galbraith, *The Great Crash,* 106n.4. See also *The Commercial & Financial Chronicle,* CXXX (March 1, 1930), 1372.
17. *The Wall Street Journal,* October 26, 1929; *The New York Times,* October 26, 1929.

cited several indications to prove that the economy was in a "healthy condition," but carefully avoided making any similar reference to the situation on the stock market, as Lamont and his group had asked him to do.[18]

The omission went unnoticed in the plethora of optimistic statements that were issued by financiers and business leaders. And even if the president had obliged the bankers, it seems highly unlikely that his words would have prevented the avalanche that hit the market on Monday, October 28. By the time the exchange closed, more than 9 million shares had been dumped at lower and lower prices. American Telephone and Westinghouse plunged 34 points, General Electric fell $47\frac{1}{2}$ points, and United States Steel, according to *The New York Times,* suffered its largest decline in recent years. It lost $17\frac{1}{2}$ points. Banking support had kept the market orderly and prevented hysteria, so reported *The Wall Street Journal,* but it had been unable to halt the disastrous decline, much less bring about a rally.[19]

That afternoon, after a two-hour meeting at the Morgan offices, Lamont announced that the purpose of the banking group was "to offer certain support to the market and to act as far as possible as a stabilizing factor." The group never was intended, he said, "to maintain prices as such, but to insure a free and open market." [20]

Subsequently the same view was expressed by Albert Wiggin. Testifying before the Senate Banking and Currency Committee two years later, he said that "we did not regard it [as our function] . . . to sustain the market." All he and the other consortium members hoped to accomplish was to provide "purchasing power at some fair price," and to do so only for certain "pivotal stocks," which he easily defined as "active-market stocks." [21] (Later, another Senate investigation uncovered the fact that at the very time the banking group was trying desperately to stabilize the market, Wiggin himself was selling short and making a handsome profit, while thousands of others were being ruined.)[22]

Lamont's statement that the pool's only purpose was to maintain orderly markets was quite different from what the press had led the

18. Galbraith, *The Great Crash,* 111.
19. *The Commercial & Financial Chronicle,* CXXIX (November 2, 1929), 2795–96 quotes *The New York Times,* October 29, 1929; *The Wall Street Journal,* October 29, 1929.
20. Quoted in *The Commercial & Financial Chronicle,* CXXIX (November 2, 1929), 2800. See also Benjamin M. Anderson, *Economics and the Public Welfare: Financial and Economic History of the United States, 1914–1946* (New York, 1949), 213.
21. U.S. Senate, Committee on Banking and Currency, 71st Cong., 3d Sess., *Operation of the National and Federal Reserve Banking Systems: Hearings* . . . (8 pts., Washington, 1931–32), pt. 1, 198–99.
22. Ferdinand Pecora, *Wall Street Under Oath: The Story of Our Modern Money Changers* (New York, 1939), 154.

public to believe was its function.²³ Speculators and investors (the two were not always distinguishable) had assumed that the pool would continue to support prices as it had done the previous Thursday, when Whitney was sent to the rescue. Now, according to Lamont, prices were to be allowed to fall. All that the pool hoped to do, Wiggin later explained, was to prevent "shrinkages," as he labeled these precipitous declines, from being "too severe at one time." ²⁴

The next day, "Tragic Tuesday," October 29, came still another and even more acute crisis. Nearly 16.5 million shares were dumped, and the bankers, who on Monday had hoped to keep subsequent liquidations orderly, proved unable to accomplish even this. "Banking support, which would have been impressive and successful under ordinary circumstances," *The New York Times* reported, "was swept violently aside, as block after block of stock, tremendous in proportions, deluged the market." Every effort to slow down the stampede to sell was "crashed through violently." By the end of "the most disastrous trading day in the stock market's history," it was impossible to determine how much money had been lost. On the New York Stock Exchange alone, 880 issues registered a loss of between $8 billion and $9 billion.²⁵ No buyers could be found for many stocks, and thousands of major accounts were liquidated.

The leaders of Wall Street, who a few days earlier had been acclaimed for having intervened successfully on Black Thursday, now were blamed for having failed to prevent the crash. Indeed, the bankers were accused of having abetted it. Rumor had it that instead of trying to alleviate the situation, the bankers actually had been selling stocks in order to save themselves.²⁶ The charge was true in the case of Wiggin, but the public did not know this, nor did Lamont, who denied it. The banking group had not been selling stocks, he assured the press that evening. It "has continued and will continue in a co-operative way to support the market." ²⁷ The crash had made reassurances of this kind worthless, however; and though the banking group was held together until February 1930, no one ever again expected much of it. The reputation of the great bankers never recovered from the October quake.

The events of the crash made a mockery of the investment bankers' much touted expertise and overoptimistic forecasts. The crash demonstrated how powerless they actually were in the face of the

23. George McCabe, "Wall Street Goes Amateur," *The Commonweal,* XI (December 11, 1929), 166.
24. *Operation of the National and Federal Reserve Banking Systems,* pt. 1, 198.
25. *The New York Times,* October 30, 1929. See also *The Wall Street Journal,* October 29, 1929.
26. *The Commercial & Financial Chronicle,* CXXIX (November 2, 1929), 2800; Galbraith, *The Great Crash,* 118.
27. *The Commercial & Financial Chronicle,* CXXIX (November 2, 1929), 2800.

disaster. This in itself the public might have overlooked if the bankers had not explained every major drop as a technical correction or temporary setback. Their seeming confidence in the face of such huge losses made them appear as either fools or liars. Public confidence in financiers generally and in Wall Street bankers particularly was shattered entirely as the stock market belied their every statement.

After Tuesday's crash the stock market coasted slowly downward for two and a half years, with occasional brief rises that were not maintained. The index of common stock prices (1941–1943 = 10), which had stood at 26.02 in 1929, fell to 6.93 in 1932.[28] The value of all common stocks declined 89.9 percent. By the summer of 1932, $75 billion of paper wealth had been wiped out, and the average price of common stocks, as measured by *The Magazine of Wall Street,* whose index included all active issues traded on the New York Stock Exchange, fell from a 1929 high of 173 to 17.20 in July 1932.[29] Nor was the bondholder spared. By the summer of 1932 nearly 20 percent of the $7.5 billion of foreign bonds outstanding in the United States were in default, according to the IBA. No other type of bond had suffered so badly. Real estate bonds were the second largest losers. Of the $6 billion outstanding, including only those issues in excess of $500,000, 14 percent were in default. Municipal bonds survived the depression better than any other type, with only 1.8 percent in default out of a total $18.2 billion outstanding. The casualty figures for the other principal bond groups were as follows: industrials, 7.2 percent; utilities, 5.4 percent; and rails, 3.5 percent.[30]

Like the rest of the country, the investment banking community did not feel the full impact of the crash for almost another two years. Corporations that had planned new issues called upon investment houses to underwrite and distribute their securities as they had done in the past. In 1930 Halsey, Stuart & Co. sold more than $200 million of bonds, notes, and debentures for Samuel Insull, who spent almost all of it to increase the generating and distributing capacities of his utility companies. Insull's credit still was so good that nearly every one of these issues was oversubscribed.[31]

Few new offerings were sold so quickly or profitably. Some did not sell at all and had to be taken up by the underwriting bankers.[32]

28. U.S. Bureau of the Census, *Historical Statistics of the United States: Colonial Times to 1957* (Washington, 1960), 657.
29. *The Magazine of Wall Street,* LI (November 12, 1932), 75.
30. IBA, *Proceedings . . . 1932,* 7.
31. Forrest McDonald, *Insull* (Chicago, 1962), 286.
32. See examples cited in Floyd F. Burtchett and Clifford M. Hicks, *Corporation Finance* (3d ed., Lincoln 1959), 381n.10; Anderson, *Economics and the Public Welfare,* 211.

Meanwhile, as the economy slowly deteriorated, and fewer and fewer corporations sought additional capital, the total volume of security offerings (new capital and refunding issues) declined from nearly $9.4 billion in 1929 to $5.0 billion in 1930.[33]

By the beginning of 1931, however, it appeared to some people that the bottom of the depression had been reached. Robert P. Lamont, Hoover's Secretary of Commerce, predicted a recovery, and James Speyer, the head of one of Wall Street's oldest and most respected investment houses, saw no cause for further pessimism.[34] Other distinguished bankers made similarly incorrect public statements.

For a few months early in 1931 business did improve, but high hope soon faded to helpless observance of deepening depression. In May the Kreditanstalt, Austria's largest bank, failed, taking down with it all Central Europe. From Vienna, the chain of disaster spread to Germany and Great Britain, and finally struck the United States. This "concatenation of catastrophes from abroad," as Hoover described these events, wiped out whatever modest economic progress had been achieved here in the twenty months since the crash and precipitated another steep business decline that lasted until July 1932. Then, after a slight recovery in the autumn, the trend turned downward again until March 1933.

It was during these twenty-one months, from July 1931 to March 1933, that the depression was at its worst. All the economic indexes plunged to unprecedented lows, and extraordinary suffering, misery, and humiliation were brought to millions and millions of Americans.

Many investment bankers, like the clients they served, both issuers and investors, also were hit hard by the prolonged business contraction. Total security offerings, which had declined by some $4.4 billion between 1929 and 1930, fell even more precipitously during the next two years. In 1931 they totaled slightly less than $2.4 billion, approximately half the volume of the previous year. The decline in 1932 was even steeper; the $644 million brought out that year was about 27 percent of the amount issued in 1931, and less than 10 percent of the all-time high of 1929. Moreover, about half of the securities offered in 1932 were brought out to refund older issues rather than to raise additional capital.[35] This huge decline in new capital issues cut deeply into one of the investment

---

33. *Historical Statistics to 1957*, 658. See also New York Stock Exchange, *Report of the President, May, 1930–May, 1931* (New York, 1931), 19–20.
34. *The Wall Street Journal*, January 1, 1931.
35. *Historical Statistics to 1957*, 658. See also New York Stock Exchange, *Report of the President, May, 1931–May, 1932* (New York, 1932), 60; William J. Shultz and M. R. Caine, *Financial Development of the United States* (New York, 1937), 648–49.

bankers' principal and most lucrative sources of profits — the fees and commissions they earned from originating, underwriting, and distributing securities.

Underwriting was not the only aspect of the investment banking business to suffer. The huge drop in the volume of shares traded on the stock exchanges shrank brokerage profits. On the New York Stock Exchange alone, sales fell from 1.1 billion shares in 1929 to 425 million in 1932.[36] Sales of other securities were even worse.

Earnings of many private investment banking houses from other sources also dropped precipitously. For example, some firms dealt heavily in foreign exchange and carried on a substantial letter of credit business. Their profits from these sources also shrank rapidly. Merchandise imports to the United States fell from $4.4 billion in 1929 to $1.3 billion in 1932, and the amount of dollars sent abroad in the form of loans and investments during the same years declined from about $7.4 billion to $2.4 billion.[37] For years, international bankers like Kidder, Peabody & Co. had relied on the income from this business to help pay for their overhead. The depression cut into it heavily when it was most needed.[38]

Many private investment houses, like Morgan, Kuhn, Loeb, and Kidder, Peabody, also were banks of deposit, holding the funds of their clients, mostly corporations, banks, and foreign governments. During the boom years the private bankers had put these deposits out on call, earning handsome profits. In 1929 the interest rate on brokers' new call loans ranged from a high of 14.4 percent to a low of 4.5 percent a year. The peak was reached during the last week of March.[39]

After the crash, depositors started to withdraw their funds. Even the most conservative and prestigious houses, like Morgan and Kuhn, Loeb, saw their deposits reduced. Most of Morgan's, after increasing by nearly $11 million in 1930, fell from $503.9 million in 1931 to $319.4 million in 1932, while those of Kuhn, Loeb dropped from $88.5 million in 1929 to $15.2 million in 1932.[40] Other private bankers suffered even more serious reductions. In some cases they were wiped out entirely, forcing the investment firms into bankruptcy.

One of the first private investment houses to suffer this fate was Caldwell & Co., the large Nashville firm established in 1917. Caldwell had started out exclusively as a municipal bond house, but after World War I, like many other small firms, it expanded its

36. *Historical Statistics to 1957,* 659.
37. Mitchell, *Depression Decade,* 60–61.
38. Alfred E. Borneman to author, December 15, 1965.
39. Board of Governors of the Federal Reserve System, *Banking and Monetary Statistics* (Washington, 1943), 456.
40. U.S. Senate, Committee on Banking and Currency, 73d Cong., 2d Sess., *Stock Exchange Practices: Report . . .* (Washington, 1934), 226.

activities to include the underwriting and distribution of real estate and industrial bonds and, subsequently, common stock. By the time of the crash, stocks had become the firm's principal offering. Many of the issues it sponsored were poorly investigated and highly speculative. During the great bull market, when the public's demand for stocks was insatiable, Caldwell had no difficulty in finding buyers, but by the end of October 1929, despite a vigorous selling campaign, the firm found it impossible to dispose of its securities.

The house also was heavily overextended, having invested considerably in the securities of several southern insurance companies. The collapse of the stock market destroyed whatever chance it had of selling these issues, and the commitments it had assumed so lightly now became increasingly burdensome. By the end of 1929 they amounted to nearly $9.8 million, of which $1.1 million represented Kidder, Peabody's interest in one of the companies. Facing difficulties of its own, Kidder, Peabody was as anxious as Caldwell to sell these holdings, but it too was unable to do so. Loaded with these and other unmarketable securities and in a dangerously weak cash position, Caldwell drew on funds deposited by the state of Tennessee in the Bank of Tennessee, a Caldwell-controlled institution.[41] The firm's vulnerability was made worse by the lack of experience of both its officers and its staff. The most pressing problem was the steady withdrawal of funds, which finally forced Caldwell to close its doors on November 14, 1930. Its collapse subsequently brought down about 120 banks.[42]

As the failure of Caldwell illustrated how the crash struck a young, inexperienced firm, the near demise of Kidder, Peabody in 1931 demonstrated the impact of that crisis upon one of the oldest, most respected investment banking houses in the United States. Neither lack of experience nor lack of knowledge of investment banking traditions explained this firm's difficulties. Its growth had paralleled the development of the securities business itself. Some of the industry's leading figures, among them George Whitney, had been apprenticed in its offices. Its long-time connection with the Barings gave it an international reputation, and its position of leadership among American investment firms was recognized even before the turn of the century.

Kidder, Peabody's difficulties in 1931 arose from a variety of sources, not all of which were immediately attributable to the stock market crash. Since the end of World War I, when Robert Winsor became Kidder, Peabody's active senior partner, the firm appears to have suffered from a lack of effective, creative leadership. The war and the stock market boom of the 1920's had seen the dyna-

41. John Berry McFerrin, *Caldwell and Company: A Southern Financial Empire* (Chapel Hill, 1939), 124–25.
42. *Ibid.*, 166, 180, 186.

mism of the old established Atlantic Coast firms pass to a new generation. Nearly all the prominent prewar banking figures with whom Winsor had developed close personal and business ties, such as the elder Morgan, Jacob Schiff, James Stillman, Henry Higginson, George F. Baker, Sr., Frank Vanderlip, and Gardiner Lane, were either dead or in retirement. Winsor was one of the last of these financiers still actively engaged in the securities business.

He was in his early sixties when he became active head of Kidder, Peabody, and he appears to have had little interest or wish to change established policies. During the 1920's Kidder, Peabody's position deteriorated markedly.[43] Its name no longer appeared among the ten leading houses of issue. Its place was taken by newer, more energetic firms, such as Halsey, Stuart and Dillon, Read.[44]

Winsor ruled his firm like an autocrat, one of his associates recalled later. He dictated policy and made all the major decisions, very often without consulting anyone. "Practically nothing was done in Kidder, Peabody & Co.," Albert H. Gordon testified later, "without Mr. Winsor's full knowledge and approval."[45] No one questioned his decisions; and no one knew the firm's exact financial condition, not even the partners, its creditors, or its correspondents. No balance sheet or any other year-end statement was distributed. Some doubted whether Winsor himself knew the real condition of the firm.[46] The stock market collapse revealed it to the world.

At the time of the crash a substantial part of Kidder, Peabody's capital was tied up in securities of companies it had financed and reorganized, many of them New England corporations. These issues, like some of those in the portfolios of other investment houses, had declined in value quickly and appreciably. Some of them proved to be unmarketable at any price, whereas others could be sold only at a considerable loss. The stock market collapse thus had frozen most of Kidder, Peabody's assets, but what proved to be even worse was that many of the securities had been "optimistically" valued on the firm's books.[47]

The firm's difficulties were aggravated further by the retirement of one partner, in August 1929, and the death of two others, in January 1930, one of whom was Winsor and the other Frank G. Webster. The latter had been with Kidder, Peabody from the time of its founding in 1865. The capital they had invested in the part-

43. Borneman to author, December 15, 1965.
44. Anna Rochester, *Rulers of America: A Study of Finance Capital* (New York, 1936), 91–92.
45. U.S. Temporary National Economic Committee, *Investigation of Concentration of Economic Power: Hearings* . . . (31 pts., Washington, 1939–1941), pt. 23, 11943.
46. Borneman to author, December 15, 1965.
47. Kidder, Peabody & Co. Records. "Arthur Young Audit," December 5, 1930. Unless otherwise noted, all references to Kidder, Peabody & Co. Records are to the firm's files in New York City.

nership was withdrawn, thus reducing Kidder, Peabody's cash reserves still further.

The full impact of these events was felt as soon as depositors, apprehensive about the firm's condition, started to withdraw their funds. The Italian government, which during World War I had maintained a deposit of nearly $100 million, closed its account early in 1930, withdrawing almost $8 million.[48] This huge withdrawal, together with other sizable ones, made it impossible for Kidder, Peabody to meet its current liabilities, and early in November 1930 the partners called on the Morgan firm for assistance.

The House of Morgan had been a close associate of Kidder, Peabody for almost a half century. The two firms had participated regularly in each other's syndicates, especially in financing the American Telephone & Telegraph Company. Close personal ties existed among the partners of the two houses.

Morgan's decision to come to Kidder, Peabody's assistance, however, was not based on just sentiment; nor was it an act of philanthropy. The country's financial situation at the end of 1930 was grim. Hundreds of banks had failed, and others were being pushed to the wall. The collapse of Kidder, Peabody, a firm with an old respected name, whose business had been closely connected with some of Morgan's major enterprises, would have been "a calamity of considerable proportions." [49]

Self-interest, the public good, and sentiment combined to persuade Morgan to assist this old Boston firm, whose New York offices then were across the street from Morgan's. This it did by arranging for a $10 million loan, of which Morgan and the Chase National Bank each subscribed to $2.5 million. The other $5 million was contributed by three New York City and four Boston banks.[50]

The loan, called a "Revolving Credit," was made contingent upon the partners' raising an additional $5 million on their own, which they did by calling upon their friends. The largest contribution ($600,000) was made by Edwin S. Webster, son of the late Frank G. Webster. As a boy Edwin Webster had worked as a clerk under his father's supervision. In 1889, after graduating from the Massachusetts Institute of Technology, he and Charles A. Stone organized Stone & Webster, Inc., a firm of consulting engineers. In

48. Albert H. Gordon to John M. Olin, November 10, 1939, in *U.S. v. Henry S. Morgan et al.,* "Plaintiff's Exhibit No. 1072" (April 6, 1949), 4215–16. During the 1920's the Italian government made its war debt payments to the United States through Kidder, Peabody. See U.S. Senate, Committee on Finance, 72d Cong., 1st Sess., *Sale of Foreign Bonds or Securities in the United States: Hearings* . . . (4 pts., Washington, 1931–32), pt. 1, 56–57.
49. *U.S. v. Henry S. Morgan et al.,* "Transcript of Trial: Defendants' Opening — Mr. [Bethuel M.] Webster" (March 6, 1951), 4024.
50. *U.S. v. Henry S. Morgan et al.,* "Plaintiff's Exhibit No. 1072," 4216, lists the names and contributors of all the participants.

1902 its activities were widened to include certain specialized investment banking services for its clients, most of whom were utility companies.[51] The rest of the money was raised by a dozen or so wealthy Bostonians. This group subsequently came to be called the Commonwealth Corporation; it was headed by Frederic C. Dumaine, a wealthy and influential Boston businessman.[52]

Soon it became apparent that the $15 million, which became available to Kidder, Peabody on December 1, 1930, was not enough to keep the firm afloat. Much of the trouble arose from the fact that it had grossly exaggerated its assets. Early that month a firm of outside auditors reported that the total decline in the value of the securities in Kidder, Peabody's portfolio amounted to about $6.2 million.[53] The volume of business was so limited that the firm was losing more than $2,000 a day, and the prospect, some of the partners feared, was that the situation would get worse. The bankers in the Revolving Credit were even more concerned with Kidder, Peabody's steadily deteriorating condition. They faced the unpleasant situation of having committed themselves to lend a large sum of money to a firm that had not only frozen assets, but also current losses that soon would require another major infusion of capital.

Despite all these risks the Morgan firm was not prepared to abandon Kidder, Peabody. It still possessed some salvageable assets. The greatest of these were its name and reputation, but it also had a few others. Some of the securities in its portfolio eventually would regain value, and the firm enjoyed the loyalty and confidence of a large clientele. With these considerations in mind, George Whitney asked Edwin Webster to rescue Kidder, Peabody by undertaking the firm's reorganization.[54]

There were many good reasons, apart from his father's long association with the firm and his own sizable investment in it, why Webster was the logical person for this task. As the largest stockholder in Stone & Webster, and one of the two senior officers, he possessed the necessary capital, experience, and ability. Moreover, as a director of more than a score of banks and corporations, he was widely known in business and financial circles.[55] Webster was unwilling, however, to assume the responsibility himself. He was then in his early sixties, sufficiently occupied with the affairs of his own firm, and he did not wish to neglect them in order to assume others. His thirty-one-year-old son, Edwin S. Webster, Jr., who was

51. *Ibid.*, "Plaintiff's Exhibit No. 1588B" (January 3, 1950), 8755, 8759.
52. Chandler Hovey to author, October 25, 1961.
53. Kidder, Peabody & Co. Records, "Arthur Young Audit," December 5, 1930.
54. *U.S. v. Henry S. Morgan et al.*, "Transcript of Trial" (March 6, 1951), 4016–25; Albert H. Gordon to John M. Olin, November 10, 1939, "Plaintiff's Exhibit No. 1072," 4216–17.
55. U.S. House, Committee on Interstate and Foreign Commerce, 73d Cong., 2d Sess., *Relation of Holding Companies to Operating Companies in Power and Gas Affecting Control: Report* . . . (6 pts., Washington, 1934–35), pt. 1, 595–96.

vice president of Stone & Webster, had been considering for some time going into business for himself, and when he indicated that he was interested in rehabilitating the firm, his father agreed to assist him.⁵⁶ At the time of the crisis in Kidder, Peabody's affairs, young Webster was in the hospital, recovering from a serious accident that kept him from returning to work for another two years.

In the meantime his father assumed the responsibility of planning the reorganization and representing his son in the negotiations. He was assisted by his brother-in-law Chandler Hovey, and Albert H. Gordon, a close friend of Edwin Webster, Jr. Hovey had been with Kidder, Peabody in Boston between 1900 and 1909, leaving to open his own brokerage firm.⁵⁷ Gordon and young Webster had been classmates at Harvard College and at the Harvard Business School. Twenty-nine years old, Gordon was then selling commercial paper for Goldman, Sachs & Co. and, like Webster, was anxious to go into business on his own.⁵⁸ These three men, Gordon, Hovey, and the elder Webster acting for his son, were the ones who planned and executed the reorganization.

Negotiations started early in December 1930, shortly after the completion of the audit of Kidder, Peabody's books. The first and most difficult question that the three men had to decide was the size, make-up, and headquarters of the new partnership. It was decided at once that the main office of the new Kidder, Peabody was to be in New York City, not Boston. The other decisions required more deliberation. Webster and Gordon were relatively unknown in financial circles. Neither one, it was feared, had the experience or commanded the respect necessary to take over a firm like Kidder, Peabody. Hovey was older and more experienced, but he too was not widely known on Wall Street. His closest ties were on State Street, where he conducted his own highly successful firm.

Indeed, it was Hovey himself who suggested bringing into the firm an older, respected, and well-known figure who would lend stature to the new partnership. Early in February he suggested to young Webster that they approach E. V. R. Thayer of Chicago, the head of the Central Trust Company and a director of several railroads and of the American Telephone & Telegraph Company. Thayer, Hovey wrote, was on a "first name" basis with many of the country's leading financiers. His addition to the firm would "practically assure its success." ⁵⁹ Thayer was, furthermore, a grandson

---

56. Albert H. Gordon to John M. Olin, November 10, 1939, in *U.S. v. Henry S. Morgan et al.,* "Plaintiff's Exhibit No. 1072" (April 6, 1949), 4217–20.

57. Hovey to author, October 25, 1961.

58. Gordon to author, November 10, 1939; Albert H. Gordon to John M. Olin, November 10, 1939, in *U.S. v. Henry S. Morgan et al.,* "Plaintiff's Exhibit No. 1072," 4217–20.

59. Chandler Hovey to Edwin S. Webster, Jr., February [?] 1931, Kidder, Peabody & Co. Records.

of Nathaniel Thayer, partner in John E. Thayer & Brother, the predecessor firm of Kidder, Peabody.

The proposal was dropped quickly, however, when it was learned that Thayer, as senior partner, intended to make policy and wanted to change the firm's name to include his own. Neither Hovey, Gordon, nor the Websters was prepared to change the firm's name in order to gain Thayer's talents and reputation, great as these were. Their decision was endorsed by most of the members of the Revolving Credit.[60]

Another possibility they considered, but only briefly, was to invite into the new firm one or two of the partners from the old one. They rejected this idea because it would mean asking older, established bankers to accept a lesser interest than the one they then held. Even more important, in Gordon's opinion, was the necessity of making it absolutely clear to the public that the new firm was in no way financially connected with the old one.[61] "We felt," Gordon said later, "that even if we had wanted to endeavor to persuade some of the partners of the old firm to become our partners that it was unsound for us to do so. We were fearful that undisclosed liabilities would rise up to haunt us. We were insistent that the new firm operate in an area completely shut off from the old firm. We wanted an iron curtain put down and kept down."[62] Once it was decided not to admit any of the old partners, no effort was made to find anyone else.

Meanwhile Hovey and Gordon, using the auditors' report of December 1930, worked with the representatives and attorneys of the Revolving Credit, the Commonwealth Corporation, and Kidder, Peabody to determine the terms of the sale. Negotiations lasted three months and involved not only the partnership, but the three Kidder, Peabody Participations and the Kidder, Peabody Acceptance Corporation as well.

The final agreement disassociated the new firm from these companies entirely. According to the bill of sale, signed March 6, 1931, the new partnership assumed the deposits of the old one, which amounted to about $8 million, and purchased its name, goodwill, accounts receivable, and certain other carefully selected assets, the most important of which were some marketable securities and the former partners' seats on the New York and Boston stock exchanges.[63]

60. Chandler Hovey to Edwin S. Webster, Jr., February 16, 1931, Kidder, Peabody & Co. Records.
61. Albert H. Gordon to John M. Olin, November 10, 1939, in *U.S. v. Henry S. Morgan et al.,* "Plaintiff's Exhibit No. 1072," 4217.
62. *U.S. v. Henry S. Morgan et al.,* "Transcript of Trial: Plaintiff's Case — Deposition of Gordon" (May 3, 1951), 6083.
63. "Bill of Sale," March 6, 1931, in *U.S. v. Henry S. Morgan et al.,* "Plaintiff's Exhibit No. 1166" (April 13, 1949), 4979–85; U.S. TNEC, *Hearings,* XXIII, 11947.

The new partners took special care, Gordon later wrote, to accept "only those assets we considered current and liquid." [64] No cash was paid at the time of the sale; Webster, Hovey, and Gordon agreed to pay the former partners, who organized themselves under the name Devonstreet & Co., 25 percent of the new firm's net earnings until they had paid $2 million. They also agreed to pay the old firm's creditors, the Commonwealth Corporation, 10 percent of their net earnings for a period of five years.[65]

Throughout these negotiations the assistance of the elder Webster proved invaluable. He advised the new partners on all important questions, offered constructive solutions to the seemingly endless flow of large and small problems that had to be resolved daily, and worked closely with Hovey and Gordon in supervising the liquidation of the old firms.[66]

The new partners assumed operational control of Kidder, Peabody early in February 1931, almost six weeks before the sale became official. "Dumaine has told Charlie Sargent [Winsor's successor as head of the old firm] to take instructions from us regarding selling of inventory of stocks & bonds and also cutting down overhead," Hovey wrote young Webster.[67] Just about the same time, Gordon also reported to his ailing partner, saying that he was spending all his time at Kidder, Peabody, helping the old partners run the business and, with the assistance of the elder Webster, preparing a comprehensive program of reforms designed to cut losses and expenses.[68]

The transfer was facilitated also by the help and cooperation of the Morgan firm. Several of its partners, notably Whitney, followed the negotiations closely, intervening frequently to reconcile differences and to protect the interests of both parties. No detail was too small for them to consider.[69]

Almost every afternoon one or two members of the old and new firms met at the Morgan offices to report on the progress of negotiations and consider ways to reduce Kidder, Peabody's continuing

64. Albert H. Gordon to John M. Olin, November 10, 1939, in *U.S. v. Henry S. Morgan et al.*, "Plaintiff's Exhibit No. 1072," 4217.
65. *U.S. v. Henry S. Morgan et al.*, "Transcript of Trial" (March 6, 1951), 4017. In 1936 the partners liquidated their $2 million obligation to Devonstreet & Co. with a cash settlement of $700,000, part of which the old partners used to meet the deficit incurred by the Revolving Credit. The new firm also reduced its liability to the Commonwealth Corporation by buying "a substantial part" of its common stock. See also Albert H. Gordon to John M. Olin, November 10, 1939, in *ibid.*, "Plaintiff's Exhibit No. 1072," 4218.
66. Albert H. Gordon to Edwin S. Webster, Jr., February 28, 1931, Kidder, Peabody & Co. Records.
67. Chandler Hovey to Edwin S. Webster, Jr., February [?] 1931, Kidder, Peabody & Co. Records.
68. Albert H. Gordon to Edwin S. Webster, Jr., February [?] 1931, Kidder, Peabody & Co. Records.
69. Chandler Hovey to Edwin S. Webster, Jr., February 16, 1931, Kidder, Peabody & Co. Records.

losses, which on some days amounted to as much as $5,000. These meetings, Gordon recalled later, were always friendly but never relaxed. Early in March, after the final terms of the sale had been agreed upon, Gordon told Webster that a welcome, perhaps even significant, change had occurred at a recent meeting at 23 Wall Street. "Incidentally," he wrote, "we [Gordon and the elder Webster] are slowly making the grade socially. Yesterday for the first time Morgan invited us to tea on our way out from the almost daily conference. Hitherto they [Morgan and his partners] have bade us goodby as they went into J. P.'s room for tea." [70]

The new Kidder, Peabody opened officially for business on March 17, 1931.[71] Its capital was $5.3 million, of which the elder Webster contributed $2.5 million in the form of 50,000 shares of Stone & Webster stock. Hovey and Gordon put up the rest.[72]

The new partners took over a firm that had been nearly bankrupted by the stock market crash and prostrated by the depression. When the new Kidder, Peabody opened its doors for business, its daily overhead expenses amounted to $5,000 and its daily income, almost entirely from brokerage commissions, averaged $1,500. These large cash losses prevented the partners from developing new business as energetically as they had hoped, since most of their time at first was devoted to internal operations. Much of this involved reducing office personnel. The staff of Kidder, Peabody's main Boston office, which had numbered about 170 in September 1929, was reduced to 100, and in New York the number of employees was cut from 300 to 120. "The whole thing — the firing and the cutting — was a somewhat unpleasant procedure. But we had to do it; otherwise Kidder, Peabody would have folded." [73] Small inactive accounts that had been entrusted to the firm for safe keeping were discontinued, and other economies introduced.

More important than any of these changes was the decision to shift the firm's main emphasis from general banking to investment banking and brokerage. Before the crash Kidder, Peabody had been an important banking and foreign exchange house. By 1931 the firm had lost most of its large foreign depositors, and it was unlikely that it would attract others. Most of these were going to commercial banks, which were competing vigorously for them.[74] The new partners also deemphasized the firm's business in foreign exchange

70. Albert H. Gordon to Edwin S. Webster, Jr., March 11, 1931, Kidder, Peabody & Co. Records.
71. *The New York Times,* March 17 and 18, 1931.
72. Hovey to author, October 25, 1961; Albert H. Gordon to John M. Olin, November 10, 1939, in *U.S. v. Henry S. Morgan et al.,* "Plaintiff's Exhibit No. 1072," 4217. Before the crash Stone & Webster stock had sold at $200 and no one expected it to go below $50, the price in March 1931. A year later it fell to $2.
73. Hovey to author, October 25, 1961. See also Albert H. Gordon to Edwin S. Webster, Jr., March 1, 1931, Kidder, Peabody & Co. Records.
74. Borneman to author, December 15, 1965.

and letters of credit, though they continued to maintain the old firm's correspondent relationship with Baring Brothers & Co., Ltd. Kidder, Peabody's business with the Barings now was limited entirely to underwriting and distributing securities.[75]

The partners' decision to emphasize the securities business and establish themselves as major underwriters and distributors of new issues was reinforced late in December 1931. At that time they took over Kissel, Kinnicutt & Co., a New York City brokerage and banking firm, founded in 1906.[76] The crash and the depression had wiped out many of this firm's assets; its capital no longer was adequate for it to remain in business; and its continuing heavy cash losses would have forced it into liquidation. G. Herman Kinnicutt, the senior partner, had worked for Morgan and, after opening his own firm, had been associated with many Morgan offerings. Whitney had suggested the merger to the elder Webster. Such a step, Whitney explained, would add Kissel, Kinnicutt's goodwill to that of Kidder, Peabody and it would assist a former employee and close associate.[77] After much discussion it was agreed to admit Kinnicutt as a general partner in Kidder, Peabody and to accept a selected number of his firm's brokerage accounts. Kinnicutt, who was then in his sixties, added seniority to the firm, which the Street believed it needed, and it freed Gordon from supervising routine office matters. Henceforth he could devote his talents to the more important job of developing new business.[78]

At the time of the merger, Kidder, Peabody still was losing money. The practices instituted nine months earlier had served only to cut losses. In 1932 the new partners made their first profits. It took almost ten years, however, before the firm was restored to the proud position it once had occupied and the reputation of its partners fully established on Wall Street.

Early in 1932, another old conservative Boston investment banking house also was plunging into financial difficulties. The reorganization of Lee, Higginson in June was precipitated by the suicide of Ivar Kreuger, the then widely respected Swedish "Match King" and international financier.[79] On March 12, 1932, just before his worldwide holding company empire collapsed, Kreuger shot himself in his

75. Albert H. Gordon to John M. Olin, November 10, 1939, in *U.S. v. Henry S. Morgan et al.*, "Plaintiff's Exhibit No. 1072," 4220; Chandler Hovey to Edwin S. Webster, Jr., March 12 [?] 1931, Kidder, Peabody & Co. Records.
76. *The New York Times*, December 24, 1931.
77. Undated, unsigned "Memorandum," Kidder, Peabody & Co. Records.
78. *U.S. v. Henry S. Morgan et al.*, "Transcript of Trial" (March 6, 1951), 4046.
79. Kreuger's career was summarized in a series of three anonymous articles in *Fortune*, subsequently revealed to have been written by Archibald MacLeish. "Ivar Kreuger," *Fortune*, VII (May 1933), 51–57, 78–84; (June 1933), 59–63, 78–95; *ibid.*, VIII (July 1933), 68–76. See also the brief account by Wilhelm Grotkopp, "Ivar Kreuger," *Encyclopedia of the Social Sciences* (15 vols., New York, 1944), VIII, 600–01.

Paris apartment. Leaders of business and finance everywhere mourned his death, and public officials, whose governments he had assisted with loans, extolled his accomplishments. A month later, when his companies' books were examined, however, the great Kreuger was exposed as a manipulator who had swindled, embezzled, and forged his way to power and affluence.[80] These shocking revelations shattered the reputation of Lee, Higginson, Kreuger's principal American bankers.

Not only had Kreuger decieved Lee, Higginson, but, even worse, that firm itself, a Senate investigation revealed, had neglected not only its own welfare but that of its customers. It had failed to take any real precautions to protect either its own interests or those of the thousands of investors who had purchased some $250 million of Kreuger's securities because they had been sponsored and recommended by this highly respected investment firm.[81] Donald Durant, a Lee, Higginson partner and, since 1929, a director of Kreuger & Toll, one of the companies whose securities his firm had sponsored, testified that he never had attended a single meeting of this corporation's board of directors until after Kreuger's death.[82] Nor did he admit that his firm had failed its clients in any way, even though in the case of the $50 million Kreuger & Toll bond issue of March 1929, Lee, Higginson had neither asked for nor received an independent audit of the company's accounts, nor investigated the quality and value of the collateral Kreuger had substituted for the one he originally had pledged.[83]

The substitution turned out to be a "gigantic deception." Sound, marketable securities were replaced by inferior ones, at great loss to the investors who had purchased Kreuger & Toll bonds. By January 1933, less than three years after they first had been offered, the price of these bonds had dropped from $1,000 to $140.[84]

Kreuger's collapse dealt such a heavy blow to Lee, Higginson's resources and reputation that on June 14, 1932, the partners announced that the firm was being liquidated and its securities business turned over to a new corporation with the same name. Unlike the old partnership, the Lee, Higginson Corporation neither accepted deposits nor provided any other banking services. Its activities were restricted exclusively to issuing and distributing securities. Capital

---

80. Arthur N. Plummer, *The Great American Swindle Incorporated* (New York, 1932), ch. xi; John L. Parker, *Unmasking Wall Street* (Boston, 1933), 156–73.

81. U.S. Senate, Committee on Banking and Currency, 72d Cong., 1st Sess. *Stock Exchange Practices: Hearings* . . . (7 pts. in 6 vols., Washington, 1932–33), pt. 4, 1313–19. See also Max Winkler, *Foreign Bonds — An Autopsy: A Study of Defaults and Repudiations of Government Obligations* (Philadelphia, 1933), 94–102.

82. U.S. Senate, *Stock Exchange Practices: Hearings,* pt. 4, 1182.

83. *Ibid.,* pt. 4, 1145–57, 1163–73, 1182–89, and 1218–23 describe fully the details of this transaction.

84. *Ibid.,* pt. 4, 1156.

was contributed entirely "from sources outside the present partnership." [85] None of the old firm's assets was transferred to the new one. The Lee, Higginson Corporation recruited most of its officers and branch managers from the old partnership. Its first president, N. P. Hallowell, had been with the old firm for more than twenty years, and Edward M. Jesup, a vice president in charge of the New York City office, had been a partner since 1925.[86]

The new corporation began operations from new headquarters and on a scale much reduced from that of its predecessor. The main office was moved to New York City, and the Boston headquarters were reorganized as a branch. This one, together with a branch in Chicago, were the corporation's only offices in the United States outside New York City. Sixteen branches of the old firm were discontinued. The organization of the Paris partnership, Lee, Higginson *et Cie.*, remained unchanged, but it dropped many of its former banking services. Only the London partnership, Higginson & Co., continued to conduct its affairs as it had in the past.[87] The interlocking partnerships that had existed between the old firm and the London and Paris houses were discontinued and no formal ties existed between them and the new Lee, Higginson, though both continued to participate in the corporation's flotations.

By the summer of 1932 the crash and the depression had wiped out a large number of investment banking houses, compelled many others to reorganize, and forced the remaining ones to retrench. According to one estimate, published in September 1932, some 2,000 investment and brokerage firms had been put out of business and many of those that survived had closed most of their branches.[88]

Membership in the exclusive IBA, which included nearly all the principal investment houses in the country, also dropped rapidly during these years. From 690 in 1928, it fell to 378 in 1933.[89] Both membership and income from dues were smaller that year than they had been in 1921. Some of these membership losses resulted from mergers and consolidations, but the largest number were resignations attributable directly, according to the IBA, to liquidations brought on by the depression.

The decline in the IBA's membership was revealed also in the number of cities with 15 or more member firms represented. In 1929 there had been 33 such cities; by 1933 the number had been

85. Quoted in *The Commercial & Financial Chronicle*, CXXXIV (June 18, 1932), 4437.
86. Edward Weeks, *Men, Money, and Responsibility: A History of Lee, Higginson Corporation, 1848–1962* (Boston, 1962), 27; Marshall W. Stevens, "History of Lee, Higginson and Company" (typescript, Baker Library), Appendix A.
87. *The Commercial & Financial Chronicle*, CXXXIV (June 18, 1932), 4437.
88. Clifford B. Reeves, "A Brief for the Bankers," *The American Mercury*, XXVII (September 1932), 21–22.
89. The information on the IBA is based upon reports in the *Proceedings* for the years 1928 through 1933.

cut by more than half. New York City and Chicago, the largest investment banking centers in the country, continued to lead with the largest number of member firms, but even in these two cities the association's losses by 1933 were considerable. In New York City alone, which in 1929 accounted for 28.6 percent of all the investment banking houses in the United States, the number of member firms declined from 233 to 145; and in Chicago the IBA's losses were relatively greater, from 134 to 73.[90] In fact, the Chicago investment banking community was especially hard hit. Fewer than one-third of the 600 investment firms that had been in business before the crash survived the depression.[91]

The casualty rate in other cities often was as large, and in a few instances even greater. In San Francisco the number of houses that belonged to the IBA fell by approximately 46 percent between 1929 and 1933. In Baltimore the decline was almost as great.[92] The steady collapse of one investment house after another during 1930 and 1931 dealt a heavy blow to the already badly shaken reputation of the investment banker.

But it was not just his professional shortcomings or lack of business acumen that blasted the image of the investment banker as a high-minded, vigilant financier with a deep sense of obligation. Even worse was the disclosure of irresponsibility, selfishness, and favoritism in the world of high finance.[93] The spring of 1932 was a more terrible time for the investment banker than the autumn of 1929. The revelations of Kreuger's gross fraud and deception; the collapse of Samuel Insull's mighty utility and holding company empire and his subsequent flight to Europe in June 1932; and the start, two months later, of a Senate investigation of stock market practices destroyed whatever confidence the public still had in the investment banker. "The so-called experts are all wrong," was the reaction of one investor. "A big front, a Saint Bernard dog's honest face and a pose — that's your investment banker." [94]

Rarely had a group lost so much status and respect so rapidly as had investment bankers in the three years following the great stock market crash. Their already badly tarnished public image was to deteriorate still further in 1932 and 1933, as congressional committees probed deeper into their business affairs during the speculative boom of the late 1920's. These investigations supplied the addi-

90. IBA, *Proceedings, 1928–1933;* Raymond W. Goldsmith, *Financial Intermediaries in the American Economy Since 1900* (Princeton, 1958), 120.
91. F. Cyril James, *The Growth of Chicago Banks* (2 vols., New York, 1938), II, 1097.
92. IBA, *Proceedings, 1928 and 1933.*
93. See, for instance, Donald R. Hanson, "Choosing an Investment Banker," *The Forum,* LXXXIII (May 1930), supp., xxxviii, xl, xlii.
94. Quoted in Stuart P. Meech, "The Investment Securities Business and the Future," *The Journal of Business,* V (July 1932), 242.

tional evidence that completed the transformation of the investment banker's image from the folk hero of the prosperity years to the scapegoat of the depression era. Apart from the investment bankers themselves, no one contributed more to this metamorphosis than Ferdinand Pecora, the fifty-one-year-old New York City attorney, who interrogated the great financiers summoned to appear before the Senate subcommittee investigating stock market and investment banking practices.

16 The Investment Banker on Trial: The Gray–Pecora Investigation

The great Wall Street probe of 1932–1934, the so-called Gray-Pecora Investigation, which destroyed the favorable public image of investment bankers, grew out of President Herbert Hoover's belief that his efforts to bring about recovery were being frustrated by a small, powerful group of bears who were depressing stock prices for their own selfish advantage. In July 1931, when European finances were collapsing, as well as several times thereafter, Hoover warned the directors of the New York Stock Exchange that unless they adopted "adequate measures to protect investors from artificial depression of the price of securities for speculative profit," he would ask Congress to investigate and, if necessary, draft legislation placing the exchange under federal control.[1] Much the same view was expressed by Senator Simeon D. Fess of Ohio, chairman of the Republican National Committee. "In New York they think short selling is all right and down here we think it is an evil," Fess told Washington reporters. "Unless the Stock Exchange does something to correct the practice of short selling, Congress will take drastic steps in that direction."[2] From such a relatively innocuous inception began the searching investigation that demolished the reputation of several eminent financiers, destroyed public confidence in investment bankers generally, and paved the way for widespread regulation of the securities business.

Neither Hoover's repeated urgings nor senatorial warnings of an impending investigation budged key officials of the exchange. "I see no evil in short selling," Richard Whitney, president of the New York Stock Exchange, announced after conferring with Senator Fess. "That has been my position . . . and I still find no reason to change it."[3]

The Senate thought otherwise. Both Republicans and Democrats, progressives as well as conservatives, were demanding an investigation and insisting upon regulatory legislation. At the very time Whitney was justifying short sales, there were four bills before senate committees designed either to supervise or to prohibit such transactions.[4] Hoover, however, was reluctant to ask for an investigation, he explained later, "as we had enough burdens to carry, without all the discouraging filth such an exposure entailed."[5]

1. Herbert Hoover, *The Memoirs of Herbert Hoover* (3 vols., New York, 1951–52), III, 126.
2. Quoted in *The Commercial & Financial Chronicle,* CXXXIII (December 26, 1931), 4255–56.
3. Quoted in *ibid.,* 4256.
4. *Ibid.,* 4256.
5. Hoover, *Memoirs,* III, 127.

Hoover finally decided to act late in February 1932. His good friend and occasional financial adviser Senator Frederic C. Walcott, a conservative Connecticut Republican and member of the Banking and Currency Committee, informed him that further bear raids were being planned. A former partner in the New York investment banking house of Bonbright & Co., Walcott was in close touch with Wall Street developments. When he heard rumors that a small group of market operators, supposedly led by such Democratic party bigwigs as John J. Raskob and Bernard Baruch, were planning to discredit the Hoover administration by "a series of bear raids" that would drive down an already badly depressed stock market still further, he warned the president.[6] It was this step, probably more than anything else, that caused Hoover to push for an investigation. He would put a stop to these damaging raids and, at the same time, frustrate his political enemies by having the Senate Banking and Currency Committee expose the culprits publicly.

A resolution authorizing the Senate to investigate short sales on the New York Stock Exchange had been introduced on December 14, 1931, by John G. Townsend, Jr., a Delaware Republican and also a member of the Banking and Currency Committee. On March 4, 1932, after Hoover had instructed Walcott and Senator Peter Norbeck of South Dakota, the progressive Republican who was chairman of the Banking and Currency Committee, to launch the investigation as soon as possible, the Townsend resolution was reported back to the Senate, but in substantially altered form. As originally introduced, the resolution had called for nothing more than an investigation of bear raids, and this was all that Hoover had intended when he ordered the probe.

Such a limited inquiry did not satisfy all those who suspected that there was much more wrong with Wall Street practices than just short sales. As a result of their efforts the resolution that was adopted authorized a far more comprehensive inquiry. It directed the Senate Banking and Currency Committee, or one of its subcommittees, "to make a thorough and complete investigation" of buying and selling practices, as well as "borrowing and lending of listed securities upon the various stock exchanges." The proposed committee was to study the effects of these practices upon interstate and foreign commerce, the operation of the national banking and the Federal Reserve systems, and upon the sale of federal government bonds and notes. Lastly, it was to report on the desirability of using the federal taxing power to regulate trading in securities.[7]

6. Ferdinand Pecora to author, May 20, 1964. See also Hillel Black, *The Watchdogs of Wall Street* (New York, 1962), 10–11; John T. Flynn, "Wall Street Medicine," *Collier's,* XCII (November 11, 1933), 12–13, 54–55; the same author's, "The Marines Land in Wall Street," *Harper's Magazine,* CLXIX (July 1934), 148–49.
7. U.S. Senate, Committee on Banking and Currency, 73d Cong., 2d Sess.,

Despite its greatly expanded authority the Senate Banking and Currency Committee, which held its first "emergency meeting" on April 11, 1932, confined itself almost exclusively to investigating short selling on the New York Stock Exchange, as Hoover had requested.[8] The great "Senate Bear Hunt," as the press quickly dubbed the hearings, failed to uncover any Democratic conspiracy or other organized raids designed to discredit Hoover and destroy public confidence in his efforts to bring about recovery. Whitney, the committee's first witness, once again defended short sales as necessary and beneficial; he denied categorically that exchange practices were in any way at fault or responsible for the depression.[9]

Most of the business and financial press agreed with him. *Business Week,* for instance, though admitting that the hearings had produced some news of untidy activities, regarded it as of a kind that had been generally known among Wall Streeters. Nevertheless, it was enough to cause Iowa's Republican Senator Smith W. Brookhart, no friend of Hoover or Wall Street, to tell a representative of *Business Week* that "before Congress adjourned there would be a law which would put an investment banker in the penitentiary for pegging the price of a security on the Stock Exchange while unloading it upon the public."[10] Spokesmen for the administration disagreed with Brookhart, and most journalists doubted that Congress would pass such a law unless the hearings disclosed "more sensational wrong-doings."

On April 25 the Senate Banking and Currency Committee organized a special subcommittee, composed of three Republicans and two Democrats, to continue the hearings.[11] It was this subcommittee

---

Stock Exchange Practices: Report . . . (Washington, 1934), 1. See also Ralph F. De Bedts, *The New Deal's SEC: The Formative Years* (New York, 1964), 17. John T. Flynn credits Norbeck and other insurgent Republicans and Democrats with the greatly broadened scope of the amended resolution. See his article in *Collier's* cited above.

8. *The Commercial & Financial Chronicle,* CXXXIV (April 9, 1932), 2634.

9. Subsequently Whitney elaborated his defense of the Stock Exchange still further in a special report to the Governing Committee of the New York Stock Exchange and in an address to the Industrial Club of St. Louis, which was broadcast nationally. See *The Commercial & Financial Chronicle,* CXXXV (August 27, 1932), 1432–34; *ibid.* (October 1, 1932), 2259–60.

10. "Heaving Bricks at Wall Street Good Politics — Poor Business," *Business Week* (May 4, 1932), 5–6.

11. *The Commercial & Financial Chronicle,* CXXXIV (April 30, 1932), 3196, quoting the New York *Journal of Commerce.* Besides Norbeck, who was chairman, the other Republicans on the subcommittee were John G. Townsend, Jr., of Delaware, and James Couzens of Michigan. The two Democrats were Carter Glass of Virginia and Duncan U. Fletcher of Florida. Walcott, the spokesman of the White House, and the man Hoover had instructed to initiate the investigation, was conspicuously absent. "Failure to select him," *The Commercial & Financial Chronicle* reported, "is taken as notice that a majority of the Committee are determined to go a good deal deeper into speculative activities on the New York Stock Exchange and in brokers' offices than was in the original purview of the President." Townsend was the only administration friend on the committee.

that first disclosed some of Wall Street's more serious sins. During April and May witnesses testified that during the 1920's, pool and market operators had employed publicity agents to push stocks on unsuspecting investors, paid newspapermen to recommend certain securities to their readers, and subsidized a radio announcer to persuade his listeners to buy stocks that were being boomed.[12] One such operation, a pool organized in March 1929 to trade in Radio Corporation of America (RCA) common, allegedly had earned its members a profit of nearly $5 million in a week.[13] Prominent businessmen and national figures of both political parties, such as Raskob, Charles M. Schwab, Percy Rockefeller, and Walter P. Chrysler, participated in these activities, along with less respected market operators like Harry F. Sinclair. In the case of the RCA pool, even the wives of the corporation's president and the head of the brokerage house conducting most of the manipulations had participated in the operation.

More damaging to the reputation of the investment banker were disclosures detailing how old respected banking houses had abused the trust and interests of investors. In May 1932, Walter E. Sachs, a general partner in Goldman, Sachs & Co., appeared before the subcommittee. He was questioned on some of the activities of the Goldman Sachs Trading Corporation, his firm's investment affiliate. The purpose of this company, of which he had been president since June 1930, Sachs explained, was "to trade, deal, and to make investments in securities of various kinds in which companies we, as a firm, participated, and in which others could participate through stock ownership if they so desired." [14]

The Trading Corporation's investments, though profitable to Goldman, Sachs, which earned handsome fees for handling them, had proved to be disastrous for investors. The extent of their losses was revealed fully when Senator James Couzens, the Michigan Republican, questioned Sachs. First offered in December 1928 and eagerly purchased at $104 a share, the stock had dropped to $1.75 in May 1932.[15] One of its investments, Frosted Foods, Inc., cost the corporation $12.7 million.

Neither the disclosure of Goldman, Sachs's poor business judgment, which proved so costly to some 40,000 investors, nor the publication of Ivar Kreuger's frauds and successful deception of Lee, Higginson & Co., which the subcommittee uncovered in January 1933, so shattered the image and reputation of the investment

12. John Kenneth Galbraith, *The Great Crash, 1929* (Boston, 1955), 78; and De Bedts, *New Deal's SEC,* 20.
13. De Bedts, *New Deal's SEC,* 21.
14. U.S. Senate, Committee on Banking and Currency, 72d Cong., 1st Sess., *Stock Exchange Practices: Hearings* . . . (7 pts. in 6 vols., Washington, 1932–33), pt. 2, 566–83.
15. *Ibid.,* pt. 2, 567.

banker as did the evidence of financial chicanery and skulduggery that was exposed after January 24, 1933. On that date Ferdinand Pecora was appointed the subcommittee's counsel.

Born in Sicily in 1882, Pecora came to the United States when he was five years old. He had intended to become an Episcopal minister, but economic circumstances forced him to find a job. Working as a junior clerk in a New York City law firm caused him to change his vocation to the law. In 1909 he was admitted to the bar; in 1918 he was appointed Assistant District Attorney for New York County, and four years later, Chief Assistant District Attorney, a position he held until December 1929, when he entered private practice.[16]

During his years with the District Attorney's office, Pecora acquired much experience as an investigator and some knowledge of Wall Street practices. His probe of the investment policies of the New York State sinking fund resulted in several indictments and a reorganization of the entire system. He was equally successful in exposing abuses in the bail-bond business; misdeeds of bucket-shop operators, who victimized thousands of small investors; and milk-graft scandals in the city Health Department. In 1929 his investigation into the failure of the City Trust Company led to the bribery conviction of the former State Superintendent of Banks.[17] These and other noteworthy prosecutions earned him widespread respect as an honest, energetic, and fearless investigator. Jacob Benton, the New York City District Attorney, wrote Norbeck that Pecora was "the best qualified lawyer in the country" for the Senate subcommittee's job.[18]

Pecora was recommended for the position, which paid $250 a month, by Bainbridge Colby, President Wilson's last Secretary of State. The two men had known each other since 1912, when they had joined the Progressive party and worked to put Theodore Roosevelt back in the White House. Pecora was the Bull Moose party's vice chairman in New York State that year, but by 1916, impressed by the magnitude of Wilson's legislative accomplishments, he joined the Democratic party. Unlike Colby, who became a conservative Democrat and in 1934 turned against the New Deal, Pecora remained a lifelong progressive and admirer of the social and legal philosophy of Oliver Wendell Holmes, Louis D. Brandeis, and Benjamin N. Cardozo.[19]

Pecora's appointment occurred as a result of a squabble between

---

16. *The New York Times*, January 25, 1933; *The Commercial & Financial Chronicle*, CXXXVI (January 28, 1933), 586, quoting the New York *Journal of Commerce*.
17. *The New York Times*, January 25, 1933.
18. *Ibid*.
19. Pecora to author, May 20, 1964; Ferdinand Pecora, "The Reminiscences of Ferdinand Pecora" (6 vols., Oral History Research Office, Columbia University, New York, 1962), III, 655. See also *The New York Times*, May 21, 1933.

the subcommittee and its counsel, Irving Ben Cooper, who resigned on January 17, one week after his appointment.[20] Cooper, who had assisted Samuel Seabury in the investigation that led to the resignation of New York City's mayor, James J. Walker, in September 1932, charged that he had been denied the authority and "free hand" promised him at the time of his appointment. He accused the subcommittee of assigning one of its staff to his New York City office for the "sole purpose" of supervising his activities and putting a "lid" on the investigation. The same Senate conservatives who had interfered with the work of William A. Gray, Cooper's predecessor, now were trying to place so many restrictions on his own activities, he asserted, as to make it impossible for him to conduct an investigation that would be "thorough, fair, and play no favorites." [21]

Reports of strong demands by members of the Senate Banking Committee to discontinue the probe had appeared in the press long before Cooper was appointed. After his resignation *The New York Times* attributed his departure to the fact that he had been "criticized by conservative members [of the committee] for undermining public confidence in market and corporation leaders and interfering with recovery by exploring personal operations instead of collecting observations on the general topics of short selling, manipulation of the market and the need of statutory regulation of the Stock Exchange." [22]

Norbeck denied all this, saying that Cooper's difficulties with the subcommittee arose from his own personal ambition. He had assumed unwarranted responsibility, Norbeck explained. Besides hiring seven assistants and renting an office in New York City's financial district — all of which the subcommittee was unwilling to approve — Cooper had demanded 500 blank subpoenas. This demand the subcommittee was unwilling to grant, especially since only 27 had been issued thus far. Cooper resigned, Norbeck concluded, not because the subcommittee had prevented him from conducting a "genuine investigation," as the New York City attorney charged, but because it "declined to delegate to him the powers of the Senate." [23] Whatever the reason, Norbeck assured the press that Pecora would have "full authority" in conducting the investigation and hearings, and that the subcommittee would "accord him its complete support and co-operation." [24]

20. *The Commercial & Financial Chronicle*, CXXXVI (January 21, 1933), 415.
21. *Ibid.*, CXXXVI (January 28, 1933), 586.
22. *The New York Times*, January 1, 19, 1933. See also *The Commercial & Financial Chronicle*, CXXXV (July 2, 1932), 49.
23. The text of Cooper's letter of resignation appears in *The Commercial & Financial Chronicle*, CXXXVI (January 28, 1933), 586–87.
24. *The New York Times*, January 25, 1933; *The Commercial & Financial Chronicle*, CXXXVI (January 28, 1933), 586.

When Pecora accepted the assignment, he had no idea that it would keep him in Washington for the next eighteen months. The Seventy-second Congress, which had authorized the investigation, was to adjourn before March 4, 1933. While Franklin Roosevelt approved of the inquiry and had used some of its findings in his campaign speeches, he had not as yet told Norbeck that he intended to ask Congress to continue the probe. Pecora's job, Norbeck explained, was to conclude the investigation and prepare the subcommittee's report, which was due before the end of that Congress.[25] Except for two sessions in January, the hearings had been suspended since the previous June. Neither the Republicans nor the Democrats had favored continuing them. The subcommittee's disclosures had been sufficiently bipartisan to prevent either party from using them to tar the other. In fact, so many Democrats had been called to testify that on one occasion Carter Glass asked his colleagues on the subcommittee whether there were any Republicans at all on Wall Street.[26]

Though Pecora had been employed to write the subcommittee's report, Norbeck was especially interested in getting the "low-down" on Samuel Insull. Many of his constituents in South Dakota had suffered heavy losses as a result of Insull's collapse, and they expected Norbeck to do something about it.[27] Investigation of the Insull failure started on February 15, 1933. For three days Pecora questioned witnesses on the many operating firms, holding companies, and super-holding companies that Insull had created and the methods Halsey, Stuart & Co. had employed in selling the securities of these corporations. Owen D. Young, the board chairman of the General Electric Company, testified that it was "impossible for any man to grasp the situation of that vast structure," referring to the Insull empire. "I should like to say here," he added, "that I believe Mr. Samuel Insull was very largely the victim of that complicated structure, which got even beyond his power, competent as he was, to understand it." [28]

The funds to finance all these companies were recruited mainly from the public, and Pecora called Harold L. Stuart, the head of Halsey, Stuart, Insull's principal bankers, to explain how this was done. In the course of his examination Pecora elicited the information that this highly respected banking house had financed a radio hour and employed a University of Chicago professor to advertise the "principles of sound investment to millions of listeners." [29]

25. Pecora to author, May 20, 1964; Pecora, "Reminiscences," III, 656–59.
26. Pecora to author, May 20, 1964.
27. *Ibid.*
28. Quoted in Ferdinand Pecora, *Wall Street under Oath: The Story of Our Modern Money Changers* (New York, 1939), 226.
29. *Stock Exchange Practices: Hearings*, pt. 5, 1611, 1614.

Neither Pecora nor the committee was convinced that the "Old Counsellor," the professor's radio name, was interested only in educating his listeners, especially since Stuart admitted that his firm wrote all the broadcasts. "He was simply the deliverer," Stuart said.[30]

Pecora also uncovered information on other common investment banking practices of the boom era that in the grim days of 1933 appeared highly unethical. Not only did the Insull probe raise once again the often-debated question of the propriety of investment bankers' serving as directors of the corporations whose securities they sold — the same old issue that the Pujo Committee had argued twenty years earlier — but it emphasized the way a very reputable investment house had pushed on unsuspecting investors the securities of a company in which it was closely associated. Halsey, Stuart had advised one of its clients to sell United States government bonds and invest part of the proceeds in one of Insull's companies, an investment trust, whose securities "to-day," Pecora asserted, "are worth practically nothing." [31] What disturbed him was not so much the fact that the firm's advice had proved bad; this could be attributed to honest error. Much more disturbing was the fact that Halsey, Stuart had failed to inform this buyer that it held "a very extensive stock interest" in the company and that several of the firm's partners also were officers of the corporation. There was nothing illegal in Halsey, Stuart's failure to provide investors with this kind of information, and other firms were just as secretive. It simply was not the custom to disclose these facts, Stuart asserted.[32] He believed it should be, and he concluded his testimony by saying that a full-disclosure law should be adopted, one similar to the English Companies Act.

The Insull revelations so shocked the country that Norbeck realized the investigation could not stop there. He immediately instructed Pecora to look into the affairs of the National City Co., the security affiliate of the National City Bank of New York, whose salesmen and representatives had peddled billions of securities across the country, victimizing, among others, many South Dakotans. Pecora started his study of these two financial giants, which "were in all but name, one institution," in the New York City offices of the bank's attorneys.[33] For four days, working from early morning until late at night, he read and took extensive notes from the records of the bank and its affiliate. The flagrant breaches of trust that he discovered in the minutes of the directors' meetings, he said later,

30. *Ibid.,* pt. 5, 1625.
31. *Ibid.,* pt. 5, 1593–94, 1626–27.
32. *Ibid.,* pt. 5, 1627, 1675.
33. Pecora, *Wall Street under Oath,* 79. The organizational structure of the National City Co. and its interlocking arrangements with the National City Bank are described in *Stock Exchange Practices, Report,* 156–59.

"amazed" him.[34] Subpoenas were issued at once, ordering high officials of the two institutions to appear before the committee.

Hearings on National City's activities started on February 21, with the questioning of Charles E. Mitchell, the fifty-six-year-old chairman of the board of both the bank and its affiliate. The ethics of the men responsible for guiding these two very widely respected institutions proved to be much worse than those of Insull or his bankers. The abuses uncovered were so gross that the financial community itself was appalled. The conservative *Commercial & Financial Chronicle,* never an admirer of the Senate investigation, admitted that the revelations were "far from pleasing to say the least," and described the testimony of National City officials as "highly sensational." [35]

When the hearings came to a close, two days before Roosevelt's inauguration, "a whole era of American financial life passed away," Pecora wrote later.[36] The investment affiliates of commercial banks were doomed. Nothing the committee uncovered in the next seventeen months revealed the "sickening story of exploitation" unfolded during the National City hearings. "The only thing that some of our great financial institutions overlooked during the years of boom," observed Heywood Broun, the noted Scripps-Howard columnist, "was the installation of a roulette-wheel for the convenience of depositors." [37]

Witnesses disclosed a wide variety of abuses and excesses. Investors were lured into buying issues sponsored by the National City Co. and were told few, if any, pertinent facts concerning the quality of the securities recommended. In March 1928, for instance, National City Co. had issued $8.5 million of bonds for Minas Geraes, a state in the Brazilian republic, whose authorities a National City official had described earlier as being lax, negligent, and entirely uninformed concerning the responsibilities of a long-term borrower. Not only was none of this information given the investor, but the prospectus for the issue, prepared by this same official, actually referred favorably to the way the state's finances had been administered. The next year Minas Geraes negotiated a second $8 million loan, one-half of which was to be used to bail out the National City Co., which had advanced some $4 million in short-term credits. Instead of disclosing this fact to the public, the prospectus stated only that the funds were "designed to increase the economic productivity of the State." When asked why National City had not given investors all the facts, Ronald M. Byrnes, a former vice president

34. Pecora to author, May 20, 1964; Pecora, "Reminiscences," III, 669–86.
35. *The Commercial & Financial Chronicle,* CXXXVI (February 25, 1933), 1243–44.
36. Pecora, *Wall Street under Oath,* 70.
37. "Big Bankers' Gambling Mania," *The Literary Digest,* CXV (March 11, 1933), 11–12. This article quotes various newspapers on Mitchell's testimony.

of this affiliate, replied: "In my opinion there is no investor that I know of who would have had the slightest interest, or whose judgment would have been in the least affected, by the fact that the moneys from this loan were to be used to pay advances which were made for these purposes." [38]

These Brazilian flotations were not isolated examples of the National City Co.'s pushing low-quality securities on unsuspecting investors, who had no way of learning their "true value." As Pecora noted, people had purchased them largely because of their "faith in the integrity and presumed conservatism of the National City Bank." [39] Notable among other instances of this kind were the three Peruvian loans of 1927 and 1928, totaling $90 million, about which the public never was told that National City's own experts had described the credit position of this government as "an adverse moral and political risk." [40] The same lack of responsibility was shown in the flotation of a $15 million loan for the Cuban Dominican Sugar Company and a $32 million bond issue for the Lautrato Nitrate Company of Chile.[41]

Methods such as these had been employed also in selling stocks of domestic corporations. As bankers of Anaconda Copper, the National City Co. "promptly sold" to its customers its own sizable holdings in this corporation's stock when the price of copper dropped sharply, while it continued to tout these shares to the public. Not satisfied with this, National City bought an additional million shares, which it resold at a profit of some $20 million. When asked about these transactions, Mitchell denied that the drop in copper prices had in any way influenced him to sell his company's holdings. He explained National City's subsequent purchases in these words: "it became our duty, or so we conceived it, so long as our customers viewed that stock as an investment stock, to buy in the market and to sell additional shares to them. Which we did." Mitchell volunteered no opinion as to the extent to which the National City Co.'s sales tactics may have influenced its "customers" to reach the conclusion that Anaconda Copper was a sound "investment stock." [42]

From the hearings the public also learned how the National City Co., the nation's largest investment banking house and the affiliate

38. *Stock Exchange Practices: Hearings,* pt. 6, 2137. See also Pecora, *Wall Street under Oath,* 96–100.
39. Pecora, *Wall Street under Oath,* 92.
40. *Ibid.,* 100. See also *Stock Exchange Practices: Hearings,* pt. 6, 2082–87, on the way the Institute of International Finance, a "supposed independent fact-finding body," sponsored by the Investment Bankers Association and conducted with the assistance of New York University, was used to assist sellers of foreign bonds, in this case the National City Co.
41. The details of these and similar transactions are discussed in Pecora, *Wall Street under Oath,* ch. v. See also "South American Loans Feature Senate Hearings," *Barron's,* XIII (March 6, 1933), 9.
42. Quoted in Pecora, *Wall Street under Oath,* 95.

of the world's second largest bank, had engaged in various other ethically dubious activities. It speculated on the stock exchange and participated in pool operations. The bank itself, of course, was barred by federal law from entering into these transactions, but there was nothing to stop it from doing so indirectly and extensively through its affiliate. Between December 1928 and March 1929 it was in three copper stock pools, which Mitchell insisted on calling "joint accounts." However labeled, these operations earned huge profits for the participants, all of whom were either executives of the corporations whose stocks were being manipulated or individuals with access to inside information not available to the public.[43]

The National City Co. also traded heavily in the stock of the National City Bank itself, driving up the price to what Pecora called "dizzy heights." In January 1928, when National City officials took the stock off the New York Stock Exchange because they feared that it might be manipulated, it sold for $785. Early in 1929, after a five-for-one split, it was selling for $585. No one was more responsible for booming this stock than the National City Co. itself; it was the single largest trader, sometimes buying and selling from 30,000 to 40,000 shares a day.[44]

While the affiliate engaged in these questionable activities, the bank assisted it by providing clients. Bank officials advised depositors seeking investment counsel to call on the affiliate's security salesmen, all of whom were exhorted to push sales by "pep talks" and special sales contests.[45] The bank assisted and cooperated with its affiliate in numerous other ways as well.

Nor were the clients of the bank's fiduciary affiliate, the City Bank Farmers Trust Co., overlooked either. It had been decided at the time the trust company was organized that it would not buy any issues from the bank's security affiliate, "except where in some specific trust it is set forth as the desire of the maker of that trust that they may buy from the National City Co." This was done for reasons of "general safety," Mitchell had testified, when interrogated on this point by a House committee in June 1930. At the time he also had said it was to the "specific advantage" of any one making a trust with the City Bank Farmers Trust Co. to put into the trust agreement a provision permitting the trust company to purchase securities from the National City Co.[46] Mitchell argued strongly for

---

43. Pecora, *Wall Street under Oath,* 105–09; *Stock Exchange Practices: Report,* 166–67.

44. Pecora, *Wall Street under Oath,* 110–12; *Stock Exchange Practices: Report,* 168–73.

45. Pecora, *Wall Street under Oath,* 91; *Stock Exchange Practices: Report,* 163–65.

46. U.S. House, Committee on Banking and Currency, 71st Cong., 2d Sess., *Branch, Chain and Group Banking: Hearings* . . . (15 pts. in 2 vols., Washington, 1930), pt. 15, 1971–76.

what he called "complete banking service" and admitted readily that the trust company's clients were given strong reasons to authorize it to use the investment facilities of the National City Co.

Such close ties as existed among these institutions, especially those between the bank and its investment affiliate, disguised bad banking practices and kept mistakse and losses from reaching the attention of the stockholders. A striking example of this deception occurred in 1927; the National City Bank, criticized by federal examiners for having made some poor sugar loans, unloaded some $25 million of these on its affiliate and did so at the expense of the bank's stockholders and without their knowledge. This was accomplished by a "legal corporate maneuver" in which National City Bank authorized and sold to its stockholders 250,000 common shares at $200, bringing in $50 million. The bank then applied half this sum to its own capital account, writing it up from $50 million to $75 million. The other half it applied to the capital and surplus of the National City Co., all of whose stock was held in trust for the benefit of the bank's stockholders. The next step in the maneuver was for the City Co. to use its $25 million to finance the General Sugar Corporation, which it then organized. This company, in turn, used the funds to buy the National City Bank's bad loans, thus saving the bank from a heavy loss and further censure but at considerable cost to the National City Co. The latter company subsequently had to put down its investment in the Sugar Corporation as being worth, Pecora asserted, "the munificent sum of exactly $1." [47] When Mitchell was asked why stockholders of National City Co. were not told that part of their money was to be used to "bail out" the bank, he replied: "I hardly think there was any necessity of it." [48]

Mitchell and other top National City executives saw themselves, he said, as "the equivalent of partners in a private banking or investment firm." They conducted the bank's and the affiliate's affairs in the same way, entirely oblivious of the fact that they were employees of a corporation and responsible to its stockholders. Besides drawing substantial salaries, they voted themselves huge annual bonuses, not reported in annual statements.[49] In addition to his annual salary of $25,000, Mitchell received very large cash bonuses from two "management funds," created especially to reward the executives of the National City Bank and the National City Co. For the three years 1927 through 1929 his compensation from these two funds alone amounted to nearly $3.5 million. In 1929, the year the bank organized its fiduciary affiliate, the City Bank Farmers Trust

---

47. *Moody's Manual of Investments: Banks* . . . *1928,* 2151–52; Pecora, *Wall Street under Oath,* 121–22.
48. Quoted in Pecora, *Wall Street under Oath,* 123.
49. *Ibid.,* 114–21; *Stock Exchange Practices: Report,* 205–08.

Co., Mitchell received nearly $16,000 from this institution's special management fund.[50]

When questioned on the propriety of permitting executives to share to such an extent in the net earnings of financial institutions without their having to bear any part of the losses, Mitchell replied that he had found the arrangement highly satisfactory in promoting a strong "esprit de corps" among the officers. "Does it not also inspire a lack of care in the handling and sale of securities to the public?" Senator Couzens asked. Mitchell replied affirmatively, saying that the practice may have had "some influence" on the fact that almost $1 billion, a fifth, of the securities issued by the National City Co. during the past ten years were in default.[51]

Large salaries and "stupendous bonuses" were only two roads to private riches. Like the partners in many private investment banking firms, the executives of the National City Co. also profited handsomely from participating individually in the affiliate's flotations. One of these transactions, in October 1928, netted a small group of "officers, directors, key men, and special friends" a profit of at least $1.6 million in a matter of weeks. When the stock market collapsed, and the speculators among National City's officers found themselves in trouble, the bank went to their rescue promptly by establishing a special "morale loan fund," from which they might borrow without interest or collateral.[52] Nearly all the "loans" made by this fund, amounting to some $2.4 million, never were repaid and, as in the case of many of its other transactions, the stockholders, whose money it was, were not told of their bank's solicitude for the morale of its executives.

Even more shocking was the disclosure that these distinguished, respected pillars of the financial community had employed every legal trick to avoid, if not evade, paying any income taxes on their huge earnings. One simple, commonly employed method of establishing a convenient tax loss was to transfer title of securities to a relative. This was the device that Mitchell used in 1929, when he sold 18,300 shares of National City Bank Stock to his wife, incurring a "paper loss" of some $2.8 million, which he deducted from his income.[53] Three years later, after a precipitous decline in the stock's price, he bought it back for the price at which he had sold it. He did so, he explained, because he was unwilling to have his wife suffer such a loss. "That sale was just really a sale of convenience, to reduce your income tax?" Senator Brookhart asked. "You can call it that if you will," the banker replied. "Well, is that

50. *Stock Exchange Practices: Report*, 206.
51. *Ibid.*, 207–08.
52. Pecora, *Wall Street under Oath*, 124–26, 127–28.
53. *Stock Exchange Practices: Report*, 322–23.

right?" Brookhart insisted. "Yes," Mitchell admitted, "it was a sale, frankly, for that purpose." [54] The government subsequently looked upon this transaction not as "tax avoidance" but "tax evasion," and instituted criminal proceedings against him. After he was acquitted the government filed a civil suit, which Mitchell fought for three years. By the time the matter was settled, in December 1938, penalties and interest had increased the amount he owed from $700,000 to nearly $1.4 million, but the Internal Revenue Bureau, in announcing the settlement, made no mention of the amount paid.[55]

These disclosures badly damaged the careers of Mitchell and Hugh B. Baker, president of the National City Co. Both men resigned their posts on February 28, 1933, two days before the hearings were concluded. It was reported at the time that Mitchell reached his decision after his long-time friend, William H. Woodin, the head of the American Car and Foundry Company, whom Roosevelt had just appointed to be his Secretary of the Treasury, learned that FDR "thought it would be best" for the banker to step down.[56] Many others shared the president-elect's view. "No banking institution," *The New York Times* editorialized, "not even the next to the largest in the world, could afford ever to approve or condone the transactions of which he [Mitchell] was a guiding spirit and one of the beneficiaries." [57]

By the time the National City hearings came to a close, March 2, it was generally accepted that the investigation would be extended. Almost a month earlier *The New York Times* had reported that Roosevelt had told Norbeck that he favored continuing the probe. Furthermore, in his inaugural address the president used the subcommittee's findings to condemn the "unscrupulous money changers," who stood "indicted in the court of public opinion, rejected by the hearts and minds of men." [58] Ten days later, Duncan U. Fletcher, the Florida Democrat who had succeeded Norbeck as chairman of the Senate Banking and Currency Committee, reassured the country that the investigation would be continued. He added that the president had authorized the Attorney General to follow the hearings closely for disclosure of violations that could be prosecuted under federal law.[59]

Fears that the banking crisis and other pressing business facing

54. *Ibid.*, 323; Pecora, *Wall Street under Oath*, 194–95.
55. Pecora, *Wall Street under Oath*, 196.
56. *The New York Times*, February 28, 1933.
57. *Ibid.* See also "Banking Versus Salesmanship: Picture of Affiliate Company Unfolded Before Inquiring Senators Led to Mitchell Resignation," *Newsweek*, I (March 4, 1933), 23–24.
58. *The New York Times*, February 7, 1933; Samuel Rosenman, ed., *The Public Papers and Addresses of Franklin D. Roosevelt* (13 vols., New York, 1938–50, II, 12.
59. *The New York Times*, March 14, 1933.

the Congress in March 1933 would cause it to sidetrack the investigation were quickly allayed. One disgruntled member of the subcommittee's staff had charged earlier that certain conservative senators, unwilling to alienate Wall Street by disclosing its past errors and abuses, would prevent it from doing its work effectively. Concern over favoritism of this type also proved unwarranted. On April 1 Fletcher introduced a resolution, which the Senate approved three days later, widening substantially the scope of the inquiry.[60] In addition to the powers granted the committee previously, the Fletcher resolution, which Pecora had assisted in preparing, authorized it to "make a thorough and complete investigation" of the operations and business practices of private bankers.[61] This extension was made, the press reported, to overcome certain objections of the Morgan firm, the first private banking house scheduled to be investigated.[62]

The question of the committee's authority to probe into the affairs of private bankers had been raised on March 22 at a conference attended by Pecora and two representatives of the Morgan firm. The meeting took place in a two-room office Pecora had rented at 285 Madison Avenue, in New York City. Here, surrounded by dirty, unpainted walls and shabby, rented furniture, Thomas W. Lamont, the very knowledgeable Morgan partner, and John W. Davis, the firm's legal adviser, who in 1924 had been the Democratic party's presidential candidate, discussed the committee's powers, procedures, and the information that Morgan needed to provide it.[63]

Some of the facts Pecora asked for were easily available; others had to be dug out of the firm's records. This did not disturb Lamont. What concerned him most was Pecora's request that Morgan submit copies of its balance sheets for the past five years. Davis questioned whether the committee had the authority to demand this information of a private bank. Pecora interpreted their reluctance to provide him with the figures as outright refusal, which was not the case at all, or so Lamont subsequently wrote President Roosevelt. "I wanted to have you know the story and to know that none of us is holding out on the Committee," the banker assured FDR. "So far as this particular item is concerned, we haven't the slightest hesitation at any time in showing our balance sheet to members of the Committee, and I may add that I think you would regard it as a highly satisfactory one. In fact, there is not one single item

60. *The Commercial & Financial Chronicle,* CXXXVI (February 25, 1933), 1289; *The New York Times,* April 1, 1933.
61. *Stock Exchange Practices: Report,* 2; *The New York Times,* April 1, 1933.
62. Pecora to author, May 20, 1964. See also "Next, Morgan & Co.," *Business Week* (April 12, 1933), 12, 14; "Morgan: Private Bankers Included in Senate Inquiry," *Newsweek,* I (April 8, 1933), 21–22.
63. Pecora to author, May 20, 1964; Pecora, "Reminiscences," III, 703–10.

in our whole business that we are not quite willing to show anybody who is entitled to see it." [64]

Morgan issued no public statement refuting the false report that it had refused to answer one of the committee's inquiries. Lamont was prepared to do so, but "wiser counsels prevailed," he wrote Roosevelt, "because it was pointed out to me that by adopting such a course we should only be getting into a public controversy which might be annoying to the Committee which, I assume, is acting in perfectly good faith." [65] Nothing further was said about the matter, and Pecora, armed with the additional authority he had requested, launched the second and longest phase of the investigation.

Public hearings resumed on May 23, and continued, with several brief interruptions, through May 4, 1934. The first witness to be called was the sixty-six-year-old J. P. Morgan, a large, heavy man, six-feet-two, with thinning gray hair and thick black eyebrows. His appearance before the committee aroused intense public interest; photographers crowded the Senate Caucus Room, where the hearings were held, and created such a commotion that the chairman ordered the sergeant at arms to stop them from disturbing the proceedings.[66] A week later, in that same room, an enterprising press agent for the Ringling Brothers and Barnum & Bailey Circus sat a twenty-seven-inch midget on the great Morgan's lap, thus giving photographers the opportunity to take a unique picture of the publicity-shy banker, about whom the public knew little but was intensely interested.[67]

It was only natural that Morgan should be first in the committee's probe into the affairs of private bankers. His was the wealthiest, most prestigious, and most influential banking partnership in the United States. His firm, and others like it, Morgan told the committee, belonged to a very old profession, dating back to the close of the Middle Ages. Unlike incorporated banks, whose affairs were regulated by the government authority that chartered them, the business of the private banker was supervised by no one. He regulated himself according to "a code of professional ethics and customs" that had evolved slowly through time, and that "could never be expressed in legislation, but has a force far greater than any law." The touchstone of this code was credit. This, Morgan said, was the

64. Thomas W. Lamont, "Memorandum for the President," April 11, 1933, "President's Personal File," Franklin D. Roosevelt Library, Hyde Park, New York. See also George Harrison, "Conversation with Messrs. Lamont and Gilbert, March 28, 1933," Confidential File, Binder 46, George Harrison Papers, Columbia University Library, New York.
65. Lamont, "Memorandum for the President."
66. U.S. Senate, Committee on Banking and Currency, 72d and 73d Congs., *Stock Exchange Practices: Hearings* (20 pts. in 9 vols., Washington, 1933–34), pt. 1, 3–4; Pecora, *Wall Street Under Oath*, 4–5.
67. Sherwin D. Smith, "Thirty Years Ago," *The New York Times Magazine*, May 26, 1963.

private banker's "most valuable possession; it is the result of years of fair and honorable dealing and, while it may be quickly lost, once lost cannot be restored for a long time, if ever." [68]

Freedom from regulation bore a price tag. In New York private bankers were forbidden to advertise themselves as bankers, solicit deposits from the general public, or pay interest on them when they amounted to less than $7,500.

The House of Morgan did not consider these limitations at all burdensome. Indeed, it approved of and adhered to them strictly. No sign of any kind proclaimed to the passerby that the four-story Renaissance building at 23 Wall Street, at the corner of Broad, housed a bank. Neither the word itself nor the name of the firm appeared on the front door. "Is your name listed among the banks?" Senator Couzens asked. "We hope not," Morgan answered. "We have taken every precaution to prevent it." [69] Its business and address were well known nonetheless.

Like other private bankers the Morgan firm restricted its services to a small, select group of clients, mostly great corporations, whose securities it had sponsored and for which it acted as fiscal or transfer agent. Some of the executives of these companies also kept personal deposit accounts with the firm, as did other prominent businessmen and financiers; all either were friends of the partners or had been recommended to them. No one opened an account at 23 Wall Street without an invitation, Morgan told the committee in his opening statement.[70]

Pecora interrogated at length not only Morgan but the other partners who appeared before the committee. He questioned them on the organization of the firm, the responsibilities of its various members, and their "rights and interests" as defined in the articles of copartnership. Disclosure of the latter's contents was not achieved without some difficulty. Neither Davis, the firm's chief counsel, nor all the partners themselves ever had seen the original agreement. Davis argued strongly that its contents were entirely private, "purely a matter between the partners themselves," and that it contained nothing that was of "public interest" or would assist the work of the committee.[71] Pecora insisted on seeing the document nonetheless, and finally the firm made it available to the committee in executive session. "It was like asking Morgan & Co. to bare its soul," Pecora recalled this incident later. The law did not require partnership agreements to be filed anywhere, and no outsider had ever before asked to see it.[72]

68. *Stock Exchange Practices: Hearings,* 73d Cong., pt. 1, 3.
69. Quoted In Pecora, *Wall Street under Oath,* 8.
70. *Ibid.,* 12–13; *Stock Exchange Practices: Hearings,* 73d Cong., pt. 1, 3–6.
71. *Stock Exchange Practices: Hearings,* 73d Cong., pt. 1, 9; Pecora to author, May 20, 1964.
72. Pecora to author, May 20, 1964.

The document, beautifully handwritten on rolled parchment and carefully tied together with ribbons, specified each partner's interest in the firm. It gave Morgan, its senior member, full and final authority to decide any and all disputes, "compel any partner at once to withdraw and retire from the partnership," determine the distribution of the firm's undivided profits, and dissolve it at any time he saw fit.[73]

Once the question of the committee's right to see the articles of copartnership had been established, the hearings proceeded without any further delays or difficulty. Morgan proved to be a friendly and cooperative witness, but a far less knowledgeable one than his partner Thomas Lamont. Lamont was a sixty-three-year-old native New Yorker who had served as a vice president of the Bankers Trust Company and the First National Bank of New York before joining Morgan in 1911. He was an exceptionally able financier, as well informed about business generally as he was about investment banking specifically. No one had a more intimate acquaintance with the firm's activities. Pecora called him the firm's "chief-of-staff." [74]

Probes into the affairs of the private bankers disclosed none of the gross abuses and flagrant violations of fiduciary trust that had so disfigured the record of the National City Co. With few exceptions, the leaders among these firms, such as the Morgan House and Kuhn, Loeb, the second private banking partnership to be investigated, were run conservatively. They eschewed speculative ventures, dealt mostly with established corporations, and usually showed a considerable sense of responsibility toward their clients, both borrowers and lenders. Morgan employed no salesmen, and Kuhn, Loeb retailed only a very few of the securities it distributed. Both firms were chiefly originators and wholesalers, dealing principally in bonds. There had been very few defaults among the securities they had sponsored. In the case of Morgan, less than 2.1 percent of all the securities it had offered publicly since 1919, amounting to some $6 billion, were in default at the time of the hearings. None of these issues was that of a foreign government or corporation; in each instance the defaulting company was an American railroad.[75] Kuhn, Loeb's record was equally good. Only one of its foreign bond issues, that of the Mortgage Bank of Chile, was in default, and only one railroad with which the firm was associated, the Wabash, was in receivership at the end of 1931.[76]

73. Pecora to author, May 20, 1964; Pecora, *Wall Street under Oath*, 6–7.
74. Pecora to author, May 20, 1964.
75. J. P. Morgan & Co., "Reprints of Statements Submitted by Members of J. P. Morgan & Co. to Senate Committee on Banking and Currency . . ." (New York [1934]), 9, 11. This pamphlet contains the complete text of the principal statements made by members of the firm at the hearings.
76. *Stock Exchange Practices: Hearings,* 73d Cong., pt. 3, 1217; U.S. Senate,

As Pecora viewed them, the sins of the private bankers were of a more subtle nature. Like Untermyer a generation earlier, Pecora and the more progressively minded members of the subcommittee were greatly disturbed with the concentration of financial power in a small number of firms in New York City. He was concerned about the many close, continuing ties that existed between a few Wall Street private investment houses and most of the country's largest railroads and industrial corporations and the great influence these bankers exercised over the security markets generally. To progressives like Pecora the "money trust" seemed just as entrenched as it had been in Pujo's day, and not a whit less powerful.[77] Pecora accused Morgan and the other interrogated investment bankers of refusing to compete with one another, using directorships to control the corporations they financed, and fighting competitive bidding in order to protect their own profits. All the talk about banking ethics, Pecora asserted, was nothing more than an excuse to allow investment houses to charge all the traffic would bear.[78]

Not satisfied with the huge profits they made in offering the securities of established corporations and the best foreign issues, Pecora believed, these eminent bankers also succumbed to and helped feed the speculative craze that seized the country in the late 1920's. Like many smaller, younger, less prominent investment houses, they too had become promoters of new corporations, engaging in questionable practices that the subcommittee found not at all in keeping with the strict code that Morgan and Otto Kahn, of Kuhn, Loeb, claimed to govern their firms' conduct.

The most disturbing revelations concerning the House of Morgan arose out of its role in launching three great holding companies, all organized in 1929. The firms in question were the United Corporation, a super-holding company designed to occupy the same position in the electric power industry that United States Steel and American Telephone & Telegraph held in theirs; the Alleghany Corporation, which brought under its control various railroad properties owned by the Van Sweringen brothers; and Standard Brands, Inc., a merger of four large food companies.[79] Each of these transactions involved issuing a large amount of common stock, a type of security Morgan never had offered before. Unwilling to distribute these issues to the general public over its own name, the firm arranged to offer them privately, at cost, to a select list of customers, people

---

Committee on Finance, 72d Cong., 1st Sess., *Sale of Foreign Bonds or Securities in the United States: Hearings* . . . (4 pts., Washington, 1931–32), pt. 1, 129.

77. *Stock Exchange Practices: Hearings*, 73d Cong., pt. 2, 904–07, 940–42. See also *U.S. v. Henry S. Morgan et al.*, "Plaintiff's Exhibit No. 112" (November 9, 1948), 266–70.

78. *Stock Exchange Practices: Report*, 83–90.

79. Pecora, *Wall Street under Oath,* ch. ii; Forrest McDonald, *Insull* (Chicago, 1962), 249–50.

"whom we know," George Whitney, a Morgan partner, testified, "and whom we have had relations with, whom we know are competent financially and mentally to undertake the risks, whatever the risk may be." [80] Whitney likened these lists to those used by English banking houses underwriting their securities. "This theory of having a list of underwriters to share an equity risk with us . . . is not new," he said. "In fact, it is very old. It goes down, traditionally, ever since there has been banking." [81]

The public did not look upon these "preferred lists," as the press labeled them, so complacently, and neither did Pecora nor a majority of the subcommittee. To them the lists appeared to be more like payoffs or a form of polite bribery, a way of providing certain favored individuals and banking firms with a convenient way to make some money without much risk. The names on the lists seemed to confirm these suspicions. They included not only important, strategically placed business firms and financial leaders, investment houses, and brokerage firms, but also many prominent figures in politics and public life. Among the latter were former President Calvin Coolidge; Charles Francis Adams, Hoover's Secretary of the Navy; Newton D. Baker, Wilson's Secretary of War; William Woodin, soon to become FDR's Secretary of the Treasury; General John J. Pershing, a close friend of a Morgan partner; Joseph Nutt, the treasurer of the Republican National Committee; John J. Raskob, the chairman of the Democratic National Committee and a director of General Motors; Charles A. Lindbergh, Jr., the son-in-law of a Morgan partner; Bernard Baruch; and Senator William Gibbs McAdoo of California, to cite but a few of the names that made headlines.[82]

At the time McAdoo was a member of the Senate Banking Committee, and he explained carefully that his name appeared on the list as a result of his friendship with Russell C. Leffingwell, a Morgan partner, whom he knew "as a young man — his family and mine having lived across the street from each other." The transactions in which he was involved, McAdoo explained further, occurred four years before he had become a senator, and resulted in his losing $2,500. He felt it necessary to make this statement, he told the committee, "because of the misleading articles which had appeared in the press, and which are attempting, through headlines and otherwise, to impart some sinister feature into perfectly proper business transactions conducted by the Morgans on the one hand and myself on the other, within our rights and not subject to the least criticism." [83]

80. *Stock Exchange Practices,* 73d Cong., pt. 2, 401.
81. *Ibid.,* pt. 2, 396.
82. *Ibid.,* pt. 2, 885–99 gives all the names on the Morgan lists. See also Pecora, *Wall Street under Oath,* 28–31; Pecora, "Reminiscences," III, 755–59.
83. *Stock Exchange Practices: Hearings,* 73d Cong., pt. 1, 153–54.

The lists also contained the names of many other less widely known figures, all of whom were included because they too were friends of the partners. In some cases these individuals were allocated no more than ten shares, such as were given to one of Morgan's clerks.[84] There were many other individuals who received allotments of fifty or fewer shares. These names attracted no attention. It was the prominent figures who made the headlines, since usually they were the ones who were allotted the largest participations and stood to gain most by the opportunity to buy these selected stocks at the price Morgan paid for them.

Buyers were not obliged to keep their shares any length of time. "There are no strings tied to this stock," wrote Morgan partner William Ewing to Woodin, informing him that 1,000 shares of Alleghany common had been set aside for him if he wanted it. The price was $20 a share, "the same price it is costing us," and "you can sell it whenever you wish." When Ewing made the offer, the stock was selling at between $35 and $37 a share, "which means very little," he wrote Woodin, "except that people wish to speculate."[85]

The same moneymaking opportunities also were granted those invited to buy stocks of United Corporation and Standard Brands. Few on the subcommittee believed that Morgan did not expect something in return for such generous courtesies. Whitney denied vehemently that such was the case, but the impression remained nevertheless.[86]

It was just as difficult to persuade the subcommittee or the public that not a single Morgan partner owed any income taxes for the years 1931 and 1932. The fact that the firm's capital had dropped from $118 million in 1929 to less than $45 million in 1932, much of which the partners attributed to capital losses rather than withdrawals, impressed very few. Disclosure of partners' failure to pay any income taxes for two years, together with the publication of the Morgan customers' lists, aroused more widespread public criticism against this firm than did any other information the subcommittee uncovered about its activities.[87]

The Morgan hearings were followed by an investigation of Kuhn, Loeb, and then, after a three-month summer recess, one of Dillon, Read & Co. Neither house escaped censure. Kuhn, Loeb

---

84. *Ibid.*, pt. 2, 399–400.
85. *Ibid.*, pt. 1, 143.
86. See, for instance, the editorial, "Mr. Morgan's Show," *The Commonweal*, XVIII (June 9, 1933), 141–42; John T. Flynn, "J. P. Morgan & Co.: A House Built on Favors," *The New Republic*, LXXV (June 28, 1933), 174–76.
87. Ernest K. Lindley, "Wall Street under the New Deal," *The Literary Digest*, CXVI (July 22, 1933), 3; "House of Morgan: Its Tales and Favored Friends Provide a National Crossfire of Agitation, and Some Sniping," *Newsweek*, I (June 3, 1933), 3–5.

was criticized for its role in organizing the Pennroad Corporation, a holding company similar to the Morgan-sponsored Alleghany Corporation. Launched in April 1929, Pennroad was designed to provide the Pennsylvania Railroad with capital to acquire properties it was afraid of losing to its rivals, particularly the Alleghany Corporation. There were other reasons as well, notably the Pennsylvania's wish to extend its own system by acquiring the Ford-owned Detroit, Toledo & Ironton Railroad, and to do so without risking disapproval by the Interstate Commerce Commission.[88] The Pennroad Corporation was to be both an offensive and defensive weapon in the Pennsylvania's battles with its competitors. It was essential, therefore, that the Pennsylvania maintain firm control of the holding company that was to own this road and any other properties Pennroad might acquire. The responsibility for organizing such a company was entrusted to Kuhn, Loeb, and the plan adopted was largely its creation.

Instead of going to the public, Kuhn, Loeb arranged to have the stockholders of the Pennsylvania provide the funds by subscribing not to the new corporation's stock but to special voting-trust certificates. The stock itself was to be held in trust for ten years, and three trustees, the president of the railroad and two of its directors, were empowered to vote it. The result was that Pennroad's owners had no control whatsoever over their own property.[89] As in the case of the Alleghany issue, Pennroad voting-trust certificates were offered to a select few, mostly customers and other friends of the Pennsylvania's officers who were not stockholders in the railroad; but unlike the Alleghany preferred list, which the Morgan firm had prepared, the Pennroad one was compiled by the directors of the Pennsylvania.[90] As it turned out, the demand for these certificates was so great that not enough were available to give the Pennsylvania's preferred friends as many as they originally had been promised.

At the time the Pennroad Corporation was organized, the voting-trust certificate appeared to be an excellent device to accomplish the Pennsylvania Railroad's purposes. Four years later Otto Kahn denounced it. He had come to realize, he told Pecora, that all schemes designed to deprive the stockholder of his rights were wrong. They were, he said, "inventions of the devil." [91]

88. U.S. Senate, Committee on Interstate Commerce, 76th Cong., 3d Sess., *Investigation of Railroads, Holding Companies and Affiliated Companies: Report No. 1182* . . . (5 pts., Washington, 1940), pt. 4, 2104–09. The full story of Pennroad's organization is told in U.S. Senate, Committee on Interstate Commerce, 76th Cong., 1st–3d Sess., *Investigation of Railroads, Holding Companies, and Affiliated Companies: Report No. 25* (27 pts., Washington, 1939–40), pt. 24, 1–26.
89. *Investigation of Railroads: Report No. 25*, pt. 24, 8; Pecora, *Wall Street under Oath*, 58–59.
90. *Investigation of Railroads: Report No. 25*, pt. 24, 16–17.
91. Cited in Pecora, *Wall Street under Oath*, 59.

Although he had acknowledged one error, Kahn was not at all disposed to admit to another. He rejected the suggestion that his firm's charges for its advice and services in launching the Pennroad Corporation might have been excessive, considering the slight risk it had assumed in underwriting and distributing the stock. He strongly denied that the $1.1 million Kuhn, Loeb had received as its share of the syndicate profits and the $2.7 million the firm realized from the sale of its stock options were at all too large.[92] Kuhn, Loeb's counsel in this instance, Kahn said, was "almost the most valuable piece of advice we ever gave them." [93]

Actually, Kuhn, Loeb got off lightly. Against another New York City private investment house the subcommittee leveled even more serious charges than excessive banking profits. Dillon, Read & Co., Inc., was the unhappy target. It was a New York joint-stock company, headed by Clarence Dillon, a native Texan, who first entered the banking business in 1913 as a salesman in the Chicago offices of Wm. Read & Co. Three years later, Dillon, then thirty-four years old, joined the firm's head office in New York, and in 1920 became its senior partner. The next year the partnership was reorganized and its name changed to Dillon, Read & Co. In October 1922 it was reconstructed as a joint-stock company, with Dillon owning a majority of the shares.[94]

Unlike most investment houses that did a general banking business, Dillon, Read dealt strictly in securities. At one time it had accepted deposits, mostly to accommodate its clients, but after 1927 it discouraged the practice. It had "no use" for such funds, Dillon told Pecora. Nor did it deal in foreign exchange, issue letters of credit, or make short-term loans of any kind. It specialized in long-term financing; its total security offerings during the fifteen years following World War I amounted to almost $4 billion.[95]

The investigation into Dillon, Read's activities in the 1920's revealed many of the same abuses, violations of fiduciary trust, and selfish profit-seeking that the subcommittee had brought to light when Pecora interrogated Mitchell of the National City Co. Many of Dillon, Read's South and Central American bonds had turned out to be nearly worthless. But it was not these nor its other foreign flotations, which altogether amounted to more than $1.5 billion,

---

92. *Investigation of Railroads: Report No. 25,* pt. 24, 20–21.
93. Cited in Pecora, *Wall Street under Oath,* 63.
94. *U.S. v. Henry S. Morgan et al.,* "Corrected Opinion of Harold R. Medina" (February 4, 1954), 93; *ibid.,* "Transcript of Trial: Defendants' Opening — Mr. [Mathias F.] Correa" (February 20, 1951), 3423; *Stock Exchange Practices: Report,* 223–24; Fritz Redlich, *The Molding of American Banking: Men and Ideas* (2 vols., New York, 1947, 1951), II, 420n.534.
95. *Stock Exchange Practices: Hearings,* pt. 4, 1541–42; *Stock Exchange Practices: Report,* 226–27.

that provoked the most criticism.[96] This went to Dillon, Read's sponsorship of two investment trusts, the United States & Foreign Securities Corporation (US&FS) organized in 1924, and its subsidiary, the United States & International Securities Corporation (US&IS) established in 1928.

These two investment trusts, primarily Dillon's handiwork, incorporated several of those "inventions of the devil" that Kahn later condemned. The US&FS was so capitalized as to give the outside stockholders little voice in its management. The trust brought out three classes of no par shares: $6 first preferred (250,000 shares), $6 second preferred (50,000 shares), and 1 million shares of common. The preferred had voting rights only if dividends were passed. Dillon, Read marketed the first preferred, selling it to the public at $100. And to make the offer attractive, gave a share of common as a bonus with each preferred share. The bankers bought the entire issue of second preferred for $5 million and took as a bonus the remainder of the common (750,000 shares), thus acquiring control. By this move, the outside investors, who had put up $25 million in cash, held only a minority of the voting stock.[97]

Dillon, Read used the same technique, refined still further, to launch the US&IS in 1928. This time the firm acted through its affiliated US&FS. By that year the latter company had built up a surplus of over $10 million, and the investment bankers had US&FS use these funds to buy controlling shares in US&IS. The new firm, like its parent, issued three classes of stock, also all no par: 500,000 shares of $5 first preferred, 100,000 shares of $5 second preferred, and 2.5 million shares of common. It sold the first preferred to the public at $100 a share, with a share-for-share bonus of common. US&FS bought the second preferred and 2 million shares of common for $10 million. Thus between 1924 and 1928, Dillon, Read, with an investment of $5 million, won almost complete control of two corporations in which the public had invested $75 million.[98]

In addition to this control leverage, Dillon, Read had profited substantially in fees for organizing these companies and distributing their securities. The sale of US&FS first preferred netted the firm $339,000 in syndicate income, and it received $1 million for launching US&IS. Individual members of the firm also profited greatly from selling their US&FS common. These shares, which had cost them $13\frac{1}{3}$ cents in 1924, eventually reached a high of $72. The sub-

---

96. Proctor W. Hansl, *Years of Plunder: A Financial Chronicle of Our Times* (New York, 1935), 249–50.
97. Pecora, *Wall Street under Oath*, 207–09; *Moody's Manual of Investments: Banks . . . 1929*, 2755–56.
98. Pecora, *Wall Street under Oath*, 211; Hansl, *Years of Plunder*, 251–52; *Moody's Banks, 1929*, 2756–57.

committee estimated the profit from the sale of some 120,000 of these shares at better than $6.8 million.[99]

Unlike Kahn, who admitted that the banking ethics of the 1920's left much to be desired and acknowledged that reforms were necessary, Dillon saw nothing wrong in any of his firm's transactions. "May I ask you, Mr. Dillon, if you were to organize two investment trusts again, would you, in view of the disclosures, follow the same procedure?" Senator Couzens wanted to know. "Yes," Dillon answered, "I do not think I should vary it, except that when I subscribe the junior money I might not have different classes of stock." And a little later, when asked whether the public had been treated fairly in receiving only 250,000 common shares of US&FS, Dillon said: "We could have taken 100 percent. We could have taken all that profit. We could have bought all the common stock for $5,000,000." Senator Alva B. Adams, a Colorado Democrat, ended the discussion by quoting Lord Clive's famous words: "When I consider my opportunities, I marvel at my moderation." [100]

Four days after the Dillon, Read hearings the subcommittee turned its attention to the Chase Securities Corporation, the affiliate of the influential Chase National Bank, the world's largest bank.[101] The Chase hearings produced the same "shocking disclosure of low standards in high places" that had been revealed eight months earlier, when the subcommittee was investigating the affairs of its rival, the National City Co.[102]

For nearly two months the country was treated to another chapter in the recent history of high finance. The errors of the private bankers, great as many of them were, came nowhere near those of the Chase Securities Corporation and its respected and admired president, Albert H. Wiggin, who also headed the Chase Bank. Wiggin had been dubbed "the most popular banker in Wall Street." [103] Like the National City Co., Chase Securities matched, if it did not exceed, its competitor in the number and variety of its "misdemeanors." Stock pools, market manipulations, "insiders' profits," large salaries and substantial bonuses, excessive trading in the bank's own stock for personal gain, short sales, "preferred lists" and other forms of favoritism, and income tax avoidance were as characteristic of the Chase as they were of the National City and its executives.[104]

Wiggin had used family-owned corporations he controlled to engage in extensive market speculations in the stock of his own bank as well as that of other companies. His activities were carried

99. Pecora, *Wall Street under Oath*, 210, 212; Hansl, *Years of Plunder*, 252.
100. Quoted in Pecora, *Wall Street under Oath*, 213–14.
101. *Stock Exchange Practices: Report*, 159–63.
102. Pecora, *Wall Street under Oath*, chs. vii–viii.
103. *Ibid.*, 134.
104. *Ibid.*, chs. vii–viii; *Stock Exchange Practices: Report*, 185–205.

on either independently or in association with the Chase Securities Corporation and its wholly owned subsidiary, the Metropolitan Corporation.[105] He conducted these highly profitable operations even during the darkest days of October and November 1929, and at the expense of his own bank. The Chase had been good to Wiggin. It had lent him and his corporations millions of dollars and given these companies syndicate participations that allowed them to reap huge profits. But Wiggin did not allow these past favors to interfere with his own personal affairs, even when it meant selling his own bank's stock short at the very time the Chase itself was a member of the banking group trying to support and stabilize the market. Wiggin's profits from his three-month operation immediately following the crash netted him $4 million.[106]

Some of Wiggin's activities proved to be as startling to the bank's top management as to the public. Winthrop W. Aldrich, who succeeded Wiggin as executive head of the Chase in January 1931, condemned many of his predecessor's actions almost as vigorously as did the subcommittee. Aldrich disapproved of bank affiliates originating, underwriting, and distributing securities; and he agreed wholeheartedly with Pecora that reforms were badly needed. On March 8, 1933, months before he had learned of Wiggin's conduct, and at the very time President Roosevelt and Congress were struggling to reopen the country's banks, Aldrich issued a public statement urging reforms designed to prevent a recurrence of the financial abuses disclosed by the subcommittee. "The spirit of speculation should be eradicated from the management of commercial banks," he declared, and investment and commercial banking should be separated completely from each other.[107] The Chase itself already had decided to get out of the securities business, and a special committee was at work preparing a plan to separate the bank from its security affiliates.

Months later, while testifying before the subcommittee, Aldrich elaborated further on the need for reform and improved banking ethics. He spoke out strongly against participation of bank officers in syndicates, either directly or through family-owned corporations, as Wiggin had done; and he disapproved of their receiving any "indirect compensation from anybody." The "only compensation they should receive," Aldrich told the subcommittee, "should be their own salary or such other compensation as is permitted by the board of directors where full disclosure is made." Bank officers

---

105. *Stock Exchange Practices: Report,* 173–84.
106. Pecora, *Wall Street under Oath,* 154.
107. Winthrop W. Aldrich, *Suggestions for Improving the Banking System* (New York, 1933), 6–7. See also, Pecora, *Wall Street under Oath,* 136–40. This statement, revised and elaborated considerably, served as the basis for Aldrich's remarks before the subcommittee, when he was called to testify on November 29, 1933. *Stock Exchange Practices: Hearings,* 73d Cong., pt. 8, 3975–92.

should be prohibited also from engaging in any kind of "speculative adventure," he declared. "When I say that, I am speaking of pools or operations in securities." [108] No bank should be permitted to "deal in its own shares," not even "indirectly in the sense of making a market." Aldrich reasserted his opposition to commercial banks functioning as investment bankers, and he acknowledged that it had been a "mistake" for the Chase's board of directors, of which he was then a member, to have voted Wiggin "a life salary of $100,000 a year." Aldrich explained this unfortunate decision on the grounds that neither he nor the other members of the board had been aware of the way Wiggin had used his position for personal profit.[109]

When it became evident that the Chase would never again call on Wiggin for "advice" affecting the "welfare and management" of the bank, he renounced his generous pension, and the bank accepted his decision. Indeed, the new management sought to disassociate itself entirely from his stewardship in the hope of restoring the Chase Bank to its former position as one of the great banking institutions of the country.

Hearings on the Chase came to an end early in December 1933 and concluded the main phase of the subcommittee's investigation. Many of the abuses that Pecora had brought out were being uncovered also by other congressional committees, and very often through the testimony of the same individuals. The Senate's Finance Committee investigated foreign bond sales and its Banking and Currency Committee also held hearings on the workings of the Federal Reserve and National Banking systems. The House Banking and Commerce committees probed into branch and group banking, collecting information used in drafting the Securities Act. Never before had the leaders of American finance been called before so many congressional groups and asked to defend the way they conducted their affairs and to explain why their activities should not be regulated in the public interest.

The investment banker did no acquit himself well in any of these proceedings, but in none did he do so badly as he did before the Pecora Committee. It was the findings of this group, more than those of any other, that did much to blast the investment banker's once proud and respected reputation. A good many Americans came to regard Wall Street financiers as being no better than John Dillinger, the notorious bank robber, who was shot to death a month before the Pecora hearings came to an end. "He wasn't any worse than the bankers and politicians who took poor people's money," one citizen remarked. "Dillinger did not rob the poor people. He robbed those who became rich by robbing the poor. I am for Johnnie." [110]

108. *Stock Exchange Practices: Hearings,* 73d Cong., pt. 8, 4119–20.
109. *Stock Exchange Practices: Report,* 209–210.
110. Quoted in William B. Fierlong, "Thirty Years Ago," *The New York Times Magazine,* August 9, 1964.

Like the Pujo investigation before it, Pecora's probe was not the impartial, dispassionate examination of the investment banking business that the subcommittee's friends claimed it to be. The times did not permit such an inquiry. There was no cross-examination, a fact that the bankers complained about then and for years thereafter.[111] Nor were they the only ones to argue that they had not received a fair hearing. Carter Glass, for personal and political reasons, expressed great annoyance with the investigation, which he labeled a "spectacle." He was reported to have been especially displeased with the way Pecora had treated the Morgan firm. Two of its partners — Russell Leffingwell and S. Parker Gilbert — had been associated with Glass in the Treasury Department and were close personal friends.[112] And there was enough other criticism of the investigation to cause its most ardent supporters to fear that even though Roosevelt had expressed his strong approval of the subcommittee's work, the bankers and their friends might succeed in persuading Congress to terminate the hearings.[113]

Some of the criticisms leveled against the subcommittee and its counsel doubtless were justified, as were a few of the subsequent ones directed against the final *Report*. Some of its conclusions were overdrawn, and the impression of Wall Street malfeasance created was too sweeping.[114] The fact remains, nonetheless, that many of the more responsible bankers who appeared before the subcommittee admitted the truth of many of Pecora's charges and acknowledged the urgent need for drastic reforms. Kahn told Pecora privately that the subcommittee was doing a much needed job of housecleaning. Wall Street's leaders, Kahn said, had been aware of the abuses and evils that existed, but were reluctant to expose friends and business associates and, like everyone else, were afraid to do or say anything that might disturb the great stock market boom. As a result, they had failed to exercise whatever authority they possessed.[115] Charles S. McCain, board chairman of the Chase National Bank, agreed with Pecora that better disclosure requirements were necessary and that investment houses should be licensed and regulated;[116]

111. *U.S. v. Henry S. Morgan et al.*, "Defendants' Opening" (February 1, 1951), 2639. See also *The New York Times*, March 28, 1954.
112. "Morgan & Co.," *Business Week* (June 7, 1933), 5–6; editorial in *ibid.*, "No Banking Is Private" (June 7, 1933), 32.
113. "Let the Banking Inquiry Go On," *The Nation*, CXXXVI (June 14, 1933), 656–57; "The Bankers at Work," *ibid.*, CXXXVII (October 4, 1933), 369; *The New York Times*, May 31, 1933.
114. Robert Winsmore, "Wall Street's Reply to the Senate's Investigation," *The Literary Digest*, CXVI (July 22, 1933), 5, 31; Peter H. Noyes, "Wall Street at the Wailing Wall," *The Nation*, CXXXVII (October 25, 1933), 485–86; "Low Spots in High Finance," *The Saturday Evening Post*, CCVI (January 13, 1934), 22; "Investment Bankers under Fire," *The Bankers' Magazine*, CXXIX (September 1934), 320–21; *The New York Times*, August 7, 1934.
115. Pecora to author, May 20, 1964.
116. *Stock Exchange Practices: Hearings*, 73d Cong., pt. 8, 4194.

and Lamont saw no real objection in requiring private bankers to submit to government examination, though he did not think that such supervision was "essential." [117]

Many of Wall Street's more responsible leaders, while quite ready to condemn manipulation, pool operations, inadequate disclosure, and the dangers from combining commercial and investment banking, were not at all prepared to admit to other charges. Notably, they rejected those accusing a few great investment houses of excessive underwriting charges and profits, monopolizing the new issues business, and using directorships to influence the policies of the corporations they financed.[118] Morgan called the private banker a "national asset" and, like his partner Leffingwell, argued that the usefulness of institutions of this type be kept intact by allowing them to accept deposits as they had in the past, though on a selected and limited basis.[119]

The close issuer-banker relationships that had developed among certain firms and corporations benefited not only these firms but the investor as well, investment bankers insisted. Kahn explained his aversion to competitive bidding partly on the ground that it destroyed this kind of valuable relationship, deprived issuers of continuing, long-term banking advice, and prevented the banker from acquiring the intimate knowledge of a corporation's affairs that was necessary in advising investors. Competitive bidding, which the liberal members of the subcommittee and Pecora endorsed, promoted the very kind of unethical competition that the Roosevelt administration was trying to eliminate through the National Industrial Recovery Act, Kahn insisted.[120]

The Pecora investigation did little to settle this question or other old ones about Wall Street banking monopoly and power. Nor did any of the other congressional inquiries of the early 1930's resolve these problems, though all these groups, like the Pujo Committee before them, were concerned with these issues. Few people still accepted seriously the existence of a "money trust," but many of the issues that once had given strength to the charge continued to be debated until the outbreak of World War II, especially by the Temporary National Economic Committee.[121] After the war they were taken up by the Justice Department. The Pecora investigation contributed to all these developments, but its greatest achievement was in focusing attention on Wall Street's errors and excesses and in marshaling public opinion in support of reform.

117. *Stock Exchange Practices: Report,* 227–28.
118. *Ibid.,* 113–50.
119. *Stock Exchange Practices: Hearings,* 73d Cong., pt. 2, 953.
120. Pecora, *Wall Street under Oath,* 45–47; *U.S. v. Henry S. Morgan et al.,* "Transcript of Trial: Defendants' Motions" (April 14, 1953), 22090–93.
121. Samuel Spring, "Whirlwinds of Speculation," *The Atlantic Monthly,* CXLVII (April 1931), 483; Lindley, "Wall Street under the New Deal," 31.

Unlike the Pujo investigation, which resulted in no specific legislation, the Pecora probe was immediately and directly responsible for several statutory reforms of far-reaching effect. Another result was important changes in the internal revenue code, designed to prevent the kind of legal tax avoidance practiced by some of the eminent financiers who had testified before the subcommittee. Two of these reforms, the Securities Act and the Glass-Steagall Banking Act, separating investment and commercial banking, were passed in 1933, a year before the hearings had come to a close. Another, the Securities Exchange Act, was signed into law on June 6, 1934, just as the subcommittee was concluding its work. These laws introduced important changes in investment banking practices. Rarely, if ever, has an industry had to face so many innovations so quickly. In February 1932, when Hoover ordered the Senate to investigate bear raids on the New York Stock Exchange, the investment banking business was almost entirely free of federal regulation. Two years later, the reverse was true.

17 The New Deal on Wall Street: I. Divorcement, Disclosure, Regulation

The new era in American finance, which the Pecora investigation helped bring about, was launched during the New Deal's first hundred days, when more legislation of far-reaching significance was enacted in a shorter period of time than ever before in the history of the United States. The banking and securities statutes passed by the Seventy-third Congress were among the New Deal's most constructive and enduring achievements. In no sense were they a "beating of management" or an attack upon the free enterprise system. On the contrary, they were a real rescue and repair of the financial system, with a few reforms.

The administration's objectives, to restore and extend public confidence in America's financial institutions and securities markets by correcting injustices and abuses, were endorsed by most of the electorate and by many of the country's leading deposit and investment bankers. It was methods not goals that precipitated the greatest conflicts and controversies. These were compromised by the increasingly effective dialogue that developed between Washington and Wall Street. The result of this cooperation was the drafting of a group of laws that embodied social control of the securities industry without altering radically the substance of the investment banking function. Considering conditions at the time and the mood of the public, the New Deal's securities laws, in spite of the protests of some financiers, were a conservative response to a widespread demand for reform.

On March 4, 1933, when Franklin D. Roosevelt was inaugurated president, most of the nation's banks were closed, the security markets near collapse, and the depression at its worst. The descent from prosperity had been rapid and precipitous, bringing heavy losses and untold suffering to millions. In less than three years, Standard and Poor's index of common stock prices (1941–1943 = 10) fell from a peak of 26.02 in 1929 to a low of 6.93 in 1932. The price per $100 of high-grade corporate bonds fell considerably less, from $89.1 in 1929 to $84.4 in 1932, the decade's high point ($91.8) having been reached the previous year. New corporate security offerings declined from almost $9.4 billion in 1929 to less than $400 million in 1933.[1] Investors had no confidence in securities and

---

1. U.S. Bureau of the Census, *Historical Statistics of the United States Colonial Times to 1957* (Washington, 1960), 657–58. See also U.S. Senate, Committee on Banking and Currency, 81st Cong., 2d Sess., *Securities Exchange Act Amendments: Hearings* . . . (Washington, 1950), 10; Robert Sobel, *The Big Board: A History of the New York Stock Market* (New York, 1965), 284.

even less in financiers. The investment banking business was at a standstill, and the reputation of its leaders never more tarnished. The public needed someone to blame, and bankers were prime candidates for the role of scapegoat.

The electorate was in an angry mood. It had decided that the bankers were responsible for its losses, and the conviction that thousands of innocent investors had been mulcted by self-serving financiers was strengthened still further by the Pecora hearings, which almost daily disclosed new evidence of financial negligence and irresponsibility. Millions of voters insisted upon reform and legislative protection; the Democratic party platform of 1932 had promised them both.

Although Roosevelt himself was less inclined than the public to punish Wall Street for its past errors, he responded to the voters' demands at once.[2] On March 29, he asked Congress for a federal securities law that would "protect the public with the least possible interference with honest business." The statute he proposed was not intended to have the federal government pass on the merits or guarantee the soundness of new securities, though some people hoped that it would do either or both. Roosevelt believed otherwise. The government's only responsibility, he told the Congress, was to require that "every issue of new securities to be sold in interstate commerce shall be accompanied by full publicity and information, and that no essentially important element attending the issue shall be concealed from the buying public. . . . What we seek," he concluded, "is a return to a clearer understanding of the ancient truth that those who manage banks, corporations, and other agencies handling or using other people's money are trustees acting for others."[3]

Much the same view was expressed a few months later by Felix Frankfurter, a Harvard Law School professor whom the administration called upon for assistance in drafting the proposed bill. "The Securities Act," Frankfurter wrote in *Fortune* three months after the bill had become law, "proceeds on the principle that when a corporation seeks funds from the public it becomes in every true sense a public corporation. Its affairs cease to be the private perquisite of its bankers and managers; its bankers and managers themselves become public functionaries."[4] This was the principle, too long ignored in the past, that FDR asked Congress to write into law.

There was little new in Roosevelt's proposal. Similar legislation

---

2. Arthur M. Schlesinger, Jr., *The Coming of the New Deal* (Boston, 1959), 434.
3. Samuel Rosenman, ed., *The Public Papers and Addresses of Franklin D. Roosevelt* (13 vols., New York, 1938–50), II, 93–94.
4. Felix Frankfurter, "The Federal Securities Act: II," *Fortune,* VIII (August 1933), 111.

for disclosure had been recommended repeatedly since the late 1880's, when the question of federal licensing and regulation of interstate corporations first started to receive wide attention.[5] In 1902 the Industrial Commission had recommended a full-publicity law similar to the British Companies Act. The idea took hold and grew during the Progressive era. The fact that the states, beginning with Kansas in 1911, started to enact their own blue-sky laws in no way diminished the demand for federal legislation. Theodore Roosevelt, William Howard Taft, and Woodrow Wilson all supported the principle of compulsory disclosure, and Associate Supreme Court Justice Louis D. Brandeis once had urged such a statute as the ideal answer to the problem of corporate and financial power. "Sunlight is said to be the best of disinfectants," he wrote in 1914, and "electric light the most effective policeman."[6]

During World War I the Capital Issues Committee (CIC) had reviewed all new security offerings in excess of $100,000 to curb nonessential issues, and in 1919 it had recommended that the Federal Trade Commission (FTC) police the sale of securities as an emergency measure. Its purpose was to prevent the "speculative orgie in 'wild cat' investments" (to use the words of Commissioner Huston Thompson) from jeopardizing the success of the Victory Loan. On the basis of its own and the FTC's experiences, the CIC reported to Congress that because of "the continuance of a considerable traffic in worthless and fraudulent securities," it was "unanimously of the opinion that Federal supervision of security issues . . . should be continued by some public agency, preferably by one of the Government departments." Never was such legislation more necessary.[7] The Liberty bond had acquainted millions of Americans with securities as a form of investment. It was the "obligation" of the federal government, the committee asserted, to "protect" these people "from financial exploitations by reckless or unscrupulous promoters."[8]

The committee's recommendation resulted in the immediate introduction in Congress of several bills, all designed in one way or another to protect investors against fraud and misrepresentation.[9] In 1919 Democratic Representative Edward T. Taylor of Colorado sponsored a disclosure law similar to the British Companies Act.

5. *Securities Exchange Act Amendments: Hearings,* 9; Louis Loss, *Securities Regulation* (2d ed., 3 vols., Boston, 1961), I, 107–08.
6. Quoted in Loss, *Securities Regulation,* I, 123.
7. Huston Thompson, "Informing the Investor," *The Magazine of Wall Street,* XXV (December 27, 1919), 234; U.S. Federal Trade Commission, *Annual Report . . . 1919* (Washington, 1920), 47–48; U.S. House, Committee on the Judiciary, 66th Cong., 1st Sess., *Proposed Federal "Blue Sky" Law: Hearings . . .* (Washington, 1919), 123–24.
8. Quoted in Loss, *Securities Regulation,* I, 116.
9. Edward T. McCormick, *Understanding the Securities Act and the S.E.C.* (New York, 1948), 13–17; Loss, *Securities Regulation,* I, 116–17.

The next year Andrew J. Volstead, a widely known Minnesota Republican and author of the national prohibition enforcement law, introduced an antifraud bill, which he claimed was intended to apply the principles of the Pure Food and Drug Act to the securities business. And in 1923, another Republican Congressman, Edward E. Denison of Illinois, sponsored the first of several bills aimed at strengthening the state blue-sky laws by authorizing the Justice Department to prosecute security dealers using the mails or the agencies of interstate commerce to circumvent state regulations. None of these bills, nor others introduced later, succeeded in getting through Congress, largely because of the opposition of investment bankers and security dealers.

Many of the same criticisms that were raised against the New Deal measure were used to defeat these bills. Paul V. Keyser, attorney for the Investment Bankers Association (IBA), told the House Judiciary Committee in October 1919 that the liability provisions of the Taylor bill not only would fail to deter fraudulent security dealers, it would compel honest and reputable investment houses to increase their fees and commissions to cover the additional risk imposed by the requirement making them "liable for the recovery of money on account of the mere accident of some mistake or misstatement." [10]

These and later bills, as well as the British Companies Act and similar statutes then in force on the Continent, were studied and considered in drafting the "Truth-in-Securities" Act of 1933. Samuel Untermyer, of Pujo fame, and Huston Thompson, the former Federal Trade Commissioner who had policed security sales in 1919, prepared drafts of the proposed law, but neither one satisfied the administration. Untermyer's bill contained constitutionally dubious provisions, and White House adviser and assistant Raymond Moley disapproved of making the overburdened Post Office Department responsible for administering the new law. Thompson's bill was too vague and violated the president's instructions that the government should neither approve nor disapprove of the quality of securities.[11]

10. *Proposed Federal "Blue Sky" Law, Hearings,* 125, 129; U.S. House, Committee on Interstate and Foreign Commerce, 73d Cong., 1st Sess., *Federal Securities Act: Hearings* . . . (Washington, 1933), 11. See also U.S. House, Committee on Interstate and Foreign Commerce, 67th Cong., 1st and 2d Sess., *"Blue-Sky" Bill: Hearings* (2 pts., Washington, 1921–22), pt. 1, 8–9, 19–20, and pt. 2, 14–15. Paul M. Warburg of Kuhn, Loeb & Co. warned the investment banking community that it was to their advantage to have a federal securities law, even if it meant a "little delay and red tape" in bringing out new issues. See *Proposed Federal "Blue-Sky" Law: Hearings,* 123.

11. Schlesinger, *Coming of the New Deal,* 440; Ralph F. De Bedts, *The New Deal's SEC: The Formative Years* (New York, 1964), 35; Raymond Moley, *The First New Deal* (New York, 1966), 306–15. See also U.S. House, Committee on Interstate and Foreign Commerce, 73d Cong., 1st Sess., *Federal Supervision of Traffic in Investment Securities: Report* . . . (Washington, 1933); U.S. Senate,

The bill finally accepted was written largely by James M. Landis and Benjamin V. Cohen, two exceptionally able young lawyers. They had been invited to Washington by Felix Frankfurter, early in April, to draft a substitute for the discarded Thompson measure. Thomas G. Corcoran, an attorney with the Reconstruction Finance Corporation and later one of FDR's close advisers, also worked on the bill.

Their draft embodied the Brandeisian philosophy of disclosure. In this respect it followed the tradition of the British Companies Act rather than the regulatory one commonly incorporated in most state blue-sky laws.[12] Its expressed purpose, to "provide full and fair disclosure of the character of securities sold in interstate and foreign commerce and through the mails, and to prevent frauds in the sale thereof," fulfilled the president's instructions to the letter. The law's objectives were to be achieved by requiring issuers to file a detailed statement with the Federal Trade Commission.[13]

The commission administered the law until July 1934, when this responsibility was taken over by the newly established Securities and Exchange Commission (SEC). Failure to file a registration statement imposed criminal and civil liabilities, as did the submission of inadequate, incorrect, or misleading information. Certain classes of securities were exempted; chief among these were federal, state, and municipal bonds, bonds of public authorities, bank stocks, short-term commercial paper, and railroad issues regulated by the Interstate Commerce Commission (ICC).[14] All other new, publicly offered security issues in excess of $100,000, including those of foreign governments and corporations, came under the act's jurisdiction.[15] Congress adopted the bill late in May, and it went into effect six weeks later, on July 7, 1933.[16]

Before a new, nonexempt issue could be sold publicly, the issuer was required to file a lengthy registration statement with the FTC, later with the SEC. Providing detailed information concerning the issuer, the securities, and the underwriters and paying a fee amount-

---

Committee on Banking and Currency, 73d Cong., 1st Sess., *Regulation of Securities: Report* . . . (Washington, 1933).

12. Loss, *Securities Regulation*, I, 121–27; Charles H. March, "Uncle Same Safeguards the Investor," *The Magazine of Wall Street*, LII (September 16, 1933), 514–15.

13. U.S. Federal Trade Commission, *Annual Report* . . . , *1933* (Washington, 1933), 11.

14. U.S. Senate, Committee on Banking and Currency, 73d Cong., 2d Sess., *Stock Exchange Practices: Report* . . . (Washington, 1934), 151.

15. In May 1945 the "exemption limit" on new offerings was raised to $300,000. Charles C. Abbott, *Financing Business During the Transition* (New York, 1946), 109.

16. U.S. Federal Trade Commission, *Annual Report, 1933*, 15. The best analysis of the Securities Act and its subsequent amendments is in Loss, *Securities Regulation*, I, 455–713. For an earlier, less detailed appraisal see Rudolph L. Weissman, *The New Wall Street* (New York, 1939), 198–247.

ing to $\frac{1}{100}$ of 1 percent of the total offering price of the securities were mandatory. The registration statement and all accompanying exhibits were kept on file, available to the public at the commission's offices in Washington. Nearly all the information that went into the registration statement also had to be made available to prospective buyers through a prospectus, whose form and content were carefully defined and supervised.

Registration statements did not become effective until twenty days after filing. No sales could be made during this waiting, or "cooling off," period. It was hoped that this enforced delay would prevent the kind of speedy distribution to dealers and high-pressure sales tactics that had been common in the 1920's, when small investment houses across the country often were asked to accept blindly their allotments of new issues.[17] The commission also was authorized to issue stop orders, preventing the distribution of an issue if the information supplied in the registration statement or prospectus was inadequate, incorrect, or misleading.

Most investment bankers and their attorneys expressed restrained and qualified approval of the law's broad purposes, and intense displeasure, if not actual alarm, with many of its specific provisions.[18] Their opinion of the law as finally enacted was almost identical with the views many responsible investment bankers had expressed when the House and Senate had started considering FDR's proposal. George W. Bovenizer, a partner in Kuhn, Loeb & Co., expressed their position succinctly. Testifying before the House Commerce Committee on April 1, 1933, Bovenizer said that his firm was "whole-heartedly in favor of the type of legislation . . . suggested by the President. We have stood by now for the past 12 years, or more, and have looked on with apprehension as the good name of the investment banker has been put into jeopardy or dragged down by the actions of some people who never should have been in the business. . . . I believe that every honest banker today will look with great favor upon the principle of this legislation as the dawn of a new era." Such a law, he concluded, would permit investment bankers once again to "raise their heads and hold them high." The bill, however, needed to be amended in order to make it effective and workable.[19]

17. In 1940 the Securities Act was amended to allow the SEC to shorten the cooling period, provided the concession in no way lessened the protection afforded investors. See David Saperstein, "Governmental Regulation of Investment Banking" in Investment Bankers Association, *Fundamentals of Investment Banking* (Englewood Cliffs, 1960), 589. "The cooling period," Frankfurter asserted, "will afford the necessary opportunity for scrutiny by state agencies, financial commentators, and investment services" and will thus help "restore sobriety to American finance." Frankfurter, "The Federal Securities Act: II," 55. Consult also Willard E. Atkins *et al., The Regulation of the Security Markets* (Washington, 1946), 120–21.

18. De Bedts, *New Deal's SEC*, 48–52, summarizes some of the contemporary opinion on the Securities Act.

19. *Federal Securities Act: Hearings,* 154.

Other prominent financiers and their official spokesmen, the officers and attorneys of the IBA, expressed similar views, as did much of the financial press. "With the general principle of enforcing soundness and honesty in security dealings, as far as it is humanly possible, there can be no dissent," wrote the editors of *The Magazine of Wall Street*. But they too cautioned great care. "Otherwise legislation which had inherently wholesome and desirable safeguards within it may offer a serious threat, rather than a protection, to legitimate investment savings. In striking down the guilty we must not harm the innocent." [20]

No sooner had the bill become law than investment bankers urged that it be amended.[21] The law was not workable, they insisted. Its terms were so poorly defined and its requirements so burdensome that it created dangerous uncertainties, imposed excessively heavy hazards on security dealers, increased expense and time of floating new issues, made it difficult for small and medium-size corporations to obtain long-term capital, and interfered with business generally. Moreover, it was a deflationary measure that would retard recovery.[22]

Financial leaders cited the "virtual stagnation in the long-term capital market" as proof of the law's ill effects.[23] "It is time for plain speaking," the president of the IBA declared, six months after the act became effective. "The law is a hindrance to national recovery. . . . Its result up to this time has been an almost complete stoppage of new . . . corporate underwritings for capital improvement and an embarrassment to refunding and readjustment of old issues." [24] Concern that this was the case, *The Commercial & Financial Chronicle* reported, had caused the administration to

---

20. "Sound Security Regulation Need Not Be Feared," *The Magazine of Wall Street*, LI (April 15, 1933), 653; Raymond F. Brown, "What the New Securities Act Means," *ibid.*, LII (April 29, 1933), 12–13. See also *Federal Securities Act: Hearings*, 158–160, 163–69, for the views of the IBA as expressed by its president and counsel.

21. Frank M. Gordon, "Benefits of Security Regulation," *Investment Banking*, IV (October 7, 1933), 4–8, summarizes many of the investment bankers' principal complaints. See also Peter H. Noyes, "Wall Street Faces the New Securities Act," *The Nation*, CXXXVII (July 5, 1933), 20; "The Securities Act: An Interim Report," *Fortune*, VIII (December 1933), 34–35, 136–37.

22. Arthur H. Dean, "The Federal Securities Act: I," *Fortune*, VIII (August 1933), 104, 106, lists the many adverse effects of the Securities Act on business and finance. See also A. E. Duncan, "My Experiences with the Securities Act," *The Magazine of Wall Street*, LVI (August 17, 1935), 435.

23. U.S. Senate, Committee on Banking and Currency, 72d and 73d Congs., *Stock Exchange Practices: Hearings* . . . (20 pts. in 9 vols., Washington, 1932–34), pt. 8, 4122. See also Bernard Flexner, "The Fight on the Securities Act," *The Atlantic Monthly*, CLIII (February 1934), 232–50; William O. Douglas and George E. Bates, "The Federal Securities Act of 1933," *Yale Law Journal*, XLIII (December 1933), 173.

24. Quoted in "The Securities Act: An Interim Report," 34.

investigate the law's workings to see whether it actually was "hampering legitimate business." [25]

Winthrop W. Aldrich of the Chase National Bank discussed many of the investment bankers' principal complaints before the Pecora hearings. No responsible banker opposed the law's full disclosure and antifraud provisions, Aldrich asserted. Nor were they much alarmed by the criminal liabilities it imposed: $5,000 fine and imprisonment for five years. What disturbed them most were the law's civil liability clause and the nature of the damages imposed on issuers, corporation directors, and underwriting houses.[26] The law held each underwriter liable for the entire amount of the issue, regardless of the size of his participation. The bankers insisted that their liability should be apportioned according to the "risk taken in the underwriting." [27]

Several of the law's other provisions also frightened investment bankers. They were especially disturbed by the fact that purchasers could sue to rescind a transaction and obtain the return of their money not only if the banker had filed false or wrong information, but also if he had failed to include in the registration statement or prospectus any "material fact" whose omission might mislead the reader. "It may easily happen," Aldrich told the Senate Banking and Currency Committee, "that what at the time of issuance was considered in entire good faith and upon confident judgment as a wholly immaterial fact, may subsequently turn out to have been a very material fact." [28] This imposed a very grave risk on responsible bankers. Although Aldrich could cite no specific examples of how such a situation might occur, he raised the problem as one that alarmed many security dealers and caused them to hesitate to bring out new issues.

Similarly, the provision holding corporation directors personally and individually responsible for misstatements also raised considerable apprehension. This was an entirely "new doctrine," Aldrich asserted. It is one thing to "hold a person liable in damages for the consequences of his wrongful act . . . but to compel him to refund money which he never received personally is a new idea." It would cause "responsible men . . . either [to] resign as directors or refuse to vote new security issues." The "burden of loss" should fall on the

---

25. *The Commercial & Financial Chronicle,* CXXXVII (December 2, 1933), 3933.

26. The original Senate version of the bill had imposed "absolute liability without opportunity for exculpation," but the House substituted a more moderate provision, "withholding absolute liability and imposing merely the standard of responsibility to which fiduciaries are held." Frankfurter, "The Federal Securities Act: II," 108.

27. *Stock Exchange Practices: Hearings,* pt. 8, 4124.

28. *Ibid.,* pt. 8, 4125.

banker, Aldrich concluded, but the act should be amended so as to make "the punishment fit the crime." [29]

Next to the liability and damage clauses, no provision of the law distressed the investment banking community more than the one imposing a twenty-day postregistration waiting period before an issue could be distributed to dealers and sold to the public. This requirement, the bankers argued, greatly increased their risks. Market conditions changed quickly, and the public, which might have bought the issue earlier, could refuse to do so at the later date. Failure to distribute an issue promptly would embarrass the issuer and impose serious hardship on bankers. It would tie up their funds in unmarketable securities or force them to sell the issue at a loss.

The head of a small San Francisco investment firm was so apprehensive about the act's effects on his business that he decided to quit even before the law went into effect. He was being "legislated out of business," he told newspapermen.[30]

Though many claimed to face the same dismal fate, there is no evidence to indicate the number of firms that actually did close their doors rather than submit to a law that many of them feared and resented. No small part of their opposition to the Securities Act stemmed from the fact that it brought about a radical change in the established order of things. What is more, the change was brought about by men they did not know and whose ideas they distrusted.[31]

Supporters of the law dismissed all these criticisms as propaganda designed to camouflage the investment bankers' real purpose — to destroy the statute's effectiveness by having it amended to death. Chairman Duncan U. Fletcher of the Senate Banking and Currency Committee accused the bankers of bad faith. Adolf A. Berle, Jr., a close White House adviser, denied the charge that the law had been drafted hastily, without much consultation and discussion with industry leaders.[32] The investment banking community, Berle declared, had shown little or no disposition to cooperate with the Congress in drafting the law. "In failing to come out publicly [with concrete suggestions], the investment bankers missed a chance to make a real contribution," Berle asserted.[33] James M. Landis, who had assisted in writing the act and subsequently helped administer it as a member of the FTC, told a group of New York certified public accountants, many of whom were as distressed with the law's liability provisions as were the investment bankers, that "if half of the energy that has been expended in fulminating against the Act and propagandizing for amendments were enlisted in the effort to advise

29. *Ibid.*, pt. 8, 4124, 4126.
30. *The New York Times*, June 10, 1933.
31. Emanuel Stein, *Government and the Investor* (New York, 1941), 102–03.
32. *The New York Times*, May 21, 1933, June 4, 1933.
33. *Ibid.*, June 4, 1933.

the Commission in the wise exercise of its powers, the government and issuers, bankers, lawyers and accountants would be far nearer to a solution of their problems." [34]

It was not the Securities Act that was responsible for the dearth of new financings, the New Dealers argued. It was the investment bankers themselves who, in the hope of frustrating a much needed reform measure, had gone on a quiet, undeclared strike. Several years later, when labor's use of the sitdown strike had made this tactic popular, Pecora accused the investment bankers of having originated this technique in 1933 in order to force Congress to liberalize the Securities Act.[35] The arguments for and against the act raged on bitterly for at least a year, until June 1934, when Congress relaxed the civil liability provisions. Even then the debate did not end.

That the Securities Act alone was the reason for the virtual cessation of new offerings during its first year does not seem entirely convincing, though at the time investment bankers and their spokesmen were as certain of it as their critics were not. Arthur H. Dean, a distinguished Wall Street attorney with Sullivan & Cromwell, whom Landis and Cohen had consulted in drafting the final version of the bill, upheld the arguments of the financiers. He asserted that the Securities Act was "seriously interfering with the flow of capital to industry at a time when it is sorely needed. Officials of corporations with impending maturities," he said, "are finding it difficult to get bankers to undertake commitments, and those seeking new capital are baffled by the complexities of the Act." [36]

Others were not so certain that this was the case. James P. Warburg, vice president of the Bank of Manhattan Co., doubted seriously whether the Securities Act was to blame for the "failure of the capital issues market to function." [37] Subsequent studies appear to support the view that lack of need of funds rather than fear of the law was the principal reason for the drastic decline in new offerings. This certainly appears to have been the explanation for the lack of new railroad securities, which did not have to be registered under the act.

On the other hand, the law did not stop corporations that wanted to take advantage of low interest rates from bringing out new reg-

34. Quoted in "The Securities Act: An Interim Report," 34.
35. *The New York Times,* March 21, 1937.
36. Arthur H. Dean, "Economic and Legal Aspects of the Federal Securities Act of 1933," *Proceedings of the Sixteenth Annual Convention of the National Association of Securities Commissioners* (Milwaukee, 1933), 161. The text of this talk was reprinted in *Investment Banking,* IV (October 7, 1933), 18–31. See also Moley, *First New Deal,* 312–13.
37. Quoted in "Warburg Points Out Faults of Securities Act," *Rand McNally Bankers Monthly,* LI (February 1934), 106. See also Robert Weidenhammer, "Control of New Investment," *The Annals,* CLXXXI (January 1934), 73–82; Charles T. Donworth, "A Review of the Securities Act of 1933," *Washington Law Review,* VIII (October 1933), 61–69.

istered issues. Refundings accounted for nearly 64 percent of all corporate securities offered in 1934. One utility company, for instance, registered and sold $15 million of bonds in March 1934, almost four months before the Securities Act was amended.[38] All in all, 1,095 registration statements were filed with the FTC during the year it administered the Securities Act, and of these 794, representing almost $1.2 billion in securities, were allowed to become effective. Of these, 62.4 percent represented new issues of financial and investment companies, and nearly 20 percent were those of industrial corporations. Common and preferred stocks accounted for 84.1 percent of the total registrations, and mortgage and debenture bonds amounted to 8.4 percent.[39] Investment bankers were not at all convinced of the law's workability, despite these FTC statistics.

While investment bankers and corporation officials attacked the Securities Act and demanded its amendment, others criticized it for what it failed to do. Many well-informed observers pointed out that disclosure and publicity afforded investors little protection; most of them lacked the time, inclination, or ability to study lengthy, detailed prospectuses, written in the technical language of lawyers, accountants, and bankers. The law, these critics argued, was based on an entirely erroneous assumption. It was not fraud, incompetence, or lack of sufficient information that had accounted for the huge losses investors had suffered in the past. Warburg attributed their misfortune to "speculative greed." [40]

The Securities Act neither outlawed speculation nor prevented the public from making bad bargains. Had it been in effect in the 1920's, it would have prevented only a very few of the scandalous transactions that Pecora had exposed and denounced. "There is nothing in the Act," William O. Douglas, a law professor at Yale University and later chairman of the SEC, wrote in December 1933, "which would control the speculative craze of the American public, or which would eliminate wholly unsound capital structures. . . .

---

38. Merwin H. Waterman, *Public Utility Financing, 1930–35* (Ann Arbor, 1936), 11.

39. U.S. Federal Trade Commission, *Annual Report, 1934,* 10, 38–39.

40. Quoted in "Warburg Points Out Faults of Securities Act," 106. See also George W. Edwards, *The Evolution of Finance Capitalism* (London, 1938), 311–16; Weissmann, *The New Wall Street,* 211, 215; the editorial, "Regulating the Speculators," *The New Republic,* LXXVIII (February 21, 1934), 33–34. In 1964 George J. Stigler, a distinguished University of Chicago economist, questioned the effectiveness of the Securities Act in protecting "the innocent (but avaricious) investor" and, on the basis of his sample studies, concluded that the law's "registration requirements had no important effect on the quality of new securities sold to the public." See his "Public Regulation of the Securities Markets," *The Journal of Business,* XXXVII (April 1964), 117–42, and the rebuttals by Irwin Friend and Edward S. Herman, "The S.E.C. through A Glass Darkly," *ibid.,* XXXVII (October 1964), 382–405, and Sidney Robbins and Walter Werner, "Professor Stigler Revisited," *ibid.,* XXXVII (October 1964), 406–13. Stigler's reply to his critics, "Comment," appears in *ibid.,* XXXVII (October 1964), 414–22.

Thus the effects of such an Act, though important, are secondary and chiefly of two kinds: (1) prevention of excesses and fraudulent transactions, which will be hampered and deterred merely by the requirement that their details be revealed; and (2) placing in the market during the early stages of the life of a security a body of facts which, operating indirectly through investment services and expert investors, will tend to produce more accurate appraisal of the worth of security if it commands a broad enough market." [41] Less than a year later, in another extensive critique of the law, Douglas labeled the Securities Act a "nineteenth-century piece of legislation," one "wholly antithetical to the programme of control envisaged in the New Deal and to the whole economy under which we are living." [42]

Despite the bitter controversy it inspired, the Securities Act did not alter significantly the role and function of the investment banker, nor did it change materially the way he conducted his business. The most it did was to force him to readjust some of his methods and practices, and some of these adjustments were in the making before 1933, whereas others grew out of the depression and subsequent New Deal legislation. The Securities Act required issuers and bankers to adhere to new, more comprehensive, and strictly defined standards of disclosure, but these did not affect significantly the behavior of the more responsible and conservative investment houses, except perhaps to make them even more cautious and careful in sponsoring new issues, if only to protect themselves against possible damage suits. [43]

The most important changes in investment banking practices resulting from the Securities Act grew out of three of the law's provisions: the filing requirement, the civil liability clause, and the twenty-day waiting period. The first was an entirely new development only insofar as the issuer was concerned. The house that originated the issue did almost all the investigating and negotiating of the issue, just as it had done in the past. In this respect the Securities Act proved to be of great assistance to the originating bankers. It made it much easier for them to conduct a thorough investigation. "Haggling over such matters," one writer noted, "is now usually ended by the bankers' statement that the information is required by the Securities Act." Nor did the law alter significantly the role of the other underwriters and purchasers who were required to sign the registration statement and were held liable for its accuracy. As

---

41. Douglas and Bates, "The Federal Securities Act of 1933," 171–72.
42. Quoted in Loss, *Securities Regulation*, I, 124–25.
43. George E. Bates, "Some Effects of the Securities Act upon Investment Banking Practices," *Law and Contemporary Problems*, IV (January 1937), 72; S. L. Miller, "Effects on Investment Banking Practices of Federal Regulation of Securities," *Investment Banking*, VII (September 22, 1937), 355.

in the past, they continued to rely almost entirely upon the findings of the originating house. Their role in the investigation was perfunctory, usually involving nothing more than what was legally necessary to defend themselves should there be a suit.[44]

Changes resulting from the civil liability provisions made more impact. In June 1934, largely because of persistent protests of investment bankers, Congress liberalized these and certain other sections of the act. The alterations were incorporated in Title II of the Securities & Exchange Act.[45] Instead of holding each underwriter liable for the entire amount of the offering, the law freed him from any damages" in excess of the total price at which the securities underwritten by him and distributed to the public were offered to the public." The net effect of this change was to put an end to the use of the joint liability syndicate in bringing out registered issues.[46] Since the law now allowed investment firms to limit their liability, it was to their advantage to contract directly with the issuer. The originating banker continued to sign the purchase agreement, but now he did so "on behalf of each of the underwriting firms severally." [47] After 1933 joint liability contracts continued to be used mostly for nonregistered issues.[48]

Actually, the Securities Act merely shares the responsibility for the simplification of syndicate structures that occurred in the 1930's. To some extent, the trend toward fewer syndicates in an offering had started even before the stock market crash and was accelerated by the depression, when most new securities were high-grade refunding issues floated to take advantage of lower interest rates. The risk in selling these issues was negligible, the demand for them greater than the supply, and the underwriting spreads were small.[49]

44. Bates, "Some Effects of the Securities Act," 77.
45. The other amendments changed the "standards of reasonableness" used in determining "what constitutes reasonable investigation and reasonable ground of belief from that required of a person occupying a fiduciary relationship" to that required of "a prudent man in the management of his own property," reduced the time limit in which purchasers could bring suit from ten years after the security had been offered to three years, and allowed the court to determine whether an investor who initiated a suit should pay the costs of the litigation if it "believes the suit or the defense to have been without merit." Critics charged that these changes rendered the law ineffective; others saw them as necessary and indispensable improvements. See Bernard J. Reis, *False Security: The Betrayal of the American Investor* (New York, 1937), 265–66; Jules I. Bogen, "Changed Conditions in the Marketing of New Issues," *Journal of the American Statistical Association,* XXXIII (March 1938), 33–34.
46. Sumner B. Emerson, "The Wholesaling of Corporate Securities" in Philipp H. Lohman and Franc M. Ricciardi, eds., *Wall Street Explains Its Operations . . .* (New York, 1951), 91. See also Arthur H. Dean, "The Federal Securities Act: I," 99.
47. Emerson, "The Wholesaling of Corporate Securities," 91.
48. *U.S. v. Henry S. Morgan et al.,* "Corrected Opinion of Harold R. Medina" (February 4, 1954), 42.
49. Bates, "Some Effects of the Securities Act," 74; Miller, "Effects on Investment Banking Practice," 356.

But the most important reason for reducing the number of syndicates was the Revenue Act of June 1932, which raised the transfer tax on stocks substantially and, for the first time, imposed a tax on bonds.[50] Thus, a combination of factors, rather than any one of them alone, brought about a significant simplification of syndicate practices, but without in any way changing greatly the substance of the system.

The Securities Act affected distribution methods even less than it did wholesale practices.[51] Retail sales continued to be supervised by the originating banker acting as the manager of a selling group, composed of dealers and brokers, who purchased the securities from the underwriters and sold them on a commission.[52] As in the past, underwriters with their own sales organizations, such as Kidder, Peabody & Co., continued to retail all or a large part of the securities they underwrote.[53] Unlike selling syndicates of the 1920's (both the limited and unlimited types), selling groups organized in the 1930's did no underwriting, and their members, except for the original underwriters in a group, were not liable for damages under the Securities Act.[54] The law drew a clear distinction between an underwriter and a dealer, defining the latter as "a person whose interest is limited to a commission from an underwriter or dealer not in excess of the usual and customary distributor's or seller's commission."[55] This distinction made selling groups rather than the older type of selling syndicate the commonly employed method of distribution.

Again, the Securities Act did not initiate this development. The trend toward separating the underwriting and sales functions, like the one toward more simplified syndicate structures, was "well advanced" when the law was passed.[56] Market conditions, declining spreads, and increased transfer taxes were more important than the Securities Act in forcing investment bankers to abandon the different types of intermediate syndicates they previously had used to spread the risk and share in the profits of originating, underwriting, and selling securities. The functions of these different groups, reported a financial observer and economist, now were performed by a purchase syndicate, composed of "a few large underwriting houses who sign the purchase contract with the issuer, dividing the liability in fixed proportions among themselves, and a far larger selling group which does no underwriting, the members receiving

50. *U.S. v. Henry S. Morgan et al.*, "Corrected Opinion," 41.
51. Miller, "Effects on Investment Banking Practice," 356.
52. Bogen, "Changed Conditions in the Marketing of New Issues," 34.
53. Alfred E. Borneman to author, December 6, 1965.
54. Bates, "Some Effects of the Securities Act," 74, 76, *passim*.
55. Quoted in *U.S. v. Henry S. Morgan et al.*, "Corrected Opinion," 134.
56. Bates, "Some Effects of the Securities Act," 74. See also Bogen, "Changed Conditions in the Marketing of New Issues," 34.

a substantial selling commission only for securities actually sold by them."[57]

Establishment of a twenty-day waiting period by the Securities Act probably was more important than any of the other provisions in affecting investment banking practices. No sales or offers to sell could be made before the registration statement became effective.[58] In the past, investment firms had arranged tentative sales of issues they underwrote while still negotiating with the issuer.[59] The Securities Act made this practice illegal. Investment bankers could solicit sales before the registration statement became effective only if they provided buyers with a complete prospectus, including all the price information required. In order to acquaint their clients with a new security before the offering date without violating the Securities Act, investment houses adopted the practice of distributing a preliminary circular or announcement known as a "red herring prospectus." It was so called because the law required that each page carry a statement, printed in red ink, saying that the information presented was subject to completion or amendment and that the document itself did not constitute an offer of sale or the solicitation of an offer to buy.[60]

The required waiting period succeeded only in stopping formal sales. It failed entirely to prevent informal, oral understandings between investors and security salesmen. "Beating the gun," as this practice was called, actually increased as a result of the enforced "cooling off" period.[61] Before 1933, one Wall Street observer noted, "beating the gun took place anywhere from one to three days before the official public offering; after the act, the period was lengthened to two to fifteen days."[62]

Disturbed by the disruption of established selling practices, underwriters sought to protect themselves against possible losses by "hedging" their commitments to issuers. The technique they commonly employed was to include in the purchase contract various provisions relieving them of their obligation to take up the securities if market conditions deteriorated, or if some serious development occurred damaging the reputation of the issuer or threatening the success of the offering. Besides termination and "market-out" clauses of this type, purchase contracts very often included others, relieving the underwriters of any liability for information in the

---

57. Bogen, "Changed Conditions in the Marketing of New Issues," 34.
58. In 1954 the Securities Act was amended, allowing bankers to make written "offers" during the registration period. Sales continued to be prohibited.
59. Merwin H. Waterman, *Investment Banking Functions: Their Evolution and Adaptation to Business Finance* (Ann Arbor, 1948), 64.
60. *U.S. v. Henry S. Morgan et al.,* "Transcript of Trial: Defendants' Opening — Mr. [W. G.] Claytor (February 28, 1951), 3782.
61. Bates, "Some Effects of the Securities Act," 73.
62. Miller, "Effects on Investment Banking Practice," 356.

registration statement supplied by the issuer. Some contracts held underwriters harmless even for the information they themselves had provided.[63] The result of all these developments was that the issuer rather than the underwriters bore the "major risks of the waiting period." [64]

By increasing the dangers and uncertainties of a public offering, the waiting period contributed directly to the growth of direct or private placements. In such transactions the borrower sold securities, mostly high-grade corporate bonds and notes, directly to a limited number of lenders, more often than not to a large insurance company or a group of them.[65] Sales of this type did not have to be registered under the Securities Act, since it was assumed that institutional buyers were knowledgeable, sophisticated investors, in no need of government protection. Corporations requiring capital as well as life insurance companies seeking suitable investments for their huge and increasing funds found direct placements a convenient and mutually satisfactory investment practice.[66]

Once corporations had overcome their initial fear of the Securities Act, probably the single most important reason why they decided on a private sale was the fact that in a direct placement they received a "firm commitment" as soon as the negotiations had been completed. Very often the entire transaction was concluded in a week.[67] Such speed was impossible in the case of a public offering. No investment house dared price an issue three weeks or more before it could be distributed. Faced with selling it in an unpredictable market, investment firms not only hedged their commitments with various escape clauses but, even more important, postponed pricing the issue until two or three days before the registration became effective.[68] Delay in fixing terms, more than the time, inconvenience, and expense of registration, risk of liability, or even the substantially higher banking charges involved in a public offering, accounted for the continued and growing popularity of private placements.[69] Between 1900 and 1933 private sales had accounted

63. Bates, "Some Effects of the Securities Act," 77–78.
64. Harold G. Moulton et al., *Capital Expansion, Employment, and Economic Stability* (Washington, 1940), 247.
65. E. Raymond Corey, "Corporate Financing by Direct Placement," *Harvard Business Review,* XXVIII (November 1950), 67–76. See also the same author's lengthier study, *Direct Placement of Corporate Securities* (Boston, 1951).
66. U.S. House, Committee on Interstate and Foreign Commerce, 77th Cong., 1st and 2d Sess., *Proposed Amendments to the Securities Act of 1933 and to the Securities Exchange Act of 1934: Hearings* . . . (6 pts., Washington, 1941–42), pt. 2, 584–85.
67. Corey, "Corporate Financing by Direct Placement," 76.
68. *Ibid.,* 69–70.
69. In November 1941, SEC Commissioner Granson Purcell testified before the House Commerce Committee that there was no evidence to indicate that corporations were using direct placements to circumvent the Securities Act. "In our considered judgment," he said, "the fundamental cause of the substantial growth in

for less than 3 percent of all security offerings. For the period 1934 to 1939 direct placements of corporate bonds and notes averaged close to 23.3 percent a year, and they grew still more after World War II, forcing investment bankers to adopt new practices specifically designed to serve corporations intent upon private sales.[70]

The Securities Act was the first of a group of laws aimed at reforming Wall Street. Its intent was to force corporations and investment firms seeking funds from the public to adopt higher standards of social responsibility. The safeguards of the law applied only to new issues; their enforcement, despite the bankers' initial alarm, did not alter seriously their business methods. Insofar as the organization of the investment banking industry itself was concerned, the Securities Act did not affect it at all. It was the Glass-Steagall Banking Act, signed June 16, 1933, that revolutionized the structure of the investment banking community by requiring the complete separation of investment and commercial banking.

This law, like the Securities Act, grew out of the stock market crash and the numerous bank failures that followed it. Demand for it existed even before Pecora's disclosure of the activities of the National City Bank and its affiliate shocked the country into insisting on financial reform. On December 3, 1929, President Hoover, in his first annual message to Congress, had recommended that it consider the advisability of separating commercial and investment banking as part of a larger study of the entire financial system.[71] Nothing came of Hoover's proposal, but during the next two years, as more and more banks closed, numerous resolutions were introduced in Congress calling for investigation and reform of the banking system.[72] One of these, first introduced by Senator William King, Democrat from Utah, was subsequently drastically amended and replaced by another, sponsored by Carter Glass, the seventy-four-

---

private placements in recent years is that the insurance companies and banks have been faced on the one hand with constantly expanding assets which must be invested, and, on the other hand, by a constantly contracting field of available investment media." *Proposed Amendments to the Securities Act of 1933 and to the Securities Exchange Act of 1934,* pt. 2, 584–85. See also Corey, "Corporate Financing by Direct Placement," 68, 73–74; "The Investment Banker: 1939," *Fortune,* XX (September 1939), 112, 115.

70. U.S. House, Committee on Interstate and Foreign Commerce, 82d Cong., 2d Sess., *Study of the Securities and Exchange Commission: Report* . . . (Washington, 1952), 127; U.S. Temporary National Economic Committee, *Investigation of Concentration of Economic Power: Final Report of the Executive Secretary* . . . (Washington, 1941), 231. See also Donald L. Kemmerer, "The Marketing of Securities, 1930–1952," *The Journal of Economic History,* XII (Fall 1952), 457–59; R. W. Goldschmidt, "Registration under the Securities Act of 1933," *Law and Contemporary Problems,* IV (January 1937), 19–31.

71. Herbert Hoover, *The Memoirs of Herbert Hoover* (3 vols., New York, 1951–52), III, 122–25.

72. Helen M. Burns, "The American Banking Community and New Deal Banking Reform, 1933–35" (unpub. diss., New York University, 1965), ch. i.

year-old Virginia Democrat. It provided for the most thorough review and study of the nation's banking system since the one conducted by the National Monetary Commission, twenty-five years earlier.[73] A special subcommittee of the Banking and Currency Committee was organized, with Glass as its chairman, and hearings were held in 1931.

Bankers and government officials were called to testify on a wide variety of subjects, including the underwriting activities of security affiliates, and whether they should be outlawed or placed under rigid federal supervision. John W. Pole, the Comptroller of the Currency, asserted that affiliates were "susceptible of a great many evils." Some of these institutions, over which the government had no jurisdiction whatsoever, were nothing more than "market operators," declared Adolph C. Miller of the Federal Reserve Board. Because of "their access to the credit facilities of the banks with which they were affiliated, and the access of the banks to the Federal reserve system," Miller explained, "it has been made very easy for investment affiliates to spread into dangerous zones."[74] He favored eliminating them altogether, but if this was not possible, then they should be subjected to careful, regular examination, and the government should be authorized to exercise "some supervision and control over [their] practices."

Officers of these companies naturally defended as essential the close ties that had developed between commercial and investment banking and fought to prevent their liquidation.[75] "I do not believe that this country could have developed industrially to the extent that it has since the war without the assistance of bank affiliates," said Allan M. Pope, the executive vice president of the First National Old Colony Corporation, "because private capital probably could not have been found in sufficient volume in so short a time as to develop private investment houses to a point where they would have been in a position to handle this enormous increase in underwriting and distribution." Pope, who also was a member of the IBA's Board of Governors, admitted that security affiliates had engaged in "a certain amount of unwise financing," but he argued that this could be corrected easily enough by requiring that they "be examined coincidentally with the examination of the parent institution." Security affiliates, Pope explained, served a useful function, not only to individual investors, but to hundreds of small banks whose officers were unfamiliar with investments. These institutions

73. *Ibid.*, 3–4, 12–13.
74. U.S. Senate, Committee on Banking and Currency, 71st Cong., 3d Sess., *Operation of the National and Federal Reserve Banking Systems: Hearings* ... (8 pts., Washington, 1931–32), pt. 1, 19–20, 147–48.
75. Marcus Nadler and Jules I. Bogen, *The Banking Crisis: The End of an Epoch* (New York, 1933), 46–47.

benefited from the advice and service of the affiliates of the large commercial banks.[76]

The next year, when the full Banking and Currency Committee held hearings on the Glass bill, Pope was called to testify again. This time he spoke as the representative of the IBA, of which he had become president. Pope started his lengthy critique of the proposed bill by saying that all the investment bankers with whom he had spoken, "numbering several hundred," opposed the measure on both general and specific grounds. He argued that it was highly dangerous to enact major banking legislation while the country was in the grip of a severe depression; the "extreme deflationary character of the Glass bill was "diametrically opposed" to the Hoover administration's chief objective, to bring about recovery.[77]

Among the bill's various provisions, Pope singled out several for specific criticism. He opposed those calling for the separation of security affiliates from their parent banks, a step that would cripple the system of distributing stocks and bonds and delay new corporate financings, as well as those increasing the authority of the Federal Reserve over the lending policies of member banks, especially loans to investment bankers with securities as collateral. He also faulted other provisions prohibiting officers of investment houses from serving as directors of banks belonging to the Federal Reserve System, thus making it illegal for the same individuals to be officers of both the parent bank and its affiliates.[78] Other bankers joined Pope in denouncing these and other provisions of the bill.

Debate on banking reform continued through the election of 1932. The Democratic party platform, though failing to endorse the Glass bill itself, supported several of its provisions, notably those calling for the separation of investment banking and commercial banking, divorcement of security affiliates from their parent banks, and "further restriction" on the use of Federal Reserve "facilities for speculative purposes." In a speech at Columbus, Ohio, Roosevelt reasserted his support of these proposals. After the election, Glass incorporated them in a revised bill that, together with other provisions introduced in a House measure sponsored by Henry B. Steagall, an Alabama Democrat, ultimately became law.[79]

Opposition to the revised bill was strong. Not only was it criticized by bankers, but the directors of the New York Federal Reserve Bank warned the Senate Banking and Currency Committee that it would be "most unfortunate" if the law should result in "any

76. *Operation of the National and Federal Reserve Banking Systems: Hearings,* pt. 3, 540–41.
77. *Ibid.,* pt. 8, 16–21.
78. *Ibid.,* pt. 8, 28–43. See also Nadler and Bogen, *The Banking Crisis,* 52–54.
79. Rosenman, ed., *Public Papers and Addresses of Franklin D. Roosevelt,* I, 682–83; *The New York Times,* August 21, 1932; Burns, "The American Banking Community," 71–73.

material disorganization" of the capital markets. "The broad question to be determined," the directors explained, "is the extent to which the capital market should be divorced from the banking system and removed from all supervision, or whether its relations with the banking system should be maintained and placed under appropriate supervision." [80] Congress's decision to separate investment banking from commercial banking was strengthened and made easier by Pecora's disclosure of the National City Co.'s affairs and Winthrop Aldrich's statement, in March 1933, that the Chase Bank was taking immediate steps to divorce itself from its security affiliates. These events, furthermore, defeated any possibility of extending the time that banks were to be allowed to divorce themselves from their affiliates.[81]

The Glass-Steagall Banking Act (also known as the Banking Act of 1933) provided for numerous other significant changes, among them the establishment of the Federal Deposit Insurance Corporation. The statute required banks belonging to the Federal Reserve System to divorce themselves of their security affiliates within one year after the law went into effect, compelled private banks to choose between deposit and investment banking, and restricted the underwriting activities of commercial banks to general obligation bonds of federal, state, and municipal bodies and of government corporations. In addition it prohibited partners and officials of security firms from serving as directors or officers of commercial banks that were members of the Federal Reserve System, increased the authority of the twelve Federal Reserve district banks to supervise and control the amount of credit extended to their members, and empowered the Federal Reserve Board to regulate bank loans secured by bonds or stock collateral.[82]

The Banking Act of 1933 effected many changes in the behavior of investment bankers. It altered both the structure and the operations of their industry, disrupted established methods of underwriting and distributing securities, upset many traditional relationships between issuers and bankers, and reduced drastically the amount of capital available to float new issues. In 1929 two security affiliates, those of the National City and the Chase banks, reported a capital and surplus of $221 million. Ten years later, according to

---

80. Quoted in Edwards, *Evolution of Finance Capitalism*, 296. See also Benjamin Anderson, *Economics and the Public Welfare: Financial and Economic History of the United States, 1914–1946* (New York, 1949), 321–23.
81. Burns, "American Banking Community," 76. See also Francis H. Sisson, "Investment Restrictions in Glass Bill," *The Bankers' Magazine*, CXXVI (March 1933), 253–55.
82. The Clayton Act of 1914 had prohibited interlocking bank directorates, but this law's effectiveness was greatly reduced by amendment in 1916. The Glass-Steagall Act's restriction was designed to correct this, but the Banking Act of 1935 again liberalized this provision. See Edwards, *Evolution of Finance Capitalism*, 296–97.

The Wall Street Journal, the "average capital employed" by the eight largest investment banking firms in the country during the period 1934 through 1939 totaled less than $75 million. These figures are admittedly imperfect, since they fail to take into account the great decline in security values that occurred after the stock market crash. Nonetheless, they illustrate the huge decline in capital at the disposal of investment firms after commercial banks were eliminated from the securities business. Private bankers, like Morgan, who had depended on their deposits not only as a source of income but as an aid to their underwriting activities, now found themselves, Arthur Dean explained later, more dependent than ever before upon commercial bank loans.[83] Security firms, Berle pointed out at the time, would have to develop and depend upon their own "pool of investment money," one "in large measure outside the usual deposit liabilities." [84]

A major reorganization of the investment banking industry immediately resulted from the Banking Act. Affiliations were eliminated; the bond departments of commercial banks were cut in size and their activities greatly reduced; and private bankers were forced to choose between deposit and investment banking. Two-thirds of these partnerships, according to one estimate, decided to stay in the securities business, a choice that was widely interpreted, according to *The Literary Digest,* as proof that "some of the country's ablest financiers" believed in a rapid recovery and an "early renewal of investment financing." [85] The Morgan firm and its Philadelphia office, Drexel & Co., as well as Brown Brothers Harriman & Co., were notable exceptions. These three old investment houses abandoned the securities business and opted for deposit banking. (Later some of the partners in each firm resigned to reenter investment banking.) All three banks continued to limit themselves almost entirely to serving the needs of large corporations, as they had done in the past, but, like all commercial banks, they were required to submit to government examination and supervision. The secrecy that once surrounded their activities was gone forever.[86]

Implementation of the Banking Act also led to the organization of new investment firms. Most of these were officered and staffed by individuals formerly associated either with security affiliates or with

83. *U.S. v. Henry S. Morgan et al.,* "Transcript of Trial: Defendants' Opening — Mr. [Arthur H.] Dean" (December 11, 1950), 745–46; Waterman, *Investment Banking Functions,* 62–63; T. Kenneth Haven, *Investment Banking under the Securities and Exchange Commission* (Ann Arbor, 1940), 135.

84. Adolf A. Berle, Jr., *The Future of American Banking* (New York, 1933), 5–6.

85. "Wall Street Accepts New Deal in Finance," *The Literary Digest,* CXVII (June 23, 1934), 36.

86. *Ibid.*; "Deadline — June 16," *Business Week* (June 16, 1934), 18; John T. Madden and Marcus Nadler, *The International Money Markets* (New York, 1935), 156.

private banks that had decided to give up the security business. The First Boston Corporation, one of the largest and leading underwriting and bond-trading houses since its establishment, is a case in point. Organized on June 16, 1934, as a publicly owned corporation, it was a rare phenomenon among investment banking firms. The First Boston grew out of the security affiliate of the First National Bank of Boston, with some key personnel also coming to it from the old Harris, Forbes organization. Six months of planning and extensive legal negotiations preceded the organization of First Boston. The chief officers of this entirely new company were experienced and able investment bankers who had held responsible positions with the disbanded affiliates and were well known on Wall Street and among corporation executives across the country. These old business relationships, together with the underwriting and distributing skills of its officers, were First Boston's greatest assets in 1934, far more important than its original capital of $9 million, large as this was.[87]

In September 1934 three Morgan partners and two from Drexel resigned and organized Morgan Stanley & Co., Inc., an investment banking corporation. They moved just at the time the securities business was starting to revive and Congress, largely at Roosevelt's insistence, had rejected Senator Glass's effort to repeal the Banking Act's prohibition against allowing commercial banks to return to the underwriting business. The five men, together with three other Morgan employees, became the new firm's directors and principal officers. The next year two more were added, both of whom formerly had been associated with either the Guaranty Trust or its affiliate, the Guaranty Co.[88] Unlike The First Boston Corporation, whose stock was publicly held, all Morgan Stanley's common (voting) shares were "owned [with one exception] entirely by stockholders who were both officers and directors." The exception was the former head of Morgan's statistical department, an officer but not a director. All the preferred (nonvoting) stock, with the exception of 4,000 shares (held by two officers and directors, Henry S. Morgan

---

87. *U.S. v. Henry S. Morgan et al.*, "Corrected Opinion," 88–92; *ibid.*, "Transcript of Trial: Plaintiff's Exhibit" (January 13, 1949), 831–34, 844–46; U.S. Temporary National Economic Committee, *Investigation of Concentration of Economic Power: Hearings* . . . (31 pts. Washington, 1939–41), pt. 22, 11512–16. See also "In the New Wall Street," *Fortune*, XII (October 1935), 78–83, 114–120. In July 1946 the Mellon Securities Corporation merged with The First Boston. See *U.S. v. Henry S. Morgan et al.*, "Transcript of Trial: Defendants' Case — Deposition of [Harry M.] Addinsell" (March 19, 1952), 21448–49.

88. *U.S. v. Henry S. Morgan et al*, "Corrected Opinion," 60–62; U.S. TNEC, *Hearings*, XXII, 11551–54; "Wall Street Expects Better Trade," *The Literary Digest*, CXX (September 14, 1935), 40; "Banking: House of Morgan Gives Up a Son, Five Partners and $7,500,000 to Return to Underwriting," *Newsweek*, VI (September 14, 1935), 31–33. On Glass's failure to amend the Banking Act of 1933, see Burns, "American Banking Community," 166–67; *The New York Times*, February 4, 1935, July 6, 1935, August 13 and 17, 1935.

and William Ewing), was owned by nine of the seventeen partners in the old Morgan bank.[89] Though legally and in other ways entirely independent of 23 Wall Street, Morgan Stanley was immediately recognized for what it was — the return of some of the Morgan firm's ablest partners to the investment banking business.

Numerous other similar changes occurred in 1934 and 1935, as former officials of security affiliates and partners in private banking houses either organized new firms or joined existing ones. The officers and directors of Brown Harriman & Co., Inc., organized in June 1934, came from the National City Co. and Brown Brothers Harriman & Co.[90] Officials of Harris, Hall & Co., founded in October 1934, came from the defunct affiliate of Chicago's Harris Trust & Savings Bank.[91] In June 1935, Charles E. Mitchell, the onetime head of the National City Co., was named board chairman of Blyth & Co., the successor to Blyth, Witter & Co., originally a San Francisco banking house founded in 1914.[92] Edward B. Smith & Co., a Philadelphia partnership established in 1892, took in four of the Guaranty Co.'s senior officers as general partners and employed some 230 other individuals formerly associated with this affiliate.[93] Other junior and senior officers of the Guaranty Co. joined Blyth, Kidder, Peabody, and Morgan Stanley, to name but a few of the principal investment firms that accommodated employees of the now defunct security affiliates.[94]

By the end of 1935, when most of the reorganizations brought about by the Banking Act had been effected, the leadership of the investment banking industry was composed of three principal groups of security houses. Old partnerships, like Kuhn, Loeb and Lehman Brothers, whose organization was only slightly, if at all, affected by the law except, of course, for the loss of their deposit business, constituted one group. New firms that owed their very existence to the statute, such as The First Boston Corporation and Morgan Stanley, comprised the second. And the third embraced houses like Edward B. Smith, Blyth, and many others whose officers and staffs included officials and employees previously associated with a security affiliate or the bond department of a large commercial bank.

Within each of these groups there was a wide variety of firms

---

89. *U.S. v. Henry S. Morgan et al.,* "Corrected Opinion," 61–62. In December 1941 Morgan Stanley was reorganized as a partnership.

90. [Harriman, Ripley & Co.] *The Investment Banking Services of Harriman Ripley & Co., Inc.* (New York, 1959), 6. In January 1939 the firm's name was changed to Harriman Ripley & Co., Inc., largely in order to distinguish it from Brown Brothers Harriman & Co., a private banking partnership engaged in commercial banking. See *U.S. v. Henry S. Morgan et al.,* "Transcript of Trial" (May 2, 1951); *ibid.,* "Corrected Opinion," 100–01.

91. *Time,* XXVI (November 11, 1935), 69.

92. *U.S. v. Henry S. Morgan et al.,* "Corrected Opinion," 94–97.

93. *Ibid.,* 66–67.

94. *Ibid.,* 67.

providing many types of investment banking services. Most of them were partnerships; a few were corporations. The only thing they all had in common was that none of them was engaged in deposit banking. Their chief business was merchandising securities, either as wholesalers, retailers, or both. Their other functions, such as providing financial advice to corporations, managing individual funds, and serving as fiscal agents, all were related to their principal role — buying and selling securities.[95] Because of this specialization, some people again questioned whether investment bankers should be called bankers at all.

The Banking Act also upset many long-established ties between issuers and investment houses. Corporations that had employed bank affiliates to manage their security offerings now had to find new firms. Investment houses competed vigorously to win these accounts. New firms like The First Boston Corporation made every effort to inherit the business formerly done by the affiliates of the First National Bank of Boston and the Chase National Bank; and firms like Edward B. Smith, four of whose fifteen partners had been officers of the Guaranty Co., fought to win the corporate clients of that defunct affiliate.[96] Other investment houses also competed for these accounts. In April 1933 Harold L. Stuart of Halsey, Stuart wrote the president of the Pacific Gas & Electric Co. that if the proposed Banking Act was "going to affect" this large California utility's "banking relationship . . . I want you to know that we are still in business and are competent and able to function in a large way and quickly on high grade bond issues such as you have." [97]

Similar letters went to other corporations planning new offerings. Even Kuhn, Loeb, which reportedly never competed for the business of corporations with established banking connections, made certain that issuers were fully aware of its existence and that it was willing to accept new business.[98] The disruption in issuer-banker relationships created by the Banking Act resulted in a general "hustling for business," in which old and new firms, small and large, sought to hold on to their clients and fought hard to win as many new ones as possible.

On June 6, 1934, ten days before the Banking Act went into effect, Roosevelt signed the Securities Exchange Act, the last of the Seventy-third Congress's major banking and securities statutes. This law supplemented the Securities Act, which was concerned chiefly with supervising new offerings. The SEC law extended federal con-

95. L. Douglas Meredith, "Financial Merchandising and Its Functions," *The Bankers' Magazine*, CXXVII (December 1933), 613–30; Bogen, "Changed Conditions in Marketing of New Issues," 31–41.
96. U.S. TNEC, *Hearings*, XXIII, 12029–30.
97. Harold L. Stuart to A. F. Hockenbeamer, April 19, 1933, in *U.S. v. Henry S. Morgan et al.*, "Defendants' Exhibits," 63.
98. *Ibid.*, "Corrected Opinion," 260–66.

trols over trading on the exchanges; it required the registration of those institutions themselves and regulated their operations and members. Together with the Banking and Securities laws, this statute fulfilled the pledges of Roosevelt and the Democratic party to protect investors and depositors against a recurrence of the abuses of the 1920's.

The SEC bill was drafted by Cohen and Corcoran with the assistance of several members of Pecora's staff and experts from other government departments. It was introduced in the Senate by Duncan Fletcher and in the House by Sam Rayburn, immediately following Roosevelt's message of February 9, 1934, asking for legislation regulating exchanges and eliminating, "so far as it may be possible . . . unnecessary, unwise and destructive speculation." [99]

The Fletcher-Rayburn bill was a lengthy, detailed measure, designed to meet the president's objectives. It prohibited such abusive practices as wash sales, matched orders, and pools; regulated other types of manipulation, such as stabilization operations, which had to be disclosed and reported; and required the registration of all securities listed on national exchanges (those registered with the SEC), thus extending the full-disclosure principle of the Securities Act to these issues as well as newly offered ones. Moreover, corporations whose securities were traded on a national exchange also had to register themselves, file detailed financial reports quarterly, and adhere to carefully specified procedures in soliciting proxies and reporting the security transactions of their officers and directors. In order to prevent excessive speculation, the act set a minimum margin requirement for brokers' loans of 55 percent of market value, and authorized the Federal Reserve Board to determine and control the use of credit for such loans. Most of these provisions, as well as many others, did not affect the investment banker directly.

Corporation executives and stock exchange officials raised the greatest outcry against the Fletcher-Rayburn bill. The former disapproved of the registration and listing requirements; the latter strongly opposed regulation of any kind. Richard Whitney, president of the New York Stock Exchange, who had told Pecora that "the Exchange is a perfect institution" quite capable of regulating itself, predicted that if the SEC bill was enacted "the security markets of the Nation will dry up." Many other business and financial leaders joined him in denouncing the measure as entirely unnecessary, unworkable, impractical, deflationary, unconstitutional,

---

99. Rosenman, ed., *Public Papers and Addresses of Franklin D. Roosevelt*, III, 91; U.S. Senate, Committee on Banking and Currency, 73d Cong., 2d Sess., *Federal Securities Exchange Act of 1934: Report* . . . (Washington, 1934), 1–11; John T. Flynn, "The Marines Land in Wall Street," *Harper's Magazine*, CLXIX (July 1934), 150; Schlesinger, *Coming of the New Deal*, 456–57; De Bedts, *New Deal's SEC*, ch. iii.

even Communist-inspired.[100] No previous New Deal measure was so bitterly fought as this one. Rayburn described the opposition to it as "the most powerful lobby ever organized against any bill which ever came up in Congress." [101]

Not all Wall Streeters shared the views of the bill's more vocal critics or agreed with Whitney. The so-called moderates were fully aware of the abuses and were far from confident that the exchanges were ready and able to end them. These men admitted the need for reform and regulation. What disturbed them and many investment bankers was the provision segregating and limiting the functions of brokers and dealers. Eugene E. Thompson, president of the Associated Stock Exchanges, a group of smaller exchanges located in sixteen cities, had strong beliefs on the subject. He testified that if this section of the bill were enacted, it would "destroy the means of livelihood of hundreds of brokers, members of local exchanges, who now act both as a broker and as a dealer in, or underwriter, or distributor of securities." No small brokerage or investment house could survive, he alleged, if it was forced to discontinue any one of these services.[102]

G. Herman Kinnicutt, a Kidder, Peabody partner since 1931 and previously head of his own underwriting and brokerage house, also opposed the proposed segregation of brokers and dealers. Speaking for eighteen firms belonging to the New York and regional exchanges, all of which were dealers, brokers, and underwriters, Kinnicutt admitted the need for regulation and, with few exceptions, approved of what the Fletcher-Rayburn bill sought to accomplish. His objections, and those of the other seventeen investment houses he represented, were with the segregation proposal; he claimed it would shatter the existing system of distributing securities, cause great financial hardship to hundreds of small and medium-size firms, limit the underwriting business to a very few houses, and provide investors with no additional protection. "We believe," Kinnicutt said, "there is much mistaken criticism of a dealer in selling from his own inventory because it is approached from the false premise that an inventory presupposes something the dealer is 'hung up' with." This was not at all the case. "As a matter of fact, in the great majority of cases, his inventory is acquired because the dealer believes it is advantageous for his customer as to quality and as to price." [103]

100. Schlesinger, *Coming of the New Deal,* 457–60; Sobel, *The Big Board,* 298–300. See also "Stock Exchange: 'Kill the Bill' Becomes Rallying Cry," *Newsweek,* III (April 7, 1934), 29–30.
101. Quoted in Schlesinger, *Coming of the New Deal,* 464.
102. *Stock Exchange Practices: Hearings,* pt. 15, 6988. See also *Stock Exchange Regulation: Hearings,* 593–95.
103. *Stock Exchange Practices: Hearings,* pt. 15, 6865.

Those who favored segregation of functions based their case principally on two grounds, one ethical and the other financial. Allegedly, the combination of broker, dealer, and underwriting services in a single firm reduced its ability to advise its customers impartially. The temptation to push issues it had underwritten or owned was too great for "ordinary humankind" to resist, Corcoran testified. Combining operations also increased substantially the risk that a firm's brokerage capital would become involved in financing its activities as a dealer and underwriter, tying it up in unmarketable or slow-selling securities. Wall Street's "biggest failures," Corcoran asserted, were houses with "perfectly solvent" brokerage accounts.[104] The collapse of these firms resulted from the fact that their "assets were involved in positions in securities which they had sponsored or in which they were interested, and when they were wiped out in their positions in such securities the bankruptcy pulled the brokerage clients down with them." [105]

Kinnicutt and other investment bankers, such as John M. Hancock of Lehman Brothers, recognized these dangers, though they questioned whether they were so serious as Corcoran claimed them to be. Kinnicutt pointed out that during the past four years the number of failures on the five largest exchanges amounted to $\frac{3}{8}$ of 1 percent per annum of their total membership.[106] The dangers of combination, Kinnicutt and Hancock argued, could be minimized still further without requiring houses of issue to give up their brokerage business, their "only bread and butter business during a depression." All that was needed, Hancock explained, was to require these firms to inform their brokerage clients of the nature of the transaction, whether the investment house acted as agent or principal. Hancock recommended requiring investment houses that did a combined business to separate their capital and "prohibit loans from the brokerage portion to the issuing portion of the business. This would be as effective as actual segregation." [107]

A few days later Kinnicutt recommended that enforcement of these regulations be entrusted to a special securities commission, as the Senate bill proposed, rather than to the FTC, as the House version provided. The newly organized commission should be given both supervisory and mandatory powers and, most important of all, it should be "left free to operate with great flexibility," thus permitting it to adjust quickly to the "constantly changing conditions" of the securities business.[108]

Late in March, as Whitney and other diehards continued their

---

104. The firms Corcoran referred to were Whiteley, Pynchon & Co., West & Co.; and Bauer, Payne, Pond & Vivian.
105. *Stock Exchange Practices: Hearings,* pt. 15, 6521–22.
106. *Ibid.,* pt. 15, 6867.
107. *Stock Exchange Regulation: Hearings,* 487–88.
108. *Stock Exchange Practices: Hearings,* pt. 15, 6868.

fight against the Fletcher-Rayburn bill, Corcoran and Cohen revised the House measure sufficiently to satisfy many of the strongest objections of Kinnicutt, Hancock, and other moderates.[109] The segregation provision was dropped and made a subject of further study, as recommended earlier by a committee of the Commerce Department.[110] On March 26 Roosevelt made it clear that he intended no further delays or concessions. "I am certain," he wrote Fletcher, "that the country as a whole will not be satisfied with legislation unless such legislation has teeth in it." The revised bill, he said, "seems to meet the minimum requirements. I do not see how any of us can afford to have it weakened in any shape, manner or form."[111] By mid-May the two houses had compromised their remaining differences, and the final bill was drafted for Roosevelt's signature.

As enacted, the SEC Act contained many provisions that had been endorsed by investment bankers. The law established an independent commission composed of five members, no more than three of whom could belong to the same party, and entrusted it with wide discretionary authority, just as Kinnicutt and others had recommended. The law also granted it numerous specific, statutory powers as well. Besides entrusting the commission with administering the Securities Act, the law required the securities exchanges to register with the SEC as national exchanges or to apply for exemption. It provided for their regulation, established rules and procedures for trading and the conduct of members, and it prohibited various manipulative practices, such as wash sales and matched orders, and placed others, like short selling and stop-loss orders, under strict control. Stabilizing operations had to be publicized, and the Federal Reserve Board was granted power to establish and regulate margin requirements. The disclosure principle of the Securities Act was extended to all issues traded on national exchanges by requiring their registration and forcing the companies that offered them to file annual reports and other periodic statements concerning their earnings and operations. The act also regulated the solicitation of proxies, and required directors, officers, and other individuals owning more than 10 percent of a corporation whose securities were traded on a national exchange to report this fact to the SEC as well as subsequent transactions involving the company's stock. These and the law's other provisions gave the SEC sweeping authority over the country's principal securities exchanges.

As the commission's first chairman, Roosevelt appointed Joseph

109. Schlesinger, *Coming of the New Deal,* 466; De Bedts, *New Deal's SEC,* 68–69.
110. U.S. Department of Commerce, *Report to Secretary of Commerce of Committee on Stock Exchange Regulation* (Washington, 1934), 19–20.
111. Rosenman, ed., *Public Papers and Addresses of Franklin D. Roosevelt,* III, 170.

P. Kennedy (father of the thirty-fifth president), a wealthy financier who once had engaged in some of the very practices now banned. The choice shocked Wall Street as much as it did Roosevelt's more liberal friends and supporters. Interior Secretary Harold L. Ickes described Kennedy as "a former stockmarket plunger" and questioned whether he should have been selected as Wall Street's chief policeman. "The President has great confidence in him," the secretary confided to his diary, "because he has made his pile, has invested all his money in Government securities, and knows all the tricks of the trade."[112] Others explained Kennedy's appointment as settlement of a political debt. Kennedy had contributed generously to FDR's campaign and was anxious to enter government service in order, so wrote Ickes, "to make a name for himself for the sake of his family."[113]

The other four commissioners included two Democrats and two Republicans. Landis and Pecora, both of whom had hoped to win the chairmanship, were the Democrats. The two regulation-minded Republicans came from the FTC — George C. Matthews of Wisconsin, an experienced administrator of his state's securities law, and Robert Healy of Vermont, who since 1928 had been in charge of the public utilities investigation Congress had ordered that year.[114]

Kennedy served as chairman until September 23, 1935, when he resigned to head the United States Maritime Commission. During his fifteen-month term he proved to be an able administrator, contributed significantly to developing the SEC into an effective regulatory body, and worked hard to win the support of Wall Street's responsible leaders by convincing them that the commission was not out to crush or punish them. What it sought was their assistance and cooperation in eliminating abuses and promoting more effective self-regulation, thus restoring public confidence in the security markets and expediting recovery.[115]

Kennedy succeeded in accomplishing these objectives to a very large extent. Even Whitney spoke approvingly of the commission's purposes, though he himself, as events were to prove, continued to run his firm's affairs as he had before the law was passed.[116] In 1938,

112. Harold L. Ickes, *The Secret Diary of Harold L. Ickes* (3 vols., New York, 1953–54), I, 173. Raymond Moley, then one of FDR's trusted advisers, recommended Kennedy for the SEC chairmanship because of his "executive ability, knowledge of habits and customs of business to be regulated and ability to moderate different points of view on Commission." See Moley, *First New Deal*, 518.
113. Ickes, *Secret Diary*, I, 173. See also Sobel, *The Big Board*, 300–01; Schlesinger, *Coming of the New Deal*, 467–69; Moley, *First New Deal*, 517–19.
114. De Bedts, *New Deal's SEC*, 92–93.
115. Washington Dodge, "What Became of the Stock Market?" *Fortune*, XXVI (December 1942), 156; Schlesinger, *Coming of the New Deal*, 469. See also Theodore M. Knappen, "SEC Surprises Both Friend and Foe," *The Magazine of Wall Street*, LVI (September 14, 1935), 538–39, 564–65.
116. Robert Winsmore, "Free Exchange Markets Indicate Stabilization," *The Literary Digest*, CXVIII (November 24, 1934), 40.

after the New York Stock Exchange had suspended Whitney's firm for insolvency, New York City District Attorney Thomas E. Dewey arrested him for grand larceny. Convicted, he was sentenced to serve five to ten years in the Sing Sing state penitentiary at Ossining.[117]

Whitney's disgrace forced the opponents of regulation and reform to their final retreat. The New York Stock Exchange quickly adopted a new constitution incorporating many of the changes recommended by Chairman Douglas of the SEC, and Wall Street's outspoken resistance to government regulation came to an end.

The SEC law, the amended Securities Act, and the Glass-Steagall Banking statute all went into effect during the summer of 1934, just when the investment banking business showed the first real signs of recovery in almost five years. The major changes brought about by these statutes were those that grew out of the Banking Act. These altered the structure of the industry itself. An indication of this was the fact that not a single firm that the Pujo Committee had listed in 1912 as being a leader of the money trust still was in the securities business in July 1934; and of their three chief allies, two had been badly crippled by the depression. Only one, Kuhn, Loeb, continued as a major house of issue, having chosen, like many other investment banking firms, to discontinue its deposit banking.

A turning point in the history of American investment banking clearly occurred in the summer of 1934. A new era began, one in which investment houses ceased to be bankers in the commonly accepted meaning of that term. Their primary function henceforth was in advising and servicing securities issuers. The way they conducted this business and the various related services they provided were, for the first time, carefully supervised by the federal government. The transition from almost total freedom to widespread regulation was abrupt, often difficult, and carried out during the worst depression in American history. The next half dozen years brought still further regulation, but none of the subsequent statutes affected the structure and operation of the investment banking business so significantly as did the banking and securities laws of 1933 and 1934.

117. *The New York Times,* March 9, 1938; De Bedts, *New Deal's SEC,* 164–66; Sobel, *The Big Board,* 305–06.

18 The New Deal on Wall Street: II. More Regulation and Further Adaptation

The years between the passage of the Securities Exchange Act and America's entry into World War II were a period of readjustment for investment bankers. Their functions, however, except for the abandoned deposit business, remained essentially the same. They continued to advise corporations planning new issues and to investigate, purchase, underwrite, and distribute securities. They still provided corporations and investors with various financial and advisory services, such as presiding over mergers and reorganizations and serving on corporate boards of directors. Very frequently they also conducted a general brokerage business, buying and selling securities for their customers on a commission basis. What changed was the way they performed these services. They discarded or revised old habits and practices and developed some new procedures.

Many factors accounted for these changes, but all were the result of either the steady growth of federal regulation or other contemporary developments that affected the way the investment banking industry recruited its capital and individuals and institutions invested their savings.[1] Some of these circumstances were economic, others political; some were external to the industry, others were generated within it. Regulation now was extended to all three types of financial institutions that had been used so extensively in the 1920's: bank affiliates, investment trusts, and public utility holding companies. Along with outside regulation came constructive efforts by the industry itself for self-policing. Changes in operating methods also came about in response to the new restrictions and to changing economic forces; among the more significant were those revising syndicate types and procedures.

Beginning in 1935 with the passage of the Public Utility Holding Company Act, the regulatory and advisory duties of the Securities and Exchange Commission (SEC) were greatly extended. This bitterly fought law grew out of the lengthy Federal Trade Commission (FTC) study that was begun in 1928 and a subsequent investigation by the House of Representatives. Its purpose was to break up the huge utility holding company empires that had been built in the 1920's and place the industry under "local management and local regulation."[2] To achieve these ends, the law required gas and electric holding companies and their subsidiaries to register with

---

1. Donald L. Kemmerer, "The Marketing of Securities, 1930–1952," *The Journal of Economic History*, XII (Fall 1952), 455–57; *U.S. v. Henry S. Morgan et al.*, "Corrected Opinion of Harold R. Medina" (February 4, 1954), 38–46.
2. Louis Loss, *Securities Regulation* (2d ed., 3 vols., Boston, 1961), I, 135.

the SEC. It was authorized to enforce the statute's famous "death sentence" provision, limiting utility holding companies to "a single, integrated . . . system." The SEC also was to review and pass upon their new security issues, determine their type, price, and method to be employed in offering them,[3] and supervise their relations with investment bankers. These and the act's provisions with respect to reporting, proxies, insider trading, and many other matters made it the most regulatory of all federal securities laws.[4]

Still other laws limited and regulated the functions of investment bankers further. In June 1938, following an extensive SEC study of protective and reorganization committees, Congress passed the Chandler Act, which added Chapter X to the federal Bankruptcy Act of 1898. This amendment to the original law greatly restricted the once dominant role of investment bankers in reorganizations of publicly held corporations. Furthermore, it assigned the task of preparing reorganization plans to disinterested trustees and authorized the SEC to examine their proposals, determine their "fairness and feasibility," and submit an advisory report.[5]

The Trust Indenture Act, like the Chandler amendment, resulted from the same SEC study. Passed in July 1939 as Title III of the Securities Act, the law was intended to protect holders of publicly issued debt securities by requiring issuing corporations to file a trust indenture with the SEC as part of their registration statements. The content of these documents was carefully defined by the commission, as were the qualifications of the trustees appointed to enforce them, all of whom were prohibited from being in any way associated with either the issuer or its investment bankers.

In November 1940 two other federal securities laws were passed. One regulated investment companies, formerly known as investment trusts; the other required the registration of investment advisers. The first of these, the Investment Company Act, grew out of a provision in the Public Utility Holding Company law authorizing the SEC to make an extensive study of these institutions and propose regulatory legislation.[6] An original version of this bill was so unpalatable to the industry's leaders that a second one, drafted with their cooperation, was admitted. The final bill, the lengthiest of the securities acts administered by the SEC, defined investment com-

---

3. In 1938 the SEC required utility companies registered under the Public Utility Holding Company Act to maintain "arms-length bargaining" with bankers, and in 1941 this rule (U-12 F-2) was discarded and competitive bidding made compulsory. See Loss, *Securities Regulation,* I, 389–90.

4. *Ibid.,* I, 131–41.

5. Arthur H. Dean, "Twenty-Five Years of Federal Securities Regulation by the Securities and Exchange Commission," *Columbia Law Review,* LIX (May 1959), 706. See also William O. Douglas, *Democracy and Finance* (New Haven, 1940), 180–81.

6. Hugh Bullock, *The Story of Investment Companies* (New York, 1959), 74–78; Loss, *Securities Regulation,* I, 144–53.

panies as publicly held corporations or trusts "engaged . . . in the business of investing, reinvesting, owning, holding, or trading in securities," and established quantitative standards to distinguish these institutions from holding companies and other corporations.[7]

The act required investment companies to file a detailed statement with the SEC disclosing most of the usual information required of other registrants, as well as considerable additional data concerning their financial and investment policies, none of which could they change substantially without the approval of the shareholders. The act limited the number of underwriters, bankers, brokers, and investment advisers who could serve as directors of these companies; prohibited corporations and trusts from transacting business with banks, companies, and firms with which their directors or employees were in any way associated, unless specifically exempted by the SEC; and restricted their activities in numerous other ways as well.[8]

The law's purpose, like that of the Public Utility Holding Company Act, was primarily regulatory. It was intended to prevent a recurrence of the abuses and conflicts of interest that had occurred in the operation and management of investment trusts during the later 1920's. The framers hoped to achieve their objectives by outlawing certain practices, reducing the influence of investment houses over affairs of these institutions, and increasing that of the shareholders.[9]

Title II of the law contained the Investment Advisers Act, requiring investment advisers to register with the SEC. The act outlawed fraudulent and deceitful practices and barred registered advisers from entering into "profit-sharing arrangements" with their clients and from assigning advisory contracts without the client's approval.[10] As originally passed, the act was, in the words of a subsequent congressional report, not much "more than a mere census taking of persons in the investment advisory business."[11] In September 1960 Congress greatly strengthened the SEC's supervisory and enforcement authority, allowing the commission, among other things, to inspect the records and accounts of firms engaged in this business and to regulate their advertising.[12]

One other regulatory statute, the 1938 Maloney Amendment to the SEC Act of 1934, was largely the product of the investment banking industry's own efforts at self-regulation, which for all practical purposes started in 1933 under the National Industrial Recovery Act (NIRA). Long aware of the abuses existing in the

7. Loss, *Securities Regulation*, I, 148.
8. Bullock, *The Story of Investment Companies*, 79–96.
9. Loss, *Securities Regulation*, I, 149–53.
10. *Ibid.*, I, 154–55.
11. Quoted in *ibid.*, II, 1393n2.
12. *Ibid.*, II, 1392–1417.

securities business and the low ethical standards of some firms, and disturbed by the disclosures of the Pecora and other contemporary investigations, the more responsible leaders of the industry welcomed the opportunity to establish an effective, enforceable code of self-regulation under the jurisdiction of the National Recovery Administration (NRA).

The Investment Bankers Association (IBA) had tried for years to improve the industry's standards of conduct, but with limited success. For one thing, not all security dealers belonged to the IBA, a fact that soon led some nonmembers to challenge its right to represent the industry. Far more important was the fact that the association did not undertake to police even its own members. What the industry needed, White House adviser Adolf A. Berle, Jr., suggested, was a "Committee of Public Safety," organized by and composed of investment bankers, which would supervise the activities of the securities business in the public interest and maintain standards of responsibility comparable with those of the most reputable firms. "This means," he said, "instituting a group of bankers who quite frankly undertake to be their brothers' keepers. But when it is realized that the reputation of their brothers is in the last analysis their own reputation, that their own life and death interests are bound up in the transactions of every member of their guild, it is plain that they have a quite definite personal interest, as well as a legitimate public interest, which must be served." [13]

At the very time Berle's advice appeared in print, the IBA was preparing to assume just such a responsibility. On June 16, 1933, the same day FDR signed the Glass-Steagall Banking Act, he also signed the NIRA into law. Title I of this statute authorized every industry to develop its own code of fair competition which, when approved, would have the force of law. The task of preparing the investment banking code fell upon the IBA, the securities industry's only national trade association, with a membership of some 440 firms with nearly a thousand offices in 118 cities.[14] A special code committee, composed of twenty-four members, represented firms in 15 cities. Headed by B. Howell Griswold, Jr., of Alex. Brown & Sons, Baltimore, it spent months consulting thousands of security dealers, as well as accountants, lawyers, and government officials.[15] Public hearings were held, and after General Hugh S. Johnson, the

13. A. A. Berle, Jr., "Action to Avoid Another 1929," *American Bankers Association Journal*, XXVI (July 1933), 16–18. Compare Bertram O. Moody "On the Other Hand —," *ibid.*, 18, 48.
14. [Investment Bankers Code Committee] *Code of Fair Competition for Investment Bankers With a Descriptive Analysis of Its Fair Practice Provisions and A History of Its Preparation* ([Washington, 1934]), 43.
15. Francis A. Bonner, "The Fair Practices Amendment," *Investment Banking*, IV (May 3, 1934), 209; [A. P. Richardson] "Investment Bankers' Code," *The Journal of Accountancy*, LVII (May 1934), 326–28.

NRA administrator, recommended the code's adoption, President Roosevelt signed it on November 27, 1933.

This was only the basic competition code. The fair trade practice rules still remained to be written.[16] This task was assigned to a special drafting committee, headed by Allan M. Pope, a West Point classmate of "Blue Eagle" Johnson, and soon to become president of The First Boston Corporation.[17] Early in January, while this group was hard at work on these regulations, Robert E. Christie, Jr., the IBA's president and a partner in Dillon, Read & Co., called at the White House to discuss them with the president. "It is our ambition," Christie later wrote Marvin H. McIntyre, the president's assistant secretary, "that this particular code of ours be the best one of all the codes, and I am sure that if we do an intelligent job of it that it will play an important and constructive role in the whole administration program."[18] Christie had hoped to discuss it with Roosevelt again, before submitting it for final approval, "to make sure it meets not only with his personal ideas, but as far as possible all of the just criticism of our business." But the president was suffering from a cold when the time came for the meeting, and no other conference was scheduled.[19] By the end of February the Pope Committee concluded its work and sent drafts to the 1,100 or more security dealers who had voted to approve the earlier competition code, inviting their comments. Public hearings were held on March 15; the president approved the rules a week later, and they went into effect on April 23, 1934.[20]

The investment bankers' code, according to *The New York Times,* was "one of the most stringent regulatory documents under the NRA." Hugh Johnson, in recommending it to the president, called its fair trade provisions "remarkable"; and Arthur D. Whiteside, one of the NRA's division administrators, who subsequently became president of Dun & Bradstreet, Inc., labeled it "a master-

---

16. U.S. National Recovery Administration, *Codes of Fair Competition: Nos. 111–150* . . . (Washington, 1934), 509–12; *The New York Times,* February 1, 1934; "Special Code Meeting of Board of Governors," *Investment Banking,* IV (December 15, 1933), 138–39; [Robert E. Christie, Jr.] "Fair Practice Rules for Investment Banking Code," *ibid.,* IV (February 3, 1934), 172–74.

17. *Investment Bankers Code,* i; "In the New Wall Street," *Fortune,* XII (October 1935), 82–83; *The New York Times,* February 12, 1934. See also "IBA Code," *Business Week* (February 10, 1934), 22–23.

18. Robert E. Christie, Jr., to Marvin H. McIntyre, January 8 and 13, 1934, Franklin D. Roosevelt Papers (President's Personal File), Franklin D. Roosevelt Library, Hyde Park, New York.

19. Robert E. Christie, Jr., to Marvin H. McIntyre, January 3, 1934, and February 8, 1934, in FDR Papers (President's Personal File).

20. *The New York Times,* February 17, 25, 26, March 16, 24, 1934. See also U.S. House, Committee on Interstate and Foreign Commerce, 73d Cong., 2d Sess., *Stock Exchange Regulation: Hearings* . . . (Washington, 1934), 595–613; *Investment Bankers Code,* 1–4.

piece." [21] With very few exceptions, most investment bankers applauded the code enthusiastically. It is "not something which has been forced unwillingly down the throat of the investment banking business," said Francis A. Bonner, a prominent Chicago investment banker and vice chairman of the IBA Code Committee. "It is something which has been desired by the industry for years. Today for the first time we have police power." [22] Others welcomed it because of the opportunity it provided to repair the investment banker's badly tarnished image, restore public confidence in high finance, standardize industry practices, and establish a sound basis of "mutual helpfulness and cooperation between Government and business" in the national interest.[23]

The code incorporated the disclosure provisions of the Securities Act and other stipulations. It required corporations with outstanding issues to provide investors with adequate periodic financial statements and established detailed rules and standards affecting the origination of new securities, syndicate procedures, and sales methods, including greater supervision of salesmen. It outlawed preferred lists and other forms of price discrimination between large and small investors and required publication, in the prospectus, of the price the bankers paid the issuing corporation for its securities, thus ending the secrecy that once surrounded bankers' "spreads." These and other rules governing the conduct of investment bankers, their relations among themselves, with issuers, and investors, all were designed "to correct the evils of the past — fraud, ignorance, lack of frankness, haste," the chairman of the IBA's Code Committee asserted at the time he presented the completed code to the NRA for approval.[24] Never before had the investment banking industry established such comprehensive, enforceable rules of self-regulation. "It is hoped," the IBA's president stated, that they "will mark the birth of a new epoch in American investment banking, in which the best traditions of the business will govern." [25]

Registration under the code was voluntary, but its rules applied to all investment bankers, whether registered or not. The code prohibited a registered investment banker from participating in syndicates or selling groups with nonregistered security dealers. This ruling, by depriving nonsigners of the usual discounts, allowances,

21. *The New York Times,* August 23, 1934; Hugh S. Johnson to FDR, March 23, 1934, in *Investment Bankers Code,* 2; Arthur D. Whiteside, "A Square Deal for the Investor," *Investment Banking,* IV (May 3, 1934), 207.
22. Bonner, "The Fair Practices Amendment," 209.
23. Samuel O. Rice, "The Investment Bankers Code," *Investment Banking,* IV (September 17, 1934), 300–05; Wallace P. Zachry, "Operations under the Investment Bankers Code," *ibid.,* IV (June 11, 1934), 264–69; Whiteside, "A Square Deal for the Investor," 200–07.
24. *Investment Bankers Code,* 39.
25. *Ibid.,* 46.

and commissions, made registration virtually compulsory for most firms. Nor could nonregistered firms be shown any other preferential treatment not accorded the public generally.[26] By September 1934, some 2,800 investment houses had signed the code and were displaying the Blue Eagle, the NRA's symbol.[27] The SEC, still undecided on its own plans to regulate the over-the-counter markets, watched these developments closely.[28]

Administration of the code was delegated to a national group, the Investment Bankers Code Committee (IBCC), composed of twenty-one members, including representatives of firms that did not belong to the IBA. This body operated directly under the NRA. To facilitate and expedite its work, the committee divided the country into sixteen districts, each with its own regional code committee. These local groups accepted registrations, investigated complaints and violations, and served as fact-finding agencies for the national committee. It alone was authorized to impose fines up to $500 and to suspend or expel a firm from registration.[29]

Most investment bankers approved and supported the regulations with enthusiasm. The exceptions were municipal bond houses, which sometimes found it difficult to comply with all the code's requirements, and smaller firms that did not belong to the IBA and resented its role in drafting and enforcing the fair trade rules. It was generally agreed that the code, by demonstrating a real effort at serious reform, had contributed substantially in getting the Securities Act amended in 1934, and industry leaders hoped that further cooperation with Washington was possible.[30] In January 1935 the IBA disclosed that more than 90 percent of its members favored retaining the code, even if Congress allowed it to expire on June 16, 1935.[31] Four months later, attorneys of the IBCC met with SEC officials to discuss transferring the code's enforcement to this organization, thus continuing the principle of self-regulation under federal supervision first introduced under the NRA. B. Howell Griswold, chairman of the IBCC, argued strongly for it, and the SEC also favored it.[32]

The Supreme Court declared the NRA unconstitutional on May 27, 1935, but the investment banking business, now dignified by

26. *Ibid.*, 26–28; Bonner, "The Fair Practices Amendment," 211–12.
27. "Bond Blue Eagle," *Business Week* (September 8, 1934), 38.
28. *The New York Times*, August 23, 1934.
29. *Investment Bankers Code,* 29–30; Bonner, "The Fair Practices Amendment," 212.
30. B. Howell Griswold, Jr., "The Future of the Investment Bankers Code," *Investment Banking,* V (June 4, 1935), 211. See also Alfred L. Bernheim and Margaret G. Schneider, eds., *The Security Markets* (New York, 1935), 94–95.
31. "Questionnaire on Investment Bankers Code," *Investment Banking,* V (February 5, 1935), 151; *The New York Times,* January 20, 1935.
32. Griswold, "Future of the Investment Bankers Code," 210–17; *The New York Times,* April 14, 1935.

the SEC as a "profession," continued to adhere to the code voluntarily. Some regional groups sought to perpetuate the NRA code on a state basis. One such effort was the organization of the California Security Dealers Association.[33] Most investment bankers, however, preferred federal supervision. On July 31, 1935, the national code committee, which had remained together at the request of the SEC, polled the 3,200 security dealers that had registered under the NRA to determine whether they wanted the old group continued on a temporary basis while plans were made to establish a new, permanent, nationwide organization under the SEC.[34] More than 90 percent replied affirmatively, and in October the IBCC reorganized itself informally as the Investment Bankers Conference Committee.[35]

For the next ten months the conference worked closely with the SEC and securities dealers in drafting a constitution and establishing uniform fair practice rules for the over-the-counter markets.[36] On July 20, 1936, at a special meeting in Chicago, investment bankers, brokers, and dealers from across the country approved a plan for a nationwide voluntary organization to police the over-the-counter markets, "standardize fair business practices and maintain high principles in the investment banking business, aiming at ultimate development of self-regulation in the securities business."[37] Early in September, with the blessing of the SEC, the group incorporated itself under the laws of Delaware as the Investment Bankers Conference, Inc. Six of the twenty-one incorporators were representatives of New York firms, including George Bovenizer of Kuhn, Loeb & Co., Sidney J. Weinberg of Goldman, Sachs & Co., George Whitney of J. P. Morgan & Co., and Joseph R. Swan of Edward B. Smith & Co.[38]

Nearly 1,200 investment bankers and brokers out of a total of some 6,000 security dealers registered with the SEC in 1936 immediately applied for membership in the conference. Within a year the number increased to almost 1,700.[39] Regional groups similar to

33. "'NRA' for Security Dealers," *Business Week* (September 21, 1935), 18.
34. *The New York Times,* June 13, 1935; "Investment Bankers Organize," *Business Week* (October 12, 1935), 23–24.
35. U.S. House, Special Subcommittee on Legislative Oversight of the Committee on Interstate and Foreign Commerce, 85th Cong., 2d Sess., *History of National Association of Securities Dealers, Inc. . . .* (Washington, 1959), 2. See also *The New York Times,* December 31, 1935.
36. *The New York Times,* October 14, 1935, December 21, 1935, April 15, 1936.
37. *The Commercial & Financial Chronicle,* CXLIII (July 25, 1936), 508–09; *The New York Times,* August 2, 1936.
38. *The Commercial & Financial Chronicle,* CXLIII (September 12, 1936), 1642–43; *The New York Times,* August 2, 1936, September 9, 1936; *U.S. v. Henry S. Morgan et al.,* "Transcript of Trial: Government's Opening — Rebuttal, Mr. [Roscoe T.] Steffen" (March 22, 1951), 4929.
39. *History of NASD,* 2; *The Commercial & Financial Chronicle,* CXLIII

those that had existed under the NRA were established and, as before, the national organization determined all major questions of policy and procedures. The IBA cooperated with the conference but chose to remain independent.[40]

The conference's most important contribution was to draft the legislation subsequently passed as the Maloney Act. For almost a year representatives of the Investment Bankers Conference worked closely with the IBA, various state and regional groups of security dealers, and the SEC in planning a national association that would continue the principles of self-regulation under government supervision first tried under the NRA.[41] William O. Douglas, then chairman of the SEC, strongly supported the establishment of such an organization, which would police its members in the same way that the stock exchanges regulated theirs. "Government would keep the shot gun, so to speak, behind the door — loaded, well-oiled, cleaned, ready for use — but with the hope that it would never have to be used." [42] Such an organization, Douglas said, should be voluntary, open to all reputable dealers, and run democratically. Its purpose should be "to promote just and equitable principles of trade, to prevent fraud and manipulative acts and practices, to eliminate unreasonable profits and commissions, to promote accuracy of quotations, and in general to protect investors by improving the character of the over-the-counter market and by insuring that it be free, open, and competitive." [43]

Members of the association would be accorded "preferential business advantages" not available to nonmembers, as had been the case under the NRA code. To assure "effective disciplining," the association was to be empowered to suspend these privileges and expel those who violated its rules.[44]

A preliminary measure incorporating many of these proposals was drafted in November 1937, one month after the SEC had issued its own over-the-counter rules.[45] The conference adopted these regu-

---

(September 12, 1936), 1642–43. The Census Bureau's 1935 count of firms "engaged primarily in the flotation, purchase, sales, and/or brokerage of stocks and bonds" was 7,224, of which 6,220 were operated by 4,445 security brokers and/or dealers who were registered with the SEC in January 1936. The SEC's registration figure for 1936 was 5,303, indicating a discrepancy of 858 firms between its count and the one conducted by the Census Bureau. See U.S. Bureau of the Census, *Census of Business: 1935, Financial Institutions Other Than Banks* (Washington, 1937), iii.

40. *The New York Times,* December 7, 1936, November 6, 1937.

41. *The New York Times,* April 16, 1937; "Offer Unlisted Code," *Business Week* (April 24, 1937), 28; *The Commercial & Financial Chronicle,* CXLIV (April 24, 1937), 2747.

42. Quoted in "Self-Regulation," *Investment Banking,* VIII (January 15, 1938), 48.

43. *Ibid.*

44. *Ibid.,* 49; *U.S. v. Henry S. Morgan et al.,* "Transcript of Trial: Defendants' Opening — Mr. [Arthur H.] Dean" (January 8, 1951), 1323–24.

45. *The New York Times,* September 29, 1937; *History of NASD,* 2.

lations and, along with additional ones of its own, included them in the bill introduced on January 18, 1938, by Senator Francis T. Maloney, Democrat from Connecticut.[46] "This program," the senator said, "is based upon cooperative regulation, in which the task [of policing the over-the-counter markets] will be largely performed by representative organizations of investment bankers, dealers, and brokers, with the Government exercising appropriate supervision in the public interest, and exercising supplementary powers of direct regulation." [47] The alternative to such a program, SEC Commissioner Robert E. Healy later warned, was direct government regulation.[48]

The Maloney bill provided for registration with the SEC of a national association of over-the-counter brokers and dealers that would have regional affiliates. Membership would be voluntary, but brokers and dealers who did not join would remain under the direct supervision of the SEC and would not enjoy any of the preferential business advantages accorded to members.[49]

While favoring regulation of the over-the-counter markets, the IBA opposed the Maloney bill's emphasis upon SEC supervision.[50] "The bill would not be self-regulation but over regulation of an already sorely harassed industry," testified Francis E. Frothingham, the association's president. "So directly and indirectly overpowered is it by commission supervision and dictation," he said, "that it does not inspire free men to put forward the enthusiastic, self-sacrificing energy without which the best results are impossible." [51] The IBA recommended several changes, some of which were subsequently accepted. After the final bill had been voted, the association, claiming credit for having improved the measure, urged its members to join the proposed new organization.[52] Reports were denied that the IBA and the Investment Bankers Conference, Inc., planned to merge and become the industry's self-regulatory body under the Maloney Act, which became law in June 25, 1938. The IBA chose to continue as the industry's independent trade association, free to carry on its educational, advisory, and lobbying activities, and the Investment Bankers Conference prepared to reorganize itself in order to qualify under the Maloney Act.[53]

46. *The New York Times*, January 18, 1938.
47. Quoted in Loss, *Securities Regulation*, II, 1362. See also Francis T. Maloney, "Cooperative Regulation," *Investment Banking*, IX (September 1939), 18–23.
48. Robert E. Healy, "Advantages of Self-Regulation," *Investment Banking*, IX (April 1939), 21–22.
49. *The New York Times*, January 18, 1938.
50. *Ibid.*, January 23, 1938.
51. [Francis E. Frothingham] "The Maloney Bill," *Investment Banking*, VIII (February 15, 1938), 81. See also *The New York Times*, February 9, 1938.
52. Investment Bankers Association, *Proceedings . . . 1937* (Chicago, 1937), 10–11; *The New York Times*, July 8, 1938.
53. *The New York Times*, June 6, 1938, July 9, 17, 1938; IBA, *Fiftieth Anni-*

The transformation of the Investment Bankers Conference into the National Association of Securities Dealers, Inc. (NASD) involved mostly drafting a new charter and preparing more extensive bylaws and fair trade rules. The basic organizational structure of the conference was retained, except that provision was made to meet the Maloney Act's emphasis upon democratic procedures and regional autonomy. The NASD made every effort to dispel the fears of small dealers that it would be controlled by "a few powerful underwriting houses." [54] All major policies were determined by a board of governors composed of twenty-one elected representatives from each of the fourteen districts into which the country was divided. Districts with unusually large memberships elected more than one member. The thirteenth district, for instance, which comprised New York, Connecticut, and northern New Jersey, elected five governors. Only two other districts elected more than one. Together with the thirteenth district, their combined representation accounted for ten members of the board of governors.

Each regional district was governed by its own elected committee, which appointed a Business Conduct Committee to police its members.[55] Violators of the association's rules were liable to fines, cancellation of membership, or suspension. Since members were barred from participating in syndicates and selling groups with nonmembers, allowing them discounts and commissions, or dealing with them on terms other than those accorded the general public, expulsion or a suspension imposed heavy financial burdens, as well as loss of prestige.

On August 7, 1939, the SEC approved the conference's application for registration under the Maloney Act. From then on, the NASD, in cooperation with the commission, assumed the responsibility of policing the over-the-counter markets, standardizing practices, and enforcing the association's lengthy fair trade rules, which were designed to protect investors against fraud and deceptive manipulation and generally promote "just and equitable principles of trade." [56] Organization of the NASD was praised by Jerome N. Frank, the new chairman of the SEC. "This event," he said, "marks the beginning of a significant attempt by an important segment of a

---

versary: 1912–1962 (n.p. [1962?]), 11–12; "Over the Counter: The IBA Votes to Cooperate for Regulation Under SEC," *Newsweek,* XII (November 7, 1938), 44. See also *U.S. v. Henry S. Morgan et al.,* "Transcript of Trial: Defendants' Opening — Mr. [Arthur H.] Dean" (January 8, 1951), 1350–54.

54. Healy, "Advantages of Self-Regulation," 21. See also Homer V. Cherrington, "National Association of Securities Dealers," *Harvard Business Review,* XXVII (November 1949), 741–59; "Securities Dealers Association," *Investment Banking,* IX (February 1939), 8–10; John C. Loeser, *The Over-the-Counter Securities Market: What It Is and How It Operates* (New York, 1940), 115–22.

55. *History of NASD,* 11–12.

56. *Ibid.,* 5; "The N.A.S.D.," *Investment Banking,* IX (June 1939), 1.

business affected with a marked public interest in regulating its own affairs in cooperation with the government." [57]

By the end of 1939 some 2,600 firms had joined the NASD. Included among these were all the leading investment houses in the country. The Maloney Act, together with the other federal and state securities laws, made investment banking one of the most thoroughly supervised and regulated service industries in the country.

Though the underlying philosophies of these laws differed, all had the same purpose: to protect the investor and eliminate past abuses with the least possible interference with the way investment bankers recruited capital and channeled it into industry. When these laws were passed, however, few investment bankers admitted that this was the government's intention. To many of them it appeared as if Washington was determined upon punishing and harassing the securities industry out of existence. Emmett F. Connely, the two-time president of the IBA, expressed the discouragement of many investment bankers over their relationship with the government. "I sometimes wonder," he said in 1941, "why we and the bureaus that regulate us see these things so differently." [58]

Much of the bankers' difficulty in adjusting to federal regulation stemmed from the fact that it came at a time when the investment banking industry was beset with a host of other problems. The protracted depression more than federal regulation made the decade of the 1930's an especially difficult one for investment bankers. Although the economy generally started to recover by the middle of 1933 and continued to improve until August 1937, when another severe setback wiped out the gains that had been made up to then, the investment banking business did not keep pace with this revival. New corporate issues stayed at depression levels throughout the decade. Although they increased from $380.0 million in 1933 to $4.4 billion in 1936, the next year they fell by 50 percent, dropping to $2.2 billion, a figure not exceeded again until 1940, when they amounted to over $2.6 billion.[59]

Most new issues were refundings. In 1936, for instance, they amounted to 74 percent of all corporate issues.[60] Large, established corporations took advantage of prevailing low interest rates to cut costs by exchanging high interest bonds for lower paying ones. Refundings, together with municipal financing, accounted for most of

57. Quoted in "The Maloney Association," *Investment Banking,* IX (September 1939), 1.
58. IBA, *Proceedings . . . 1941,* 11.
59. U.S. Bureau of the Census, *Historical Statistics of the United States: Colonial Times to 1957* (Washington, 1960), 658. See also Harold G. Moulton *et al., Capital Expansion, Employment, and Economic Stability* (Washington, 1940), 328–29.
60. "The Investment Banker: 1939," *Fortune,* XX (September 1939), 78–79; *Time,* XXX (November 15, 1937), 84.

the underwriting that was done during the 1930's. Because of this and the fact that investors distrusted stocks, bonds dominated the new issues business.

Not all investment houses, however, benefited from refundings. Those that profited most were the larger ones that had financed these corporations in the first place, or new and reorganized firms with partners and officers formerly associated with the now defunct security affiliates of the large metropolitan commercial banks, such as The First Boston Corporation and Blyth & Co. Years later, Albert H. Gordon, the young, energetic head of the new Kidder, Peabody firm, testified to the mad scramble that existed for this business and to the time and effort he and his partners expended to win as much of it as possible.[61] The same competitive pattern prevailed in financing municipalities, with Halsey, Stuart & Co. fighting hard to secure the leadership of these issues.[62] Even after Adolf Hitler's armies invaded Poland and the United States stepped up its defense program, the underwriting business still remained depressed.

What disturbed investment bankers during the 1930's even more than the continued low level of new offerings was the fact that many borrowers and institutional investors no longer found their services essential. Large, established corporations, once the investment bankers' most important clients and their chief source of profits, relied increasingly on financing themselves, placing securities directly with institutions, or negotiating long-term commercial bank loans. Direct placements alone accounted for $2.8 billion of all corporate bonds and notes issued between 1934 and 1939. The gross loss to investment bankers in these transactions, according to a conservative Temporary National Economic Committee (TNEC) estimate, amounted to $60 million.[63]

Not only was the investment banker being circumvented by many of his former customers, but his chief function, providing capital to industry, often was performed by the federal government. The most important federal agency making loans to business was the Reconstruction Finance Corporation (RFC), established in February

61. *U.S. v. Henry S. Morgan et al.*, "Transcript of Trial: Defendants' Opening — Mr. [W. G.] Claytor" (March 1, 1951), 3882–83.
62. A. E. Bryson, *Halsey, Stuart & Co., Inc., 1901–1937, 1938–1944: A History* . . . ([Chicago 1937, 1945]?), 66. Late in 1938 the Treasury proposed eliminating the tax exemption on municipal bonds, but the Congress failed to support the administration's plan and, after a lengthy court battle, the Supreme Court, in January 1945, refused to accept the government's test case. See *ibid.*, 8–10, suppl.; *Time*, XXXII (November 7, 1938), 56.
63. U.S. Temporary National Economic Committee, *Investigation of Concentration of Economic Power: Final Report of the Executive Secretary* . . . (Washington, 1941), 231. According to one estimate, private placements increased from 19 percent of all corporate issues in 1932 to 33 percent in 1939, and their growing importance was "dramatically illustrated" the next year, when the American Telephone and Telegraph Co. sold a $140 million issue privately. See *Newsweek*, XVI (December 23, 1940), 37.

1932. At first most of its loans went to railroads, but after 1934 many were made to industrial and other companies as well. By the end of 1932 the value of the RFC's outstanding loans amounted to some $272 million, and the amount rose steadily thereafter, reaching a peak of nearly $795 million by the end of 1942, when the agency was actively involved in financing defense plants. "There can be little doubt," a partner in Harriman, Ripley & Co. told the House Commerce Committee in November 1941, "that through the Reconstruction Finance Corporation today, and through other agencies of government, a great part of the functions of what in an economic sense is investment banking is now being conducted by Government." [64]

All these developments made corporations and institutional investors less and less dependent upon the services of investment bankers. The severe drop in the rate of the economy's growth and the virtual cessation of large corporate mergers and promotions reduced still further the business and profits of investment bankers. Many knowledgeable observers, appraising these developments, concluded that the once dominant position of the investment banker as the principal channel through which savings were turned into investments had come to an end. Like other middlemen, the investment banker either was being bypassed or his functions were being taken over by others, and his future seemed to be one of declining importance.[65]

The low volume of new issues and alternative methods of financing available to borrowers, other than negotiated public offerings, caused a marked decline in underwriting profits.[66] With few exceptions, underwriting spreads and commissions had been falling steadily since the immediate pre–World War I years (1912–1915). At that time, according to one estimate, the gross profits of an investment house selling different types and qualities of bonds and preferred stock averaged about 4 percent for bonds and 5 percent for both bonds and preferred stock.[67] There are very few accurate figures for the 1920's, but what little evidence there is suggests that gross under-

64. U.S. House, Committee on Interstate and Foreign Commerce, 77th Cong., 1st and 2d Sess., *Proposed Amendments to the Securities Act of 1933 and to the Securities Exchange Act of 1934: Hearings* . . . (6 pts., Washington, 1941–42), pt. 2, 403–04; Stewart Johnson, "Statistics on Federal Lending and Loan Insurance Programs in the United States, 1929–1958," in Stewart Johnson et al., *Federal Credit Programs* (Englewood Cliffs, 1963), 81–82.

65. Paul M. Sweezy, "The Decline of the Investment Banker," *The Antioch Review*, I (March 1941), 63–68; Stuart Chase, "Shadow over Wall Street," *Harper's Magazine*, CLXXX (March 1940), 367–74; Kemmerer, "The Marketing of Securities, 1930–1952," 454–68.

66. George A. Eddy, "The Present Status of New Security Issues," *The Review of Economic Statistics*, XXI (August 1939), 116–21; Avery B. Cohan, "The Price of Underwriting Services on Corporate Debt, 1935–1952," *The Journal of Finance*, XV (September 1960), 407–08.

67. T. Kenneth Haven, *Investment Banking under the Securities and Exchange Commission* (Ann Arbor, 1940), 31–33.

writing profits shrank considerably during that decade. A study of 104 bond issues offered publicly during the years 1926 to 1929 disclosed that commissions "on the actual amount of capital raised" averaged 3.088 percent. Since most of the issues analyzed were large offerings, many of them high-quality railroad bonds sponsored by four of the nation's leading and most respected private banking houses, the commissions were doubtless lower than the average. Even so, the figure is an indication of the marked drop in underwriting commissions since the time of the Pujo investigation.[68]

During the 1930's, commissions fell still further. Cash underwriting commissions paid to bankers between 1934 and 1937 averaged 2.683 percent of the capital raised, according to a study of 665 publicly underwritten bond and stock issues prepared by T. Kenneth Haven of the University of Michigan's Bureau of Business Research. As in the past, the amount of the bankers' commissions increased as the quality of the security decreased. The underwriting commission on the 313 bond issues Haven analyzed ranged from a low of 1.659 percent of the capital raised to as much as 4.128 percent; those for 120 issues of preferred stock ranged between 2.362 percent and 15.0 percent; and those for 232 common stock offerings were still higher, ranging from 2.932 percent to as much as 17.577 percent.[69] For common stocks sold directly to the public without first being offered to old holders, the underwriting commissions were even higher, reaching more than 22.3 percent.[70] Where privilege provision was made, commissions were lower, since such subscriptions greatly reduced the investment banker's risk and expenses. The "average underwriting commissions" bankers received, including expenses, between 1934 and 1937, on all 665 issues Haven studied, were as follows: bonds, 2.232 percent; preferred stock, 3.030 percent; and common stock, 8.833 percent. Comparable figures for securities "offered by privilege subscriptions" were: bonds, 1.942 percent; preferred stock, 2.150 percent; and common stock, 3.810 percent. Those charged for securities issued directly to the public without a prior offering to old holders were higher: bonds, 2.241 percent; preferred stock, 3.576 percent; and common stock, 14.396 percent. On the basis of his findings, Haven concluded that underwriting commissions during these years had dropped by more than 50 percent since the immediate pre–World War I era. They dropped still further during the next twenty years.[71]

Decline in underwriting profits was accompanied by a sharp drop

68. *Ibid.,* 33–34.
69. *Ibid.,* 20.
70. *Ibid.,* 23; Merwin H. Waterman, *Investment Banking Functions: Their Evolution and Adaptation to Business Finance* (Ann Arbor, 1958), 76.
71. Haven, *Investment Banking,* 20–23, 35–39; Cohan, "The Price of Underwriting Services," 407–08. See also *U.S. v. Henry S. Morgan et al.,* "Brief on General Points in Support of Motion to Dismiss . . . ," Appendix A, Table 1.

in brokerage commissions, a further significant factor accounting for generally low profits in the investment banking business during the 1930's. In 1929 these commissions had totaled $227 million; in 1938 they amounted to only $43 million.[72] Most investment banking houses relied on them to pay a substantial part of their overhead and other expenses, often amounting to several thousand dollars a day. In the case of Kidder, Peabody, for instance, brokerage commissions accounted for almost one-third of its gross income during most of these years, and the firm's partners worked as hard to promote this business as they did to increase their underwritings.[73]

Throughout the 1930's investment banking profits were "exceedingly spotty," according to a *Fortune* survey. Only a few of the larger houses showed a reasonably good return on capital, and even they occasionally suffered deficits.[74] During the years between 1935 and 1939 The First Boston Corporation averaged about a 10 percent return on its capital. Except for 1937, when it incurred a deficit of nearly $2.5 million, this firm's earnings on capital invested ranged from a high of 27.4 percent in 1935 to a low of 5.4 percent in 1938. Haven, who compiled these figures, also studied the earnings record of four other investment banking houses which, together with First Boston, represented "a better than average cross section of the industry." [75] For these five firms the average earnings on capital invested during the years 1935 to 1939 was 8 percent.[76] Most of the smaller firms, along with some of the larger houses, made nowhere near so much.

The low rate of return on investment banking capital was attributed to other causes. Some leading Wall Street figures blamed it on the fact that there were too many firms in the industry for the amount of business available. This explanation was especially popular after the severe market break of August 1937, which brought heavy losses to several firms and, in the case of one major house, Edward B. Smith, led to its reorganization.[77] Charles E. Mitchell later testified before the TNEC that in October 1937 Harold Stanley, of Morgan Stanley, had told him that "it was the view of his firm and of the 'corner' that there were too many houses in the business now, that there ought to be a smaller number and that number ought to be stronger." [78]

72. Chase, "Shadow over Wall Street," 364.
73. Kidder, Peabody & Co. Records, New York City.
74. "Investment Banker: 1939," 110.
75. Haven, *Investment Banking*, 135. The other four firms, and their average invested capital for the years 1935 to 1939, were: Blair & Co. $3.6 million; Schoellkopf, Hutton & Pomeroy $3.7 million; Central Republic Co. $1.9 million; and Harris, Hall & Co. $1.2 million. See *ibid.*, 133–34, 136–37.
76. *Ibid.*, 140.
77. "Investment Bankers' Famine," *Business Week* (October 30, 1937), 20, 22; "Investment Banker: 1939," 110.
78. U.S. Temporary National Economic Committee, *Investigation of Concen-*

Others attributed the slump in the investment banking business to different causes. They cited alternative methods of long-term financing, the fear of federal regulation, and higher income taxes.

John W. Hanes, a former partner in Charles D. Barney & Co. whom FDR appointed to the SEC in January 1938, blamed the investment bankers themselves for their poor profits, accusing them of lacking energy and creativity. Hanes charged them with failing to develop new business, especially the financing of smaller corporations, and avoiding the risk-bearing function by using various types of "market-out" clauses in their agreements with issuers. Such devices, he asserted, limited the usefulness of investment bankers to industry and accounted for many of their financial troubles.[79] Still others, interested principally in protecting investors, were concerned that declining spreads and commissions on highly rated securities would result in bankers pushing the sale of less meritorious issues, where the profit margin was largest.[80]

Low earnings, declining spreads and commissions, higher transfer taxes, increased competition, and federal regulation led to a radical streamlining of syndicate procedures, a trend already evident late in the 1920's. The various intermediate groups once commonly employed to originate, purchase, underwrite, subunderwrite, and sell an issue were eliminated entirely. Their functions now were assigned at most to two groups: one to purchase or underwrite the issue and sell it, in whole or in part, and, at times, another, a so-called selling group, to assist in marketing it.[81] These changes in no way altered the investment banker's traditional role in the "substance" of the several transactions necessary to bring out a new issue.

In a privately negotiated issue the originating banker acted much as he had prior to 1933. Assisted by lawyers, accountants, and other experts, he conducted the investigation and negotiated with the issuer a preliminary, informal agreement that specified the amount and type of security to be sold, the tentative offering price, the size of the bankers' spread, and as many other details concerning the issue, registration statement, and prospectus as could be agreed upon.[82] Except for the extensive and costly additional paperwork

---

tration of Economic Power: Hearings . . . (31 pts., Washington, 1939–41), pt. 22, 11587–88, 11782.

79. John W. Hanes, "The Lifeblood of Our Industrial Machine: The Capital Market and the Investment Banker," *Vital Speeches of the Day*, IV (May 1, 1938), 421–24. See also John W. Hanes and Francis E. Frothingham, "Two Viewpoints on Investment Banking," *Business Week* (March 26, 1938), 56; Willard E. Atkins et al., *The Regulation of the Security Markets* (Washington, 1946), 37–41.

80. Rudolph L. Weissmann, *The New Wall Street* (New York, 1939), 275–81.

81. *U.S. v. Henry S. Morgan et al.*, "Corrected Opinion," 42. See also Harold G. Moulton et al., *Capital Expansion*, 198–227.

82. John H. Prime, "Private Negotiation in the Origination of Securities" in

necessary to satisfy the disclosure requirements of the Securities Act and the provisions of other relevant federal statutes, such as those of the Trust Indenture Act in the case of debt issues, the preliminary job of an originating house in preparing a privately negotiated offering hardly changed.

The most significant and obvious departure from previous practice occurred after completion of the preliminary negotiations that gave birth to a new issue. Nearly all these changes involved methods, and most of them were concerned with the way the securities were purchased from the issuer, the liability of syndicate members, and selling group practices.

As in the past, unless the offering was small enough for the originating banker to take up entirely alone, the usual practice after 1933 was for him to organize an underwriting or purchase syndicate to share the liability and assist in the distribution. Both types commonly were called underwriting syndicates, but in fact nearly all were purchase groups, in which each member bought and paid for his share of the issue. Pure underwriting, the exclusive risk-bearing function, usually was employed now only when an established corporation made a rights offering to its stockholders and arranged with a group of investment houses to take up whatever securities remained unsold after the close of the subscription. This was true underwriting, in the classic sense of the term.[83]

As in the past, the underwriting or purchase group was organized by the originating banker, who customarily became its manager. If more than one firm participated in investigating and planning the issue, the management was divided, and the participating firms agreed among themselves as to the way their names would appear on the prospectus and in newspaper advertisements.[84] When there was more than one originating house, they sometimes agreed to continue their joint relationship in financing that corporation's subsequent issues, but as a rule these so-called "nucleus groups" rarely lasted for any considerable length of time.[85]

The number of houses to be included in a syndicate depended upon the character and size of the issue and the risk involved in selling it. After 1937, when several firms incurred heavy losses as the result of two "conspicuously unsuccessful" flotations, syndicates were enlarged substantially. Firms that previously had not partici-

---

Investment Bankers Association, *Fundamentals of Investment Banking* (Englewood Cliffs, 1960), 477–92.

83. Moulton *et al., Capital Expansion*, 210–11.

84. See, for instance, the "Understanding between Kuhn, Loeb & Co. and Lehman Brothers with Respect to Tide Water Associated Oil Co. Financing," dated June 22, 1945, in *U.S. v. Henry S. Morgan et al.*, "Plaintiff's Exhibit, No. 222-B." See also U.S. TNEC, *Hearings*, pt. 24, 12391–93.

85. *U.S. v. Henry S. Morgan et al.*, "Corrected Opinion," 53.

pated regularly in purchasing and underwriting groups were asked to become members. Their addition doubled the size of many syndicates.[86]

The choice of syndicate members was left almost entirely to the manager and the issuer. During the 1930's, unlike earlier periods, corporation executives assumed an increasingly active role in determining the make-up of these groups. Their decisions on these matters were tantamount to a "royal command," a banker testified. It was not at all uncommon for investment houses to write company officials and ask for participations.[87]

Numerous other factors determined the selection of syndicate members. Special consideration was given to firms that had participated in a corporation's previous flotations. After the Banking Act of 1933 went into effect, requiring the separation of investment from commercial banking, this practice raised numerous difficult problems. Who was to "inherit" the business of the defunct security affiliates and the few private bankers, like J. P. Morgan & Co., that had decided to give up investment banking? In the case of the latter, the problem was resolved in 1935 with the organization of Morgan Stanley. Insofar as the others were concerned, the policy followed by most syndicate managers was to offer participations to firms they believed had inherited the personnel and business of the former affiliates. In December 1939, while testifying before the TNEC, George W. Bovenizer of Kuhn, Loeb explained why this firm had decided in 1939 to invite Brown, Harriman to participate in underwriting a $16 million bond issue for the Chicago Union Station Co. The National City Co., one of Kuhn, Loeb's long-time associates in these offerings, was no longer in business, but all its "principal officers" and the "better part" of its selling organization had joined Brown, Harriman. "Our original partner in the business," Bovenizer said, "was the National City Bank which became the National City Co., and later on in our eyes became Brown Harriman & Co." [88] This policy, employed by many leading investment houses, subsequently was used by the government as part of its conspiracy charges against seventeen of these firms.[89]

Besides "historical position," as the practice of recognizing past participations in choosing syndicate partners came to be known, several other considerations also weighed heavily. One was financial responsibility. Nearly all the leading originating houses were kept informed of the financial capacity of firms they considered likely

---

86. *Ibid.*, "Transcript of Trial: Plaintiff's Case — Deposition of [Walter E.] Sachs" (May 14, 1951), 6858–59.

87. U.S. TNEC, *Hearings*, pt. 22, 11542; *U.S. v. Henry S. Morgan et al.*, "Plaintiff's Exhibit, No. 235-B."

88. U.S. TNEC, *Hearings*, pt. 22, 11442–43.

89. *U.S. v. Henry S. Morgan et al.*, "Transcript of Trial: Plaintiff's Case — Deposition of [Charles E.] Mitchell" (November 2, 1951), 10395–402.

syndicate partners, though the methods they employed in securing this information varied widely, from hearsay to requests for formal financial statements.[90] The latter method was used by Morgan Stanley after the 1937 market break, when it became apparent that several houses might suffer serious losses.[91] Ability to distribute securities, as measured by past performance, not only determined whether a firm was invited, but very often the size of its participation as well. A firm's selling ability frequently depended on the type of security that was offered. Houses specializing in a certain kind of issue were invited to join syndicates offering that type, not only because they could sell it quickly, but also because their names on the prospectus added prestige.

Geographical considerations also were taken into account, since usually it was advantageous to include firms located where the issuer conducted its business. Finally, invitations were extended to firms that were themselves able to grant participations. Although Charles E. Mitchell testified before the TNEC that reciprocal arrangements of this kind were the least important factor in determining the make-up of a syndicate, the practice was nonetheless widely employed.[92]

Organization of the purchase group occurred in the interval between the time when the originating banker concluded preliminary negotiations with the issuer and the SEC declared the registration statement effective, usually a period of some 30 to 60 days. This was a busy time for the originating house. While some of its staff worked with the issuer, its attorneys, and independent accountants preparing the registration statement, prospectus, and their accompanying documents, other members of the originating house conferred with the lawyers who were preparing the purchase agreement. This lengthy, detailed document contained most of the information that had been incorporated in the earlier, informal agreement between the originating house and the issuer, such as the amount and type of securities to offer, whether they were to be listed on an exchange, and many other provisions affecting their value and marketability. In addition, the purchase agreement included the corporation's guarantee that the securities had been registered with the SEC; that the information in the registration statement and prospectus was correct, complete, and complied with the requirements of the Securities Act; and that the issue had been qualified under the blue-sky laws of the states in which it was to be sold.[93]

90. U.S. TNEC, *Hearings,* pt. 22, 11544–45, XXIV, 12661.
91. *U.S. v. Henry S. Morgan et al.,* "Plaintiff's Exhibits," Nos. 687, 690–91, 959.
92. U.S. TNEC, *Hearings,* pt. 22, 11569, 11602–04.
93. Prime, "Private Negotiation," 478–84.

The agreement, furthermore, encompassed several other provisions as well. It listed the names of the purchasers and the amount that each agreed to buy, set the time and method of payment, and included various stipulations designed to limit the liability of the purchasers and particularly a market-out clause, permitting them to terminate the contract in the case of unfavorable market conditions. The final pricing of the issue, including the determination of the bankers' spread, usually was delayed until the last possible moment, sometimes as late as the morning of the day the registration statement became effective. This information, submitted in the form of an amendment, became part of the registration statement and purchase agreement, and was added also to the prospectus.[94]

Many of the most significant changes that occurred in the investment banking business after 1933 were observable in the various provisions of the document. Some of them involved only the compulsory disclosure of information once held confidential, such as the price the syndicate paid the corporation for the securities, the price at which they were sold to the public, and the profit the bankers made in the transaction. Others indicated more fundamental changes in methods. Perhaps the most important of these was the statement that the members of the syndicate purchased the issue severally and not jointly, as had been customary before 1933.[95]

Changes in purchase agreements also reflected changes in the way the syndicate manager negotiated the sale of securities. He no longer bought and took title to the entire issue himself, reselling it immediately to the purchase group at a step-up in the price. He now signed the agreement on behalf of each member of the syndicate. Except for the share of the issue that the manager kept for himself, title passed directly from the corporation to the individual members of the group, each according to the amount of his participation. The principal reason for adopting this procedure was to avoid the new federal transfer tax on bonds, enacted in the Revenue Act of June 1932, and the additional levies that law imposed on stock sales. The civil liability provisions of the Securities Act provided further reason to continue the practice. The change, however, in no way altered the manager's function. Even the management fee, the syndicate's payment to the manager for his services, was not an entirely new development. After 1932 it was employed regularly, and provision for it usually was incorporated in the "purchase group agreement," also commonly called the "agreement among underwriters." [96]

This document, signed by each member of the syndicate, spelled

---

94. Ibid., 482–84.
95. U.S. v. Henry S. Morgan et al., "Corrected Opinion," 42.
96. U.S. v. Henry S. Morgan et al., "Transcript of Trial: Plaintiff's Case" (February 18, 1953), 20343–54; "Deposition of [Charles E.] Mitchell" (May 14, 1951), 6881–85; "Corrected Opinion," 42.

out the numerous phases of the selling operation. It specified the amount of each signer's participation, established the time and method of payment, and fixed the length of the initial distribution period and provided for its extension or earlier termination. It also conferred broad powers on the manager, charging him with the entire responsibility of supervising every aspect of the distribution.[97] It authorized him to sell an agreed portion of the issue to institutional investors and dealers, the former at the public offering price, and the latter at a discount or concession. The proceeds from these group and dealer sales were credited to the account of the members according to their individual participations.

Moreover, the purchase-group agreement often conferred other powers on the manager. It authorized him to enforce the public offering price by withholding commissions and discounts to dealers who violated it during the initial distribution. And it also empowered him to stabilize the price by buying and selling securities on the open market on behalf of the group, according to the strictly defined stabilization rules laid down by the SEC.[98]

The provisions of these clauses differed widely, as did the extent to which they were employed. Morgan Stanley, which specialized in high-grade corporate bonds, much in demand by institutional investors, stopped using price maintenance and penalty clauses in its agreements in 1938. Harriman, Ripley did so in 1943, but Halsey, Stuart, after dropping them for "a year or so," reinstated them.[99]

Purchase-group agreements also contained provisions for organizing and controlling selling groups, composed of hundreds of dealers scattered across the country, and selected by the manager and the other purchasers or underwriters. The function of these groups was to retail a portion of the securities to the public. Selling groups were largest when the amount of effort needed to distribute the issue quickly and successfully was greatest.

The amount of any issue available to individuals as investors varied considerably, but it was never substantial. In the case of high-grade bonds, it usually was small, especially during the 1930's, since syndicate managers could place them easily with institutional investors anxious to buy this type of security. Moreover, since the profit margin on these issues was small, purchase-group members with retail sales organizations of their own, such as Kidder, Peabody, preferred to distribute their allotments themselves, thus increasing their share of the spread.[100]

97. Prime, "Private Negotiation," 484–86; *U.S. v. Henry S. Morgan et al.,* "Corrected Opinion," 42–43.
98. U.S. TNEC, *Hearings,* pt. 24, 12364–65; "Permissible Stabilization," *Investment Banking,* IX (April 1939), 27–30.
99. *U.S. v. Henry S. Morgan et al.,* "Corrected Opinion," 117–18.
100. Prime, "Private Negotiation," 488; Waterman, *Investment Banking Functions* 77; U.S. TNEC, *Hearings,* pt. 23, 11991–92; Sumner B. Emerson, "The

Originating bankers usually initiated the organization of the selling group as soon as the registration statement was filed. Sometimes they acted even earlier if they were reasonably certain that the preliminary negotiations with the issuer, especially those concerning the pricing of the securities, would be concluded successfully.[101] The Securities Act prohibited offering the securities before the SEC declared the registration statement effective, but it did not prevent the manager of the purchasing or underwriting syndicate from inviting selected dealers to join a selling group. He did this by writing them that a registration statement had been filed, and he included with the invitation a preliminary, or "red herring," prospectus, containing most of the essential facts about the issue, but usually excluding the price the issuer was to be paid, the price to the public, and the amount of the dealers' discount. This information, together with the final, completed prospectus and a selling-group agreement, the manager sent out on the day the registration became effective.[102]

The "offering to selected dealers," as this agreement sometimes was called, often contained other data as well. It usually stipulated the amount to be allotted, the time allowed for replies (usually three days at most), the method and time of payment, and other provisions setting forth the manager's powers. These included maintaining and stabilizing the price of the securities during the initial distribution, whether the syndicate could be extended and for how long, and the nature of the penalties imposed on dealers who violated the agreement. Sometimes, when a distribution proved "sticky," the manager asked certain syndicate members or dealers to take up an additional share of the issue if they thought they could sell it. If the securities were of the type then popular with investors, the issue was quickly oversubscribed, sometimes within an hour or two after the invitation to the dealers. The manager then had to decide how much to assign to each one.[103]

All the principal houses of issue, such as Morgan Stanley, Kuhn, Loeb, First Boston, and Kidder, Peabody, kept lists of dealers they regularly invited, with detailed information on their previous performance. The largest subsequent allotments were granted to houses with the best sales records. Firms that repeatedly refused to accept invitations or accepted only those requiring little sales effort were dropped from the list and replaced by others. Dealers anxious to be added to the list of a prestigious issuing house frequently applied for allotments, either directly or through the corporation that was offering the securities, but the surest way to obtain an invitation to

Wholesaling of Corporate Securities" in Philipp H. Lohman and Franc M. Ricciardi, eds., *Wall Street Explains Its Operations* . . . (New York, 1951), 92–93.

101. U.S. TNEC, *Hearings,* pt. 24, 12669–72.
102. Prime, "Private Negotiation," 487–91.
103. *Ibid.,* 490–91.

an underwriting as well as a selling group was to develop a strong sales record, as Kidder, Peabody did after 1931.[104]

The various changes that occurred in syndicate procedures during the 1930's had "a profound effect" on the way investment bankers conducted their affairs but, Judge Medina said later, they in no way "altered the basic function of the syndicate operation as a unitary, integrated means of underwriting and distributing a security issue, under the direction of a manager. . . . Such changes as had taken place from first to last were the normal and natural reactions of business men with common problems, to the course of economic events and the legislation" of the times.[105]

During the 1930's and after, investment houses assisted issuers much as they had done before, but, in order to meet the dual threat posed by the growth of competitive bidding and the pronounced increase in private placements, they introduced new services designed specifically to assist corporations intent upon raising capital by methods other than the traditional, negotiated, registered public offering. By the end of the decade some of the major investment houses were maintaining specialized groups to work with corporations in planning issues to offer at competitive bids. Many more firms devoted substantial efforts to preparing issues to be placed privately, finding institutional buyers, and negotiating special sales. In arranging private placements, the investment banker acted as the agent of the seller. Financial services of this kind became an increasingly important source of revenue for investment firms, and many of them, such as Kidder, Peabody and Lehman Brothers, expended sizable sums and considerable energy in advertising them.[106]

None of these many changes and developments, however, affected the basic structure of the industry. New York City remained the investment banking center of the country. Nearly all the leading firms were concentrated there, with Chicago occupying second place, followed by Philadelphia and Boston. A few other cities, no more than twenty in 1939 according to the IBA, counted a dozen or more member firms. Some of these smaller houses were important as originators of local issues, and many of them participated regularly in underwriting syndicates headed by New York and Chicago firms.[107]

There are no reliable figures on the aggregate amount of capital invested in these firms, but the total for the entire industry at the

104. Albert H. Gordon to author, December 15, 1965. See also *U.S. v. Henry S. Morgan et al.*, "Transcript of Trial: Defendants' Opening" (March 1, 1951), 3882–83.
105. *U.S. v. Henry S. Morgan et al.*, "Corrected Opinion," 46.
106. Alfred E. Borneman to author, March 10, 1966; [Lehman Brothers] *Private Placements: A Means of Raising Capital in a Changing Economy* (n.p., n.d.).
107. "Investment Banker: 1939," 79–80. See also Douglas, *Democracy and Finance*, 22–24.

end of 1939 has been variously estimated at between $200 million and $330 million.[108] According to *The Wall Street Journal,* the "average capital employed" by the eight largest houses in the years 1934 to 1939 ranged between $4 million for Blyth and $16 million for Kuhn, Loeb. Three other firms had a capital of $10 million or more.[109]

The size and type of firms varied widely during the 1930's as before, but most of them fell into three major groups: (1) a very select few, like Morgan Stanley, were primarily originators of bond issues, managers of underwriting syndicates, and wholesalers; (2) several hundred firms, both wholesalers and retailers, were anxious to win managerships but also strove to obtain participations in syndicates led by others; (3) the largest group of all embraced thousands of retailers scattered across the country, some of whom on occasion also accepted syndicate participations. Within each of these major classifications there were numerous subdivisions. Some firms specialized in municipals; others, such as Halsey, Stuart, limited themselves to bonds. In 1938 this firm was second only to Morgan Stanley in the number of issues it managed and sixth in the amount of its syndicate participations.[110]

During the 1930's approximately 700 houses originated and underwrote securities, and more than 2,500 participated in selling groups. The total number of firms in the industry, however, was considerably larger. In 1934, according to one compilation, there were 6,800 security dealers in the United States, or some 350 more than there had been before the stock market crash.[111] Most of the country's investment banking business, however, still was conducted by a very few firms.

Many reasons accounted for this high degree of concentration.

---

108. "Investment Banker: 1939," 79; Haven, *Investment Banking,* 133; IBA, *Fiftieth Anniversary, 1912–1962,* 15.

109. *The Wall Street Journal,* March 18, 1940. The "average capital employed 1934–1939" of the eight firms was listed as follows: Kuhn, Loeb & Co. $16 million, Mellon Securities Corp. $12 million, The First Boston Corp. $11 million; Smith, Barney, & Co. $10 million, Morgan Stanley & Co., Inc. $8 million, Harriman, Ripley & Co. $7 million, Dillon, Read & Co. $6 million, and Blyth & Co. $4 million.

110. "Investment Banker: 1939," 80, 115. In 1938 issues managed by Morgan Stanley and Halsey, Stuart amounted to $456.3 million and $296.8 million, respectively. The top syndicate participant that year was The First Boston Corp., $87.9 million, followed by Morgan Stanley, $83.8 million; Harriman, Ripley, $81.5 million; Smith, Barney, $66.3 million; Bonbright, $51.4 million; and Halsey, Stuart, $50.9 million. See also "Wall Street, Itself," *Fortune,* XV (June 1937), 74.

111. There are few exact figures on the number of firms. Membership in the IBA, which included most of the principal houses, ranged from a low of 495 in 1934 to a high of 796 in 1937, dropping slightly to 754 in 1938 and 734 in 1939. See IBA, *Proceedings* for these years; "Investment Banker: 1939," 79. Consult also *History of NASD,* 19; Irwin Friend, James R. Longstreet *et al., Investment Banking and the New Issues Market* (Cleveland, 1967), 94. See also other references in n. 39 of this chapter.

One of the more important and obvious reasons was that many of the largest corporations were domiciled in New York City; another was the oligopolistic structure of American industry generally.[112] Not everyone, however, was persuaded by these explanations. Some highly knowledgeable observers, including a few investment bankers outside New York City, attributed this concentration to investment banking practices and the close business and personal relationships that existed among the leading bankers and between them and the heads of the great corporations they served.[113] On March 24, 1937, Commissioner William O. Douglas of the SEC, in what came to be one of his most famous speeches, told the Bond Club of New York, much to the discomfiture of its members, that there was too little competition in the investment banking industry.[114] Many others shared this view. The legislative changes brought about by the New Deal, these critics argued, had been too slight and too few. Not surprisingly, therefore, by the end of the decade investment bankers were under investigation once again.

112. J. Fred Weston, *The Economics of Competitive Bidding in the Sale of Securities* (Chicago, 1943), 6–7.
113. *Ibid.*, 8–17. See also Donald J. Emblen, *Competitive Bidding for Corporate Securities* (Canton, N.Y., 1944), 26–33; Jacob O. Kamm, *The Decentralization of Securities Exchanges* (Boston, 1942), 130–32.
114. Douglas, *Democracy and Finance,* 32–45. See also *The New York Times,* March 25, 1937.

19 Pujo Revisited: The TNEC

Early in 1938 investment bankers again faced federal probers. This time, however, they played a relatively minor role in the drama. Big business generally, rather than Wall Street specifically, occupied the center of the stage. The inquiry, moreover, was not concerned with disclosing wrongdoings, though some were uncovered. Its primary purpose was to investigate monopoly. Brandeisian liberals among the New Dealers blamed big business and its Wall Street allies for the acute economic decline of August 1937. These monopolists, it was claimed, had restrained capital investments (contemporaries called it a "strike of capital") in order to embarrass the administration and stymie needed reforms. The Temporary National Economic Committee (TNEC), which conducted the probe, the most comprehensive since those of the Industrial Commission and Pujo, reflected many of the same fears and suspicions that had motivated the earlier scrutinies. Some of the questions TNEC examiners asked investment bankers were almost identical to those Samuel Untermyer and his staff had asked the elder Morgan twenty-five years before. The replies often were similar.

The most striking difference between Pujo and the TNEC was, of course, the political and economic environment in which the two investigations were conducted. Unlike 1912, the climate of 1938 was one of depression, government regulation, partisan politics, and the airing of some flagrant business and financial abuses. Many of the New Deal's regulatory statutes were being implemented, amended, or protested.

One of the major areas of controversy between Washington and Wall Street concerned the stock exchanges. Since its establishment, the Securities and Exchange Commission (SEC) had urged the exchanges to revise and improve their practices. In 1937 Commissioner William O. Douglas warned that there would be federal administration unless the exchanges were managed in the public interest. He condemned "high finance" as practiced by "financial termites" interested only in immediate profits and engaged in siphoning off money from investors and business. And he extended his list of guilty even to include teachers. "Academic economists have tried to endow cycles and crises . . . with natural attributes. In this way they have cleverly washed the hands of high finance and excused it from social responsibility." [1]

Winthrop W. Aldrich of the Chase National Bank, on the other hand, blamed government policies for the recent stock market break. Taxes and regulation both were at fault. New margin requirements

1. William O. Douglas, *Democracy and Finance* (New Haven, 1940), 8–11.

were excessive and were having the opposite effect from the one intended, for they were increasing speculation rather than curbing it. "Few informed investors," he said, "are free from apprehension regarding the long-run consequences of policies already inaugurated or of policies proposed." [2]

Although some regional exchanges had revised certain of their procedures, the Old Guard on the New York Stock Exchange refused to adopt similar measures to increase the protection of investors or to police its members more effectively. Led by Richard Whitney, the exchange's five-time president, the conservatives on its board believed further reform unnecessary and that Washington was too weak to enforce changes. In January 1938 a proposed new constitution was opposed by Whitney.

Events then moved quickly and spectacularly. On March 11 Whitney was indicted for grand larceny; a week later the exchange adopted a new constitution incorporating the SEC's suggested reforms.

The reorganization of the exchange brought to an end the "small private club" atmosphere that Douglas said had dominated this market. The leadership was democratized and provision was made for public representation on the board of governors and for a salaried president. The first man to occupy this post was William McChesney Martin, Jr., a thirty-four-year-old St. Louis investment banker, who had participated in drafting the constitution.[3]

Reorganization of the New York Stock Exchange occurred just at the time the White House decided to revive the antitrust laws. On April 29, President Roosevelt asked Congress to establish the TNEC. It found a receptive climate on Capitol Hill, where similar proposals already had been introduced.

The investigation's objectives received widely differing interpretations. Liberals hoped it would lead to an overall attack on monopoly and bigness. Others placed the probe in the context of depression and politics. They described it as "the product of a mood of deep despair over both the justice and the efficiency of our economic arrangements. . . . There can be little doubt that, in the hands of a powerful party representing the interests of workers and farmers, this official portrait of our economy would be a powerful, perhaps decisive, political instrument of reform." [4] The president

2. Winthrop W. Aldrich, "The Stock Market from the Viewpoint of a Commercial Banker," an address at a meeting of the Rochester Chamber of Commerce, October 14, 1937, 6.
3. Robert Sobel, *The Big Board* (New York, 1965), 307; Ralph F. De Bedts, *The New Deal's SEC* (New York, 1964), 163–66.
4. Moses Abramovitz, "Savings and Investment: Profits *vs.* Prosperity?" *American Economic Review,* Suppl., XXXII (June 1942), 53. On the origins of the TNEC see also Ellis W. Hawley, *The New Deal and the Problem of Monopoly: A Study in Economic Ambivalence* (Princeton, 1966), 402–06, 409–15.

himself, however, had made no broad commitments of any kind.

Roosevelt's message indicated the range of subjects he believed required examination. Included among these were several directly affecting investment banking practices. He cited the following for specific criticism:[5]

Industrial empire building, unfortunately, has evolved into banker control of industry. We oppose that.

Such control does not offer safety for the investing public. Investment judgment requires the disinterested appraisal of other people's management. It becomes blurred and distorted if it is combined with the conflicting duty of controlling the management it is supposed to judge.

Interlocking financial controls have taken from American business much of its traditional virility, independence, adaptability, and daring — without compensating advantages. They have not given the stability they promised.

Business enterprise needs new vitality and the flexibility that comes from the diversified efforts, independent judgments, and vibrant energies of thousands upon thousands of independent businessmen.

The individual must be encouraged to exercise his own judgment and to venture his own small savings, not in stock gambling but in new enterprise investment. Men will dare to compete against men but not against giants.

Participating in the overall TNEC investigation were congressmen and several federal departments and commissions. Among these were the Justice, Treasury, Labor, and Commerce departments, the SEC, and the Federal Trade Commission (FTC).[6] The TNEC held hearings in 1939 and 1940 which, when published (1940–41), filled tens of thousands of pages. In addition, two *Reports* on the hearings were published in 1941. Furthermore, in order to provide supplementary and reportorial material, the committee had forty-three monographs prepared, based in part on the hearings.

Interrogation of investment bankers received relatively little publicity. The hearings were staged under the auspices of the SEC in December 1939 and January 1940. Although over 1,600 pages of testimony and exhibits resulted, the final report contained little specific reference to investment banking, and none of the monographs was devoted to it. The one titled *Savings, Investment, and National Income,* however, did give about four pages to the subject, partly based on the hearings.[7] Moreover, when the hearings were completed, in the spring of 1940, Senator Joseph O'Mahoney, the Wyoming Democrat who headed the TNEC, announced that final

---

5. U.S. Temporary National Economic Committee, *Investigation of Concentration of Economic Power: Final Report and Recommendations . . .* (Washington, 1941), 13.
6. *Ibid.,* 735.
7. U.S. TNEC, *Monograph No. 37: Saving, Investment, and National Income* (Washington, 1941), 61–65.

reports would not be published until late fall so as to avoid involvement in the political campaign.[8]

Questioning of investment bankers by the committee revealed much about the conduct of the industry and the attitudes of the interrogators. It was conducted chiefly by Peter R. Nehemkis, Jr., a young graduate of the Yale Law School. He was the committee's special counsel for this part of the investigation. In anticipation of the hearings, he prepared a summary of his intended approach to the issue of monopoly and the scope of his questioning. The focal point of the inquiry, he believed, should be the financial mechanism of the country's economic system, which he assumed had failed to function properly in the recent depression and even in the more distant past. His chief purpose, he said, would be to lay a foundation for the creation of a system that would accomplish the objective of supplying funds for the production of capital goods through the sale of securities. He anticipated that public hearings revealing "incidental abuses of the banking business" would be interesting "only as drama and should remain subordinate to the primary objectives." [9]

For his investigation, Nehemkis prepared the following outline of the facts he intended to elicit:[10]

(1) The actual flow of capital through the capital markets from 1922 to the present. . . .
(2) The sources from which capital obtained through such financing were derived. . . .
(3) The stream of capital financing dropped rapidly commencing in 1932 and has never recovered full volume. . . . [why?]
(4) The amount and the source of government spending which went to fill the gap. . . .
(5) The analysis as of today: where does existing financing go. . . . ?
(6) The functions performed by the investment banker with particular reference to the following:
   (a) The judgment exercised by the investment banker when his aid is sought. Does he look for new construction? Or for the economic value of the construction? Or for the strategic position of the enterprise which he is asked to finance? Or for its real productivity? Or merely for the probability that the bonds can be sold?
   (b) Does the banker play any part in working up and assembling a productive enterprise? In some cases he did for better or for worse; in some cases he did not but merely passed judgment upon projects brought to him.

8. *The Commercial & Financial Chronicle*, CL (February 10, 1940), 923.
9. Peter R. Nehemkis, Jr., "Confidential Memorandum to Benjamin V. Cohen," February 7, 1939. National Archives, Record Group No. 48, Office File of Benjamin V. Cohen, General Counsel, National Power Policy Committee, 1934–1941, Box 10 — Legislative Projects, Folder: "Monopoly Studies," 1.
10. *Ibid.*, 2–6.

(c) It is said that the bankers provide management. Did they? To the extent that they do, is there any other method by which management can be provided?
(d) What of underwriting spreads and competitive bidding?
(7) The relation of investment banking to commercial banks. . . .

Leon Henderson, the SEC lawyer who initiated the hearings, indicated the investigation would be far less comprehensive and that the focus would be different from what Nehemkis originally had intended. Henderson defined the extent of coverage of data and testimony as limited to the following three categories: "(1) The manner in which the investment banking processes have been adjusted to conform with the provisions of the Banking Act of 1933, (2) the extent to which concentration exists in the industry, and (3) the manner in which business is negotiated between underwriters and issuers and among underwriters." He emphasized that the industry and not individuals or firms would be discussed and that activities of small dealers would be excluded. One aspect for special investigation would be the measures investment bankers had taken to separate from their affiliates as of June 1934, the effective date under the Banking Act of 1933.[11]

Individuals from twenty-one commercial banks, trust companies, and investment firms were called to testify. They were examined on documents that had been taken from their private files by the federal investigators after exhaustive searches. Present were men from parent and spun-off firms.[12]

The questioners gave a kind of testimonial to the cooperation of the bankers in making documents available to the investigators. Henderson said, and Nehemkis concurred, "I think one other thing might be said at this time which I have wanted to say. Generally there has been associated with the banking inquiries, with anything banking, a certain amount of feeling about exercise of influence upon the investigators and upon the people responsible for the presentation. . . . Despite the fact that we have touched many of the most important investment banking houses in this country, no improper influence or pressure of any kind whatsoever, political or economic, has been attempted to be exercised on this staff." [13]

Although three major topics for exploration were specified, they

11. U.S. Temporary National Economic Committee, *Investigation of Concentration of Economic Power: Hearings* . . . (31 pts., Washington, 1939–41), pt. 22, 11383–84.
12. The list of firms was as follows: Bankers Trust Co.; Blyth & Co., Inc.; Bonbright & Co.; Brown Bros. Harriman & Co.; H. M. Byllesby & Co.; Dillon, Read & Co.; The First Boston Corp.; The First National Bank of N. Y.; Glore, Forgan & Co.; Goldman, Sachs & Co.; Halsey, Stuart & Co., Inc.; Harriman, Ripley & Co.; Kidder, Peabody & Co.; Kuhn, Loeb & Co.; Lazard Frères & Co.; Lee, Higginson Corp.; Lehman Bros.; J. P. Morgan & Co.; Morgan Stanley & Co., Inc.; Schroder, Rockefeller & Co., Inc.; Smith, Barney & Co.
13. U.S. TNEC, *Hearings*, pt. 24, 12546.

really overlapped. One test for conformance was whether spun-off firms "inherited proprietary interests" in accounts from predecessor firms. Such inheritance also tied in with the question of concentration within a few firms as well as relations with issuers and fellow investment bankers—maintenance of "historical positions" in flotations. Other phrases that became the catchwords of the hearings and were believed to carry connotations of concentration were "frozen accounts," "crystallized accounts," and "traditional bankers"; even "gentlemen's agreements" became sinister.

One thoroughly explored aspect of conformance was whether investment banking functions had been separated from commercial banking after 1934. Witnesses were quizzed exhaustively about technical, as contrasted with the actual, divorcement. Questioners used four criteria to test the actuality of separation: Did individuals in a predecessor firm hold a substantial investment in a spun-off firm, even if the two were separate legal entities and investment was not accompanied by exercise of potential control? Had new investment banking firms inherited, or did they expect to inherit, clients (issuers) of predecessor firms? Was a traditional-banker relationship continued? Had new firms maintained deposit accounts with former affiliates, and did they still have access to their files?

Many of the documents cited by TNEC lawyers tended to show that bankers did indeed hold the concept of inheritance and believed that they *should*. But the bankers protested that competition among new (and old) firms actually had become intense, in part because there were conflicting claimant heirs. Since there had been a considerable amount of shuffling of displaced individuals among new firms, the lines of inheritance had become blurred, and many witnesses asserted that if there was an inheritor, it was the man who had done the negotiating with clients and not his former firm.

Of the two more important, old established firms, J. P. Morgan & Co. and Kuhn, Loeb & Co., the latter had elected to remain an investment banker and the separateness issue did not arise. For the Morgan firm, however, the question was pursued at length over the separateness of Morgan Stanley & Co., Inc., and J. P. Morgan & Co., a partnership. The two new firms were headed by partners of the former Morgan and Drexel houses, but there was no overlapping in directors or officers. Ownership of the stock of Morgan Stanley, however, the investigators contended, indicated that control still lay with the Morgan house at 23 Wall Street, despite the latter firm's legal opinion asserting separateness.[14] The controversy arose over the ownership of preferred stock in the Morgan Stanley corporation. Its outstanding capital at its organization in September 1935 consisted of 70,000 shares of 6 percent preferred ($100 par) and

14. *Ibid.*, pt. 23, 12318–20. Letter of Davis Polk Wardwell Gardiner & Reed to J. P. Morgan & Co., September 13, 1935.

50,000 shares of common ($5 par). Partners in J. P. Morgan had taken 66,000 shares of preferred, and Henry S. Morgan, treasurer and secretary of Morgan Stanley, and William Ewing, a director, had taken the remainder. The preferred stock carried no voting rights except as provided by the New York Stock Corporation law. All the common stock was held by directors and officers of the corporation.

Legal opinion also asserted that business divorcement was complete and that the corporation should be considered free to use the banking services of the partnership as it was free to use those of any other commercial bank. The questioners, however, offered exhibits showing that in the trade there were individuals who believed that the new corporation was a continuation of the original Morgan partnership and, furthermore, that it would "fall heir" to important accounts.[15]

The issue of continuing control through stock ownership in a spun-off company arose in other instances, as in the case of Brown Brothers, Harriman & Co., and Brown, Harriman & Co., later Harriman Ripley & Co., Inc. Again the principles maintained that they did not exercise the potential control that went with stock ownership.

In contrast to the relatively clear split of individuals of the Morgan firm was the situation of the National City Co., affiliate of the National City Bank. Here the question of separation was tied to inheritance of accounts. Partners of National City Co. scattered; some went to Blyth & Co., some to Brown, Harriman, and some to Lazard Frères. Acceptance of the theory of inheritance, but question of its application, were indicated in this excerpt from a letter from a vice president of Blyth in 1936, offered as evidence at the hearing:[16]

As a matter of fact, no New York firm has inherited the right to the National City Company business. Brown, Harriman & Co. have in their organization a number of former National City men, but Brown Bros., Harriman & Co., the banking firm who started their investment banking business with a union of former Brown Bros. and National City men, paid nothing to the National City stockholders for the Company's good will, and have positively no claim of inheritance. Other investment banking firms, also, are now manned by former National City men, including our own firm—not only in New York but scattered across the country. . . . Mr. Mitchell, the Chairman of our Board, was formerly the head of the National City Company and of the National City Bank, and is responsible for the development of the National City Company from a three man personnel to a point where it had become the largest organization of its kind in the country, all of which was entirely under his leadership. He, in fact, was ultimately responsible for the negotiation and consummation of the pieces of financing which the National City Company did. It would defi-

15. *Ibid.*, pt. 22, 11553–54.
16. *Ibid.*, pt. 22, 11492.

nitely appear, therefore, that if there is any claim for the National City business as a heritage, that we could make such a claim — perhaps on better grounds than any other investment banking firm.

Still another opinion was that inheritance existed, but that the heirs to National City Co.'s business were Brown, Harriman and Lazard Frères. Joseph Ripley, formerly executive vice president of National City Co., which he described as the "finest investment banking organization" existing, went to Brown, Harriman. He was one who believed that corporations issuing securities would do business with "people with whom they had successfully and satisfactorily done business in the past." [17]

Other bankers were inclined to scoff at quoted documents that referred to inheritance. They insisted that the word meant little and that getting a client now was a highly competitive process in which use of such an argument was only a form of sales pressure or a matter of no significance.[18]

Queries concerning the extent of concentration of the investment banking business in the hands of a few firms attempted to bring out that a virtual monopoly was held by a small group. Proof of the validity of the claim included demonstrations that certain firms tended to continue to underwrite securities for certain issuers or appeared to dictate who should be invited to serve. The point was closely related to inheritance.

As examples of continuing control by a few bankers over certain issuers' flotations, the cases of American Telephone and Telegraph Company (AT&T) and Pacific Gas and Electric Company (PG&E) were cited, among others. A small group of firms over a long period had, in fact, held the same or nearly the same percentages of participations in the bond issues of AT&T and its affiliated companies. Some of the supporting data offered in evidence was carried back to the 1870's. "Proprietary interests" had been a phrase used by Kidder, Peabody & Co. to apply to the percentage allotments to the seven principal underwriters of AT&T issues, shown as follows in a list for September 19, 1918, taken from Kidder, Peabody files and produced by the questioners.[19]

J. P. Morgan & Co.	25
First National Bank [of N.Y.]	10
Kuhn, Loeb & Co.	$13\frac{1}{2}$
National City Bank	10
Harris, Forbes & Co., Inc.	5
Lee, Higginson & Co.	5
Kidder, Peabody & Co.	$31\frac{1}{2}$
	100

17. *Ibid.*, pt. 22, 11417.
18. *Ibid.*, pt. 22, 11494–95.
19. *Ibid.*, pt. 23, 12211, Exhibit No. 1672.

The document also gave Kidder, Peabody's subdistribution of its share.

The phrase "proprietary interest" apparently had limited circulation, however. George Whitney, who had been a clerk with Kidder, Peabody before going to Morgan in 1916, testified that he had not heard the expression before it came up at the hearings and did not know where it came from. Nor was Albert H. Gordon, partner of the new Kidder, Peabody firm, familiar with the phrase, but he thought it might have been a colorful invention of Robert Winsor, the house's former head. And Gordon had not been aware of its practical application. On the other hand, it was not new to John R. Chapin, who had been a partner in the old Kidder, Peabody firm. He said the phrase was customarily applied there to the percentage participations in AT&T issues.[20]

The continuing fixed nature of the percentages was documented with an impressive collection of figures. The compilation indicated that between 1920 and 1930 the Morgan firm had headed fourteen issues for AT&T and its associated companies, totaling nearly $800 million. For each of these syndicates, the following underwriting percentages had applied:[21]

J. P. Morgan & Co.	20.00
First National Bank	10.00
National City Co.	10.00
Kuhn, Loeb & Co.	10.75
Harris, Forbes & Co.	5.00
Lee, Higginson & Co.	5.00
Guaranty Co.	4.75
Bankers Trust Co.	4.75
Kidder, Peabody & Co.	29.75
	100.00

TNEC interrogators contended that the pre-1934 relationships had continued thereafter. One witness held that after 1934 some groups were "more frozen" than others and that AT&T underwriters were one of these. There had been so-called "crystallization" of groups under Morgan Stanley comparable with those under Morgan.[22]

The seven firms listed in Exhibit 15 held the seven top positions in advertisements offering the securities. They were not the sole underwriters, however; for one issue there had been 9, and for another, 97. This list reflected changes in firms resulting from the 1934 divorces and lines of inheritance. Morgan Stanley replaced J. P. Morgan; Kuhn, Loeb was unchanged; Kidder, Peabody and Lee,

---

20. *Ibid.*, pt. 23, 11876, 11942–43, 11865.
21. *Ibid.*, pt. 23, 12234, Exhibit No. 1687.
22. *Ibid.*, pt. 22, 11570–71.

Exhibit 15. Financing of American Telephone and Telegraph Company and associated companies by Morgan Stanley & Co., Inc., 1935-1938

Firm	Ten issues of AT&T and associated companies									
A. Percentage allocations of the seven principal underwriters										
Morgan Stanley & Co., Inc.	31.0	30.4	30.0	16.6	14.3	30.0	17.6	32.0	18.0	18.0
Kuhn, Loeb & Co.	15.5	15.2	15.0	8.3	7.1	15.0	8.8	16.0	9.0	9.0
Kidder, Peabody & Co.	12.1	11.6	10.0	6.7	5.7	10.0	7.1	12.8	7.2	7.4
Lee, Higginson Corp.	5.7	5.2	5.0	4.0	3.4	5.0	3.5	6.4	3.6	3.6
First Boston Corp.	10.4	9.8	7.7	6.0	5.1	7.6	5.9	10.4	6.3	6.2
Brown, Harriman & Co., Inc.	9.2	8.6	7.7	6.0	5.1	7.6	5.9	10.4	6.3	6.2
Edward B. Smith & Co. (Smith, Barney & Co.)	9.2	8.6	7.7	6.0	5.1	7.6	5.9	10.4	6.3	6.2
B. Participation of the seven principal underwriters in relation to participation of Morgan Stanley & Co., Inc.										
Morgan Stanley & Co., Inc.	100.0	100.0	100.0	100.0	100.0	100.0	100.0	100.0	100.0	100.0
Kuhn, Loeb & Co.	50.0	50.0	50.0	50.0	50.0	50.0	50.0	50.0	50.0	50.0
Kidder, Peabody & Co.	39.0	38.0	33.3	40.0	40.0	33.3	40.0	40.0	40.0	40.4
Lee, Higginson Corp.	18.4	17.2	16.7	24.0	24.0	16.7	20.0	20.0	20.0	20.2
First Boston Corp.	33.1	32.1	25.6	36.0	36.0	25.4	33.3	32.5	35.0	34.6
Brown, Harriman & Co., Inc.	29.4	28.3	25.6	36.0	36.0	25.4	33.3	32.5	35.0	34.6
Edward B. Smith & Co. (Smith, Barney & Co.)	29.4	28.3	25.6	36.0	36.0	25.4	33.3	32.5	35.0	34.6

Source: U.S. TNEC, *Hearings*, pt. 23, 12244–49. Compiled from Exhibit Nos. 1703 and 1704.

Higginson were the old firms renewed; The First Boston Corporation had taken in some of the Harris, Forbes personnel. To Brown, Harriman had gone many individuals from National City Co. And a large number of individuals from the dissolved Guaranty Co. had gone to Edward B. Smith & Co., which merged with Charles D. Barney & Co. in December 1937 to become Smith, Barney & Co. If this was inheritance, the questioners made the most of it.

The formidable display of documentation relating to inheritance of the business of floating securities for PG&E, the large West Coast utility, raised some similar and some different issues. For several years the company's underwriters had been headed by Blyth, originally a San Francisco firm. Then National City Co. had obtained leadership and still held it when it was dissolved. Since National City's personnel were dispersed, lines of inheritance were not clear. A test case rose in an issue of $45 million 4 percent PG&E bonds in 1935. Stanley A. Russell, previously vice president of National City and its chief negotiator for industrial and public utility securities, had joined Lazard Frères and obtained leadership in this financing for his firm. He did not "claim" the account, he said, but he had hoped to get it. He had had close relations with the past and current presidents of PG&E in negotiating issues for National City.

Actively competing for this business in 1935 was Blyth, which hoped to regain its former position and was now headed by Charles E. Mitchell, former head of National City. Of particular importance to Blyth at this time was restoration of its top position in this business, as well as public recognition as a house of issue in the post-1934 financial world. Furthermore, Blyth executives believed that the make-up of the underwriting syndicate for this issue and the relative positions of members would set a pattern for future syndicates. A letter from George Lieb, vice president of Blyth, to James Black, vice president of North American Company, a substantial stockholder in PG&E, used many of the now familiar phrases and implied relationships. Two participants in former syndicates, he said, wanted Blyth to be "heirs to their sixteen per cent interest in the Pacific Gas business. This, coupled with our historic connection with the business, would appear to entitle us to head this account, particularly in view of the fact that the old National City Company has no heir (according to public statement of its president, James Perkins); and further in view of the fact that even if there is an heir, the legacy has been split between Brown Harriman and Lazard Frères." [23]

Lieb offered the following list of firms and percentages as the most logical and most likely the best to serve PG&E for the new issue: [24]

Blyth & Co., Inc.	37
Brown, Harriman & Co.	19
Lazard Frères	19
First Boston Corp.	$7\frac{1}{2}$
E. B. Smith & Co.	$7\frac{1}{2}$
Witter & Co.	5
E. H. Rollins & Sons	5

He also offered a revised allocation that would recognize the acknowledged friendship of the president and Russell, and gave the top three 25 percent apiece. His letter added more sales arguments for Blyth. When questioned about it at the hearings, he described the letter as merely sales pressure.

In the distribution of an issue of $25 million PG&E bonds in 1930 and another in 1931, the underwriters and percentages had been as follows: [25]

	1930	1931
National City Co. (Manager)	32.50	35.00
Blyth & Co., Inc., N.Y.	20.00	22.50
American Securities Co., S. F.	16.25	16.25
H. M. Byllesby & Co., Chicago	16.25	16.25
E. H. Rollins & Sons, N.Y.	7.50	5.00
Peirce Fair & Co., S. F.	7.50	5.00

23. *Ibid.*, pt. 22, 11666–67, Exhibit 1606.
24. *Ibid.*, pt. 22, 11495.
25. *Ibid.*, pt. 22, 11662–63, Exhibits 1602 and 1603. The figure for Blyth given in text page 11495 is 37 percent Exhibit 1602 gives 29 percent.

Although the concepts of inheritance and frozen accounts appeared to be held by various individuals concerned, Blyth executives also recognized that direct pressure on the issuer was necessary in order to make the concepts effective. The direct pressures of Russell on the president of PG&E won out, for Lazard Frères headed the syndicate, with Blyth and Brown, Harriman fighting for second place and finally sharing it: Blyth in the West and Brown, Harriman in the East. But a different set of direct pressures succeeded in Blyth's displacing Lazard in the subsequent issue. There also was some turnover in the make-up of that syndicate.

Exploring the question of the traditional-banker relationships and segregation of functions in successor firms brought out evidence concerning continued contacts of issuers with both the commercial and the investment banking groups after 1934. Commercial bankers were asked whether they continued to give their services to customers and the nature of such services. George Whitney described the functions that a commercial banker could be expected to perform for former clients while still complying with the 1933 act. He could recommend to them the names of underwriting houses "best equipped to handle their business," he believed; this was as much a function of a banker as giving advice is that of a physician. The banker also should keep track of customers' day-to-day financial needs and know when to call in a specialist. After the passage of the Banking Act, issuers especially needed such services because the investment banking business had been "torn to pieces" — new firms had been organized and their capabilities and capitals were untried. It had become routine for bankers to give clients advice regarding issues and suitable investment bankers. He believed that it was apparent that such advice to a client in no way put the banker in the business of "issuing, underwriting, selling, or distributing securities," functions prohibited by the act.[26]

Many of the testifying investment bankers also chose to liken their advisory functions to those of lawyers or other professional men and to draw the analogy of the importance of continuing relationships. Some were intent on showing also that the business was highly competitive; they answered the apparent ethical conflict with the argument that the client should continue relations with his banker as long as they were satisfactory, as with a lawyer.

Harold L. Stuart's view of changed competitive circumstances after 1933 was that formerly it had been the custom for a corporation to choose the investment banking firm it wanted to do business with and to stay with it. After 1933, he said, "it has been anybody's business."[27] And Mitchell testified: "This is a monopoly investiga-

---

26. *Ibid.*, pt. 23, 12317–18. Letter of George Whitney to Leon Henderson, January 25, 1940, amplifying earlier testimony.
27. *Ibid.*, pt. 23, 11938.

tion. My long experience on the Street tells me that the investment banking business is a dog fight. There is no monopoly about it, gentlemen." [28]

Witnesses presented much evidence of real competition for accounts; yet there also was evidence of "reciprocal obligations" honored by firms that customarily had been in syndicates together in the past. The questioners probed this aspect of the alleged concentration of financing among a few firms, holding that a system of reciprocity gave firms a proprietary interest in one another's flotations. At the first session in January 1940, Leon Henderson indicated the tenor of the questioners' understanding of what the evidence showed. He said, in part: "[Earlier] evidence was offered with respect to a number of 'understandings' existing between various underwriting firms. . . . In my considered opinion, the testimony on agreements and understandings . . . is highly significant. These treaties, agreements, and understandings are the sinews of the prevailing method of doing business; they form the framework of banker-issuer relations and are the essence of the system of negotiated prices." [29]

To demonstrate domination by bankers of a corporation's financial policy, examiners explored situations in which investment bankers sat on directorates of client companies. Some committee members held this traditional practice to be one way in which the money power was concentrated in investment banking firms. The point remained moot, however, some witnesses asserting their impartiality although the opportunity for using influence was clearly present. Walter E. Sachs of Goldman, Sachs & Co., when asked whether it was the policy of his partners never to participate in discussions of financial matters on the boards on which they served, replied: "It seems to me that is absolutely a, b, c." [30] He previously had stated that bankers had taken directorships because they had sold the securities of the issuers and felt that they represented the interests of the public. "In many instances," he said, "we probably could not have sold the securities as successfully if we had not indicated that we were going on the board because the general American public in these early years was not as investment minded." This was especially true in the case of stock offerings, Sachs said. "We considered it an element of strength all around to go onto these boards, and it became a very common practice in our instance." [31]

The Cluett, Peabody Company, whose bankers had been Lehman Brothers and Goldman, Sachs, expressed a different view of issuer-banker interaction. These two investment banking firms for years

28. *Ibid.,* pt. 22, 11566.
29. *Ibid.,* pt. 24, 12343–44.
30. *Ibid.,* pt. 24, 12401.
31. *Ibid.,* pt. 24, 12357.

had maintained traditional bankers' relationships with clients and with one another in an agreement for joint managements of issues of specified corporations, including Cluett, Peabody, manufacturer of famous Arrow shirts and other men's wear. Inherent in this situation was the practice of having representatives of the two investment banking firms on the directorates. "At the time the present company was organized through the joint efforts of Lehman Brothers and Goldman, Sachs and Co., a representative of each banking firm was elected to the board," George A. Cluett recalled. "It was clearly understood at the time that each firm would have a voice in the financial affairs of the company and that any new financing that the company might be called upon to do in the future would be handled by both firms." [32]

This long-standing arrangement between Goldman, Sachs and Lehman Brothers was broken in 1936 for a variety of reasons, some attributable to the 1933 banking law. It appeared now that a single manager was more efficient for handling registration procedures, and Goldman, Sachs won out. Lehman Brothers made a strong effort to hold joint management and refused to take second place because it would lose prestige as well as the management fee. Relations between the firms became strained. But in 1938 the bankers reached a new agreement under which the allocation of position in advertisements and management fee again were specified for issues of the several corporations for which the firms were expecting to continue to act as investment bankers. Charging a management fee for placing issues had become increasingly common after passage of the 1933 act; the amount of work preparatory to registration now became large and generally was centered in one firm.[33]

Although competitive bidding was not a stated issue in the TNEC investigation, the subject arose frequently. There was a theory that if it were used it could break the alleged monopoly in investment banking. Henderson had assured several bankers, who currently were in controversy with the SEC or one another, that the subject would not be brought up before the committee, since it was being reviewed by other federal agencies. He objected strenuously when Harold Stanley wished to present a memorandum on the subject. Stanley, however, was prepared to debate the issue and presented a few arguments against it in his testimony on the AT&T accounts. Other bankers did the same in other instances.

Stanley believed that both the issuing corporation and the investor were better off without competitive bidding. When it was used, he declared, "casual intermittent connections" between issuer and banker resulted; issuers failed to receive the professional advice

32. *Ibid.*, pt. 24, 12738–39, Exhibit No. 1815. Letter from George A. Cluett to Sanford L. Cluett, May 13, 1937.
33. *Ibid.*, pt. 24, 12382.

of bankers; bankers had to take an issue as presented or pass it up; and it tended to overprice issues and result in poorer securities. As for its relation to concentration, competitive bidding would rule out small dealers and tend to concentrate business in the larger ones.[34] Joseph R. Swan, of Smith, Barney, held that competitive bidding would materially lower the standards of the investment business and increase concentration; furthermore, it would increase the price and lower the quality of the goods. Making use of the professional services of investment bankers, he believed, was much to be preferred.[35]

Chicago Union Station Company provided an example of the failure of an attempt to use competitive bidding. In 1940 it wished to market a $16 million bond issue. At the suggestion of the ICC, it tried this method and invited bids from 107 banking, insurance, and savings funds companies, but only one firm, Halsey, Stuart, accepted. Terms of the bid being unsatisfactory to the issuer, it rejected the bid. The company at once negotiated the sale through Kuhn, Loeb, from whom it already had received advice about terms for such an issue suitable for that particular time and purpose. Several letters were introduced at the hearings from bankers who had declined the offer to submit a bid. One reply stated that it was the firm's policy not to engage in competitive bidding except for state and municipal obligations; and one was "definitely opposed" to the procedure. Among the firms that did not reply were all those that subsequently joined with Kuhn, Loeb to market the bonds. There was an implication that there was collusion in their refraining from bidding.

A long statistical presentation, prepared by SEC experts, closed the hearings. It showed a high degree of concentration in the investment banking industry. In October 1938, when the IBA's membership numbered some 730 firms, 38 of these had headed almost 91 percent of the $9.2 billion of registered, managed issues offered in the period January 1934 to June 1939.[36] More important, 6 New York City firms alone managed 57.3 percent ($5.3 billion) of all registered issues sold by investment bankers, and 14 other New York City houses headed issues amounting to an additional 21.3 percent ($2.0 billion).[37] All in all, 20 New York City houses

34. *Ibid.*, pt. 23, 11970.
35. *Ibid.*, pt. 24, 12538.
36. U.S. TNEC, *Hearings*, pt. 24, 12690–91. Total cash offerings of securities during this period amounted to $36.1 billion, of which $9.6 billion was registered with the SEC. Of the latter amount, $9.2 billion was sold through investment banking firms. The $26.5 billion of nonregistered issues was composed chiefly of securities offered by the federal government and its agencies, $16 billion; state and local governments, $6 billion; common carriers regulated by the ICC, $1.6 billion; and banks, educational, religious, and nonprofit organizations, $1 billion.
37. *Ibid.*, pt. 24, 12691, 12991. The six leading New York City houses and the individual percentage they managed were: Morgan Stanley 23.2 percent, First

managed 78.6 percent of all publicly offered issues registered with the SEC. Of the 21.4 percent ($1.9 billion) managed by firms outside New York City, more than half, 12.1 percent ($1.1 billion), was managed by 18 firms.[38]

In terms of quality of securities offered, as determined by rating organizations like Moody's, the degree of investment banking concentration in New York City was even more pronounced. During the period from January 1, 1934, to June 30, 1939, the country's thirty-eight leading investment houses managed $7.3 billion of bond issues, of which $1.3 billion received top-quality rating. Not a single investment house outside of New York City managed one of these first-grade issues. All of them were headed by the principal New York City firms, eighteen houses in all.[39] One firm alone, Morgan Stanley, accounted for 65 percent of the entire amount; and if allowance is made for the fact that this house did not start in business until September 16, 1934, more than eighteen months after the beginning of this period, its share of the top-quality managements would have been 81 percent.[40]

According to TNEC studies, the importance of non-New York City investment bankers as syndicate managers increased as the quality of the securities decreased. Thus, while eighteen leading firms outside New York City managed only 13.3 percent ($311.2 million) of second-quality bonds, they headed issues amounting to 21.7 percent ($65.5 million) of those rated below fourth grade. Their total bond managements for the entire period, however, amounted only to 13.6 percent ($1.0 billion). The other 86.4 percent ($6.4 billion) was managed by twenty New York City houses, the top six accounting for 65.3 percent.[41] The leadership of these twenty firms was demonstrated further by the TNEC disclosure that they had managed 97.1 percent ($760 million) of the bonds issued by transportation and communication companies; 91.6 percent ($1.8 billion) of those brought out by manufacturing companies; 91.3 percent ($814.8 million) of those offered by companies other than manufacturing or public utilities, but including foreign governments; and 80.3 percent ($3.0 billion) of those issued by electric light and power, gas, and water companies.[42]

A similar degree of concentration existed in the distribution of syndicate participations. During the period from June 1934 to June 1939, the country's eight leading investment houses, all but one

---

Boston 10.7 percent, Dillon, Read 7.4 percent, Kuhn, Loeb 6.7 percent, Smith Barney (E. B. Smith) 5.1 percent, and Blyth 4.2 percent.

38. *Ibid.*, pt. 24, 12991.
39. *Ibid.*, pt. 24, 12695, 12993. Two of the top six New York City houses, Kuhn, Loeb and Blyth, did not manage any first-grade bond issues during these years.
40. *Ibid.*, pt. 24, 12695, 12993.
41. *Ibid.*, pt. 24, 12993.
42. *Ibid.*, pt. 24, 12996–99.

located in New York City, retained for themselves underwriting participations averaging 86 percent of the group's total originations. The participations these firms reserved for themselves in their own managements during these years averaged 56 percent.[43]

The IBA argued that these figures, and other statistics compiled by the SEC, exaggerated the degree of underwriting concentration and minimized the role played by the smaller firms, but its claims were unconvincing.[44] The fact remained, the SEC disclosed in 1939, that in the four and a half years between January 1, 1934, and June 30, 1938, forty investment banking houses headed 94.2 percent in terms of value of all managed issues and held 82.6 percent in terms of value of all underwriting participations.[45]

In contrast to the startling statistical disclosures and the apparent tone of the background and conduct of the hearings, the part of TNEC *Monograph 37* that dealt with investment banking played down the importance of this business in the total machinery of financing American industry. "Investment banking has done its part," it said, "but this part has been subordinate to internal financing and direct investment by individuals." It had done little financing of small or new enterprises, for one thing. Even in 1929, the author estimated, the industry probably was responsible for only a tenth of the total investment in capital goods. And the more recent tendency was for it to be decreasingly important, being superseded by private placement, chiefly with life insurance companies. Investment bankers naturally regretted this cut in their business opportunities and contended that it destroyed capital markets, retarded investment, and fostered unemployment. They blamed the Securities Act of 1933, provisions of which were being found too onerous by issuers. The extent of the change was measured by estimates that 25 percent of all corporate bonds and notes had been placed privately in 1934, whereas in 1940 the proportion had risen to more than 56 percent (see Exhibit 16).[46]

Although private placement of securities was a matter of great current concern to investment bankers, it was not pursued directly at the hearings. It came up only occasionally and incidentally, as in Stanley's testimony on AT&T's private placements. This company had sold many issues to its own stockholders or directly to insurance companies. Since 1935, Stanley reported, the company had sold

43. *Ibid.*, pt. 24, 12706, 12710, 13001–04. The Mellon Securities Corporation of Pittsburgh was the only non-New York City firm in this group. The other seven houses were Morgan Stanley, Kuhn, Loeb, The First Boston Corporation, Blyth, Dillon, Read, Harriman, Ripley, and Smith, Barney.

44. J. Fred Weston, *The Economics of Competitive Bidding in the Sale of Securities* (Chicago, 1943), 1–7.

45. U.S. Securities and Exchange Commission, *Selected Statistics on Securities and on Exchange Markets* (Washington, 1939), A-34, *passim*. See also Weston, *Economics of Competitive Bidding*, 4.

46. U.S. TNEC, *Monograph No. 37*, 61–65.

Exhibit 16. Corporate bonds and notes issued and placed privately, 1934–1940

Year	Aggregate corporate bond and note financing	Private placements	Percentage of aggregate privately placed
	(millions)		
1934 (est.)	456	115	25.2
1935	2,117	335	15.8
1936	4,026	287	7.1
1937	1,673	285	17.0
1938	2,043	802	39.3
1939	1,871	818	43.7
1940 (est.)	2,300	1,300	56.5

Source: U.S. TNEC, *Monograph No. 37, Saving, Investment, and National Income,* 63.

$150 million of securities without the assistance of investment bankers and $580 million through such bankers, namely, Morgan Stanley.[47] In a letter to the committee's special counsel, sent after the hearings were closed, he gave his reasons for believing that the trend to more private placements was resulting from the present securities laws, rather than from the "coming of age of the corporation," as the TNEC staff had asserted. Stanley cited issues totaling $125 million that he knew had been privately placed because of the market risk involved in registration delays, and he referred to others also for substantial amounts.[48]

This letter developed at some length the arguments for and against private placement, but concluded that the *con* arguments were by far the controlling ones. For example, the advantage of time saving, among other things, was offset by such benefits of negotiated sale as the advertising value of wider distribution and the advisory services of investment bankers. He attributed the current lag in investment to both taxation and various other government policies,

47. U.S. TNEC, *Hearings,* pt. 23, 11970–71.
48. The Stanley pamphlet was prepared to submit to the TNEC, but the committee refused to make it part of the record. His firm then circulated 20,000 copies of it to banks, other institutional investors, newspapers, business and financial journals, and individuals who might be called upon by the SEC or other government agencies, such as the FCC, which had come out in favor of regulating the issue of telephone securities. See *U.S. v. Henry S. Morgan et al.,* "Transcript of Trial: Defendants' Motions" (April 16, 1953), 22281–86; *ibid.,* "Plaintiff's Case" (June 18, 1951), 8374–86; U.S. Federal Communications Commission, *Report on Telephone Investigation* (2 vols. Washington, 1939), II, 583–85. Consult also Francis E. Frothingham, "Public Bidding *vs.* Private Sales," *Investment Banking,* IX (June 1939), 19–22; Franklin T. McClintock, "Competitive Bidding," *ibid.,* IX (September 1939), 24–29. The Stanley piece is summarized in "Shop Talk in Public," *Investment Banking,* X (January 1940), 6–11.

including those causing fear of a trend toward socialism in the United States.

Ironically, though the government was once again concerned over concentration of money power in the hands of investment houses and banks, the IBA was expressing great concern over concentration of economic power in Washington. The association saw this trend as not only dangerous, but actually "foreign." And while the TNEC was assuming that syndicate participations were frozen, the IBA was recognizing interfirm conflicts and was trying to improve relationships.

Individuals in the association, furthermore, were constantly being consulted by, and giving advice to, lawmakers and administrators of regulatory agencies in Washington and elsewhere. Yet the association's president in 1938 quoted with strong approval the following remark of Bernard Baruch: "The single missing element is a feeling of security — a belief that money can be spent or invested without confiscation of reasonable profits by inordinate taxation; that American assets will not again be subject to some great arbitrary change in the value of money; that there are to be no further disturbing assaults on business either by some statutory change in the existing business pattern or a general governmental hostility or governmental competitive invasion of existing fields of private enterprise." [49] The president went on to pledge full cooperation of the association with the SEC and other government agencies "to accomplish results beneficial to our country."

At the time of the TNEC hearings the IBA was quite aware of faults in its public image and in the practices of some members. It was critical of certain procedures for placing securities that were being discussed by regulators. In 1938 it adopted a new constitution and bylaws, tightening up on requirements for membership, but it gave up its long-established Business Conduct Committee because it had so little to do. It was only in 1939 that the IBA set up a Committee on Stock Exchange Relations, apparently at this late date feeling not only the need for better communication with the New York exchange but better understanding of common problems. The two groups exchanged views on questions arising as a result of the securities laws as well as other matters. After the New York Stock Exchange adopted its new constitution, the IBA had strong representation on its governing board.

In 1940, with the TNEC investigation well under way, the association recognized its failure to gain public confidence and started a large-scale public relations program. It used professionals and a variety of media. The next year one convention session was broadcast over a nationwide radio network. In efforts to improve internal

---

49. Investment Bankers Association, *Proceedings . . . 1938* (Chicago, 1938), 15.

operations the association tried to deal with such things as complaints of overcompetition among members. One topic at a 1941 IBA "Forum," for instance, focused on improving relations between participants and managers of big syndicates, especially on how to take care of grievances resulting from pressures on investment firms to participate in issues that they did not want. The association vigorously opposed competitive bidding and private placement.

Although the IBA had feared that the public would believe that the TNEC hearings were telling the whole story of investment banking and had sought to be heard, only its president, Emmett F. Connely, had an opportunity to make a brief statement. In March 1940, he wrote Jerome N. Frank, chairman of the SEC, again putting the case for investment bankers. Since the SEC had given its side, he said, the investment bankers should have the same chance. He pointed out that it was "a matter of keen disappointment and much astonishment to this Association and to those who are engaged in investment banking that neither the Securities and Exchange Commission nor the Temporary National Economic Committee has seen to it that investment banking should have a full and free opportunity publicly to present the facts derived from its experience and knowledge of these matters, in its own words and through witnesses of its own choosing." [50]

Responding to some of the criticisms being leveled, Connely pointed out that the profession did compete for clients and customers, but when satisfactory relationships with bankers were established, they were likely to continue because of mutual trust "like most satisfactory relationships in human affairs." Information about most security flotations was not secret, but known to the public quite promptly; successes and failures also were generally known, and reputations were affected accordingly. Many security issues, furthermore, were evaluated by rating services. He also wrote in opposition to competitive bidding except for municipals.[51]

Subsequently, in June 1940, the SEC and the IBA agreed to a joint review of securities legislation in the hope of simplifying the laws and making their operation less costly. They intended to have a bill ready for the next Congress. The emphasis, again, was promotion of the flow of private capital into industry, but the two new elements of competitive bidding and private placement continued to worry the investment bankers.[52]

Later in the year, President Connely had occasion to comment on

50. Emmett F. Connely, *A Reply to the Securities and Exchange Commission Concerning the Underwriting and Sale of Certain Issues of Public Utility Securities, the Law Appertaining Thereto, "Maintenance of Competitive Conditions," Rule U-12 F-2 and Related Matters* (Chicago, 1940), 41.
51. *Ibid.*
52. IBA, *Proceedings . . . 1940*, 7.

TNEC matters, this time in relation to a proposal for government financial aid to small business. He contended that not only were facilities for such aid not needed, but actually would deter the employment of private capital.[53]

In 1940 the IBA expanded its public relations activities to counteract the publicity given the TNEC hearings. It cooperated with the United States Chamber of Commerce to distribute copies of a pamphlet the Chamber had prepared for a nationwide campaign under the general theme "What Helps Business Helps You," and specifically on "The Case for Investment Banking." [54]

The Nation's Business, the Chamber's official publication, came to the defense of investment banking. The periodical presented a series of surveys on this same topic, "The Case for Investment Banking." One of these, quoted at length in the IBA publication *Investment Banking,* spelled out the many service functions of investment bankers and gave the background of voluntary as well as legislative regulation. It put particular emphasis on the investment banker's role of putting savings to work and raised the question of whether government or private enterprise should be responsible for doing this. *The Nation's Business* questioned whether safeguards had proceeded too far and were interfering with the operations of investment banking. It feared that Congress had written the 1933 and 1934 laws too hastily and pointed to the five-year deliberations of a British committee before it had recommended amendments to Britain's Companies laws in 1930. This committee had said: "It appears to us, as a matter of general principle, most undesirable, in order to defeat an occasional wrong-doer, to impose restrictions which would seriously hamper the activities of honest men and would inevitably react upon the prosperity and commerce of the country." [55]

The Nation's Business also criticized several other aspects of the investigation. It denied the validity of the views expressed by Leon Henderson and Adolf A. Berle, Jr., to the TNEC, namely, that private investment no longer could keep the economy functioning and that government banks were needed to supply capital and direct its investment. It belabored the TNEC, furthermore, for the incompleteness of its study of the functioning of investment banking. In addition, the magazine expressed fear that government harassment would stifle private initiative: "The issue at the core of all the issues now facing the American people comes inevitably to the question of the future of free enterprise." [56]

When Stuart Chase, in articles in *Harper's* drew on the hearings

53. *The New York Times,* September 10, 1940.
54. "The Case for Investment Banking," *Investment Banking,* X (March 1940), 4.
55. *Ibid.,* 1–4.
56. *Ibid.,* 4.

to "spin a dismal yarn about a futureless economy and an early demise of investment banking," President Connely replied in the same magazine. He again pointed out the one-sidedness of the hearings. Evidence was readily available, he showed, to demonstrate plans made by industry for placing substantial security issues for productive investment.[57]

Among other comments, two important detailed appraisals of the TNEC's monographs appeared in 1941 and 1942. One was a book sponsored by the National Association of Manufacturers; the second, a series of articles published in the *American Economic Review*.[58] They both found much to criticize in the coverage and points of view of the authors of the monographs. Even the more impartial views shown in the *Review* articles found oversimplifications and distortions. Recommendations, they said, were not consistent with the scope of the testimony or the problems raised. Of the proceedings as a whole, one comment was the inevitable one that the work was completed when the country was "particularly unready to use it," and thus it was better to treat the various findings "not as the political document which it was meant to be, but as a set of academic materials." [59]

The broad outlines of Nehemkis's planned procedures were not perhaps reached, but Leon Henderson's modest three points for inquiry seemed far exceeded. Although the hearings on investment banking and the documents of the TNEC and the responses they brought from critics and defenders did much to expose and explain the inner workings of the industry, the committee made no special report on investment banking and no new laws stemmed from the hearings. The *Final Report* did, however, include some generalizations on the continued nature of monopoly and urged "the vigorous and vigilant enforcement of the antitrust laws, confident that an awakening business conscience will realize the necessity of complete cooperation in the elimination of monopolistic practice." [60]

Despite the mass of business and financial information it collected, the TNEC inquiry proved a disappointment to almost everyone. Foes of monopoly and big business were dissatisfied by the inconclusiveness of the committee's recommendations and its failure to call for forceful antibigness legislation. Businessmen generally and investment bankers particularly were disturbed by the one-

57. "President Connely Answers Chase," *Investment Banking*, X (May 1940), 22–23.
58. John Scoville and Noel Sargent, comps., *Fact and Fancy in the T.N.E.C. Monographs* (New York, 1942); "Temporary National Economic Committee: Reviews of Monographs," *American Economic Review*, XXXI (September 1941), 573–601; "Papers Relating to the Temporary National Economic Committee," *ibid.*, suppl., XXXII (June 1942), 1–132.
59. Abramovitz, "Savings and Investment: Profits *vs.* Prosperity?", 53.
60. U.S. TNEC, *Final Report*, 9.

sidedness of the hearings and the lack of opportunity to present their case to the country more fully and effectively.

Actually, the probe was not entirely valueless. For one thing, it documented several important contemporary business developments. This was made especially apparent during the investment banking phase of the hearings. The ability of the great corporations to finance themselves and the growth of private placements had diminished significantly the role and influence of investment bankers in the economy. Few seemed to appreciate this at the time. What attracted the attention of liberals was the evidence on underwriting concentration, interlocking directorships, and the number of issuers that supposedly were captives of the bankers that financed them. The TNEC's recommendations did nothing to dispel the fears of Brandeisian liberals concerning financial concentration and the alleged abuses of the money power. The evidence amassed during the probe, together with other data accumulated during the debate over the merits of competitive bidding, later were used by the Justice Department in preparing its antitrust suit against seventeen leading investment houses. The TNEC played a significant part in preparing the way for that trial and in sparking the competitive bidding battles of the 1940's.

20 Compulsory Competitive Bidding: Perennial Controversy

Suspicion of and resentment at alleged Wall Street monopolists lay at the bottom of the competitive bidding controversy, the most bitterly fought issue facing investment bankers since the passage of the Securities Act, if not in the entire history of the industry. Proponents held that competitive bidding, whereby issuers sold their securities to the highest bidder, would prevent disposition of new issues from being preempted by a group of monopolists. The controversy reached major dimensions in the late 1930's, was dragged into the TNEC hearings, and was only partially resolved by the 1950's. The battle was fought in several arenas, generally by three ardent advocates facing the united opposition of nearly all other investment bankers.

Neither the practice of competitive bidding nor the arguments about it were new. The method had been used before the Civil War by federal, state, and municipal governments as well as some railroads, and during the latter part of the nineteenth century it also was employed in marketing other securities.[1] As early as 1870 Massachusetts required gas and electric companies to sell their stock at public auction if the shareholders failed to subscribe to them, and in 1919 it required these companies to sell their bonds at competitive bids.[2] Until 1905 the American Telephone & Telegraph Company (AT&T) offered nearly all its bonds by this method.[3] Just about the time the directors of this company were abandoning the practice in favor of establishing a more permanent investment banking relationship, the critics of the money power were urging legislation requiring compulsory bidding as the best solution to end the New York City bankers' supposed stranglehold over the economy. The Pujo Committee, like several witnesses before the Industrial Commission in 1900, recommended that the Interstate Commerce Commission (ICC) require railroads to sell their bonds competitively. In 1922, after lengthy hearings in which Otto Kahn of Kuhn, Loeb & Co. presented many of the same arguments against competitive bidding that investment bankers used

---

1. Fritz Redlich, *The Molding of American Banking: Men and Ideas* (2 vols., New York, 1947, 1951), II, 344, 348.

2. Charles Christenson, *Strategic Aspects of Competitive Bidding for Corporate Securities* (Boston, 1965), 19; *U.S. v. Henry S. Morgan et al.*, "Transcript of Trial: Defendants' Opening — Mr. [Ralph M.] Carson" (January 22, 1951), 2082–83.

3. U.S. Temporary National Economic Committee, *Investigation of Concentration of Economic Power: Hearing* . . . (31 pts., Washington, 1939–41), pt. 23, 11838–41. See also U.S. Federal Communications Commission, *Report on Telephone Investigation* (2 vols., Washington, 1939), II, 607–08.

repeatedly thereafter, the ICC dropped the subject until 1926; it then imposed the practice for the sale of equipment trust certificates.[4]

The issue was raised again during the Pecora investigation and at subsequent congressional hearings on the federal securities bills and the Public Utility Holding Company Act, but it was not until 1937 that competitive bidding came to be the single most important question facing the country's investment bankers. In January of that year Joseph P. Kennedy, writing in *The Saturday Evening Post,* argued strongly that investment bankers "should be eliminated from control and management of corporations." Two months later William O. Douglas, speaking before the Bond Club of New York, told Wall Street's leading financiers that "the economic utility of continuity of banking relationships is of unestablished value to anyone except the banker."[5] Competitive bidding, Douglas said, would put an end to bankers' domination of industry, excessive underwriting charges, overissuance of securities, and many other related evils — all to the great advantage of investors and issuers alike.

At the time Douglas delivered this now famous talk, a small group of very determined individuals were conducting their own highly effective campaign for compulsory public sealed bidding. The principal leaders of this group were Robert R. Young, chairman of the Alleghany Corporation and a director of the Chesapeake & Ohio Railroad (C&O) and soon to become the chairman of its board; Cyrus Eaton, the head of Otis & Co., an important Cleveland investment banking house; and Harold Stuart of Halsey, Stuart & Co.

Whereas these three men all doubtless believed, as they repeatedly asserted, that this method of offering securities was in the best interests of both issuers and investors, each also had his own personal reasons for urging its adoption. Included among these reasons, Judge Harold R. Medina later observed, "revenge for real or fancied wrongs played no small part."[6] To Young, the diminutive but imaginative and forceful railroad leader, who after World War II won nationwide attention for his efforts to get transcontinental rail service for passengers without their having to change cars at Chicago, competitive bidding was an excellent club to strike at the Morgan interests, with which he had been feuding for control of

4. For the complete text of Otto Kahn's 1922 memorandum to the ICC see U.S. Senate, Committee on Banking and Currency, 72d Cong., 1st and 2d Sess., and 73d Cong., 1st and 2d Sess., *Stock Exchange Practices: Hearings* . . . (26 pts. in 9 vols., Washington, 1932–34), pt. 3, 1034–58.

5. Joseph P. Kennedy, "Big Business, What Now?" *The Saturday Evening Post,* CCIX (January 16, 1937), 10–11; William O. Douglas, *Democracy and Finance* (New Haven, 1940), 37. See also J. Fred Weston, *The Economics of Competitive Bidding in the Sale of Securities* (Chicago, 1943), 18–24.

6. *U.S. v. Henry S. Morgan et al.,* "Corrected Opinion of Harold R. Medina," (February 4, 1954), 393.

the Alleghany Corporation.[7] For Eaton, compulsory bidding was the means to break the alleged New York City investment banking monopoly, promote the growth of regional capital markets, and, as he liked to say, bring democracy to high finance. All these results would add considerably to the business of his firm. "Mr. Eaton is not interested in public sealed bidding for getting cheaper money for the issuer," Arthur H. Dean, one of the defense attorneys in the investment banking antitrust trial, told the court in 1952; "he is interested . . . in only getting a larger position for Mr. Eaton." [8]

Much the same was true of Stuart. He was interested in competitive bidding as a device to win new business for his firm. In 1926, after the ICC's ruling on equipment trust certificates, Stuart tried to persuade the commission to extend the requirement to other railroad securities; and in 1933, after the collapse of the Insull empire, whose financing he admitted to having monopolized for a quarter of a century, he launched his campaign for public sealed bidding for utility issues.[9] From then on, Stuart carried on his fight consistently. He discussed the merits of competitive bids for utility issues with nearly all the SEC commissioners, including Douglas, with whom he conferred on numerous occasions, beginning early in 1936, shortly after Douglas had been appointed to the commission.[10]

To Stuart the use of public sealed bidding was the best way by which his firm might hope to win some of the large utility accounts then held by the major New York City houses, thus compensating for the losses it had suffered from the Insull failure.[11] "Did you ever suggest to Mr. Insull . . . that he ought to put his securities up at public sealed bidding?" Dean asked Stuart in 1952. "No, sir," the banker replied. "Why not?" Dean continued. "Well," Stuart said, "because we had the business." [12] Two months later, while being questioned by another defense attorney, the following colloquy took place: "The fact that you did not have in 1939 the investment business you used to have was your principal reason for pushing competitive bidding, wasn't it?" "I think it was; yes, sir," Stuart replied. "To be fair and frank about it, we will have to say that was true, wasn't it," the attorney insisted. "I think it is true," Stuart admitted.[13]

7. "The Investment Banker: 1939," *Fortune*, XX (September, 1939), 112; "Mr. Young and His C&O," in J. Fred Weston, ed., *Readings in Finance from Fortune* (New York, 1958), 88–90.
8. *U.S. v. Henry S. Morgan et al.*, "Transcript of Trial: Plaintiff's Case" (February 14, 1952), 12593.
9. *Ibid.*, "Transcript of Trial: Testimony of Harold L. Stuart-Cross" (March 13, 1952), 13790–91; *ibid.* (May 14, 1952), 15830–43.
10. *Ibid.* (May 5, 1952), 15429–36; (May 6, 1952), 15469–78.
11. *Ibid.*, "Colloquy" (May 2, 1952), 15358; *ibid.*, "Harold L. Stuart-Cross" (May 7, 1952), 15535–56.
12. *Ibid.* (March 13, 1952), 13751.
13. *Ibid.*, "Testimony of Harold L. Stuart-Cross" (May 8, 1952), 15663. See also *ibid.* (May 15, 1952), 15896; *ibid.*, "Plaintiff's Case" (February 7, 1952), 12415–24; A. E. Bryson, *Halsey, Stuart & Co., Inc., 1901–1944: A History* . . .

Young struck one of the first major blows in the rapidly growing competitive bidding controversy in December 1938, when he persuaded the C&O board to sell a $30 million refunding issue to the Halsey, Stuart and Otis firms. The road's previous bankers had been Morgan Stanley and Kuhn, Loeb. On December 2, at a meeting of the C&O finance committee, which Harold Stanley of the Morgan firm and Elisha Walker of Kuhn, Loeb had been asked to attend, Young told the New Yorkers, with no small amount of pleasure, that the company had received a "firm offer" for the proposed issue. Then he invited them to make a competing bid. Stanley, speaking for himself and Walker, refused, saying that their firms did not bid on issues and that it would be premature to set a price before the ICC had approved the offering. Later that day, after making it clearly understood that in mentioning a price they were not making a bid, Stanley indicated that if the sale were to take place then, he and Walker would be prepared to pay $95\frac{1}{2}$. Halsey, Stuart and Otis had offered 100, and they got the bonds at that price, but only after Young had urged two of the railroad's directors, who disapproved of Otis's cosponsoring the issue, to change their votes.[14] Young later stated that he was proud of having deprived Morgan Stanley of this business; he had saved the railroad $1.35 million.[15] This figure subsequently was disproved. "I am absolutely convinced," Judge Medina declared after reviewing the evidence, "that there was no such saving, and to go around telling people that there was was just making an inaccurate statement."[16]

Following this victory, Young, Eaton, and Stuart intensified their efforts to require public sealed bidding, a campaign that Young later referred to as "putting the heat on."[17] They employed every tactic that promised success, including misinformation and political pressure. Issuers were importuned to put their securities up for auction and harassed into doing so when they insisted upon nego-

---

(Chicago [1945]), 11–14, suppl. Victor Perlo, a writer with strong Marxist views, also claimed that the major impetus for competitive bidding came from "the pressure of midwestern banking groups, largely excluded from the investment banking business after the collapse of the Insull utilities empire." See his *The Empire of High Finance* (New York, 1957), 75.

14. *U.S. v. Henry S. Morgan et al.,* "Transcript of Trial: Testimony of Robert R. Young" (December 4, 1951), 11459–76; *ibid.* (December 5, 1951), 11486–88; *ibid.* (December 6, 1951), 11664–76; *ibid.* (December 7, 1951), 11681–85, 11696–707.

15. *Ibid.* (December 6, 1951), 11673; *ibid.,* "Testimony of Harold L. Stuart — Colloquy" (May 6, 1952), 15489; U.S. Senate, Committee on Banking and Currency, 84th Cong., 1st Sess., *Stock Market Study: Hearings* . . . (3 pts., Washington, 1955–56), pt. 3, 1497–98.

16. *U.S. v. Henry S. Morgan et al.,* "Transcript of Trial—Colloquy" (May 6, 1952), 15491. See also *ibid.* (April 3, 1952), 14580–91.

17. *Ibid.,* "Transcript of Trial: Testimony of Robert R. Young" (December 11, 1951), 11832.

tiating privately with bankers of their own choice. The result was that several issuers succumbed to this ingenious and skillfully conducted campaign.[18]

One of the principal losers in this fight was Morgan, Stanley, the firm against which Young and Eaton focused most of their fire.[19] In February 1939 the Cincinnati Union Terminal Company was negotiating a $12 million bond issue with Morgan Stanley and Kuhn, Loeb, when Young and Eaton protested that the company would be served better if it called upon "independent bankers." They made public their claims by telegrams to the company's directors, one of whom was Ohio's Republican Senator, Robert A. Taft. They also appealed to the presidents of the terminal's proprietary railroads, the ICC, and Jesse Jones, chairman of the Reconstruction Finance Corporation. To avoid further controversy and embarrassment, the company decided to offer the bonds competitively. Morgan Stanley and Kuhn, Loeb refused to bid, and the issue went to a syndicate headed by Lehman Brothers, with Halsey, Stuart and Otis submitting the lowest of the four bids received.[20]

Many of the same tactics were employed again in the summer of 1939. At that time the Terminal Railroad Association of St. Louis was preparing to offer a $7 million refunding issue. Morgan Stanley and the company had been at work on the offering since the beginning of February. Early in June, just as the negotiations were about to be completed, Young denounced the proposed transaction; in letters to the association's president, members of the finance committee, and the heads of the terminal company's guaranteeing railroads he urged that the bonds be sold competitively, citing the large savings that had resulted from his "active intervention" in the recent C&O and Cincinnati Union Terminal offerings. He also informed public officials and the press. *The St. Louis Post-Dispatch* wrote a strongly worded editorial in favor of competitive bidding, which Eaton later claimed had had "considerable influence" on the decision of the company's directors to offer the bonds by this method. Morgan Stanley withdrew from the negotiations, declined to accept a fee for its work in preparing the issue, and refused to submit a bid. The company subsequently sold the issue to Halsey, Stuart, the higher of two bidders.[21]

Not all these interventions were successful. Some backfired. One such instance occurred in January 1940. On that occasion the ICC

18. *Ibid.*, "Colloquy" (May 6, 1952), 15486–501.
19. *Ibid.*, "Transcript of Trial: Defendants' Motions" (April 16, 1953), 22281–86.
20. *Ibid.*, "Plaintiff's Exhibit," No. 764, 9213–14; *ibid.*, No. 907, 3498–99.
21. *Ibid.*, "Defendants' Exhibit," No. MS-50, No. MS-130; *ibid.*, "Plaintiff's Exhibit," No. 765, No. 772, No. 919, No. 922. See also *ibid.*, "Corrected Opinion," 394; "The Investment Banker: 1939," 112.

set aside a petition signed by two "old ladies" (also described as two "girls of uncertain age") protesting the Louisville & Nashville Railroad Co.'s (L&N) sale of a $60 million bond issue to Morgan Stanley. The women, both small L&N shareholders, subsequently stated in affidavits that they had been "high-pressured" into signing the petition at a bridge party, had been misinformed about its content, and "knew nothing of the transaction in question." The ICC approved the sale to Morgan Stanley, and later it was learned that the individual who had solicited the women's signatures was representing Eaton.[22] Tactics such as these led Judge Medina to label the fight for competitive bidding an "unsavory subject." [23]

While Young, Eaton, and, to a lesser degree, Stuart were "putting the heat on" issuers and appealing to public officials to require public sealed bidding, the SEC had assumed the responsibility of enforcing "competitive conditions" in the financing of gas and electric companies. In March 1935, when the Roosevelt administration was at work on the public utility holding company bill, the National Power Policy Committee reported: "Fundamentally, the holding company problem always has been, and still is, as much a problem of regulating investment bankers as a problem of regulating the power industry." [24] Congress agreed with this view, and the following August, when it passed the Public Utility Holding Company Act, charged the SEC with supervising the security issues of these companies and their operating subsidiaries. The objective was to prevent a recurrence of past evils, including those that "result from an absence of arm's-length bargaining or from restraint of free and independent competition." [25]

The SEC enforced this provision by refusing to allow registration statements to become effective if "the fees, commissions, or other remuneration, to whomsoever paid, directly or indirectly, in connection with the issue, sale, or distribution of the security" were "not reasonable." [26] Determining the reasonableness of banking charges for each issue that came before it proved to be so time-consuming and burdensome that in December 1938, at the very time the Young-Eaton-Stuart campaign was in full swing, the SEC adopted a general rule (U-12 F-2) designed to prevent excessive

---

22. *U.S. v. Henry S. Morgan et al.,* "Plaintiff's Exhibit," No. 907, 3501–02. See also *ibid.,* "Defendants' Exhibit," No. KL-17; *ibid.,* "Transcript of Trial: Testimony of Robert R. Young" (December 11, 1951), 11828–29. Many of the Young-Eaton-Stuart interventions between 1935 and 1943 are summarized in *ibid.,* "Plaintiff's Exhibit," No. 907, 3497–3518.

23. *Ibid.,* "Corrected Opinion," 392.

24. Quoted in Louis Loss, *Securities Regulation* (2d ed., 3 vols., Boston, 1961), I, 389.

25. Quoted in *ibid.*

26. Quoted in Twentieth Century Fund, *Electric Power and Government Policy: A Survey of the Relations between the Government and the Electric Power Industry* (New York, 1948), 298.

underwriting charges and to ensure arm's-length bargaining in the security transactions of utility companies under its jurisdiction.

The "affiliate" or "arm's-length bargaining" rule, as U-12 F-2 soon came to be known, went into effect on March 1, 1939. It immediately struck snags. Under its provisions utility companies were prohibited from paying underwriting fees to investment houses with which they were affiliated if there was "liable to be or to have been an absence of arm's-length bargaining with respect to the transaction." [27] The rule was waived if the issue was awarded competitively, if the affiliated banking firm's participation was less than 5 percent of the entire offering, or if it was impracticable to require bids.[28] Experience quickly proved that U-12 F-2 was difficult to administer and easily evaded. According to the SEC, the rule did not increase competition in the underwriting of utility issues, and very often it necessitated a lengthy and costly investigation to determine whether an affiliation existed. Since neither the SEC nor investment bankers found the rule satisfactory, the commission invited the Investment Bankers Association (IBA) and "other interested organizations" to recommend procedures that would "best insure the reasonableness of fees and commissions, and the fairness of the terms and conditions of any proposed issue and sale of utility securities." [29]

Shortly thereafter the IBA submitted a lengthy memorandum in which it strongly opposed compulsory sealed bidding or the imposition of any rule that required issuers to prove that they had " 'shopped around' among investment bankers for the most favorable terms." The association, moreover, questioned the SEC's authority under the Public Utility Holding Company Act to require competitive bidding. It also denied the existence of any investment banking monopoly and challenged the TNEC's findings on underwriting concentration. It argued, furthermore, that "free and independent competition" prevailed throughout the investment banking industry and asserted that large and small houses competed "actively with each other for positions in underwriting and selling syndicates," as well as in searching for new clients. The memorandum pointed to the growth of direct placements and long-term commercial bank loans as examples of the alternatives available to issuers and defended vigorously the continuity of relationships that existed be-

---

27. Quoted in Loss, *Securities Regulation*, I, 390.
28. Twentieth Century Fund, *Electric Power and Government Policy*, 299–300.
29. Emmett F. Connely, *A Reply to the Securities and Exchange Commission Concerning the Underwriting and Sale of Certain Issues of Public Utility Securities, the Law Appertaining Thereto, "Maintenance of Competitive Conditions," Rule U-12 F-2 and Related Matters* (Chicago, 1940), 1. The drafting of this document and its submission is discussed in *U.S. v. Henry S. Morgan et al.*, "Transcript of Trial: Defendants' Opening — Mr. [Hugh B.] Cox (March 13, 1951), 4396–415. See also Weston, *Economics of Competitive Bidding*, 29–30; Ernest R. Abrams, "Is Competitive Bidding for Utility Issues Ahead?" *The Commercial & Financial Chronicle*, CXLVIII (April 1, 1939), 1862–66.

tween corporations and investment houses as being based on "mutual trust" and in the best interests of issuers and investors. Finally, the association warned that compulsory bidding "would tend greatly to concentrate in relatively few hands the business of underwriting and distributing issues of corporate securities and virtually eliminate from this business the hundreds of selling group dealers who are currently engaged in the distribution of corporate issues." [30]

These arguments fell on deaf ears at the SEC. Many of them had been used before, most recently in two widely quoted memoranda, one written by Stanley and another by Franklin T. McClintock, vice president of Harriman Ripley & Co., Inc.[31] The SEC criticized the IBA, as did the more liberal journals of opinion, for using the commission's invitation "to repeat its customary opposition not only to the Holding Company Act, but to all statutes which Congress had adopted for the protection of investors and consumers." It ordered its Public Utilities Division to make a comprehensive study of utility financing and recommend new regulatory procedures to replace rule U-12 F-2.[32]

In a report of December 18, 1940, the division recommended the repeal of U-12 F-2. It asserted that the rule had been "demonstrably deficient in achieving the statutory objective of assuring maintenance of arm's-length bargaining and competitive conditions in the sale and distribution of securities of registered holding companies and their subsidiaries." Moreover, it urged the adoption of another "requiring competitive bidding in connection with the issuance or sale of utility securities subject to the Commission's jurisdiction under the provisions of the Public Utility Holding Company Act." [33]

The division explained its decision on several grounds. Compulsory competitive bidding for utility issues, it held, would put an end to bankers' domination of these companies, lessen the concentration of underwriting managements, reduce banking charges, allow for improvements in the capital structure of these companies, and ease "the administrative problems of governmental regulatory agencies." [34]

At a public conference, held at the SEC's Washington headquar-

30. Connely, *Reply to SEC*, 2–20.
31. Harold Stanley, *Competitive Bidding for New Issues of Corporate Securities* (New York, 1939), 1–14; Franklin T. McClintock, *Competitive Bidding for New Issues of Securities* (New York, 1939), 3–8.
32. *The New York Times,* March 20, 1940. See also Keith Hutchison, "Arm's-Length Bargaining," *The Nation,* CL (March 30, 1940), 421–22; John T. Flynn, "The Investment Bankers Again," *The New Republic,* CII (April 1, 1940), 441.
33. U.S. Securities and Exchange Commission, Public Utilities Division, *The Problem of Maintaining Arm's-Length Bargaining and Competitive Conditions in the Sale and Distribution of Securities of Registered Public Utility Holding Companies and their Subsidiaries* (Washington, 1940), 45.
34. *Ibid.,* 41. See also Sidney M. Robbins, "Competitive Bidding in Sale of Securities," *Harvard Business Review,* XXVII (September 1949), 646–64.

ters, beginning January 27, 1941, the report became the subject of a week-long debate. Never before had the commission called a "town meeting" of this kind to discuss one of its staff reports. The proceedings, attended by some 125 investment bankers and dealers, insurance company representatives, and public officials, were reported extensively in the press.[35] Harry S Truman, then a senator, "made a very spirited defense of compulsory competitive bidding." [36] Years later, while testifying before the Senate Banking and Currency Committee, Eaton claimed credit for having enlisted Truman's assistance in the fight, and explained how the two of them had worked "shoulder to shoulder" in persuading the SEC to require compulsory bidding for utility issues under its jurisdiction." [37]

As was to be expected, the IBA and most of the leading investment houses condemned the report and opposed compulsory competitive bidding, using all the familiar arguments. "It is in fact clearly demonstrable from experience," the IBA asserted in its prepared statement, "that there is no greater concentration in the underwriting of corporate securities through direct negotiations than in the purchase of municipal securities in compulsory competitive bidding." The pressure of competition in the investment banking business was relentless. There were no captive corporations, and examples of issuers' changing from one underwriter to another were numerous.[38] Stanley and other leading bankers, among them George Woods of The First Boston Corporation, R. H. Bollard of Dillon, Read & Co., and John W. Cutler of Smith, Barney & Co., asserted vigorously the many advantages that derived from long-continuing relationships between investment bankers and issuers, and they denied that the existence of these associations eliminated competition. Stanley testified that he considered himself "free to solicit business without responsibility to anyone excepting myself. . . . I would be very glad to say now that if any person who came to me who had been doing business with any other good bankers in the business and wanted me to do the business, I would do it right away, and I would expect them to do it right away with any client of ours."

Other bankers agreed that while competition among investment houses was not so obvious as in certain other industries, there was nonetheless plenty of it. Woods said that his firm "would not ag-

35. *The New York Times,* January 26, 1941; "Challenges to SEC," *Business Week* (January 25, 1941), 50; "Competitive Arguing," *Time,* XXXVII (February 17, 1941), 80–82.
36. *U.S. v. Henry S. Morgan et al.,* "Transcript of Trial: Defendants' Opening — Mr. [Hugh B.] Cox" (March 13, 1951), 4407.
37. U.S. Senate, Committee on Banking and Currency, 81st Cong., 2d Sess., *Securities Exchange Acts Amendments: Hearings . . .* (Washington, 1950), 165.
38. Investment Bankers Association, *An Examination of the proposal of the S.E.C. Staff for Compulsory Competitive Bidding in the Sale of Certain Public Utility Securities* (New York, 1941), 5–13.

gressively go out and try to get a piece of business from another party," but that it would do so "subtly and by that I mean . . . we would endeavor to get ourselves in a position where the management, the principal executive officers and directors of the proposed issuer, would invite us to do the business." [39]

Other bankers opposed compulsory bidding on the grounds that it would lead to overpricing and the sale of poorly investigated securities. "I am opposed to the theory of compulsory competitive bidding in principle," John F. Fennelly of Chicago's Glore, Forgan & Co. wrote to SEC chairman Jerome Frank, who conducted the hearings, "but it seems to me particularly unsound if the theory is applied to second-grade securities and equities. I am certain that such a requirement will make impossible the careful investigation which every reputable investment banker feels compelled to undertake in connection with the issuance of any but the most high grade securities. I feel that the proposed rule will cause a general lowering of investment banking standards, will increase the cost of financing, and in the end, the chief sufferer will be the investing public." [40]

Everyone expected the major originating houses to oppose competitive bidding. The surprise came when many of the small firms outside New York City, the very ones Stuart, Eaton, and others claimed would profit most by putting an end to Wall Street's underwriting monopoly, also expressed themselves unequivocally against the practice. What the smaller houses feared most was that the underwriters, forced to pay higher prices, would sell the securities themselves and bypass the independent, out-of-town dealers entirely. Stanley and others had said repeatedly that competitive bidding would eliminate the small dealers and bring about an even greater underwriting concentration, since many houses of issue, in order to increase their profits, would develop or expand their own selling organizations, a trend that already was well under way.[41] Stanley intimated that his own firm might have to start retailing issues it

---

39. *U.S. v. Henry S. Morgan et al.*, "Plaintiff's Exhibit," Nos. 930–937, 958. These documents are reproductions of the original testimony before the SEC.

40. John F. Fennelly to Jerome Frank, January 13, 1941, in *U.S. v. Henry S. Morgan et al.*, "Plaintiff's Exhibit," No. 1260. See also *ibid.*, No. 656, for an earlier criticism of competitive bidding prepared by Eugene Bashore of Blyth & Co.; *ibid.*, No. 1242, in which Sidney J. Weinberg of Goldman, Sachs & Co. expressed many of the same views. See also *ibid.*, "Transcript of Trial" (February 7, 1951), 2817; *ibid.*, "Plaintiff's Case" (May 14, 1951), 6859–69; *ibid.*, "Deposition of [Joseph P.] Ripley" (December 3, 1951), 11323–24. These and other arguments against competitive bidding are summarized in Weston, *Economics of Competitive Bidding*, 35–44; Donald J. Emblen. *Competitive Bidding for Corporate Securities* (Canton, N.Y., 1944), 70–100; Ernest R. Abrams, "Fallacy of Competitive Bidding for Public Utility Securities, Part II," *Public Utilities Fortnightly*, XIX (April 15, 1937), 476–85. Consult also "New Money for Industry: The Investment Banker's Job for Industry," *Business Week* (November 30, 1940), 41–52.

41. See, for instance, Stanley's testimony before the TNEC, *Hearings*, pt. 23, 11970.

originated. "Where does that leave us?" the head of one small house asked. "I don't welcome Mr. Stanley's competition in Pittsburgh." [42]

Advocates of competitive bidding attributed the opposition of small dealers to pressure from the larger houses. *Time* magazine noted that the fact that the "little men were much better at reading prepared statements than answering questions" seemed to suggest "that their arguments had been partly prepared by the Wall Street tyrants they were supposed to fear." [43] Stuart implied as much when he said that the reason why many of these firms had refused to join his accounts was that they were afraid of being "shut out of New York syndicates if they attempted to put in a bid." He dismissed "the great love of the big issuing houses for the small dealer" as sheer nonsense. "I never knew that it existed before, and it doesn't really exist in any event." [44] Nor did he consider very important any of the arguments advanced against competitive bidding. The value of detailed investigations was greatly overrated, especially in the case of top-quality bonds, as were the claims presented to support the existence of continuing issuer-banker relationships. Competitive bidding, Stuart argued, would reduce underwriting spreads and remove one of the main reasons for the growth of private placements. "If the insurance companies and the other great aggregates of funds are aggressive, and decide they want to buy, and they have the money to do it, that is just too bad for the rest of us who are in business and have to make a profit." [45]

Eaton's firm was the only other major investment house to support the SEC's proposed compulsory bidding rule. Two months before the hearings, one of the firm's partners, a former governor of the IBA, sent a letter to all the association's members urging them to endorse competitive bidding, saying that it would strengthen the investment banking business and forestall the possibility of the government's organizing publicly owned underwriting banks to provide funds to industry at reasonable cost.[46] Later, in a lengthy statement to the SEC, copies of which were distributed also to all members of the IBA, Congress, the ICC, state regulatory commissions, and institutional investors, the Otis firm explained the many advantages to be gained by requiring competitive bidding. This statement stressed especially the decline in banking charges that would follow its adoption, the principal argument advanced by all

---

42. Quoted in "Competitive Arguing," 80–82.
43. *Ibid.*, 80–82.
44. *U.S. v. Henry S. Morgan et al.*, "Plaintiff's Exhibit," No. 1036; *ibid.*, "Transcript of Trial: Testimony of Harold L. Stuart-Cross" (May 13, 1952), 15733–36.
45. *Ibid.*, "Plaintiff's Exhibit," No. 1036. These and other arguments advanced in favor of competitive bidding are summarized in Weston, *Economics of Competitive Bidding*, 31–34; Emblen, *Competitive Bidding*, 34–55.
46. *The New York Times*, November 30, 1940.

those supporting the practice, and the pressing need to destroy the investment banking monopoly.[47]

Otis & Co. rejected the view widely held among investment bankers that the securities business was a profession, governed by a code of ethics similar to the ones adhered to by doctors and lawyers. The investment banker, the memorandum asserted, was a merchant, a middleman "who buys securities at wholesale for resale at a profit."[48] Concern that competitive bidding would lead to overpricing, as its opponents argued, was groundless. Overpricing could, and did, occur in private negotiations, though more often than not the latter method resulted in underpricing. The memorandum concluded with a blast against the "super-middlemen" in the industry, obviously aimed at Morgan Stanley, and the few other firms like it that had no retail selling organizations. They were the ones, according to Otis & Co., that had "instituted the practice of exacting a management fee from the other bankers included in the underwriting. Such super-middlemen serve no useful purpose; their going would be no loss to issuer, investor or the investment banking business itself."[49]

The officials of the utility companies, whose securities were directly involved in the controversy, said almost nothing, obviously preferring to let the bankers fight it out among themselves.[50] The utilities had fought and lost the battle over the Holding Company Act, and they were not at all disposed to alienate further the commissions that regulated them by opposing something many regulatory bodies strongly endorsed. Most managements of utility companies, like those of other corporations, Stuart testified, much preferred to negotiate privately than to offer their securities competitively. They resented the practice and avoided it, even when, according to Stuart, it was to their and the stockholders' interest.[51]

Nor were the large institutional investors in favor of compulsory bidding, if the views of the Metropolitan Life Insurance Company were at all indicative. At the request of the SEC, this company, one of the largest bond buyers in the nation, submitted a lengthy letter against the practice; it argued that though large institutional investors like itself might very well gain from such a requirement, its long-term effects would "result in ultimate harm to investors."[52]

47. Otis & Co., *Investors, Dealers and Issuers Would Benefit by Competitive Bidding for the Securities of Public Utilities: A Reply to the Opponents of Competitive Bidding* ([Cleveland, 1941]), 1–16.
48. *Ibid.,* 5. See also Emblen, *Competitive Bidding,* 5–8.
49. Otis & Co., *A Reply to the Opponents of Competitive Bidding,* 13.
50. *The New York Times,* January 26, 1941.
51. *U.S. v. Henry S. Morgan et al.,* "Transcript of Trial: Testimony of Harold L. Stuart-Cross" (May 1, 1952), 15269–72.
52. F. W. Ecker, vice president, Metropolitan Life Insurance Co., to SEC, January 18, 1941, in *U.S. v. Henry S. Morgan et al.,* "Defendants' Exhibits," No. 4888.

Whatever immediate price advantage was derived, its benefit would be offset by the fact that competitive bidding "would enable and indeed require the issuer to write its own terms." This might be of little consequence in the case of high-grade issues, whose terms generally had been standardized. This was not true of securities of lesser quality. Indentures for these issues had to be carefully drawn, if the investors' interests were to be protected. The terms of these documents often were more important than the price of the issue, and the responsibility for drafting them should rest with able, independent bankers rather than the issuer or its attorneys. To perform this essential and highly desirable service might require months of investigation and considerable expense. No reputable investment banker dared risk either if the issue was to be put up for bids.[53]

Like the IBA and most investment bankers, Metropolitan Life also repeated all the other arguments advanced against competitive bidding; and it rejected the claim that its adoption would lessen concentration in the underwriting business or result in more reasonable prices. To prove the latter point, this giant insurance company cited the policy of the federal government. "It is to be noted that securities of the federal government other than Treasury bills have with few exceptions not been offered for competitive bidding. Moreover it is a familiar fact that government securities are invariably slightly underpaid, or intended so to be, and that this represents unquestionably good business judgment on the part of the Treasury officials." [54]

SEC officials took nearly three months to decide whether to adopt the compulsory bidding rule recommended by its Public Utilities Division. Very few financial observers expected the commission to ignore the division's proposal entirely. Their prognostications were confirmed on April 8, 1941; the SEC then promulgated its now famous rule U-50, requiring competitive public sealed bidding for all issues of registered holding companies and their subsidiaries under its jurisdiction. Issues of $1 million or less were exempted from the requirement, as were those offered to existing stockholders or sold "in connection with a liquidation or reorganization." Bonds and other debt issues sold directly to banks, insurance companies, or other institutions without the assistance of any third parties also were exempted. The commission was authorized to waive the rule in other cases as well. Most of these, as it turned out, were private placements, rights offerings, and either exceptionally large or very small common stock issues.[55]

---

53. *Ibid.* See also Arthur Dean's discussion of the shortcomings of competitive bidding in *ibid.,* "Transcript of Trial: Defendants' Opening — Mr. Dean" (December 11, 1950), 751–52.
54. Ecker to SEC, January 18, 1941. See also *U.S. v. Henry S. Morgan et al.,* "Transcript of Trial: Defendants' Opening—Mr. Dean" (January 15, 1951), 1710–12.
55. Loss, *Securities Regulation,* I, 390–91.

Concerned trade associations reacted at once. The National Association of Securities Dealers (NASD) deplored the commission's decision, claiming that U-50 interfered with free enterprise and would lead to government control of the capital markets. The IBA asserted that compulsory bidding would deprive "widows and orphans" of an opportunity to buy top-quality bonds.

SEC officials dismissed these claims. The commission pointed out how few senior securities were made available to small investors. "The truth is that in at least several of the issues [offered in 1941 after U-50 went into effect] the bankers had commitments from insurance companies for the entire issue in their back pockets when they submitted their bids," the SEC's chairman stated. "And a check would undoubtedly show that in all the other issues, only a very small percentage got beyond the very large institutional investors — and almost none to the widows and orphans." [56]

To the advocates of competitive bidding, the SEC's new rule was a major victory, and they immediately launched another campaign to persuade the ICC to adopt a similar requirement for railroad securities. Since 1926, when it required equipment trust certificates to be sold competitively, the ICC had repeatedly refused to extend the practice to other types of railroad issues.[57] The decision of the SEC to require competitive bidding for utilities attracted wide public attention and much favorable comment in the press, but even more important in persuading the ICC to reverse its previous position was the ably organized and energetically conducted campaign of propaganda and pressure led by Young, Eaton, and Stuart.[58]

In June 1943, when the Pennsylvania Railroad was negotiating a $28 million bond issue with Kuhn, Loeb, Eaton denounced the transaction in a telegram to President Roosevelt. "If you favor competitive bidding in the sale of standard railroad bonds," Eaton asked FDR, "are you willing to make a statement to that effect at your press conference tomorrow or to wire me and permit me to make your telegram public?" A week later he sent the president another telegram in which he called this refunding "a public scandal" and accused the ICC of refusing "to protect the public interest, as required by law." [59]

56. *The New York Times,* December 5, 1941; Keith Hutchison, "Bankers Hate Competition," *The Nation,* CLII (April 19, 1941), 472–73.
57. *U.S. v. Henry S. Morgan et al.,* "Transcript of Trial: Defendants' Opening — Mr. [Wm. Dwight] Whitney" (February 15, 1951), 3151–52. Joseph Eastman, a member of the ICC since 1919, was one of the Commissioners who had consistently favored competitive bidding for railroad securities.
58. *Ibid.,* 3150–57; *ibid.,* "Testimony of Harold L. Stuart-Cross" (May 12, 1952), 15711–16; *ibid.,* "Testimony of Robert R. Young" (December 11, 1951), 11830–32. See also *The New York Times,* August 31, 1943, November 6, 1943.
59. Cyrus Eaton to Franklin D. Roosevelt, June 24, 1943; July 1, 1943, in *U.S. v. Henry S. Morgan et al.,* "Defendants' Exhibits," Nos. KL-48, KL-49. See also *ibid.,* "Colloquy" and "Testimony of Harold L. Stuart-Cross" (May 26, 1952), 16033–47.

A year later the Burlington Railroad asked the ICC to approve a $30 million privately negotiated issue through Morgan Stanley, and the Pennsylvania applied for permission to sell $35 million of its securities privately, with Kuhn, Loeb acting as the road's agent. Eaton complained to the president again. The fees these bankers were charging for their services ($75,000 in the case of Morgan Stanley and $87,500 for Kuhn, Loeb), Eaton asserted, were "an outright steal." He told Roosevelt: the "Administration has nothing to gain by continuing to let the ICC countenance scandalous deals like these between the railroads and Wall Street." Eaton concluded his appeal for White House intervention by saying that New York's Governor Thomas E. Dewey, then the leading Republican contender for his party's presidential nomination, had "an offensive and defensive alliance" with the anticompetitive bidding crowd, and he reminded FDR that there were no votes for him among those people. The president, then occupied with the final planning for the Allied invasion of France, wrote Eaton on May 27, 1944, saying that he assumed the ICC was reviewing the proposed offerings.[60]

One week before FDR's letter to Eaton, the ICC had ruled that all railroad securities should be sold competitively, except for stock issues and certain other types of offerings similar to those exempted by the SEC's rule U-50. The commission explained that while Morgan Stanley and Kuhn, Loeb had sponsored most of the country's railroad securities, there was no evidence at all to indicate that these two houses dominated the roads they financed. "The record indicates," the ICC reported, "that railroads have given and continue to give the bulk of their business to the two firms because of the quality of service rendered and because the railroads have seen no reason to make a change. Nor have proponents [of competitive bidding] called to our attention any facts showing or tending to show that the bankers maintain their position in railroad financing by distribution of patronage, coercion of other investment bankers or favoritism of such bankers because of interlocking relationships."[61]

Advocates of competitive bidding celebrated the ICC's action, but to men like Eaton, convinced of the existence of an investment banking monopoly, the commission's ruling was only a tactical victory in the long struggle to destroy "the eastern money ring." They continued their campaign until the Justice Department brought suit against the seventeen alleged leaders of the monopoly.[62]

60. Eaton to FDR, May 9, 10, and 11, 1944, FDR to Eaton, May 27, 1941, in *U.S. v. Henry S. Morgan et al.*, "Defendants' Exhibits," Nos. KL-9 through KL-12, inclusive.
61. Quoted in *U.S. v. Henry S. Morgan et al.*, "Corrected Opinion," 396–97.
62. See, for example, Eaton's telegram and letter to Interior Secretary Harold L. Ickes, dated October 24 and November 8, 1944, and the Secretary's replies, dated October 27 and November 14, 1944, in *U.S. v. Henry S. Morgan et al.*, "Defend-

Expanded use of competitive bidding brought about radical changes in investment banking procedures. In privately negotiated transactions the originating banker conducted the investigation, planned the provisions of the issue, and assisted in preparing the registration statement, prospectus application to state regulatory bodies, and other necessary documents. Under competitive bidding all this work was done by the issuer, sometimes with the assistance of an investment banker to whom it paid a fee. The detailed legal work required in preparing indentures or contracts, bidding forms, and statements was assigned to independent attorneys specializing in these matters, hired by the issuer, and paid by the successful bidder. The fears expressed by investment houses that competitive bidding would result in poorly executed indentures and careless investigations proved greatly exaggerated. Preliminary studies in competitive offerings, though generally less exhaustive than those conducted for a private negotiation, did not cause any great hardship to investors, largely because of the high quality of the securities usually sold by this method. Prospective bidders reviewed all relevant documents, and issuers almost always held "due diligence" meetings, at which company officials and their hired experts gave any further information the bidders asked for. Very often bidders visited issuers to look over the property and interview the management.[63]

As soon as they learned that an issuer was planning a competitive offering, the larger investment houses, those experienced in originating and managing privately negotiated transactions, organized and led bidding accounts or syndicates. Any firm could submit an individual bid, but this occurred rarely, and then only in the case of very small issues, $1 million or less, for which a single house could afford the risk of taking the entire issue itself.

Under competitive bidding account managers started recruiting syndicate associates as early as possible. They wanted to put together a strong, well-balanced group, one able to distribute an issue quickly and, at the same time, have sufficient strength to carry the securities, if necessary. Moreover, they wanted to have the best and largest

---

ants' Exhibits," Nos. KL-13 through KL-16. Consult also *ibid.*, "Colloquy" (December 11, 1951), 11907–11, in which Young asserts that he had always opposed private negotiations and proudly claimed credit for having "broken up 85 per cent" of that business.

63. Franklin T. McClintock, "Competitive Bidding in the Origination of Securities" in Investment Bankers Association, *Fundamentals of Investment Banking* (Englewood Cliffs, 1960), 502–03; Albert B. Hager, Jr., "Competitive Bidding for Corporate Debt Securities" in [Yale Daily News] *Wall Street: 20th Century* (New Haven, 1960), 100–03. See also the testimony of SEC Commissioner Ganson Purcell in U.S. House, Committee on Interstate and Foreign Commerce, 77th Cong., 1st and 2d Sess., *Proposed Amendments to the Securities Act of 1933 and to the Securities Exchange Act of 1934: Hearings* . . . (6 pts., Washington 1941–42), pt. 3, 738.

possible choice of potential partners. Account managers extended invitations even before they knew the size or terms of the issue. All that was expected of those invited at the time was a written indication that they were interested in being included in the account.

Identical considerations that governed the choice of syndicate members in a privately negotiated offering — distributing ability, underwriting strength, previous association with the issuer — also determined the selection of firms to include in a bidding group. It was customary for an issuer's former banker to submit a bid when his client decided or was required to make a competitive offering. In such cases the bidding account usually was composed of the same firms that had belonged to earlier underwriting or purchase syndicates.[64]

The number and size of accounts organized for any one offering depended upon a variety of factors, the most important of which were the amount and quality of the issue and the condition of the market at the time. More than a dozen accounts might be formed to bid on a $5 million issue of top-grade, highly prized corporate bonds, whereas fewer than five might be organized for a $50 million offering of lesser quality. Sometimes, if the issue was exceptionally large, $100 million or more, it was difficult to put together even two independent accounts. There simply were not enough firms to organize more, especially since some houses did not bid for stock issues. The greater the risk, the smaller the number of bidding groups and the larger the membership in each account, since individual firms usually took smaller participations if it appeared that the securities might prove "sticky."[65]

Each firm's participation generally was determined by the manager after the issuer had made available all the necessary information and documents. The largest participations always were reserved for the so-called "majors," a group of fewer than two dozen leading houses, whose capital and reputation were such that they often headed bidding groups of their own. In a negotiated transaction the individual participations assigned these firms usually were smaller than the amount the originating house kept for itself, but in a competitive account the share allotted to each of the majors generally was as large as the manager's, and it always was equal to that of any other member of the group. Firms below the majors also were arranged in groups, depending upon their capital and selling ability; each received the same participation as every other house in its group. Managers observed these classifications carefully, since a firm's syndicate position was regarded as an index of its status in the industry. To ignore the "customs of the business" invited dis-

---

64. McClintock, "Competitive Bidding in the Origination of Securities," 501.
65. *Ibid.*, 500.

satisfaction in the account, dropouts, and refusals of future invitations.[66]

When the issuer announced that bidding papers were available, the account leaders, after being qualified to bid, were given copies to distribute to their syndicate members. These documents usually included, besides the formal invitation for bids, the terms and conditions of the sale, a preliminary prospectus and registration statement, and a proposed purchase contract, as well as copies of the indenture (if it was a bond offering) and various memoranda indicating that all the legal requirements had been satisfied. Not all those that qualified and asked for papers always submitted bids. Some dropped out, others were absorbed by competitors, and still others merged to form joint accounts, with the head of each acting as co-manager of the enlarged group. Whatever changes occurred, the leading houses almost always knew with whom they were competing.[67]

Every member of each group, especially the managers, studied the bidding papers carefully. They and their syndicate associates attended the "due diligence" meeting conducted by the issuer for the purpose of providing them with whatever additional information they wanted; analyzed the current market prices and yields of comparable outstanding issues; and investigated the potential interest of institutional investors and, in some cases, solicited their views on prices. Every effort was made to secure all the information relevant for pricing. Each group then discussed its findings at a preliminary price meeting, usually held a day before it had to submit the bid.[68]

The account manager usually opened proceedings with a report on market conditions, the status of recent offerings of similar size and quality, and the extent to which institutional buyers had expressed an interest in the securities. The members then were asked to express their own views as to price, spread, and yield, and the results of the poll were announced so that every participant could learn the views of all his partners, though not always those of the manager, since he might delay making a recommendation at this time. If there was considerable uncertainty regarding a "proper bid," the manager worked to narrow the range of difference. Members who refused to accept these limitations dropped out, and others who could not attend the final price meeting were allowed to file bidding limits with the manager, stipulating the highest bid they

---

66. *Ibid.*, 502; Christenson, *Strategic Aspects of Competitive Bidding for Corporate Securities*, 12.

67. *U.S. v. Henry S. Morgan et al.*, "Testimony of Harold L. Stuart-Cross" (April 2, 1952), 14442–43; Hager, "Competitive Bidding for Corporate Debt Securities," 102.

68. Hager, "Competitive Bidding for Corporate Debt Securities," 102; Christenson, *Strategic Aspects of Competitive Bidding for Corporate Securities*, 23–24.

were willing to make. If the final one exceeded their limits, the manager dropped them from the group. Usually these firms were required to file their bidding limits at the close of the preliminary price meeting or very shortly thereafter.[69]

Commitments of the dropouts, known as the "slack," were taken up by the remaining participants and the manager, since it was too late at this point to admit other firms into the group. If the slack amounted to less than 10 percent of the entire issue, the manager was authorized to allocate it as he saw fit, without consulting the members; but if it exceeded this amount, he had to absorb it himself or persuade others, usually the majors, to increase their participations.[70]

At the final price meeting, usually held a few hours before the time bids had to be submitted, the manager again reported on market conditions and institutional interest in the issue, but the main order of business often was deciding upon the public offering price and the one to be paid the issuer. The latter, in the case of bond offerings, was expressed as the "cost of money" to the issuer, figured on an annual basis to maturity. It represented a combination of the manager's judgment of the market and his estimate of the spread required to sell the issue.[71] The manager's suggested price was discussed by the entire group or, if the membership was too large to do so conveniently, by a price committee, usually composed of the majors or other houses with an agreed-upon minimum participation.

The price committee, or the entire group if no committee was formed, might be polled several times before the final bid was determined. Those who disagreed with it could withdraw at the last roll call, and firms that wanted to increase their participations could declare the additional amount they were willing to take. The manager's representatives then recorded these in the purchase contract, completed all the other paper work necessary, and rushed to submit the bid to the issuer, very often arriving at the company's headquarters only minutes before the deadline.

After the bids were opened, the winning account immediately decided upon the public offering price, if it had not already been determined or needed to be revised. Sometimes the group's original ideas as to a proper offering price and spread were affected by the

---

69. McClintock, "Competitive Bidding in the Origination of Securities," 505–06; Christenson, *Strategic Aspects of Competitive Bidding for Corporate Securities*, 24–25. See also *U.S. v. Henry S. Morgan et al.*, "Testimony of Harold L. Stuart-Cross" (April 30, 1952), 15220–27.

70. McClintock, "Competitive Bidding in the Origination of Securities," 506.

71. *U.S. v. Henry S. Morgan et al.*, "Testimony of Harold L. Stuart-Cross" (April 30, 1952), 15227. The cost of money to the issuer is equal to the interest rate as evidenced by the coupon, less any premium received over par or, rarely, plus any discount from par over the life of the bond.

"cover," the difference between the winning and losing bids. If the bids were very close, the winners might decide to increase the spread a little, thus adding to their profit and the concession allowed dealers.[72]

The distribution of the securities, once they had been purchased, was the same in a competitive account as in a privately negotiated one. The manager retained a portion of the issue to sell to institutional investors on behalf of the entire group and to selected dealers, if a selling group was formed. He kept the syndicate records, stabilized the market if necessary, and supervised the entire flotation, just as he would do if he had originated the issue.

With very few exceptions, competitive bidding has been employed only when required by law. Not many issuers have adopted it voluntarily. AT&T did so in September 1941, when it broke its long-standing ties with the Morgans and for the first time since the turn of the century decided to put up for bids a $90 million issue of debentures. Some financial observers attributed the decision to the fact that the FCC, the company's regulatory authority, recently had recommended that it sell its securities competitively; others explained it as a move to avoid the criticism of Halsey, Stuart and other advocates of competitive bidding. Whatever the reason, the sale attracted widespread attention, especially when the winners turned out to be three insurance companies. The IBA protested to the New York Superintendent of Insurance, saying that the winning companies had joined together to form a bidding group in violation of the state's famous Armstrong law. *The New York Times,* in an editorial criticizing compulsory bidding, warned that "a new kind of monopoly" was in the offing, one in which the large insurance companies would take up "any high-grade issue they desire, shutting out not merely the investment banker but also all other investors."[73]

These fears were quickly laid to rest. Executives of these companies made it quite clear that they found competitive bidding almost as "unpalatable" as did the investment bankers. Since their companies usually were unwilling to buy entire issues, they rarely appeared as competing bidders against investment houses, a fact that the Justice Department later used as evidence of conspiracy against seventeen New York City firms.[74]

72. *Ibid.* (April 30, 1952), 15222; McClintock, "Competitive Bidding in the Origination of Securities," 506.
73. *The New York Times,* October 3, 1941; *U.S. v. Henry S. Morgan et al.,* "Plaintiff's Exhibit," Nos. 564, 569–71, 573–75, 942B–946B. These documents include copies of the correspondence between the IBA's president and the New York Superintendent of Insurance, as well as other letters and memoranda relating to the AT&T offering of September 1941. The three insurance companies that purchased the issue were the Mutual, Metropolitan, and New York Life. See also *The New York Times,* November 10, 1941; Emblen, *Competitive Bidding,* 109–12.
74. *U.S. v. Henry S. Morgan et al.,* "Transcript of Trial: Government's Opening — Rebuttal — Mr. [Roscoe T.] Steffen" (March 22, 1951), 4972–78; *ibid.,* "Plaintiff's Case" (February 9, 1953), 19907; *ibid.* (February 10, 1953), 19925–28.

AT&T continued to sell its debt issues competitively, but few other corporations that had a choice did so. Not a single industrial corporation opted to offer its bonds or stocks by this method in the years 1942 through 1946. When the Cudahy Packing Co. did so in April 1947, Leslie Gould, financial editor of the New York *Journal American,* interpreted the move as "the opening gun" in Halsey, Stuart's "drive to force competitive bidding on industrial companies." [75]

By the end of the 1940's, as the controversy over competitive bidding continued to rage, it was becoming increasingly apparent that some of the claims of its advocates had been grossly exaggerated.[76] The anticipated growth of regional capital markets at the expense of New York City did not occur to any significant extent; nor was the concentration of underwriting managements reduced appreciably.[77] In 1939, according to a reliable study, the top fifteen investment houses managed 90 percent of all registered, publicly offered issues; in 1948 their share of the business had been cut to 81 percent. This decline, however, did not apply to the top three firms in the group. They actually increased the amount of their managements, from 41 percent in 1939 to 56 percent in 1948. Nor did the membership of the group change significantly. Eleven of the fifteen leading managers in 1939, mostly New York City houses, continued to head the list in 1949. Probably the chief beneficiary of compulsory bidding was Halsey, Stuart, which increased its share of managements from less than 1 percent in 1940 to 29 percent in 1948.[78] The smaller investment banking firms across the country, which the SEC had declared would profit considerably from compulsory bidding, gained nothing from this requirement. Managements were even more concentrated after the SEC and ICC rulings than they had been before.[79]

Compulsory bidding appeared to have contributed significantly to the marked decline in bankers' gross spreads that occurred in the 1940's. Whether this was the only factor, however, remained to be proved, just as it was uncertain whether the issuer or the investor was the chief beneficiary of this drop in fees, though it was generally assumed that it was the former.[80] Since there were very few privately

75. Quoted in *U.S. v. Henry S. Morgan et al.,* "Plaintiff's Exhibit," No. 1166. See also Merwin H. Waterman, *Investment Banking Functions: Their Evolution and Adaptation to Business Finance* (Ann Arbor, 1958), 111.
76. On the results of competitive bidding see the excellent article by Robbins, "Competitive Bidding in Sale of Securities," 646–64. Consult also Emblen, *Competitive Bidding,* 113–42; McClintock, "Competitive Bidding in the Origination of Securities," 508–16; "Review of Competitive Bidding on Public Service Securities," *Investment Banking,* XVI (June 1948), 15–18.
77. McClintock, "Competitive Bidding in the Origination of Securities," 507–08; Jacob O. Kamm, *Decentralization of Securities Exchanges* (Boston, 1942), 139–41.
78. Robbins, "Competitive Bidding in Sale of Securities," 648–52.
79. McClintock, "Competitive Bidding in the Origination of Securities," 509.
80. Robbins, "Competitive Bidding in Sale of Securities," 652.

negotiated utility issues after May 1941, when rule U-50 went into effect, meaningful comparisons between the spreads on these offerings with those sold competitively were difficult to make. Franklin McClintock claimed that before the SEC's ruling the average gross spread on most utility bonds was about 2 percent, or $20 for each $1,000 bond. In 1942 it fell to 1.1 percent, and by 1945 and 1946 it was down to 0.7 of 1 percent.[81] The average gross spread on preferred stock during the same period was cut almost in half, from 3.4 percent in 1942 to 1.78 percent in 1946. The latter figure represented a slight increase from what it had been in 1945. No similar decline occurred in common stock offerings. The average gross spread on these issues actually increased, from roughly 4 percent in 1943 to 4.88 percent in 1946.[82] McClintock's figures are not very dissimilar from those compiled during the antitrust suit, as is shown in Exhibit 17, which includes comparative data on the spreads earned on railroad bonds and debentures.

Several factors, apart from competitive bidding, contributed to the decline in bankers' spreads. For one thing, the expense involved in investigating a competitive offering was considerably less than that entailed in shaping up a privately negotiated issue. Even more important was the fact that utility and other top-quality corporate bonds were highly prized by institutional investors, especially life insurance companies. Underwriters had no difficulty in selling these issues. Very often they sold the entire amount within a few hours after they had purchased them. During the immediate postwar years the underwriting risk on high-grade corporate bonds was negligible. Merwin H. Waterman of the University of Michigan's Bureau of Business Research reported that the life companies' investments in corporate securities, principally bonds, rose rapidly. They stood at slightly less than $1.1 billion in 1942, dropped to $896 million in 1943, then jumped to $1.9 billion in 1944 and to almost $5 billion in 1948. The next year they fell to $3.9 billion, but in 1950 they were up again to $4.2 billion.[83]

Decline in banking spreads was not limited to issues sold at competitive bidding. "Your regular clients know what size spread you take on competitive issues, because all the figures are published," a Kuhn, Loeb partner explained. "And you can't charge your friends more than you charge strangers."[84] More important reasons for the drop in spreads of noncompetitively sold issues were the availability of capital and the institutionalization of savings, which lessened underwriting risks and reduced the selling task. The average gross spread on privately negotiated industrial and certain other corporate

81. McClintock, "Competitive Bidding in the Origination of Securities," 512–13.
82. Ibid., 513.
83. Waterman, *Investment Banking Functions,* 116–17.
84. Quoted in Martin Mayer, *Wall Street: Men and Money* (New York, 1959), 177.

Exhibit 17. Arithmetic averages of percentage gross spread for public utility and railroad debt, issues of $1 million or more, 1936, 1946

	Quality ratings	Number of issues 1936	Gross spread	Number of issues 1946	Gross spread
Public utilities privately negotiated	AAA	10	2.02	–	–
	AA	16	2.07	1	0.73
	A	12	2.43	2	1.10
	BAA	6	2.86	1	1.16
Public utilities competitively bid	AAA	1	1.05	2	0.76
	AA	2	1.07	5	0.50
	A	–	–	11	0.66
	BAA	–	–	3	0.58
Rails privately negotiated	AAA	–	–	–	–
	AA	8	1.97	–	–
	A	4	2.04	–	–
	BAA	1	2.00	–	–
Rails competitively bid	AAA	–	–	1	0.90
	AA	–	–	1	1.19
	A	–	–	4	0.75
	BAA	–	–	5	1.00

Source: U.S. v. Henry S. Morgan et al., "Brief on General Points in Support of Motions to Dismiss . . . ," Appendix A, Table 1.

Exhibit 18. Arithmetic averages of contemplated gross spreads on privately negotiated bonds of industrial, financial, and service corporations, issues of $1 million or more

Quality ratings	Number of issues 1936	Gross spread	Number of issues 1946	Gross spread
AAA	3	1.94	3	0.92
AA	2	2.18	3	1.12
A	5	2.55	3	1.21
BAA	10	2.89	9	1.74

Source: U.S. v. Henry S. Morgan et al., "Brief on General Points in Support of Motions to Dismiss," Appendix A, Table 1.

bonds fell by approximately 50 percent between 1936 and 1946, as shown in Exhibit 18.

The drop was not so great for stock offerings. The average gross spread on nonconvertible preferreds during these years fell from 5.71 percent to 3.29 percent, while that for common stock dropped from 13.06 percent to 8.68 percent. Spreads on convertible preferreds, on the other hand, increased by more than a point, from 4.52 percent in 1936 to 5.91 percent in 1946 (see Exhibit 19).[85]

Exhibit 19. Average percentage gross spread and average percentage selling concessions industrial, financial, and service corporations (underwritten, negotiated public offerings of $1 million or more, 1936, 1946)

	Number of issues 1936	Percent gross spread	Number of issues 1936	Percent selling concessions	Number of issues 1946	Percent gross spread	Number of issues 1946	Percent selling concessions
Nonconvertible preferred stock	11	5.71	9	2.28	55	3.29	52	1.63
Convertible preferred stock	10	4.52	9	1.80	44	5.91	43	2.88
Common stock	11	13.06	10	5.41	67	8.68	64	4.26

Source: U.S. v. Henry S. Morgan et al., "Brief on General Points in Support of Motions to Dismiss," Appendix A, Tables 3–5.

Small dealers were the hardest hit by these reduced spreads, as the opponents of competitive bidding had predicted. Selling groups, when organized, were smaller, the amount allotted dealers was reduced, and the selling concessions allowed them were drastically cut, as indicated in Exhibits 19 and 20. In November 1941, six months after the SEC's rule U-50 went into effect, John K. Starkweather, the head of a small New York City House, testified before the House Commerce Committee that his firm's profits had been cut by at least one-third and that the same was true of most other dealers with whom he had spoken.[86]

85. *U.S. v. Henry S. Morgan et al.*, "Brief on General Points in Support of Motions to Dismiss . . . ," Appendix A, Tables 1, 3–5.
86. *Proposed Amendments to the Securities Act of 1933 and to the Securities Exchange Act of 1934: Hearings*, pt. 3, 697. See also McClintock, "Competitive

Exhibit 20. Arithmetic averages of percentage of selling concessions, underwritten bonds and debentures of $1 million or more, maturing ten years or more after date of issue, 1936, 1946

		1936		1946	
	Quality ratings	Number of issues	Average percent selling concessions	Number of issues	Average percent selling concessions
Industrial, financial and service corporations (negotiated issues)	AAA	4	0.81	3	0.29
	AA	2	0.88	3	0.46
	A	6	1.09	3	0.54
	BAA	11	1.27	11	0.63
	BA	4	1.54	7	0.80
Public utilities (negotiated issues)	AAA	11	0.73	–	–
	AA	19	0.86	1	0.25
	A	20	1.12	2	0.31
	BAA	18	1.33	1	0.49
	BA	3	1.69	–	–
Rails (negotiated issues)	AAA	2	0.66	–	–
	AA	7	0.75	–	–
	A	3	0.82	–	–
	BAA	2	1.26	–	–
	BA	–	–	–	–
Public utilities (public sealed bidding)	AAA	1	0.36	4	0.24
	AA	2	0.24	10	0.16
	A	1	0.74	15	0.23
	BAA	–	–	5	0.39
	BA	–	–	3	0.24

Source: U.S. v. Henry S. Morgan et al., "Brief on General Points in Support of Motions to Dismiss," Appendix A, Table 2.

Underwriters, who previously had reserved anywhere from 30 percent to 70 percent of an issue for resale to dealers, now sought to make up for the decline in spreads by increasing their own syndicate participations and retailing the securities they received.[87]

Bidding in the Origination of Securities," 513–14; *The New York Times,* January 2, 1942.
87. *U.S. v. Henry S. Morgan et al.,* "Plaintiff's Exhibit," No. 769; McClintock, "Competitive Bidding in the Origination of Securities," 513–14.

Morgan Stanley started retailing some of its own issues in May 1941, immediately after rule U-50 first went into effect.[88] "The distribution of high-grade public utility bonds to investors . . . under the competitive bidding system," a *New York Times* financial writer reported a decade later, has provided "little opportunity for the nation's hundreds of small bond dealers to share even in the crumbs." [89] The same view was expressed by Judge Medina. Competitive bidding had resulted, he said, in making "the big firms bigger, and the little fellow is worse off than he was before." [90]

To offset their losses from smaller concessions, many dealers sought underwriting participations. The result was that during the 1940's purchase syndicates grew substantially in size, while separate selling groups, composed of retail houses, virtually ceased to exist. Sumner B. Emerson, a Morgan Stanley partner, pointed this out in comparing two top-quality debenture offerings of the same size, one in 1936, and the other in 1949. The former, a $150 million issue for AT&T, was brought out with 47 underwriters; the latter, for the Standard Oil Company (New Jersey), was purchased by a syndicate of 187 underwriters.[91]

However influential competitive bidding may have been in some of the foregoing respects, it did bring about other changes in investment banking practices. It altered and restricted the banker's role as a financial adviser to corporations that sold their securities competitively, disrupted some very old banker-issuer relationships, and contributed to many new syndicate alignments.[92] Most investment bankers, though strongly opposed to compulsory bidding, nonetheless organized and joined such accounts regularly. Only a very few firms consistently refused to submit bids or accept participations in bidding groups. Morgan Stanley and Kuhn, Loeb were two of the longest holdouts. The former did not organize its first bidding account until 1941, after the SEC had adopted rule U-50; and the latter, whose partners were as opposed to competitive bidding as were Morgan Stanley's, competed only for state and municipal issues until 1944.[93]

Compulsory bidding for utility and railroad debt issues forced

88. *Ibid.*, "Corrected Opinion," 63; Mayer, *Wall Street: Men and Money*, 174.
89. *The New York Times*, July 21, 1952.
90. *U.S. v. Henry S. Morgan et al.*, "Corrected Opinion," 401.
91. Sumner B. Emerson, "The Wholesaling of Corporate Securities," in Philipp H. Lohman and Franc M. Ricciardi, eds., *Wall Street Explains Its Operations* . . . (New York, 1951), 92–93.
92. Waterman, *Investment Banking Functions*, 112–14; *The New York Times*, January 2, 1942. In March 1953, when Morgan Stanley and Halsey, Stuart joined to co-manage a $200 million issue of debentures for the Allied Chemical & Dye Corporation, the event was hailed as the end of an eighteen-year feud over the merits of competitive bidding. See *The New York Times*, March 28, 1953.
93. *U.S. v. Henry S. Morgan et al.*, "Corrected Opinion," 63–65; *ibid.*, "Transcript of Trial: Plaintiff's Case — Deposition of Schiff" (May 29, 1951), 7879–80.

both firms to change some of their practices. Morgan Stanley's emergence as a limited retailer in the New York City market was occasioned largely by the SEC's ruling, which also appears to have contributed to the firm's decision, late in 1941, to reorganize itself as a partnership, qualify for membership on the New York Stock Exchange, and develop a specialized brokerage business.[94] In the case of Kuhn, Loeb the most radical departure from previous policy occurred in 1944, when the ICC required railroad debt issues to be sold competitively. Up to this time this firm had sold only bonds, principally for railroads. In April 1944, three months before the ICC's ruling went into effect, Kuhn, Loeb sponsored its first common stock issue. It based its decision to develop this business almost entirely on the anticipated ICC requirement.[95] Competitive bidding also provoked one of the very few real fights within the IBA's ranks, with the Otis firm charging publicly that the association had "recklessly compromised" itself by submitting to the ICC a brief against compulsory bidding for railroad securities.[96]

Although the bankers suffered only a partial defeat in their fight against compulsory competitive bidding, they did not succeed in persuading much of the public that they were not a group of financial monopolists, intent upon preserving their privileged position. Nor did they succeed in disproving the alleged advantages of the practice. The controversy persisted during World War II, when the investment banking business was nearly stalled. In 1945 the president of the IBA warned the membership that investment bankers still faced powerful critics and the possibility of still another government inquiry. "Rumor has it there is one more investigation left in the barrel, to go back 25 years in the relations between business and finance. Business being already numb from filling out blanks can no doubt survive." [97] Two years later the competitive bidding question was raised again in the most serious form thus far — the antitrust suit starting in 1947. These proceedings against seventeen of the industry's leaders and the IBA launched the lengthiest and most comprehensive review of the investment banking industry in American history.

94. *Ibid.*, "Corrected Opinion," 64; *The New York Times*, January 2, 1942; Mayer, *Wall Street: Men and Money*, 171, 174.
95. *U.S. v. Henry S. Morgan et al.*, "Transcript of Trial: Defendants' Opening — Mr. [Wm. Dwight] Whitney" (February 15, 1951), 3145–46.
96. Investment Bankers Association, *Proceedings . . . 1943* (Chicago, 1943), 11–14; *The New York Times*, August 31, 1943.
97. IBA, *Proceedings . . . 1945*, 8.

21   Antitrust

On October 30, 1947, the Justice Department filed a fifty-six-page complaint against seventeen top investment banking firms and the Investment Bankers Association (IBA). In the words of Attorney General Tom Clark, this was "one of the biggest" and "most important" cases ever initiated under the Sherman Act.[1] It was the first suit to be brought against the alleged money monopolists, and it dragged on for six years.

Charges by the Justice Department closely resembled those leveled at investment bankers in earlier investigations, even as far back as the New York life insurance (Armstrong) probe of 1905. As in previous inquiries, the testimony brought out much that was informative about changing patterns in the business of issuing and distributing securities. Furthermore, the trial also served to reveal serious lapses, if not abuses, by some individuals in the industry.

The investment bankers had to meet this costly, prolonged court action after a long depression and the very lean war years. During the period of American participation in World War II, business was prosperous for almost everyone except the investment banker. New corporate issues fell from $2.6 billion in 1941 to less than $1.1 billion in 1942, and long-term state and municipal offerings dropped from $1.2 billion in 1940 to less than $450 million in 1943.[2] Public offerings, mostly refundings, were carefully timed so as to avoid interfering with the government's war loans. The Treasury requested that investment houses not issue new securities during a bond drive. The government, furthermore, directly financed approximately two-thirds of the plant expansion necessary to win the war, much of it through the Defense Plant Corporation, established in 1940 as a subsidiary of the Reconstruction Finance Corporation.[3]

The principal contribution of investment bankers to the war effort was selling war bonds. That job earned them little money (to be sure, sellers' risks were negligible) but won them widespread

---

1. Quoted in "U.S. v. Investment Houses," *Newsweek*, XXX (November 10, 1947), 58. The seventeen firms were Morgan Stanley & Co.; Kuhn, Loeb & Co.; Smith, Barney & Co.; Lehman Brothers; Glore, Forgan & Co.; Kidder, Peabody & Co.; Goldman, Sachs & Co.; White, Weld & Co.; Eastman, Dillon & Co.; Drexel & Co.; The First Boston Corporation; Dillon, Read & Co. Inc.; Blyth & Co. Inc.; Harriman Ripley & Co. Inc.; Stone & Webster Securities Corporation; Harris Hall & Co. Inc.; and Union Securities Corporation.

2. U.S. Bureau of the Census, *Historical Statistics of the United States: Colonial Times to 1957* (Washington, 1960), 658; Investment Bankers Association, *Proceedings . . . 1943* (Chicago, 1943), 144.

3. *U.S. v. Henry S. Morgan et al.*, "Transcript of Trial: Testimony of Harold L. Stuart-Cross" (May 14, 1952), 15806–07; Gerald T. White, "Financing Industrial Expansion for War: The Origin of the Defense Plant Corporation Leases," *The Journal of Economic History*, IX (November 1949), 156–83.

praise from Treasury and other government officials, just as in World War I. "Everyone is shouting our story from the housetops," the president of the IBA reported in 1944. "Can it be that investment banking, the ugly duckling, stoned so long, may possibly become a swan?"[4]

For most firms, wartime investment banking was mostly routine. Most houses depended upon brokerage commissions, advisory services, and a few private placements as their chief sources of income. Profits generally were down. Many firms closed or merged; nearly all operated with reduced staffs; and some houses, such as Kuhn, Loeb & Co. and Lehman Brothers, lost more than half of their partners to the war effort. Many of them joined the armed forces, and others took government jobs.[5] Membership in the IBA steadily declined, from 653 at the time of the Pearl Harbor attack to 578 at the end of 1943, when a modest membership drive brought the figure back up to 628 by the end of 1944.[6] The National Association of Securities Dealers (NASD), which included many firms that did not belong to the IBA, also suffered a substantial decline in membership, from 2,974 in 1941 to 2,193 in 1944.[7]

Throughout the war years the principal concern of investment bankers, like that of everyone else in the country, was to defeat the Axis. The IBA dedicated itself to this task, and most of the speakers at its annual conventions spoke about distributing war bonds or other aspects of war finance, with an occasional complaint that the administration was not making better use of the industry's specialized training and experience. At the same time many of its leaders continued to voice concern over the growing threat of "big government" to business in general and to investment banking in particular, through controls, regulation, and the spread of competitive bidding.

Investment bankers also looked ahead to the problems of postwar reconversion. Beginning in 1943 the IBA offered numerous suggestions designed to help the government make orderly contract terminations and satisfactory arrangements to turn government-owned war plants over to private operators. It also called for a balanced budget and revision of the tax and securities laws to encourage the flow of private capital into industry, and thus to maintain maximum employment. Foreseeing a great postwar expansion, it was optimistic about the future growth of the investment banking business,

4. IBA, *Proceedings* . . . *1944*, 1–8.
5. [Kuhn, Loeb & Co.] *Investment Banking through Four Generations* (New York, 1955), 25; [Lehman Brothers] *A Centennial: Lehman Brothers, 1850–1950* (New York, 1950), 43.
6. IBA, *Proceedings* . . . *1948*, 44.
7. U.S. House, Special Subcommittee on Legislative Oversight of the Committee on Interstate and Foreign Commerce, 85th Cong., 2d Sess., *History of National Association of Securities Dealers, Inc.* . . . (Washington, 1959), 38.

citing the 85 million Americans who had invested in war bonds as potential clients of the future.

Despite such cheering forecasts and wartime talk of the investment bankers' much improved image, some top financiers retained doubts and worries about the future. Industry leaders continued to express concern with lingering prejudices and misconceptions about investment banking's role and methods and the seemingly hostile attitude of some government officials. Their fears proved to be well founded, for two years after Japan had surrendered, the Justice Department instituted its suit, and the investment banking industry was under investigation once again.

The trial itself lasted two and a half years, from November 28, 1950, through May 19, 1953; and its documentation was massive. The stenographic transcript filled 23,962 printed pages; the documents and stipulations introduced added another 33,609 pages to the record. The total amount of material printed for the entire case exceeded 100,000 pages.[8] A dozen attorneys appeared on behalf of the government, and eleven of New York City's most prominent law firms represented the defendants. Dr. Bertrand Fox (until recently Director of Research at the Harvard Graduate School of Business Administration) and a small group of researchers and assistants devoted almost three years to preparing detailed charts and tables analyzing some 10,000 security offerings, including private placements, issued between January 1935 and December 1949. These compilations, together with numerous special studies of pre-1933 offerings, public sealed bidding accounts, syndicate managements and participations, spreads and selling concessions were based on quantitative data as to each security issued during the fifteen years 1935–1949. Both the government and the defendants accepted these data as the foundation of summary statistical tabulations to be used during the trial.[9] The cost of preparing and trying the case was estimated at from $1.5 million to $3 million for the government and between $5 million and $7 million for the defendants.[10]

Public announcement of the start of the case revived many memories of earlier charges against the Wall Street money trust. Some of them went as far back as the beginning of the twentieth century, when Thomas W. Lawson published his "Frenzied Finance" in *Everybody's*. More specifically, many repeated the same allegations of the Pujo investigation and Louis Brandeis's condemnation of the financial oligarchs who supposedly controlled the country's economic life. To all those who agreed with the findings of these

8. *U.S. v. Henry S. Morgan et al.,* "Corrected Opinion of Harold R. Medina" (February 4, 1954), 413–15.

9. *Ibid.,* 419–24; Bertrand Fox to author, February 17, 1967. See also [National Bureau of Economic Research, Financial Research Program] *Research in the Capital and Securities Markets* (New York, 1954), 5–7.

10. *The New York Times,* September 23, 1953.

exposés and investigations, and whose earlier suspicions of Wall Street bankers had been strengthened considerably by the Pecora and other congressional disclosures of the early 1930's, the government's action promised to be the anticipated final chapter in the people's long struggle to destroy the mightiest monopoly of them all — the New York City money ring. The great financial houses that repeatedly had been indicted by Lawson, Untermyer, Pujo, Brandeis, and Pecora finally were to be brought to trial, and the sources and machinery of their power exposed and effectively curtailed.

Both the substance and the language of the government's complaint were reminiscent of these earlier investigations, as well as those conducted more recently by the TNEC.[11] The findings of all these inquiries were brought up and argued over repeatedly during the trial. But the distinguishing feature of this case, the defense attorneys stressed, was the fact that for the first time the accused were allowed to challenge the evidence cited against them and to cross-examine witnesses. Every investigation from Pujo through the TNEC, Arthur H. Dean, one of the principal defense attorneys, told the court, was stacked with anti-investment banking members who were intent upon finding fault rather than disclosing truth.[12]

The case had several roots. Its immediate origins stemmed from the TNEC's report on investment banking concentration. The strong, concerted opposition of the leading Wall Street houses to compulsory public sealed bidding, which the government cited as evidence of lack of competition in the new issues business, also played an important part in persuading the government to bring suit, as did the continuing complaints of Cyrus Eaton, of Otis & Co. Some defense attorneys traced the source of the case to the prejudices, lack of practical business knowledge, misinformation, and political bias of the legal theoreticians and academicians in the Justice Department's Antitrust Division.[13] Others interpreted the government's action as an effort to accomplish by court decision what the critics of investment banking had failed to achieve through legislation or SEC rulings.[14]

---

11. *U.S. v. Henry S. Morgan et al.*, "Transcript of Trial: Testimony of Harold L. Stuart — Colloquy" (April 7, 1952), 14676–80; *ibid.*, "Copy of Complaint," *passim*.

12. *Ibid.*, "Defendants' Opening — Mr. Dean" (December 11, 1950), 707–13; *The New York Times*, December 12, 1950, March 28, 1954.

13. *U.S. v. Henry S. Morgan et al.*, "Transcript of Trial: Defendants' Opening — Mr. Dean" (January 9, 1951), 1455–57; *ibid.*, "Defendants' Opening — Mr. Whitney" (February 15, 1951), 3222–25; *ibid.*, "Defendants' Case" (March 19, 1953), 21432–35; *ibid.*, "Defendants' Motions" (April 16, 1953), 22317–25. See also *The New York Times*, December 14, 20, 1950; Marcus Gleisser, *The World of Cyrus Eaton* (New York, 1965), ch. x.

14. "Antitrust Case Silver Lining," *Business Week* (November 8, 1947), 86; *The New York Times*, October 12, 1953.

Since the close of the TNEC hearings the Justice Department had been collecting data on the investment banking business. Although the national defense program and American participation in World War II delayed formal proceedings, they did not prevent the department from continuing its investigation. In February 1944 it filed a brief with the SEC declaring price-fixing clauses commonly used in underwriting agreements illegal under the Sherman Antitrust Act. This news hit investment firms "like a bombshell." The IBA immediately sought to counter the government's attack on syndicate contracts by having Congressman Carroll Reece, a conservative Tennessee Republican, introduce an amendment to the Securities Act formally legalizing price-fixing agreements during the time a new offering was being distributed. Nothing came of this proposal, nor of a second, similar one, introduced in January 1945, except to provide still further evidence for the government's attorneys.[15]

Harry S Truman's accession to the presidency, on April 12, 1945, spurred the hopes of Wall Street's critics. He had been a strong advocate of compulsory bidding and, a year earlier, at the request of Harold L. Ickes, had argued persuasively for it before the ICC, using many of the same arguments that had been employed earlier by Robert R. Young and Cyrus Eaton.[16]

The first indication that the government was ready to proceed against certain investment houses occurred late in July 1945, when the Justice Department filed its criminal conspiracy charges before a federal grand jury in the Southern District of New York. The purpose of these proceedings was to allow the government to subpoena the records of these firms and those of their clients.[17]

While the grand jury was conducting its investigation, Eaton stepped up his campaign against the New York bankers. As on previous occasions, he sought to enlist the assistance of Ickes, who had resigned from the cabinet in February 1946.[18] The "Old Curmudgeon" had helped Eaton before, arranging meetings for him with Jerome Frank of the SEC and other government officials. Ickes shared Eaton's dislike for Wall Street, and the Cleveland banker hoped that the former Secretary would join him in arousing public opinion against the alleged monopolists.[19]

15. *U.S. v. Henry S. Morgan et al.,* "Plaintiff's Exhibits," Nos. 1369-B, 1370-B, 1371-B; ibid., "Corrected Opinion," 146–49. See also *The New York Times,* February 13, 1944.

16. *U.S. v. Henry S. Morgan et al.,* "Transcript of Trial: Defendants' Motions" (April 16, 1953), 22317–25.

17. Ibid., "Transcript of Trial: Plaintiff's Case" (February 13, 1952), 12492–95; Arthur H. Dean to author, May 13, 1964. See also "Antitrust Case Silver Lining," 86; *The New York Times,* October 16, 1947; Gleisser, *The World of Cyrus Eaton,* 155–57.

18. Harry S Truman, *Memoirs* (2 vols., New York, 1955–56), I, 553–54.

19. Harold L. Ickes, *The Secret Diary of Harold L. Ickes* (3 vols., New York, 1953–54), III, 41.

Eaton also may have sought Ickes's support because of the prominent Wall Streeters in the Truman administration. These included Commerce Secretary W. Averell Harriman and Under Secretary of State Robert A. Lovett, both formerly with Brown Brothers Harriman & Co., and Defense Secretary James V. Forrestal, a long-time member of Dillon, Read & Co. Fear that these men might persuade the grand jury to drop, delay, or soften its charges probably influenced the Cleveland banker's behavior too.[20]

Meanwhile, Eaton himself appears to have supplied the government with information to prepare its suit. During the course of the trial one of the defense lawyers cited an article in *The Cleveland Plain Dealer* to show Eaton's role in instigating the action. This item asserted that "the bulk of the government's case had been drawn from Otis & Co."[21] Months later, when the subject came up again, the government's attorney neither admitted nor denied the fact. "It would be the grossest breach of my duty to reveal whether Mr. Eaton did or did not" provide such information, he said.[22]

On October 30, 1947, Attorney General Clark announced that the government had filed a civil suit against seventeen investment houses and the IBA, charging them with violation of Sections 1 and 2 of the Sherman Act. The defendants, the complaint charged, had "entered into a combination, conspiracy and agreement to restrain and monopolize the securities business of the United States and that such business was thereby unreasonably restrained and in part monopolized."[23] The reason why the Justice Department had decided upon civil rather than criminal proceedings, Clark explained, was that the practices employed by the defendants had been in use for many years and were well known.[24] Dean attributed the decision to the fact that the grand jury hearings had exposed the weakness of the government's case, a view that was shared by many other knowledgeable observers.[25]

Eaton applauded the suit as "an absolute necessity." "The nation simply will no longer stand for the continued concentration of financial control in a few hands and in one place, because it has been amply demonstrated that such control militates against the creative and constructive finance that is the keystone of our free enterprise system."[26]

20. No doubt the Ickes manuscripts in the Library of Congress contain information on Eaton's activities in pushing the trial. Permission to use and cite from this collection was not granted.
21. *U.S. v. Henry S. Morgan et al.*, "Transcript of Trial: Defendants' Opening — Mr. [Ralph M.] Carson" (January 18, 1951), 2012.
22. *Ibid.*, "Plaintiff's Case" (November 14, 1951), 10686.
23. *Ibid.*, "Corrected Opinion," 1.
24. "U.S. v. Investment Houses," 58; "Antitrust Case Silver Lining," 86.
25. Dean to author, May 13, 1964. See also "$14,357,000,000.00," *The Commonweal*, XLVII (November 14, 1947), 108.
26. Quoted in *The New York Times*, October 31, 1947.

Although probably more responsible than any other single individual for having instigated the case, Eaton never was called to testify as a government witness.[27] The government, it appears, was aware that Eaton's charges were difficult, if not impossible, to substantiate, and it was concerned too that his appearance on the witness stand might prove more embarrassing to its case than to the defendants'.[28]

Wall Street accepted Attorney General Clark's announcement with great calm. The defendants denied the conspiracy charges; cited the competition that existed in the investment banking business; suggested that the case was politically motivated and, in the words of Harold Stanley, that the Justice Department had been "misled" in bringing the action. Many of the defendants actually welcomed it. Since "attacks on Wall Street are still popular in certain quarters for political reasons," a Kuhn, Loeb spokesman observed, "it should prove constructive to have the issues in this case decided by our courts," and thus put an end to "the long-continued efforts to harass a business which plays so vital a part in our economy." John Hancock of Lehman Brothers asserted that the government's charges stemmed from "ignorance of how the business is done," and that they "will not stand the light of day."[29] Similar views were expressed by other defendants. Harry M. Addinsell of The First Boston Corporation testified that on reading the complaint his reaction was "sort of like old Hans Andersen Fairy Tales that referred to people that didn't exist because I didn't recognize all the conspirators who were described therein or all the conspiracies."[30]

Many Wall Streeters were puzzled by the Justice Department's choice of the seventeen firms, and some prominent investment bankers considered it a slight not to have been included. "It made them feel like second-class citizens," Dean said.[31] Nor was the choice entirely clear to Judge Medina. "I just cannot figure it out," he said nearly two and a half years after the beginning of the trial. For a time he had thought that the government had picked the seventeen solely because their total underwritings during the years 1935 through 1949, when added together, resulted in a figure that the Justice Department wanted to arrive at in order to prove its concentration and monopoly charges. This, Judge Medina believed, might explain why several houses with very small underwriting percentages had been included. Drexel & Co. and Union Securities Cor-

27. *U.S. v. Henry S. Morgan et al.*, "Transcript of Trial: Defendants' Opening — Mr. Carson" (January 18, 1951), 2012–13; *ibid.* (November 14, 1951), 10686.
28. Dean to author, May 13, 1964.
29. *The New York Times,* October 31, 1947.
30. *U. S. v. Henry S. Morgan et al.*, "Transcript of Trial: Plaintiff's Case — Deposition of [Harry M.] Addinsell" (May 22, 1951), 7481.
31. Dean to author, May 13, 1964.

poration, for instance, had underwritten less than 1 percent of the total offerings brought out during the fifteen-year period under investigation, and two other defendants, Eastman, Dillon & Co. and White, Weld & Co., had underwritten less than 1.5 percent.[32]

A careful analysis of the underwriting statistics for these years quickly disproved the theory that the defendants had been chosen because they constituted what Dean called "a ranked list" of the top seventeen underwriters. In the period from January 1, 1938, through April 30, 1947, Halsey, Stuart, a nondefendant, managed more underwritten issues registered with the SEC (11.5 percent) than any of the defendants except Morgan Stanley (15.4 percent) and The First Boston Corporation (14.3 percent).[33] In 1950, according to the *Investment Dealers Digest,* Halsey, Stuart surpassed these two firms, sponsoring $723 million of new issues as compared with $644 million for Morgan Stanley and $555 million for The First Boston Corporation, the next two leading syndicate managers. Exhibit 21,

Exhibit 21. Leading syndicate heads, 1950 (in millions)

Firm	Amount	Firm	Amount
Halsey Stuart & Co.[a]	723	Stone & Webster Securities Corp.	169
Morgan Stanley & Co.	644	Salomon Bros. & Hutzler[a]	145
The First Boston Corp.	555	Dillon, Read & Co.	120
Merrill Lynch, Pierce Fenner & Beane[a]	338	Harriman, Ripley & Co.	102
Kidder, Peabody & Co.	289	Kuhn, Loeb & Co.	97
Blyth & Co.	265	Glore, Forgan & Co.	79
Lehman Brothers	232	Equitable Securities Corp.[a]	50
White, Weld & Co.	210	Drexel & Co.	40
Union Securities Corp.	182		

Source: U.S. v. Henry S. Morgan et al., "Transcript of Trial, Reply Opening Statement — Mr. Whitney" (March 29, 1951), 5356–57.
[a] Nondefendants.

taken from this publication and read into the transcript of the trial, lists the "Leading Syndicate Heads" for 1950 and the dollar amount of all underwritten issues of $1 million or more sponsored by them, except municipals, private placements, and agency transactions.[34]

The defense attorneys claimed that the choice of the seventeen

32. *U.S. v. Henry S. Morgan et al.,* "Transcript of Trial: Defendants' Case" (March 19, 1953), 21429.
33. *U.S. v. Henry S. Morgan et al.,* "Copy of Complaint," 49; Paul L. Howell, "Competition in the Capital Markets," *Harvard Business Review,* XXXI (May–June 1953), 89.
34. *U.S. v. Henry S. Morgan et al.,* "Transcript of Trial: Reply Opening Statement — Mr. Whitney" (March 29, 1951), 5355–57.

was an entirely artificial one, which had little relation to the amount of their underwritings and even less to the size of their capital. There were some twenty other investment houses that had greater financial resources than the defendants.[35] The real reason, the defense argued, was to be found in the histories of these firms and the way they had conducted their affairs. Some were included because they or their predecessors had been accused of monopoly previously, either by Pujo or the TNEC; others, such as Lehman Brothers and Goldman, Sachs, were selected because they had worked together closely in underwriting many issues. Drexel, organized on April 1, 1940, was included among the seventeen, according to the defense attorneys, for no other reason than that of its name, which happened to be exactly the same as that of the pre-1934 Philadelphia house of J. P. Morgan.[36]

Harris, Hall & Co., Inc., was made a defendant because of its former connection with the Harris Trust & Savings Bank of Chicago and the Harris, Forbes organizations in Boston and New York; Blyth, because it was alleged to have succeeded to the investment banking business of the National City Co. The fact that in June 1935 Charles E. Mitchell, the former head of this affiliate, joined Blyth as chairman of its board appeared to confirm the government's reliance on the successorship theory still further. These and other similar historic relationships, the defense claimed, constituted the principal criteria of selection.[37]

The government not only asserted the importance of these historic relationships, some of which first were disclosed by the TNEC, but sought to show how the defendants had used them, together with certain other business practices, to monopolize the investment banking business in violation of the Sherman Act. These seventeen houses, the government charged, had engaged in price fixing, refused to compete with one another for managements, and divided underwriting participations among themselves. The net effect of their policies was to exclude from the "cream of the business" some two hundred houses with the capital and expertise to underwrite issues of $1 million or more. Occasionally, when one of these outsiders posed a competitive threat, the defendants bought it off with an offer of a participation or, more rarely and only when it was absolutely necessary, by granting it a co-managership.[38] Consistent refusal to compete, the government argued, was what distinguished

35. *Ibid.* (March 29, 1951), 5353–55; *ibid.,* "Government's Opening (Rebuttal — Mr. Baldridge)" (March 21, 1951), 4903.
36. *Ibid.,* "Transcript of Trial: Reply Opening Statement — Mr. Dean" (March 30, 1951), 5402–05; *ibid.,* "Defendants' Case" (March 19, 1953), 21430.
37. *Ibid.,* "Transcript of Trial: Reply Opening Statement — Mr. Whitney" (March 29, 1951), 5349–61; *ibid.* (March 30, 1951), 5398–5413; *ibid.,* "Defendants' Case" (March 19, 1953), 21428–32.
38. *Ibid.,* "Government's Opening (Rebuttal — Mr. Baldridge)" (March 21, 1951), 4902–11.

the seventeen from other investment houses; and this, more than anything else, was the reason why they had been indicted.

One argument centered on the Halsey, Stuart firm. That house, whose capital and number of syndicate managements since 1935 greatly exceeded those of nearly all the seventeen, was not made a defendant, the prosecution said, because it "competes for the business it handles," and because Harold Stuart had been "a leader in the fight for public sealed bidding, whether . . . required by a government agency or not."[39] The fact that Halsey, Stuart was exclusively a bond house, dealing mostly in issues that since 1941 had to be offered competitively, was cited by the defense as proof that the real reason why the seventeen were chosen was because they had opposed compulsory bidding; that, and nothing else, was what distinguished the defendants from other firms. Even more important, "the only time that you can identify the defendants, or most of them, all on one side and on one subject and all working together," one of the defense attorneys told Medina, "was in the campaign against public sealed bidding."[40]

Because of its role in this fight, and its lobbying activities against other regulatory legislation, the IBA also was made a defendant, the defense maintained. The government sought its dissolution on the grounds that the defendants had used the association to further the alleged conspiracy.[41]

Pretrial proceedings lasted thirty-seven months. During this time the defendants filed their answers to the complaint and asked the court to require the government to answer 160 interrogatories, all designed to force the Justice Department to make its charges more specific.[42] Government attorneys asked the court to deny all of them, saying they were intended only to "hamstring" the department's preparation of the case. After considering each interrogatory separately, Medina ordered the government to answer 51 of them. This was no small victory for the defendants, since it forced the government to specify, among other things, when and by whom the alleged conspiracy was started, give the names of the co-conspirators, and describe how the conspiracy was effected and continued.[43]

It took the government almost ten months to answer the interrogatories. Much of the material came from the files of the defendants themselves. It included correspondence and various syndicate and other agreements illustrating the way the defendants organized purchase and selling groups, fixed and controlled the public offering price of new issues, allocated underwriting participations to one

39. *Ibid.*, 4907–11.
40. *Ibid.*, "Reply Opening Statement — Mr. Whitney" (March 29, 1951), 5352.
41. *The New York Times,* October 31, 1947, December 6, 1947; Investment Bankers Association, *Fiftieth Anniversary: 1912–1962* (n.p. [1962?]), 25.
42. *The New York Times,* January 24, 1948, May 18, 1948.
43. *Ibid.,* August 8, 1963.

another, decided upon management fees, and in other ways supposedly conspired to restrain competition and monopolize the securities business. The agreement relating to Morgan's organization of the syndicate to distribute the huge Anglo-French loan of 1915 was considered especially significant, since the government used it to establish the beginning of the alleged conspiracy.[44]

The case finally came to trial on November 28, 1950, before United States Circuit Judge Medina. He had just finished presiding over the widely publicized trial of eleven top officials of the Communist party, which resulted in their imprisonment for violation of the Smith Act of 1940. Born in Brooklyn, New York, on February 16, 1888, Medina was graduated from Princeton University in 1909 and from Columbia University Law School in 1912. A few years later he returned to Columbia as a part-time law instructor, a post he held until 1940. His own practice, meanwhile, grew steadily, and in 1947, when Truman appointed him to the federal bench, Medina headed a firm of some twenty attorneys and was earning an estimated $100,000 a year.[45]

Medina was assigned the investment banking case at the suggestion of Learned Hand, the distinguished jurist whom Medina later succeeded on the Court of Appeals for the Second Circuit. Hand believed that Medina's experience and record qualified him to preside over what everyone acknowledged would be a difficult and complicated case. The trial proved these predictions. The investment banking case, Medina recalled later, "took more out of me" than the Communist trial.[46] His forbearance during those proceedings won him the title of the "patient" judge, a quality Medina possessed in abundance, as he demonstrated repeatedly during the many heated legal arguments that erupted during the investment banking case. What was wearing him out, he told the attorneys on both sides, only six months after the start of the trial, was their constant wrangling. "Twenty-five years ago I could have sat and listened to that sort of thing until the cows came home, and it just rolled off my back like water off a duck's, but now it doesn't. So just let us try to avoid it where we can." [47]

Though an expert in neither antitrust law nor investment bank-

44. *U.S. v. Henry S. Morgan et al.*, "Corrected Opinion," 4, 239; *ibid.*, "Defendants' Opening — Mr. Whitney" (February 1, 1951), 2620–26. See also *The New York Times*, October 16, 1948. In order to keep the case within "reasonable bounds" and prevent it from dragging on for years, Judge Medina later ruled out all evidence having to do with transactions prior to January 1, 1935. See also *U.S. v. Henry S. Morgan et al.*, "Plaintiff's Case" (October 3, 1951), 9075–77.

45. Hawthorne Daniel, *Judge Medina* (New York, 1952), chs. i–iii; *The New York Times*, October 10, 1966; *New York World-Telegram and Sun*, February 8, 1966; Harold R. Medina to author, September 2, 1966.

46. Medina to author, September 2, 1966. See also *U.S. v. Henry S. Morgan et al.*, "Transcript of Trial: Defendants' Opening — Mr. Whitney" (February 1, 1951), 2586–90.

47. *U.S. v. Henry S. Morgan et al.*, "Transcript of Trial — Plaintiff's Case" (May 18, 1951), 7233.

ing, Medina quickly came to grips with the core of the case. "I see difficulties in proof. I see many of those, but as to the theory on which they [the government attorneys] are proceeding, I think I have a pretty good notion of it," he told one of the defense lawyers.[48] Medina made it clear from the very beginning that there were two things with which he was chiefly concerned: (1) whether the evidence applied only to one or to all the defendants, and (2) even more important, whether there actually was a conspiracy. "I am going to be thinking about that right from the drop of the hat every minute of the time that we are trying this case." Learning the way the defendants had conducted their business was, in his opinion, far more important than the rhetoric they used to explain their actions, and he cautioned both sides that he intended to scrutinize and test the evidence with that in mind.[49] "I am from Missouri on every single phase of this case," he said. He was as skeptical of the claims of the defendants as he was of the government's charges. "I think that is what I ought to be." [50]

To prove its charge that the defendants had conspired successfully to monopolize the securities business, the government submitted statistics showing that in the ten years between January 1938 and April 1947 the seventeen firms had managed 68.9 percent of all publicly offered securities, amounting to $14.4 billion. These issues represented some 85 percent of the "prime" securities merchandised during this period. The government charged that the dominance exercised by these firms had "arbitrarily and unreasonably limited and restricted" the activities of hundreds of other investment bankers, with the result that 258 major houses were forced to scramble for the remaining 31.1 percent ($6.4 billion) of the country's underwriting business; and of this amount, slightly less than one-half, 15.1 percent ($3.1 billion), had been sponsored by the largest of the nondefendants, Halsey, Stuart. The other 257 nondefendants had to settle for the remaining 16 percent of the business, amounting to $3.3 billion out of a total of $20.8 billion (see Exhibit 22).[51]

48. *Ibid.*, "Defendants' Opening — Mr. Whitney" (February 1, 1951), 2586–90. See also *ibid.*, "Government's Opening" (December 5, 1950), 359–60.
49. *Ibid.*, "Hearing before Judge Medina" (November 8, 1950), 47–53. See also *ibid.*, "Transcript of Trial: Plaintiff's Case" (May 18, 1951), 7244–45 (October 15, 1952), 17699–703.
50. *Ibid.*, "Defendants' Opening" (December 8, 1950), 637.
51. *U.S. v. Henry S. Morgan et al.*, "Copy of Complaint," 21, 24, 49. See also *The New York Times*, October 31, 1947; Howell, "Competition in the Capital Markets," 88–90. During the course of the trial, one of the government's attorneys stated that if the "statistical period" was extended to cover all the years under review, from January 1935 to the end of 1949, the extent of the defendants' control over the industry would have appeared even greater. These firms, he charged, actually had "managed 82 per cent of all new security issues and registered secondaries sold on a negotiated basis." See *U.S. v. Henry S. Morgan et al.*, "Transcript of Trial: Government's Opening" (December 5, 1950), 403–04; *The New York Times*, November 29, 1950.

Exhibit 22. Concentration of control in the investment banking business: security issues managed[a] January 1, 1938, to April 30, 1947 (in millions)

	Issues registered with SEC	Rail issues (exclusive of equipment trust issues)	Total issues managed	Percent of all issues
Morgan Stanley & Co.	2,783.6	578.8	3,362.4	16.1
First Boston Corporation[b]	2,592.4	133.6	2,726.0	13.1
Dillon, Read & Co., Inc.	1,460.1	26.0	1,486.1	7.1
Kuhn, Loeb & Co.	762.1	618.0	1,380.1	6.6
Blyth & Co.	838.9	63.3	902.2	4.3
Smith, Barney & Co.	804.0	–	804.0	3.9
Lehman Brothers	604.3	36.0	640.3	3.1
Harriman, Ripley & Co., Inc.	611.6	6.7	618.3	3.0
Glore, Forgan & Co.	418.7	–	418.7	2.0
Kidder, Peabody & Co.	364.0	28.9	392.9	1.9
Stone & Webster Securities Corporation	352.1	–	352.1	1.7
Goldman, Sachs & Co.	287.8	–	287.8	1.4
Harris, Hall & Co. (Incorporated)	240.6	–	240.6	1.2
White, Weld & Co.	233.5	4.8	238.3	1.1
Eastman, Dillon & Co.	212.0	–	212.0	1.0
Union Securities Corporation	181.8	–	181.8	0.9
Drexel & Co.	90.2	23.4	113.6	0.5
Total — 17 defendant banking firms	12,837.7	1,519.5	14,357.2	68.9
Total — 1 nondefendant investment banking firm	2,097.7	1,050.3	3,148.0	15.1
Total — 257 nondefendant investment banking firms	3,190.8	146.2	3,337.0	16.0
Total — 275 investment banking firms	18,126.2	2,716.0	20,842.2	100.0

Source: U.S. v. Henry S. Morgan et al., "Copy of Complaint," 49.
[a] Co-managed issues shown pro-rata for each co-manager.
[b] Includes issues managed by Mellon Securities Corporation.

Not only did the defendants monopolize the management of new issues, but they also effectively excluded most other investment houses from participating in their buying groups and underwriting syndicates. During the ten years between January 1938 and April 1947, according to the government's tabulations, the total buying

Exhibit 23. Total amount of buying group participations of seventeen defendant banking firms in buying groups managed by one of their number from January 1, 1938, through April 30, 1947

Year	Buying group participations	Defendant banking firms' participations	Percent
	(millions)	(millions)	
1938	715.7	596.0	83.3
1939	619.7	563.2	90.9
1940	811.2	703.9	86.8
1941	607.8	598.7	98.5
1942	265.4	246.1	92.7
1943	377.9	356.7	94.4
1944	688.0	616.1	89.5
1945	1,413.9	1,348.0	95.3
1946	1,760.9	1,675.4	95.1
1947[a]	411.0	396.7	96.5

Source: U.S. v. Henry S. Morgan et al., "Copy of Complaint," 50.
[a] From January 1 through April 30.

group participations of the defendants in syndicates managed by them never fell below 83.3 percent of their total purchases or underwriting commitments. More often than not they exceeded 90 percent, as Exhibit 23 indicates.[52] Competitors thus were deprived of the opportunity to participate in selling many of the choicest securities offered during these years.

The conspiracy, the complaint charged, also damaged the interests of issuers and investors. The former were forced to sell their bonds and stocks at noncompetitive prices, and the latter had to buy them on equally disadvantageous terms. "Issuers and investors have been deprived of freedom of choice with respect to the method by which, the terms upon which, and the investment bankers through which they respectively may dispose of and may purchase security issues." [53]

Allegedly the conspiracy was effected by the defendants and their predecessors "in or about" 1915, at the time of the great Anglo-French loan. It was continued and enforced through a variety of formal and informal agreements and practices designed to eliminate competition among themselves and from other investment bankers in violation of the Sherman Act.[54] The "core, the heart, the very

52. *U.S. v. Henry S. Morgan et al.,* "Copy of Complaint," 21, 50.
53. *Ibid.,* 42; *The New York Times,* November 29, 1950.
54. *U.S. v. Henry S. Morgan et al.,* "Copy of Complaint," 24–25; *ibid.,* "Transcript of Trial; Government's Opening" (November 28, 1950), 3–24. See also *ibid.* (March 14, 1951), 4505–07; *ibid.,* "Hearing before Judge Medina" (April 26, 1951), 5556–65.

essence" of the case, Medina asserted, rested on the claim that the defendants "by their various combinations and machinations" had stifled competition, monopolized the merchandising of securities, restrained issuers, and deprived investors of the opportunity to buy securities in a competitive market under conditions of free competition.[55]

In effecting and preserving their monopoly of the securities business, all the defendants followed identical policies and employed similar practices, prosecutors asserted. Some practices, such as fixing and controlling the price of new offerings, were outright violations of the law; others, such as the campaign against competitive bidding and the use of directorships to control issuers, though not illegal in themselves, had been intentionally subverted and abused to sustain and promote "a wrongful and unlawful conspiracy."[56]

The government did not rest its case on any specific abuses or illegalities, important as these were. The "gravamen of the complaint," one observer noted at the close of the trial, was the existence among the defendants of "an unwritten code of ethics, a custom, a pattern, or mode of operation which, when viewed in its entirety, amounts to and has the effect of restraining active competition in the investment banking business and monopolizing said business."[57] The "continuing agreement and concert of action" that distinguished the policies and practices of these firms from those of other investment bankers constituted an unlawful and harmful conspiracy.

Charges against the defendants filled sixteen pages of the complaint. Some of them were dropped as the trial progressed, whereas others were narrowed or revised. One of the first to be abandoned was the accusation that the IBA had conspired and cooperated with the defendant bankers in conducting "intensive pressure and propaganda campaigns" against compulsory public sealed bidding for certain types of securities. Very early in the trial Medina criticized the government's attorneys severely for citing the IBA and the other defendants' opposition to public sealed bidding as evidence against them; the charge smacked of "totalitarianism" and infringed the freedoms guaranteed by the Bill of Rights, he said. "It positively shocks me," he told the government's chief attorney at the time, "that men who openly press their views on public bodies in the open should be accused of wrongdoing."[58]

A few days later, speaking again on the subject, Medina added:

55. *Ibid.*, "Transcript of Trial: Government's Opening" (December 5, 1950), 402; *ibid.*, "Defendants' Opening—Mr. Whitney" (February 16, 1951), 3280–81.
56. *Ibid.*, "Copy of Complaint," 25; "Transcript of Trial: Government's Opening" (December 5, 1950), 374, 380–82. See also *The New York Times*, December 2, 5, 1950.
57. Howell, "Competition in the Capital Markets," 90–91. See also *U.S. v. Henry S. Morgan et al.*, "Transcript of Trial: Plaintiff's Case" (March 13, 1953), 21247–60.
58. Quoted in *The New York Times*, December 1, 1950.

"Now I see a big difference between some kind of sneaky, furtive lobbying that you can't put your finger on so that influence is brought to bear on committees of Congress or administrative bodies or whatever it may be in a way that is not plain to the public. That doesn't seem to me to be quite in the American tradition. But to come right out in the open where everybody can see who the man is, that he is frankly furthering his own economic interest — that seems different to me, and that is a thing that I just bristle up at every time you get down to it." [59]

Medina returned to this question again in March 1951, when he asked the government to drop the charge against the IBA, saying that the defendants' opposition to competitive bidding was protected by the Bill of Rights' guarantee of free speech.[60] The prosecution demurred, but eight months later, on November 19, 1951, it withdrew the charges.[61]

Prosecuting attorneys also chose this occasion to drop several charges against the remaining defendants. Among the most important of those dropped were the ones accusing the seventeen bankers of coercing other investment houses and security dealers to refuse to accept agency transactions, whereby they acted as agents of either the purchaser or the issuer, receiving a commission for their services. The government also discarded the charges that the defendants had refused to advise and finance their clients' competitors without prior approval, encouraged and promoted reorganizations, consolidations, and refinancings in order to create more business for themselves, and neglected to assist small companies in need of capital. Also excluded was the accusation that the conspirators had infiltrated protective committees of insolvent and reorganized companies in order to protect or extend their influence over the management of these enterprises. And lastly, the government withdrew the charge that the accused had plotted to concentrate the securities business "in a single market where," according to the complaint, "sales are made to large institutional investors upon terms and conditions favorable to such buyers and with a minimum of risk to the defendant banking firms." [62]

In May 1952 the government yielded on two other major issues. It withdrew its original demand that the court issue an injunction requiring the defendants to function either as financial advisers to issuing corporations or as merchandisers of their securities, but

---

59. *U.S. v. Henry S. Morgan et al.*, "Transcript of Trial: Government's Opening" (December 5, 1950), 384–85. See also *ibid.*, "Defendants' Opening — Mr. [Arthur H.] Dean" (December 12, 1950), 838–40.
60. *The New York Times*, March 15, 1951.
61. *U.S. v. Henry S. Morgan et al.*, "Plaintiff's Case" (November 19, 1951), 10775–87, 10791–93; *The New York Times*, November 20, 1951.
62. *U.S. v. Henry S. Morgan et al.*, "Copy of Complaint," 28–30; *The New York Times*, April 6, 1951, November 20, 1951.

not as both; and it no longer asked that the officers of these seventeen firms be enjoined from acting as financial advisers to issuers.[63] Neither these nor subsequent deletions from the original complaint altered the central issue on which the case was fought.

The "heart" of the government's case, Medina stated repeatedly, rested on certain alleged "customs and practices" collectively labeled the "triple concept." [64] The three parts of this concept, or code of behavior, to which all the defendants supposedly adhered and around which the government's attorneys tied all their other charges were those of "traditional banker," "historical position," and "reciprocity." The term traditional banker itself was coined at the time of the TNEC hearings, and several of the others used in the case also came out of that and earlier investigations, as did much of the ideology upon which the triple concept charge was based.

Traditional banker described the practice whereby the defendants recognized the investment house that first managed an issuer's offering as being entitled to head all its subsequent issues. Although the Glass-Steagall Banking Act of 1933 required the separation of commercial and investment banking, government attorneys maintained that the defendants, even after splitting up, had agreed to recognize that certain of their number had succeeded to or inherited the business previously done by their predecessors.[65] Recognition of these so-called "predecessor-successor" relationships, as the government labeled them, allowed the defendants to continue their illegal conspiracy and confirmed the vital importance of the traditional banker concept in the case.[66] It was rigid adherence to this principle that enabled these seventeen firms to eliminate competition among themselves and preserve their hold over the financial affairs of their clients. "When one of the defendant banking firms is the traditional banker for an issuer," the government charged, "none of the other defendants will discuss or undertake the merchandising of new security issues for that issuer." [67]

Historical position referred to the allegedly restrictive practices the defendants used in selecting their syndicate partners. Once a defendant firm had participated in a buying or underwriting group to merchandise the securities of a particular issuer, it was entitled, according to the unwritten code that supposedly governed the relations of the members of "Club 17," to "participate on substantially the same terms" in all future syndicates established to distribute

63. *U.S. v. Henry S. Morgan et al.*, "Transcript of Trial: Government's Opening" (December 5, 1950), 383–84; *The New York Times*, May 30, 1952.
64. *The New York Times*, December 21, 1950.
65. *U.S. v. Henry S. Morgan et al.*, "Corrected Opinion," 5–6. See also *ibid.*, "Transcript of Trial: Plaintiff's Case" (February 4, 1952), 12177–82.
66. *Ibid.*, "Plaintiff's Case" (February 16, 1953), 20145–48.
67. *Ibid.*, "Copy of Complaint," 31. See also *ibid.*, "Corrected Opinion," 3.

that issuer's securities.[68] The historical position concept was used by the defendants, the government charged, to exclude rival firms from their syndicates, thus depriving them of the opportunity to compete for most of the "prime" offerings.

Reciprocity was the policy whereby the defendants agreed to exchange participations in syndicates on an agreed-upon formula. Specifically, in any given period of time, "the amount of gross spreads which one of such firms enables another to earn by selecting it for participation in buying groups is substantially equivalent (with due allowance for differentials in prestige and underwriting strength) to the amount of gross spreads it has earned in the same period of time as a participant in buying groups formed and managed by such other firm." [69] Each of the defendants kept a detailed "reciprocity record," indicating exactly the amount of business it had received from and granted to every other member of the group. This practice, the government charged, deprived nondefendant firms of the opportunity to participate in merchandising nearly all the better quality issues, with the result that the "cream of the business" remained the exclusive monopoly of the members of "Club 17."

The traditional banker charge was the most important of the three. Moreover, Medina noted during the trial, it was the only feature of the triple concept that, if proved, was "patently artificial and could not reasonably be accounted for as a normal and to-be-anticipated result of the ebb and flow of natural, unrestrained competitive effort." The other two, if proved, did not violate the Sherman Act. They were nothing more than a form of "pay-off," as Medina put it, the reward the traditional banker paid his co-conspirators for recognizing his special relationship with a particular issuer. If the government failed to prove its traditional banker charges, the others, he said, had "no significance." [70]

Price fixing was the other principal offense charged in the complaint. The government held that the various restrictive clauses commonly found in almost all syndicate agreements violated Section 1 of the Sherman Act. These included, among others, provisions fixing and controlling the public offering price of securities, establishing the concessions and discounts allowed dealers, imposing penalties on brokers whose securities had to be repurchased by the group, and authorizing the manager to stabilize the price of the issue during its initial distribution. The SEC, which supervised these practices closely, did not consider them illegal restraints on competition. Indeed, it endorsed them as highly necessary. "Our views on the application of the antitrust laws to the securities field

68. *Ibid.,* "Corrected Opinion," 3; *ibid.,* "Copy of Complaint," 32.
69. *Ibid.,* "Copy of Complaint," 31–32.
70. *Ibid.,* "Corrected Opinion," 222–23, 228.

may be summarized as follows," the SEC had declared almost a decade earlier: "the mere making of agreements containing provisions for a fixed offering price, price maintenance and stabilization is not per se unlawful. But, like many other contracts, these may be entered into and performed under circumstances that amount to an unlawful suppression of competition." [71]

On the other hand, the Justice Department contended that these agreements were per se violations of the Sherman Act. This was the position it had taken in 1945, when it first had raised the antitrust question before the SEC; and though the department's views on the illegality of syndicate price-fixing practices had not changed since then, it had not incorporated them in its original complaint. "We are not asking for relief . . . outside the over-all conspiracy," the government told the court. "We are pressing our over-all charge of conspiracy among those who have been named defendants." [72]

The government maintained that it was not attacking the syndicate system itself, which the complaint asserted had been "invented by defendant banking firms and their predecessors." "It is the syndicate system as abused and not the syndicate system as not abused that we are talking about, and that has been made clear time and time again," the government's attorney asserted in January 1951.[73] This was, in Medina's words, "the government's first position on the subject of the syndicate system." [74]

Months later, when it became apparent that the evidence did not support this charge, the government shifted its ground and proceeded to do the very thing, according to Medina, it previously had denied was its intention. It attacked the syndicate system itself and "the entire investment banking industry." [75]

If the court had upheld the government's contention that price-fixing clauses and other tradewide practices usually found in syndicate contracts violated the Sherman Act, the entire existing syndicate system of security distribution would have been disrupted, if not destroyed.[76] "The plain truth of the matter," Medina observed, is that they "form an area of head-on collision between the SEC on the one hand and the Antitrust Division of the Justice Department on the other." [77]

It was not up to him, he said, to resolve this conflict. Neither

71. Quoted in *ibid.*, 149. See also *The New York Times*, December 8, 1950.
72. Quoted in *U.S. v. Henry S. Morgan et al.*, "Corrected Opinion," 111–12. See also *ibid.*, 4–5, 112–13.
73. *Ibid.*, "Defendants' Opening" (January 25, 1951), 2233. See also *ibid.*, "Government's Opening (Rebuttal — Mr. Baldridge)" (March 14, 1951), 4507–08; *ibid.*, "Hearing before Judge Medina" (April 26, 1951), 5556–65.
74. *Ibid.*, "Corrected Opinion," 112.
75. *Ibid.*, 114.
76. *Ibid.*, 113–16. See also *The New York Times*, November 25, 1951.
77. *U.S. v. Henry S. Morgan et al.*, "Corrected Opinion," 138. See also *The New York Times*, May 24, 26, 1951.

Congress, which drafted the SEC Act, nor the commission, which was authorized to enforce that law, intended any "exemption to the Sherman Act; and it is hardly probable that they would inadvertently accomplish such a result. The real point," he went on, "is that all those who worked together on the formulation of this most significant and beneficial legislation went about their task of integrating into the statutory pattern the current modes of bringing out new security issues then in common use by investment bankers generally, with complete assurance that no violation of the Sherman Act was even remotely involved. This recognition by the Congress of the legality and utility to the American economy of the general features of the syndicate system cannot lightly be disregarded by any court or judge." [78] The price-fixing charge, therefore, was relevant only as it applied to the overall conspiracy.

The government marshaled an impressive collection of documents to support its charges. Thousands of items — letters, papers, memoranda, syndicate records — taken from the files of the defendants were received in evidence. And the government added still more from the public record, much of it culled from the long series of investigations at which investment bankers had been called to testify, from the time of the Armstrong investigation of 1905 down through the TNEC, as well as from many other congressional, ICC, and SEC hearings. This huge collection, all of it documentary and circumstantial, was so imposing at first glance that during the first year of the trial Medina thought it highly probable that the government would win its case.[79]

To all the charges the defendants entered strong denials. They attacked the government's evidence as incomplete, inaccurate, misleading, inferential, argumentative, and based on a few isolated instances that had occurred years earlier, when the needs of the economy and the conduct of the investment banking business were entirely different.[80] The defense argued that the conspiracy theory, upon which the government rested its case, was a myth, born at the time of the Pujo hearings and perpetuated since then by misinformed and prejudiced individuals in and out of government. Much the same view was shared by a financial writer for *The New York Times,* who accused the Justice Department of beating a dead horse. "Many figures in the financial community who were supposed to have directed the 'conspiracy' have long since passed from the scene, the type of securities handled by some firms has been radically changed, and even many of the bright young men who laid the

78. *U.S. v. Henry S. Morgan et al.,* "Corrected Opinion," 145.
79. Medina to author, September 2, 1966.
80. *U.S. v. Henry S. Morgan et al.,* "Defendants' Opening" (January 25, 1951), 2231–51; *ibid.* (January 31, 1951), 2514–16; *ibid.,* "Plaintiff's Case" (May 28, 1951), 778–83.

groundwork for the government's case have transferred to more profitable undertakings."[81]

Defense witnesses and attorneys criticized the government's statistical tables at length and in great detail, charging that they gave an entirely false impression of the relative position of the defendant and nondefendant firms in the industry. Dean stressed this fact repeatedly throughout the trial; and he accused the government attorneys of having compiled their statistics according to the age-old recipe for horse and rabbit stew — fifty horses and fifty rabbits.[82] At first, Medina was not at all persuaded by Dean's rhetoric or his complaints against the government's statistics, but later, when the defense submitted its own extensive charts and tables, prepared under Fox's direction, Medina changed his mind. "I would not have believed it possible that so many misleading charts could be gotten up and submitted to a court," he said. "Human ingenuity seems to know no bounds when it comes to getting up this statistical matter so as to fool you."[83]

Defense strategy, effectively executed by some of Wall Street's most able and experienced attorneys, aimed at disproving the existence of the alleged conspiracy. They offered voluminous evidence that the defendants did not monopolize the securities business and, even more important, that they competed vigorously among themselves for the leadership of new issues.[84] To prove there was no "concert of action" among them, that each of the seventeen firms determined its own policies independently of the others, the defense submitted extensive statistical tables analyzing the managements and underwritings of these houses, and comparing their performance and position in the industry with that of the leading nondefendants. These tables, covering the years 1935 through 1949, together with other statistical charts and compilations dealing with different aspects of the securities business, were used with telling effect to refute the government's charges.[85]

The most important tables presented by the defense, the ones that made the greatest impression upon Medina, were those proving beyond all doubt that there was no conspiracy, no common action among the defendants. Not only did these tables reveal "a pattern of no pattern," he wrote later, but the rankings of the defendants, in terms of their positions as managers or agents of privately negotiated issues of $1 million or more, varied widely from one period to another, showing the existence of a lively competition among

81. *The New York Times,* May 29, 1949.
82. *U.S. v. Henry S. Morgan et al.,* "Transcript of Trial: Plaintiff's Case" (May 28, 1951), 7779.
83. *Ibid.* (February 20, 1953), 20542.
84. *The New York Times,* December 6, 13, 1950.
85. *U.S. v. Henry S. Morgan et al.,* "Corrected Opinion," 419–24.

them, as well as with other firms in the industry.[86] Apart from Morgan Stanley, which, with one exception (during the triennial 1941–1943), consistently ranked first in the dollar amount of negotiated issues managed, the position of the defendants, as shown in Exhibit 24, changed often and radically. The First Boston Corporation, for example, started out in third place during the period 1935–1937, fell to tenth place in the triennial 1941–1943, and climbed to second place by the end of 1949. Other firms, Dean stressed, showed even more "dramatically dynamic shifts" in position. Such changes in rankings were true not only of the defendants, but of most other investment banking houses as well. An even greater competitive situation prevailed among firms that managed smaller issues, those between $100,000 and $1 million, a fact the government charts had ignored entirely.[87]

To refute the monopoly charge, defendants used the same statistical tables and charts that were cited to show competition. Defense lawyers elicited the fact that there were a half dozen or more nondefendant investment houses whose total dollar amount of managements during the years 1935 through 1949 exceeded that of several of the alleged monopolists. Twelve nondefendant firms had managed more negotiated issues of $1 million or more, in terms of dollar amounts, than had Drexel, one of the supposed conspirators; and in the case of four of these nondefendant bankers, each sponsored issues valued at twice the amount offered by this defendant. The dollar volume of negotiated issues headed by each of these four houses actually was larger than that of three other defendants.[88]

The defense disclosed, furthermore, that during the years 1935 through 1949 the defendants had managed 59.7 percent of the total dollar value of all privately negotiated issues of $1 million or more, amounting almost to $26 billion. Measured in terms of the total number of issues sponsored, the defendants' share of the business amounted to only 38.5 percent.

Even these figures, the defense lawyers insisted, did not provide an entirely accurate picture of the defendants' position in the industry. Much more indicative were the statistics on all privately negotiated offerings of $100,000 or more, excluding domestic railroad trust certificates. According to these figures, which included many more issues (7,624) than those in the larger dollar-amount category (4,596), and involved more than twice as many firms (850 as compared with 340), the defendants managed 51.6 percent of the total dollar value of these issues, amounting to $23.1 billion, but only 27.1 percent of the entire number.

---

86. *Ibid.*, 12; *ibid.*, "Defendants' Case" (March 19, 1953), 21403–06.
87. *Ibid.*, "Defendants' Case" (March 19, 1953), 21403–06.
88. *Ibid.*, "Defendants' Tables," M-1, M-2.

Exhibit 24. Investment bankers as managers or agents: negotiated issues only[a] (dollar amount of issues, 1935–1949)

Manager or agent	1935–1949 Dollar amount of issues (millions)	1935–1949 Rank	1935–1949 Percent of total	1935–1937 Dollar amount of issues (millions)	1935–1937 Rank	1935–1937 Percent of total	1938–1940 Dollar amount of issues (millions)	1938–1940 Rank	1938–1940 Percent of total	1941–1943 Dollar amount of issues (millions)	1941–1943 Rank	1941–1943 Percent of total	1944–1946 Dollar amount of issues (millions)	1944–1946 Rank	1944–1946 Percent of total	1947–1949 Dollar amount of issues (millions)	1947–1949 Rank	1947–1949 Percent of total
Total (340 managers or agents)	43,507.3		100.00	9,141.9		100.00	6,962.8		100.00	3,860.9		100.00	10,203.0		100.00	13,338.8		100.00
MORGAN STANLEY	5,142.0	1	11.82	1,891.3	1	20.69	849.9	1	12.21	338.6	2	8.77	809.6	1	7.94	1,252.6	1	9.39
Halsey Stuart	1,048.7	8	2.41	173.2	12	1.89	633.0	3	9.09	15.1	24	0.39	198.7	10	1.95	28.8	34	0.22
FIRST BOSTON	2,826.9	2	6.50	771.4	3	8.44	445.2	4	6.39	107.9	10	2.79	471.8	5	4.62	1,030.7	2	7.73
DILLON, READ	2,796.7	3	6.43	403.2	5	4.41	716.0	2	10.28	343.7	1	8.90	590.8	2	5.79	743.0	3	5.57
KUHN, LOEB	2,360.2	4	5.42	922.6	2	10.09	336.4	6	4.83	208.0	4	5.39	499.3	4	4.89	393.9	4	2.95
BLYTH	1,558.6	5	3.58	387.0	6	4.23	117.2	13	1.68	143.4	6	3.71	530.3	3	5.20	380.6	5	2.85
LEHMAN	1,313.6	7	3.02	189.0	9	2.07	211.4	8	3.04	135.6	7	3.51	411.2	6	4.03	366.4	6	2.75
SMITH BARNEY	1,403.6	6	3.23	445.1	4	4.87	236.4	7	3.40	170.2	5	4.41	276.2	8	2.71	275.7	8	2.07
Mellon	753.8	12	1.73	169.3	13	1.85	159.5	9	2.29	245.3	3	6.37	178.7	14	1.75	—	—	—
HARRIMAN, RIPLEY	1,005.6	9	2.31	210.1	7	2.30	101.8	15	1.46	112.7	8	2.92	331.3	7	3.25	249.7	9	1.87
WHITE, WELD	827.2	10	1.90	79.3	21	.87	140.9	10	2.02	82.6	11	2.14	175.1	15	1.72	349.4	7	2.62
KIDDER, PEABODY	615.1	14	1.41	103.1	18	1.13	17.6	28	.25	19.3	21	0.50	256.5	9	2.51	218.6	11	1.64
GOLDMAN, SACHS	789.1	11	1.81	197.7	8	2.16	122.8	12	1.76	52.5	12	1.36	195.7	12	1.92	220.4	10	1.65
GLORE, FORGAN	616.0	13	1.42	157.0	14	1.72	95.6	16	1.37	108.7	9	2.81	183.2	13	1.80	71.6	20	0.54
STONE & WEBSTER	505.0	16	1.16	103.5	17	1.13	116.8	14	1.68	6.6	43	0.17	75.7	21	0.74	202.4	12	1.52
Bonbright	574.1	15	1.32	180.6	11	1.98	374.9	5	5.38	18.6	22	.48	—	—	—	—	—	—
Merrill Lynch, Pierce Fenner & Beane	434.5	17	1.00	37.7	28	0.41	42.2	20	.61	37.3	14	.97	131.5	17	1.29	185.8	13	1.39
UNION	338.8	19	0.78	50.9	26	.56	19.6	27	.28	15.6	23	.40	145.2	16	1.42	107.5	16	0.81
HARRIS, HALL	312.7	20	.72	20.4	37	.22	130.4	11	1.87	13.8	26	.36	35.4	34	0.35	112.8	15	.85
EASTMAN, DILLON	398.5	18	.92	—	—	—	40.2	21	.58	25.7	16	.66	198.3	11	1.94	134.4	14	1.01
Salomon Bros. & Hutzler	256.5	22	.59	93.0	19	1.02	50.0	18	.72	25.0	17	.65	—	—	—	88.5	18	0.66
Lazard Frères	290.2	21	.67	188.7	10	2.06	—	—	—	14.5	25	.38	35.7	31	0.35	51.3	24	.38
W C Langley	148.1	31	.34	—	—	—	49.2	19	.71	5.0	49	.13	2.6	104	.03	20.0	40	.15
DREXEL	172.7	29	.40	71.4	22	0.78	1.5	71	.02	47.4	13	1.23	61.7	23	.60	62.1	21	.47
Paine, Webber, Jackson & Curtis	216.2	23	.50	32.1	31	.35	23.3	25	.33	13.5	27	0.35	92.7	18	.91	54.6	23	.41

		Firm															
185.4	25	.43	Coffin & Burr	85.3	20	.93	71.2	17	1.03	8.3	36	.21	16.0	54	.16	4.6	74	.03
193.6	24	.44	A G Becker	42.4	27	.46	10.4	35	0.15	22.4	19	.58	86.1	19	.84	32.3	29	.24
182.5	26	.42	Blair & Co	148.4	16	1.62	—	—	—	—	—	—	24.9	45	.24	9.2	56	.07
137.4	34	.32	W. E. Hutton	5.8	25	0.63	23.2	26	.34	9.0	35	.23	30.8	39	.30	16.4	45	.12
178.0	27	.41	Lee, Higginson	58.3	24	.64	15.3	29	.22	10.5	30	.27	78.5	20	.77	15.4	46	.12
156.3	30	.36	Otis	2.7	75	.03	29.7	23	.43	27.2	15	.71	73.2	22	.72	23.4	37	.18
177.5	28	.41	Hayden, Stone	150.5	15	1.65	—	—	—	5.0	49	.13	14.6	56	.14	7.4	63	.06
141.3	33	.32	F. S. Moseley	27.0	33	0.29	7.2	41	.10	13.4	28	.35	35.6	32	.35	58.0	22	.43
146.2	32	.34	Reynolds	5.0	56	.05	2.2	61	.03	2.6	59	.07	45.7	27	.45	90.7	17	.68
42.3	58	.10	Shields	1.2	103	.01	—	—	—	5.2	47	.13	28.2	42	.28	7.8	61	.06
128.9	36	.30	Dean, Witter	25.5	34	.28	5.6	45	.08	—	—	—	13.4	61	.13	84.5	19	.63
131.8	35	.30	Hornblower & Weeks	71.2	23	.78	11.9	33	.17	9.9	33	.26	19.8	48	.19	18.9	43	.14
126.9	37	.29	Scranton	37.2	29	.41	8.0	39	.11	6.6	42	.17	39.3	30	.39	35.8	26	.27
123.2	38	.28	F. Eberstadt	10.4	48	.11	8.3	37	.12	21.6	20	.56	53.7	24	.53	29.3	32	.22
113.2	40	.26	Hemphill, Noyes	29.7	32	.33	11.1	34	.16	3.0	57	.08	46.6	26	.46	22.7	38	.17
2,581.3		5.93	All other firms (300 managers or agents)	434.7		4.76	246.9		3.55	196.6		5.09	948.2		9.29	754.7		5.66
12,057.7		27.71	No investment banker	1,077.1		11.78	1,480.0		21.26	1,212.5		31.40	2,761.3		27.06	5,526.8		41.43

Source: U.S. v. Henry S. Morgan et al., "Defendants' Tables," M-2, 1.

[a] Underwritten new and registered secondary issues, non-underwritten public offerings of new issues, and private placements of new issues, $1,000,000 and larger of domestic and foreign business corporations and foreign governments (excluding domestic railroad equipment trust certificates).

Exhibit 25. Investment bankers as managers or agents: public sealed bidding issues only[a] (number of issues 1935–1949)

1935–1949					1935–1937				1938–1940	
Number of issues		Pro-rated number of issues			Number of issues		Pro-rated number of issues		Number of issues	
Sole manager or agent	Co-manager or co-agent	Number of issues	Rank	Percent of total	Manager or agent	Sole manager or agent	Co-manager or co-agent	Number of issues	Rank	Percent of total	Sole manager or agent	Co-manager or co-agent
		660		100.00	Total (62 managers or agents)			16		100.00		
32	5	34.5	4	5.23	MORGAN STANLEY	–	–	–	–	–	–	–
178	8	181.3	1	27.47	Halsey Stuart	5	–	5.0	1	31.25	1	–
74	40	92.2	2	13.96	FIRST BOSTON	1	–	1.0		6.25	2	–
15	2	15.7	11	2.37	DILLON, READ	1	–	1.0		6.25	–	–
16	6	18.5	7	2.80	KUHN, LOEB	–	–	–	–	–	–	–
23	25	35.0	3	5.30	BLYTH	–	–	–	–	–	–	–
19	17	26.5	6	4.02	LEHMAN	2	–	2.0	2	12.50	1	–
4	12	9.3	17	1.41	SMITH BARNEY	–	–	–	–	–	–	–
13	8	17.0	9	2.58	Mellon	–	–	–	–	–	–	–
12	8	15.8	10	2.40	HARRIMAN, RIPLEY	1	–	1.0		6.25	–	–
9	18	17.7	8	2.68	WHITE, WELD	–	–	–	–	–	–	–
19	25	30.5	5	4.62	KIDDER, PEABODY	–	–	–	–	–	–	–
–	6	2.7	26	0.40	GOLDMAN, SACHS	–	–	–	–	–	–	–
3	13	9.2	18	1.39	GLORE, FORGAN	–	–	–	–	–	–	–
7	8	10.3	15	1.57	STONE & WEBSTER	–	–	–	–	–	–	–
–	1	0.5		0.08	Bonbright	–	–	–	–	–	–	–
3	8	7.0	20	1.06	Merrill Lynch, Pierce Fenner & Beane	–	–	–	–	–	–	–
6	8	9.8	16	1.49	UNION	–	–	–	–	–	–	–
4	7	7.2	19	1.09	HARRIS, HALL	–	–	–	–	–	–	–
–	–	–	–	–	EASTMAN, DILLON	–	–	–	–	–	–	–
10	3	11.5	13	1.74	Salomon Bros. & Hutzler	–	–	–	–	–	–	–
–	5	2.0	32	0.30	Lazard Frères	–	–	–	–	–	–	–
7	13	13.2	12	1.99	W. C. Langley	–	–	–	–	–	–	–
–	7	3.3	25	0.51	DREXEL	–	–	–	–	–	–	–
2	–	2.0	32	.30	Paine, Webber, Jackson & Curtis[b]	1	–	1.0		6.25	–	–
–	3	1.5	36	.23	Coffin & Burr	–	–	–	–	–	–	–
1	1	1.3	40	.20	A. G. Becker	–	–	–	–	–	–	–
–	–	–	–	–	Blair & Co.	–	–	–	–	–	–	–
–	3	1.5	36	.23	W. E. Hutton	–	–	–	–	–	–	–
1	–	1.0		.15	Lee, Higginson	–	–	–	–	–	1	–
5	1	5.5	23	.83	Otis	–	–	–	–	–	–	–
–	–	–	–	–	Hayden, Stone	–	–	–	–	–	–	–
2	2	2.7	26	.40	F. S. Moseley[b]	1	–	1.0		6.25	1	–
–	–	–	–	–	Reynolds	–	–	–	–	–	–	–
5	13	11.2	14	1.69	Shields	–	–	–	–	–	–	–
2	1	2.5	31	0.38	Dean, Witter	–	–	–	–	–	–	–
–	–	–	–	–	Hornblower & Weeks	–	–	–	–	–	–	–
–	–	–	–	–	Scranton	–	–	–	–	–	–	–
–	–	–	–	–	F. Eberstadt	–	–	–	–	–	–	–
–	2	1.0		.15	Hemphill, Noyes	–	–	–	–	–	–	–
7	–	7.0	20	1.06	Equitable	–	–	–	–	–	–	–
2	–	2.0	32	0.30	Dick & Merle Smith	–	–	–	–	–	–	–
3	1	3.5	24	.53	C. M. Loeb, Rhoades	–	–	–	–	–	–	–
4	4	6.0	22	.91	Bear, Stearns	–	–	–	–	–	–	–
		26.7		4.05	All other firms (25 managers or agents)			4.0		25.00		
		14		2.12	Direct institutional purchases — no investment banker			–		–		

Source: U.S. v. Henry S. Morgan et al., "Defendants' Tables" M-1, 2.

[a] New and registered secondary issues, $1,000,000 and larger of domestic and foreign business corporations and foreign governments (excluding domestic railroad equipment trust certificates).

[b] Aggregate of data for the two or more firms which combined during the period into this single firm.

Antitrust | 483

1938–1940			1941–1943						1944–1946						1947–1949					
Pro-rated number of issues			Number of issues		Pro-rated number of issues				Number of issues		Pro-rated number of issues				Number of issues		Pro-rated number of issues				
Number of issues	Rank	Percent of total	Sole manager or agent	Co-manager or co-agent	Number of issues	Rank	Percent of total		Sole manager or agent	Co-manager or co-agent	Number of issues	Rank	Percent of total		Sole manager or agent	Co-manager or co-agent	Number of issues	Rank	Percent of total		
6		100.00			55		100.00				261		100.00				322		100.00		
–	–	–	–	–	–	–	–		22	3	23.5	3	9.00		10	2	11.0	7	3.42		
1.0		16.67			–	–	–		61	2	62.0	1	23.75		103	2	104.0	1	32.30		
2.0	1	33.33	8	4	9.3	2	16.97		35	17	42.7	2	16.35		31	13	37.0	2	11.49		
–	–	–	5	10	9.5	1	17.27		10	2	10.7	8	4.09		4	–	4.0	16	1.24		
–	–	–	1	2	2.0	8	3.64		11	3	12.0	7	4.60		4	1	4.5	13	1.40		
–	–	–	1	3	2.3	7	4.24		7	11	12.3	6	4.73		15	11	20.3	3	6.31		
1.0		16.67	1	2	1.8	10	3.33		2	4	3.5	15	1.34		13	11	18.2	4	5.64		
–	–	–	1	2	1.8	10	3.33		1	6	3.7	13	1.40		2	4	3.8	17	1.19		
–	–	–	4	1	4.5	3	8.18		9	7	12.5	5	4.79		–	–	–	–	–		
–	–	–	1	1	1.5	12	2.73		2	2	3.0	18	1.15		8	5	10.3	8	3.21		
–	–	–	–	1	0.5		0.91		1	6	3.8	12	1.47		8	11	13.3	5	4.14		
–	–	–	–	8	3.2	5	5.76		11	8	14.8	4	5.68		8	9	12.5	6	3.88		
–	–	–	–	–	–	–	–		–	2	0.8		0.32		–	4	1.8	26	0.57		
–	–	–	–	5	2.5	6	4.55		2	3	3.3	17	1.28		1	5	3.3	21	1.04		
–	–	–	–	4	1.3	13	2.42		5	1	5.5	10	2.11		2	3	3.5	18	1.09		
–	–	–	–	1	0.5		0.91		–	–	–	–	–		–	–	–	–	–		
–	–	–	–	–	–	–	–		–	5	2.5	19	0.96		3	3	4.5	13	1.40		
–	–	–	–	–	–	–	–		–	2	1.0		.38		6	6	8.8	9	2.74		
–	–	–	–	1	.5		.91		2	4	3.7	13	1.40		2	2	3.0	22	0.93		
–	–	–	4	–	4.0	4	7.27		–	–	–	–	–		6	3	7.5	10	2.33		
–	–	–	–	3	1.0		1.82		–	–	–	–	–		–	2	1.0		0.31		
–	–	–	–	–	–	–	–		3	6	6.0	9	2.30		4	7	7.2	11	2.23		
–	–	–	–	–	–	–	–		–	2	0.8		0.32		–	5	2.5	23	0.78		
–	–	–	–	–	–	–	–		1	–	1.0		.38		–	–	–	–	–		
–	–	–	–	1	0.5		0.91		–	–	–	–	–		–	2	1.0		.31		
–	–	–	–	–	–	–	–		–	–	–	–	–		1	1	1.3	28	.41		
–	–	–	–	–	–	–	–		–	2	1.0		.38		–	1	0.5		.16		
1.0		16.67	–	–	–	–	–		2	–	2.0	20	.77		3	1	3.5	18	1.09		
1.0		16.67	–	2	.7		1.21		–	–	–	–	–		–	–	–	–	–		
–	–	–	2	–	2.0	8	3.64		1	8	4.8	11	1.85		2	5	4.3	15	1.35		
–	–	–	–	–	–	–	–		–	1	0.5		0.19		2	–	2.0	25	0.62		
–	–	–	–	–	–	–	–		–	–	–	–	–		–	2	1.0		.31		
–	–	–	–	–	–	–	–		1	–	1.0		.38		6	–	6.0	12	1.86		
–	–	–	–	–	–	–	–		2	–	2.0	20	.77		3	1	3.5	18	1.09		
–	–	–	–	–	–	–	–		3	1	3.5	15	1.34		1	3	2.5	23	0.78		
–					1.5		2.73				10.0		3.83				11.2		3.47		
–					4		7.27				7		2.68				3		.93		

These figures, like those disclosing the dollar value and size of the defendants' business in heading issues of $1 million or more, accomplished two important results. They shattered the monopoly charged and they showed that whereas the seventeen firms had managed a relatively small proportion of the total number of issues distributed during the stipulated period, the value of the offerings they headed amounted to more than half of the entire dollar amount merchandised.[89] In the case of issues of $1 million and larger, this accounted for 59.7 percent of the entire amount ($43.5 billion), whereas the aggregate dollar volume of issues of $100,000 or more sponsored by the defendants represented 51.7 percent of the total value of all these offerings ($44.7 billion).

The offering of securities by public sealed bidding, the method that the Justice Department asserted provided the greatest opportunities for smaller, non-New York City houses, did not alter significantly the leadership position occupied by most of the defendants, but there were a few exceptions. Eastman, Dillon, for instance, did not participate in a single public sealed bidding account throughout the entire fifteen-year period. Several other defendants did not engage in this business until 1941, when the SEC put into effect rule U-50. Still others joined these accounts only occasionally. As in the case of privately negotiated issues, several nondefendant firms, most notably Halsey, Stuart, managed more dollar amounts of public sealed issues than three of the alleged conspirators.[90]

Despite these exceptions, and the supposedly more competitive situation that prevailed when offerings were made by sealed bids, the defendants won for themselves only a slightly smaller share (54.4 percent) of the total dollar amount of such issues of $1 million or more than the amount (59.7 percent) of negotiated offerings in the same category (see Exhibit 25). If leadership was measured in terms of the number of issues, the defendants actually managed a larger percentage of public sealed offerings of $1 million or more than they did of privately negotiated issues of this size, 51.2 percent of the former as compared with 38.5 percent of the latter.[91]

These statistics, together with others submitted by the defense, not only refuted the government's monopoly charge, but, as Medina observed, they also disproved the widely held idea, strongly put forth by the Justice Department, that compulsory public sealed bidding reduced investment banking concentration, promoted the growth of regional capital markets, and provided "the little fellow" with the opportunity to compete successfully for the larger issues.[92] The facts clearly were otherwise. Regardless of the way these issues

89. Ibid., M-1, M-2, M-13.
90. Ibid., "Plaintiff's Case" (May 28, 1951), 7789–804.
91. Ibid., "Defendants' Tables," M-1, M-2.
92. Ibid., "Transcript of Trial" (March 27, 1951), 5115.

were sold, the evidence proved that they were handled almost exclusively by the larger houses — those with the capital, personnel, and expertise to merchandise them quickly and effectively.[93]

Other documentary evidence presented by the government also failed to survive close examination. Some of it proved to be inaccurate, and much of it was subject to several interpretations. Medina severely criticized its poor quality and the careless manner in which the prosecution used it.[94] When the Justice Department's attorneys sought to substantiate the all-important traditional banker charge, they relied on testimony of prominent investment bankers taken from earlier hearings, such as Otto Kahn's classic statement that Kuhn, Loeb did not compete for business.[95] Other similar remarks were cited, some of them taken from the defendants' depositions, and interpreted to suit the government's purposes, as were numerous examples of certain issuers' being repeatedly served by the same investment banker.[96] None of this voluminous evidence proved to be impressive or relevant. Some of it did not apply to conditions after 1933, if it ever had; much of it proved to be based on incomplete or inaccurate information; and not a small amount of it turned out to be more advantageous to the defense than it did to the plaintiff. "The further I get along in the case," Medina said, "the more evidence I see accumulating of the lack of any agreement." So far as he could tell, the defendants were "just a set of individual firms that are going their separate ways doing business as they think it is best for them to do it . . . for the purpose of making money." [97]

An even more important consideration, one that Medina was quick to appreciate, was that none of the miscellaneous documents taken from the files of the defendants contained the term "traditional banker." Only two of the bankers questioned admitted to ever having heard of it before 1939, when it was given wide currency by the TNEC.[98] Still more damaging, so far as this phase of the government's case was concerned, was the fact that examination of hundreds of thousands of documents did not reveal a single one suggesting in any way whatsoever that Morgan Stanley, the alleged "master mind," ever recognized or deferred to traditional banker practices, or for that matter, any of the other features of the so-called triple concept. "No amount of argument or explanation," Medina asserted, "can supply this significant absence of documen-

93. *Ibid.,* "Corrected Opinion," 247, 401.
94. *Ibid.,* "Transcript of Trial: Plaintiff's Case" (January 13, 1953), 18797–802.
95. *Ibid.,* "Corrected Opinion," 260–66. See also *ibid.,* "Transcript of Trial: Plaintiff's Case" (January 12, 1953), 18677–79.
96. *Ibid.,* "Plaintiff's Case" (January 12, 1953), 18668–70, 18685–90.
97. *Ibid.* (June 19, 1951), 8390–94.
98. *Ibid.,* "Corrected Opinion," 220–22.

tary evidence admitted testimonially against Morgan Stanley." [99] Except for Kuhn, Loeb, from whose files the government collected most of its traditional banker documents, none of the defendants adhered to this practice, and even Kuhn, Loeb used the practice as a competitive device, regardless of Kahn's oft-repeated statement to the contrary.[100]

The defense's devastatingly successful assault upon the traditional banker concept as originally defined forced the government to dilute its claims on this crucial issue so drastically that it came very close to abandoning them entirely. The revised claim, labeled "this lesser charge," marked a major shift in the government's theory of the case.[101]

According to this newer claim, the traditional banker concept applied only when a satisfactory banker-issuer relationship existed. The determining factor in an investment firm's decision to compete for a new security offering was whether or not the investment house that previously had served that issuer still enjoyed a "satisfactory relationship" with that client. When this existed, the government argued, there was no competition, and to prove that this was the case it cited, among others, the testimony of Henry L. Bogert, a partner in Eastman, Dillon since 1922. Bogert admitted that it was not customary for investment firms to solicit the business of issuers with satisfactory banking relations. "Courtesy generally requires that you conduct your business in a way so as not to make enemies, and if you think that a man, firm, friend of yours is engaged in doing a piece of business, it is not quite the polite thing to muscle in and upset the applecart." [102] Government counsel labeled this statement "one of the most convincing admissions that have been made in this trial," adding that "in Wall Street courtesy had been substituted for competition." They also used it to argue that "satisfactory relationships" stood at the very center of the conspiracy, that they determined the informal code of ethics and mutual understandings that governed the defendants' business conduct, not only among themselves, but toward other investment bankers as well.[103]

Unfortunately for the government, it was no more able to substantiate the "lesser charge" than it had been able to prove the original one. The defendants argued that it was futile for investment houses to compete for offerings they had no chance at all of winning. "We advertise, we do everything we can to get business," Albert Gordon of Kidder, Peabody testified. "In addition to that, we go after any

99. *Ibid.*, 238. See also *ibid.*, "Defendants' Motions" (April 10, 1953), 21929–38.
100. *Ibid.*, "Corrected Opinion," 260–66.
101. *Ibid.*, 222–25; *ibid.*, "Transcript of Trial: Defendants' Motions" (April 13, 1953), 21976–81.
102. *Ibid.*, "Plaintiff's Case" (January 12, 1953), 18668.
103. *Ibid.*, 18667–70, 18675–77. See also *ibid.*, "Defendants' Motions" (April 13, 1953), 21976–77.

piece of business we think we have much chance of getting." [104] Stuart, the government's chief witness and one of the country's most experienced and knowledgeable investment bankers, concurred fully with Gordon's and the other defendants' views. It was useless, Stuart said, to chase after business unless "invited" to do so by the issuer. To do otherwise was a total waste of money, time, and energy. Issuers resented the "ringing-door-bell type of approach." [105]

This attitude was made very clear in the financing of the American Telephone & Telegraph Company (AT&T) and its subsidiaries, one of the largest and most famous of the so-called "frozen accounts." The government charged that Morgan Stanley's leadership between 1935 and 1949 showed the working of the conspiracy in all its varied manifestations. The defense proved otherwise. Morgan Stanley did not, as the government claimed, inherit this account from Morgan, AT&T's principal bankers since 1906.

In September 1935 Walter S. Gifford, AT&T's president, chose Morgan Stanley shortly after this firm had been organized to take over the investment banking business formerly done by the old Morgan partnership. Very early that year AT&T had decided to bring out a $43.7 million issue of the Illinois Bell Telephone Company, the first offering of telephone securities in more than four years. Many of the country's major investment houses, including several of the defendants as well as Halsey, Stuart, sought to win this prime account. Nothing came of their efforts, nor of any of the other various plans that AT&T officials discussed, including one calling for the company to sell the issue itself through an old subsidiary. As soon as he learned that Morgan Stanley was to be organized, Gifford told Stanley, "that solves my problems," and assigned him the entire responsibility of registering the issue with the SEC and organizing the underwriting and distributing groups.[106]

Government attorneys were unable to uncover a single piece of evidence to prove that Morgan Stanley achieved and maintained leadership of this business by any other means than the free choice of the Telephone Company's executives. Nor was the government any more successful in supporting its traditional banker allegations against any of the other defendants. "It is difficult to put out of one's mind the thought that this 'lesser charge,' " Medina concluded, "is nothing more than a maneuver to cover up the lack of evidence to support the charge as formulated in the complaint." [107]

Government retreat on the traditional banker charge undermined

104. *U.S. v. Henry S. Morgan et al.,* "Corrected Opinion," 328.
105. *Ibid.,* 225; *ibid.,* "Transcript of Trial: Plaintiff's Case" (April 13, 1953), 21977.
106. *Ibid.,* "Defendants' Opening — Mr. Carson" (January 18, 1951), 1954–69; *ibid.,* "Corrected Opinion," 250–54.
107. *Ibid.,* "Corrected Opinion," 225.

the entire structure upon which it had built its case. The predecessor-successorship claim was made meaningless by the satisfactory relationship argument. How was a potential competitor to determine whether to go after a piece of business if the decision to do so depended upon whether that issuer's relationships with its previous banker had been satisfactory? What constituted a satisfactory relationship and, even more important, how was it passed on from one investment house to another? The "adoption of the satisfactory relationship formula," the defense argued, "is an implicit abandonment of the whole successorship foundation in this case." To this Medina added: "I think there is a lot in that." [108]

The unconvincing, very often inaccurate, nature of the government's evidence on the predecessor-successorship phase of the case was demonstrated repeatedly but never more so than with respect to Blyth's post-1936 leadership of the choice Pacific Gas & Electric Company (PG&E) account. The government used material from the TNEC investigation to show that Blyth had inherited the management of this business from the defunct National City Co. Other evidence, however, proved that there was, in Judge Medina's words, "no succession of any kind, either *de jure* or *de facto*, from the National City Company to Blyth by reason of the fact that Mitchell joined the Blyth organization, or for any other reason." [109] Blyth had won the management of PG&E's underwritings only after a fierce two-year struggle against two strong rivals. Its victory was due to what Medina called its "sheer tenacity" in continuing the fight, even after it had lost the first issue to Lazard Frères, and to the fact that it was a strong California-based house with a large, effective sales organization.[110] Other similar instances of alleged traditional banker and successorship practices proved just as unconvincing.

Nor was the government any more successful in documenting claims subsidiary to the traditional banker charge, namely, historical position, reciprocity, and the defendants' use of directorships to dominate and control issuers. Not a single piece of evidence did it submit to show that Morgan Stanley had employed any of these practices. Indeed, the facts proved the very opposite. Morgan Stanley determined its choice of syndicate associates for the Illinois Bell Telephone issue, mentioned above, "strictly on the merits," Medina asserted, "without perfunctory or other adherence to any 'practice' of 'historical position'." It told every firm to which it offered an underwriting participation that the invitation established

108. *Ibid.,* "Defendants' Motions" (April 13, 1953), 21978; *ibid.,* "Corrected Opinion," 224–28.
109. *Ibid.,* "Corrected Opinion," 97.
110. *Ibid.,* 367.

"no precedent for any other underwriting of the Telephone Company." [111]

The historical position and reciprocity charges were exploded finally by a series of statistical tables. These showed the many significant changes that had occurred during the fifteen years after 1935 in the relative rankings of the country's seventy-five top investment houses, including the defendants.[112] Changes disclosed by these charts did much more than disprove the existence of a conspiracy; they confirmed what the defense had argued from the beginning: that competition among the seventeen and between them and other investment houses was continuous and spirited.

If the alleged conspiracy had existed, if the defendants had adhered to the practices of the triple concept, as the government charged, frequent and sharp changes in firm standings never would have occurred, since the very purpose of the combination was to prevent just such fluctuations.[113] During the years 1935 to 1937, to cite just one example among many, Kidder, Peabody ranked seventh in terms of the dollar amount of negotiated issues of $1 million and larger that it had underwritten; during the next triennial it fell to twelfth place; and, after moving up to tenth place in the period 1941–1943, it made a dramatic comeback, jumping to second place in the next triennial, where it remained until 1949, the last year for which figures were compiled. More important still, if the conspiracy had been in effect, there would have been no increase in the proportion of the total dollar volume of underwriting participations going to nondefendant houses. The reverse was true; the combined share of these participations going to fifteen smaller, nondefendant firms between 1935 and 1949 just about tripled, increasing from 7.6 percent to almost 22.7 percent.[114]

Measured in terms of the number of participations, the statistics disclosed an equally vigorous pattern of change and competitive behavior. Both large and small houses, defendants as well as nondefendants, experienced significant ups and downs, disproving "any notion of a stable relationship among investment banking firms." [115] Merrill Lynch, Pierce, Fenner & Beane's percentage of syndicate participations in all negotiated underwritings in excess of $1 million more than doubled between the first (1935–1937) and fifth (1947–

111. *Ibid.*, 252–53; *ibid.*, "Defendants' Opening" (January 18, 1951), 1962.
112. *Ibid.*, "Defendants' Tables," P-1, P-2. See also *ibid.*, "Brief on General Points in Support of Motions to Dismiss . . . ," 254–60; *ibid.*, "Transcript of Trial: Statistical Analysis by Mr. Dean" (April 6, 1953), 21544–47, 21556–57, 21564–67, 21578–79, 21586–87.
113. *Ibid.*, "Transcript of Trial: Statistical Analysis by Mr. Dean" (April 6, 1953), 21557.
114. *Ibid.*, "Defendants' Tables," P-2; *ibid.*, "Transcript of Trial; Statistical Analysis by Mr. Dean" (April 6, 1953), 21557.
115. *Ibid.*, "Brief on General Points in Support of Motions to Dismiss," 255.

1949) triennials, increasing from 16.88 percent to 39.34 percent. Other nondefendant firms registered significant gains during these years: Paine, Webber, Jackson & Curtis increased from 18.53 percent (1935–1937) to 38.39 percent (1947–1949), and Hornblower & Weeks, from 20.37 percent to 42.89 percent. Some of the most striking advances were made by the smaller houses. Carl M. Loeb, Rhoades, for instance, jumped from 0.37 percent to 16.36 percent, and R. W. Baird & Co., Equitable Securities, and G. H. Walker also made impressive increases. Some of the more notable declines, furthermore, were registered by the supposed conspirators. Kuhn, Loeb, for instance, suffered a drop of 6 percentage points in the number of its underwriting participations, from 21.65 percent (1935–1937) to 15.64 percent (1944–1949), while those of Smith, Barney fell by an even greater proportion, 8.28 points, from 37.43 percent to 29.15 percent.[116]

Several factors accounted for these striking alterations in the rankings of firms. Fear of compulsory bidding and the Justice Department's growing concern with monopoly no doubt played a part, but they were not the principal reasons, Dean asserted. He attributed these shifts to the "tremendous increase" in the number of investment bankers with the capital, staffs, and expertise necessary to manage and underwrite; the serious losses suffered by the participants in the Pure Oil and Bethlehem Steel syndicates in the autumn of 1937; and the failure of Richard Whitney & Co. the following spring.[117] As a result of these developments many firms reduced the amount of capital they had set aside purely for underwriting purposes and increased the number of syndicate participants to take up the share of the risk they formerly would have kept themselves.

On the subject of the defendants' use of directorships to dominate issuers, the government also was forced to trim its original charge substantially. The evidence again disclosed that the defendants' policies toward this practice varied widely. Goldman, Sachs and Lehman Brothers often were represented on the boards of companies they sponsored; Morgan Stanley, on the other hand, rarely sought or accepted directorships.[118] Their usefulness as a competitive device remained unproved; nor did the many colloquies that occurred on this subject settle the propriety of these relationships. By the end of the trial the directorship question had become relatively insignificant. The government was forced to admit that the defendants had not obtained these positions in concert or used them to stifle competition in violation of the Sherman Act.[119]

116. *Ibid.*, 254–58; *ibid.*, "Defendants' Tables," P-2.
117. *Ibid.*, "Transcript of Trial: Statistical Analysis by Mr. Dean" (April 6, 1953), 21565–66.
118. *Ibid.*, "Corrected Opinion," 153–58; *ibid.*, "Defendants' Motions" (April 13, 1953), 21981.
119. *Ibid.*, "Defendants' Motions" (April 13, 1953), 21981.

From the start the government had hoped to win its case entirely on documentary evidence, and it was extremely reluctant to call witnesses and subject them to cross-examination.[120] Medina, on the other hand, was anxious to have "live witnesses," qualified to discuss investment banking practices and able to interpret the many documents entered in evidence. "Some day I hope to see a man sitting there," he said, pointing to the witness stand, "that I can listen to and ask questions of, and watch him and tell whether I believe him or not."[121] Finally, after much prodding, the government "crossed the Rubicon," as one of the defense attorneys labeled the event, and, in December 1951, called to the stand Robert R. Young of Chesapeake & Ohio fame.

He was to be the Justice Department's "anti-Morgan machine gun," but, as events quickly proved, his appearance turned out to be far more damaging to the government's case than it was to the defendants'. Young gave the impression of being not at all interested in presenting evidence to get at the truth; he seemed to have determined what "the truth" was long before and now refused to be influenced by facts. Nor did he care to answer questions; what he wanted was a platform from which to voice his prejudices. He had to be reminded repeatedly that he was in a court of law and that he was expected to answer questions asked him without "sounding off" whenever he felt his credibility was being challenged. "So bear in mind," Medina cautioned him, "that this is a court in which we are trying to be just as fair as we can, but that does not mean letting people who are witnesses hold forth."[122] Medina became so annoyed with Young's courtroom behavior, by his vindictive and venomous remarks, gratuitously offered, that at the end of his appearance, when, stepping down from the witness stand, Young offered the judge his hand, the jurist refused to accept it.[123]

The government's other star witness was Stuart. The career of this veteran Chicago banker, who at the time of the trial was nearing his seventy-first birthday, spanned more than a half century. Few men knew more about the investment banking business than he did. Dean called him the "dean of investment bankers."[124] Unlike Young, Stuart made an "excellent impression" on the stand.[125] Medina paid tribute to Stuart's knowledge and integrity on several occasions, and in dismissing the case, wrote that Stuart was a man "upon whose testimony I could rely with confidence."[126]

120. Medina to author, September 2, 1966.
121. *U.S. v. Henry S. Morgan et al.,* "Plaintiff's Case" (October 3, 1951), 9131; ibid., "Defendants' Motions" (April 10, 1953), 21937.
122. *Ibid.,* "Transcript of Trial: Testimony of Robert R. Young—Colloquy" (December 11, 1951), 11869–71.
123. Medina to author, September 2, 1966.
124. Dean to author, May 13, 1964; *The New York Times,* March 8, 1952.
125. *The New York Times,* March 6, 1952.
126. Medina to author, September 2, 1966; *U.S. v. Henry S. Morgan et al.,*

Stuart was too well informed not to see the many serious weaknesses in the government's case, and from the beginning he was not at all sanguine about the outcome. He knew full well that the conspiracy charge was impossible to uphold. He also realized that if the defendants succeeded in explaining the way investment houses actually conducted their affairs (which they did), the charges against them would fall apart.[127]

Stuart's views proved to be correct, and it seems probable that by the time he was called to testify, early in March 1952, the government's attorneys also were beginning to share some of his doubts. This may explain why the government did not plan to question him extensively or to use his testimony to prove the conspiracy charge.[128] Its examination of Stuart was so ineffective and unrewarding that Medina called it "a most tremendous waste of time." [129]

The same certainly could not be said of the defense's questioning. Dean and the other defense attorneys appreciated the importance of Stuart's testimony, and when it came time for them to cross-examine, they made every use possible of his intimate knowledge of the investment banking business to demolish the government's case. "He is the man," Medina said later, "who broke the case for the government." [130]

Stuart denied any knowledge of an investment banking conspiracy. The first time he had ever heard that one existed, he said, was when the Justice Department's attorneys told him of it. His first reaction on learning about it was to ask whether his firm was one of the conspirators.[131] Nor was he aware of any traditional banker or reciprocity arrangements among investment houses. "On the basis of your observation and experience," he was asked, "do you know of any understanding or arrangement among investment bankers by which when one investment banker manages an issue for a company the others agree not to seek subsequent issues of the same issuer?" "No, sir, I do not," Stuart replied. "Do you know on the basis of your experience of an arrangement among investment bankers by which whenever an investment banker receives a participation in the underwriting of some issuer, he is entitled in any way to have a similar position in future business of the same issuer?" Stuart again replied that he had no knowledge of such practices or of historically "frozen" syndicates.[132]

"Corrected Opinion," 47; *ibid.*, "Transcript of Trial: Plaintiff's Case" (January 13, 1953), 18848–49.
127. Dean to author, May 13, 1964.
128. *The New York Times,* March 7, 1952.
129. Quoted in *The New York Times,* March 8, 1952.
130. *U.S. v. Henry S. Morgan et al.,* "Statistical Analysis by Mr. Dean" (April 8, 1953), 21755; *The New York Times,* March 20, 1952.
131. *U.S. v. Henry S. Morgan et al.,* "Testimony of Harold L. Stuart-Cross" (April 9, 1952), 14818–23. See also *The New York Times,* April 10, 1952.
132. *U.S. vs. Henry S. Morgan et al.,* "Transcript of Trial: Testimony of Har-

As Stuart's cross-examination continued, the government's other major charges collapsed as quickly as those included in the triple concept. He testified that the underwriting syndicate, with its price-fixing arrangements, which the defendants supposedly had invented in 1915, was in common use at the turn of the century, if not earlier, and he explained that the changes in syndicate structure and procedures since then were natural developments, dictated by the needs of the times. None of them was the result of concerted deliberation or action by the defendants or any other investment bankers. Nor was it uncommon, much less conspiratorial, for an investment banker to try to get an issuer he had served once to agree to employ his firm to head subsequent financings. Stuart said that his own firm had sought to win such preferential agreements as late as 1938.[133]

The more Stuart explained the way investment bankers conducted their business and the reasons why they employed certain practices to which the government objected, such as price fixing during syndication, the more difficult it became for government counsel to substantiate its charges against the defendants. Attorneys for the Justice Department admitted the damaging effects of Stuart's testimony to their side of the case even before the defense had completed its cross-examination. By the time Stuart left the stand, several months later, the conspiracy charge had been totally disproved.[134]

Government lawyers rested their case in March 1953, and two months later the defense concluded its presentation of motions to dismiss. It was now up to Medina to decide whether to dismiss the charges or to require the defendants to present their side of the case, which very probably would have extended the trial another several years. Medina worked on his decision throughout the summer, often as long as eleven hours a day; and he announced it unexpectedly on September 22, 1953, at a "procedural conference" of attorneys for both sides. The final, revised, and corrected opinion he presented three weeks later, and filed on February 4, 1954.[135]

Medina dismissed the charges against the defendants on the grounds of insufficient evidence. "I have come to the settled conviction and accordingly find," he wrote, "that no such combination, conspiracy and agreement as is alleged in the complaint, nor any part thereof, was ever made, entered into, conceived, constructed, continued or participated in by these defendants, or any of them.

---

old L. Stuart-Cross" (May 14, 1952), 15858–59. See also *The New York Times*, May 15, 1952.

133. *The New York Times*, March 12, 13, 1952, May 3, 1952.

134. *U.S. v. Henry S. Morgan et al.*, Statistical Analysis by Mr. Dean" (April 8, 1953), 21753–59; *The New York Times*, May 19, 1952.

135. *The New York Times*, March 14, 1953, May 20, 1953, September 19, 23, 1953.

Since there was no combination, the monopoly charges fall of their own weight."[136] So convinced was he of this, that he not only dismissed the complaint "on the merits," but did so "with prejudice," thus making it impossible for the Justice Department to retry the case. If it wanted to bring suit against the defendants, it would have to prepare an entirely new complaint.[137] The government, of course, could appeal Medina's decision, but it did not do so.

The trial had resulted in an exhaustive examination of the investment banking business. No pertinent evidence had been overlooked. Witnesses had been examined and cross-examined fully, and their credibility and the probative value of the documentary material carefully tested. Medina's closely reasoned and tightly written opinion, moreover, demonstrated clearly the "fictional foundation" upon which the government had built its conspiracy and monopoly charges. Had the suit been filed before 1933, Medina observed, the government might have uncovered conditions and practices that violated the Sherman Act, but the trial had made evident that those days, when investment banking was surrounded by an aura of "dignity and mystery," had long since passed. The Justice Department, recognizing the extent to which its case had been demolished, was reluctant to invest more time and money in an appeal that it had little, if any, chance of winning.[138]

Medina also denied a government motion to amend the complaint to include, entirely apart from the original charges, the additional one of illegal price fixing. This widely employed practice, Medina said, was not a justiciable issue. Nor were the other restrictive clauses commonly found in syndicate agreements. If these practices violated the Sherman Act, it was up to the Congress, not the courts, to outlaw them.

Having said this, he set forth his views on modern syndicate practices in a lengthy obiter dictum. He explained their widespread use as "a gradual, natural and normal" development, dictated by need and recognized as essential by the authors of the Securities Exchange Act and the SEC commissioners. "No court can turn back the hand of time; and the plain unvarnished truth of the matter is that the intricate, highly sensitive and flexible system which now serves its purpose so well, is perhaps to a large extent the product of legislation by the Congress and administrative rulings by those functioning under the authority of the Congress."[139]

Judge Medina's opinion was more than an important legal docu-

136. *U.S. v. Henry S. Morgan et al.*, "Corrected Opinion," 416. See also *The New York Times,* September 23, 1953.
137. Medina to author, September 2, 1966.
138. *Ibid.;* Dean to author, May 13, 1964; *The New York Times,* May 6, October 15, 1953, April 8, 1954.
139. *U.S. v. Henry S. Morgan et al.*, "Corrected Opinion," 125–26. See also *The New York Times,* March 15, April 24, October 15, 1953.

ment, setting aside one of the longest, most complex antitrust suits ever to be brought under the Sherman Act. It also was a major treatise on the history of investment banking. A *New York Times* editorial said, "it must be reckoned as at least 'must' supplementary reading to any textbook on the subject of investment banking." [140]

Medina's careful summation and critical appraisal of the trial evidence provided an authoritative account of the way investment bankers actually conducted their business. Their affairs had been investigated at length on several occasions before, but never in such depth or detail. "I felt as though I had run down Wall Street naked," Stuart said after many hours of questioning.[141] He was not the only one who felt that way. Never before had investment bankers been required to divulge so much confidential information concerning their operations and business relationships.

The image of the investment banker that emerged from these disclosures was entirely different from the one that had existed before the trial started. At that time, the generally held view of the role and function of the investment banker was the one made popular by Pujo and Brandeis a generation earlier and reaffirmed by the Pecora and TNEC hearings. It was largely on the basis of their findings, which had become part of the accepted folklore, that the government rested its complaint and hoped to win its case. The trial disproved many of the misconceptions that had grown out of these earlier investigations and shattered the old myth of a Wall Street money monopoly.

140. *The New York Times*, October 15, 19, 1953. Robert R. Young did not share *The Times*'s high regard for Medina's opinion. In June 1955, while testifying before the Senate Banking and Currency Committee, he implied that Medina had been biased in favor of the defendants, and he criticized government attorneys for not objecting to his hearing the case. Young's criticism of the judicial ethics in this case stemmed from the fact that Medina's two sons were employed by two New York City law firms representing four of the defendants. Everyone associated with the case was aware of this. The very first thing Medina did upon being assigned the case was to call all the lawyers together and announce the fact publicly in the courtroom. No one objected, since both men had just graduated from law school, were beginning their clerkships, and were in no way concerned with the work their firms were doing on this case. Young, however, was not at all persuaded that there had been no favoritism. "We do not know who was responsible for this magnanimous decision," he said, referring to the government attorneys' refusal to protest Medina's assignment to the case, "but we do know that the head of the Antitrust Division, who certainly should have interested himself in all matters pertaining to one of the most important cases ever to come before his Division, shortly thereafter went back to work for one of the law firms which was defending the banks, leaving his assistants and Government witnesses to take the rap in court." See U.S. Senate, Committee on Banking and Currency, 84th Cong., 1st Sess., *Stock Market Study: Hearings* . . . (3 pts., Washington, 1955–56), pt. 3, 1458–59. Young's views subsequently were given wider currency by Victor Perlo, *The Empire of High Finance* (New York, 1957), 77–79.

141. As quoted in *The New York Times*, April 4, 1953.

Epilogue: Mid-Century and Later

The antitrust trial against the nation's top seventeen investment houses documented both the change and continuity that marked American investment banking after the turn of the century. In response to government investigations, recurring political pressure, increasing federal regulation, and widespread alterations in the demand for and supply of capital, the investment banker modified many of his practices to conform to the changes that had occurred in American business and society. Traditional methods of operation were discarded and new ones adopted, some to satisfy the demands of government regulators, others to meet new economic requirements. Despite the many changes and innovations, the investment banker's primary function remained essentially what it had been in 1900. What changed was the way he performed that function and his own status in American society.

At the beginning of the century the investment banker was the central figure in the economy. His exploits and pronouncements were front-page news, and the names of Wall Street's chieftains were almost as well known as those of the nation's political leaders. There was good reason for this. Capital then still was a relatively scarce resource, and the men who could recruit it wielded great power and influence. The elder J. Pierpont Morgan and the heads of the other great investment houses presided over much of the country's financial and business activity. Through formal and informal arrangements they had access to the funds of the great urban commercial and savings banks, trust companies, and life insurance concerns, and through their overseas ties to foreign capital as well.

Provision of investment and commercial banking services by the same institutions added further to the image of Wall Street's power. Private banks like the House of Morgan accepted deposits, and many commercial banks and trust companies originated and distributed stocks and bonds, either directly or through wholly owned or controlled security affiliates. The intermingling of these two different and separate functions put the investment banker at the vital center of American finance, able to influence the flow of both long- and short-term credit. The elder Morgan's role in the panic of 1907 epitomized not only his own great influence, but that of investment and commercial bankers generally. His leading associates in that drama were engaged as much in the securities business as in commercial banking.

To the large users of capital, the great railroad and industrial corporations, the investment banker then was as indispensable as he was to individual and institutional investors. Not only were large borrowers dependent upon him for the funds they could not generate themselves, but in the case of many of the great reorganizations, mergers, and consolidations of the late nineteenth and early twentieth centuries, they relied on him for promoting, organizing, and financing these giant enterprises.

Sixty years later the demand for investment banking services had changed radically. Railroads, once the chief customers of investment firms, had ceased to be major borrowers. At the beginning of the century new railroad bond issues had accounted for 51.3 percent of an annual total of slightly less than $1 billion of all new corporate offerings of this type. In the triennial 1959–1961 new railroad bond issues amounted only to 2.5 percent of yearly corporate bond offerings of $8.1 billion. And the only reason rail issues amounted to what they did in that three-year period was because of the sale of equipment trust certificates.[1]

After 1913 the position of prime corporate borrower, once held by the railroads, passed to the public utilities. From then on these companies remained the major issuers of new corporate bonds. During the years 1950–1958, when the total of such offerings amounted to $7.5 billion annually, public utility bonds accounted for almost 44 percent of all such issues, followed by industrials (38.0 percent) and, trailing at a distance, finance and real estate companies (12.0 percent) and railroads (6.1 percent).[2]

Equally significant changes occurred in the percentage distribution of corporate stock. During the years 1901–1912 total annual stock offerings amounted to some $500 million. Slightly more than 82 percent of this amount was issued by three groups of companies. Industrials led the list (29.7 percent), followed closely by rails (28.8 percent), and finance and real estate companies (23.9 percent). The balance, almost 18 percent, was made up of public utility issues. In the years 1959–1961 total volume of new stock issues amounted to $6.2 billion annually. During that triennial there were no new railroad stock issues, and those of finance and real estate companies also suffered a major decline, falling to 8.2 percent of all such offerings. Sales of new public utility and industrial stock during the same three year period accounted for 26.8 percent and 22.1 percent, respectively, of all annual offerings of this type. The remainder, almost 43 percent, represented equities of investment companies.[3]

During the years 1959–1963 investment companies were the leading issuers of new corporate equities. Before 1927 these offerings had accounted for less than 5 percent of all new corporate stock issues. In 1962 and 1963 they amounted to 56 percent of all

1. Irwin Friend, James R. Longstreet et al., *Investment Banking and the New Issues Market* (Cleveland, 1967), 68–69. See also John Lintner, "The Financing of Corporations," in Edward S. Mason, ed., *The Corporation in Modern Society* (New York, 1966), 165–201.
2. Friend, Longstreet et al., *Investment Banking and New Issues Market*, 68–69.
3. *Ibid.*

new equities sold.[4] Investment companies, unlike most other corporations, used the proceeds from stock sales to buy other existing securities rather than for new capital expenditures. It was probably for this reason that the Securities and Exchange Commission (SEC) excluded the offerings of these companies from its tabulations of new security offerings.

The choice clients of the investment banker at the turn of the century were the large established corporations and those being consolidated into still greater units. After World War II it was the smaller and newer companies that were most in need of outside financing and required the assistance of investment firms to find buyers for their securities. The future of the investment banking industry, some Wall Street commentators of the 1960's insisted, rested upon its ability to service young, expanding companies, with limited knowledge of the capital markets and the different methods of selling securities.[5]

Important changes also occurred among long-term borrowers. In 1900 corporations were the major issuers of publicly sold bonds. State and local governments issues were relatively inconsequential. By the end of the 1950's and early 1960's the corporation's long-held leadership in this type of offering was being challenged by the states and their political subdivisions. In 1959, for instance, the dollar volume of state and municipal issues exceeded that of corporate bonds (see Exhibit 26).[6]

Underwriting and distributing state and local securities, unlike corporate offerings, were not the functions of investment bankers exclusively. Although they sold many of these issues, they shared the business in tax exempt securities with commercial banks, which could, and increasingly did, underwrite and deal in general obligation bonds. It was only in the sale of revenue bonds that investment bankers did not have to compete with the great metropolitan banks. This in itself was reason enough for the Investment Bankers Association (IBA) to oppose vigorously all efforts to amend the Glass-Steagall Banking Act of 1933 so as to allow commercial banks to deal in revenue bonds. The debate on this question was prolonged and bitter. It was being argued as strongly at the end of the 1960's as it had been at the beginning of the decade.[7]

4. *Ibid.*
5. Rudolph L. Weissman, "America's Giant Investors," *Challenge,* VI (October 1957), 11.
6. U.S. Securities and Exchange Commission, *Annual Report, 1956* (Washington, 1956), 233–36; *ibid., 1960,* 233–36; *ibid., 1964,* 169–72.
7. *The New York Times,* August 26, October 8, 1963, January 15, February 6, 1966, October 5, 1967. See also Frank C. Carr, "Statement . . . before the Subcommittee on Financial Institutions, Senate Committee on Banking and Currency" (August 29, 1967). Carr was a member of the IBA's Municipal Council Division and the president of John Nuveen & Co., a Chicago investment house specializing in tax-exempt offerings.

Exhibit 26. New securities offered for cash sale in the United States 1951–1963 (in billions)

Year	Total corporate bonds (including debentures and notes)	Total state and municipals
1951	5.7	3.2
1952	7.6	4.4
1953	7.1	5.6
1954	7.5	7.0
1955	7.4	6.0
1956	8.0	5.4
1957	10.0	7.0
1958	9.7	7.4
1959	7.2	7.7
1960	8.1	7.2
1961	9.4	8.4
1962	9.0	8.6
1963	10.9	10.1

Source: U.S. Securities and Exchange Commission, *Annual Report, 1956* (Washington, 1956), 233–36; *ibid., 1960*, 233–36; *ibid., 1964*, 169–72.

Equally significant changes also occurred over the past sixty years among the suppliers of capital. The prime sources of external corporate funds after World War II were the great institutional investors, investment and life insurance companies and pension and mutual funds. In 1960 new corporate bonds, excluding retirements, totaled $5 billion. Of this amount, 84 percent ($4.2 billion) was held by three groups of institutions: life insurance companies ($1.4 billion), private noninsured pension funds ($1.6 billion), and state and local government retirement funds ($1.2 billion). Institutional buyers also held most of the new corporate stock and new state and local bond offerings, the former going largely to noninsured pension funds and the latter to commercial banks.[8] The growth in number and resources of these institutions and the marked rise in personal income taxes brought to an end the era when wealthy individuals and estates were major buyers of new securities. Nor did the impressive growth in the nation's shareholding population, some 22 million in 1966, according to the New York Stock Exchange, have much effect on the new issues market, especially the one for corporate bonds. The buyers of these securities were almost exclusively institutions.[9]

8. Bankers Trust Company, *The Investment Outlook, 1968* (New York, 1968), Tables 2, 10–12.
9. Weissman, "America's Giant Investors," 8–11.

Whereas individuals acquired practically all their securities through public offerings, institutions, on the other hand, bought their stocks and bonds both through public and private sales. After the 1933 Securities Act went into effect the latter increased markedly. By the early 1950's private placements accounted for nearly 50 percent of the dollar value of all corporate securities sold for cash.[10]

The tremendous growth in the volume of direct sales forced investment bankers to adopt new methods and revise old ones. Some firms, appreciating the significance of the trend toward private placements, cultivated the business and developed specialized services designed to serve corporations intent upon this type of sale. Kidder, Peabody & Co. was such a house. During the years 1960–1965 this firm arranged 412 private placements, ranging in size from $95,000 to $100 million. In one year alone (1965) it acted as the agent of issuers in private sales amounting to $509 million.[11] Other firms also solicited this business. In the 1961–1963 triennial, investment bankers as agents participated in almost 64 percent of all privately sold debt issues, measured by dollar volume.[12]

Unlike direct placements, which issuers found so attractive, competitive bidding never won wide acceptance. For the most part, sales of this type were employed only when they were required by state or federal law, and primarily in connection with debt offerings. Variations between the volume of competitive and negotiated transactions stemmed almost exclusively from alterations in the composition of issuers and changes in the proportion of stock offerings as compared to bonds. Public utility bonds and railroad equipment trust certificates were the principal issues sold at bids. Whenever the amount of these offerings dropped, so did the volume of competitive sales.[13]

Underwriting common stock became an increasingly important activity of investment bankers after World War II. Annual public cash sales of these issues, which had ranged from a low of $13 million in 1932 to a high of $397 million in 1945, increased substantially during the mid-century decade. In 1951 they amounted to $1.2 billion, a level not reached since 1929. The high point for the decade was reached in 1957. In that year $2.5 billion of new common stock was sold. That figure was topped in 1961, with sales of almost $3.3 billion (see Exhibit 27).[14]

10. Friend, Longstreet et al., *Investment Banking and New Issues Market*, 339.
11. Kidder, Peabody & Co., Inc., "Annual Report . . . 1966."
12. Friend, Longstreet et al., *Investment Banking and New Issues Market*, 349.
13. *Ibid.*, 385–93. See also Roland I. Robinson, *Postwar Market for State and Local Government Securities* (Princeton, 1960), 28.
14. U.S. Bureau of the Census, *Historical Statistics of the United States, Colonial Times to 1957* (Washington, 1960), 658; U.S. Securities and Exchange Commission, *Annual Report, 1964*, 170.

Exhibit 27. New common and preferred stock offerings sold for cash (in millions)

Year	Common	Preferred
1951	1,212	838
1952	1,369	564
1953	1,326	489
1954	1,213	816
1955	2,185	635
1956	2,301	636
1957	2,516	411
1958	1,334	571
1959	2,027	531
1960	1,664	408
1961	3,294	450

Source: U.S. Bureau of the Census, *Historical Statistics of the United States, Colonial Times to 1957* (Washington, 1960), 658; SEC, *Annual Report, 1960,* 234; ibid., *1964,* 170.

Offerings of new preferreds, on the other hand, suffered a sizable decline after 1946. That year total new issues of this type amounted to $1.1 billion. That level was not reached again, and during the next fifteen years new preferred issues exceeded $800 million only on two occasions, in 1951 and 1954 (see Exhibit 27).[15]

The growing importance of new common stock offerings at mid-century was only one indication of the changes that had occurred in the activities of investment firms since 1900. At that time the major houses looked upon themselves primarily as bond dealers — underwriters and distributors of senior corporate securities. In the 1950's and 1960's these issues, while still important, no longer dominated the new issues market as they had earlier. The method of placing them, moreover, also had changed radically over the years. In 1900 direct placements were virtually unknown, and compulsory competitive bidding for corporate issues was largely a subject of discussion by reformers who urged it and bankers who dismissed it as impractical, dangerous, or both. These and many other commonly accepted investment banking practices of the 1960's, notably those growing out of the New Deal's banking and securities laws, indicated the extent of the transformation that had occurred in the investment banking business since the beginning of the century.

Differences between the two eras were so striking that they obscured the similarities. The investment banker of the 1960's, like

15. U.S. Securities and Exchange Commission, *Annual Report, 1960,* 234; ibid., *1964.* 170.

his predecessor of 1900, was a generalist, providing a wide variety of financial services to users and suppliers of capital. Legal and economic necessity forced him to drop some functions and add others. The New Deal put an end to his days as a deposit banker, and the great commercial banks took over the foreign exchange and letter of credit business that once had belonged to him. Despite these changes the investment banker's primary function remained the same: to provide financial advice and services to corporations and governments. As in the past, investment bankers advised issuers on the method to employ in raising capital, whether to arrange for a public offering of new securities and determine the terms on which it could be accomplished successfully, or to place them privately with institutional investors.

Investment firms provided corporations with other services as well. One of the most important of these after 1960 was to investigate, evaluate, and negotiate acquisitions and mergers. This was not an entirely new function. Investment bankers had performed some of these services before, at the turn of the century, for instance, when they participated in launching some of the new industrial giants of that era. The mergers of the 1950's usually were less spectacular than some of the earlier ones. Often they involved smaller companies seeking to diversify or others planning to turn themselves into conglomerates.

In mergers and acquisitions, investment bankers acted as consultants, financial advisers, or agents. Their job was to prepare detailed plans of diversification, analyze companies which appeared to meet their client's requirements and, once a merger or acquisition was decided upon, negotiate terms satisfactory to both parties. One of the investment banker's most important services involved valuing the securities of the companies concerned to determine a fair basis of share exchange. Acquisitions and mergers required extensive, detailed investigations of the companies being combined and, for legal and tax purposes, expert determination of the type of consolidation to be effected. "An essential part of our job is to fill the role of professional negotiator," a Kidder, Peabody & Co. executive explained. "We try to get the parties to look beyond the merger to the new company." Once the terms have been approved by all concerned, the investment banker may be asked to raise all or a part of the money to effect the reorganization. This he does in the traditional way: placing the securities privately or offering them to the public through an underwriting group. The increase in the number of corporate mergers and the growth of conglomerates provided investment bankers with new, promising opportunities. Many of the larger houses, such as Kidder, Peabody, added mergers and acquisitions to their list of specialties.[16]

16. Alfred E. Borneman to author, January 10, 1969.

In performing their many financial and advisory services, investment bankers retained some of their long-established practices, modified others, and added new ones. The present-day syndicate system, to cite an outstanding example, illustrates the mix of old and new that continues to prevail in the securities business. Despite significant innovations and changes in methods of organizing and operating a syndicate, its substance and purpose have remained essentially the same. This is as true of the bidding groups as it is of those set up for a negotiated offering.

The structure of the investment banking industry in the 1960's also reflected the same pattern of continuity and change. One of the most obvious differences, of course, was the number of firms in the industry. In 1900, according to one estimate, there were approximately 1,000; in 1960 the number registered with the SEC stood at 5,239. The number of underwriters at both times, however, was considerably smaller. In 1900 there were only some 250 such firms. Sixty years later, according to the SEC, only 424, or approximately 9 percent of its registrants reported underwriting as their primary activity. The figure increased almost to 15 percent if the 313 houses that claimed this function as a secondary activity are included with those that reported it as their primary concern.[17]

New York, of course, remained the chief center of investment banking activity. Of the 9,484 offices operated by members of the National Association of Securities Dealers, Inc. (NASD) at the end of 1962, almost 26 percent were in the Empire State. New York City alone accounted for slightly more than 19 percent of the national total. The next largest number was in California, with its growing population and rising level of income. All told, fifteen states accounted for slightly more than 76 percent of all NASD offices.

The size, type, and functions of firms in the 1960's varied as widely as they always had. They ranged all the way from small single offices, owned and operated by one man with very limited capital, to a very few large corporations with far-flung branches throughout the United States and abroad, employing thousands of individuals and with capital in the tens of millions. Almost one-half of the country's security houses in 1962 had an estimated "book capital" of less than $25,000; at the other extreme, those in the $10 million or more category, accounted for only 1 percent of the total.[18]

In 1962, according to a study prepared by the staff of the Uni-

---

17. U.S. House, *Report of Special Study of Securities Markets of the Securities and Exchange Commission* (5 pts., Washington, 1963), pt. 1, 17. The authors of the Wharton School study reported a higher percentage of underwriters, 15 percent primary activity and 25 percent secondary activity. They arrived at these figures by excluding from total houses in the industry all mutual-fund firms and "others whose primary and principal secondary activities are largely peripheral." See Friend, Longstreet *et al., Investment Banking and New Issues Market,* 104.

18. Friend, Longstreet *et al., Investment Banking and New Issues Market,* 115.

versity of Pennsylvania's Wharton School of Finance and Commerce, the industry's total capital was estimated at $2 billion. Of this amount approximately 40 percent was held by thirty-nine firms, representing roughly 1 percent of the industry. Some 45 percent of the country's investment houses had about 1 percent of the capital, and approximately 70 percent of the firms held some 5 percent of it.[19]

The same wide differences that prevailed among investment houses in terms of capital also existed in the types of securities they handled and the kinds of services they provided. Firm size generally determined the degree of specialization. The smaller the firm the more likely it was to specialize, both in the type of securities it sold and in the number of its activities.[20]

Least specialized were the larger houses, those with a capital of $1 million or more, the so-called financial department stores of the investment banking community. Most of these firms (80 percent) sold both corporate and tax exempt issues and provided a variety of financial services.

Kidder, Peabody is an example of a large, diversified investment house. This firm acts as underwriter, distributor, dealer, wholesaler, and retailer, and provides financial advisory services to corporations. During the 1950's and 1960's underwriting generally accounted for between 30 percent and 40 percent of its total annual gross income; occasionally it rose to as much as 50 percent. In 1966, for example, Kidder, Peabody managed or co-managed syndicates for 34 corporate offerings amounting to $600 million, and it participated in 193 underwriting groups that distributed more than $7 billion of these securities. In addition it managed or co-managed groups offering almost $888 million of tax exempt bonds and accepted participations in others that sold another $2.7 billion of these issues. For individuals and institutional clients it executed stock exchange transactions involving more than 35 million shares. Arranging 109 private placements of $509 million of securities also was among its functions. In addition the firm maintained national trading markets in industrial, utility, bank, and mutual fund shares, and arranged block and secondary distributions. The same diversified services were provided by other major houses, such as The First Boston Corporation, Merrill, Lynch, Pierce, Fenner & Smith, Inc., and Lehman Brothers, to name three of the top ten underwriters of the early 1960's.[21]

Some major firms conducted a more restricted business. Morgan Stanley & Co., for instance, remained chiefly a wholesale house,

19. *Ibid.,* 114–15, 141.
20. *Ibid.,* 126–27. See also *Special Study of Securities Markets,* I, 69.
21. Borneman to author, September 21, 1967; Kidder, Peabody & Co., Inc., "Annual Report, Year Ending December 31, 1965"; *ibid.,* 1966; "Bankers — Wall Street Style," *Financial World* (June 28, 1967), 8–10.

limiting its activities largely to originating new issues, managing syndicates, underwriting, and providing financial advice to corporations. This firm's brokerage activities also were designed to satisfy the special needs of corporations, institutional investors, and foreign governments.[22] The same generally was true of Kuhn, Loeb & Co. Before World War II it had specialized in originating and wholesaling railroad securities; after 1945 it became active in financing foreign governments and corporations. And Halsey, Stuart & Co., Inc., continued to restrict its underwritings to debt issues.

Despite the number and types of firms, investment banking in the 1960's was as highly concentrated as it had been sixty years earlier. In some respects it was even more so. No matter how measured — firm size, capital employed, underwritings, syndicate managements — a relatively few large houses, mostly located in New York City, conducted most of the nation's new issues business. As was to be expected, concentration remained most apparent in syndicate managements. The number of houses that headed most offerings, measured in terms of volume of issues managed, was small and their rankings within this select group changed from year to year. The composition of the group itself, moreover, also changed, depending on the type of flotation. In the years 1947–1949, for instance, ten firms managed 62 percent (dollar value) of all privately negotiated corporate offerings sold publicly and 87 percent of those offered competitively. The top ten firms' share of this business in the 1961–1963 triennial fell to 58 percent, for privately negotiated corporate offerings, and increased slightly, to 88 percent, for issues sold at bids.[23]

Another indication of concentration was distribution of income. In 1963, after the most comprehensive examination of the securities industry since the antitrust trial, the SEC estimated that in 1961 and 1962 slightly more than 5 percent of the firms in the industry earned almost 61 percent of the gross income from securities transactions of various kinds, underwriting, trading, and brokerage. The firms in this small group were all major houses, those with gross annual incomes in excess of $500,000.[24]

In the years after the antitrust trial, as in those before it, traditional investment banking functions were the concern of a relatively few firms. The business of underwriting and distributing original and secondary issues, maintaining markets in outstanding securities, executing orders on the stock exchanges, and providing advice to corporations and other borrowers was carried on by some 2,900 firms. And of these, fewer than 750 made up the "core of the indus-

22. [Morgan Stanley & Co.] *A Summary of Financing, 1935–1960* (New York, 1961), 14.
23. Friend, Longstreet *et al., Investment Banking and New Issues Market,* 156.
24. *Special Study of Securities Markets,* I, 18, 35, 175–76.

try," the IBA's president testified before the Senate Committee on Banking and Currency in August 1967.[25]

The industry's continuing high degree of concentration did not mean lack of competition. There was much hustling for business among firms, and significant changes occurred in their rankings, measured in terms of the number and dollar value of their syndicate managements and participations. Every year *Finance* magazine, a widely read monthly, reported the net worth and performance of the nation's "Top 400" underwriters. Its findings, together with those of the SEC and other federal agencies, disclosed the shifts in standing, as well as the turnover of firms in the industry.

Throughout the post-trial decade there were numerous dissolutions and mergers. Most of the turnover occurred among the smaller and younger houses, but it was not limited to them. The IBA, with its relatively high admission requirements ($50,000 net worth and three years in the securities business), also registered a sizable reduction in membership, most of it attributable to mergers.

Need for greater capital to meet the growing demands of both issuers and investors prompted many mergers. Institutional buyers insisted that their bankers furnish extensive, detailed information on issues that interested them. To provide it often required considerable research. Gathering this information was costly. Similarly, the use of computers to facilitate handling the growing volume of brokerage transactions, improve stock-clearing facilities, and expedite back-office operations, such as billing and delivery, added to already high operating costs. For many small and medium-size firms, mergers were an attractive, convenient solution to these problems. There also were other reasons for the increase in mergers, such as the death or retirement of a partner.[26]

The trend toward mergers was paralleled by another organizational change. During the 1950's many firms abandoned the industry's traditional forms of organization (sole proprietorships and partnerships) and incorporated. In 1950 securities corporations accounted for only 28 percent of all broker-dealers registered with the SEC; by the end of 1960 they represented almost 42 percent.[27] Tax benefits for the partners, continuity of the firm, and greater opportunity to spread ownership were the principal reasons that prompted incorporation. The latter was especially important, since it made it easier to give able young men an interest in the firm, and thus to reduce the amount of raiding of promising executives by competitors with more attractive employee benefit plans. Incorpora-

---

25. H. Lawrence Bogert, "Statement Submitted to the Senate Committee on Banking and Currency" (August 3, 1967).
26. Borneman to author, September 21, 1967.
27. *Special Study of Securities Markets,* I, 37.

tion was made still more attractive after 1953, when the New York Stock Exchange abolished its old rule prohibiting corporate officers and directors from holding seats on the exchange.[28]

Incorporation usually involved little more than a change in legal entity. A firm's partners became the corporation's officers and stockholders. Their financial interest in the business generally remained the same, as did their duties and responsibilities. Nor did significant changes occur in the firm's functions.

One result of the incorporation movement was the publication of more annual reports by security houses. Probably this would have occurred anyway. The trend was in this direction. Incorporated houses, of course, already published them, and some of the larger partnerships, such as Kidder, Peabody (incorporated in 1964), had been doing so for several years. Increased financial disclosure, moreover, was being urged by the SEC. Speaking at the IBA's annual convention in November 1965, SEC chairman Manuel F. Cohen suggested that investment firms be required to supply the commission with detailed annual reports indicating their "profits and losses on each separate aspect of their business." The information Cohen asked of them was no more than they demanded of their corporate clients.[29]

Most investment bankers were unwilling to oppose Cohen's proposal openly. Some executives of large houses refused to comment on it, others admitted to the SEC's right to demand more financial information, and many more hoped that a compromise solution might be worked out. Almost everyone realized that investment bankers hardly could object to full disclosure. To do so, a financial writer for *The New York Times* observed, "would make the securities industry look like the one overdressed figure in a nudist colony that it helped to create."[30] More than a half century earlier the elder Morgan confided to a friend that disclosure was becoming the rule of the day. Cohen's proposal confirmed Morgan's prediction and underscored the extent to which the securities business had changed since then. The "dignity and mystery" of that earlier day had long since ended.

Unlike the few great houses of Morgan's era, whose prestige, status, and influence stemmed from their close ties and interlocking relationships with the principal users and suppliers of capital, the strength, vigor, and future of investment bankers in the 1960's rested with the entire industry, not with any single individual or small group of firms. The antitrust trial demonstrated beyond cavil that

28. Friend, Longstreet *et al., Investment Banking and New Issues Market,* 112; Borneman to author, September 21, 1967.
29. *The New York Times,* February 8, 1966.
30. *Ibid.,* February 9, 1966.

there was no investment banking monopoly and, just as important, the extent to which the new issues business had been changed by federal regulation and economic need.

In 1963 the SEC released its lengthy study of the securities industry. It found much to praise and some "serious shortcomings" that remained to be corrected. The commission recommended changes in practices designed to increase the public's protection, such as requiring underwriters to maintain a certain minimum net capital, establishing effective procedures to keep out unqualified persons from entering the industry, and correcting other inadequacies in the regulatory system. Despite these and other deficiencies, the *Report* concluded that "neither the fundamental structure of the securities markets nor of the regulatory pattern of the securities acts requires dramatic reconstruction." [31]

At the time the SEC made public its findings, there were investment bankers still active who remembered the Wall Street of Morgan's day. To the generation born after World War I, the world of Old Jupiter was as remote as the one of Nicholas Biddle or Jay Cooke. The economic, social, and legal environment in which investment bankers functioned in the 1960's was so radically different from what it had been at the time of Morgan's death that it seemed as if eons separated the two eras.

One indication of the transformation that had occurred was in the public's image of the investment banker. In 1913 he was feared and looked upon as the head of a powerful and sinister conspiracy; by the 1960's he had become an accepted figure on the nation's economic landscape. The evils Louis D. Brandeis had warned against at the time of the Pujo investigation never materialized, and violations of fiduciary trust of the type disclosed by the Pecora hearings a generation later had become rare occurrences.[32] Federal regulation and the investment banking community's own "heightened sense of obligation" did much to rehabilitate Wall Street's reputation and restore public confidence in financiers.

By the 1960's the position of the investment banker in the national economy was considerably less than it had been at the beginning of the century. No investment banker since then has occupied the place once held by the elder Morgan or any of the other great financiers of his era. No one could. Fundamental changes in the availability of capital and in the relative size of investment houses vis-à-vis their issuer clients greatly diminished the bankers' bargaining power. Their influence was reduced further by the 1933 separation provisions of the Glass-Steagall law, which deprived investment firms of their banking functions, and by the New Deal's securities

---

31. *Special Study of Securities Markets*, I, iii.
32. Richard Hofstadter, *The Paranoid Style in American Politics and Other Essays* (New York, 1967), 215.

laws, which circumscribed their freedom of action in originating and distributing securities. Continued growth of the SEC's regulatory powers since then limited the investment banker's activities still further. None of these developments, however, altered his primary role or diminished his importance. What had changed was his clientele and how he serviced its needs.

Bibliography

Primary Sources

Manuscripts, Typescripts, and Private Papers

Clark, E. W., & Co. Brief typescript "History." In possession of Professor Henrietta M. Larson.
Corcoran, William Wilson. Papers, Library of Congress, Washington, D.C.
Harrison, George. "Conversation with Messrs. Lamont and Gilbert, March 28, 1933." Confidential File, Binder 46, George Harrison Papers, Columbia University Library, New York.
Kidder, Peabody & Co., "Bank Consolidation of 1898" in Kidder, Peabody & Co., Miscellaneous Records, Baker Library, Harvard Graduate School of Business Administration.
——— "Circulars" (1895–1927), 10 vols., Baker Library.
——— "Confidential Letters" (1883–1929), 6 vols., Baker Library.
——— "Histories" (1911–1943), 16 vols., Baker Library.
——— Miscellaneous Business Records, Kidder, Peabody & Co., Inc., New York.
——— Miscellaneous Records, Baker Library.
——— "Record of Clerks" (1880–1927 [?]), 5 vols., Baker Library.
Lamont, Thomas W. "Memorandum to R. Gordon Wasson," dated March 27, 1939. In possession of Professor Henrietta M. Larson.
——— "Memorandum for the President," April 11, 1933. (President's Personal File), Franklin D. Roosevelt Library, Hyde Park, New York.
Larson, Henrietta M. Typescript of Interview with George W. Bovenizer, dated December 18, 1951. In possession of author.
Morgan, J. P., & Co., "Reprints of Statements Submitted by Members of J. P. Morgan & Co. to Senate Committee on Banking and Currency . . ." (New York, 1934), Baker Library.
——— "Letter from Messrs. J. P. Morgan & Co. in Response to the Invitation of the Sub-Committee (Hon. A. P. Pujo, chairman) of the Committee on Banking and Currency of the House of Representatives" (New York, 1913), Baker Library.
Nehemkis, Peter R., Jr. "Confidential Memorandum to Benjamin V. Cohen," February 7, 1939. National Archives, Record Group No. 48, Office File of Benjamin V. Cohen, General Counsel, National Power Policy Committee, 1934–1941, Box 10 — Legislative Projects, Folder: "Monopoly Studies."
Stevens, Marshall W. "History of Lee, Higginson and Company," Typescript, Baker Library.
Thayer, John E. *et al.* Miscellaneous Business Manuscripts, Baker Library.

Memoirs, Diaries, and Letters

Adler, Cyrus. *Jacob H. Schiff: His Life and Letters* (2 vols., New York, 1929).

512 | Bibliography

Aldrich, Winthrop W. *Suggestions for Improving the Banking System* (New York, 1933).
[Babson, Roger W.] *Actions and Reactions: An Autobiography* . . . (New York, 1935).
Baker, Ray Stannard. *Woodrow Wilson: Life and Letters* (8 vols., Garden City, 1927–1939).
Carpenter, Frances, ed. *Carp's Washington* . . . (New York, 1960).
Clews, Henry. *Fifty Years in Wall Street* (New York, 1908).
Ellis, George E. *Memoir of Nathaniel Thayer, A.M.* (Cambridge, Mass., 1885).
Forgan, James B. *Recollections of a Busy Life* (New York, 1924).
Griscom, Lloyd C. *Diplomatically Speaking* (Boston, 1940).
Hoover, Herbert. *The Memoirs of Herbert Hoover* (3 vols., New York, 1951–52).
Ickes, Harold L. *The Secret Diary of Harold L. Ickes* (3 vols., New York, 1953–54).
Lamont, Thomas W. *Across World Frontiers* (New York, 1951).
Lanier, J. F. D. *Sketch of the Life of J. F. D. Lanier* (New York, 1870).
Lefevre, Edwin. *Reminiscences of a Stock Operator* (New York, 1923).
Noyes, Alexander D. *The Market Place: Reminiscences of a Financial Editor* (Boston, 1938).
Perry, Bliss. *Life and Letters of Henry Lee Higginson* (Boston, 1921).
Roosevelt, Theodore. *An Autobiography* (New York, 1926).
Rosenman, Samuel, ed. *The Public Papers and Addresses of Franklin D. Roosevelt* (13 vols., New York, 1938–1950).
Smith, Matthew Hale. *Twenty Years Among the Bulls and Bears of Wall Street* (Hartford, 1870).
Truman, Harry S. *Memoirs* (2 vols., New York, 1955–56).
Wyckoff, Richard D. *Wall Street Ventures and Adventures Through Forty Years* (New York, 1930).

Government Documents: Federal and State

New York, Committee on Speculation in Securities and Commodities, *Report* . . . *June 7, 1909* (Albany, 1910).
New York, *Joint Committee of the Senate and Assembly of the State of New York to Investigate and Examine into the Business and Affairs of Life Insurance Companies Doing Business in the State of New York* (7 vols., Albany, 1906).
U.S. Board of Governors of the Federal Reserve System, *Banking and Monetary Statistics* (Washington, 1943).
U.S. Bureau of Corporations. *Report* . . . *on the Steel Industry* (3 vols., Washington, 1911–1913).
U.S. Bureau of Foreign and Domestic Commerce. "A New Estimate of American Investment Abroad," *Trade Information Bulletin, No. 767* (Washington, 1931).
U.S. Bureau of the Census. *Census of Business: 1935. Financial Institutions Other Than Banks* (Washington, 1937).
——— *Historical Statistics of the United States, Colonial Times to 1957* (Washington, 1960).

U.S. Comptroller of the Currency. *Annual Report . . . 1898* (2 vols., Washington, 1899).
U.S. Department of Commerce. *Report to Secretary of Commerce of Committee on Stock Exchange Regulation* (Washington, 1934).
U.S. District Court, Southern District of New York (Civil No. 43-757), *United States of America v. Henry S. Morgan et al.* The specific references to various parts of the trial are indicated in the footnotes.
U.S. Federal Communications Commission. *Report on Telephone Investigation* (2 vols., Washington, 1939).
U.S. Federal Trade Commission. *Annual Report . . . 1919* (Washington, 1920). Also other years.
——— *Electric-Power Industry, Control of Power Companies . . . : A Report Relative to the Organization, Control and Ownership of Commercial Electric Power Companies* (Washington, 1927).
——— *Utility Corporations: Summary Report . . . on Economic; Financial and Corporate Phases of Holding and Operating Companies of Electric and Gas Utilities* (96 pts., Washington, 1928–1937).
U.S. House, Committee on Banking and Currency, 71st Cong., 2d Sess. *Branch, Chain and Group Banking: Hearings . . .* (15 pts. in 2 vols., Washington, 1930).
U.S. House, Committee on Interstate and Foreign Commerce, 67th Cong., 1st and 2d Sess. *"Blue-Sky" Bill: Hearings . . .* (2 pts., Washington, 1921–22).
——— 73d Cong., 1st Sess. *Federal Securities Act: Hearings . . .* (Washington, 1933).
——— 73d Cong., 1st Sess. *Federal Supervision of Traffic in Investment Securities: Report . . .* (Washington, 1933).
——— 77th Cong., 1st and 2d Sess. *Proposed Amendments to the Securities Act of 1933 and to the Securities Exchange Act of 1934: Hearings . . .* (6 pts., Washington, 1941–42).
——— *Regulation of Stock Ownership in Railroads* (3 vols., Washington, 1931).
——— 73d Cong., 2d Sess. *Relation of Holding Companies to Operating Companies in Power and Gas Affecting Control: Report . . .* (6 pts., Washington, 1934–35).
——— 73d Cong., 2d Sess. *Stock Exchange Regulation: Hearings . . .* (Washington, 1934).
——— 82d Cong., 2d Sess. *Study of the Securities and Exchange Commission: Report . . .* (Washington, 1952).
U.S. House, Committee on Investigation of United States Steel Corporation. *United States Steel Corporation: Hearings . . .* (Washington, 1912).
U.S. House, Committee on the Judiciary, 66th Cong., 1st Sess. *Proposed Federal "Blue Sky" Law: Hearings . . .* (Washington, 1919).
U.S. House, Special Committee to Investigate Violations of Antitrust Act of 1890 and Other Acts, 62d Cong., 2d Sess. *Investigation of United States Steel Corporation, Report . . .* (Washington, 1912).
U.S. House, Special Subcommittee on Legislative Oversight of the Committee on Interstate and Foreign Commerce, 85th Cong., 2d Sess.

History of National Association of Securities Dealers, Inc. . . . (Washington, 1959).

U.S. House, 62nd Cong., 3d Sess. *Investigation of Financial and Monetary Conditions in the United States* . . . (3 vols., Washington, 1913).

U.S. House, *Report of Special Study of Securities Markets of the Securities and Exchange Commission* (5 pts., Washington, 1963).

U.S. House, 62d Cong., 3d Sess. *Report of the Committee Appointed . . . to Investigate the Concentration of Control of Money and Credit* (Washington, 1913).

U.S. Industrial Commission. *Report* . . . (19 vols., Washington, 1900–1902).

U.S. National Recovery Administration. *Codes of Fair Competition, Nos. 111–150* . . . (Washington, 1934).

U.S. Pacific Railway Commission. *Report* . . . (10 vols., Washington, 1887).

U.S. Securities and Exchange Commission. *Annual Report* (Washington, 1956). Also other years.

——— *Investment Trusts and Investment Companies: Report* . . . (5 pts., Washington, 1939–1942).

——— *Investment Trusts and Investment Companies: Report [on] Investment Counsel, Investment Management, Investment Supervisory, and Investment Advisory Services* (Washington, 1939).

——— Public Utilities Division. *The Problem of Maintaining Arm's Length Bargaining and Competitive Conditions in the Sale and Distribution of Securities of Registered Public Utility Holding Companies and Their Subsidiaries* (Washington, 1940).

——— *Selected Statistics on Securities and on Exchange Markets* (Washington, 1939).

U.S. Senate, Committee on Banking and Currency, 73d Cong., 2 Sess. *Federal Securities Exchange Act of 1934: Report* . . . (Washington, 1934).

——— 71st Cong., 3d Sess. *Operation of the National and Federal Reserve Banking Systems: Hearings* . . . (8 pts., Washington, 1931–32).

——— 73d Cong., 1st Sess. *Regulation of Securities: Report* . . . (Washington, 1933).

——— 63d Cong., 2d Sess. *Regulation of the Stock Exchange: Hearings* . . . (Washington, 1914).

——— 81st Cong., 2d Sess. *Securities Exchange Acts Amendments: Hearings* . . . (Washington, 1950).

——— 72d Cong., 1st Sess. *Stock Exchange Practices: Hearings* . . . (7 pts., in 6 vols., Washington, 1932–33).

——— 72d and 73d Congs., *Stock Exchange Practices: Hearings* . . . (20 pts., in 9 vols., Washington, 1933–34).

——— 73d Cong., 2d Sess. *Stock Exchange Practices: Report* . . . (Washington, 1934).

——— 84th Cong., 1st and 2d Sess. *Stock Market Study: Hearings* . . . (3 pts., Washington, 1955–56).

U.S. Senate, Committee on Finance, 72d Cong., 1st Sess. *Sale of Foreign*

Bonds or Securities in the United States: Hearings . . . (4 pts., Washington, 1931–32).

U.S. Senate, Committee on Interstate Commerce, 74th Cong., 2d Sess., 75th Cong., 3d Sess. *Investigation of Railroads, Holding Companies, and Affiliated Companies: Hearings* . . . (29 pts., Washington, 1937–1942).

——— 76th Cong., 1st-3d Sess. *Investigation of Railroads, Holding Companies . . . Report No. 25* (27 pts., Washington, 1939–40).

——— 76th Cong., 3d Sess. *Investigation of Railroads, Holding Companies and Affiliated Companies: Report No. 1182* . . . (5 pts., Washington, 1940).

U.S. Senate, Special Committee Investigating the Munitions Industry, 73d and 74th Congs. *Munitions Industry: Hearings* . . . (40 pts., Washington, 1934–1943).

U.S. Temporary National Economic Committee. *Investigation of Concentration of Economic Power, Final Report and Recommendations* . . . (Washington, 1941).

——— *Investigation of Concentration of Economic Power: Final Report of the Executive Secretary* (Washington, 1941).

——— *Investigation of Concentration of Economic Power: Hearings* . . . (31 pts., Washington, 1939–1941).

——— *Monograph No. 37, Saving, Investment, and National Income* (Washington, 1941).

U.S. Treasury, *Annual Report . . . 1914* (Washington, 1915). Also other years.

U.S. v. United States Steel Corporation and Others (1911–1920).

Other Sources and Unpublished Works

Aldrich, Winthrop W. "The Stock Market from the Viewpoint of a Commercial Banker," An address at a meeting of the Rochester Chamber of Commerce, October 14, 1937.

Burns, Helen M. "The American Banking Community and New Deal Banking Reform, 1933–1935" (unpublished Ph.D. dissertation, New York University, 1965).

Bogert, H. Lawrence. "Statement Submitted to the Senate Committee on Banking and Currency" (August 3, 1967). Text supplied to author by Investment Bankers Association.

Carr, Frank C. "Statement . . . before the Subcommittee on Financial Institutions, Senate Committee on Banking and Currency" (August 29, 1967). Text supplied to author by Investment Bankers Association.

Connely, Emmet F. *A Reply to the Securities and Exchange Commission Concerning the Underwriting and Sale of Certain Issues of Public Utility Securities, the Law Appertaining Thereto, "Maintenance of Competitive Conditions," Rule U-12 F-2 and Related Matters* (Chicago, 1940).

Donham, Wallace B. "Underwriting Syndicates and the Purchase and Sale of Securities Through Banking Houses" in Harvard Graduate School of Business Administration, "Corporation Finance" (mimeographed lecture notes, Baker Library, 1908).

The First National Bank of Boston. *The First National Corporation* Boston, May 25, 1918).
The First National Bank of Boston. *Report to the Stockholders* (January 14, 1919, April 16, 1921).
Harvard University, Graduate School of Business Administration. "Corporation Finance" (mimeographed lecture notes, Baker Library, 1908).
Hidy, Muriel E. "George Peabody. Merchant and Financier, 1759–1869" (unpublished Ph.D. dissertation, Harvard University, 1939).
Investment Bankers Association of America, *An Examination of the Proposal of the S.E.C. Staff for Compulsory Competitive Bidding in the Sale of Certain Public Utility Securities* (New York, 1941).
[Investment Bankers Code Committee] *Code of Fair Competition for Investment Bankers With a Descriptive Analysis of its Fair Practice Provisions and a History of its Preparation* (Washington, 1934).
Joline, A. H. "Reorganization of Corporations — Reorganization and Underwriting Syndicates" in Harvard Graduate School of Business Administration, "Corporation Finance" (mimeographed lecture notes, Baker Library, 1908).
Katz, Irving. "Investment Bankers in American Government and Politics" (unpublished Ph.D. dissertation, New York University, 1964).
Lanston Monotype-Machine Company, *Annual Report, Year Ending April 17, 1902.*
[Lehman Brothers] *Private Placements: A Means of Raising Capital in a Changing Economy* (n.p., n.d.).
Macy, George Oliver. "Flotation" in Harvard Graduate School of Business Administration, "Corporation Finance" (mimeographed lecture notes, Baker Library, 1908).
Meade, Edward S. "Initial Stages of Organization" in Harvard Graduate School of Business Administration "Corporation Finance" (mimeographed lecture notes, Baker Library, 1908).
——— "The Private Banker as a Bond Distributor" in Harvard Graduate School of Business Administration, "Corporation Finance" (mimeographed lecture notes, Baker Library, 1908).
Morgan, J. P., & Co., [*Letter*] *To the Stockholders of the Federal Steel Company, National Steel Company, National Tube Company, American Steel and Wire Company of New Jersey, American Tin Plate Company, American Steel Hoop Company, American Sheet Steel Company* (March 2, 1901).
[New York Stock Exchange] *Answers of the New York Stock Exchange to the Questions of Governor Hughes' Committee* (New York, 1909).
New York Stock Exchange, *Report of the President, May, 1930–May, 1931* (New York, 1931). Also other years.
Otis & Co. *Investors, Dealers, and Issuers Would Benefit by Competitive Bidding for the Securities of Public Utilities: A Reply to the Opponents of Competitive Bidding* (Cleveland, 1941).
Pecora, Ferdinand. "The Reminiscences of Ferdinand Pecora" (6 vols., 1962). Oral History Research Office, Columbia University, New York.

Seligman, Isaac. "Reminiscences." typescript dated July 1925. In possession of Professor Henrietta M. Larson.
Storrow, James J. "Management of Capital Account" in Harvard Graduate School of Business Administration, "Corporation Finance" (mimeographed lecture notes, Baker Library, 1908).
——— "The Purchase, Syndicating, and Distributing of an Issue" in Harvard Graduate School of Business Administration, "Corporation Finance" (mimeographed lecture notes, Baker Library, 1908).
Warburg, Paul M. "Some Problems of the Investment Banker," An address delivered before the Bond Club of New York, May 23, 1919.

Author Interviews and Correspondents.

   Ames, Amyas
   Borneman, Alfred E.
   Calvert, Gordon L.
   Chapin, John R.
   Dean, Arthur H.
   de Blasi, Gerard
   Fox, Bertrand D.
   Gordon, Albert H.
   Hovey, Chandler
   Medina, Judge Harold R.
   Pecora, Judge Ferdinand
   Rae, Edward L.
   Webster, Bethuel M.

Secondary Works

Abbott, Charles C. *Financing Business During the Transition* (New York, 1946).
——— *The New York Bond Market: 1920–1930* (Cambridge, Mass., 1937).
Allen, Frederick Lewis. *The Great Pierpont Morgan* (New York, 1949).
——— *The Lords of Creation* (New York, 1935).
——— *Only Yesterday* (New York, 1931).
——— *Since Yesterday: The Nineteen-Thirties in America* . . . (New York, 1940).
American Council on Education. *A Study of Investment Banking* (n.p., 1927).
Anderson, Benjamin M. *Economics and the Public Welfare: Financial and Economic History of the United States, 1914–1946* (New York, 1949).
Ashby, Forrest Bee. *The Economic Effect of Blue Sky Laws* (Philadelphia, 1926).
Atkins, Willard E. et al. *The Regulation of the Security Markets* (Washington, 1946).
Bankers Trust Company. *The Investment Outlook* (New York, 1968).
Barron, Clarence W. and Joseph G. Martin. *The Boston Stock Exchange* Boston, 1893).

Beckhart, Benjamin H., ed. *The New York Money Market* (4 vols., New York, 1931–32).
Bell, David. *The End of Ideology* (new rev. ed., New York 1962).
Berle, Adolf A., Jr. *The Future of American Banking* (New York, 1933).
Bernheim, Alfred L. and Margaret G. Schneider, eds. *The Security Markets* (New York, 1935).
Black, Hillel. *The Watchdogs of Wall Street* (New York, 1962).
Bonbright, James C. and Gardiner C. Means. *The Holding Company: Its Public Significance and Its Regulation* (New York, 1932).
Boston Stock Exchange. *The Boston Stock Exchange* (Boston, 1930).
Brandeis, Louis D. *Other People's Money and How the Bankers Use It* (New York, 1914).
Brandes, Joseph. *Herbert Hoover and Economic Diplomacy: Department of Commerce Policy, 1921–1928* (Pittsburgh, 1962).
Brown Brothers & Company. *Experiences of a Century, 1818–1918* (Philadelphia, 1919).
Brown, John Crosby. *A Hundred Years of Merchant Banking: A History of Brown Brothers and Company . . .* (New York, 1909).
Bryson, A. E. *Halsey, Stuart & Co., Inc., 1901–1937, 1938–1944: A History . . .* (Chicago, 1937–1945 [?]).
Buley, R. Carlyle. *The Equitable Life Assurance Society of the United States, 1859–1964* (2 vols., New York, 1967).
Bullock, Hugh. *The Story of Investment Companies* (New York, 1959).
Burr, Anna R. *The Portrait of a Banker: James Stillman, 1850–1918* (New York, 1927).
Burtchett, Floyd F. and Clifford M. Hicks. *Corporation Finance* (3d ed., Lincoln, 1959).
Campbell, Edward G. *The Reorganization of the American Railroad System, 1893–1900* (New York, 1938).
Chamberlain, Lawrence and George W. Edwards. *The Principles of Bond Investment* (rev. ed., New York, 1927).
Chandler, Alfred D., Jr. *Henry Varnum Poor: Business Editor, Analyst, and Reformer* (Cambridge, Mass., 1956).
Christenson, Charles. *Strategic Aspects of Competitive Bidding for Corporate Securities* (Boston, 1965).
Clews, Henry, & Co. *Railroad Investments* (New York, 1870).
Cochran, Thomas C. *The American Business System: A Historical Perspective, 1900–1955* (Cambridge, Mass., 1960).
——— *Railroad Leaders, 1845–1890: The Business Mind in Action* (Cambridge, Mass., 1953).
Cooper, Francis [Conyngton, Hugh R.] *Financing an Enterprise* (2 vols., New York, 1906).
Corey, E. Raymond. *Direct Placement of Corporate Securities* (Boston, 1951).
Corey, Lewis. *The House of Morgan* (New York, 1930).
Corwin, Edward S., ed. *The Constitution of the United States of America, Analysis and Interpretation, Annotation of Cases Decided by the Supreme Court of the United States to June 30, 1952* (Washington, 1953).

Curtiss, Frederic Haines. *Fifty Years of Boston Finance, 1880–1930* (Boston, 1930).
Daniel, Hawthorne. *Judge Medina* (New York, 1952).
Danielian, Noobar R. *A.T.&T.: The Story of Industrial Conquest* (New York, 1939).
De Bedts, Ralph F. *The New Deal's SEC: The Formative Years* (New York, 1964).
Diamond, Sigmund. *The Reputation of the American Businessman* (Cambridge, Mass., 1955).
Doane, Robert R. *The Anatomy of American Wealth* (New York, 1940).
Douglas, William O. *Democracy and Finance* (New Haven, 1940).
Dowrie, George W. *Money and Banking* (New York, 1936).
[Drexel & Co.] *A New Home for an Old House* (Philadelphia, 1927).
Dunn, Robert W. *American Foreign Investments* (New York, 1926).
Edelman, Jacob Murray. *Securities Regulation in the 48 States* (Chicago, 1942).
Edwards, George W. *The Evolution of Finance Capitalism* (London, 1938).
Emblen, Donald J. *Competitive Bidding for Corporate Securities* (Canton, New York, 1944).
Emden, Paul H. *Money Powers of Europe in the Nineteenth and Twentieth Centuries* (New York, 1938).
Ezell, John S. *Fortune's Merry Wheel: The Lottery in America* (Cambridge, Mass., 1960).
Faulkner, Harold U. *The Decline of Laissez Faire, 1897–1917* (New York, 1951).
Federal Reserve Bank of Boston. *Annual Report for 1960: A History of Investment Banking in New England* (Boston, 1961).
Filler, Louis. *Crusaders for American Liberalism: The Story of the Muckrakers* (New York, 1961).
Finance and Indusry; The New York Stock Exchange: Banks, Bankers, Business Houses, and Moneyed Institutions of the Great Metropolis of the United States (New York, 1886).
Financial Advertisers Association, Investment Research Committee. *Advertising Investment Securities* (New York, 1928).
Flynn, John T. *Investment Trusts Gone Wrong!* (New York, 1931).
——— *Security Speculation: Its Economic Effects* (New York, 1934).
[Forbes, Abner] *The Rich Men of Massachusetts . . .* (2d ed., Boston, 1852).
Forbes, Bertie C. *Men Who Are Making America* (New York, 1921).
——— *Men Who Built America* (New York, 1927).
Fowler, John F. *American Investment Trusts* (New York, 1928).
Frankfurter, Felix. *The Public and Its Government* (New Haven, 1930).
Friend, Irwin, James R. Longstreet et al. *Investment Banking and the New Issues Market* (Cleveland, 1967).
Galbraith, John Kenneth. *The Great Crash, 1929* (Boston 1955).
Galston, Arthur. *Security Syndicate Operations: Organization, Management and Accounting* (rev. enl. ed., New York, 1928).
Garraty, John A. *Right-Hand Man: The Life of George W. Perkins* (New York, 1957).

Garrett, Garet. *Where the Money Grows* (New York, 1911).
Gibb, George S. *The Saco-Lowell Shops: Textile Machinery Building in New England, 1813–1949* (Cambridge, Mass., 1950).
Gleisser, Marcus. *The World of Cyrus Eaton* (New York, 1965).
Goldschmidt [Goldsmith], Raymond W. *The Changing Structure of American Banking* (London, 1933).
——— *Financial Intermediaries in the American Economy Since 1900* (Princeton, 1958).
——— *A Study of Saving in the United States* (3 vols., Princeton, 1955).
Govan, Thomas Payne. *Nicholas Biddle: Nationalist and Public Banker, 1786–1844* (Chicago, 1959).
Graham, Benjamin and David L. Dodd. *Security Analysis: Principle and Technique* (2d ed., New York, 1940).
Gras, N. S. B. *The Massachusetts First National Bank of Boston, 1784–1934* (Cambridge, Mass., 1957).
Gras, N. S. B. and Henrietta M. Larson, *Casebook in American Business History* (New York, 1939).
Hammond, Bray. *Banks and Politics in America from the Revolution to the Civil War* (Princeton, 1957).
Hansl, Proctor W. *Years of Plunder: A Financial Chronicle of Our Times* (New York, 1935).
[Harriman, Ripley & Co.] *The Investment Banking Services of Harriman Ripley & Co., Inc.* (New York, 1959).
[Harris Trust & Savings Bank] *Forty Years of Investment Banking* (Chicago, 1922).
Haven, T. Kenneth. *Investment Banking Under the Securities and Exchange Commission* (Ann Arbor, 1940).
Hawley, Ellis W. *The New Deal and the Monopoly Problem: A Study in Ambivalence* (Princeton, 1966).
Hedges, Joseph E. *Commercial Banking and the Stock Market before 1863* (Baltimore, 1938).
Hendrick, Burton J. *The Story of Life Insurance* (New York, 1907).
Hidy, Ralph W. *The House of Baring in American Trade and Finance . . . 1763–1861* (Cambridge, Mass., 1949).
Hidy, Ralph W. and Muriel E. Hidy, *Pioneering in Big Business, 1882–1911: History of the Standard Oil Company (New Jersey)* (New York, 1955).
Hofstadter, Richard. *The Paranoid Style in American Politics and Other Essays* (New York, 1967).
Holbrook, Stewart H. *The Age of the Moguls* (New York, 1954).
Hovey, Carl. *The Life Story of J. Pierpont Morgan* (New York, 1912).
Investment Bankers Association of America. *Fiftieth Anniversary: 1912–1962* (n.p. 1962[?]).
——— *Fundamentals of Investment Banking* (Englewood Cliffs, 1960).
James, F. Cyril. *The Growth of Chicago Banks* (2 vols., New York, 1938).
James, Marquis and Bessie R. James. *Biography of a Bank: The Story of Bank of America, N.T. & S.A.* (New York, 1954).

Johnson, Arthur M. and Barry E. Supple. *Boston Capitalists and Western Railroads* (Cambridge, Mass., 1967).
Jolliffe, M. F. *The United States as a Financial Centre, 1919–1933* Cardiff, Wales, 1935).
Kahn, Otto H. *Our Economic and Other Problems: A Financier's Point of View* (New York, 1920).
Kamm, Jacob O. *Decentralization of Securities Exchanges* (Boston, 1942).
Katz, Irving. *August Belmont, A Political Biography* (New York, 1968).
Keister, Albert S. *Our Financial System: An Introductory Text* (New York, 1930).
Keller, Morton. *The Life Insurance Enterprise, 1885–1910: A Study in the Limits of Corporate Power* (Cambridge, Mass., 1963).
Kennan, George. *E. H. Harriman: A Biography* (2 vols., Boston, 1922).
Kent, Frank R. *The Story of Alexander Brown & Sons* (Baltimore, 1925).
Kirkland, Edward C. *Industry Comes of Age: Business, Labor, and Public Policy, 1860–1897* (New York, 1961).
——— *Men, Cities and Transportation* (2 vols., Cambridge, Mass., 1948).
Klein, Henry H. *Dynastic America and Those Who Own It* (New York, 1921).
Kouwenhoven, John A. *Partners in Banking: An Historical Portrait of a Great Private Bank, Brown Brothers Harriman & Co., 1818–1968* (Garden City, 1968).
[Kuhn, Loeb & Co.] *Investment Banking Through Four Generations* (New York, 1955).
Lamont, Thomas W. *Henry P. Davison: The Record of a Useful Life* (New York, 1933).
Larson, Henrietta M. *Jay Cooke: Private Banker* (Cambridge, Mass., 1936).
[Lehman Brothers] *A Centennial: Lehman Brothers, 1850–1950* (New York, 1950).
Lewis, Cleona. *America's Stake in International Investments* (Washington, 1938).
Link, Arthur S. *Wilson: The New Freedom* (Princeton, 1956).
——— *Wilson: The Struggle for Neutrality, 1914–1915* (Princeton, 1960).
——— *Woodrow Wilson and the Progressive Era, 1910–1917* (New York, 1954).
Loeser, John C. *The Over-the-Counter Securities Market: What It Is and How It Operates* (New York, 1940).
Loss, Louis. *Securities Regulation* (2d ed., 3 vols., Boston, 1961).
Loss, Louis and Edward M. Cowett. *Blue Sky Law* (Boston, 1958).
Lowenthal, Max. *The Investor Pays* (New York, 1933).
Lundberg, Ferdinand. *America's 60 Families* (New York, 1937).
Madden, John T. and Marcus Nadler. *The International Money Markets* (New York, 1935).
Martin, Joseph G. *A Century of Finance* (Boston, 1898).

——— *Martin's Boston Stock Market* (Boston, 1886).
——— *Twenty-One Years in the Boston Stock Market . . .* (Boston, 1856).
Mason, Alpheus T. *Brandeis: A Free Man's Life* (New York, 1946).
Matz, Mary Jane. *The Many Lives of Otto Kahn* (New York, 1963).
May, Henry F. *The End of American Innocence: A Study of the First Years of Our Own Time* (New York, 1959).
Mayer, Martin. *Wall Street: Men and Money* (rev. ed., New York, 1962).
McClintock, Franklin T. *Competitive Bidding for New Issues of Securities* (New York, 1939).
McCormick, Edward T. *Understanding the Securities Act and the S.E.C.* (New York, 1948).
McDonald, Forrest. *Insull* (Chicago, 1962).
McElroy, Robert. *Levi Parsons Morton: Banker, Diplomat and Statesman* (New York, 1930).
McFerrin, John B. *Caldwell and Company: A Southern Financial Empire* (Chapel Hill, 1939).
McGrane, Reginald C. *Foreign Bondholders and American State Debts* (New York, 1935).
Meade, Edward S. *The Careful Investor* (Philadelphia, 1914).
Mintz, Ilse S. *Deterioration in the Quality of Foreign Bonds Issued in the United States, 1920–1930* (New York, 1951).
Mitchell, Broadus. *Depression Decade: From New Era through New Deal, 1929–1941* (New York, 1947).
Moley, Raymond. *The First New Deal* (New York, 1966).
Moody, John. *The Masters of Capital: A Chronicle of Wall Street* (New Haven, 1921).
[Morgan Stanley & Co.] *A Summary of Financing, 1935–1960* (New York, 1961).
Moulton, Harold G. et al. *Capital Expansion, Employment, and Economic Stability* (Washington, 1940).
Mowry, George E. *The Era of Theodore Roosevelt, 1900–1912* (New York, 1958).
Mulvey, Thomas. *Report Upon Existing Registration in Canada and Elsewhere Prepared by the Under Secretary of State* (Ottawa, 1913).
Myers, Gustavus. *History of the Great American Fortunes* (New York, 1936).
Myers, Margaret G. "Origins and Development" in Benjamin H. Beckhart, ed. *The New York Money Market* (4 vols., New York, 1931–32).
Nadler, Marcus and Jules I. Bogen. *The Banking Crisis: The End of an Epoch* (New York, 1933).
Nadler, Marcus, Sipa Heller, and Samuel S. Shipman, *The Money Market and Its Institutions* (New York, 1955).
Nash, Bradley D. *Investment Banking in England* (Chicago, 1924).
[National Bureau of Economic Research, Financial Research Program] *Research in the Capital and Securities Markets* (New York, 1954).

Neill, Humphrey B. *The Inside Story of the Stock Exchange* (New York, 1950).
Nelson, Samuel A., ed. *The Bond Buyers' Dictionary* (New York, 1907).
Nettels, Curtis P. *The Emergence of a National Economy, 1775–1815* (New York, 1962).
Nevins, Allan. *The Emergence of Modern America, 1865–1878* (New York, 1927).
——— *Grover Cleveland: A Study in Courage* (New York, 1944).
Nicolson, Harold. *Dwight Morrow* (New York, 1935).
Noyes, Alexander D. *The War Period of American Finance, 1908–1925* (New York, 1926).
[James H. Oliphant & Co.] *The Problem of Depreciated Investment Securities* (New York, 1920).
Osborne, Algernon A. *Speculation on the New York Stock Exchange: September 1904—March 1907* (New York, 1913).
Parker, John L. *Unmasking Wall Street* (Boston, 1933).
Peach, W. Nelson. *The Security Affiliates of National Banks* (Baltimore, 1941).
Pecora, Ferdinand. *Wall Street Under Oath: The Story of Our Modern Money Changers* (New York, 1939).
Pearson, Henry G. *Son of New England: James Jackson Storrow, 1864–1926* (Boston, 1932).
Perlo, Victor. *The Empire of High Finance* (New York, 1957).
Pierce, Bessie Louise. *A History of Chicago* (3 vols., New York, 1937–1957).
Plummer, Arthur N. *The Great American Swindle Incorporated* (New York, 1932).
Poor, Henry V. *Manual of the Railroads* (New York, 1887)
Pringle, Henry F. *The Life and Times of William Howard Taft* (2 vols., New York, 1939).
Redlich, Fritz. *The Molding of American Banking: Men and Ideas* (2 vols., New York, 1947, 1951).
Redmond, George F. *Financial Giants of America* (2 vols., Boston, 1922).
Reis, Bernard J. *False Security: The Betrayal of the American Investor* (New York, 1937).
Ripley, William Z. *Railroads: Finance & Organization* (New York, 1915).
Robbins, Sidney M. and Nestor E. Terleckyj. *Money Metropolis: A Locational Study of Financial Activities in the New York Region* (Cambridge, Mass., 1960).
Robinson, Leland R. *Investment Trust Organizations and Management* (rev. ed., New York, 1929).
Robinson, Roland I. *Postwar Market for State and Local Government Securities* (Princeton, 1960).
Rochester, Anna. *Rulers of America: A Study of Finance Capital* (New York, 1936).
Satterlee, Herbert L. *J. Pierpont Morgan: An Intimate Portrait* (New York, 1939).

Schlesinger, Arthur M., Jr. *The Coming of the New Deal* (Boston, 1959).
Scoville, John and Noel Sargent, comps. *Fact and Fancy in the T.N.E.C. Monographs* (New York, 1942).
Shultz, William J. and M. R. Caine. *Financial Development of the United States* (New York, 1937).
Simmons, Edward H. H. *"Financing American Industry" and other Addresses* (n.p., 1930).
———— *Modern Capitalism and Other Addresses* (n.p., 1927).
Sites, Henry W. *Investment Bankers and Brokers in the United States and Canada* (New York, 1916).
Smith, Arthur D. Howden. *Men Who Run America* (New York, 1935).
Sobel, Robert. *The Big Board: A History of the New York Stock Market* (New York, 1965).
Soule, George. *Prosperity Decade, From War to Depression: 1917–1929* (New York, 1947).
Sparling, Earl. *Mystery Men of Wall Street: The Powers Behind the Market* (New York, 1930).
Staley, Eugene. *War and the Private Investor: A Study in the Relations of International Politics and International Private Placement* (Garden City, 1935).
Stanley, Harold. *Competitive Bidding for New Issues of Corporate Securities* (New York, 1939).
Stedman, Clarence E., ed. *The New York Stock Exchange* (New York, 1905).
Stehman, James W. *The Financial History of the American Telephone and Telegraph Company* (Bosotn, 1925).
Stein, Emanuel. *Government and the Investor* (New York, 1941).
Steiner, William H. *Investment Trusts: American Experience* (New York, 1929).
Stover, John F. *American Railroads* (Chicago, 1961).
Studenski, Paul and Herman E. Krooss. *Financial History of the United States* (2d ed., New York, 1963).
Swaine, Robert Taylor. *The Cravath Firm and Its Predecessors, 1819–1948* (3 vols., New York, 1946–1948).
Taylor, George R. *The Transportation Revolution, 1815–1860* (New York, 1951).
Trescott, Paul B. *Financing American Enterprise: The Story of Commercial Banking* (New York, 1963).
Twentieth Century Fund. *Electric Power and Government Policy: A Survey of the Relations Between the Government and the Electric Power Industry* (New York, 1948).
University of Illinois, Bureau of Economic and Business Research, Bulletin No. 39. *Investment Banking in Chicago* (Urbana, 1931).
Washburn, Charles G. *The Life of John W. Weeks* (Boston, 1928).
Wesson, R. Gordon. *The Hall Carbine Affair: A Study in Contemporary Folklore* (New York, 1948).
Waterman, Merwin H. *Investment Banking Functions: Their Evolution and Adaptation to Business Finance* (Ann Arbor, 1958).
———— *Public Utility Financing, 1930–1935* (Ann Arbor, 1936).

Weeks, Edward. *Men, Money, and Responsibility: A History of Lee, Higginson Corporation, 1848–1962* (Boston, 1962).
Weissman, Rudolph L. *The New Wall Street* (New York, 1939).
Weston, John F. *The Economics of Competitive Bidding in the Sale of Securities* (Chicago, 1943).
Weston, John F., ed. *Readings in Finance from Fortune* (New York, 1958).
Wiebe, Robert H. *Businessmen and Reform: A Study of the Progressive Movement* (Cambridge, Mass., 1962).
Williamson, Harold F. *Winchester, The Gun that Won the West* (Washington, 1952).
Williamson, Harold F. and Orange A. Smalley. *Northwestern Mutual Life: A Century of Trusteeship* (Evanston, 1957).
Willis, H. Parker. *The Federal Reserve System: Legislation, Organization and Operation* (New York, 1923).
Willis H. Parker and Jules I. Bogen. *Investment Banking* (rev. ed., New York, 1936).
Winkler, John K. *Morgan the Magnificent: The Life of J. Pierpont Morgan (1837–1913)* (New York, 1930).
Winkler, Max. *Foreign Bonds — An Autopsy: A Study of Defaults and Repudiations of Government Obligations* (Philadelphia, 1933).
Writers' Program, Massachusetts. *Boston Looks Seaward, The Story of the Port, 1630–1940* (Boston, 1941).
Willoughby, Woodbury. *The Capital Issues Committee and the War Finance Corporation* (Baltimore, 1934).
[Yale Daily News] *Wall Street: 20th Century* (New Haven, 1960).
Young, Ralph A. *Handbook on American Underwriting of Foreign Securities* (Washington, 1930).

Periodical and Other Articles

Abramowitz, Moses. "Savings and Investment: Profits *vs.* Prosperity?" *American Economic Review,* Suppl., XXXII (June 1942), 53.
Abrams, Ernest R. "Is Competitive Bidding for Utility Issues Ahead?" *The Commercial & Financial Chronicle,* CXLVIII (April 1, 1939), 1862–66.
——— "Fallacy of Competitive Bidding for Public Utility Securities, Part II" *Public Utilities Fortnightly,* XIX (April 15, 1937), 476–85.
Abrams, Richard M. "Brandeis and the New Haven-Boston & Maine Merger Battle Revisited," *Business History Review,* XXXVI (Winter 1962), 408–09.
Adler, Cyrus. "Jacob Henry Schiff," *Dictionary of American Biography* (22 vols., New York, 1928–1958), XVI, 430–32.
Ames, Amyas. "An Approach to the Securities Business," *Career Guide,* I (Winter 1961), 2.
"The Amsterdam Stock Exchange," *The Ticker,* I (February 1908), 4.
Anderson, Gordon Blythe. "The Effect of the War on New Security Issues in the United States," America's Changing Investment Market, *The Annals,* LXVIII (November 1916), 120–30.

"Antitrust Case Silver Lining," *Business Week* (November 8, 1947), 86.
Ashmead, Graham. "Syndicate Management and Operation: The Machinery for Distribution and Marketing of Industrial Securities," *Trust Companies,* XXXIII (September 1921), 232.
Atwood, Albert W. "John Pierpont Morgan," *Dictionary of American Biography,* (22 vols., New York, 1928–1958), XIII, 175–80.
Bacon, Nathaniel. "American International Indebtedness," *The Yale Review,* IX (November 1900), 265–85.
Balgue, George L. "The Big Panics Since 1837," *The Magazine of Wall Street* XIV (September 1914), 480–81.
"The Bank Investigation — What it Might Reveal," *The Bankers' Magazine,* LXXXIV (June 1912), 751–52.
"The Bankers At Work," *The Nation,* CXXXVII (October 4, 1933), 369.
"Bankers — Wall Street Style," *Financial World* (June 28, 1967), 8–10.
"Banking: House of Morgan Gives Up a Son, Five Partners and $7,500,000 to Return to Underwriting," *Newsweek,* VI (September 14, 1935), 31–33.
"Banking Versus Salesmanship: Picture of Affiliate Company Unfolded Before Inquiring Senators Led to Mitchell Resignation," *Newsweek,* I (March 4, 1933), 23–24.
"The Barren Money Trust Inquiry," *American Banker,* LXXVII (June 22, 1912), 2022.
Barron, Mary L. "State Regulation of the Securities of Railroads and Public Service Companies," *The Annals,* LXXVI (March 1918), 167–90.
Bates, George E. "Some Effects of the Securities Act Upon Investment Banking Practices," *Law and Contemporary Problems,* IV (January 1937), 72.
Berle, Adolf A., Jr. "Action to Avoid Another 1929," *American Bankers Association Journal,* XXVI (July 1933), 16–18.
"Big Bankers' Gambling Mania," *The Literary Digest,* CXV (March 11, 1933), 11–12.
"The Bill for the Control of the Stock Exchanges," *The Magazine of Wall Street,* XIII (March 1914), 351–54.
Blauss, John L. "Commercial Banking and the Financing of Industry," *American Banker,* LXVI (March 2, 1901), 441.
"Blue Sky Laws," *American Banker,* LXXVIII (April 12, 1913), 1158–59.
"The 'Blue-Sky' Laws," *The Bankers' Magazine,* LXXXIV (May 1912), 635–37.
"Blue Sky Laws in New York," *American Banker,* LXXVIII (March 29, 1913), 1000.
Bogen, Jules I. "Changed Conditions in the Marketing of New Issues," *Journal of the American Statistical Association,* XXXIII (March 1938), 31–41.
———. "A New Era of Investment Banking," *Investment Banking,* VIII (March 23, 1938), 124.
"That Bond Dealers' Organization" *American Banker,* LXXVI (September 30, 1911), 3284.

"Bonds Becoming Popular in the West," *American Banker,* LXXIV (August 14, 1910), 2917.
"Bond Blue Eagle," *Business Week* (September 8, 1934), 38.
Bonner, Francis A. "The Fair Practice Amendment," *Investment Banking,* IV (May 3, 1934), 209.
Borne, John E. "The Proper Conservative Attitude of Trust Companies Toward Corporate Enterprises," *The Commercial & Financial Chronicle: Bankers' and Trust Supplement,* LXXI (October 13, 1900), 94–95.
Bowden, Witt. Biographical sketches of Anthony J., Francis M., and Joseph W. Drexel in *Dictionary of American Biography* (22 vols., New York, 1928–1958), V, 455–57.
Breed, William C. "Public Regulation in Origination and Distribution of Securities," *Investment Banking,* III (February 21, 1933), 183–96.
"Broadening the Bond Market," *The Bankers' Magazine,* LXXXIX (December 1914), 609.
Brown, Raymond F. "What the New Securities Act Means," *The Magazine of Wall Street,* LII (April 29, 1933), 12–13.
"Bucket Shops," *The Ticker,* II (May 1908), 12–23.
Bullock, Charles J. "The Concentration of Banking Interests in the United States," *The Atlantic Monthly,* XCII (August 1903), 182–92.
"Capital Issues Committee Terminates Its Work," *Federal Reserve Bulletin,* V (January 1, 1919), 18–19.
Carey, George. "The Investment Banker as an Educator," *Gunton's Magazine,* XXIII (December 1902), 511.
"The Case for Investment Banking," *Investment Banking,* X (March 1940), 4.
"Challenges to SEC." *Business Week* (January 25, 1941), 50.
Chamberlain, Lawrence. "Are Investment Bankers Public Servants?" *The Outlook,* CVI (March 14, 1914), 604–05.
——— "A Reply to Mr. Brandeis," *Harper's Weekly,* LVIII (April 4, 1914), 22.
Chase, Stuart. "Shadow Over Wall Street," *Harper's Magazine,* CLXXX (March 1940), 367–74.
Cherrington, Homer V. "National Association of Securities Dealers," *Harvard Business Review,* XXVII (November 1949), 741–59.
[Christie, Robert E., Jr.] "Fair Practice Rules for Investment Banking Code," *Investment Banking,* IV (February 3, 1934), 172–74.
Clay, Paul. "American Business and The Great War," *The Magazine of Wall Street,* XVI (May 1, 1915), 6–9.
Clews, Henry. "Current Concentration of Industrial Capital," *Lippincott's Monthly Magazine,* XLVI (September 1890), 382.
——— "The Overcapitalization of Railroads," *The Bankers' Magazine,* LXXV (July 1907), 123.
——— "Wall Street's Wild Speculation: 1900–1904," *The Cosmopolitan,* XXXVII (August 1904), 410.
Coard, Robert D. "Services Rendered to Investors by a Properly Conducted Bond Department," *The Bankers' Magazine,* LXXXIV (January 1912), 44–45.

Cochran, Thomas C. "The Entrepreneur in American Capital Formation" in National Bureau Committee for Economic Research, *Capital Formation and Economic Growth* (Princeton, 1955).
Cohan, Avery B. "The Price of Underwriting Services on Corporate Debt, 1935–1952," *The Journal of Finance,* XV (September 1960), 407–08.
"The Coming Meeting of the Investment Bankers," *The Commercial & Financial Chronicle,* XCV (August 3, 1912), 268–69.
"Competitive Arguing," *Time,* XXXVII (February 17, 1941), 80–82.
"Competitive Bidding," *Investment Banking,* IX (September 1939), 24–29.
Conant, Charles A. "The Existing Mechanism of the New York Money Market," *The Bankers' Magazine,* LXXV (July 1907), 20.
——— "Selling American Securities Abroad," *North American Review,* CLXXXIII (September 21, 1906), 508.
Conant, Luther, Jr. "Industrial Consolidations in the United States," *Quarterly Publications of the American Statistical Association,* n.s., VII (March 1901), 1–20.
Connors, William T. "The Day of the Small Investor," *The Magazine of Wall Street,* X (September 1912), 284.
——— "Striking Features of the New Liberty Loan," *The Magazine of Wall Street,* XX (September 29, 1917), 857.
Conway, Thomas, Jr. "Financing American War Orders," America's Changing Investment Market, *The Annals,* LXVIII (November 1916), 131–50.
Corey, E. Raymond. "Corporate Financing by Direct Placement," *Harvard Business Review,* XXVIII (November 1950), 67–76.
Corey, Lewis. "How Is Ownership Distributed?", *The New Republic,* XLVI (May 5, 1926), 323–24.
Crump, Arthur. "The Baring Financial Crisis," *The Economic Journal,* I (June 1891), 392.
Dakin, Allin W. "Foreign Securities in the American Money Market, 1914–1930," *Harvard Business Review,* X (January 1932), 233–35.
Davis, Arthur G. "A Multiplicity of Laws," *Investment Banking,* 1 (September 1931), 30–31, 41.
Davis, Lance E. "Capital Immobilities and Finance Capitalism: A Study of Economic Evolution in the United States, 1820–1920," *Explorations in Entrepreneurial History,* 2d Ser., I (Fall 1963), 88–105.
"Deadline — June 16," *Business Week* (June 16, 1934), 18.
Dean, Arthur H. "Economic and Legal Aspects of the Federal Securities Act of 1933," *Proceedings of the Sixteenth Annual Convention of the National Association of Securities Commissioners* (Milwaukee, 1933), 161.
——— "The Federal Securities Act: I," *Fortune,* VIII (August 1933), 104, 106.
——— "Twenty-Five Years of Federal Securities Regulation by the Securities and Exchange Commission," *Columbia Law Review,* LIX (May 1959), 706.

DeVilliers, Victor. "The Growing Army of 'Small Investors'," *The Magazine of Wall Street,* XXVII (November 13, 1920), 30.
Dewing, Arthur S. "Investment Trusts," *Harvard Business Review,* X (October 1931), 24–25.
Dill, James B. "Industrials as Investments," *American Banker,* XLV (June 6, 1900), 995–96.
Dodge, Washington, "What Became of the Stock Market?" *Fortune,* XXVI (December 1942), 156.
Donworth, Charles T. "A Review of the Securities Act of 1933," *Washington Law Review,* VIII (October 1933), 61–69.
Douglas, William O. and George E. Bates. "The Federal Securities Act of 1933," *Yale Law Journal,* XLIII (December 1933), 173.
Dresser, Gardiner S. "The Liberty Loan and the Partial Payment Plan," *The Magazine of Wall Street,* XX (July 7, 1917), 461.
Duncan, A. E. "My Experiences With the Securities Act," *The Magazine of Wall Street,* LVI (August 17, 1935), 435.
Eddy, George A. "The Present Status of New Security Issues," *The Review of Economic Statistics,* XXI (August 1939), 116–21.
"The Elusive Bogey — The Money Trust," *Current Literature,* LII (March 1912), 298.
Emerson, Sumner B. "The Wholesaling of Corporate Securities" in Philipp H. Lohman and Franc M. Ricciardi, eds., *Wall Street Explains its Operations* . . . (New York, 1951).
Escher, Franklin. "The Bond Broker's Hard Lot," *The Bankers' Magazine,* LXXIX (December 1909), 925–26.
——— "Finance: The Wall Street Investigation," *Harper's Weekly,* LII (July 3, 1909), 28.
——— "The Great Open Market for Bonds," *The Bankers' Magazine,* LXXXIII (July 1911), 46.
——— "Investments," *The Bankers' Magazine,* LXXVIII (June 1909), 1025.
——— "New England: The Home of Investment Capital," *Harper's Weekly,* LIV (May 28, 1910), 34.
"Federal Control of Railroad Securities," *American Banker,* LXXVI (December 16, 1911), 4338–39.
Fierlong, William B. "Thirty Years Ago," *The New York Times Magazine,* August 9, 1964.
"The Financial Centre of the World," *The Bankers' Magazine,* LXIV (February 1902), 172–75.
Fisk, Harvey E. "Fisk & Hatch, Bankers and Dealers in Government Securities, 1862–1885," *Journal of Economic and Business History,* II (August 1930), 706–10.
Flexner, Bernard. "The Fight on the Securities Act," *The Atlantic Monthly,* CLIII (February 1934), 232–50.
Flynn, John T. "The Investment Bankers Again," *The New Republic,* CII (April 1, 1940), 441.
——— "J. P. Morgan & Co.: A House Built on Favors," *The New Republic,* LXXV (June 28, 1933), 174–76.

——— "The Marines Land on Wall Street," *Harper's Magazine,* CLXIX (July 1934), 148–50.
——— "Wall Street Medicine," *Collier's,* XCII (November 11, 1933), 12–13, 54–55.
Forbes, Allen B. "Supervision of Security Issues by the United States," *The Nation,* CVI (March 28, 1918), 372.
"$14,357,000,000.00," *The Commonweal,* XLVII (November 14, 1947), 108.
Frankfurter, Felix. "The Federal Securities Act: II," *Fortune,* VIII (August 1933), 108, 111.
Franklin, Lewis B. "The Formation of Syndicates," *The Magazine of Wall Street,* XV (March 20, 1915), 452–53.
——— "Syndicates," *The Bankers' Magazine,* LXXXVII (December 1913), 664–69.
"French Investors and American Securities," *American Banker,* LXX (May 13, 1905), 871.
Friend, Irwin and Edward S. Herman, "The S.E.C. Through a Glass Darkly," *The Journal of Business,* XXXVII (October 1964), 382–405.
[Frothingham, Francis E.] "The Maloney Bill," *Investment Banking,* VIII (February 15, 1938), 79–82.
——— "Public Bidding *vs.* Private Sales, *Investment Banking,* IX (June 1939), 19–22.
Garraty, John A. "Lion in the Street," *American Heritage,* VIII (June 1957), 32–35, 97–101.
Gay, Edwin F. "The Great Depression," *Foreign Affairs,* X (July 1932), 533–34.
Gerstenberg, Charles W. "The Underwriting of Securities by Syndicates," *Trust Companies,* X (June 1910), 328.
Ginzburg, Benjamin. "Wall Street Under the New Deal," *The North American Review,* CCXLV (Spring 1938), 70.
Goldschmidt [Goldsmith] Raymond W. "Registration Under the Securities Act of 1933," *Law and Contemporary Problems,* IV (January 1937), 19–31.
"A Good Example," *Harper's Weekly,* LVIII (January 17, 1914), 3.
Gordon, Frank M. "Benefits of Security Regulation," *Investment Banking,* IV (October 7, 1933), 4–8.
Gourrich, Paul P. "Investment Banking Methods Prior to and Since the Securities Act of 1933," *Law and Contemporary Problems,* IV (January 1937), 44–71.
"Government Regulation of Bond and Stock Issue," *Moody's Magazine,* XI (January 1911), 53–54.
Gras, N. S. B. "George Fisher Baker," *Dictionary of American Biography* (22 vols., New York. 1928–1958) XXI, 44–45.
Greenwood, Frederick. "What Modern Underwriting Accomplished," *The Magazine of Wall Street,* XII (September 1913), 353–56.
Griswold, B. Howell, Jr. "The Future of the Investment Bankers Code," *Investment Banking,* V (June 4, 1935), 211.
Grotkopp, Wilhelm. "Ivar Kreuger," *Encyclopedia of the Social Sciences* (15 vols., New York, 1944), VIII, 600–01.

"Growth and Expansion of Trust Companies," *The Commercial & Financial Chronicle,* LXVII (August 6, 1898), 251–52.

Hager, Albert B., Jr. "Competitive Bidding for Corporate Debt Securities" in [Yale Daily News] *Wall Street: 20th Century* (New Haven, 1960), 100–03.

Hammond, Bray. "Long and Short Term Credit in Early American Banking," *Quarterly Journal of Economics,* XLIX (November 1934), 79–103.

Hanes, John W. "The Lifeblood of Our Industrial Machine: The Capital Market and the Investment Banker," *Vital Speeches of the Day,* IV (May 1, 1938), 421–24.

Hanes, John W. and Francis E. Frothingham. "Two Viewpoints on Investment Banking," *Business Week* (March 26, 1938), 56.

Hanson, Donald R. "Choosing an Investment Banker," *The Forum,* LXXXIII (May 1930), supp. xxxviii, xl, xlii.

Harlow, Alvin F. "Thomas W. Lawson," *Dictionary of American Biography* (22 vols., New York, 1928–1958), XI, 59–60.

Hawkins, David F. "The Development of Modern Financial Reporting Practices Among American Manufacturing Corporations," *Business History Review,* XXXVII (Autumn 1963), 144.

Hayes, Henry R. "Public Aspects of the Securities Business," *Investment Banking,* I (October 1931), 27–29, 41–42.

Healy, Robert E. "Advantages of Self-Regulation," *Investment Banking,* IX (April 1939), 21–22.

"Heaving Bricks at Wall Street Good Politics — Poor Business," *Business Week* (May 4, 1932), 5–6.

Herrick, Myron T. "The Government and the Bankers," *American Banker,* LXXV (June 25, 1910), 7712.

Hidy, Muriel E. "The Capital Markets, 1789–1865" in Harold F. Williamson, ed. *The Growth of the American Economy* (2d ed., New York, 1951), 256–78.

Hidy, Ralph W. "The Organization and Functions of Anglo-American Merchant Bankers, 1815–1860," *The Journal of Economic History,* I (December 1941), 53–66.

Higginson, H. L. "The Real 'Money Trust' Consists of the Trust of One's Fellow-Men," *The Bankers' Magazine,* LXXXVI (April 1913), 450.

"House of Morgan: Its Tales and Favored Friends Provide a National Crossfire of Agitation, and Some Sniping," *Newsweek,* I (June 3, 1933), 3–5.

Howard, Samuel F., Jr. "Samuel Untermyer," *Dictionary of American Biography* (22 vols., New York, 1928–1958) XXII, 674–76.

Howell, Paul L. "Competition in the Capital Markets," *Harvard Business Review,* XXXI (May–June 1953), 89.

Huebner, S. S. "The American Security Market During the War," America's Changing Investment Market, *The Annals,* LXVIII (November 1916), 93–107.

Hume, John F. "The Heart of Speculation," *The Forum,* II (October 1886), 130–41.

Hutchison, Keith. "Arm's-Length Bargaining," *The Nation,* CL (March 30, 1940), 421–22.
——— "Bankers Hate Competition," *The Nation,* CLII (April 19, 1941), 472–73.
"IBA Code," *Business Week* (February 10, 1934), 22–23.
"In the New Wall Street," *Fortune,* XII (October 1935), 78–83, 120.
"Investigating the Money Trust," *American Banker,* LXXVII (May 4, 1912), 1382–83.
"Investigating the Money Trust," *The Bankers' Magazine,* LXXXIV (March 1912), 285–86.
"The Investment Banker: 1939," *Fortune,* XX (September 1939), 78–80, 109–116.
"Investment Bankers and Bankers' Association," *The Literary Digest,* XLIV (May 25, 1912), 1126.
"Investment Bankers and the Stock Exchange," *The Literary Digest,* XLVI (April 26, 1913), 982.
"The Investment Bankers' Association: What It Proposes To Do," *The Magazine of Wall Street,* XI (January 1913), 184.
"Investment Bankers' Famine," *Business Week* (October 30, 1937), 20, 22.
"Investment Bankers Organize," *American Banker,* LXXVII (August 10, 1912), 2694.
"Investment Bankers Organize," *The Bankers' Magazine,* LXXXV (September 1912), 281–91.
"Investment Bankers Organize," *Business Week* (October 12, 1935), 23–24.
"Investment Bankers Under Fire," *The Bankers' Magazine,* CXXIX (September 1934), 320–21.
"Investment Business of Trust Companies," *The Bankers' Magazine,* LXXXIII (August 1911), 158–59.
"The Investment Security Business," *The Ticker,* III (January 1909), 119.
"Is It Safe to Buy Foreign Securities?" *The Magazine of Wall Street,* XXXIII (April 26, 1924), 1112–13.
"Is Speculation Declining?" *The Bankers' Magazine,* XLVII (December 1892), 415.
"Issues of Bonds in Place of Stocks," *American Banker,* LXVI (June 22, 1901), 2062.
"Ivar Kreuger," *Fortune,* VIII (May 1933), 51–57, 78–84; (June 1933), 59–63, 78–95; (July 1933), 68–76.
Johnson, Stewart. "Statistics on Federal Lending and Loan Insurance Programs in the United States, 1929–1958" in Stewart Johnson *et al., Federal Credit Programs* (Englewood Cliffs, 1963).
Kemmerer, Donald L. "The Marketing of Securities, 1930–1952," *The Journal of Economic History,* XII (Fall 1952), 455–59.
Kennedy, Joseph P. "Big Business, What Now?" *The Saturday Evening Post,* CCIX (January 16, 1937), 10–11.
Keys, C. M. "Ten Years Growth of the Investment Market," *The World's Work,* XXI (January 1911), 13843–45.

"Kidder, Peabody & Co.," *The Bankers' Magazine,* LXXVI (February 1908), 263–70.
Kilborne, Russell D. "American Investment Trusts," *Harvard Business Review,* III (January 1925), 160–61.
Knappen, Theodore M. "A New Deal in Banking," *The Magazine of Wall Street* LI (March 18, 1933), 566.
───── "SEC Surprises Both Friend and Foe," *The Magazine of Wall Street,* LVI (September 14, 1935), 538–39, 564–65.
───── "The Silent Revolution in American Finance," *The Magazine of Wall Street,* XXXV (December 20, 1924), 262.
Kuhn, C. John. "The Securities Act and its Effect Upon the Institutional Investor," *Law and Contemporary Problems,* IV (January 1937), 83.
Larson, Henrietta M. "S. & M. Allen — Lottery, Exchange, and Stock Brokerage," *Journal of Economic and Business History,* III (May 1931), 424–45.
"The Late Pujo Committee," *The Outlook,* CIII (March 15, 1913), 568–69.
Lawson, W. R. "The Financial Outlook in 1892," *The Bankers', Insurance Managers' and Agents' Magazine,* LIII (January 1892), 45–47.
"Lee Higginson & Co., Boston," *The Bankers' Magazine,* LXXIV (May 1907), 813–14.
"Legal Developments Significant in Business: The Relationship of Syndicate Managers and Members," *Harvard Business Review,* VIII (October 1929), 92.
"Let the Banking Inquiry Go On," *The Nation,* CXXXVI (June 14, 1933), 656–57.
Lewis, M. Frederick. "Europe's Golden Flood." *The Magazine of Wall Street,* XVII (November 27, 1915), 219–21, 277–78.
Lindley, Ernest K. "Wall Street Under the New Deal," *The Literary Digest,* CXVI (July 22, 1933), 3–4, 31.
Lintner, John. "The Financing of Corporations" in Edward S. Mason, ed., *The Corporation in Modern Society* (New York, 1966).
Logan, James A. "The Vice of Fictitious Corporate Capitalizations," *The American Journal of Politics,* II (February 1893), 203–10.
"Low Spots in High Finance," *The Saturday Evening Post,* CCVI (January 13, 1934), 22.
Lyons, Hastings. "The Work of an Investment Banking House," *The Annals,* LXXXVIII (March 1920), 34–42.
"The Maloney Association," *Investment Banking,* IX (September 1939), 1–3.
Maloney, Francis T. "Cooperative Regulation," *Investment Banking,* IX (September 1939), 18–23.
March, Charles H. "Uncle Sam Safeguards the Investor," *The Magazine of Wall Street,* LII (September 16, 1933), 514–15.
McCabe, George. "Wall Street Goes Amateur," *The Commonweal,* XI (December 11, 1929), 165–67.
McClintock, Franklin T. "Competitive Bidding," *Investment Banking,* IX (September 1939), 24–29.

——— "Competitive Bidding in the Origination of Securities" in Investment Bankers Association, *Fundamentals of Investment Banking* (Englewood Cliffs, 1960), 502–16.
McCoy, Joseph S. "The U.S. Legion of Capitalists," *American Bankers Association Journal,* XIX (February 1927), 560, 626–28.
McNaughton, Walter. "Organizing the Railroad Investor," *The Magazine of Wall Street,* XX (June 9, 1917), 307–09.
Mead, Edward S. "How the Investment Banker Investigates Public Utilities," *Lippincott's Monthly Magazine,* XC (October 1912), 508–12.
Means, D. M. "A New Profession," *The Nation,* LXV (August 26, 1897), 162–63.
Means, Gardiner C. "The Diffusion of Stock Ownership in the United States," *The Quarterly Journal of Economics,* XLIV (August 1930), 591.
Meech, Stuart P. "The Investment Securities Business and the Future," *The Journal of Business,* V (July 1932), 241–56.
"Merchants of Credit and the Pirates of Promotion," *The World's Work,* XXXVI (September 1918), 538–41
Meredith, L. Douglas. "Financial Merchandising and Its Functions," *The Bankers' Magazine,* CXXVII (December 1933), 613–30.
Merriman, Norman. "The Big Loan: Its Probable Effect on Security Markets," *The Magazine of Wall Street,* XVI (October 2, 1915), 762–64.
Miller, S. L. "Effects on Investment Banking Practice of Federal Regulation of Securities," *Investment Banking* VII (September 22, 1937), 355.
Mitchell, Charles E. "Sound Inflation," *The Magazine of Wall Street,* XX (June 9, 1917), 295–96.
"Modern Bond Houses and Their Clients," *The Ticker,* I (March 1908), 2–4.
"The Money Trust," *American Banker,* LXXVII (February 3, 1912), 326–27.
"The 'Money Trust,'" *The Nation,* XLV (December 19, 1912), 599.
"The Money-Trust Evidence," *The Literary Digest,* XLVI (January 4, 1913), 1–3.
"The 'Money Trust' Inquiry," *American Banker,* LXXVII (May 18, 1912), 1559.
"The 'Money Trust' Inquiry," *The Nation,* XCIV (June 6, 1912), 575.
"The 'Money Trust' Investigation," *The Outlook,* CIII (January 4, 1913), 2.
"The 'Money Trust' Recommendations," *The Journal of Political Economy,* XXI (April 1913), 355–57.
Moody, Bertram O. "On the Other Hand ———," *American Bankers Association Journal,* XXVI (July 1933), 18, 48.
Moody, John and George K. Turner. "Masters of Capital in America — Wall Street — The City Bank: The Federation of Great Merchants," *McClure's Magazine,* XXXVII (May 1911), 73–87.
——— "Wall Street: How Morgan Built the Money Power," *McClure's Magazine,* XXXVIII (June 1911), 186–89, 201–02.

Moore, Terris. "Security Affiliates Versus Private Investment Banker — A Study in Security Originations," *Harvard Business Review,* XII (July 1934), 478–84.
"More Work than Profits," *Business Week* (December 29, 1951), 86–87.
"Morgan & Co.," *Business Week* (June 7, 1933), 5–6.
"J. P. Morgan Before the Pujo Committee," *Current Opinion,* LIV (February 1913), 90–92.
"Morgan: Private Bankers Included in Senate Inquiry," *Newsweek,* I (April 8, 1933), 21–22.
"Mr. Kuhn and Mr. Loeb," *Fortune,* I (March 1930), 89, 116, 118.
"Mr. Morgan's Denial of a Money Trust," *The Literary Digest,* XLV (December 28, 1912), 1213–14.
"Mr. Morgan's Show," *The Commonweal,* XVIII (June 9, 1933), 141–42.
"Mr. Young and His C&O" in John F. Weston, ed., *Readings in Finance From Fortune* (New York, 1958), 88–90.
"The N.A.S.D.," *Investment Banking,* IX (June 1939), 1.
" 'NRA' for Security Dealers," *Business Week* (September 21, 1935), 18.
Nash, Gerald D. "Government and Business: A Case Study of State Regulation of Corporate Securities, 1850–1933," *Business History Review,* XXXVIII (Summer 1964), 144–62.
"National Bond Dealers' Association," *American Banker,* LXXVI (June 17, 1911), 1941, (July 22, 1911), 2484.
Navin, Thomas R. "Investment Banking Since 1900: An Unexplored Field in American Financial History," *Bulletin of the Business Historical Society,* XXVII (March 1953), 60–65.
Navin, Thomas R. and Marian V. Sears. "The Rise of a Market for Industrial Securities, 1887–1902," *Business History Review,* XXIX (June 1955), 105–38.
——— "A Study in Merger: Formation of the International Mercantile Marine Company," *Business History Review,* XXVIII (December 1954), 291–328.
Nelson, Samuel A. "Wall Street As It Is," *The World's Work,* IX (February 1905), 5823.
"The New Bucket Shop Law in New York State," *The Ticker,* II (August 1908), 177–78.
"The New Currency Law," *The Bankers' Magazine,* LXXVI (June 1908), 1817–19.
"New Money for Industry: The Investment Banker's Job for Industry," *Business Week* (November 30, 1940), 41–52.
"The 'New Idea' in Bond Advertising," *The Bankers' Magazine,* LXXV (August 1907), 251–52.
"Next, Morgan & Co.," *Business Week* (April 12, 1933), 12–14.
"No Banking is Private," *Business Week* (June 7, 1933), 32.
North, Douglass C. "Life Insurance and Investment Banking at the Time of the Armstrong Investigation, 1905–1906," *The Journal of Economic History,* XIV (Summer 1954), 212–28.

Noyes, Alexander D. "The Course of a Great Stock-Exchange Speculation," reprint from *Scribner's Magazine* (July 1928), n.p.
——— "Finance," *The Forum,* XXXV (January 1904), 368.
——— "Financial Signs of the Times," *The Nation,* LXXIV (May 1, 1902), 340.
——— "The Future of High Finance," *The Atlantic Monthly,* CV (February 1910), 229–39.
——— "Wall Street," *The Independent,* LVIII (January 26, 1905), 185.
——— "Why There Has Been No Financial Crisis," *Yale Review,* XIII (November 1904).
Noyes, Peter H. "Wall Street at the Wailing Wall," *The Nation,* CXXXVII (October 25, 1933), 485–86.
——— "Wall Street Faces the New Securities Act," *The Nation,* CXXXVII (July 5, 1933), 20.
"Offer Unlisted Code," *Business Week* (April 24, 1937), 28.
"The Old and the New Year," *American Banker,* LXV (January 3, 1900), 9.
Oppenheimer, Francis J. "James Speyer on Money and Railroad Problems," *The Magazine of Wall Street,* XXV (February 7, 1920), 435–38.
Osterweis, Steven L. "'Security Affiliates and Security Operations of Commercial Banks," *Harvard Business Review,* XI (October 1932), 126–29.
"Over the Counter: The IBA Votes to Cooperate for Regulation Under SEC," *Newsweek,* XII (November 7, 1938), 44.
Palgrave, R. H. Inglis. "An English View of Investments in the United States," *The Forum,* XV (April 1893), 198.
"Papers Relating to the Temporary National Economic Committee," *American Economic Review,* suppl., XXXII (June 1942), 1–132.
"Paul M. Warburg Says: 'Immigrants Are Potential Capitalists'," *The Magazine of Wall Street,* XXVI (June 26, 1920), 226.
Paxson, Frederic L. "Levi Parsons Morton," *Dictionary of American Biography* (22 vols., New York, 1928–1958), XIII, 258–59.
"Peculiar State of the Bond Market," *American Banker,* LXXII (June 15, 1907), 1997.
Perine, Edward T. "Trust Company Resources and Revenues: A Five-Year Summary," *The Commercial & Financial Chronicle, Bankers' Convention Section,* LXXXIX (September 25, 1909), 178.
"Permissible Stabilization," *Investment Banking,* IX (April 1939), 27–30.
Pomroy, Henry K. "An Ex-president of the Stock Exchange Replies to Miss Tarbell," *The American Magazine,* LXXV (June 1913), 29–32.
Powers, Barnard. "Wall Street's Patriotism," *The Magazine of Wall Street* XX (June 23, 1917), 363.
——— "Who Are the Real Owners of Wall Street?" *The Magazine of Wall Street,* XXXIII (April 26, 1924), 1106.
Pratt, Sereno S. "New York's Great Financial Institutions and Their

Presidents," *The Independent,* LVII (December 22, 1904), 1435–36.
"President Connely Answers Chase," *Investment Banking,* X (May 1940), 22–23.
Preston, H. H. and Allan R. Finlay. "Era Favors Investment Affiliates," *American Bankers Association Journal,* XXII (June 1930), 1153–54.
———— "Investment Affiliates Thrive," *American Bankers Association Journal,* XXII (May 1930), 1027–28.
Price, William H. "Life Insurance Reform in New York," *American Economic Association Quarterly,* X (December 1909), 22–23.
Prime, John H. "Private Negotiation in the Origination of Securities" in Investment Bankers Association of America, *Fundamentals of Investment Banking* (Englewood Cliffs, 1960), 477–92.
"Probable Stock Exchange Legislation," *The Magazine of Wall Street,* XIII (November 1913), 24–27.
"Prospects of the Investment Bankers' Association," *The Magazine of Wall Street,* X (September 1912), 250–51.
"The Public and the Banks," *The Bankers' Magazine,* LXXXVI (February 1913), 135–36.
"The Public Bond Market," *American Banker,* LXX (August 26, 1905), 1921.
"The Public Bond Market," *American Banker,* LXXIII (June 20, 1908), 2184.
"Public Utility Bonds," *American Banker,* LXXI (October 1906), 3291.
"The Pujo Committee Inquiry," *American Banker* LXXVII (December 21, 1912), 4360–61.
"The Pujo Report," *The Nation,* XCVI (March 6, 1913), 224–25.
"Questionnaire on Investment Bankers Code," *Investment Banking,* V (February 5, 1935), 151.
Raymond, William L. "Investment Banking in the United States: Its Historical Background and Development — The Wholesalers," *Barron's,* VI (May 31, 1926), 7, 20.
Read, John. "Bringing Wall Street to the People," *The Magazine of Wall Street,* XXVIII (June 11, 1921), 153, 211–12.
[Reed, Robert R.] "Regulation of the Business of the Investment Banker," *I.B.A. of A. Bulletin,* II (July 15, 1914), 9–17.
Reeves, Clifford B. "A Brief for the Bankers," *The American Mercury,* XXVII (September 1932), 21–22.
"Reforming the Stock Exchange," *Current Opinion,* LIV (March 1913), 246.
"Regulating the Sale of Securities," *The Magazine of Wall Street,* XI (March 1913), 326.
"Regulating the Speculators," *The New Republic,* LXXVIII (February 21, 1934), 33–34.
"Regulation of the Sale of Securities," *The Bankers' Magazine,* LXXXVI (April 1913), 418–19.
"Report of the Capital Issues Committee," *Federal Reserve Bulletin,* IV (August 1, 1918), 704–08.

"Review of Competitive Bidding on Public Service Securities," *Investment Banking,* XVI (June 1948), 15–18.
Rice, Samuel O. "The Investment Bankers Code," *Investment Banking,* IV (September 17, 1934), 300–05.
[Richardson, A. P.] "Investment Bankers' Code," *The Journal of Accountancy,* LVII (May 1934), 326–28.
[Richberg, Donald R.] "Mr. Brandeis and Investment Banking," *Harper's Weekly,* LVIII (January 17, 1914), 25.
Riggs, Edward G. et al. "Wall Street," *Munsey's Magazine,* X (January 1894).
Robbins, Sidney M. "Competitive Bidding in Sale of Securities," *Harvard Business Review,* XXVII (September 1949), 646–64.
Robbins, Sidney and Walter Werner. "Professor Stigler, Revisited," *The Journal of Business,* XXXVII (October 1964), 406–13.
Robertson, Ross M. "St. Louis as a Central Reserve City, 1887–1922," *Monthly Review,* Federal Reserve Bank of St. Louis, XXXVI (August 1954), 85–92.
Rollins, Montgomery. "Underwritings," *The Magazine of Wall Street,* XVII (December 11, 1915), 288–92.
Saperstein, David. "Government Regulation of Investment Banking" in Investment Bankers Association, *Fundamentals of Investment Banking* (Englewood Cliffs, 1960), 573–631.
"Jacob H. Schiff," *The Magazine of Wall Street,* XXVI (October 16, 1920), 837–38, 869.
Sears, Marian V. "The National Shawmut Bank Consolidation of 1898," *Business History Review,* XXXIX (Autumn 1965), 368–90.
"The Securities Act: An Interim Report," *Fortune,* VIII (December 1933), 33–35, 136–37.
"Securities Dealers Association," *Investment Banking,* IX (February 1939), 8–10.
Selden, G. C. "Striking England's Balance Sheet," *The Magazine of Wall Street,* XVII (January 8, 1916), 434.
"Self-Regulation," *Investment Banking,* VIII (January 15, 1938), 48.
Sheldon, Paul S. "Buying Stocks on the Partial Payment Plan," *The Magazine of Wall Street,* XIV (September 1914), 455–57.
"Shop Talk in Public," *Investment Banking,* X (January 1940), 6–11.
"Should the Government Regulate the Exchange?" *The Magazine of Wall Street,* XV (January 23, 1915), 224.
Simon, Matthew. "The Morgan-Belmont Syndicate of 1895 and Intervention in the Foreign-Exchange Market," *Business History Review,* XLII (Winter 1968), 385–417.
Sisson, Francis H. "Investment Restrictions in Glass Bill," *The Bankers' Magazine,* CXXVI (March 1933), 253–55.
Smitley, Robert L. "Wall Street's Red Tape," *The Magazine of Wall Street,* XIX (February 3, 1917), 592–93.
Smith, Sherwin D. "Thirty Years Ago," *The New York Times Magazine,* May 26, 1963.
Snider, Joseph L. "Security Issues in the United States, 1909–1920," *The Review of Economic Statistics,* III (May 25, 1921), 100.

"Some Good Bond Advertising," *The Bankers' Magazine*, LXXIV (March 1907), 425.
"Sound Security Regulation Need Not Be Feared," *The Magazine of Wall Street*, LI (April 15, 1933).
"South American Loans Feature Senate Hearings," *Barron's*, XIII (March 6, 1933), 9.
Speare, Charles F. "Wall Street's Crisis and the Country," *The American Monthly Review of Reviews*, XXXV (May 1907), 558–60.
Speare, Charles F. and Paul Clay. "Foreign War Loans and the Investor," *The Magazine of Wall Street*, XVI (July 24, 1915), 415–19.
"Special Code Meeting of the Board of Governors," *Investment Banking*, IV (December 15, 1933), 138–39.
Spring, Samuel. "Whirlwinds of Speculation," *The Atlantic Monthly*, CXLVII (April 1931), 483.
Steiner, William H. "The Functions of the Investment Banker," *The Annals*, CLXXI (January 1934), 64.
Stern, S. "Has the Time Come for the American Banker to Help Finance Europe?" *The Magazine of Wall Street*, XXXII (September 29, 1923), 1013, 1056.
Stewart, Percy M. "Underwriting Syndicates" in Investment Bankers Association, *Fundamentals of Investment Banking* (Englewood Cliffs, 1960), ch. xviii.
Stigler, George J. "Public Regulation of the Securities Markets," *The Journal of Business*, XXXVII (April 1964), 117–42.
——— "Comment," *The Journal of Business*, XXXVII (October 1964), 414–22.
"The Stock Exchange and the Pujo Committee," *The Magazine of Wall Street*, XI (February 1913), 221–26.
"Stock Exchange: 'Kill the Bill' Becomes Rallying Cry," *Newsweek*, III (April 7, 1934), 29–30.
Straus, S. W. "The Ethics of Investment Banking," *The Bankers' Magazine*, LXXXVII (October 1913), 412–13.
Strauss, Siegfried. "Profits in 'Interned' Securities; How the Investor Who Is Willing to Wait for the End of the War May Make Money — Securities Interned in Germany," *The Magazine of Wall Street*, XIX (December 23, 1916), 385–86.
——— "Safety of War Loans," *The Magazine of Wall Street*, XVI (October 2, 1915), 765.
——— "The War Loans," *The Magazine of Wall Street*, XVII (January 8, 1916), 453.
Supple, Barry E. "A Business Elite: German-Jewish Financiers in Nineteenth-Century New York," *Business History Review*, XXXI (Summer 1957), 143–51.
Sweezy, Paul M. "The Decline of the Investment Banker," *The Antioch Review*, I (March 1941), 63–68.
"Syndicates as Promoters of Financial Enterprises," *The Bankers' Magazine*, LXVI (July 1903), 15–17.
"Temporary National Economic Committee: Reviews of Monographs," *American Economic Review*, XXXI (September 1941), 573–601.

Ten Eyck, Andrew. "Some Precedents in British Law and Practice for Safeguarding Securities," *Harvard Business Review,* II (July 1924), 385–97.
Terret, John. "New York as a Bond Center," *Harper's Weekly,* LV (November 18, 1911), 13.
Thomas, Joseph A. "Ten Investment Trusts in America — A Three-Year Record," *Harvard Business Review,* IX (October 1930), 83.
Thompson, Howard. "When Stocks Are Better than Bonds," *The Magazine of Wall Street,* XVI (September 18, 1951), 726–30.
Thompson, Huston. "Informing the Investor," *The Magazine of Wall Street,* XXV (December 27, 1919), 234.
Tindall, George B. "Arsène Paulin Pujo," *Dictionary of American Biography* (22 vols., New York, 1928–1958), XXII, 544–45.
Tingley, Richard H. "Lessons of Other Wars," *The Magazine of Wall Street,* XX (June 9, 1917), 297–300.
"Trust Companies," *United States Investor,* IX (October 1, 1898), 1422.
"Trust Companies as Banks," *United States Investor,* X (January 14, 1899), 71.
Turner, George K. "Morgan's Partners," *McClure's Magazine,* XL (April 1913), 34–35.
"U.S. v. Investment Houses," *Newsweek,* XXX (November 10, 1947), 58.
"The Untermyer Inquiry," *The American Review of Reviews,* XLVII (February 1913), 136–37.
Untermyer, Samuel. "Speculation on the Stock Exchanges and Public Regulation of the Exchanges," *The American Economic Review,* V, suppl. (March 1915), 24–68.
Valeur, Robert, "Foreign Investments in Germany and the Problem of Inter-Governmental Debts," *The Annals,* CLXXIV (July 1934), 32–33.
Van Deusen, Edgar. "The Stock Exchange as the Investment Center," *The Bankers' Magazine,* LXXXIII (July 1911), 60–61.
"Wall Street Accepts New Deal in Finance," *The Literary Digest,* CXVII (June 23, 1934), 36.
"Wall Street Expects Better Trade," *The Literary Digest,* CXX (September 14, 1935), 40–41.
"Wall Street, Itself," *Fortune,* XV (June 1937), 68–75, 156–68.
"Warburg Points Out Faults of Securities Act," *Rand-McNally Bankers Monthly,* LI (February 1934), 106.
Warshaw, H. T. "The Distribution of Corporate Ownership in the United States," *The Quarterly Journal of Economics,* XXXIX (November 1924), 15–38.
Weidenhammer, Robert. "Control of New Investment," *The Annals,* CLXXI (January 1934), 73–82.
Weissman, Rudolph. "America's Giant Investors," *Challenge,* VI (October 1957), 8–11.
"Western Farm Loans," *The Bankers' Magazine,* XL (January 1886), 489–94.

"What Constitutes Strength in a Brokerage House?" *The Ticker,* III (February 1909), 173–77.
White, Gerald T. "Financing Industrial Expansion for War: The Origin of the Defense Plant Corporation Leases," *The Journal of Economic History,* IX (November 1949), 156–83.
White, Horace. "The Hughes Investigation," *The Journal of Political Economy,* XVII (October 1909), 528–40.
Whiteside, Arthur D. "A Square Deal for the Investor," *Investment Banking,* IV (May 3, 1934), 200–07.
"Why Not a Federal Law?" *The Magazine of Wall Street,* XII (May 1913), 12–13.
Wiebe, Robert H. "The House of Morgan and the Executive, 1905–1913," *American Historical Review,* LXV (October 1959), 49–60.
Williams, Carl. "Investment Trusts Under the Microscope," *The Magazine of Wall Street,* LI (October 29, 1932), 26.
Willis, H. Parker. "George Bliss," *Dictionary of American Biography* (22 vols., New York, 1928–1958), II, 372–73.
Winsmore, Robert. "Free Exchange Markets Indicate Stabilization," *The Literary Digest,* XCVIII (November 24, 1934), 40.
——— "Wall Street's Reply to the Senate's Investigation," *The Literary Digest,* CXVI (July 22, 1933), 5, 31.
Woods, Roger H. "Investment Situation and the Small Investor," *The Magazine of Wall Street,* XIX (December 23, 1916), 369–71.
"Would It Pay to be Honest in Company Promotion?" *The Statist,* XXXV (February 9, 1895), 185; (February 23, 1895), 245–46; (April 27, 1895), 537–38.
Wyckoff, Richard D. "Looking Forward — And Backward After Thirty-five Years in Wall Street," *The Magazine of Wall Street,* XXXIII (December 22, 1923), 300.
——— "The Old *vs.* the New Idea in Capitalizing an Enterprise," *The Magazine of Wall Street,* XV (December 1914), 93.
Youngman, Anna. "The Growth of Financial Banking," *The Journal of Political Economy,* XIV (July 1906), 438–39.
Zachry, Wallace P. "Operations Under the Investment Bankers Code," *Investment Banking,* IV (June 11, 1934), 264–69.
Zimmer, George. "Foreign Exchange During the War," America's Changing Investment Market, *The Annals,* LXVIII (November 1916), 156–57.

Index

Abbott, Edwin H., 36n
Acceptances, bankers', 89, 274–275; and Kidder, Peabody, 291
Acquisitions, 502
Adams, Alva B., 346
Adams, Charles Francis, 39
Adams, Charles Francis, Jr., 158, 341
Adamson Act, 228
Addinsell, Harry M., 464
Advertising, 63–64, 77, 92, 104–105, 260; Liberty Loans, 225–226; of investment trusts, 285
"Affiliate" rule, *see* Securities and Exchange Commission, U-*12* F-*2*
Affiliates, *see* Security affiliates
Airplane companies, 253
Aldrich, Winthrop W., 347–348, 359–360, 371; blames government policies for market break of *1937,* 408
Aldrich-Vreeland Act, 131, 135
Alexander, James, W., 114, 207n
Alleghany Corporation, 340, 342, 343, 432–433
Allen, Frederick Lewis, 131
Allen, Solomon, 11
Allen, S. and M., 4, 11
Alliances, financial, 112, 145
Allied powers, World War I, 201–207, 211, 213; involvement of investment bankers in purchases of, 208–209. *See also* World War I
Amalgamated Copper Company, 45, 112
American Banker, The, 44, 46, 128; welcomes proposed national association of security dealers, 164; criticism of Pujo *Report,* 175
American Bankers Association (ABA), 165–166, 231
American Bell Telephone Company, 67
American Can, 69n
American Car & Foundry, 69n, 335
American Cities Power and Light Company, 290
American Cotton Oil Company, 43
American Economic Review, 429
American Express, 197
American Foreign Securities Company, 206–207
American International Corporation (AIC), 215–216
American Securities Company, 290
American Smelting and Refining Company, 70n

American Telephone and Telegraph Company (AT&T), 59n, 63, 146, 340, 456; and Kidder, Peabody, 67, 92, 313, 415–416; *1905* bond issue, 92; in crash of *1929,* 304; in TNEC investigation, 415–417, 421, 424; private placement of issues, 424–425; and competitive bids on bonds, 431, 450–451; in antitrust investigation, 487
American Tin Plate Company, 45
American Woolen Company, 160
Amsterdam, 18
Anaconda Copper Company, 45, 112, 331
Anglo-American settlement of *1871–1872,* 22
Anglo-American trade, 9
Anglo-French loan (October *1915*), 204–205, 211, 212, 471; aloofness of general public toward, 206; agreement relating to Morgan's organization of syndicate, 468
Antifraud laws, 156, 181–182, 188; and full-disclosure laws, 183, 359; and IBA-NASBS "Proposed Blue Sky Act," 185; IBA urges adoption of, 189; and Volstead, 355
Anti-stock watering act, Massachusetts (*1894*), 158
Antitrust laws, 409, 429; and security affiliates, 272
Antitrust suit, federal, 73, 200; of *1947,* 181, 457, 458–495, 505, 507–508; trial, 433, 460–461; roots of, 461; conspiracy charge, 463–464, 467, 469, 471; defendants, 464–467; pretrial proceedings, 467; monopoly charge, 469–472, 484–485; charges against defendants, 472–475, 488; traditional banker charge, 474–475, 485, 486, 487; price-fixing issue, 475–477; government's evidence in, 477; defense strategy in, 477–484; satisfactory relationship argument, 487–488; refutation of historical position and reciprocity charges, 488–489; trimming of directorship-use charge, 490; and cross-examination of live witnesses, 491–493; Medina's opinion, 493–495
Annual reports, 507
Appomattox, 22
Argentina, 207
Armaments, World War I, 208

Armistice, World War I, 246
Armour & Co., 251, 259
"Arm's-length bargaining" rule, see Securities and Exchange Commission, U-12 F-2
Armstrong, William W., 115
Armstrong Committee, 66, 115, 117–119, 122, 138, 458, 477; condemnation of life companies' underwriting activities, 124–125; recommendations effected by New York State legislature, 125–126
Armstrong law, 450
Arrow shirts, 421
Asset realization company, 276
Associated Gas & Electric Securities Company, Inc., 297
Associated Stock Exchanges, 377
Association of Stock Exchange Brokers, 185–186
Astor, John Jacob, 1, 52
Astor, Vincent, 205
Atchison, Topeka & Santa Fe Railroad, 34–37, 88; bonded debt (1885–1888), 35; reorganization of management and financial structure, 36, 40
AT&T, see American Telephone and Telegraph Company
Atlantic Monthly, 110
Atlas National Bank of Cincinnati, 277
Auctioneer, professional, 4–5, 7, 13, 85; at outbreak of World War I, 196
Austria, 210, 307
Automobile industry, 133

Babson, Roger W., 77n, 93; on crash of *1929,* 300, 301
Bacon, Robert, 71, 87; and American Foreign Securities Company, 207
Baird, R. W. & Co., 490
Baker, George Fisher, 23, 49, 100, 108, 122, 124, 130, 153, 191, 310; and panic of *1907,* 129; and Pujo Committee, 140, 142, 144, 152; and voting trust, 143; and community of interest among syndicate participants, 145; voluntary withdrawal from directorships, 180; and Anglo-French loan (*1915*), 205; and Liberty Loan committees, 227; and security affiliate (First Security Company), 273–274
Baker, George Fisher, Jr., 303
Baker, Hugh B., 335
Baker, Newton D., 341
Baltimore, 13, 320
Baltimore & Ohio Railroad, 37, 41, 219
Bank affiliates, see Security affiliates

Bank failures (*1920*'s), 242; and Great Depression, 308–309, 313; and Glass-Steagall Act, 368
Bank Note Detector, 23
Bank of America, 242
Bank of England, 12, 51, 197, 199; and U.S. subscription to loans, 80–81
Bank of France, 206
Bank of Italy, San Francisco, see Bank of America
Bank of Manhattan, 361
Bank of Tennessee, 236, 309
Bank of the United States, second (BUS), 2, 6, 9; security affiliates, 272; failure of, 279
Bankers' Magazine, The, 3, 96, 100, 108, 111; criticism of Aldrich-Vreeland Act, 135; on security regulation, 161, 181; on efficacy of IBA-type disclosure-and-fraud law, 186
Bankers Trust Company, 141, 143, 207n, 339
Banking Act of *1933,* see Glass-Steagall Banking Act
Banking Act of *1935,* 371n
Banking laws, 174
Banking services, 1
Banking syndicates, 64. See also Syndicate
Banking system, 3, 151
Bankruptcy Act (*1898*), 383
Banks, 1, 29; assets, 84; post–World War I, 241–242
Baring, Thomas, 36; and Kidder, Peabody, 91n
Baring & Co., 91n
Baring Brothers & Co., 1, 2, 6, 7, 24, 25n, 39; and international finance, 9–10; and Kidder, Peabody, 26, 30, 91, 209, 210, 258, 309, 317; and Santa Fe Railroad, 34–36; and banking alliances, 52; "red lists," 60n; and syndicate manager's fees, 63; and World War I, 210
Baring, Magoun & Co., 44; and National Shawmut Bank of Boston, 71; and foreign issues, 80
Barney, Charles D., 25n
Barney, Charles D., & Co., 398
Baruch, Bernard, 201, 237, 323, 426; and Morgan's "preferred list," 341
Bates, Joshua, 9
Bear raids, Senate investigation of, 323
Beebe & Co., Boston, 10
Bell, David, 49–50
Belmont, August, 9–10
Belmont, August, & Co., 10, 37n, 91; and Northern Pacific, 37; and distribution of industrial securities, 44

Index | 545

Bemis, Edward W., 76
Benedict, William L., 200
Benton, Jacob, 326
Berle, Adolf A., Jr., 360, 372, 385, 428
Berlin, 18
Bertron, Griscom & Co., 215
Bertron, Griscom & Co., 215
Bethlehem Steel, 205, 490; during World War I, 218, 222, 232
Biddle, John, 8
Biddle, Nicholas, 2–3, 6, 110, 508
Biddle, Thomas, & Co., 8
Big business: public suspicion of, 133; and Pujo investigation, 137–155; and TNEC, 408–430; and antitrust investigation, 458–495
Big Five meat packers, 214
Black, James, 418
Black Friday (September *24, 1869*), 25
Black Thursday (October *24, 1929*), 300, 302–303, 305
Blake Brothers, 43
Bliss, George, 22, 38
Blue Eagle, *see* National Recovery Administration
Blue Ridge Company, 290
Blue Ridge Corporation, 290
Blue-sky laws, 156–164, 174–192, 234, 268, 288; evolution of movement, 156–157, 354; and prosperity of *1900–1910*, 162; constitutionality challenged by IBA, 182; model law drafted by IBA, 182–185; and state courts, 186–188; effectiveness of, 189–190; New Deal strengthening of, 355, 356; and syndicate procedures (*1930*'s), 401
Blyth, Charles R., 260
Blyth & Co., San Francisco, 259, 260–261, 374, 394; capital employed (*1934–1939*), 406; and TNEC's theory of inheritance, 414; and PG&E, 417–419; in antitrust case of *1950*'s, 466, 488
Blyth, Witter & Co., 260, 374
Board of Railroad Commissioners, New York, 159
Bogen, Jules I., 27
Bogert, Henry L., 486
Bollard, R. H., 439
Bonbright, William P., 208, 209n
Bonbright & Co., 281, 297, 323
Bond Club of New York, 407, 432
Bonds, 1, 84–85, 240, 243, 258, 301; American investment in foreign (*1920*'s), 246, 248; and Great Crash of *1929*, 306; transfer tax on, 401
Bonner, Francis A., 387

Boston, 13, 405; immigrant population, 90
Boston & Maine Railroad, 132
Boston Daily Advertiser, 4
Boston Evening Transcript, 4
Boston Stock and Exchange Board, 4–5; and Degrand, 5; and Thayer, 7
Boston Stock Exchange, 34; and industrial securities (*1890*'s), 42, 44; investment houses' representative on, 87
Bovenizer, George W., 389, 400; describes Schiff, 88; and Securities Act of *1933,* 357
Bowden, Witt, 15n
Branch banking, 242; federal investigation, 348
Brandeis, Louis D., 122, 152, 156, 161, 174, 326, 460–461, 495, 508; his *Other People's Money,* 110, 180; on plight of New Haven (*1913*), 132; and interlocking directorates, 144; article interpreting Pujo findings, 175; and creation of Federal Reserve Board, 177; and Rayburn bill, 179; advocate of full-disclosure law, 182–183, 354, 356
Brazil, 207; National City Co. flotation for, 330–331
Britain, *see* England; Great Britain
British Companies Act, *see* English Companies Act
British Exchequer loan (*1900*), 80
British National War Loan (*1900*), 80, 82
British Treasury Bills, 232
Brokerage, 4, 13, 16; and private banking, 6, 9
Brokerage houses: German-Jewish houses, 17–20, 26, 86; "Yankee houses," 20–22, 26; inefficiency of, 234–235; changes in during war years (*1917–1918*), 235–237; during *1920*'s, 255–270
Brookhart, Smith W., 324, 334–335
Brooklyn Rapid Transit system, 219
Broun, Heywood, 330
Brown, Alexander, & Sons, 8–9, 229, 385
Brown, Franklin Q., 215
Brown, James, 207n, 215
Brown, John A., 8
Brown, John Crosby, 9n, 38, 39
Brown, William, 8
Brown, W. & J., & Co., Liverpool, 8
Brown Brothers & Co. (Baltimore), 8, 38, 91, 229; during World War I, 197, 207
Brown Brothers Harriman & Co., 372, 374, 414, 419

Brown Harriman & Co., 374, 400, 414–415, 417, 418
Brown, Shipley & Co. (London), 8–9, 91
Bryan, William Jennings, 137, 177
Bucket-shops, 127, 326
Budge, Schiff & Co., 19
Budget, federal, 301
Bullock, Charles J., 110, 124
Burlington Railroad, 445
Burns, Walter H., 22
Burton, Theodore E., 202
BUS, *see* Bank of the United States
Business Conduct Committee: IBA, 269–270, 426; NASD, 392
Business Week, 324
Byllesby, H. M., & Co., 296
Byrnes, Ronald M., 330–331

Caldwell, George B., 165–167, 169, 171, 172; on securities legislation, 181–182; on ideal blue-sky law, 182; on European loans (*1914*), 202
Caldwell & Co., 236, 308–309
California, 260, 503
California Petroleum Co., 140, 145n
California Security Dealers Association, 389
Call market, 99
Canada, 80, 246, 248
Capital, 1, 499; domestic, 15, 84; foreign, and German-Jewish brokerage houses, 20; late nineteenth century, 29–30; short-term, 48; mobilization of long-term, 49–50; change in market, 80, 83; need for conservation of (World War I), 231; low rate of return (*1930*'s), 397; in TNEC investigation, 411
Capital Issues Committee (CIC), 231–233, 244–245, 354; and control of sales of fraudulent securities, 233–234
Capital markets, 58, 108; and New York City, 30, 105, 151, 153, 340, 405, 407, 423; late nineteenth century, 29–30, 49; foreign, 84, 108; and TNEC investigation, 411
Capitalism, 49–50
Capitalization, regulation concerning, 157
Cardozo, Benjamin N., 326
Carnegie, Andrew, 42, 73; and Anglo-French loan (*1915*), 205
Cassel, Sir Ernest, 92
Central America, 215, 246; AIC activities in, 216
Central Europe, 307
Central Life Insurance Company, 106
Central Pacific Railroad, 27

Central Powers, World War I, 210–212. *See also* World War I
Central reserve city banks, 48
Central States Electric Corporation, 290
Central Trust Company, Chicago, 205, 207n, 313
Central Trust Company, New York, 210, 219
Central Wharf, Boston, 7
Chain Stores, Inc., 290
Chamber of Commerce, U.S., *see* United States Chamber of Commerce
Chamberlain, Lawrence, 176
Chandler Act (*1938*), 383
Chandler & Co., 210
Chapin, John R., 416
Chapman, E. R., 46
Chase, Salmon P., 14–15
Chase, Stuart, 428–429
Chase National Bank, 142, 207n, 214, 371; security affiliate, 278, 346–347; aids Kidder, Peabody (*1930*), 311; and Pecora hearings, 346, 348; and Glass-Steagall Act, 371–372, 375
Chase Securities Corporation, 278, 346–347
Chesapeake & Ohio Railroad (C&O), 27, 37, 38, 491; and competitive bidding controversy, 432, 434, 435
Chicago, 16–17, 32, 320; capital markets in, 30, 405; central reserve city, 48; Atlantic Coast firms' branches in, 90; growth of investment banking community in, 105–108, 191; and origination of IBA, 165; during financial crisis of *1914,* 196
Chicago, Burlington, & Quincy, 28, 110
Chicago, Milwaukee, and St. Paul Railroad, 257
Chicago Stock Exchange, 105
Chicago Tribune, 133
Chicago Union Station Co., 400, 422
Chilean bank issue (*1925*), 264–265
China, 80n
Christie, Robert E., Jr., 386
Chrysler, Walter P., 325
Cincinnati Union Terminal Company, 435
Cisco, John J., & Son, 27
City Bank Farmers Trust Company, New York, 276–277; in Pecora investigation, 332–334
City Trust Company, New York, 326
Civil War, 10, 11, 17, 27, 51, 105, 225; government financing of, 13–15; growth of new banking and brokerage houses, 17–18
Claflin, H. B., & Co., 42

Claflin, John, 42
Clark, Champ, 137n
Clark, Dodge & Co., 11, 90
Clark, Edward W., 11
Clark, Enoch W., 11
Clark, E. W., & Co., 11, 24, 25, 52, 197
Clark, Harold Ben, 94, 103
Clark, Thomas C., 463-464
Clay, Paul, 203
Clayton Antitrust Act (*1914*), 176-177, 371n
Cleveland Plain Dealer, The, 463
Clews, Henry, 27, 113; on overcapitalization, 161
Clews, Henry, & Co., 17, 24n, 25, 161
"Club 17," 474-475. *See also* Antitrust suits
Cluett, George A., 421
Cluett, Peabody Company, 420-421
Coercion, 473
Cohen, Benjamin V., 356, 361, 376, 379
Cohen, Manuel F., 507
Colby, Bainbridge, 326
Commerce, U.S. Department of, 248-249, 379; and TNEC, 410
Commercial banks, 2, 13, 23, 32, 55, 502; and industrial common stock, 44; and financing industrial combinations, 45; and insurance companies, 48; and investment houses, 48-49; and syndicates, 58, 64; changes in (*1901-1914*), 96-97; bond departments, 97-98; role in security markets, 108; establishment of affiliates for investment function, 236; during *1920*'s, 242-243; and security affiliates, 271, 274-276, 278-279, 281; and investment trusts, 283, 292; and public utility holding companies, 298; and Glass-Steagall Banking Act, 368-371, 373, 413
Commercial bank credit, 217
Commercial paper, 19, 89; and Kidder, Peabody, 90
Commercial Trust Co., Philadelphia, 207
Commercial & Financial Chronicle, The, 37, 80, 104, 207; on investment market of *1906*, 127; on crisis of *1907*, 128; criticism of Pujo report, 174-175; hails report of New York investigating committee (*1908*), 135; and formation of IBA, 166; and Morgan's withdrawal from twenty-seven boards, 180; on financial crisis of *1914*, 193-194, 197, 198; advertises German war loans (World War I), 211; on commercial bank credit (*1914-1917*), 217; on depressed

Commercial & Financial Chronicle (cont.)
railroad securities (*1915*), 220; on investigation of National City Co., 330; on Securities Act of *1933*, 358-359
Commission, broker's, 145, 235; in *1948*, 5; and watered stock, 77; and private bank, 89; on foreign issues, 262; during *1930*'s, 395-397
Commissioners, banking, 6
Commissions, regulatory, 156-158; variation in authority and effectiveness of, 159
Committee of Five, New York Stock Exchange, 195
Committee of Seven, bankers', 195, 197
Committee on Business Practice, IBA proposal, 265
Committee on Foreign Securities, IBA, 209
Committee on Industrial Trusts, IBA, 268
Committee on Industrials, IBA, 268
Committee on Stock Exchange Relations, IBA, 426
Committee on Syndicate Agreements, IBA, 265
Commodity brokers, 7
Common stock, 43-44, 500-501; during *1920*'s, 255, 258; and House of Morgan, 256, 340; and investment trust, 285; and Great Crash of *1929*, 306
Commonwealth Corporation, 312, 314, 315
Communist party, 468
Competition, 25, 407, 439-440; and rules of interfirm behavior, 100-103; and Pujo investigation, 138-139, 152; and syndicate, 145-146, 265-266; and bidding on securities of interstate corporations, 146-147 (*see also* Competitive bidding, compulsory); Morgan on, 149-150; and underwriting and distribution of foreign loans, 248; during *1920*'s, 255, 257, 258; for foreign securities flotation, 261; and Glass-Steagall Act, 374-375; and investment banking code, 385-394 *passim;* for new issues (*1930*'s), 394, 413; in TNEC investigation, 420, 426, 427; in underwriting of utility issues, 432-438; cited in antitrust suit (*1950*'s), 464, 467, 484; in the *1960*'s, 506
Competitive bidding, compulsory, 159, 490, 500; and ICC, 177; during *1930*'s, 405; and TNEC hearings, 421-422, 430; controversy, 431-

548 | Index

Competitive bidding (*cont.*) 457; and public utility issues, 432–439; and IBA, 439; bankers' opposition to, 439–441; endorsed by Eaton's firm, 441; and the large institutional investor, 442–443; trade's reaction to SEC's U-*50,* 444; and railroad issues, 444–445, 456–457; changes in investment banking procedures, 446–456; and syndicate, 446–450; little voluntary adherence to, 450–451; and decline in bankers' gross spread (*1940*'s), 451–452; criticism of, 456; and Truman, 462; in government's conspiracy charge (*1950*'s), 472
Comptroller of the Currency, federal, 97, 140, 154, 218; and depressed railroad securities (*1917*), 220; on characteristics of nation's banks (*1920*'s), 242
Comptroller of the Currency, New York, 49, 277
Conant, Charles A., 84
Congress, U.S., 45, 154, 223; and investigation of money trust, 136; and reform concerning financial concentration, 156; Sixty-third (*1913*), and Pujo recommendations, 176–179; appropriates gold to ship to London (August *1914*), 197; and crisis in cotton market (*1914*), 200; and Pan American Financial Conference (*1914*), 215; and fraudulent securities, 234; and investor protection (*1931*), 322; Seventy-second, 328; and Pecora investigation, 336; Seventy-third, 352, 375; FDR asks for federal securities law (*1933*), 353; and Securities Act of *1933,* 356, 364; and Glass-Steagall Act, 368, 373; and SEC powers, 384; and establishment of TNEC, 409; and Public Utility Holding Company Act, 436. *See also* House of Representatives, U.S.; Senate, U.S.
Connecticut, 161, 163
Connely, Emmett F., 393, 427–429
Conspiracy, 400, 463–464, 467, 469, 471, 477, 487; and traditional banker relationship, 474; in antitrust suit defense strategy, 478; refutation of charge, 489; Stuart's testimony on, 492–493. *See also* Antitrust suit
Construction, railroad, 29, 32
Continental & Commercial National Bank, 107, 141n
Continental & Commercial Trust and Savings Bank, Chicago, 165

Continental Trust Company of Baltimore, 221
Cooke, Jay, 11, 14–15, 17, 21, 22, 23, 27, 225, 508; and Civil War five-twenty loan, 15–16; and seven-thirties, 16; and Northern Pacific Railroad, 23–25, 27, 28; and underwriting, 52–53
Cooke, Jay, & Co., 25, 52, 92
Coolidge, Calvin, 241, 254, 341
Cooper, Irving Ben, 327
Corcoran, Thomas G., 356, 376, 378, 379
Corcoran, William Wilson, 10
Corcoran & Riggs, 10, 52
Corporate bonds, 49; foreign, 262
Corporate loans, 123
Corporate shares, 30
Corporation laws, 157–158
Corporation Securities Company, 259
Corporations, 29, 42–49, 51; of *1890*'s, 42; investigation of, by investment bankers, 56–57; in *1920*'s, 244–245, 263; overseas, 262
Cortelyou, George B., 129
Coster, Charles H., 40
Cotton market, crisis in (*1914*), 200
Cotton oil refining trust, 43
Counselors, investment, 5
Couzens, James, 324n, 325, 334, 338, 346
Crash of *1929,* see Great Crash of *1929*
Credit: mercantile, 20; national, 128; during World War I, 201–203, 207, 211, 224; and sale of repatriated securities, World War I, 212; and WFC, 229
Crisis, financial: *1914–1917,* 193–223; closing of stock exchanges, 193–194; compared to *1895* and *1907,* 194. *See also* Depression; Panic
Cromwell, Frederic, 62, 117, 118, 123
Cromwell, William Nelson, 74
Cuba, 80n, 82n
Cuban Dominican Sugar Company, 331
Cudahy Packing Co., 451
Currency, 20, 128, 131, 174; and crisis in cotton market (*1914*), 200; stabilization of European (*1920*'s), 248
Curtis, James F., 230
Cutter, John W., 439
Cuyler, T. DeWitt, 207n

Dabney, Charles H., 21
Dabney, Morgan & Co., 21
Davis, John H., & Co., 43
Davis, John W., 336, 338

Davison, Henry P., 143, 146, 147, 151, 152, 198; during World War I, 204, 212; and Pan American Financial Conference (*1914*), 215
Dawes, Charles G., 205, 207n
Dawes Plan loan, 261
Day, R. L., 71
Day, R. L., & Co., 67
Dealer-licensing laws, 188
Dean, Arthur H., 361, 372, 433, 461, 463, 491; and choice of antitrust defendants, 464–465; complaints against government's statistics, 478–490; and Stuart's testimony, 492. *See also* Antitrust suit
Debt, government, 301
Debt issues, 243
DeCoppett & Doremus, 195
Defense Plant Corporation, 458
Degrand, Peter P. F., 4–5
Delano, Moreau, 209n
Delaware, 272, 283, 289, 389
Democratic party, 162, 376
Denison, Edward E., 355
Denmark, 207
Deposit accounts, 209
Depression, 25, 40, 44; post–World War I, 241. *See also* Great Depression
Detroit, Toledo & Ironton Railroad, 343
Deutsche Bank of Berlin, 214
Devonstreet & Co., 315
Dewey, Thomas E., 381; and competitive bidding controversy, 445
Dillinger, John, 348
Dillon, Clarence, 207n, 209n; and Pecora investigation, 344, 346
Dillon, Read & Co., 289–291, 310; and Pecora investigation, 342, 344–346; its investment trusts, 345–346
Directorships, interlocking, 113, 116–117, 179–180, 256, 340; and Pujo investigation, 143–144, 147, 151; and Clayton Act, 177; and TNEC investigation, 420, 430; in antitrust hearings, 490
Disclosure, 156, 160–161, 163, 177, 185, 401; and Brandeis, 182–183, 354, 356; and federal legislation, 233, 329, 349; regulation urged by Aldrich, 347; and Securities Act of *1933,* 351, 353–356, 359, 363, 376, 387, 398; and IBA code of conduct, 387; during *1960*'s, 507
Diversification, investors', 55, 502
Divorcement, and TNEC investigation, 413–414. *See also* Glass-Steagall Banking Act
Doane, Robert R., 249
Dodge, Edward, 11

Dollar, in terms of sterling (*1914*), 197–199
Dolley, J. N., 163, 189
Donham, Wallace B., 54
Douglas, William O., 362, 363, 381, 390, 407, 408; and reorganization of NYSE, 409; and competitive bidding, 432, 433. *See also* Securities and Exchange Commission
Drexel, Anthony J., 26; and J. P. Morgan, 21
Drexel, Francis A., 15n
Drexel, Francis M., 15n
Drexel, Francis W., 91n
Drexel, Joseph William, 21
Drexel & Co., Philadelphia, 15, 21, 27, 33, 91, 255, 413; and recruitment of foreign capital, 30; and foreign issues, 80; and Anglo-French loan (*1915*), 205; and public utility holding companies, 297; and Glass-Steagall Act, 372; and antitrust suit, 464, 466, 479
Drexel, Harjes & Co., 91n
Drexel, Morgan & Co., 21–22, 37
Dumaine, Frederic C., 312, 315
Dun & Bradstreet, Inc., 386
Duncan, Sherman & Co., 11, 20, 21
Du Pont de Nemours, E. I., 208
Du Pont family, 205
Durant, Donald, 317

Eastman, Dillon & Co., 465, 484, 486
Eaton, Cyrus, 432–433, 434–436, 439, 440, 441, 462; and competitive bidding for railroad issues, 444–445; and government antitrust case, 461, 462–464
Economic Vigilance Committee, proposed, 233
Economist, The (London), 128n
Edison Electric Company, 43
Egypt, 207
Electric Bond & Share Company (EB&S), 296
Electrical Shareholdings Corporation, 297
Ellis, George E., 7n
Emerson, Sumner B., 456
Engineers Public Service Company, 296
England, 1, 15, 52, 82, 84, 211; and sale of repatriated securities, World War I, 212–213. *See also* Great Britain
English Companies Act (*1900*), 160, 164, 171, 329, 428; model for Securities Act of *1933,* 354, 355, 356
Equipment trust certificate, 245, 432, 433, 444, 500

Equitable Life Assurance Society, 58, 116–117, 121, 122; and foreign issues, 81; disclosure of mismanagement (*1903*), 113; fight for control of, 114–115; and Kuhn, Loeb, 122, 143; and Union Pacific stock, 122; services provided by investment house for, 123; Morgan influence with, 142
Equitable Securities, 490
Equity issues, 30, 243, 258, 285, 301, 497–498
Erie Railroad, 41, 101
Escher, Franklin, 100n
Estabrook & Co., 67
Ethics, bankers', *see* Pecora investigation
European Merchants Banking Co., Ltd., 257
Evans, John, 209n
Everybody's Magazine, 112, 127, 460
Ewing, William, 342, 374, 414
Excess-profits taxes, 192
Exchange rates, World War I, 213
Expansion, economic, 51; during *1920*'s, 240–270; post–World War II, 459–460

Fahnestock, Harris C., 23
Far East, 82, 246, 262; AIC activities in, 216
Farm mortgages, 84
Farmers, 229
Farmers' Loan & Trust Co., 207n, 280
Federal Communication Commission (FCC), 450
Federal Deposit Insurance Corporation, 371
Federal Farm Loan Act (*1916*), 229
Federal loan: of *1843*, 10; of *1813*, 52
Federal Reserve Act of *1913*, 176–177
Federal Reserve Board, 177, 200, 211, 229, 371; and placement of Liberty Loans, 228; and CIC, 231; attempts to restrain speculation (March *1929*), 301; and Securities Exchange Act (*1934*), 376, 379
Federal Reserve System, 208, 229, 348; and distribution of Liberty Loans, 226–228; fails to curb speculation (*1920*'s), 253; and Glass bill, 370, 371
Federal Securities Corporation, 236
Federal Steel Company, 44
Federal Trade Commission (FTC), 252, 354; and Securities Act of *1933*, 356–357, 362; and Fletcher-Rayburn bill (*1934*), 378; and Public Utility Holding Company Act (*1935*), 382; and TNEC, 410

Fennelly, John F., 440
Fess, Simeon D., 322
Fidelity Trust Co., 123
Field, Marshall, 74
Finance companies, 276, 288, 290
Finance Forum, West Side YMCA, New York City, 139
Finance magazine, 506
Financial and Industrial Securities Corporation, 289
Financial crisis, December *1861*, 14. *See also* Depression; Panic
First Boston Corporation, 275, 373, 374, 375, 386, 394; return on capital (*1935–1939*), 397; and choice of syndicate participants, 404; and TNEC inheritance issue, 417; and antitrust case, 465, 479
First National Bank of Boston, 143, 375; security affiliate, 274–275, 373
First National Bank of Chicago, 32, 106, 141n; security affiliate, 97, 275; New York ties, 107
First National Bank of New York, 23, 31, 47, 100, 207n, 339; and launching of United States Steel, 73, 144; and panic of *1907*, 129; Morgan influence, 142; and Pujo investigation, 140, 145; security affiliate, 273–274
First National Bank of St. Paul, 207n
First National Corporation, 274–275
First National Investment Company of Chicago, 275
First National Old Colony Corporation, 369
First Security Co., 142, 273–274, 278
First Trust and Savings Bank of Chicago, 97, 251
First Wisconsin Co., 275
First Wisconsin National Bank, 275
First Wisconsin Trust Company, 275
Fisher, Irving, 300, 301, 302
Fisk, Harvey, 17
Fisk, Harvey & Sons, 17n, 141
Fisk, Pliny, 17n
Fisk & Hatch, 17, 25, 27
Five-twenty loan, 14, 15–16
Fleishacker, Herbert, 209n
Fleming, Robert, 92
Fletcher, Duncan U., 324n, 335, 336, 360; and Securities Exchange Act, 376, 379
Fletcher-Rayburn bill, *see* Securities Exchange Act (*1934*)
Flint, Charles R., 160
Florida, 3
Flynn, John T., 290
Forbes, Allen B., 207n, 209n, 231
Forbes, Bertie Charles, 215
Forbes, John Murray, 13, 27, 28, 168
Forbes Magazine, 215

Foreign acceptance, *see* Acceptances, bankers'
Foreign exchange, 6, 7, 317, 502; and "Yankee houses," 20–21; at outbreak of World War I, 197–199, 200; and Anglo-French loans, 204–206; during *1920*'s, 246, 255; during Great Depression, 308
Foreign issues, 79–82, 259; decrease in number and size (*1906-1913*), 82; American investment in, 84; during World War I, 202–203, 208–209, 240; during *1920*'s, 245–247, 256–257, 261–262, 264; sale of endorsed by government and financial leaders, 248; State Department review of private, 249; and small investor, 251; expectation of large profits, 262; and investment trust, 284
Forrestal, James V., 463
Fortune, 353, 397
Fourth National Bank of New York, 143
Fox, Dr. Bertrand, 460, 478
France, 51, 259, 261–262; interest in American issues, 84; American investment aid to (*1915-1917*), 204–207, 210, 211 (*see also* Anglo-French loan, *1915*); cities loan of *1916,* 211; and sale of repatriated securities, World War I, 212–213
Franco-Prussian War, 25
Frank, Jerome N., 392, 427, 440, 462
Frankfurt, Germany, 18
Frankfurter, Felix, 353, 356
Franklin, Lewis B., 202, 219, 225, 230
Franz Ferdinand, Austrian archduke, 193
Fraud: in "Proposed Blue Sky Act," 185; and Liberty bonds, 233–234. *See also* Antifraud laws; Securities, fraudulent
Free banks, 3
French cities loan (*1916*), 216
Frick, Henry Clay, 131
Frosted Foods, Inc., 325
Frothingham, Francis E., 391
Fuel Administration, 234

Gary, Elbert H., 131
Gas and Electric Commission, New York, 159
Gaston, William A., 70
Gaston, Snow & Saltonstall, 70
Gay, Edwin F., 238–239
Gay, E. H., & Co., 80, 93
General Electric Company, 43, 296; in crash of *1929,* 304; and Pecora investigation, 328

General Public Service Corporation, 296
General Sugar Corporation, 333
Georgia, 185
German-Jewish brokerage houses, 17–20, 26, 86
German Treasury notes, World War I, 210–211
Germany, 18, 210–211, 213, 259; issues floated in U.S., 81, 82, 261–262; and Great Depression, 307. *See also* Central Powers
Giannini, A. P., 242
Gifford, Walter S., 487
Gilbert S., & Sons, 5
Gilbert, S. Parker, 349
Girard, Stephen, 1, 2, 52
Glass, Carter, 209, 240–241, 249, 324n; and CIC, 232, 234; on exchange rate of *1920*'s, 246; and Pecora investigation, 328, 349; and Glass-Steagall Act, 368–369, 373; subcommittee, 369
Glass-Steagall Banking Act, 351, 368–375, 381, 385, 412–413, 419, 421, 508; and FDIC, 371; and behavior of investment bankers, 371, 474; results of, 372–375; implementation of, 372–373; and selection of syndicate members, 400
Glore, Forgan & Co., 440
Glyn, Mills, Currie & Co., London, 91
Gold, 20, 21, 197–199, 201
Gold Fund Committee, 199–200
Goldman, Henry, 82–83
Goldman, Marcus, 19
Goldman, M., & Sachs, 19
Goldman, Sachs & Co., 19, 63, 313, 325; and underwriting of small enterprises, 82; and investment trust, 289–290; and public utility holding companies, 297; arrangement with Lehman Brothers, 420–421; and antitrust case, 466, 490
Goldman Sachs Trading Corporation, 289–290, 325
Goodrich, B. F., Rubber Co., 83
Gordon, Albert H., 88n, 310, 317; and reorganization of Kidder, Peabody, 313–316; and competition for new issues (*1930*'s), 394; and TNEC investigation, 416; and antitrust investigations, 486–487
Gould, Jay, 36
Gould, Leslie, 451
Government: as investor, 1; and Civil War, 13–14, 17; foreign borrowing in U.S., 79–80, 261; in financial crisis of *1914-1917,* 199–200; provides capital to industry (*1930*'s),

Government (cont.)
394–395, 428. *See also* United States Government
Government securities, 23–24, 30; and competitive bidding controversy, 443
Graham, George S., 252
Grangers, 157
Gras, N. S. B., 27
Gray, William A., 327
Gray-Pecora investigation, *see* Pecora investigation
Great Britain, 14, 51, 259; securities law (*1900*), 160; at outbreak of World War I, 197–198, 202; and Winchester Repeating Arms Company, 208; investment trust in, 284, 288; and Great Depression, 307. *See also* England
Great Crash of *1929*, 109, 238–239, 240, 300–321; and appraisal of security affiliates, 277–279; and appraisal of investment trusts, 288, 293–294; Black Thursday, 300, 302–305; Tragic Tuesday, 305, 306; new issues following, 306
Great Depression, 307, 393, 411; investment firms forced into bankruptcy, 308–309; effect on Kidder, Peabody, 309–317; effect on Lee, Higginson, 317–319; and Senate investigation of short sales, 322–324
Great Northern Railroad, 110, 161
Gridiron Club, 178
Griffiths, William, 45
Griswold, B. Howell, Jr., 385, 388
Griswold, Benjamin H., 229
Guaranty Co., 264, 272, 274, 373–375, 417
Guaranty Trust Company, 58n, 141, 202, 207n, 214, 216, 225, 373; and Liberty Loans, 236; and French national loans, 261; its security affiliate, 272, 274
Guggenheim family, 205

Hadley, Arthur T., 178
Hadley Commission, 178–179
Hall Carbine affair, 21
Hallgarten & Co., 11, 214
Hallowell, Norwood P., 94, 319
Halsey, Noah W., 96
Halsey, N. W., & Co., 68, 96, 259; sales organization, 102, 103, 108; "informative" advertising, 105, 260; absorbed by National City Bank, 274, 275
Halsey, Stuart & Co., Inc., Chicago, 259, 261, 310, 375; aggressive sales methods, 260; staff growth, 260; during Great Crash, 306; and Pecora investigation, 328–329; and municipal issues, 394, 406; and price maintenance and penalty clauses, 403; and Chicago Union Station Company, 422; and competitive bidding controversy, 432–435, 451; and antitrust case of *1950*'s, 465, 467, 484, 487; after *1945*, 505
Hanauer, Jerome H., 88n
Hancock, John M., 378, 379, 464
Hand, Learned, 468
Hanes, John W., 398
Hanover National Bank, 207n
Hapgood, Norman, 176
Harding, Warren G., 241, 248
Harding, William P. G., 229
Harjes, Herman, 91n
Harper's Weekly, 105, 175–176, 180, 428
Harriman, Edward H., 100, 110–111, 122
Harriman, Ripley & Co., 395, 414; and price maintenance and penalty clauses, 403
Harriman, W. Averell, 463
Harris, Forbes & Co., 96n, 108, 196–197, 207n, 229, 373, 466; and public utility holding companies, 297; and AT&T issues, 417
Harris, Hall & Co., 374; and antitrust suit of *1950*'s, 466
Harris, Norman W., 106
Harris, N. W. & Co., 95–96, 102–103, 106
Harris Trust and Savings Bank, 96n, 374, 466
Harvard Business Review, 280–281; definition of investment trust, 281–282
Hatch, Alfrederick, 17
Haven, T. Kenneth, 396
Hayden, Miller & Co., 183
Hayden, Warren S., 183–185, 228, 230–231, 237
Healy, Robert E., 380, 391
Hegeman, John R., 118n
Heidelbach, Ickelheimer & Co., 200
Henderson, Leon, 412, 420, 421, 428, 429
Henry, George G., 140
Henry, Robert L., 176n
Hepburn Act (*1906*), 178
Higgins, Frank W., 115
Higginson, Francis L., Jr., 209n
Higginson, Henry Lee, 175, 191, 207n, 310; during cotton market crisis of *1914*, 200–201
Higginson & Co., London, 319
Hill, James Jerome, 100, 110–111, 114
Hill, Louis W., 207n
Hitler, Adolf, 394

Holding companies, 43, 274, 276, 289–290; affiliates as, 278; compared to investment trust, 282; and House of Morgan, 340–342; and Kuhn, Loeb's organization of Pennroad Corp., 343. *See also* Public Utility holding companies
Holding Company Act, *see* Public Utility Holding Company Act
Holland, 207
Holmes, Oliver Wendell, 326
Hoover, Herbert, 248, 303–304; and Great Depression, 307; and protection of investor, 322–323, 324, 351; and separation of commercial and investment banking, 368, 370
Hope & Co., Amsterdam, 12
Hornblower & Weeks, 49n
Hottinguer & Co., Paris, 91, 258
House, Colonel Edward M., 180, 211
House of Morgan, *see* Morgan, J. P. & Co.
House of Representatives, U.S., 137, 382; Banking and Currency Committee, 137; Banking Committee, 348; Commerce Committee, 348, 357, 395, 454; Judiciary Committee, 355. *See also* Congress, U.S.
Hovey, Chandler, 313–314, 315
Hudson, C. I., & Co., 81
Hughes, Charles Evans, 66, 115, 117, 118, 119, 120, 121; and life companies' stock purchases, 122–123; and life companies' underwriting of new issues, 124–125; governor of New York, 128; appoints committee to investigate speculation, 132, 138; and passage of public service commission laws, 159; at White House Conference (*1921*), 248
Hughes Committee, *see* New York State, investigation of *1908*
Hyde, James H., 114, 122

Ickelheimer, H. L., 200
Ickes, Harold L., 380, 462
Illinois, 157
Illinois Bell Telephone Company, 487, 488
Illinois Central Railroad, 219
Illinois Trust and Savings Bank, 107, 141n
Imports, 308
"Improvement banks," 3
Income taxes, 192, 227; investment bankers' evasion of, disclosed at Pecora investigation, 334–335, 342, 346. *See also* Taxes
Incorporation, investment firm, 506–507

Incorporation laws, 157; Delaware, 272, 283, 289
Indebtedness, limits on, 157
Indiana, 157
Industrial combinations, 29, 44, 53; and Chicago bankers, 106, 107
Industrial Commission, *see* United States Industrial Commission
Industrial relations, 251
Industrials, 42–50, 259; financing of, 43–44; distribution of, 44–45; public acceptance of, 44; overcapitalization of, 46; growth of, 79; and small investor, 93, 94
Inflation, 228
Inheritance, account, 412–420; and AT&T issues, 415–417; and PG&E issues, 417–419; and antitrust case of *1950*'s, 474, 487, 488
Installment buying and first Liberty Loan, 225. *See also* Partial-payment plan
Insull, Samuel, 251, 259, 306, 320, 330, 433; and Pecora investigation, 328–329
Insurance companies, 47–49, 55, 424, 499; and investment bankers, 48, 49, 115–123, 126, 127; and syndicates, 58, 117–119; and Armstrong Committee, 66, 115, 117–119, 122; expansion of assets, 85, 117; Lawson's attack on financial practices of, 113; reform of, 114–115, 125–126; investment policies, 117–121; stock purchases, 122–123; services provided investment houses by, 123–124; prohibited from underwriting securities, 126; decline in securities held in portfolios, 126; effect of reform laws on, 126–127; and competitive bidding, 450
Intermediary, investment, 1, 13; professional auctioneer, 4–5, 7, 13, 85, 196
Internal improvements, state-sponsored, 1, 3, 158; and serial bonds, 245
Internal Revenue Bureau, U.S., 335
Internal revenue code, 351
International finance, 202–203, 249; American ascendency in, 216, 222–223, 238
International Harvester, 69n
International High Commission, 215
International Mercantile Marine Company (IMM), 74–75, 119–120; and AIC, 215
International Securities Corporation, 291
International Securities Corporation of America, 283

554 | Index

International Securities Trust of America (ISTA), 283
International Silver Company, 45, 69n
Interstate Commerce Act, 39
Interstate Commerce Commission (ICC), 41, 177–179, 221, 343, 422, 477; and New Haven Railroad, 132–133; and regulation of investment banking activities, 154; and issuance of railroad securities, 177–178; and railroad equipment trust certificates, 245; and Securities Act of *1933*, 356; and competitive bidding controversy, 431–435, 436, 444–445, 451, 457
Interstate Commerce Railway Association, 39–40
Investigation, Federal and state, 110–136; Armstrong Committee, 116–124; effect on insurance companies, 126–127. *See also* Pujo investigation
Investment Advisers Act, 384
Investment bankers: origins and developments (pre-*1873*), 1–28; and the railroads, 29–42; and industrials, 43–50; and insurance companies, 48, 49, 115, 116–123, 126, 127; and commercial banks, 48–49, 96–97; and syndicates, 53–60, 69–70; investigation of borrower, 56; traditional relationships, 59, 112; and mergers, 76–78; *1900–1914*, 79–109; categories of functions, 89–90; foreign connections, 91–92; and small investor, 92–94; counseling function, 94; classified on strength as underwriters, 95; national banks, 97; security affiliates, 98; trust company, 98–99; rules of interfirm behavior, 100–101; young, "progressive" houses, 102–108; sales organizations, 102–103; and use of advertising, 104–105; in Chicago (*1900–1914*), 105–108; and money trust, 110; and conflict of interest, 115, 116; effect of reform laws on, 125–126; role of, and Pujo Committee, 139, 154; and control of "other people's money," 142; and interlocking directorates, 144–147; practices defended by Morgan, 147–150; and ICC regulation, 154; and securities regulation (blue-sky laws), 156, 174, 181–192; federal criticism, 174–181; state legislatures' criticism, 181–192 (*see also* Blue-sky laws); during World War I, 193–223; after U.S. entry into World War I, 224–239; in the *1920*'s, 240–270; growth of new, young, aggressive firms, 258–261; criticism of (after *1929*

Investment bankers (*cont.*)
crash), 279; and investment trusts, 285–287, 292; and crash of *1929*, 299, 300–306; and Great Depression, 307–321 *passim;* and Pecora investigation, 322–351; and New Deal reform, 352–381; reaction to Security Act of *1933*, 357; and Glass-Steagall Act, 368–375; adaptation to regulation, 382–407; competition for new issues (*1930*'s), 393–394; slump (*1930*'s), 394–398; and TNEC, 408–430; FDR's criticism of, 410; and compulsory competitive bidding, 431–457; decline in spreads (*1940*'s), 451–454; during World War II, 458–459; and antitrust suit, 460–495, modification of procedures, 496–508
Investment Bankers Association of America (IBA), 165–173, 225, 271, 306, 355, 405; initial membership, 167–169; finances, 169; "creed," 170; concern for plight of railroads, 171–172; education and service function for members, 171–172; roster of officials, 172; protests Pujo report, 175–176; and state legislation (blue-sky laws), 181–192; and model blue-sky law, 182–185; "Proposed Blue Sky Act" (with NASBS), 185; fights spread of state regulation, 186–188; urges adoption of antifraud laws, 189; and settling of joint syndicate accounts, 191–192; and Committee of Seven (*1914*), 195; ambivalence in attitude during World War I, 201–202; Committee on Foreign Securities, 209; Committee on Railroad Securities, 221; and Liberty Loans, 226, 233; and capital conservation, 231, 232; urges congressional protection of investor, 234; participation of members in patriotic activities (*1917*), 237; in the *1920*'s, 255–270; deplores irresponsible syndicate practices (*1920*'s), 265; Committee on Syndicate Agreements, 265–266; attitude of exclusiveness (*1920*'s), 267; Board of Governors, 267; function and activities of committees, 267–268; and lobbying, 269; policing function, 269–270, 385–389; leadership (*1920*'s), 270; confusion of perceptions before *1929* crash, 300–301; during Great Depression, 319–321; and securities legislation, 358; and improvement of industry's standard of conduct, 385–389; fair trade practice rules, 386; and Invest-

Index | 555

Investment Bankers Association (*cont.*) ment Bankers Conference, Inc., 389–390; and Maloney bill, 391; fears government concentration of economic power, 426; *1938* constitution and bylaws, 426; public relations program, 426–427; and compulsory sealed bids, 437–438, 439, 450, 457, 472–473; and SEC's U-*50* role, 444; and antitrust case (*1950*'s), 457, 463, 467, 472–473; during World War II, 458–459; and legalization of price-fixing agreements, 462; and Glass-Steagall Act, 498; in *1960*'s, 506

Investment Bankers Code Committee (IBCC), 388, 389

Investment Bankers Conference Committee, 389

Investment Bankers Conference, Inc., 389–391; and IBA, 390; and Maloney Act, 391; transformed into NASD, 392

Investment Banking, IBA publication, 428

Investment Company Act (*1940*), 383–384; Title II, 384

Investment counseling, 94, 383

Investment Dealers Digest, 465

Investment trusts, 258, 271, 276, 298; growth of, 281, 287–288; defined, 281–282; management, 282; fixed, 282, 283; organization of, 283; four types, 283–284; and acquisition of foreign securities, 284; factors contributing to launching of movement, 284–286; sponsors, 285–287; and publication of holdings, 288; regulation, 288; and Great Crash of *1929,* 288–289; abuses, 289–292; pyramiding, 289–290; Marxist view, 293; appraisal of, 293–294; return on invested capital, 294; doomed by Pecora investigations, 330, 332–333; and Dillon, Read, 345; regulation, 382, 383–384

Investments: foreign, in U.S., 30; *1900–1914,* 79–109; increase in funds for, 85

Investors, 1, 499–500; small, 14–16, 26, 79–109 *passim,* 250–252; and syndicate distribution function, 65–66; and installment buying ("partial payment plan"), 103–104; and World War I war loans, 211; shift in preference of (*1917–1919*), 227–228; catering to foreign-born, 236–237; increase in (*1920*'s), 240, 263; and investment trust, 293

Iowa, 187

Italy, 259, 313

Japan, 80n, 81–82, 460

Jefferson, Thomas, 3

Jesup, Edward M., 319

Johnson, General Hugh S., 385–386

Joint-account transactions, *see* Syndicate

Jones, Jesse, 435

Joseph, J. L., and S. I., & Co., 10

Justice, U.S. Department of, 59, 234, 350; and New Deal securities legislation, 355; and TNEC, 410; and monopoly, 445, 450, 490; and antitrust case (*1950*'s), 458, 460, 463, 476, 484–485, 494; Antitrust Division, 461, 476; collection of data on investment banking business, 462–463; choice of seventeen firms, 464–467

Kahn, Otto H., 47; 88n; on security legislation, 186; and Anglo-French loan (*1915*), 204, 205; on personal service of Kuhn, Loeb, 257; and Pecora investigation, 340, 343–344, 349; condemns investment trusts, 343, 345, 346; on aversion to competitive bidding, 350, 431, 485–486

Kansas, 156, 162; blue-sky laws, 163–164, 174, 181, 183, 185, 186, 188, 189, 354

Keene, James R., 145n

Kennedy, John F., 380

Kennedy, Joseph P., 379–380, 432

Kent, Frank R., 9

Keyser, Paul V., 355

Kidder, A. M., & Co., 43

Kidder, Henry P., 34n

Kidder Participations, Inc., 283

Kidder, Peabody & Co., 7n, 26–27, 39, 69, 95, 139, 191, 232, 365, 374, 486, 502; formation of (*1865*), 8; and Baring Brothers, 26, 30, 91, 209, 258, 309, 317; and Union Pacific, 28; and recruitment of foreign capital, 30; and Atchison, Topeka & Santa Fe, 34–37, 40; and incorporation of sugar trust, 43; and distribution of industrial securities, 44; syndicate managers' fee, 63; distribution to small investor, 65; and AT&T, 67, 92, 313, 415–416; and National Shawmut Bank of Boston, 70–72, 143; and launching of U.S. Steel, 73, 144; and foreign issues, 80, 90, 92, 316–317; organizational structure (pre–World War I), 86–87; functions performed by, 90; retail business, 93; and Mexican Central Railroad, 120–121; and Pujo Committee, 140, 141, 176; influence on Boston's banking resources, 143;

Kidder, Peabody & Co. (*cont.*)
and interlocking directorates, 144; during World War I, 197, 216, 217, 237; and French loans of *1914–1915,* 207; and Winchester Repeating Arms Company, 208–209; and Central Powers, World War I, 210; and railroad offerings (*1914–1917*), 219; and promotion of sale of Liberty bonds, 227; and Caldwell & Co., 236; during *1920*'s, 258; investment trusts, 258, 283, 289, 291–292; during Great Depression, 308, 309–318; and House of Morgan, 311; reorganization of, 312–317; and profits (*1930*'s), 397, 403; and choice of syndicate participants (*1930*'s), 404–405; and private placements, 405, 500; and "proprietary interest" in AT&T issues, 415–416; in antitrust suit, 486, 489; diversification (*1960*'s), 504; incorporation, 507
Kidder, Peabody Acceptance Corporation, 291, 314
Kidder, Peabody Participations, Inc., 292, 314
Kidder, Peabody Trust Company, Inc., 292
King, William, 368
Kinnicutt, G. Herman, 317, 377, 378, 379
Kissel, Kinnicutt & Co., 141, 317
Knickerbocker Trust Company, 129
Knox, Philander C., Secretary of State, 98
Krech, Alvin W., 209n
Kreditanstalt, failure of, 307. *See also* Austria
Kreuger, Ivar, 317–318, 320, 325
Kreuger & Toll, 318
Kuhn, Abraham, 19
Kuhn, Loeb & Co., 19, 27, 40, 95, 281, 416; and Pennsylvania Railroad, 33, 37, 220, 257; and Atchison, Topeka & Santa Fe, 34; and financing of industrial corporations, 44, 47; policy concerning syndicates, 57, 58, 59–60, 65, 69; manager's step-up fee, 63; profitablility of syndicates managed by, 75; and underwriting of foreign securities, 81, 82, 256–257, 261; and foreign market for American securities, 84; and Pujo investigation, 86, 140–143, 176, 180; organizational structure (pre–World War I), 87, 88n; as general bankers, 89; no brokerage branches, 92; no retail function, 93, 108; and control of Northern Pacific, 100, 110; and

Kuhn, Loeb & Co. (*cont.*)
Union Pacific, 101, 152–153; and Equitable, 121, 122; interlocking directorates, 144; choice of underwriting partners, 145; and blue-sky laws, 185–186; in financial crisis of *1914,* 198, 201; and Anglo-French loan (*1915*), 204; and Central Powers, World War I, 210, 211; and AIC, 215; and railroad issues (*1914-1917*), 219; during *1920*'s, 256–257; and gold bond issue for Mortgage Bank of Chile, 264; during Great Depression, 308; and Pecora investigation, 339, 342–344; and Glass-Steagall Act, 374, 375, 381; and choice of syndicate participants (*1930*'s), 404; capital employed (*1934–1939*), 406; and TNEC's separateness issue, 413; and Chicago Union Station Company, 422; and competitive bidding controversy, 434, 435, 445, 456–457; during World War II, 459; and antitrust case (*1950*'s), 485, 486, 490; post-*1945,* 505

Labor, 250–251
Labor, U.S. Department of, 410
Ladenburg, Thalmann & Co., 90
La Follette, Robert M., 131, 241
Lake Superior & Mississippi Railroad, 24, 52
Lamont, Robert P., 307
Lamont, Thomas W., 60–61, 129, 143, 207, 209n; and Liberty Loan committees, 227; and "Black Thursday," 302–303, 304–305; and Pecora investigation, 336–337, 339, 350
Landis, James M., 356, 360, 380
Lane, Gardiner M., 139, 191, 310
Lanier, Charles, 13
Lanier, James F. D., 12
Lanston Monotype-Machine Company, 68
Latin America, 80n, 82n, 214, 248
Lautrato Nitrate Company of Chile, 331
Lawson, Thomas W., 45, 112–113, 460–461
Lazard Frères, 414–415, 417–419, 488
Leach, A. B., 213
Ledyard, Lewis Cass, 130, 131
Lee, Higginson & Co., 11, 26, 30, 69, 95, 103, 139, 175, 207n; and Santa Fe Railroad, 34, 35; and General Electric Company consolidation, 43; and distribution of industrial securities, 44; policy concerning syndicate formation, 57, 59n; and small investor, 65, 93–94; and AT&T, 67,

Lee, Higginson & Co. (*cont.*) 416–417; and creation of National Shawmut Bank of Boston, 72; assignment of brokerage function to other houses, 90; outlets abroad, 91–92; and Pujo Committee, 140, 142, 176; influence on Boston banking resources, 143; and interlocking directorates, 144; during *1914–1917*, 216; and distribution of land banks' bonds, 229; reorganization (*1932*), 317–318; and death of Ivar Kreuger, 317–318; and Pecora investigation, 325–326
Lee, Higginson Corporation, 318–319
Lee, Higginson *et Cie*, 319
Leffingwell, Russell C., 225, 341, 349, 350
Legal Tender Act, 14
Legislation, 156, 171, 181–192; and IBA, 268–269; New Deal, 352–381
Lehman, Emanuel, 20
Lehman, Henry, 20
Lehman, Herbert H., 237
Lehman, Mayer, 20
Lehman, Philip, 83
Lehman Brothers, 20, 63, 237, 264, 420–421; and underwriting small enterprises, 82–83; and Glass-Steagall Act, 374; and private placements, 405; and competitive bidding controversy, 435; during World War II, 459; and antitrust suit of *1950*'s, 466, 490
Lehman Corporation, 289
Lehmann, Frederick W., U.S. Solicitor General, 98
Letters of credit, 89, 90, 255, 274, 317, 502; during Great Depression, 308
Liberty Loan Act (April *1917*), 224
Liberty Loan Committees, 226–227; New York, 230
Liberty loans (*1917–1918*), 224–226, 233–234, 238, 250, 354; partial-payment plan, 225, 260; distribution of, 226, 236–237, 273; and depressed prices of nongovernment securities, 227–228; disturbance of normal capital flow, 228–229; protection of, 230–232, 234; and Guaranty Trust Company, 236, 274
Licenses, 183–184, 187; and "Blue Sky Cases," 187–188
Licensing, security, 156, 182, 354
Lieb, George, 418
Life insurance companies, *see* Insurance companies
Light industry, 47, 82, 152
Lincoln, Abraham, 14
Lindbergh, Charles A., Jr., 341

Lindbergh, Charles A., Sr., 136
Literary Digest, The, 372
Livermore & Clews, 17
Lobbying, 269
Loeb, Carl M., Rhoades, 490
Loeb, Solomon, 19, 88n
Loeb, William, Jr., 215
London, 18; financing of subway construction, 82
Long Wharf, Boston, 5
Lorillard, P., 42
Louisville & Nashville Railroad Co. (L&N), 436
Lovett, Robert A., 463
Lusitania, 193

McAdoo, William G., 200, 201, 209, 214–215, 233; and U.S. war loans (*1917*), 224; and control of capital flow (*1917*), 230; and Morgan's "preferred list," 341
McCain, Charles S., 349
McCall, John A., 116
McCalmont & Co., 7
McClintock, Franklin T., 438, 452
McClure's Magazine, 105
McCoy, Joseph S., 249
McCurdy, Richard A., 118
McEldowney, H. C., 209n
McFadden Act of *1927*, 273
McIntyre, Marvin H., 386
McLane, Louis, 3
McMorran, Henry, 151
MacVeagh, Franklin, Secretary of Treasury, 98
Magazine of Wall Street, The, 173, 217, 224, 306; and Pujo report, 175; on financial crisis of *1914–1917*, 193, 202; and Anglo-French loan (*1915*), 205; on World War I "War Brides," 222; on investment bankers and Liberty loans, 227, 228; on industrial relations, 251; defends Wall Street financial practices (*1920*'s), 252–253; on New Deal securities legislation, 358
Magoun, George C., 35, 36, 39
Maine, 185, 188
Maine Central Railroad, 132
Maloney, Francis T., 391
Maloney Amendment, SEC Act of *1934*, 384–385, 391, 392; and Investment Bankers Conference, 390; and NASD, 392–393
Mann-Elkins Act, 178
Manufacturers Trust Company, New York, 290
Manufacturing companies, 30; capitalization of, 43–45
Margin accounts, 134, 230; and Federal Reserve Board, 379; require-

Margin accounts (*cont.*)
ments, and market break of *1937*, 408–409
Market crash of *1929*, see Great Crash of *1929*
Marston, Edwin S., 207n
Martin, William McChesney, Jr., 409
Maryland, 283
Massachusetts, 157, 431; and railroad commissions, 158
Massachusetts National Bank, 49n
Matched orders, 376, 379
Matthews, George C., 380
Meade, Edward S., 51, 202
Medina, Judge Harold R., 63–64, 464, 475; on high syndicate charges of early *1900*'s, 68; on evolution of syndicate system, 78; on evolution of investment banking, 79; on effect of streamlined syndicate procedures of *1930*'s, 405; and compulsory competitive bidding, 432, 434, 436, 456; and antitrust case, 467–469; background of, 468; and government's monopoly charge, 472–473, 484–485; and "heart" of government's case, 474; states government's position on syndicate system, 476; and defense strategy, 478; on traditional-banker charge, 487–488; and satisfactory relationship charge, 488; and cross-examination of live witnesses, 491–492; his opinion in antitrust case, 493–495
Mellen, Charles S., 132–133
Mellon, Andrew W., 207n, 241, 245, 248; on small investor, 250; warns against fraudulent investment banking practices, 253
Mellon National Bank of Pittsburgh, 97, 207n
Mercantile Trust Company, 123
Merchants, 1, 7; as bankers, 8–9
Mergers, 43, 44, 46–47, 502; and syndicates, 51, 69, 74–75; increase in risk, 76; and promoter's profit, 77–78; bank, 278; among investment houses, 506
Merrill, Edwin G., 207n
Merrill Lynch, Pierce, Fenner & Beane, 489–490
Metropolitan Chain Stores, New York, 290
Metropolitan Corporation, 347
Metropolitan Edison Company, 297
Metropolitan Life Insurance Company, 118n; and Vermilye & Co., 122; and compulsory bidding controversy, 442–443
Mexican Central Railroad, 120–121
Mexican War, 10, 11, 52

Mexico: U.S. investments in, 80, 82
Michigan, 186–187, 272
Middle West, 105–108
Miller, Adolph C., 369
Minas Geraes, 330
Missouri Pacific Railroad, 257
Mitchell, Charles E., 59n, 209n, 228, 274, 301, 302, 414–415, 466; and Pecora investigation, 330–335, 344; compensation received for bank duties (*1927–1929*), 333–334; and Blyth & Co., 374; testimony before TNEC, 397, 401, 419–420; and PG&E, 417–418, 488
Mitchum, Tully & Co., San Francisco, 258
Mitchum Tully Participations, Inc., 292
Moffat & White, 95
Moley, Raymond, 355
"Money trust," 110, 131, 136, 177, 350; and Pujo investigation, 138, 139; Untermyer on, 139, 149–151, 174; existence of denied by Morgan, 149–150; existence asserted by Pujo Committee, 151, 174; Pecora's view, 340. *See also* Pujo investigation
Monopoly, 110, 111–112, 132; public's fear of, 133, 160; and TNEC investigation, 408, 419–420, 421, 429; in antitrust suit of *1950*'s, 463, 466, 469–472, 478–479, 484
Monticello, 3
Moody, John, 104
Moody, William H., 132
Moody's Investors Service, 250, 298, 423
Moody's Manual of Investments, 281
Moore & Schley, 130
Moorhead, William, 24–25
Morgan, Henry S., 22n, 373–374, 414
Morgan, J. P. (John Pierpont), 11, 19, 20–22, 23, 26, 49, 108, 191, 300, 496, 508; as railroad financier, 37–38; and reorganization of roads, 38–41; and Edison Electric Company, 43; single-handed rule of firm, 88; and "money trust," 100, 113–114; and conflict of interest, 116; in crisis of *1907*, 127, 129–131, 194, 303, 496; and New Haven Railroad, 132–133; and Pujo Committee, 140, 143, 408; and voting trusts, 143; on competitive bidding on interstate securities, 146; defends investment banking practices, 147–152, 153; on increasing demand for reform, 155; death of, 174, 310; in financial crisis of *1895*, 194; and First Security Company, 273–274; foresees increased disclosure, 507

Morgan, J. P., Jr., 91n, 179–180, 207n; and closing of New York Stock Exchange (July *30, 1914*), 194; and Anglo-French loan (*1915*), 204–205; and Pecora investigation, 337, 340; calls private banker a "national asset," 350

Morgan, J. P., & Co., 20–21, 47, 67, 91, 95, 117, 194, 281, 372, 496; and recruitment of foreign capital, 30; and Federal Steel Company, 44–45; and syndicates, 60, 65, 69, 145, 256, 261; and manager's fees, 63; and creation of National Shawmut Bank of Boston, 71; and United States Steel Corporation, 73, 74, 144; and IMM, 74–75, 119–120; and foreign issues, 80–81; 255; and Pujo investigation, 86, 140, 142, 145, 176; staff (pre-*1914*), 87; as general bankers, 89, 256; firm name changes, 91n; no retail function, 92–93, 108; and interfirm competition, 100, 101; battle for control of Northern Pacific, 100, 110; and "other people's money," 142; and voting trust, 143; New York Central Railroad issue (*1914*), 195–196; during World War I crisis, 197–199, 200, 201, 204–205, 208–209, 216; services performed for France, 206–207, 212, 468; and Winchester Repeating Arms Company, 208; during *1920*'s, 255–256, 261–262; and public utility holding companies, 297; during Great Depression, 308, 311; and Kidder, Peabody, 311–312, 315; and Pecora investigation, 336–338, 340–342; and holding companies, 340–341; "preferred list" of underwriters, 341–342; and Glass-Steagall Act, 372, 400; and TNEC's separateness issue, 413–414; and AT&T issues, 416, 487

Morgan, Junius Spencer, 10, 20, 21, 22

Morgan, J. S., & Co. Ltd., 10, 21, 37, 120

Morgan-Belmont Syndicate, 53

Morgan *et Cie*, 91n, 255

Morgan, Grenfell & Co., Ltd. (London), 91, 199, 255

Morgan, Harjes & Co. (Paris), 84, 91, 206

Morgan Stanley & Co., Inc., 373–374, 397, 400–401, 406, 423; and price maintenance and penalty clauses, 403; and choice of syndicate participants, 404; and TNEC, 413, 416; and AT&T issues' private placement, 425, 487; and competitive

Morgan Stanley & Co., Inc. (*cont.*) bidding controversy, 434–435, 436, 442, 456–457; and railroad issues, 445; and antitrust case, 465, 479, 485–486, 488, 490; in *1960*'s, 504–505

Morris & Company, 214

Morris Canal and Banking Company, 2–3

Morrow, Dwight, 198

Mortgage Bank of Chile, 264, 339

Morton, Bliss & Co., 22, 37n, 38

Morton, Levi Parsons, 22

Morton, L. P., & Co., 22

Morton, L. P., Burns & Co., London, 22

Morton, Rose & Co., 22

Moseley, F. S., 70; and creation of National Shawmut Bank of Boston, 71, 72

Motion picture companies, 259

Muckrakers, 112, 127

Municipal bonds, 32, 49, 95, 102, 245, 498; Harris's innovation in sale of, 106; at outbreak of World War I, 197, 218; tax-free feature, 245; small denomination (*1920*'s), 250; in Great Crash of *1929*, 306; and IBCC, 388; competition for new issues (*1930*'s), 394

Mutual funds, 499

Mutual Life Insurance Company, 62, 113, 114; and foreign issues, 81; investment policies, 117–118, 122, 123; syndicate activities and Armstrong Committee, 124

Nation, The, 175

Nation's Business, The, 428

National Association of Attorneys-General, 187

National Association of Manufacturers, 429

National Association of Owners of Railroad Securities, 220

National Association of Securities Dealers, Inc. (NASD), 392, 503; membership (*1939*), 393; reaction to SEC's U-*50* rule, 444; decline in membership during World War II, 459

National Association of State Bank Supervisors (NASBS), 184; "Proposed Blue Sky Act" (with IBA), 185

National Bank of Commerce, 143, 207n

National Banking Act, 48, 49, 176n

National Banking system, 348

National banks: and security affiliates, 97, 98, 100, 272–273, 277; and

560 | Index

National banks (*cont.*)
  Pujo Committee recommendations, 154
National City Bank of New York, 45, 81, 98, 100, 112, 191, 207n, 216, 228; and foreign issues, 80–81; and New York Life Insurance Company, 113; and panic of *1907,* 129; and Pujo Committee, 140; Morgan influence, 142; Schiff influence, 143; Kidder, Peabody holdings in, 143; and Central Powers, World War I, 210; and AIC, 215; security affiliate, 274, 276; and Pecora investigation, 329–331, 332, 333, 368–371; and Glass-Steagall Act, 371–372; and TNEC's investigation, 414
National City Co., 98, 229, 261, 278, 374, 466; and IBA code, 267; absorption of N.W. Halsey, 274, 275; service capacity for parent bank, 276–277; and Pecora investigations, 329–335, 339, 344, 346, 368, 371; and stock of National City Bank, 332; compensation for officers, 333–334; officers join Brown, Harriman, 400; and TNEC investigation, 414–415, 417; and PG&E, 417–418, 488
National Industrial Recovery Act (NIRA), 350, 384, 385; Title I (competition code), 385
National Monetary Commission, 137, 369
National Power Policy Committee, 436
National prohibition enforcement law (Volstead Act), 355
National Recovery Administration, 184, 385–386, 390; and IBA code of conduct, 387; and Investment Bankers Code Committee, 388; declared unconstitutional, 388–389
National Shawmut Bank of Boston, 70–73; and Kidder, Peabody, 70–72, 143; problems created by consolidation (*1898*), 72; directorate, 72, 88; and Lee, Higginson, 143; investment trust, 283
National War Savings Committee, 226
Nehemkis, Peter R., Jr., 411–412, 429
Nevada, 161, 163, 188
New Deal legislation, 326, 408, 502, 508; Securities Act of *1933,* 352–368; strengthening of blue-sky laws, 355, 356; Glass-Steagall Act, 368–375; Securities Exchange Act (*1934*), 375–376
New England Cotton Yarn Company, 291
New England Investment Corporation, 291

New Freedom legislation, 190
New Haven Railroad, *see* New York, New Haven, and Hartford Railroad
New Jersey, incorporation laws, 43
New Orleans, 18
New York, New Haven, and Hartford Railroad, 132–133, 180
New York Central Railroad, 37, 195
New York City, 7, 13, 320; centralization of capital markets in, 30, 105, 151, 153, 340, 405, 407, 423; central reserve banks, 48–49; Bureau of Economic Research, 76; and panic of *1907,* 130; public service commission laws, 159; and financial crisis of *1914,* 197–199; still center of financial activities (*1960*'s), 503, 505
New York City syndicate, 198–199
New York Clearing House Association, 129
New York Consolidated Exchange, 195
New York Curb Exchange, 195
New York Financier, 96
New York *Journal American,* 451
New York Life Insurance Company, 48, 66, 115; and foreign issues, 80–81; and National City Bank, 113; and Morgan-sponsored securities, 116, 122; syndicate participations, 119–120, 124; and Mexican Central Railroad, 120–121
New York Security & Trust Company, 74, 124n
New York State, 6, 99; Superintendent of Insurance, 114–115, 120, 122, 450; legislature, 125; investigation of *1908,* 134–135, 138; Board of Railroad Commissioners, 159; gas and electric commission bill (*1906*), 159; Stock Corporation law, 414
New York State Investigating Committee, *see* Armstrong Committee
New York Stock Exchange, 19, 79, 87, 103, 105, 231, 499; and panic of *1907,* 130, 131; and New York state investigation of *1908,* 134–135; response to outbreak of World War I, 193–195, 196; and Pan American Conference (*1914*), 215; urges congressional protection of investor, 234; shares traded (*1920*'s), 243–244; in *1928,* 253; and investment trust shares, 285, 287–288; and crash of *1929,* 302, 304, 305; "Black Thursday," 303; during Great Depression, 308; and President Hoover, 322–323, 351; short sales, 323–324; and stock of National City Bank, 332; and SEC law, 381; reorganiza-

Index | 561

New York Stock Exchange (*cont.*)
tion (*1938*), 409, 426; IBA representation on board of, 426; and incorporation of investment houses, 507
New York Times, 39, 51, 59, 60, 75, 114, 300; and majority report of Pujo Committee, 174; on bankers' withdrawal from interlocking boards, 180; and crash of *1929,* 302, 303, 304, 305; on Cooper's resignation, 327; on Pecora investigation, 335; on IBA code of conduct, 386; criticism of compulsory bidding, 450, 456; on antitrust case (*1950*'s), 477–478; on Medina's opinion in antitrust trial, 495; on increased disclosure (*1960*'s), 507
Newspapers, *see* Press
Newsprint corporations, 259
Noble, H. G. S., 195
Noetzlin, Edouard, 92
Norbeck, Peter, 323, 324n, 326, 327, 328, 329, 335
North American Company, 290, 418
Northern Pacific Railroad, 23–25, 27, 28, 37, 41, 132; power struggle for control of, 100, 110–111
Northern Securities Company, 111
Norway, 207, 262
Notification, in "Proposed Blue Sky Act," 185
Notification laws, 161–162, 163
Noyes, Alexander Dana, 145n, 193; warns against speculative excesses (*1920*'s), 253
Nutt, Joseph, 341
Nylic, 120–121

Ohio, 183, 187
Ohio Bankers' Association, 110
Old Colony Trust Company, Boston, 51n, 143
O'Mahoney, Joseph, 410–411
Otis & Co., 432, 434, 435, 461; and SEC's proposed compulsory bidding rule, 441–442, 457; and antitrust case (*1950*'s), 463
Ottawa, 199
Outlook, The, 105, 176
Overcapitalization, 45–46; and New York Public Service Commission, 159
Overseas loans, *see* Foreign issues
"Over-the-counter" transactions, 6, 103; and SEC, 388, 389, 390–391; and NASD, 392
Owen, Robert L., 177

Pacific American Associates, 290
Pacific Coast, 260

Pacific Gas & Electric Co. (PG&E), 375, 415, 488; and TNEC inheritance issue, 417–419
Page, Walter Hines, 174
Paine, Webber, Jackson & Curtis, 490
Paish, Sir George, 202
Pan American Financial Conference (*1914*), 215
Panama Canal, 74
Panic: of *1837,* 3, 6–7, 10; of *1857,* 11, 23; of *1873,* 22, 25–26, 29, 30; of *1893,* 29, 40, 53, 56; of *1901* (May 9), 110, 111, 159; of *1903* (trust panic), 113, 114, 159; of *1907,* 76, 127–131, 194; of *1914,* 179
Paris, 18; Bourse, 220
Paris loan (*1916*), 216
Parish, David, 1, 52
Parsons, Lewis H., 209n
"Partial-payment plan," 103–104; and Liberty Loan (*1917*), 225, 260. *See also* Installment buying
Partnership, 42, 85–88; financial arrangements of, 87; duties and responsibilities of, 88
Peabody, Francis H., 34, 35n, 36, 37n, 86; directorships held by, 88
Peabody, Frank E., 237
Peabody, George, 10, 11; and J. P. Morgan, 21
Peabody, George, & Co., 20
Peabody, Oliver W., 34, 35n
Pearl Harbor, 459
Pecora, Ferdinand, 321, 326–327, 347, 348, 361, 362, 376; accepts assignment with Senate Banking subcommittee, 328; and investigation of National City Co., 329–335, 368, 371; and Fletcher resolution, 336; investigates private banking, 336–351; interrogates Morgan, 337–339; and SEC, 380
Pecora investigation, 322–351, 359, 385, 460–461, 495, 508; investigates Insull's activities, 328–329; and National City Co., 329–335; and House of Morgan, 336–342; and Kuhn, Loeb, 339, 342–344; and Dillon, Read, 342, 344–346; and Chase Securities Corporation, 346–347; reforms urged by Aldrich, 347; criticism of, 349–350; *Report,* 349; and election of *1932,* 353; and issue of competitive bidding, 432
Penalties, 184
Pennroad Corporation, 343–344; voting-trust certificates, 343
Pennsylvania, state defense issue (*1861*), 15
Pennsylvania Coal Co., 101

Pennsylvania Railroad, 27, 100; and Kuhn, Loeb, 33, 37, 220, 257; underwriting of bond issue (*1870*), 52–53; bond issue placed in Paris (*1906*), 84; and Pennroad Corporation, 343; and compulsory competitive bidding controversy, 444
Pension funds, 499
Perkins, George W., 48; and Armstrong Committee, 115–120, 124; and Mexican Central Railroad issue, 120–121; and panic of *1907*, 130; on competition, 138
Perkins, James, 418
Perlo, Victor, 434n
Pershing, General John J., 341
Peru, 331
Philadelphia, 7, 13, 405
Philadelphia & Reading Railroad, 37, 38, 41
Pole, John W., 369
Pool operations, 325, 348; and National City Co., 332; and Chase Securities Corporation, 346; and Securities Exchange Act, 376
Pope, Allan M., 369–370, 386
Populists, 157, 162; and blue-sky laws, 189
Porter, William H., 143
Post Office Department, U.S., 355
Postal fraud laws, 156, 185
Potter, William C., 303
Power and light companies, 260
Power struggles, interfirm, 100
Predecessor-successor relationship, *see* Inheritance, account
Preferred lists, 341–342, 346; and IBA code of conduct, 387
Preferred stock, 45, 259; decline (after *1946*), 501
Press, 77, 127; financial, 56, 59, 60, 93, 104–105, 125; daily, 104–105
Price, McCormick & Co., 71
Price index: (*1914–1917*), 218; (*1920*'s), 244; (*1929–1932*), 306
Price manipulation, 134–135; issue in antitrust trial, 475–477, 494
Prime, Nathaniel, 6
Prime, Ward & King, 6, 8, 9, 10
Private bank, 6–8, 13, 16–23, 108; and brokers, 6–8; and merchants, 8–9; representatives of foreign in U.S., 9; and railroad securities, 30; dominant force before World War I, 85; avoidance of incorporation, 86–88; described (*1910*), 88–89; functions of, 89–90; brokerage business of, 90; foreign agents and correspondents, 91; categories of, 95; and financing municipalities and public utilities, 95–96; and trust com-

Private bank (*cont.*)
panies, 99–100; and J. P. Morgan & Co., 255; and Pecora investigation, 336–351; and Glass-Steagall Act, 371, 372
Private placements, 405, 424, 427, 430, 500; and competitive bids, 441
Proctor & Gamble, 42
Promoters' fee, 45–46, profit, and watered stock, 77
Prospectuses, 77
Prosperity, *1920*'s, 240; and sound government, 241
Prosser, Seward, 207n, 209n; and "Black Thursday," 303
Providence, Rhode Island, 7
Prudential Life Insurance Company, 123
Prussing, Eugene E., 167
Public interest, 111–112, 280
Public projects, *see* Internal improvements
Public relations, & IBA, 426–428
Public Service Commission, New York, 159
Public service commission laws, 159
Public utility companies, 47, 102, 106–107, 497, 500; growth of, 79; and small investor, 93, 94; financing of, 95–96, 152; and state regulation, 156, 159; *1914–1917*, 221–222; urban concentration of, 242; and Halsey, Stuart, 259, 433; and public sealed bidding for issues, 432–433, 442; and SEC's U-*50* rule, 443
Public utility holding companies, 271, 294–298; main classes of, 295; pyramiding of, 297; regulation of, 382–383
Public Utility Holding Company Act, 382–383, 432; and SEC, 382–384, 436–437, 438; and utility company officials, 442
Publication corporations, 259
Publicity, 184, 185
Publicly owned enterprises, 53; and Chandler Act, 383
Pujo, Arsène P., 137
Pujo Committee, 107–108, 137–138, 156, 190, 227, 267, 350, 381, 495; report submitted, 150–151; conclusions, 153; recommendations, 153; *Report* released, 174–176, 181; lack of congressional action on recommendations of, 176–177; public reaction to, 180–181, 192; and competitive bidding, 431
Pujo investigation, 86, 126, 131, 137–155, 175, 340, 349, 351, 396, 408, 477, 508; questionnaire to New York and Boston bankers, 139–140;

Pujo investigation (*cont.*)
  investment bankers called to testify, 140, 145; identification of leaders in control of money and credit, 140–142, 144–145; and voting trusts, 143; and interlocking directorships, 143–144, 329; and competitive bidding on interstate securities, 146–147; Morgan's testimony at, 147–150, 152; relation to antitrust suit of *1950*'s, 460–461, 466
Pullman Palace Car Company, 42
Purchase-group agreements, 402–403
Pure Food and Drug Act, 355
Pure Oil syndicate, 490
Pyramiding, 134

Quebec province, 207

Radio companies, 253
Radio Corporation of America (RCA), 325
Railroad commissions, 158
Railroad equipment trust certificates, *see* Equipment trust certificate
Railroad issues, 2, 30, 109, 497; and Winslow, Lanier, 12; and Drexel & Co., 15n; and Jay Cooke, 23–25; and syndicate, 32, 53; and investment banker, 32–33; decline in importance of, 79; and small investor, 93–94; and ICC, 177–178; regulation of, 178–179; repatriated during World War I, 213; during *1914–1917* period, 219–221; after World War I, 240; in *1920's*, 256; and competitive bidding controversy, 444–445, 456–457
Railroad Securities Commission, 178–179
Railroads, 1, 7, 29–42, 49, 496–497; and their exclusive banker, 27–28; investment bankers' principal customer (*1870–1900*), 29, 32; bank representation on directorates of, 32–33; banker-instituted rescue operations, 40–42; and syndicate, 54; and Chicago bankers, 106, 107; and state regulation, 156, 158; IBA concern for, 171–172; *1914–1917*, 219; and WFC, 230; and Reconstruction Finance Corporation, 394–395
Randolph, Edmund B., 66, 118
Raskob, John J., 323, 325, 341
Rate wars, railroad, 38–39
Rayburn, Sam, 178–179; and Securities Exchange Act, 376, 377
Read, William A., 198
Read, Wm. A., & Co., 207n, 344

Real estate, 7; holding company, 276; speculation, and security affiliates, 279
Receivership, 257
Reconstruction Finance Corporation (RFC), 356, 394–395, 435; and Defense Plant Corporation of World War II, 458
Recovery, economic: of *1840*'s, 5–6; of *1878*, 29; of *1897*, 44
Redmond & Co., 215
Reece, Carroll, 462
Reed, Drexel & Co., 21
Reed, Robert R., 205n
Reform, banking, 3, 125–126; and panic of *1907*, 131; and New York investigating committee of *1908*, 133–135; Blue Sky, 156–164; and Pecora investigation, 347, 350–351; New Deal, 352–381; and investment bankers code of conduct, 385–389. *See also* Armstrong Committee; Pujo investigation
Refunding issues, 393–394, 434; syndicates, 23
Registration: statements, 357, 361–362, 366, 383, 401, 436; and Securities Exchange Act of *1934*, 376–377; and IBA code of conduct, 387–389
Regulation, 138, 151, 154–155, 322, 351, 382–407; Blue Sky movement, 156–164, 181–192; difficulty of enforcement, 157; growth in demand for, 159–161; and formation of IBA, 165–173; of railroad securities, 178–179; and Liberty Loans, 227–228; in *1920*'s, 240, 252; of security affiliates, 279; of investment trusts, 288; of stock exchanges, 375–381; and market break of *1937*, 408
Remick, Frank W., 87n, 139–140
Republican party, 162; National Committee, 322
Reserves, bank, 48–49
Retailers, security, 102–103
Revenue Act (June *1932*), 365, 401
Revolving Credit, and Kidder, Peabody, 311–312, 314
Rhode Island, 158; general notification statute, 162, 163, 187
Richberg, Donald R., 184–185
Ringling Brothers and Barnum & Bailey Circus, 337
Ripley, Joseph, 415
Roberts, George B., 40
Rock Island Railroad, 27
Rockefeller, John D., 42
Rockefeller, Percy, 325
Rockefeller, William, 45, 74, 112
Rockefeller interests, 215

Rogers, Henry H., 112
Rogers, N. Burton, 45
Rogers, William H., 45
Roosevelt, Franklin D., 184, 347, 376, 436; and Pecora investigation, 328, 330, 335, 336–337, 349, 350; state of economy at first inauguration of, 351–353; and Glass-Steagall bill, 370, 373; and Securities Exchange Act (*1934*), 375, 379; appoints Kennedy SEC chairman, 380; and IBA code of conduct, 386; and establishment of TNEC, 409–410; and compulsory competitive bidding controversy, 444–445. *See also* New Deal
Roosevelt, Theodore, 111–112, 128, 131, 163, 326; and Charles Mellen, 132; requests legislation to police stock market (*1908*), 133, 354; and legislation to regulate interstate corporations, 178
Root, Elihu, 131
Rose, John, 22
Rothschild, N. M., & Sons, 9, 10, 91
Rothschild banks, 12, 18; and Cooke's Northern Pacific Railroad bond issue, 24
Russell, Stanley A., 417, 418, 419
Russia, 81, 193, 204–205, 211; government loan (*1916*), 216
Russo-Japanese War (*1905*), 81–82
Ryan, Thomas Fortune, 74

Sabin, Charles H., 207n, 209n
Sachs, Samuel, 19, 82–83
Sachs, Walter E., 83, 325, 420
St. Louis, 48, 435
St. Louis & San Francisco Railroad, 84
St. Louis Post-Dispatch, The, 435
Salem, Mass., 7
Salomon, William, & Co., 140, 214
San Francisco, 18, 90, 320
Santa Fe Railroad, *see* Atchison, Topika & Santa Fe Railroad
Sargent, Charles S., 208, 315
Sargent, Charles S., Jr., 209n
Saturday Evening Post, The, 105, 432
Savings banks, 7; and creation of National Shawmut Bank of Boston, 70–71
Savings, Investment, and National Income, TNEC report, 410
Scandinavia, 259
Schiff, Jacob H., 19, 32, 43–44, 57, 108, 191, 310; on growth of investment banking, 49; and syndicate membership, 58, 59–60; on profitability of syndicates managed by Kuhn, Loeb, 75; and flotation of foreign issues, 81; domination of

Schiff, Jacob H. (*cont.*)
Kuhn, Loeb, 88; European connections, 92; on interfirm competition, 101, 146, 152; and Armstrong Committee, 116, 124; as Equitable director, 116, 121, 122; warns against financial abuses and speculation, 128; and Pujo Committee, 140, 143; and voting trusts, 143–144; on choice of Kuhn, Loeb's underwriting partners, 145; on interlocking directorates, 147; and federally supervised railroad securities law, 178; and financial crisis of *1914*, 198; and Anglo-French loan (*1915*), 204–205; and Central Powers, World War I, 210, 211; and Pan American Financial Conference (*1914*), 215; and Liberty Loan committees, 227
Schiff, Mortimer L., 88n, 209n; and Anglo-French loan (*1915*), 204
Schley, Grant B., 130
Schwab, Charles M., 325
Scribner's, 105
Seaboard National Bank of New York, 249
Seabury, Samuel, 327
Sears, Roebuck & Co., 82–83
Securities, fraudulent, 233–234; and disclosure legislation, 354–355
Securities Act of *1933*, 177, 188, 279, 348, 351–368, 381, 387, 500; and Frankfurter, 353–354; disclosure requirement, 353–356, 359, 363–376, 387, 398; drafting of, 355–356; registration statement, 357, 361–362, 366, 383, 401; amendments, 357n, 358, 364n, 388; criticism of, 358–362; and the economy, 361–362; effects of, 363–368; and syndicate structure, 364–366; and private placement of issues, 367–368, 424; supplemented by SEC law (*1934*), 375–376, 379; Title III, 383; prohibits offering of securities before registration statement declared effective, 404; amendment to legalize price-fixing agreements, 462
Securities and Exchange Commission (SEC), 285, 378–379, 426, 477, 494, 498; and Securities Act of *1933*, 356–357; extension of regulatory and advisory duties, 382–383; and Investment Company Act, 383–384; and Investment Advisers Act, 384; and regulation of over-the-counter securities, 388, 389, 390–391; and administration of investment bankers code of conduct, 388–389, 390; and stock exchanges, 408; and

Index | 565

Securities and Exchange Commission (*cont.*)
TNEC, 410, 424, 427; and trend toward private placement, 424–425; and competitive bidding, 436–438, 442, 451; and Public Utilities Holding Company Act, 436–437; U-*12 F-2* rule, 436–438; Public Utilities Division, 438, 443; U-*50* rule, 443–444, 452, 454, 456–457, 484; and price-fixing issue, 475–476; examination of securities industry (*1960*'s), 505–506; and increased financial disclosure (*1960*'s), 507; study of securities industry released (*1963*), 508; growth in powers of, 509
Securities Exchange Act (*1934*), 62n, 351, 375–376, 381, 477, 494; Title II, 364; and Fletcher-Rayburn bill, 376–379; enactment of, 379, 382; Maloney Amendment, 384–385
Securities legislation, 187; New Deal, 352–381; asked for by FDR, 353; adaptation to, 382–407; purpose of, 393; IBA-SEC joint review of, 427
Security affiliates, 100, 108, 259, 271–281, 298; and national banks, 97–98, 100, 272–273, 277; sales methods, 103; defined, 271; methods for organizing of, 271–272; regulation concerning, 272–273, 382; evolution of, 273–275; factors contributing to growth of, 275–276; functions of, 276–277; and syndicate participation, 277; appraisal of, 277–278; growth of (*1920*'s), 278–279; criticism of, 279; and *1929* crash, 279; lack of regard for public interest, 280; and investment trusts, 283; and Glass-Steagall Act, 369–371, 372, 374–375
Security analysts, 87
Security issues, domestic, 1–2; and banking system, 3; and auctioneer, 4; underwriting of, 47, 52–54, 56–58, 61–62, 64, 68; and syndicate, 51, 52–68, 75; increase in number and size, 54, 108; involving several syndicates, 55, 57; origination, 56–60; underwriting agreement, 57–58; foreign, 60; distribution of, 65–66, 68; syndicating costs and problems, 68; foreign market for American, 84–85; and trust company, 100; retailing of, 102–105; "indigestible," 114, 126, 135, 159; and sluggish market of *1906*, 126–127; state regulation, 156–164; and IBA, 171; repatriated, World War I, 212–213, 216, 240, 245–246; domestic (*1914–1917*), 217–223; during *1920*'s, 240–

Security issues (*cont.*)
254; ownership spread (*1920*'s), 249–250; and security affiliates, 276, 280–281; and SEC, 383; during *1930*'s, 393–395
Seligman, Henry, 207n
Seligman, Isaac, 18n
Seligman, James, 19
Seligman, Joseph, 18, 26
Seligman, J. & W., & Co., 18–19, 91, 207n; and recruitment of foreign capital, 30
Seligman & Stettheimer (Frankfurt), 91
Seligman Brothers, London, 91
Seligman Frères *et Cie,* Paris, 91
Senate, U.S.: Finance Committee, 60, 348; Banking and Currency Committee, 271, 323–324, 327, 335, 348, 359, 369–370, 439, 506; investigates stock market practices (*1932*), 320, 322–351; investigation of short sales (*1932*), 323–324. *See also* Congress, U.S.
Serial bonds, 245
Shawmut Association, of Boston, 283
Shawmut National Bank, *see* National Shawmut Bank of Boston
Shenandoah Corporation, 290
Sherman Antitrust Act, 111, 457, 463, 466, 471, 475, 490, 494, 495; and price-fixing in underwriting agreement clauses, 462, 472, 475–476
Short sales, 134, 322; Senate investigation of (*1932*), 323–324
Sinclair, Harry F., 325
Smith, Adam, 138
Smith, Barney & Co., 25n, 417, 422, 490
Smith, Edward B., & Co., 25n, 374–375, 417; reorganization of (*1937*), 397
Smith Act of *1940,* 468
Society of Railway Financial Officers, 219
South Africa, 80
South America, 215, 246, 259; AIC activities in, 216
South Dakota, 187
Southern District of New York, 462
Southern Pacific Railroad, 84, 110
Southern Railway, 41
Spain, 207
Specific-approval laws, 188
Speculation, 1, 77, 94, 113, 128; New York State investigation of (*1908*), 133–136, 138; of *1920*'s, 253–254, 255, 271; and *1929* crash, 300–301; and National City Co., 332; and Pecora investigation, 340, 346; and Securities Act of *1933,* 362; and

566 | Index

Speculation (*cont.*)
  Securities Exchange Act (*1934*), 376; and market break of *1937*, 409
Spencer, Trask & Co., 104
Speyer, Sir Edgar, 210
Speyer, James, 26n, 116, 122, 200, 215, 307
Speyer, Philip, 18, 26
Speyer & Co., 11, 95, 146, 261; and railroad financing, 33; and Mexican railroads, 82; loans floated in Paris, 84; and retail function, 93, 108; and Central Powers, World War I, 210
Standard and Poor's index, 352
Standard Brands, Inc., 340, 342
Standard Oil combination, 42, 45, 112, 113, 162, 456
Stanley, Harold, 397, 421, 424, 434, 438, 439, 440–441; and antitrust suit of *1950*'s, 464, 487
Starkweather, John K., 454
State Department, U.S., 25n, 210; and refinancing of Sulzberger & Sons, 214; and foreign financing, 248–249
State financing, 245, 498
State Street, Boston, 7
State Street Investment Corporation, 294
Statist, The, 202
Statistics, 104
Steagall, Henry B., 370. *See also* Glass-Steagall Banking Act
Stern, Siegfried, 249
Stetson, Francis Lynde, 178
Stillman, James, 100, 108, 112, 129, 191, 310; and Anglo-French loan (*1915*), 205
Stock and Bond Law, Texas (*1893*), 158
Stock and exchange boards, 5
Stock exchanges, 13, 408; private bank representation on, 90; reform, 153; response to outbreak of World War I, 196; and Securities Exchange Act (*1934*), 375–379
Stock market: boom of *1916*, 234; break (August *1937*), 397, 401, 408. *See also* Great Crash of *1929*
Stock watering, 76–77, 113, 158, 161
Stocks, 497; post–World War I, 240; in *1929*, 243, 301; American investment in foreign (*1920*'s), 246
Stone, Charles A., 215, 311
Stone & Webster, 215, 296, 311–312, 313, 316
Storrow, James Jackson, 57, 94
Straight, Willard D., 215
Strauss, Siegfried, 211, 213
Street railway bonds, 32
Streyckmans, Felix J., 236

Stuart, Harold L., 96, 102–103, 209n, 259, 375; describes selling syndicates during *1920*'s, 263–264; and Pecora investigation, 328–329; on competitive circumstances after *1933*, 419; and compulsory competitive bidding, 432–433, 436, 440, 441, 442, 444; and antitrust investigation, 487, 491–493
Stubbs, Walter R., 163
Subscription, popular, 51–52, 53n; through newspaper advertising, 92
Suez Canal Company, 207
Sugar trust, 43
Sullivan & Cromwell, 361
Sulzberger & Sons, Chicago, 214
Supreme Court, U.S., 111; and constitutionality of state blue-sky laws, 187, 189–190; declares NRA unconstitutional, 388–389
Swan, Joseph R., 389, 422
Sweden, 81, 82, 207
Switzerland, 207
Syndicate, 1, 50, 51–78, 191, 256, 347; and railroad bonds, 32, 37, 53; and industrial combinations, 44–45; and mergers, 51, 69, 74–75; European origins of, 51–52; earliest use in U.S., 52–53; underwriting commitment, 52–53, 56, 64; "reorganizing," 53; factors influencing changes in, 54–55; participation advantages, 55; services performed by, 55–65; agreement, 57–58, 61–62; participants, 58–60; and insurance companies, 58, 117–119, 124; size of members' participations, 60, 61; managers' functions and powers, 61–64, 68, 109, 118; borrowing capacity, 64–65; distribution of issue, 65–66; termination of, 66; and issuer's interests, 66–67; advantages to large borrowers, 68; and United States Steel Corporation, 73–74; and IMM, 74–75; fees and commissions earned by members, 75; increase in risk, 76; and stock watering, 76–77; and foreign issues, 81, 261; and Chicago bankers, 107; increase in size after reform laws of *1906*, 126; and stifling of competition, 145, 265–266; and Pujo Committee, 145–146; settling of joint accounts, 191–192; for Anglo-French loan (*1915*), 204–205; expansion in size (*1917–1918*), 235; modification of system (*1920*'s), 262–264; limited liability selling, 263–264; methods of price stabilization, 264; and Chilean bank issue (*1925*), 264–265; criticism of practices (*1920*'s), 265–267; and secu-

Syndicate (cont.)
  rity affiliates, 277; and Securities Act of *1933,* 364–366; revision of type and procedure, 382; streamlining of procedures (*1930*'s), 398–406; and compulsory bidding, 446–450, 456; in antitrust suit, 474–476, 493; Medina's view, 494; present-day, 503

Taft, Robert A., 435
Taft, William Howard, 98, 140, 272; and regulation of interstate corporations, 178, 354
Tatlock, John, 118–119, 123
Taxes, 224, 238, 351, 401; on foreign securities in France, 84; excess-profits, 192; and Liberty Loans, 227–228; and municipal bonds, 245; and rise of small investor, 251; to regulate trading in securities, 323; and Revenue Act of *1932,* 365; and market break of *1937,* 408; and lag in investment (*1930*'s), 425, 426. *See also* Income taxes
Taylor, Edward T., 354–355
Temporary National Economic Committee (TNEC), (*1939*), 181, 350, 394, 400–401, 408–430; establishment of, 409–410; participants, 410; *Reports,* 410; interrogation of investment bankers, 410–411; topics of exploration, 412–413; and divorcement issue, 413–414; and account-inheritance issue, 412–419, 466, 488; and traditional-banker relationships, 419–420, 485; and bankers' domination of corporation's financial policy, 420–421; and issue of competitive bidding, 421; shows degree of concentration in investment banking, 422–424; and IBA, 426–428, criticism of hearings, 428–430; *Final Report,* 429; relation to antitrust suit of *1950*'s, 461, 462, 466, 474, 477, 495
Tennessee, U.S.S., 197
Tennessee Coal, Iron & Railroad Co. (TCI&R), 130
Terminal Railroad Association of St. Louis, 435
Terret, John, 95n
Texas, 157, 272; Stock and Bond Law, 158
Thayer, E. V. R., 313–314
Thayer, John Eliot, 7, 8, 10, 11, 13
Thayer, John E., & Brother, 7–8, 314
Thayer, Nathaniel, 7, 8, 314
Thompson, Eugene E., 377
Thompson, Huston, 354; and Securities Act of *1933,* 355–356

Thompson, Samuel C., 23
Thomson-Houston Electric Company, 43
Time magazine, 441
"Tombstone ads," 63–64
Townsend, John G., Jr., 323, 324n
Trade, international, 207, 240
Trade acceptances, 207–208
Trade associations, 165, 169, 172, 190
Trafford, Bernard W., 280
Transfer tax, 401. *See also* Taxes
Transportation Act of *1920,* 179
Traylor, M. A., 251
Treasury, U.S. Department of, 1; and Civil War bond issues, 14–16; and L. P. Morton & Co., 22; and underwriting commitment, 53; and restoring confidence of dollar (*1914*), 199, 201; and private flotation of Allied loans (*1917*), 209; war loans (*1917–1919*), 224–225; and distribution of Liberty Loans, 226–227; and WFC, 229; and foreign financing, 249; and exploitation of small investor, 251–252; rulings, and IBA representative in Washington, 269; and TNEC, 410; and World War II 458–459
Trent affair, 14
Truman, Harry S, 439, 462; Wall Streeters in administration of, 463; and Judge Medina, 468
Trust companies, 48, 49; in investment banking, 98–99, 108; differences among, 99; auxiliary services provided by, 99–100; service provided to by insurance companies, 123–124; and panic of *1907,* 129–131; and security affiliates, 274, 278; and investment trusts, 283
Trust Company of America, 129, 131, 303
Trust Indenture Act (*1939*), 383, 399
Trusts, 29, 76; and holding companies, 43; and T. Roosevelt, 111
"Truth-in-Securities" Act, *see* Securities Act of *1933*
Tumulty, Joseph P., 180

Underwriting, security, 47, 56–57, 64, 68, 498; agreement, 57–58, 61–62; fees and commissions earned by syndicate members, 75; increase in risk, 76–78; of small enterprises, 82–83; during Great Depression, 307–308; "preferred lists," 341; and Security Act of *1933,* 360, 366–367; depressed state (*1930*'s), 394–396; and syndicate procedure (*1930*'s), 398–399, 430; common stock, 500–501

568 | Index

Union Commerce Investment Company, 272
Union Pacific, 27, 28, 33, 39, 75, 110; loyalty to Kuhn, Loeb, 101, 152-153; and Equitable, 122
Union Securities Corporation, 464-465
Union Trust Co., 207n; security affiliate, 272
United Cigar Manufacturers, 82
United Corporation, 297, 340, 342
United Fruit, 69n; and AIC, 216
United States & Foreign Securities Company (US&FS), 290-291, 345-346
United States & International Securities Corporation (US&IS), 345-346
United States Bank of Pennsylvania, 2, 3
United States Chamber of Commerce, 428
United States Government, 110-136; and Northern Securities Company, 111; in financial crisis of *1914-1917*, 199-200; first war loan (World War I), 207; leases railroads (*1917*), 221; demand for funds (*1917*), 224; during World War II, 458. *See also* name of specific department or agency
United States Industrial Commission, 45, 46, 145n, 160, 177, 408; *Final Report,* 76; describes "financiering" of mergers, 77-78; and disclosure legislation, 354; and competitive bidding, 431
United States Investor, 47, 75, 76, 99, 100
United States Maritime Commission, 380
United States Railroad Administration, 228, 234
United States Rubber Company, 160
United States Senate, *see* Senate, U.S.
United States Steel Corporation, 69n, 73, 303, 340; directorate, 73, 88, 144; underwriting syndicate, 73-74, 119n, 124n; and TIC&R stock in panic of *1907,* 130-131; stock price decline at outbreak of World War I, 195; in crash of *1929,* 304
Untermyer, Samuel, 137-153 *passim,* 175, 177, 180, 181, 340, 408, 461; on existence of money trust, 139, 149-151, 174; on Morgan's control of "other people's money," 142; and voting trust, 143; and interlocking directorships, 144; and use of syndicate, 145-146; questions Morgan on investment banking practices, 147-150; conclusions, 153-154; and rail-

Untermyer, Samuel (*cont.*)
road securities law, 178; and Anglo-French loan (*1915*), 205; and Securities Act of *1933,* 355
Uruguay, 207

Van Sweringen brothers, 340
Vanderbilt, William H., 37
Vanderbilt, William K., 74
Vanderlip, Frank A., 191, 207n, 310; AIC board chairman, 215; and National War Savings Committee, 227
Vermilye & Co., 17, 30, 118n, 122
Victory Loan (April *1919*), 224, 226, 354
Volstead, Andrew J., 355
Voting trust: railroad, 38, 40; and Pujo investigation, 143, 154
Voting-trust certificate, 343
Vreeland act, *see* Aldrich-Vreeland Act

Wabash Mining Company, 157
Wabash Railroad, 339
Walcott, Frederic C., 323, 324n
Walker, Elisha, 434
Walker, G. H., 490
Walker, James J., 327
Wall Street, 6. *See also* Investment bankers
Wall Street Employees' Relief Committee, 196
Wall Street Journal, The, 302, 303, 304, 372, 406
War bonds, 23; World War I, 224-239, 240; World War II, 458-460
"War Brides," World War I, 222
War Finance Corporation (WFC), 229-230, 232, 284
War Finance Corporation Act, 231
War industries, 229
War Industries Board, 234, 237
War loans (World War I), 207-209, 211
War Loan Organization (WLO), 225, 226
War of *1812,* 8
War savings stamps, 225
Warburg, Felix M., 88n
Warburg, James P., 361
Warburg, Max, 210
Warburg, M. M., & Co., 88n
Warburg, Paul M., 88n, 238; and small investor, 251; urges federal regulation of securities, 252; and investment trust, 284; predicts crash and depression (*1929*), 301
Ward, Thomas Wren, 9
Warfield, S. Davies, 221
Wash sales, 134, 376, 379

Washington Life Insurance Company, 118, 123
Waterman, Merwin H., 75n, 452
Webster, Edwin S., 311, 317; and reorganization of Kidder, Peabody, 312–316
Webster, Edwin S., Jr., 312–313, 314, 315
Webster, Frank G., 72, 87; and interlocking directorates, 88; death of, 310–311
Weinberg, Sidney J., 389
West Virginia, 186–187
Western Securities Company, 259
Western Union Telegraph Company, 105
Westinghouse Electric, 42, 205; in crash of *1929*, 304
Wharton School of Finance and Commerce, University of Pennsylvania, 504
White, F. Edson, 251
White, Horace, 133
White, Weld, and Co., 94, 95, 103, 141; and antitrust case (*1950*'s), 465
White House Conference (*1921*), 248
Whiteside, Arthur D., 386
Whitney, George, 87, 102, 309, 312, 389; and reorganization of Kidder, Peabody, 315; and merger with Kissel, Kinnicutt, 317; at Pecora investigation, 341, 342; and TNEC investigation, 416; and traditional banker relationships, 419
Whitney, Richard, 303, 305, 322, 324, 380–381, 409; opposes Securities Exchange bill, 376–379
Whitney, Richard, & Co., 490
Wickersham, George W., U.S. Attorney General, 98
Wiggin, Albert H., 207n, 209n, 305; and Black Thursday, 302–304; and Pecora investigation, 346–347, 348
Wildcat securities, 252, 354
Williams, John Skelton, 272
Wilson, Thomas E., 214
Wilson & Company, Inc., 214
Wilson, Woodrow, 136, 137n, 174, 176, 191, 202, 223, 241, 326, 354; and Clayton Act, 177; antitrust message (*1914*), 180; and Brandeis, 183; New Freedom legislation, 190; opposes German cities loan of *1916*,

Wilson, Woodrow (*cont.*)
211; and Pan American Financial Conference (*1914*), 215
Winchester Repeating Arms Company, Connecticut, 208
Winslow, Lanier & Co., 12, 13, 27, 28, 30, 34, 146; and Northern Pacific, 37; and cotton oil trust, 43; foreign agents and correspondents, 91
Winsor, Robert, 67n, 70, 71, 86, 87, 88, 191, 207n, 416; and Mexican Central Railroad issue, 120; and Pujo Committee, 140, 147; and competition for new underwritings (*1920*'s), 258; during Great Depression, 309–310
Wisconsin, 159
Witter, Dean, 260
Witter, Dean, & Co., 260
Wolff, Abraham, 88n
Wolff, Adelaide (Mrs. Otto Kahn), 88n
Women's Liberty Loan organization, 236
Woodin, William H., 335, 341, 342
Woods, George, 439–440
Woodward, William, 207n
Working Men's Savings Banks, 16
World War I, 27, 174, 179, 190, 191; outbreak precipitates financial crisis, 193–195; ambivalence toward investment in foreign issues, 201–203; American entry, 207, 223, 224–239; armaments, 208; and investment bankers' relations with Central Powers, 210–211; and domestic corporate securities, 216–218; need for capital conservation, 231; maladjustments in brokerage houses, 234–237; Armistice, 246
World War II, 382, 457, 458, 462, 498–499
World's Work, The, 238

"Yankee" brokerage houses, 20–22, 26
Yates & McIntyre, 4
Young, Owen D., 328
Young, Robert R., 432–433; and competitive bidding controversy, 434–435, 436, 444, 462; antitrust investigation, 491, 495n

Zimmerman & Forshay, 211

Harvard Studies in Business History

1. JOHN JACOB ASTOR, BUSINESS MAN, by Kenneth Wiggins Porter
2. JAY COOKE, PRIVATE BANKER, by Henrietta M. Larson
3. THE JACKSONS AND THE LEES: TWO GENERATIONS OF MASSACHUSETTS MERCHANTS, 1765–1844, by Kenneth Wiggins Porter
4. THE MASSACHUSETTS–FIRST NATIONAL BANK OF BOSTON, 1784–1934, by N. S. B. Gras
5. THE HISTORY OF AN ADVERTISING AGENCY: N. W. AYER & SON AT WORK, 1869–1949, revised edition, by Ralph M. Hower
6. MARKETING LIFE INSURANCE: ITS HISTORY IN AMERICA, by J. Owen Stalson
7. HISTORY OF MACY'S OF NEW YORK, 1858–1919: CHAPTERS IN THE EVOLUTION OF THE DEPARTMENT STORE, by Ralph M. Hower
8. THE WHITESMITHS OF TAUNTON: A HISTORY OF REED & BARTON, 1824–1943, by George Sweet Gibb
9. DEVELOPMENT OF TWO BANK GROUPS IN THE CENTRAL NORTHWEST: A STUDY IN BANK POLICY AND ORGANIZATION, by Charles Sterling Popple
10. THE HOUSE OF HANCOCK: BUSINESS IN BOSTON, 1724–1775, by W. T. Baxter
11. TIMING A CENTURY: HISTORY OF THE WALTHAM WATCH COMPANY, by C. W. Moore
12. GUIDE TO BUSINESS HISTORY: MATERIALS FOR THE STUDY OF AMERICAN BUSINESS AND SUGGESTIONS FOR THEIR USE, by Henrietta M. Larson
13. PEPPERELL'S PROGRESS: HISTORY OF A COTTON TEXTILE COMPANY, 1844–1945, by Evelyn H. Knowlton
14. THE HOUSE OF BARING IN AMERICAN TRADE AND FINANCE: ENGLISH MERCHANT BANKERS AT WORK, 1763–1861, by Ralph W. Hidy
15. THE WHITIN MACHINE WORKS SINCE 1831: A TEXTILE MACHINERY COMPANY IN AN INDUSTRIAL VILLAGE, by Thomas R. Navin
16. THE SACO-LOWELL SHOPS: TEXTILE MACHINERY BUILDING IN NEW ENGLAND, 1813–1949, by George Sweet Gibb
17. BROADLOOMS AND BUSINESSMEN: A HISTORY OF THE BIGELOW–SANFORD CARPET COMPANY, 1825–1953, by John S. Ewing and Nancy P. Norton
18. NATHAN TROTTER: PHILADELPHIA MERCHANT, 1787–1853, by Elva Tooker
19. A HISTORY OF THE MASSACHUSETTS HOSPITAL LIFE INSURANCE COMPANY, by Gerald T. White
20. THE CHARLES ILFELD COMPANY: A STUDY OF THE RISE AND DECLINE OF MERCANTILE CAPITALISM IN NEW MEXICO, by William J. Parish
21. THE RISE AND DECLINE OF THE MEDICI BANK, 1397–1494, by Raymond de Roover
22. ISAAC HICKS: NEW YORK MERCHANT AND QUAKER, 1767–1820, by Robert A. Davison
23. BOSTON CAPITALISTS AND WESTERN RAILROADS: A STUDY IN THE NINETEENTH-CENTURY RAILROAD INVESTMENT PROCESS, by Arthur M. Johnson and Barry E. Supple
24. PETROLEUM PIPELINES AND PUBLIC POLICY, 1906–1959, by Arthur M. Johnson
25. INVESTMENT BANKING IN AMERICA: A HISTORY, by Vincent P. Carosso